# SEAFARING IN ANCIENT EGYPT

Published by Periplus Publishing London Ltd
Publisher: Danièle Juncqua Naveau
Academic editor: Dr Mark Merrony
Managing editor: Nick Easterbrook
Assistant editors: Jenny Finch, Christelle Yeyet-Jacquot
Production manager: Sophie Chéry
Production assistant: Arvind Shah
Rights manager: Jane Lowry
Picture researcher: Aline da Silva Cerqueira
English translation: Andrew Brown

Reprographics: Periplus Publishing London Ltd
Printed in Italy by L.E.G.O. S.p.A., Vicenza

ISBN: 1-902699-33-5

# SEAFARING IN ANCIENT EGYPT

David Fabre

Periplus

London

# Foreword and Acknowledgements

*This tranquil roof on which the doves walk,*
*Glimmers between the pine trees and the tombs.*
*High noon composes with an equal fire*
*The sea that always begins again anew.*
*Ah, rich reward after hard thought –*
*A long gaze on the calm of the gods!*

It is doubtless a sign of destiny that this study was partly conceived in the University that bears the name of that great poet of the sea, Paul Valéry. These famous lines from 'The Cemetery By the Sea' were without any doubt the inspiration for these thoughts on the maritime universe of the Ancient Egyptians.

Before setting off for the seas of Egypt, it is my pleasure and duty to thank all those who helped me in this work, first and foremost M. Jean-Claude Grenier, Professor at the Université Paul Valéry – Montpellier III, who was willing to supervise my thesis entitled 'The organisation of maritime trade in Ancient Egypt', which has fed into the present book: I always found him to be the source of the wisest advice and a very friendly ear. My thanks also go to M. Bernard Mathieu, Director of the IFAO and Lecturer at the Université Paul Valéry – Montpellier III, for his judicious and reliable advice and his permanent encouragement. Thanks also to the members of the Montpellier team, especially M. Marc Gabolde, Lecturer at the same university.

My respect and gratitude for the pleasant memory of my time at the Mission Française des Fouilles de Tanis go to Mme Christiane Zivie-Coche, Director of Studies at the École pratique des hautes études, and M. Philippe Brissaud, Director of the MFFT, for their constant support. Thanks to Mme Susanne Bickel, Lecturer at the University of Fribourg and Associate Lecturer at the University of Basle, for her encouragement and her trust. I must also say how much I owe to M. André Bernand, Professor Emeritus, from whose work I have learnt so much and whose correspondence with me has always been such a constant source of encouragement.

Thanks also to M. Michel Passelac, head of research at the CNRS, who first taught me how to conduct research into archaeology and the study of pottery, as well as the problems of commercial exchanges in the (western) Mediterranean, in the course of excavations in my native Aude. Thanks to Luc Madiec, teaching assistant at the École française de voile, for his expert advice in sailing, and for having revealed the genius of all those who go down to the sea in ships, and turned me, as much as he was able, from a 'landlubber' into a sailor.

Thanks to all those who, from near or far, have supported me over these years: Alexandra Brouillet, Hélène Bret, Florent Cros, Jean-Yves Domper, Sylvie Donnat, Khaled el-Enany, Emmanuelle Galtié, Alexis Gorgues, Yves Guichard, Nadine Guilhou, Olivier Lavigne, Gérard Lenfant, Isabelle Régen, Vanessa Ritter, Thomas Sagory, Anna Scott, Frédéric Servajean, Claire Somaglino, Christophe Thiers. For their unwavering support, I would like to thank my brothers, Sébastien and Jean-Christophe, my grandparents, and the people without whom none of this would have happened – my parents.

I must express my deepest gratitude to the Conseil scientifique of the IFAO, who granted me a scholarship so that I could take advantage of the Institute's Library and complete my research. I also thank the Académie des Inscriptions et Belles-Lettres which granted me the Vandier Bursary, thereby assisting me to pursue my studies in Egyptology.

For kindly allowing the reproduction of certain images, I would like to thank Dominique Valbelle, Alessandra Nibbi, Jean Rougé, Lucien Basch, Peter Clayton, Robert Partridge, Patrice Pomey, Steve Vinson, and The Egypt Exploration Society.

Finally, thanks are due to all the members of the team at Periplus London; without their tireless energy and their love of the sea, this book would never had got beyond the manuscript stage.

*I had a longing for the wide open sea, but I could not bring*

*myself to set off aimlessly to make a few circles in the water.*

*The sea seemed to me to be worth more than*

*a mere plaything. I wanted it to be my reason for living.*

Henry de Monfreid

# Contents

Introduction    xiii

## PART ONE: EGYPT AND THE SEA

### Chapter I: The Bordering Seas

## I. The maritime space of the Ancient Egyptians    12

I.1. *Wadj Wer* and *Ym*    12
I.2. *Haunebut, chen-rekhyt, ra-haout, henet*    13

## II. The Mediterranean Sea    20

II. 1. The conditions of Mediterranean navigation    20
    *II. 1. 1. Climatic conditions*
    *II. 1. 2. Local climatic phenomena*
    *II. 1. 3. Currents*
    *II. 1. 4. The seasons for navigation*
    *II. 1. 5. The coast, navigation and piracy*
II. 2. One or two? The divisions and maritime spaces of the Mediterranean    27
    *II. 2. 1. The 'Egyptian Sea'*
    *II. 2. 2. The 'Phoenician' or 'Syrian Sea', and 'the Great Sea of Kharu'*
    *II. 2. 3. The 'Cypriot Sea'*
    *II. 2. 4. The 'Carpathic' or 'Rhodian' Sea*

## III. The Red Sea    36

III. 1. General conditions of navigation in the Red Sea    36
III. 2. Remarks on the seasons of navigation in the Red Sea    39

### Chapter II: The Ports

## I. Ports, moorings, quays and *emporion*    45

## II. The Ports of the Delta and the Mediterranean coastline    50

II. 1. Between land and sea    50
II. 2. The western coastal fringe of Egypt    60
    *II. 2. 1. Thonis and Naukratis: frontier police post and* emporion
    *II. 2. 2. The Libyan coast and Mersa Mathruh*
II. 3. The eastern coastal fringe of Egypt    65
    *II. 3. 1. Avaris, Piramesse and Tanis: the harbour capitals of the eastern Delta*
    *II. 3. 2. Tjaru*
    *II. 3. 3. Pelusium*
    *II. 3. 4. The coastline of North Sinai*
    *II. 3. 5. Tell Ruqueich*
    *II. 3. 6. The Bardawil sites*

# III. The Red Sea ports 76

### III. 1. Access routes to the Red Sea 76
### III. 2. Harbour infrastructure 76

## Chapter III: The Ships

# I. The Egyptian navy 91

# II. Egyptian naval architecture 102

### II. 1. The hulls 102
#### II. 1. 1. The skeleton
#### II. 1. 2. The planking
#### II. 1. 3. The materials and the sheathing
#### II. 1. 4. The berthing
### II. 2. Rigging and outfitting 110
#### II. 2. 1. The girdles
#### II. 2. 2. The means of propulsion
#### II. 2. 3. The steering mechanism
#### II. 2. 4. The anchors
### II. 3. Ballast, stowage and tonnage 123
#### II. 3. 1. Ballast
#### II. 3. 2. Stowage
#### II. 3. 3. Tonnage
### II. 4. The naming of ships 128

# PART TWO: THE PROFESSIONALS OF MARITIME VOYAGING

## Chapter I: The Personnel of Ports and Ships

### I. The port personnel — 137

I. 1. Stevedores and allied professions — 137
I. 2. Measurers and weighers — 139
I. 3. Shipbuilders — 140
I. 4. The port 'officials' — 141

### II. The sailing personnel — 143

II. 1. The crew — 143
II. 2. The ship's guardian — 145
II. 3. The 'officers of transport' — 146
II. 4. The officials of the crew — 147
II. 5. 'The man at the prow' or *proreutes* — 148
II. 6. 'The man at the poop' — 149
II. 7. The navigator — 149
II. 8. The captain or the 'head of the ship' — 151

## Chapter II: The Traders

### I. Ship's operators and commercial associations — 155

### II. Brokers, merchants, traders, traffickers — 158

II. 1. Trade as a profession? — 158
II. 2. Traders and internal trade — 160
II. 3. Traders and external trade — 160
II. 4. Foreign traders in Egypt — 161
II. 5. The juridicial and institutional status of traders — 162
II. 6. The way of life and social status of traders — 165
II. 7. By way of comparison: *Emporoi, Kapeloi, Naucleroi* and other merchants — 168
II. 7. 1. Emporoi *and* Kapeloi
II. 7. 2. Naucleroi

### III. Messengers, ambassadors, diplomats and wholesalers — 174

III. 1. *Bidalu* and *tamkaru*: the 'businessmen' in the Ancient Near East — 174
III. 2. 'Messengers' and 'explorers' — 175
III. 3. Wenamun: 'messenger, ambassador' and 'keeper of the porch of the temple of Amun' — 184

### IV. 'Market women' and neighbourhood trade — 188

Chapter III: Religion and Beliefs

## I. Superstitions, beliefs and religion                                191

## II. Ceremonies and thank-offerings                                     195

## III. Egyptian religion and the beliefs of the Phoenician traders       196

## Conclusion                                                             205

## Chronology                                                             209

## Lexicon of nautical terms                                              213

## Glossary                                                               219

    I. General vocabulary                             219
        I. 1. In Egyptian transliteration
        I. 2. In Semitic transliteration
    II. Proper Names                                   221
        II. 1. In Egyptian transliteration
    III. Names of Places and Peoples                   221
        III. 1. In Egyptian transliteration
        II. 2. In Semitic transliteration

## Index                                                                  223

    I. Greek and Latin terms
    II. Proper names                                   223
        II. 1. Divinities and divine beings
        II. 2. Kings and queens
        II. 3. Individuals
        II. 4. Places and peoples
    III. *Res notabiles*: economy, institutions, law, society, history,
    natural sciences, techniques, religion, worship and intellectual conceptions    230

## Sources                                                                233

    I. Egyptian sources                                233
    II. Biblical sources                               235
    III. Texts from Ugarit, classical authors and various sources    236

## Bibliography                                                           239

# Introduction

## From monumental Egypt to maritime Egypt

In the eyes of ordinary, educated people, travellers with a taste for exoticism or visitors filled with curiosity about its monuments, but with no specialist knowledge about the country they are discovering, Egypt is above all the land of the pyramids. Not only the three great pyramids of Giza, those of Khufu, Khafra and Menkaura, but also the Step Pyramid of Djoser at Saqqara or the rhomboidal pyramid of Meidun and the little pyramids dotting the valley, all quite justifiably arouse admiration. The imposing bulk of the Sphinx dominating Cairo, the colossi that rise in front of the temples or in the plain, such as the celebrated Colossus of Memnon which sang at daybreak, give mere mortals a sense of how insignificant they are. We are awestruck – and understandably so – when we stand in the forest of pillars stretching up within the temple of Karnak or in front of the obelisk of Luxor whose false twin now rises on the Place de la Concorde in Paris. Jean-François Champollion in person oversaw in detail, towards the very end of his short life, the long journey undertaken to France by this monument, a gift of the Khedive. Visitors gazing at the foot of the statue of Rameses II that rises in front of his temple at Abu Simbel feel a kind of speechless awe in the face of such imposing majesty. There is no temple in Egypt as enormous as the temple of Angkor Wat in Cambodia, but the line of temples that extends along the Valley of the Nile arouses an admiration beyond comprehension: those huge masses form such a sharp contrast with the tranquil plain of the valley or the threatening uniformity of the desert.

To the more informed eyes of scholars who study Egyptian civilisation not only in its extension on land, but also at sea, there is, too, an Egypt that exists on water – and sometimes beneath it. That Egypt is not static, but full of movement. It is the boatmen and sailors who work on it, navigating not only on the river, but also on the Mediterranean and the Red Sea.

Commerce, war, the exploration and exploitation of more or less distant lands led the Egyptians to shores that were at times very far away and sometimes unknown. On ships propelled by sails and/or oars, the Ancient Egyptians practised ocean navigation and coastal

The pyramids of Giza. © Bettmann/CORBIS. Photo: Philip Gendreau

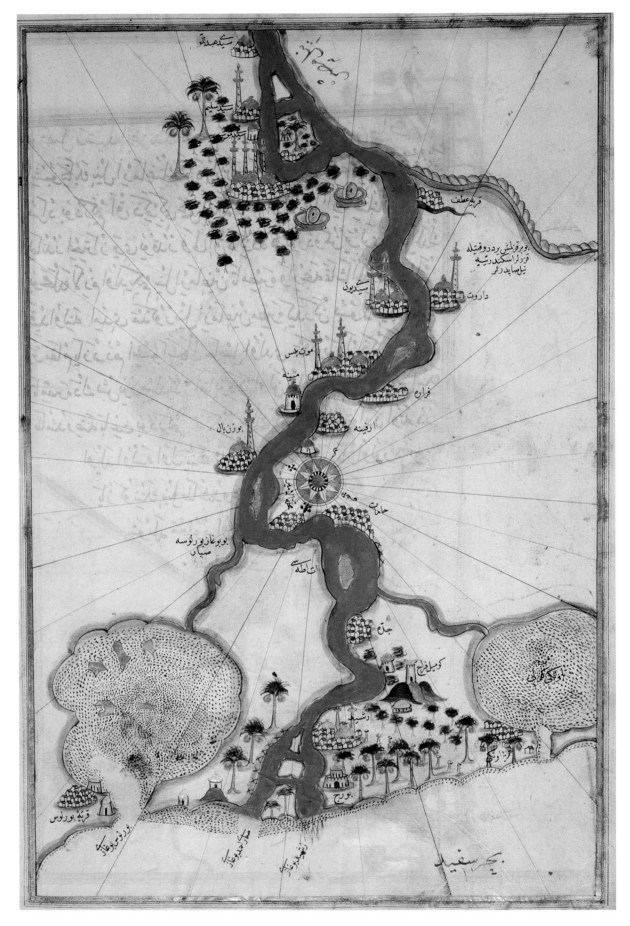

Map of the Nile Valley from the *Kitab-i-Bahriyye* ('Book of the Sea') of the Turkish sailor Piri Reis (manuscript copy from the 16th century, Walters Art Museum, Baltimore, USA). The lower part represents the Nile Delta and its coast: mouths of the Nile, Lake Menzala, Lake Borollos and the port of Damietta. © Walters Art Museum/The Bridgeman Art Library

shipping. Given the precariousness of these boats and the insecurity that reigned at sea, where storms would often blow up suddenly and where pirates lurked, these voyages were exploits that had to be undertaken again and again. 'Going to Egypt means a long and difficult journey,' wrote Homer. Much has been written about the 'Greek adventure', but we also ought not to forget 'the Egyptian adventure'. It could draw on the privilege of that thousand-year history that filled the Ancient Greeks with such admiration. This mobile, daring and ambitious Egypt brings out the enterprising spirit of the Ancient Egyptians. They were not just a land-dwelling, sedentary, peasant people, but also a nation of sailors, navigators and explorers.

A stopover on the banks of the Nile helps us to understand how Ancient Egypt's maritime destiny was played out not only on the high seas, but also and especially on this river which the Arabs designated by the same word – el-Bahr – as the one they applied to the sea. This Nile which, unlike all other rivers, grows wider the closer you come to its sources, was one of the natural routes taken by all expeditions towards the south. In the north, it fans out and flows into the Mediterranean in the shape of a blossoming lotus. Egypt, the 'gift of the Nile', was also dependent on the river's whims. The years when the Nile misbehaved were also years of famine: not enough water, and many of the fields were left arid; too much water, and the villages made of unbaked bricks crumbled away, the dikes were breached and the irrigation system destroyed. Everything was arranged around the river, and the Nile and its channels were the best of roads. The land of *Aegyptos* is a narrow stretch of land along a broad river, and boats were an essential part of its whole life.

## From the origins of Pharaonic Egypt to the conquest of Alexander

The point of departure for this Egyptian maritime adventure was the beginning of the history of Egypt and the formation of the Pharaonic state (at the beginning of the 3rd millennium BC). Its end point was the conquest of Alexander (332 BC), since the arrival of the Macedonians marked the end of Egypt's political autonomy at the same time as it inaugurated a new economic and fiscal structure within which Alexandria became the great commercial city of the eastern Mediterranean. Even if Egypt continued to play an international role, it was within the context of a Near East and a Mediterranean that were no longer in charge of their own destiny. Their new masters, Alexander and the Diadochi, and then the Caesars, shifted the world's centre of gravity westwards. When Alexandria was founded its Macedonian conqueror wished to make it the second pole of his empire, and this accelerated the movement towards a more cosmopolitan character within this society, although it had already begun to lean this way in the 6th century BC.

The new capital took advantage of its political and commercial role to become one of the main intellectual centres of a Mediterranean in which East and West met. Alexandria was the destination of the caravans that brought, from far-away Gerrha via Petra, products from India over the Persian Sea, as well as those which, coming through Dura Europus and the Phoenician bridgehead, put Egypt in contact with Asia Minor and the Silk Road. The Nile Valley was more than ever before a thoroughfare; towards Africa via Syene and the oases, towards the Red Sea by the traditional

roads and the new link between the port of Berenice and Coptos and Ptolemais in Ancient Egypt. Alexandria was the melting-pot in which these imports from the East could be found next to those sent out from the West along the great maritime routes, from Rhodes, Carthage or Rome. This was a 'worldwide' commerce. The temptation shall not be resisted to refer to this period at times, if only to make a few comparisons and to highlight certain developments.

## The maritime destiny of Ancient Egypt is a voyage...

The sea is simultaneously a source of food, an arena for navigation and a place of exchange. The techniques, conditions and procedures of navigation, the transport of merchandise, and shipbuilding: each of these themes invites us to gain a better understanding of maritime space, with its broad horizons for further study. Through the maritime travels of the Ancient Egyptians, the sea appears as a space of navigation and exchange. The way the sea was used can then be distinguished in its technical and economic dimensions, highlighted as they are by the recent contributions of archaeology to our knowledge of maritime history. The main sea bordering Egypt is the Mediterranean. To speak of the Mediterranean 'thus means – and this is our first concern and our most constant endeavour – to restore its proper dimensions. By itself, it was at one time a universe, a planet.'[1] 'A vast source of food; navigating against the distances; navigating against bad weather; ships that sink to the bottom; the Mediterranean is a set of routes': the titles of the chapters in which Fernand Braudel sets out his vision of 'planet Mediterranean' are, in reality, a summons to be immersed in the rich, multiple and hybrid realities of its past, and an invitation to a journey.

'Happy the man who, like Ulysses, has had a good journey...' The sea is a formidable stake for power-struggles, an area over which wealth and armies pass. It is an extraordinary domain for the imagination to expand into, and it has inspired the dreams of generations of sailors and landlubbers. The sea represents thousands of years rich in amazing adventures, technical innovations and bloody confrontations. Right from the prehistoric period, navigators launched out into the Mediterranean.[2] The sea is a space that was gradually 'mastered' by people, who saw brilliant maritime civilisations flourish and leave their mark on its shores. And yet for centuries it remained an unpredictable and deadly immensity. In the encounter between people and the sea, if we view this maritime space as merely a place of transit for merchandise, we forget what is said, often in a rather understated way, by certain texts: the sea is the occasion for human suffering, it is a place of shipwreck and death. So the sea is a space which divides and unites at one and the same time. It is a frontier and a link, a 'liquid cement' which conveys men, products and ideas. It is in unequal symmetry with the great deserts, being an empty space in the middle, on which converge the gazes and the thoughts of the men of antiquity: it lures men, who have always known – or have known since at least the Neolithic – that

1   F. Braudel, *La Méditerranée. L'espace et l'histoire*, 1977.

2   G. Camps, *L'Histoire 13*, 1979, pp. 6-13; id.; in *3000 ans sur la mer, Les collections de L'Histoire 8*, 2000, p. 12; id., *Chronologie et synchronisme dans la préhistoire circum-méditerranéenne*, 1976; J. Guilaine, *Premiers bergers et paysans de l'Occident méditerranéen*, 1976; id., *La mer partagée*, 1994; G. Schule, in *IX Congresso nacional de Arqueologia*, 1968, p. 449.

mastery of the earth by agriculture is but one of the two objectives to be attained. Mastery of the sea requires other tactics and other techniques.

The study of maritime exchanges cannot be limited to a history of the means of transport – in this case, boats – based on navigation routes and the merchandise carried on the boats. It is also the history of a change in mentality, since maritime commerce is first and foremost a voyage, and, what is more, a voyage abroad. The Egyptian who sets off 'to exchange goods' becomes confronted by a local organisation that is different from his own. In spite of its institutional and ideological framework, its infrastructure, and its stereotyped character, is the everyday voyage faithfully represented in its lived reality by tales of expedition and exploration? In *The Tale of the Shipwrecked Sailor*, as in *The Report of Wenamun*, the vicissitudes, discoveries and miseries of the voyage are sometimes related. Although these texts are not travel journals, the reader is lured across the oceans and into fabulous regions. While Wenamun or the sailors of Hatshepsut experience the maritime space as a place of transit and displacement, the Shipwrecked Sailor seems to experience the sea as a fateful trial he must undergo if he is to complete his mission successfully, but exile is the absolute punishment.

For every Egyptian (and every ancient) traveller, there is no happy departure without the hope and expectation of a return. The voyage constitutes for Egyptian people an existential experience, whose many various implications can be read only over what Braudel calls the *longue durée*, since by gradually mastering the sea, he exorcises the fears that in prehistory had lurked there.

The theme of the Egyptian abroad is one of the favourites of Egyptian fiction. In the Middle Kingdom (2040-1782 BC) it occurs in *The Tale of the Shipwrecked Sailor* who is cast ashore on an island in the Red Sea where a giant serpent reigns. In the New Kingdom (1570-1070 BC) we also come across variants of the same subject in *The Story of the Two Brothers* whose hero Bata is an exile on the coast of Libya; in *The Tale of the Predestined Prince*, where the young man, fleeing his destiny, takes refuge in northern Syria. *The Report of Wenamun*, for its part, is set on the coasts of the eastern Mediterranean. Later on, we know of the story of a statue of Khonsu which is sent into the depths of Asia to cure the daughter of the Prince of Bakhtan and which is kept by the latter for nearly four years. Different legends refer to the goddesses who leave Egypt and go abroad, while Plutarch recounts that Osiris, shut up in a casket and thrown into the water, landed at Byblos. In short, 'for a sedentary people like the Egyptians, adventure lay abroad.'[3]

At the same time, the love of their native land that was so highly developed in the inhabitants of the Nile Valley meant that the highest wish of an expatriated Egyptian was to be able to return home. We find this wish expressed in a New Kingdom hymn to Amun, where we read, 'He who is in Syria [says]: 'Come and take me back to Egypt!''[4] and two characters of the 4th century relate how divine intervention has enabled them to realise their desire to return from Asia to Egypt.[5] The Desperate Man is already comparing the death that he longs for to returning from an expedition. So, in order to be fully satisfying, a travel narrative had to end with the successful return of the exile, and thus it is that the Shipwrecked Sailor returns safe and sound to the residence of the Pharaoh, that Bata ends up as king of Egypt, that the healing statue of Khonsu returns to Thebes, that the 'distant goddess' is restored to her father and that Isis brings Osiris's body to the shores of the Nile. For the two texts whose endings we have lost, the same conclusion is a certainty: in *The Report of Wenamun*, as proven by the existence of his narrative of the voyage; and it is also probable in the case of the Predestined Prince. What then are we to say of that masterpiece of Egyptian literature, *The Tale of Sinuhe*?[6]

Voyaging is thus not one of the privileges of modernity, but the voyage is always a dramatic change that enables people to escape from the destiny of their everyday life and discover the mystery of unknown lands, the fresh air of wide open spaces, the marvellous aspect of some ideal city. Voyagers of yesteryear, like those of today, have the same ambiguous relations, half fascination, half fear, with the elements; the sun, the sea, the mountains, the sky, the forests, the distant island, the forbidden city.[7] Very early on, people travelled out from the frontiers of their daily lives. The discovery of strange worlds, the attendant risks, and the confrontation with different peoples and customs all contributed to the enrichment of their vision of the world and of people. Indeed, travel was a powerful – the most powerful? – factor in the broadening of horizons and thus the extension of knowledge in antiquity. Initially motivated by economic factors, travel gave birth to curiosity and a certain sense of relativism. The Assyriologist G. Contenau is surely right in stating that 'every period has had its El Dorado, stuffed to overflowing with everything that its neighbours lacked – or at least, that was how it was imagined…' He adds, 'The notion of countries developing in isolation, lacking any communication with the exterior, a notion that was more or less that of the first historians of antiquity, has been gradually replaced by a more accurate understanding of the permeability of the ancient world.

The steady tread of asses, and then of the camels that comprised the caravan, was the same 3,000 years ago as it is today, and security on the trails they followed was hardly any better. The great barques with relatively few sails that still travel from one Syrian port to the next, watching the big ships that will link Beirut to Alexandria in a single night disappearing into the distance, used in bygone times to travel between those same points, at a slower but regular speed, without leaving the coasts and taking care to stop off at night in the shelter of a cape. The different parts of the ancient oriental world could be reached from one another as can those of the modern East – less quickly, of course, but without much more difficulty. The Silk Road that Marco Polo followed was already supplying Sassanid Iran and Byzantium with precious fabrics.

3    G. Posener, *Littérature et politique*, 1956, p. 90. On the representation of the relations between Egypt and foreigners in literature, see the analyses of A. Loprieno, *Annuaire de l'EPHE V (Section des sciences religieuses)* 108, 1999-2000, pp. 163-165; id., *la pensée et l'écriture*, 2001, pp. 51-88.

4    Ostrakon in the Cairo Museum, cited by G. Posener, *op. cit.*, p. 90.

5    *Urk.* II, 4; J. J. Clère, *RdÉ* 6, pp. 148, 153.

6    On the notion of the voyage in Ancient Egypt, see, for instance, the reflections of J. Yoyotte, in *Les Pèlerinages, Sources Orientales* III, 1960, pp. 19-74; M. Malaise, in J. Chélini, H. Branthomme (ed.), *Histoire des pèlerinages non chrétiens*, 1987, pp. 55-82; É. Bernand, in M. M. Mactoux, E. Geny, *Mélanges Pierre Lévêque*, 1988, pp. 49-63; H. Beinlich, in *LÄ* VI, 1986, *s.v.* 'Wallfahrt', col. 1145-1146; M. Valloggia, *Recherche sur les « Messagers » (Wpwtyw)*, 1976; Y. Volokhine, in D. Frankfurter (ed.), *Pilgrimage and Holy Space in Late Antique Egypt, Religions in the Graeco-Roman World* 134, 1998, pp. 51-97; C. Cannuyer, in Chr. Cannuyer, J. Ries, A. Van Tongerloo (ed.), *les voyages dans les civilisations orientales, Acta Orientalia Belgica* XI, 1998, pp. 6-7; G. Moers, in G. Moers (ed.), *Definitel : Egyptian Literature, Lingua Aegyptia. Studia monographica* 2, 1999, pp. 43-61.

7    J.-P. Laurent, *Le voyage*, 1995.

*'Egypt is the gift of the Nile.'* Hapy, a divine manifestation of the Nile flood, discovered out at sea in the Bay of Aboukir.
© HILTI Foundation/Franck Goddio. Photo: Christoph Gerigk

Relief on the Mastaba of Ifi at Saqqara, Old Kingdom, middle of the 3<sup>rd</sup> millennium BC. © Archivo Iconografico, S.A./CORBIS

There was a powerful motive behind all this commercial expansionism, one whose importance tends to be forgotten in the modern era: the need for spices (a need that has survived) and for incense, which every cult used in large quantities and which, thanks to the general religiosity, constituted a vital product of major importance; and it was the Egyptians who went to Punt and brought back the incense trees represented on the temple of Deir el-Bahari. To answer this need, nomadic peoples became sedentary, protectors and organisers of the caravans that they had previously pillaged: this is the secret that explains the rise of the Nabataeans and Palmyra, the wealth of Himyar and Hadramut, the only countries to possess gold when their neighbours in Arabia had none. At first sight, it seems as if the driving forces of history had totally changed since antiquity; this is not correct, since they seem to be the same. This becomes evident when, by chance, certain clues put us on the trail of the reasons that lay behind all the great expeditions of the past.' [8]

Originally arising from the necessities of trade or the desire for conquest, 'voyaging thus became a constitutive part of the culture of the ancient Orient, and it soon became laden with didactic, symbolic and even religious values. Nostalgia for one's native land, the excitement of departure, the lure of the open sea, and the disappointments encountered en route inspired writers and poets, and suggested maxims and practical advice to sages. Sometimes the voyage appeared as a special time, in which people learned and grew, but more often, it inspired fear, since it exposed sailors to every fatigue, to uncertainty, to accidents, to a thousand unknown dangers, and even death... As an experience of life or as a training in danger,

8    G. Conteneau, *La vie quotidienne à Babylone et en Assyrie*, 1950, pp. 87-90.

voyaging bore its fruits only if it was nourished by a certain ethic. It is understandable, in these conditions, that voyaging and the state of 'dramatic change' it entailed were experienced as a means of rejecting the world, society and even religion. The voyager thus becomes a crook and his wanderings are transformed into rebellion [...]'[9]

This leads us to ponder the particular world of the professionals of voyaging. A ship at sea is an enclosed realm, an autonomous space and time of life; it is total in the sense that in this space, and in it alone, during a definite time (that which a crew spends on board), they must count only on their own strength to the exclusion of all external help. Life on board ship is subject to a specific religious rule, as well a juridical, moral, political and ethical rule, which to a great extent escape our grasp. The length of the journey – the period of enclosure – is a fundamental factor in the way different categories of sailors may be discerned. In the long term, two successive types of life are associated, the one at sea, the other on land: two concomitant periods with two different spaces.

Another factor is linked to the first; the ever-present risk in peoples' lives as soon as they embark. This risk is physical, social and psychological. These crews have a particular relationship to risk, and they develop means of coming to terms with it consciously or not, such as the establishment of what the ethnographer calls a 'formal consensus' within the framework of highly hierarchical relations. In this high-risk universe, peoples' beliefs enable them to protect themselves from the sea. In maritime writings, as well as those of historians and sailors, we often come across this quotation generally attributed to Plato: 'There are the living, the dead, and sailors.'[10] In reality, it seems to have been attributed to Bias, one of the seven sages of Greece, whom Plato claims to be quoting:[11] 'Let us take the sailor who navigates through so many perils and who is, as Bias has said, neither among the dead nor among the living; for man who is made for the earth launches out on to the sea like an amphibian and places himself entirely at the mercy of fortune.'

It is the meaning of this quotation that matters, since it demonstrates the continuity in the place sailors have occupied in collective representations for several millennia. They are 'neither dead, nor living', so they are on the world's margins. But there is also a continuity in the risks they run. 'Neither dead, nor living' means they are between, they are no longer altogether living, and not yet dead, for 'man [...] is made for the earth'.

## ... a commercial voyage

The Mediterranean, like the Red Sea, was never, particularly during the epochs under consideration, a unified space under the sole domination of one cultural and political power. The study of travel and displacement conceived within the framework of commercial exchange will lead us inexorably along the routes of frontiers, border countries that served as a background for certain major episodes in the history of Ancient Egypt: population movements, military campaigns, mining expeditions and pilgrimages. But also, economic circuits linking Africa and Asia and extending from the Mediterranean Basin to the Red Sea. Embracing the wide variety of aspects that sprang from commercial activity, it is necessary to reflect on the economic world that constituted, so to speak, the area in which juridical structures acted as the framework for exchange, and at the same time it must be borne in mind that all the interlocking

political aspects that linked different peoples in a way that, these days, we would call international. The documentation bears witness to the fact that commerce was a daily activity.

From prehistory onwards the reality of exchange was unquestionable; it is highly probable that the practice of reciprocating presents, the existence of traders, and the sealing of jars or bundles are all signs of their growing importance. The long slow evolution of prehistory, far from occurring in a closed environment, was studded with fruitful exchanges with cultural zones that were often very far away. The Egypt of the time before history was included within the circuits of an intercontinental circulation of raw or fabricated goods (Afghan lapis, Abyssinian obsidian, Syrian and Nubian vases, Mesopotamian cylinders, and so on) and also of techniques. From Palestine, wheat and barley (4500 BC at the latest), the vine and metallurgy (4th millennium BC) were imported, either by migrations or by gradually spreading from one region to the next.

It was around the middle of the 3rd millennium BC that the influence Egypt's greatness had over the Near East can be glimpsed in concrete form. Over 20 or more centuries, from the time of the first Pharaohs to that of the Persians, following the rhythm of empires as they waxed and waned, there was a succession of ideas and techniques that were exchanged in a confused and fruitful way across Asia. Egypt, conquering and conquered, found itself inevitably involved in this first concert of the peoples. Asia was to present it with some noteworthy gifts: bronze, the olive tree, the horse, the lyre, palm-leaf mouldings, and international law. Going in the other direction, exchanges of gifts, princesses and experts, and the gradual growth of trade, spread an appreciation of the gilded values of Egypt among its peers: Babylon, the Hittites, the Assyrians, later on the Lydians and the Persians; and in Palestine and the Lebanon, across which periodically tramped the soldiers and scribes of the Pharaohs, 'colonising' Egypt yielded its 'secrets' to the Asiatics. Scarabs, amulets, bronze, vases and caskets were imported in their thousands, counterfeited and re-exported throughout the Mediterranean world. On the ivories that decorated the royal furniture of Phoenicia and Syria, on the paterae, the steles and buildings of Phoenicia, many Egyptian motifs, some of which became popular across Assyria and Persia, were copied, with varying degrees of skill.

It is also true that wars and far-flung expeditions were often motivated by the desire or need to acquire products one did not have. So the system of exchange was complex and cannot be reduced to an over-schematic and thus simplistic picture. Certainly, urbanisation itself cannot be explained without realising that a growing commercial activity intervened in the process. Not only is it indispensable to realise that the mere development of agriculture, even on a large scale, can lead to the urban stage, but the very life of cities is based on a diversification of activities and a system of extended relations that characterise the development of the network of exchanges. In Egypt these exchanges were to a great extent under the supervision of the centralised state that came into being at the

9    C. Cannuyer, *op. cit.*, pp. 6-7.

10   This is the title of the work by the ethnologist M. Duval, *Ni morts, ni vivants : marins!* (1999) [i.e., *Neither dead, nor living: sailors!*]

11   See E. Chambry, in *Platon, Œuvres complètes*, vol. 8, 1950, p. 252; translation, p. 260.

end of the 4$^{th}$ millennium BC. They mobilised a significant proportion of the administration that controlled and managed the raw materials, from the time they were produced and/or imported to the stage of their transformation and delivery. The officials and personnel of the expeditions of production or trade, as well as the elite of the craftsmen, were agents of the state. In this system, the question of the existence of private maritime activities raises itself in an acute form, as does that of the place that fell to individuals in different types of exchange, as they were deemed to be under the total control of the state. It thus becomes easy to understand why we need to set this investigation within a particular political, geopolitical, social, cultural and chronological framework and see it as part of a twofold scheme of things, belonging to internal and external trade.

The internal trade of Ancient Egypt developed on two levels: first, the short-range trade that concerned individual exchange; then, state-owned trade, controlled by the officials of the temple (or of the property granted in exchange for service), exercised over the entire territory by specialised state agents, and involving vast quantities of specific products.

External trade, for its part, met the need for commodities, merchandise and various goods that were not produced or happened to be in short supply in Egyptian territory.

The evolution and developments that can be seen in commercial exchanges on the inter-state level are conclusive. Above, the great antiquity of commercial practices in the west of Asia and the east of Africa, converging on Egypt and its opening on to the Mediterranean and the Red Sea was stressed. As a consequence of this vast historical framework and geographical space the Egyptian maritime venture must be placed at the heart of a broader question: that of the role played by the Egyptian state and that of the great economic intermediaries (for instance, the temples and the real estate held by the dignitaries) in the organisation, regulation and taxation of commerce. Other questions derive from this: what was the margin for manoeuvre of traders, both in relation to Egypt and to their original country, if they were foreigners? To what period are we to attribute the great juridical interventions bearing on the risks of large-scale naval commerce? To what extent did the state intervene in international commerce: economic structures, institutional framework, juridical instruments, land taxes, river taxes, harbour taxes, toll fees, customs, and so on? As a result, in which places were customs dues exacted and what strategic and economic roles could certain cities play?

Of course, in ancient times, there was a circulation and exchange of products between Egypt and Asia Minor, Cyprus, Syro-Palestine and Babylonia – in accordance with complex and manifold processes and circuits. In addition, the study of products and varieties of merchandise constitutes over and above the analysis of their production and diffusion, a means of observing the relations between the institutional structures and the daily life of the Ancient Egyptians. The links between agents, commercial activities and legal rules appear infinitely complex.

By investigating the circumstances of, and the different forms assumed by, maritime relations between Egypt and the countries on its borders – sometimes under its economic, political or cultural influence – and between Egypt and 'distant' countries, we may then analyse the rules and the legal precedents that could be applied to the progress of a commercial voyage: the procedures to be followed in order to gain access to commerce within the Mediterranean or outside it, the hiring of ship's captains, the commercial associations, the right of embargo, judicial procedures in foreign *emporia*, the diplomatic immunity of commercial intermediaries, the right of shipwreck, and so on.

This leads to the question: what were the major routes of maritime navigation and the itineraries followed by merchants and their merchandise? What was the role played by ports, mooring grounds and the different infrastructures underlying the logistics involved in shifting goods (naval shipyards, cradles for laying up ships over the winter, entrepots for merchandise, markets, and so on) in the organisation of those commercial lines? How did people travel 'commercially': many transits, numerous transhipments, journeys with short stages or long stopovers? How was business organised to follow the paths laid open by conquest and exploration, and how did it react when the inhabited world known to the Egyptians expanded, and when their representation of the world changed scale?

The circulation of goods and persons raises several questions. First of all, the role of foreigners, and especially that of resident foreigners; then the inevitable subject of war and conquest that both make commerce dependent on the new rules emerging from the relations between the native administration and that of the occupant; finally, the definition of the economic systems used by the different protagonists in commerce and the means that authorise exchange, for instance, coinage or its equivalent in heavy goods.

Moreover, in order to describe commerce, we need to define the notions at our disposal, and this is no easy thing. The theme of commerce offers perspectives that could not be more contemporary – too much so, at times! When certain people draw a comparison, setting the relations between Egypt and the Near East on one side and those between the great powers and the Third World on the other, they are referring to problems that are current in ways that are often painful. Might it be that commercial links, such as the relationship in which 'money' occupies the central place, can lead, in the international domain, to nothing more than one group controlling another? In Ancient Egypt, the civil servant was considered superior to the trader; today, with globalisation, the merchant tends to occupy first place. That's another story – but a story that concerns us all, and this human community indubitably leads us to forge links with men who lived thousands of years ago.

The social implications go some way to explaining the permanence of the questions that may be raised about commercial activities. Furthermore, the modernisation of concepts hits us very hard. Today's words are not necessarily well adapted to describe and explain yesterday's realities. Thus we are rather hesitant to use even such a term as 'commerce' without due caution, insofar as this word refers in our daily life to a set of economic transactions that do not correspond to the reality of ancient systems of exchange.

Commerce opens up two different aspects of the same economic and social reality, one which impels a civilisation to embark on seafaring in order to seek something it cannot find at home. The very themes of voyage and displacement imply a questioning of intercultural, interregional and inter-state relations. Are the decisive moments of progress in a civilisation necessarily to be explained in terms of 'movements' or vague cultural 'influences', whose origin is always external to the culture in question and often, indeed, lies outside the country under consideration? Migrations, the displacement of populations, and the spread of ideas lay behind certain changes. Nonetheless, it remains indispensable and necessary to explain the very ideas of voyage and displacement – of persons, objects and ideas – in terms of social and economic processes that are fully visible in the main metamorphoses that Egypt underwent.

One of the interests in the maritime destiny of Pharaonic Egypt is crystallised in establishing that a contact between two populations was established, in showing that goods, and without any doubt ideas with them, circulated from one point to another. Commerce would then be an indicator of displacements and influences. The influence of one culture on another, or even the diffusion of the progress brought about by a civilisation along the axes of circulation, should not be exaggerated. It will therefore be necessary to consider the phenomenon of the circulation of goods and persons as both a proof of contacts between more or less distant countries, and as a sign that new social relations have been created within the society itself. In other words, the circulation of objects, of raw materials (as of persons and ideas) reveals the internal developments of society as much as the external influences on it. The circulation and probably the exchange of goods, and the transport of merchandise over greater or lesser distances, leads us to think about the way commercial relations came into being, about their organisation, their social significance, and the consequences that they entailed for society itself. On the other hand, it must be repeated, 'commerce' remains an ambiguous and imprecise term, so long as it is not known exactly how the objects and raw materials were transported or exchanged. The organisation of the social set-up may happen in small stages – the object passes from village to village, from town to town, and further afield, – with each place keeping part of what it acquires and putting the rest back into distribution; or it may happen over longer distances, with the trader bringing a cargo to a distant destination to sell it. But these types of distribution are many and varied and depend on the political, economic, and cultural structure of the society or societies envisaged.[12]

## … and a history of techniques

The importance of ships as instruments for fishing, migration, commerce, war and discovery is so great that it justifies the constant interest that has been shown in them for centuries. Likewise, 'the particularities of structure, and the shapes and modes of construction of ancient ships are the elements of one of the most exciting chapters in the history of technology'.[13] To try and sketch out the maritime history of Ancient Egypt also involves taking an interest in the history of techniques, one which touches on numerous domains in archaeology and history in general. This is a rapidly evolving discipline in which the debate bears fundamentally on the nature of technological innovation, the way it is made manifest and the role it plays in society.

There was a period when envisaging the study of innovation in antiquity was considered to be an absurdity. Until the 1980s, many specialists in antiquity had endeavoured, on the contrary, to try and explain why the ancient world would have been incapable of evolving in this domain, marked by what is suitably called a 'technological block'. The men of ancient times – so the argument ran – added little to the stock of technical knowledge or to people's set of tools. And it was fashionable to come out with a few clichés in

the wake of Captain G. Lefebvre des Noëttes: it was in the Middle Ages that navigation was transformed by the discovery of the stern post rudder and the triangular lateen sail, while the ancient oar and the square sail had previously made only coastal trade possible.

This view corresponded to a liberal modernist conception of the economy, which deemed that unfavourable economic conditions (the size of business enterprises, the dimension of cities, the lack of capital) necessarily blocked all technological development. Also, for the proponents of Marxist theses, the mode of production and class struggle explained the embargo on technological development. Now, an ethnological approach has shown that innovations may develop in tandem with factors that remain the same, and that the reasons that lie behind technological conservatism do not reside in any block on development or reliance on routine. The interest taken by certain specialists in specific areas has placed a question mark over earlier assertions about technology. Thus, very quickly in the history of ships and sailing, the role of the stern post rudder was qualified. The latest contribution, one which has completely renewed the approach to the history of technology, is that made by archaeology.[14]

Recent research has made clear the diversity and wealth of transportation, the originality of certain techniques, and an efficiency and technical accomplishment that render traditional ideas about low yield and inadequacy obsolete. The minimalist model described above demonstrates that every pre-industrial economy is by nature and by virtue of its situation 'primitive' with regard to the western industrial economies of the last two centuries. A re-examination of the sources, pragmatic approaches, and the accumulation of evidence leads us to realise that there are significant contradictions between the facts on the one hand and received ideas on the other, and tend to demonstrate the technological validity of the means of transport.[15]

Generally speaking, recent work emphasises the adequacy of the responses and the technological solutions to the problems encountered. During antiquity, heavy loads could be transported, sometimes in great quantities, and the necessary logistical means could be deployed. People were quite able to show great inventiveness in resolving a new difficulty or coming to terms with an original problem. In short, innovation had its own place in Ancient Egypt.

12  See C. Renfrew, *The Emergence of Civilization*, 1972; *id.*, *The Explanation of Culture Change, Models in Prehistory*, 1973; *id.*, in J. A. Sabloff, C. C. Lamberg-Karlowsky (ed.), *Ancient Civilizations and Trade*, 1975, pp. 3-60; *id.*, in T. K. Earle, J. E. Ericson, *Exchange systems in Prehistory*, 1977, pp. 71-90; *id.*, *La Recherche* n° 331, 2000, pp. 48-50; B. C. Renfrew, P. Bahn, *Archaeology – Theories, Methods and Practice*, 1996, pp. 351-384; B. B. Sternquist, *Models of Commercial Diffusion in Prehistoric Times*, 1965-1966; B. D. Clarke, *Models in Archaeology*, 1972.

13  L. Basch, *Le Musée imaginaire de la marine*, 1987, p. 17.

14  For all these questions: M-C. Amouretti, in D. Meeks, D. Garcia (ed.), *Techniques et économie antiques et médiévales*, 1997, pp. 7-12. See also M.-C. Amouretti, J.-P. Brun (ed.), *La production du vin et de l'huile en Méditerranée*, BCH suppl. 26, 1993; M. Daumas, (dir.), *Histoire générale des techniques*, vol. 1, 1962. B. Jacomy, *Une histoire des techniques*, 1990. A. Pauly, G. Wissowa, W. Kroll, *Paulys Real-Encyclopädie der classischen Altertumswissenschaft*, 1894-1951.

15  *cf.* G. Raepsaet, in D. Meeks, D. Garcia (ed.), *op. cit.*, pp. 137-138. Such re-evaluation has already been applied to Roman history; see P. Pomey, *L'Histoire* 36, 1981, pp. 96-101.

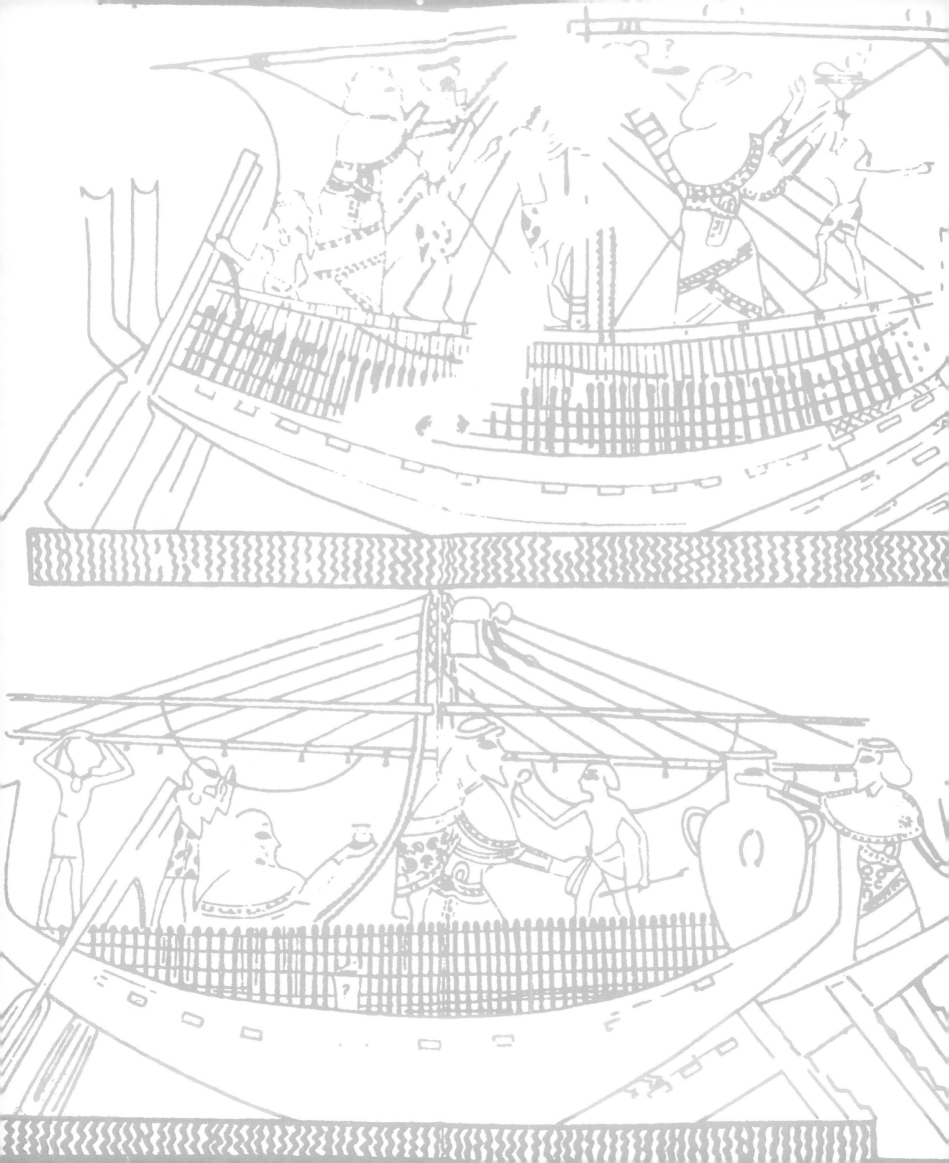

# 1
# EGYPT AND THE SEA

# From Snefru to underwater archaeology

From an early date, Pharaonic Egypt was in contact with countries outside it; this much is proved by the products discovered there that originated from abroad, such as the spices from Africa or the wood from Lebanon, but also by the monuments and by various literary texts. From the Old Kingdom (2686-2181 BC) onwards maritime relations between Egypt and Syro-Palestine were clearly established. Snefru, Userkaf, Sahure, Djekara-Isesi, Unas, Teti, and Pepi II all sent their ships out to the coasts of Asia. They were followed by the ships of the Amenemhats and the Senusrets. Maritime expeditions across the Red Sea, in the direction of Punt, are also attested, from the Old and Middle Kingdom (2040-1782 BC) onwards: the texts mention those that set out in the reigns of Sahure, Djekara-Isesi, Unas, Teti, Pepi II, Mentuhotep III, Senusret I and Amenemhat II.[1]

Among the 'traditional' sources that help to provide us with information about the Egyptian maritime adventure, there figure literary, papyrological, epigraphical, and archaeological sources. Detailed drawings, reduced-scale models and originals, an entire technical vocabulary specifying the various different types of boat and listing the details of their frames, all comprise a resource offered by Egypt to the historians of river navigation. Sources referring to maritime ships and sailing are less full and detailed. They raise all the usual questions of interpretation, in some cases because we never know how far to trust them, in others because the data with which they provide us are difficult to understand.

Maritime tales, such as the famous *Tale of the Shipwrecked Sailor*,[2] being semi-fictional, raise problems of interpretation that apparently stem from well worn themes, or *topoi*.[3] This tale, half exotic novel, half mythological narrative, prefigures the voyages of Sinbad the Sailor, and is the story of a shipwreck that occurred perhaps in the Red Sea, as related by a travelling companion to an official who has been cast ashore during his mission. The shipwrecked man has found himself on a marvellous island that belongs to a serpent. We learn that this serpent, endowed with supernatural powers, was the sole survivor of a celestial catastrophe. He is the possessor of various valuable products from the land of Punt, and predicts to the unfortunate Egyptian that he will be saved, while showering him with presents. The extraordinary wealth of themes in this (short) text means that it has been one of the most commented-on and translated works in Egyptian literature. Despite the fictional character of the narrative, the everyday realities of the period sometimes slip into the *topos* and enrich our knowledge of the ships of the period and the conditions of sea voyages.

*The Report of Wenamun* is precise when it comes to the itinerary followed by the boat through the eastern Mediterranean, but this does little to describe conditions and techniques of navigation. Nonetheless, a piece of evidence such as this, by its very nature, will keep us company all through this book. The text describes an expedition led by the 'keeper of the porch' of Amun's domain, Wenamun, who has been given the task of fetching wood from Byblos, to rebuild the great river barque of Amun. He leaves Upper Egypt, goes first to Tanis, the new capital of Lower Egypt, and from there is sent on a ship towards the Levant. During a stopover in the port of Dor, some of the goods entrusted to Wenamun are stolen by one of the crew members. Finally reaching Byblos, after many adventures and vicissitudes, he embarks on commercial negotiations

that are concluded by a sale. He sets off with his cargo, but a storm drives him on to the shore at Alasia. The text breaks off when Wenamun is negotiating with the authorities in Alasia so as to avoid falling victim to the right of shipwreck. A certain number of points about the authenticity of the tale need to be established.[4]

Agreement about the degree of credibility of the document has not yet been reached. The idea that it was an authentic report drawn up by Wenamun on his return from his mission was already defended by W. Golenischeff, the text's first editor,[5] and it has been supported by J. Cerny.[6] The Czech Egyptologist believes that the way the manuscript is set out, with lines of writing following a direction perpendicular to that of the fibres of the papyrus rather than being parallel to it, allows us to distinguish it from literary works and to identify it as an administrative document. However, G. Möller drew on palaeography to date the document to the 22nd Dynasty (c. 950–730 BC),[7] at least a century later than the supposed period of the voyage. Indeed, A. Korostovcev considers that the manuscript we possess is merely a copy of the original.[8] H. Goedicke has also spoken out in favour of assigning this manuscript to the 22nd Dynasty.[9] According to this author, this is a copy that was drawn up with relation to a similar expedition whose course is briefly summarised on the reverse side of the document. It seems rather difficult to believe that the papyrus preserved constitutes the original of a report, since the error in the date committed at the head of the manuscript is barely conceivable in a piece of writing of this sort.[10] Furthermore, the picaresque feel of the story (as J. A. Wilson called it),[11] the anecdotal nature of certain passages, and the extraordinary aspect of others, would hardly be appropriate in an official's report. *The Report of Wenamun* more closely resembles a historical novel – and this indeed is how G. Lefebvre describes it[12] – than an archival document. This problem in defining the nature of the text has been compounded by a debate relative to the geographical space circumscribed by the voyage of Amun's envoy, and we need to take

---

1   See, for example, the lists drawn up by J. Degas, *Égypte. Afrique & Orient* 1, 1996, pp. 18-22; S. Aufrère, *Égypte. Afrique & Orient* 1, 1996, pp. 23-27. Numerous historical works mention these maritime contacts: for example J. Vercoutter, *L'Égypte et la vallée du Nil*, 1992; N. Grimal, *Histoire de l'Égypte ancienne*, 1988.

2   *The Shipwrecked Man*: P. Saint Petersburg 1115, unknown origin, preserved in Moscow. See for instance G. Lefebvre, *Romans et contes*, 1949, pp. 29-40; M. Lichtheim, *Ancient Egyptian Literature*, I, 1975, pp. 211-215; W. K. Simpson, *LÄ* V, 1983, s. v. 'Schiffbrüchiger', col. 619-622; J. Baines, *JEA* 76, 1990, p. 55; C. Vandersleyen, in *Studies in Egyptology presented to M. Lichtheim*, II, 1990, pp. 1023-1024; C. Cannuyer, in C. Cannuyer, J. Ries, A. Van Tongerloo (ed.), *Les voyages dans les civilisations orientales*, Acta Orientalia Belgica XI, 1998, pp. 27-42; P. Grandet, *Contes*, 1998.

3   These *topoi* are very well known in classical Greek and Roman literature; *cf.* J. Rougé, *La marine dans l'Antiquité*, 1975, pp. 10-11.

4   G. Bunnens, *Revista di Studi Fenici* 6, 1978, pp. 2-3.

5   W. Golenischeff, *RT* 21, 1899, p. 74.

6   J. Cerny quoted by G. Lefebvre, *RdÉ* 6, 1951, p. 41, n. 8, and particularly J. Cerny, *Paper and Books in Ancient Egypt*, 1952, pp. 21-22; *id.*, in S. Donadoni (ed.), *Le fonti indirette della storia egiziana*, 1963, pp. 54-55.

7   G. Möller, *Hieratische Lesestücke*, II, 1910, p. 29.

8   M. A. Korostovcev, *Putesestviye Un-Amuna v Bibl*, 1960, pp. 16-17.

9   H. Goedicke, *The Report of Wenamun*, 1975, p. 7.

10  M. A. Korostovcev, *Putesestviye Un-Amuna v Bibl*, 1960, p. 16. See G. Lefebvre, *CdÉ* XXI, 1936, pp. 97-99; *id.*, *Romans et contes*, 1949, pp. 207-208, suggested correcting the text. On the other hand, H. Goedicke, *The Report of Wenamun*, 1975, pp. 17-18, 24-25, 27, tries to justify it.

11  J. A. Wilson, in J. B. Pritchard, *ANET*, 1969, p. 25.

12  G. Lefebvre, *op. cit.*, p. 205; *cf.* J. Leclant, in W. A. Ward (ed.), *The Role of the Phoenicians in the Interaction of Mediterranean Civilizations*, 1968, p. 9.

Gigantic head of a Ptolemaic ruler, ancient coast of the Portus Magnus of Alexandria.
© HILTI Foundation/Franck Goddio. Photo: Christoph Gerigk

up a position vis-à-vis this question. Whatever the truth of the matter, nothing obliges us to think that the sea voyage of Wenamun described in this document is very different from those that were really carried out. It will be possible to make use of this text, and read between its lines with the help of other sources, to shed light on the conditions of navigation in that highly particular maritime space, the eastern Mediterranean.

Papyrological and epigraphical texts sometimes raise problems of interpretation due to their poor state of preservation, and the way we fill in the gaps is, in spite of everything, subject to a degree of uncertainty. These sources often refer to technical terms (names of individuals involved in maritime business, names of ships and parts of ships, and so on) that are difficult to understand. But the literary and thematic wealth of the texts from Pharaonic Egypt always makes them texts of the greatest interest.

As well as the numerous documents relating to trade routes and objects of commerce that archaeology provides, the study of the documents permits an idea of that essential instrument of the sea voyage, the ship. This 'traditional' archaeology comprises representations of ships: bas-reliefs, paintings, graffiti, small-scale models, and so on, that will be presented below. These media also pose problems of preservation, dating, and so on. Morover, when a monument can be dated, this does not mean that it represents a contemporary reality, so we need to be wary of the *topoi* of representations of parts or elements of ships. Furthermore, the greater or lesser skill of the artist has to be taken into account.[13] L. Basch is quite right to quote this comment by A. Jal: 'On every painted or sculpted naval representation, of whatever period, we need to perform a labour of critical interpretation analogous to that which is applied to the words of a historian or poet who describes or relates something, and may have been poorly informed about the fact he is reporting, or may not use the proper terms, for lack of understanding or precise information. The same applies to documents, works that issue from the artist's hands, as applies to any work in which imagination and discernment play a part: error is always to be presumed, until we find proof of the contrary.'[14] The importance of ethnographic relativism should also be stressed, along with the long maritime tradition that can at times be extremely valuable in understanding naval constructions.

'Almost all the beauties of a ship are below the water; the rest is dead works,' said Paul Valéry.[15] It is now obvious, as J. Rougé realised already in 1975, that underwater archaeology increasingly tends to be one of our best sources of information, but it also has its limits. In coming to the aid of texts and illustrated documents, the analysis of wrecks has renewed those controversial questions of the tonnage and the seafaring capabilities of the merchant ships of antiquity. Although no wreck of an Egyptian type has been found thus far, the fact remains that underwater archaeology has already enabled us to solve a number of unresolved questions about naval construction in Egypt and elsewhere. The main problem is still that of the preservation of submerged wrecks, and the study of the stowage of cargoes is difficult because, more often than not, shipwrecks are the consequence of intemperate weather or reefs; the ships have keeled over or have been so thoroughly gutted that the cargoes have not been left in place. In addition, the ships have often sunk on sloping ground; so the cargo often smashed through the deck, when there was one, and was scattered over a broad area.

An ideal situation, as J. Rougé has so clearly pointed out, is to find the wreck of a ship (Egyptian if possible) that sank vertically on to a flat sea bottom as a result of being overloaded in excess of the permitted limits. Even in that situation, 'certain pieces of necessary information would still be unattainable, since there is little chance that the rigging could have been preserved, due to the nature of its constituent parts, which are essentially biodegradable materials. There may be a possibility of discovering the position of the mast in relation to the centre of the ship, an essential item of information to shed light on how far it was possible for ancient ships to sail into the wind and to tack.

One of the main contributions of underwater archaeology, once more data is available, concerns the economic relations between one country and another: the merchandise transported, its origin and

---

13   J. Rougé, *La marine dans l'Antiquité*, 1975, p. 13.

14   A. Jal, *Archéologie navale*, 1840, quoted by L. Basch, *Le Musée imaginaire de la marine*, 1987, p. 17.

15   P. Valéry, *Mer, Marines, Marins. Regards sur la mer*, 1930.

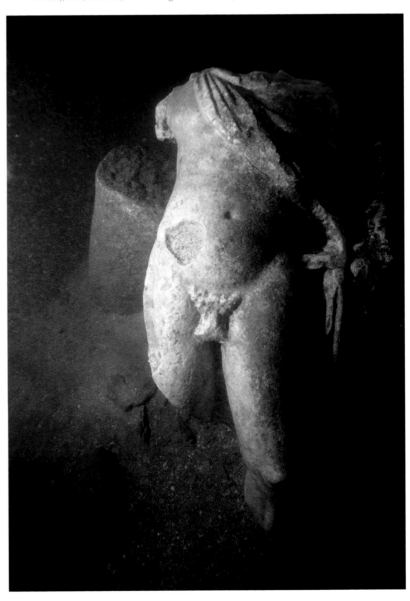

Headless statue of Hermes, Roman period, Portus Magnus of Alexandria.
© HILTI Foundation/Franck Goddio. Photo: Jérôme Delafosse

3

destination, the routes followed. Regarding the last point, there is always the reality that only wrecks near the coast can be studied and that routes out on the high seas may always remain unknown.'[16]

In Egypt, for the time being, underwater archaeology has enabled light to be shed on a range of data, sometimes spectacular, relative to the ports established on the western fringe of the Nile Delta. Even if they do not entirely concern the historical period dealt with in this book, it is pertinent to take stock of one of the largest underwater excavations ever undertaken.

In the Portus Magnus of Alexandria and the roadstead of Aboukir, the research went beyond anyone's expectations. The history of Alexandria has assumed a new dimension – or rather a new 'depth' – ever since the European Institute of Underwater Archaeology (Institut Européen d'Archéologie Sous-Marine: IEASM), established in 1995, explored that part of the city founded by Alexander the Great that today lies submerged.[17] In 1988 Franck Goddio made contact with the team of the Atomic Energy Authority, specialised in nuclear magnetic resonance. Applying these methods to archaeology, the IEASM was able to use state-of-the-art magnetometers. In *Sunken Egypt*, the discoverer explains the underwater archaeology methods that he applied. The data gathered from the sea floor were processed by computers on board the research catamaran. Splendid photographs enabled observers to follow the minute charts that were drawn up and the systematic study of the remains that were found.

It is not possible to list here all the antiquities discovered and brought to light or left under the protecting waters. Diving down into the sea and diving back in time like this has revealed the most diverse monuments. For example, the head of the Roman emperor Claudius (AD 41-54), the headless body of a figure of Hermes recognisable by its mantle fastened at the right shoulder, remains of a Sphinx, the headless statue of a priest of Isis, a gigantic head which has been interpreted as that of one of the Ptolemies, a field of pillars broken and strewn about, as it were, by some giant hand, a falcon's head with a human ear, a Pharaoh's head-dress and a lion's body. A whole lyrical catalogue could be drawn up in this way. The most moving discovery was perhaps that of a golden ring found on the site of the Poseidium. It inspired many thoughts. Might this jewel have belonged to the celebrated Cleopatra? We knew the length of her nose – why not the thickness of her finger? It is safe to assume that Cleopatra's palace has not been discovered and never can be discovered, since this whole part of the ancient city vanished at the time when the modern corniche was built.

Thanks to a new procedure, which employs a membrane of silicon applied on to the submerged stone, casts can be made for epigraphists to study on dry land. It was in this way that inscriptions dating from the reigns of Commodus (AD 180-92) and Caracalla (AD 211-17) have been brought to light.

Egyptologists were overwhelmed by the discovery of a black granite stele at Herakleion, which has been studied by Jean Yoyotte.[18] He has established, with his customary exactness, that 'what may be read, on the faces of the stele, of the titles borne by the divinity whose image dwelt in this *naos*, enables the observer to recognise his original functions. This god, the inscription informs us, was the one who brought the king to power. It is also stated that he held the object called the *mekes*, and that he resided in the House of Rejoicing; this is the palace where the pharaoh's throne is set up and where he appears in glory. The *mekes* is the receptacle which the pharaohs grasp, having taken possession of it when they acceded to the throne.' Jean Yoyotte emphasises that 'the most amazing of the discoveries and the most decisive of them all resides in another stele, that which is a twin, or almost a twin, of the stele from Year Two of the reign of Nekhtnebef, which had been found in Naukratis in 1890: the same material, the same quality of execution.' He concludes, 'Here is a case of two versions of the same document, concerning two cities distant from one another, having been by chance preserved in the very places where they had been exhibited in antiquity, very close to the point where each of them had been initially erected.' These artefacts will be examined in more detail below.

In the shallow but vast Bay of Aboukir, the IEASM team discovered the quays and basins of a great ancient port. We are starting to think that the real port of Alexandria was perhaps not in the city, but in this bay. All these discoveries, founded on reliable information, and carried out on the basis of ultra-modern methods (which it would be a good idea for contemporary technocrats to place at the disposal of public research), show the derisory nature of the recent fanciful stories circulating about one of the Seven Wonders of the Ancient World.

## On various stereotypes

Natural, technical and economic conditions have always acted as obstacles and factors in sea voyages. The fact remains that some of them, having become a sort of psychological 'block', are nothing other than modern *topoi*, as J. Rougé defined them, and they have harmed, and continue to harm, the understanding and study of navigation.[19]

The notion of 'maritime peoples' is one of these stereotypes. There are, it would appear, peoples who are naturally inclined to the sea and others who are just as naturally distrustful of the sea and navigation. For example, the Greek and Phoenician peoples were maritime peoples and the Egyptians were an earthbound or at best 'river-dwelling' people.

The poor quality of ancient sailors and their fear of the sea, obliging them, as soon as they could, to take a route on dry land; the very low tonnage of the ships; the impossibility of navigating at night and/or out on the open sea, and so on – all these fuel other clichés about ancient navigation.

It is claimed that the responsibility for this situation should be imputed to the steering apparatus. This at least is the 'scientific' explanation for the different assertions put forward, in 1935, by Captain Lefebvre des Nöettes.[20] For him, in fact, the ancient rudder, consisting of one or two big oars at the stern of the ship, was a rudimentary device, ill-suited to navigation on the high seas, with the exception of a few well known routes that could take advantage of the existence of favourable regular winds. So, 'logically', it ensued that only coasting and low tonnages could be envisaged. The appearance

---

16    J. Rougé, *op. cit.*, p. 16.

17    Periplus Publishing has already published two superb volumes: *The Submerged Royal Quarters* in 1998 and *Sunken Egypt* in 2002.

18    J. Yoyotte, *Égypte. Afrique & Orient* 24, 2001, pp. 24-34.

19    We are summarising here the findings of J. Rougé, *La Marine dans l'Antiquité*, 1975, p. 18 *et seq.*

20    C⁽ᵈ⁾ Lefebvre des Nöettes, *De la marine antique à la marine moderne*, 1935.

of the stern post rudder at the end of the Middle Ages was, in short, the only thing that enabled these deficiencies to be made good; so it was thanks to this invention, and to a lesser degree to the compass – since ancient navigators were quite unable to plot a course – that navigation on the open seas was able to develop.

J. Rougé has shown that this line of reasoning relied merely on preconceived ideas. 'In fact, the Ancients used maritime routes, as they did river routes, wherever they could, since it enabled them, more cheaply and less onerously than land routes, to transport a greater quantity of merchandise and travellers. As for the dangers, they were more or less equivalent: storms and shipwrecks at sea, and accidents of every kind on dry land, especially when the route led through the mountains; on the one hand, pirates, and on the other, highway bandits. Even supposing this was true for the early stages of navigation, which is far from being certain, during the classical periods of history, sailors navigated at day and at night – if this were not so, what would be the explanation for the *topos* that shows us the pilot steering his ship by the stars and ensuring the safety of the crossing while everyone else is asleep? The modern cliché stems from an over-generalisation based on certain passages in the *Odyssey* and the practices followed by warships. If one takes the trouble to read Homer's poem properly, then it becomes apparent that the ships are not systematically drawn up, and when they are, they are first unloaded before being hauled up on to the beach, which makes it necessary to reload them after they have been floated off. In other words, this can only be done with small vessels and not with big, heavily-laden ships.'[21]

There is a major contradiction in the outdated assertions of Captain Lefebvre des Noëttes: how could such a crude steering apparatus be suitable for coasting, which after all requires a certain sensitivity in handling? Furthermore, studies that appeared in the wake of the ideas put forward by Captain des Noëttes showed almost immediately that the ancient rudder possessed a sensitivity at least equal to that of stern post rudders.[22] Finally, 'how, even at a time when underwater archaeology had not led to the discovery of significant cargoes, could anyone suggest that ancient ships were small, when a certain number of texts showed, at least in the Hellenistic and Roman periods, that boats were navigating regularly across the Mediterranean, transporting 600 persons in addition to their cargoes,[23] or 50,000 bushels of grain, equivalent to 4,500 hectolitres.'[24] This series of traditional clichés needs to be abandoned. Nonetheless, a certain number of factors that held back navigation – natural or human circumstances – persisted until the appearance of the steam ship, governing both the times and the routes of navigation.

Other stereotypes exist: diffusionist ideas, which suggest a common origin for different types of ships.[25] Paradoxically, while certain people in the modern era deny that the Egyptians were ever involved in maritime navigation, Egypt was at one time considered to be one of the most prestigious cultural centres from which shipbuilding spread. Thus, in 1948, in a study of models of ships from the Old Kingdom, J. Poujade found that the influence of Egypt extended as far as the Land of the Rising Sun. He thought that there were significant resemblances between certain particularities in Egyptian boats and the junks of the Yangtse Jiang, the sampans of the Bay of Along, and the ships of Japan.[26] For A. Köster, Phoenician ships were indeed copies of Egyptian models,[27] while E. Marx suggested

Granite sphinx discovered on the west shore of the island of Antirhodos, Ptolemaic period. © HILTI Foundation/Franck Goddio. Photo: Christoph Gerigk

that Greek and Roman ships were directly descended from the galleys of Rameses III represented on the relief of Medinet Habu.[28] In short, these diffusionist ideas 'tend to underestimate the spirit of intervention of most peoples, who are implicitly judged to be incapable of independently attaining a relatively advanced stage of technical evolution: technical progress is attributed, instead, first and

21  J. Rougé, *op. cit.*, pp. 20-21.
22  C<sup>dt</sup> Guilleux de la Roerie, *Les transformations du gouvernail*, 1935, pp. 564-583.
23  Flavius Josephus, *Life*, 3.
24  J. Rougé, *op. cit.*, p. 21. See for example Flavuis Josephus, *Life*, 3; *Digest*, L, 5, 3.
25  This is a summary of the chapter by L. Basch devoted to these diffusionist ideas, in *Le Musée imaginaire de la marine*, pp. 33-35.
26  J. Poujade, *Trois flotilles de la VI<sup>e</sup> dynastie des Pharaons*, 1948, p. 41.
27  A. Köster, *Das Antike Seewasen*, 1923, p. 48.
28  E. Marx, *The Mariner's Mirror 33*, 1947, p. 157.

Priest of Isis, island of Antirhodos. © HILTI Foundation/Franck Goddio. Photo: Christoph Gerigk

foremost, to the intervention of a foreign influence... It is clear that influences were indeed transmitted from one point of the Mediterranean to another during antiquity, but as the sources of figurative representations increase in number, we are less struck by the similarity of forms than by their diversity, which bears witness to the tireless ingenuity of people.'[29]

## The art of ancient navigation

*Consider, my dear, the pilot: it seems to me that one is not mistaken in calling him the king of the ship. When night has come, does he not sit at the rudder, ceaselessly fixing his eyes on the stars; [...] by not sleeping himself, he ensures that everyone else can rest.*
(Libanus, *Progymnastica, sententiae*, I, 13)

*Ancient navigation was more than a science, being, rather, an art resting on the capacity to interpret natural phenomena. But this art was so well adapted to the particularities of the Mediterranean that it underwent practically no evolution throughout antiquity and almost none subsequently. In its configuration, the Mediterranean lends itself to coasting, interspersed with crossings in which land is lost sight of for generally a matter of days rather than months.*[30]

How, with the means at their disposal, did ancient navigators manage to establish their routes? First of all, there is one point that needs to be established, although it is in fact a truism: at sea, when navigating under sail, the most direct route is not necessarily a straight line. So tracing on a chart the lines of navigation by sail is practically impossible, since everything depends on the winds you encounter *en route*. In these conditions one cannot and should not speak of speed but only of the length of a crossing, which is not the same thing even though the two are often confused.

Various texts from the Roman period give us a glimpse of the difficulty navigators had in following their routes. One of the best-known of these voyages dependent on the wind is that of the Isis, that hero-ship in Lucian's fantasy. Travelling from Alexandria to Rome, during a period of irregular winds, it finds itself obliged to sail into the waters off the island of Rhodes to find favourable winds that will enable it to take the south coast of Crete and thus reach the west. But at this point it loses its way and after crossing the Aegean finds itself in the port of Piraeus where it causes a real stir. We could also cite the numerous travels reported in the story of Saint Paul's sea voyage to Italy, as it is related by the author of the Acts of the Apostles.[31]

In the absence of a chart or any instrument, the good pilot is the one who possesses a profound knowledge of his surroundings and the natural elements, the description of the coasts, the movement of the stars and the science of the winds. Because of the shape of the seas in question (the Mediterranean and Red Sea), every maritime journey started and ended with a significant stretch of coasting, with all the risks that this entailed: 'the knowledge of reefs and shallows, and of the capes difficult to round, but also of the landmarks and the distances between them, the places of shelter and anchorage, and the places for watering and picking up fresh supplies, was a fundamental necessity. This knowledge rested on the accumulation of experiences that were transmitted orally to begin with then written down in

collections entitled Voyages that have been compared to our *Sailing Directions*.'[32]

When the ship's captain had to leave sight of land to make a crossing over open seas he was obliged, since he could not take bearings in a scientific way (with the help of a sextant, comparing times), to resort to the practice of navigating 'by dead reckoning'. This art consists of evaluating as well as one can the direction followed and the distance covered thanks to the science of the wind and the stars. By day, the route could be checked by the sun, whose position and direction were known at sunrise, sunset and the zenith. By night, necessary on certain journeys and numerous texts attest this, since Homer at least, in that they show the helmsman keeping watch alone over the ship's direction – this reckoning was maintained with reference to the position of the stars and the movements of the constellations.[33] The direction of the dominant wind provided the navigator with a way of orienting himself and this enabled him to set a course. The reckoning of the distance covered 'rested exclusively on the pilot's experience and intimate knowledge of the seafaring qualities of his ship, which would travel at different speeds depending on the strength and direction of the wind and the sea conditions.'[34]

If the geography particular to the Mediterranean could to some extent correct the rather haphazard effects of dead reckoning in this way, determining the boat's trajectory could often be an imprecise matter, especially as the storms or the periods of flat calm could cause many detours and wanderings. The navigator, reaching land within a more or less broad sector in relation to his final destination, could then finish his journey by coasting.

Crossings were normally made at fair speeds, running free before a following wind, which best suited the ancient square sail. Various Greek and Roman texts refer to ships being blown off course by contrary winds, which shows clearly that they did not try to carry out any long journeys sailing into the wind. All the same, it cannot

29  L. Basch, *op. cit.*, pp. 33, 35.
30  P. Pomey, in P. Pomey (ed.), *la navigation dans l'Antiquité*, 1997, p. 32.
31  J. Rougé, *Vigiliae Christianae* XIV, 1960, pp. 193-203; P. Pomey, A. Tchernia, in P. Pomey (ed.), *op. cit.*, pp. 10-17.
32  P. Pomey, *op. cit.*, p. 32.
33  See for instance Homer, *Odyssey*, V, 270-278.
34  P. Pomey, in P. Pomey (ed.), *la navigation dans l'Antiquité*, p. 33.

Gold ring, island of Antirhodos, site of the Poseidium.
© HILTI Foundation/Franck Goddio. Photo: Christoph Gerigk

be concluded from this, as it often has been, that ancient ships were incapable of sailing against the wind. From early times, no doubt, by combining the action of the sail and the rudder, ancient ships were able to run with a cross wind or a quartering wind, since it is a classical *topos* in ancient literature to express amazement that the same wind can allow ships to go in different directions. Even then, not every route was permissible, so that the great problem posed by ancient navigation is that of knowing the extent to which a ship could pick up the wind and start tacking, by sailing successively in different directions to make headway against the wind. It all depended on the disposition of the sails and the position of the mast in relation to the ship's centre of gravity. The analysis of certain narratives shows that the Ancients were acquainted with these manoeuvres and that the real problem was not so much of knowing whether they could tack, but of realising how much headway could be made against the wind when they had learned to do so.

In the Pharaonic era, certain signs suggest that when the ship was struck by a headwind, the captain could to some extent manoeuvre the sails to make his vessel tack and thus sail into the wind. The practice of tacking into the wind at the nearest point – equivalent to 'sailing close to the wind' in modern terminology (around 45 to 50° in relation to the eye of the wind) – was more frequently used near the coasts, especially to round a cape, reach shelter, and enter or leave a port.[35] On the high seas, this manoeuvre could not be performed for too long and could only be used to enable the sailors not to get too far behind while waiting for a favourable wind. On the other hand, when contrary winds really did set in, the ship would inevitably be blown off course. This was especially true when there were storms: the only solution was to run with the wind, or allow the ship to drift. It was for this reason that Wenamun foundered on the island of Cyprus on his return from the Lebanon, and Kolaios of Samos was the first Greek to reach Tartessos in the 7th century BC, beyond the Strait of Gibraltar, having been blown off course by storms *en route* to Egypt.

As far as working out the distances that were covered, there is little information relating to the ancient periods. To gain some idea, it is necessary again to refer to classical authors. According to the most widely accepted estimate of Herodotus,[36] a day's journey (17 hours) of navigation in a straight line and with a favourable wind corresponded to a distance of 700 stadia. The analysis of the texts of ancient geographers by P. Arnaud[37] has enabled us to distinguish two units of reference to measure the distance covered on the high seas: a day's journey (with an average distance of 700 stadia) and the 24-hour day (with an average distance of 1,000 stadia).[38] Such a system of measurement, based on empirical factors, nonetheless remains imprecise and does not take into account the different speeds at which ships could travel. These figures correspond to average speeds of the order of 3 to 4 knots (3 to 4 nautical miles per hour), which are very decent for square-rigged boats. This speed was reduced, of course, by an unfavourable wind (average speeds of 1.5 to 2 knots). In conditions of favourable wind, certain crossings could be made at an average speed of 6 knots, which was still exceptional in the 18th century. It should be borne in mind that these are record crossings, and it is probable that such speeds were not normally achieved by all ships, but only by the swiftest vessels in favourable conditions.[39] Thus, Pliny reports a crossing between the strait of Sicily and Alexandria in six days.[40] Although this indication does not give an average length,

but a record, whose exceptional character alone is the reason for which it is mentioned. In any case, this is a route between two provinces, one of which is merely a staging post on the corn route from Egypt to the capital of the empire.

A reading of the ancient geographers suggests interpretative precautions, since they give only a few markers relating to the maritime voyages of ancient times, and these cannot be systematically applied to the Pharaonic era. Then the coded data of ancient geography should not be expected to produce a chart, however partial, of port-to-port routes. Nonetheless, 'these itineraries do not result from a purely intellectual theoretical construction but are the fruit of multiple, varied, and sometimes discordant experiences, gathered and set down by ancient geographers.'[41] Geographers did, however, indeed provide reference points, variable in nature, on that 'long and difficult route'.[42] When precise details of port-to-port routes are given, there is a tendency to give a route from cape to cape or from cape to port. It seems clear that capes played a leading role in ancient navigation. They seem to have constituted not just the landmarks by which the navigators would steer, but also the point from which the pilots knew they had to set their course following a given bearing if they were to reach their final destination. So capes appeared as centres of communication and were merely staging posts on navigations that were carried out over much more significant distances than those that have been preserved for us by the geographers. Furthermore, these distances, deduced from the lengths of the voyages, are not 'abstract lines'; they are 'vectors'. They have a meaning, and 'measurements taken in two different directions on the same route may have given rise to different figures, either, perhaps, because the dominant meteorological conditions were less favourable in one direction than in the other, or because currents contributed to slowing down or accelerating the course of a ship travelling under such favourable conditions. The tendency to reduce the distances to simple fractions of a day's navigation, generally a half, together with the apparent absence of taking into account the currents when estimating the distances, is enough to explain the sometimes significant errors made by this totally empirical method of reckoning, which nonetheless could yield acceptable approximations.

For the modern researcher, navigation practised by ancient mariners has the merit of its empirical character, based simply on the length of the journey from place to place, a length which has usually been scrupulously preserved, independently of the parameters involved, in estimating the distances.'[43]

The evidence provided by classical authors allows us to distinguish between two groups of documents: those which refer to

35    *Id.*, p. 35.
36    Herodotus, IV, 85-86.
37    P. Arnaud, in *Entre Égypte et Grèce, Cahiers de la villa 'Kérylos'* 5, 1995, pp. 94-107.
38    See the methodological problems raised by these calculations: P. Arnaud, in É. Rieth (ed.), *Méditerranée antique*, 1998, pp. 75-87.
39    See P. Pomey, *L'Histoire* 36, 1981, pp. 96-101; *id.*, in *3000 ans sur la mer, Les collections de L'Histoire* 8, 2000, pp. 24-27.
40    Pliny, *Natural History*, 19, 3-4. See L. Casson, *Ships and Seamanship*, 1971, pp. 281-296.
41    P. Arnaud, in É. Rieth (ed.), *Méditerranée antique*, 1998, pp. 75-87. pp. 75-87. The reader will be interested to examine the evidence from classical authors concerning the distances between the Mediterranean coasts and Egypt in J.-Y. Carrez-Maratray, *Péluse, BiÉtud* 124, 1999, pp. 41-47.
42    *Odyssey*, IV, 483.
43    P. Arnaud, in *Entre Égypte et Grèce, Cahiers de la villa 'Kérylos'* 5, 1995, pp. 96-97.

Egypt generically and those which include Alexandria.[44] The latter as a whole go back to Hellenistic sources that pre-date the Battle of Actium in 31 BC. The former may go back to sources that precede the foundation of the future capital of the Ptolemies by Alexander. They are represented by two complementary passages in Strabo that refer to the same route between Crete and Egypt. According to the first of these, Cape Samonium (Cape Sidero), at the north-eastern tip of the island of Crete, 'bends towards Egypt and towards the islands of the Rhodians.'[45] The second confirms this and adds more details. Indeed, it gives us the distance from Cape Samonium to Egypt: 'four days and four nights – three, according to some people. Some say it is a journey of 5,000 stadia, others that it is less.'[46] Strabo's note is inserted into a discussion of the routes between Cyrene and Crete. As the passage is in some ways contradictory, it is possible that this is an interpretative gloss. Nonetheless, the presence of at least one figure for the length of the journey, a figure that is viewed as accurate, militates in favour of the age of the source that has been selected; as for the variation in the figures, it is probably the sign of the longevity and popularity of this itinerary, the only one which *stricto sensu* links Greece to Egypt. It is indeed remarkable that its point of departure is not a port, but a cape, one of the crossroads of maritime traffic in the eastern Mediterranean.[47]

Other evidence from classical authors includes references to the route between Cyprus and Alexandria. Cyprus was very important because it limits the sea of Egypt on the northern side. Strabo and Agathemera have both reported the distance between Paphos and Alexandria: 3,600 stadia according to the former, 3,800 with a north wind, according to the latter. Although these figures cannot be reduced to complete days of sailing, the fact that Agathemera specifies the direction of the wind guarantees that the measurement is indeed drawn from a maritime route. The disagreement between the two geographers is minimal: it corresponds to a length of more than four days and three nights, and less than four days and four nights, and it also refers to a length not exceeding five days.[48]

The great crossings over the open seas did not have any monopoly over interregional journeys. Navigation that kept close to the coasts certainly played an important role. It is not necessary to discuss here the offshore coastal traffic on a local scale as practised by boats of lesser quality, but of ocean navigation lasting several days and following the line of the coasts, out of sight of land (or just within sight), out of reach of their dangers, but in the zone where land breezes and sea breezes, alternating by night and day, have always been the staple diet of sailing vessels in the Mediterranean.

The itinerary from Rhodes to Alexandria, following the coast, constitutes a good example.[49] Next to the direct itinerary mentioned by our sources, Strabo refers to the same journey but this time following the coastal route. According to him, the distance was then twice as long as in a straight line, about 8,000 stadia, equivalent to eight days and eight nights of navigation. In reality, the distance is almost three times greater than in a straight line. In other words, the speed of the ships was one and a half times greater than the speed of vessels taken by the direct route. This poses the question, also raised

by P. Arnaud, what the reason for this greater speed was, unthinkable of small offshore vessels whose seafaring weaknesses are well known. This was a speed normally reserved for ocean going vessels. Should it be attributed to the currents, and should this relation be taken as referring to a journey from Alexandria to Rhodes, or should it be seen as caused by an alliance between the winds from the western sector and the breezes, and then imagine that the voyage in fact went from Rhodes to Alexandria? 'All things considered, the second solution seems the most likely, but it is certain that, like most routes *a fortiori*, those subject to the changing coastal breezes were followed in both directions. Navigation along the coasts of Syria and Asia Minor, with Egypt as their destination or their point of departure, was doubtless no exception to the rule. It would be justifiable to think that there were similar routes heading towards Cyrene, but in Strabo as in Pliny, the figures without question betray the addition of figures originating from offshore sailing, corresponding to short distances as usually found in the Voyages.'[50]

Whatever the risks of navigation, travelling by sea came with many advantages over the usual means of land transport, with their slowness, discomfort and dangers, even leaving aside the unrivalled loading capacity they could offer: several hundred kilos for a caravan of donkeys; several tens of tonnes for a ship. As for sailing conditions, they were to change relatively little during the whole period of sailing ships. Progress did not in any case free sailing vessels from storms and contrary winds. The vicissitudes of Chateaubriand, who set out from Alexandria and took 50 days to reach Tunis after being blown off course via the coasts of Asia Minor and the islands of the Aegean, show how much navigation by sail has always been subject to the same precarious conditions.

44    *Id.*, p. 99.
45    Strabo, X, 4, 3: '*The town of Hierapytna is situated on the gulf. Beyond it, the island stretches out in a sharp cape, Samonium (cape Sidero), that bends towards Egypt and towards the islands of the Rhodians.*' It has been shown that Greek and Latin geographical descriptive terms such as 'turned towards', 'facing', 'opposite' or others terms of the same kind did not suppose any bearing in the sense we would give the term today, but a principle of orientation both relative and subjective; here we have a good example: even an inexperienced sailor would note that the 'islands of the Rhodians' (Casso and Scarpanto) and Egypt do not lie in the same direction. Strabo knows this better than anyone – for him, Rhodes and Alexandria are situated on the same meridian. These words mean in reality that starting from a certain point there was a habitual route by land or sea towards the place which the first point is 'turned' towards. Our text also indicates the point from which travellers could strike out for Casso and Scarpanto, to the north-east, or alternatively head south-east, towards Egypt. So this itinerary is seen from the point of view of someone coming from the west, from Cape Malea, thus from mainland Greece, or even the canal of Otranto, less probably from the north and the Aegean Sea, the usual itineraries northwards passing, at that period, via Rhodes. Alexandria, Rhodes and the straits are all imagined to lie on the same meridian. These three points would thus represent the itinerary that was supposedly the most direct towards the Black Sea and Egypt. So there was not normally any need to take an illogical detour by way of Crete. P. Arnaud, *op. cit.*, p. 100 and n. 22 p. 101.
46    Strabo, X, 4, 5.
47    P. Arnaud, *op. cit.*, p. 101.
48    *Id.*, p. 103.
49    *Id.*, p. 101.
50    *Id.*, pp. 104-105. Strabo, XVII, 1, 14; Pliny, *Natural History*, V, 32, 39: Cape Chersonesos-Catabathmos: 1,730 stadia (Pliny); Catabathmos-Paraetonium: 900 stadia (Strabo); 690 stadia (Pliny) Paraetonium-Alexandria: 1,300 stadia (Strabo); 1,600 stadia (Pliny). The distance between the Canopic and Pelusiac mouths of the Nile is for its part the object of relative agreement: 1,300 for Strabo and Scylax, 1,360 for Pliny.

# Chapter I: The Bordering Seas

Plutarch relates in his treatise on Isis and Osiris that the Egyptian priests hated the sea. He interprets this in a physical sense, so that the gods are physical realities that refer to the elements of the world and the way they are organised. The Greek author contrasts Osiris, god of fertility and vegetation, with Seth-Typhon, who is none other than the sea or the arid desert:[1]

> *In Egypt, Osiris would then be the Nile which unites with Isis the earth, and Typhon the sea, into which the Nile runs, disappears and is dispersed.*

Seth-Typhon, identified with the sea, seems to stem from the sphere of sterility, which is opposed to the sphere of fertility, with its overflowing Nile. The fertile god is contrasted with the sterile and death-dealing figure.[2] For the priest Chaeremon, navigation was impious, unless it was a matter of 'duties to the State'.[3] This belated vision may reflect the reality of more ancient times. In any case, did it constitute any major obstacle to the conquest of maritime space by a people whose habitual means of travel was, after all, the boat? It is notable that in the legend of the insatiable god of the sea (the legend of Astarte), it is Seth who is chosen to defend the gods against the sea.[4] It is also worth pointing out the role played by Seth in the solar barque: he stands at the prow and victoriously fights against the enemy of Ra, Apophis, who opposes the navigation of the sun. A

Stele of the thunder god Baal from Ugarit in Syria, 13<sup>th</sup> century BC, limestone, 142cm, Louvre, Paris, AO 15775. © Photo RMN/Hervé Lewandowski

poem from Ugarit also describes a struggle between Yam, the god of the sea, and Baal, with whom Seth was identified during the New Kingdom. Seth, introduced at a certain moment into the prestigious role of adversary of the sea, was deprived of that role later on, after his proscription, and was finally identified with the sea, according to Plutarch's treatise.[5]

Stele of Rameses II making an offering to the goddess Astarte, New Kingdom, 19<sup>th</sup> Dynasty, c. 1290-1224, limestone, Louvre, Paris, E26017. The creature depicted at the top of the stele is the 'Seth animal'.
© Photo RMN/Franck Raux

1   Plutarch, *Isis and Osiris*, 32.
2   J. Hani, *La religion égyptienne dans la pensée de Plutarque*, 1971, p. 205. See also D. Fabre, *Le dieu Seth*, 1999, p. 365; id., *Égypte, Afrique & Orient* 22, 2001, pp. 41-55.
3   See P. W. van der Horst (ed.), *Chaeremon*, 1987, pp. 21-23; id., *Studies in the History of Religions* XLIII, 1982, p. 69; G. Fowden, *The Egyptian Hermes*, 1986, pp. 54-55.
4   G. Lefebvre, *Romans et contes*, 1949, pp. 106-113; G. Posener, *Annuaire de l'Institut de Philologie et d'Histoire Orientales et Slaves* XIII, 1953, pp. 461-478.
5   On the proscription of Seth in the 1<sup>st</sup> millennium BC, see D. Fabre, *Le dieu Seth*, 1999; id., *Égypte, Afrique & Orient* 22, 2001, pp. 19-40.

# I.   The maritime space of the ancient Egyptians

Studies from the beginning of the 20th century onwards had reached a sort of Egyptological consensus concerning sea-going vessels, access to the maritime space, and the definition of the fundamental principles of navigation.[6] It was accepted that the Egyptians had practised this type of navigation since at least the Old Kingdom (2686-2181 BC) and perhaps even before that. Nonetheless, discussion of navigation was hampered by disagreement over the term *Wadj Wer*, the 'Great Green' – did it or did it not designate the sea? Those who went for a categorically negative answer felt that their opinion meant the Egyptians could not have been navigators, since they were now deprived of a significant philological piece of evidence.[7] More measured analyses concluded that 'while this expression never designates the sea in religious texts, the fact remains that Egyptian vocabulary ceaselessly made readjustments to take into account the new realities that resulted from the expansion of the Pharaonic state outside its most immediate frontiers.'[8] All the peoples who dwelt on the shores of the Mediterranean and the Red Sea practised navigation: 'the Egyptians, who can be considered just as good at this as anyone else, able to rely on their long experience of the Nile, cannot be excluded from the practice merely on the pretext that a certain word does not perhaps have the meaning that is usually attributed to it.'[9] Refusing to accept that the expression 'the Great Green' in Egyptian texts might refer to the sea does not modify in any fundamental way the ideas we may have of Egyptian navigation in the Pharaonic era: 'this leads us in particular to give a relative value to purely philological arguments if we want to use them in isolation or to give them a credit that goes beyond any other type of argument. The historians of ancient navigation who have been justifiably excited by Egypt and the vast field of research offered by these pictorial and archaeological traces have performed some remarkable work that considerations of a lexical kind cannot destroy.'[10]

The Egyptians navigated on the sea, and their fleets may have had a more flattering reputation than people have imagined, since their boats were logically capable of confronting the dangers of the sea's expanses. It is necessary to re-examine the Egyptian conception of the maritime space itself before envisaging it as a space for travel.

## I.1. *Wadj Wer* and *Ym*

The term *Wadj Wer*, literally 'the Great Green', is recognised as a designation of the sea in general, but may be applied to very different realities, such as Lake Fayum, and stretches of the waters of the Nile, among others. Now the debate aroused by *Wadj Wer* is almost exclusively linked to Pharaonic expeditions to the land of Punt.[11] As the ethnologist R. Herzog decided, in a wide-ranging work devoted to the region of Punt, huts built on piles, and the presence of several black-skinned individuals as well as a giraffe, meant that Punt could be situated only on the upper Nile, in the south of present-day Sudan.[12] The ships of Hatshepsut would have sailed only on the river, and thus the expression *Wadj Wer*, 'the Great Green', could not refer to a maritime space but only to a stretch of the River Nile.[13] As the author did not mention the fishes and marine animals represented in these scenes, this site proposed for Punt was generally criticised and

rejected,[14] especially since the way the ships of Hatshepsut could have managed to cross the cataracts without difficulty was not really explained.[15] K. A. Kitchen strengthened the work of R. Herzog[16] by reintroducing the principle of maritime navigation demanded by the presence of marine animals in the representations of Hatshepsut.

Subsequently, A. Nibbi, persuaded by the arguments of Herzog, studied the question in greater detail and likewise came to the conclusion that the expression 'the Great Green' cannot normally refer to the sea.[17] In her view, this designates an aquatic zone of the Nile Delta, or near it, where ships could be built and from which it was possible to reach the Gulf of Suez. She emphasises the fact that such a solution explains the presence of freshwater, brackish water and saltwater animals in the scenes of Hatshepsut.[18] More radically, C. Vandersleyen endeavoured to demonstrate that the Egyptians were unacquainted with the maritime space, had no name to designate it by, and had never navigated on the sea.[19] At most he concedes that navigators setting out from Palestine and Syria may have come to Egypt to trade. The Egyptian fleet, if it existed, could have come into being only at the time of Nekau II (610-595 BC) at the earliest and would have been entirely reliant on the practical skills of Phoenician carpenters and sailors, since those from Egypt had no experience of shipbuilding or maritime navigation.[20]

C. Favard-Meeks in turn examined the attestations of *Wadj Wer* in the *Pyramid Texts*, the *Coffin Texts*, the *Book of the Dead* and other, later literature.[21] In this corpus, 'Great Green' is never perceived as a maritime space but always designates a green, fertile and regenerative space frequently linked to the Delta. The same author also specifies the routes between *Wadj Wer* and *Ym*. This latter term designates a stretch of open water that the 'Great Green', both aquatic and vegetal, may occasionally border, as at Fayum.

A sufficient number of arguments mean that it is possible to maintain that the term *Ym* may designate the Mediterranean just as much as the Red Sea.[22] *Ym* is a word of Semitic origin that is met only from the 28th Dynasty onwards (1570-1293 BC), and even then,

---

6   A. Köster, *ZÄS* 58, 1923, pp. 125-132; C. Boreux, *Études de nautique égyptienne*, MIFAO L, 1925.

7   C. Vandersleyen, *Ouadj our*, 1999.

8   D. Meeks, in *Autour de Coptos*, Topoi suppl. 3, 2002, p. 319, which refers to C. Favard-Meeks, in *Herausgegeben von H. Altenmüller und D. Wildung*, SAK 16, 1989, pp. 39-63.

9   D. Meeks, op. cit., p. 319. See *id.*, in D. Meeks, D. Garcia (ed.), *Techniques et économie antiques et médiévales*, 1997, pp. 175-194.

10  *Id.*, p. 175.

11  It is not necessary to go into the debate on the location of Punt at this point; instead a separate study will be devoted to it in vol. 2 of the present work.

12  R. Herzog, *Punt*, 1968.

13  *Id.*, pp. 79-80.

14  See the remarks in K.A. Kitchen, *Orientalia* 40, 1971, pp. 193 n. 42.

15  For a bibliographical list of the different editions of this work, see G. Posener, *Ägypten und Kusch, Schriften zur Geschichte und Kultur des Alten Orients* 13, 1977, pp. 341 n. 32.

16  K. A. Kitchen, *Orientalia* 40, 1971, pp. 184-207.

17  A. Nibbi, *The Sea Peoples*, 1972.

18  *Id.*, *Ancient Egypt and Some Eastern Neighbours*, 1981.

19  C. Vandersleyen, in S. Schoske (ed.), *Akten des Vierten Internationalen Ägyptologen Kongresses, München*, vol. 4, 1985, p. 345-352; *id.*, GM 103, 1988, p. 75-80; *id.*, DE 12, 1988, pp. 75-80; *id.*, RdÉ 47, 1996, pp. 107-115, *id.*, *Ouadj our*, 1999.

20  It is on this position that the two authors finally agreed. The only thing that separates them now – it appears – is the geographical situation of the land of Punt: somewhere in the Sinai for A. Nibbi, in the Upper Nile region for C. Vandersleyen.

21  C. Favard-Meeks, SAK 16, 1989, pp. 39-63.

22  For more detail on this and 'the state of the question' concerning *Wadj Wer*: D. Meeks, in D. Meeks, D. Garcia (ed.), *Techniques et économie antiques et médiévales*, 1997, pp. 175-178.

only rarely.[23] The form *Ym* ʿȝ meaning 'sea' has been attested by the translation into Egyptian of a well known formula in the Hittite treaties drawn up with foreign powers.[24] The term appears in the sequence *pȝ Ym* ʿȝ *n ȝrw*[25] when Wenamun leaves Tanis, and sails towards Byblos: it designates 'the great sea of Kharu', the maritime space which washes the coasts of Palestine and Syro-Lebanon. In the discourse of Rameses III (1182-1151 BC) relating the story of the expedition sent into Punt, the king indicates that the ships have sailed on *Ym* ʿȝ *n Mw-qd*, 'the great sea of *Mou-qed*',[26] to reach the land of spices. This expression has led to the spilling of great quantities of ink. Almost unanimously, the expression *mw-qd*, in two words, is understood to mean 'the backward water' (the water that flows backwards). For those who deny the possibility or the use of maritime navigation, this refers to a bend of the Nile between the 3rd and 5th cataracts, where the river flows partly from north to south and not from south to north. But it is worth remembering that the bend in the Nile at the level of Amada, between the first and the second cataracts, bears the name *tȝ-qʿḥ.t*, meaning literally 'the bend'.[27] For others, the expression alludes to currents in the Red Sea that head southwards and thus go in the other direction to the Nile.[28] According to D. Meeks[29] two essential elements seem to have been neglected. Principally, *Mou-qed* is a toponym habitually designating the name of regions outside Egypt.[30] In addition, *Mou-qed* appears in toponymic sequences at Aksha, Amara and Soleb devoted to Syro-Palestine, either at the beginning or the end of these sequences. Now, these lists are closely associated with the name of Punt. That *Mou-qed* may hypothetically also be mentioned at the end of a list enumerating regions of Nubia[31] can only highlight its character as a bridge, relative to Egypt, between north and south. A papyrus from the reign of Rameses IX (1126-1108 BC) also confirms that this region was bordered by the sea, and tells us that it was inhabited by Shosou Bedouins.[32] Collectively, this information points to Sinai, and *Mou-qed* must then designate one or more of its coastal zones.

## I.2. *Haunebut, chen-rekhyt, ra-haout, henet*

Another term frequently associated with *Wadj Wer* is *Haunebut*. This terms provides an opportunity to study the Egyptian conception of the occupation of the Delta land, its coastline, and even its development over time, following the geopolitical and geo-economic changes in the lands around the Mediterranean.[33]

Two points need to be made. First of all, the terms *Wadj Wer* and *Haunebut*[34] had coexisted since the *Pyramid Texts*[35] since the 5th Dynasty (2498-2345 BC) without a break. Then, during the Ptolemaic period, *Wadj Wer* and *Haunebut* are the terms used by hieroglyphic texts to designate the Mediterranean Sea and the Greeks, among others. Bilingual texts from the Ptolemaic period permit no doubt on this subject.[36]

Two extreme opinions have since been expressed about them. On the one hand, *Wadj Wer* and *Haunebut* designate the Mediterranean and the inhabitants of the Aegean Sea from the Old Kingdom onwards (2686-2181 BC).[37] On the other hand, *Wadj Wer* and *Haunebut* designate a region and a population of the Egyptian Delta exclusively.[38]

As far as the *Haunebut* are concerned, J. Vercoutter has suggested a mediating position: the term, he says, designates an Egyptian reality during the Predynastic period, but from the end of the Old Kingdom

it may have started to designate a form of territory or any ethnic group from the north or north-east of Egypt, its usage varying at different periods.[39] C. Vandersleyen however, after attempting to locate the *Haunebut* in Syro-Palestine, now agrees with A. Nibbi in localising them in Egypt.[40]

The study of the simultaneous use of the two terms *Wadj Wer* and *Haunebut* seems to be a useful procedure when attempting to determine how they may be interpreted in such different ways. During the Ptolemaic period in the Temple of Edfu, these expressions might have designated part of the Delta, and the hydrological system of its coastal regions, whereas, again in the Ptolemaic period and in royal bilingual documents, they designate without any doubt the Greek world and the Mediterranean.

This original ambivalence in the use of these terms might stem from a twofold and sometimes contradictory necessity. Firstly there is the necessity of transcribing historical, geographical, and political (and so on) developments. Secondly, there is the necessity of referring to and repeating the foundational myths that establish a static vision of the world.[41] Indeed, in spite of their variant forms, they connote in their way an awareness – even one that is merely visual – of the environment of the Egyptian world and establish the way in which it was apprehended: the earth emerged from the primordial waters. Chaos was thus a liquid element which, thanks to the creation of the demiurge, was driven to the periphery of the created world, and the seas around the land may have been a manifestation of it. The maritime space bordering the Egyptian world had certainly been observed since the most remote antiquity.

23    The references to the texts can be found in the *Wb* I, 78, 11, to which can be added D. Meeks, *AnLex*, I, 77.0285; II, 78.0313; III, 79.0215.

24    See E. Edel, *Der Vertrag zwischen Ramses II. von Ägypten und Hattusil III. von Hatti*, 1997, pp. 72-73 (d 16); G. Kestermont, *Orientalia* 45, 1976, pp. 153 (36), 169; *id.*, *OLP* 12, 1981, pp. 54-55.

25    *Wenamun*, 1, 7-8. *Ḫȝrw*, originally 'the land of the Hurrites', is one of the names for Egypt in Syro-Palestine from the 28th Dynasty onwards, though it no longer refers to any real specific ethnic reality after the Amarna period; see *GDG* IV, 151; A. H. Gardiner, *AEO* I, 148*-149*, 180*; R. A. Caminos, *Late-Egyptian Miscellanies*, 1954, p. 17; *LÄ* III, *s.v.* "Hurriter", col. 86-87; *LÄ* VI, *s.v.* "Syrien", col. 132-133. Despite the rather unconvincing conclusions of C. Vandersleyen, see the textual and bibliographical documentation relative to *Ḫȝrw* collected by the author in *Ouadj our*, 1999, pp. 115-127.

26    P. Grandet, *Le papyrus Harris I*, *BiÉtud* 109, 1994, vol. 1, pp. 338-339. This is a quotation from the text, pp. 133-34. In the important bibliography relative to *pȝ Ym* ʿȝ *n Mw-qd*, see for example, J. H. Breasted, *Ancient records of Egypt*, IV, 1906, p. 203, n. c; Abdel-Aziz Saleh, *BIFAO* 72, 1972, p. 261; I. Hoffmann, *GM* 4, 1973, pp. 19-22; L. Störk, *GM* 9, 1974, pp. 39-40; H. Goedicke, *GM* 10, 1974, pp. 13-17; G. Posener, *GM* 11, 1974, p. 39; A. Nibbi, *GM* 16, 1975, pp. 33-38; M. Görg, *GM* 32, 1979, pp. 21-22; *LÄ* I, col. 77; *LÄ* V, col. 311-312, *s.v.* 'Rotes Meer'; D. B. Redford, *JSSEA* 10, 1979, pp. 68-69; W. Spiegelberg, *ZÄS* 66, 1931, pp. 38 and nn. 8-9.

27    M. Dewachter, *RdÉ* 38, 1987, pp.192-193.

28    K. A. Kitchen, in T. Shaw, *et al.* (ed.), *The Archaeology of Africa*, 1993, pp. 587-608.

29    D. Meeks, in *Autour de Coptos*, *Topoi*, suppl. 3, 2002, pp. 328-329.

30    P. Grandet, *Le papyrus Harris I*, *BiÉtud* 109, 1994, vol. 1, p. 257.

31    G. Posener, *GM* 11, 1974, p. 39.

32    W. Helck, *JARCE* 6, 1967, p. 148 (46), 150 (72); R. Giveon, *JARCE* 8, 1969-1970, pp. 51-53.

33    C. Favard-Meeks has been drawn to discuss this particular association: C. Favard-Meeks.

34    See J. Vercoutter, *BIFAO* XLVI, 1947, p. 137; C. Vandersleyen, in E. Lipinski (ed.), *The Land of Israel*, *OLA* 19, 1985, pp. 39-53.

35    See C. Favard-Meeks, *SAK* 16, 1989, p. 39 n. 4.

36    See *inter alia Urk.* II, 179.

37    P. Montet, *Revue Archéologique* 28, 2, 1947, pp. 129-144; *id.*, *Revue Archéologique* 34, 2, 1949, p. 129; *id.*, *Revue Archéologique* 48, 2, 1956, pp. 1-11.

38    A. Nibbi, *The Sea Peoples*, 1972, pp. 11-32; C. Vandersleyen, *GM* 103, 1988, pp. 75-80.

39    J. Vercoutter, *BIFAO* XLVIII, 1949, pp. 189-209.

40    C. Vandersleyen, *Les guerres d'Amosis*, 1971, pp. 139-176; *id.*, in E. Lipinski (ed.), *The Land of Israel*, *OLA* 19, 1985, p. 44; *id.*, *GM* 103, 1988, pp. 75-80; *id.*, *DE* 12, 1988, p. 75 n. 1.

41    See C. Favard-Meeks, *SAK* 16, 1989, pp. 40-41.

Tomb painting of Nebamun (catching birds) at Thebes, New Kingdom, 18th Dynasty, c. 1400–1425 BC. © The British Museum/Heritage Images

This ambivalence necessitates the re-examination of the constantly evolving physical geography of Ancient Egypt.[42] C. Favard–Meeks has clearly emphasized the way the geography of the Nile Delta was integrated into Egyptian thinking. Far from being a permanent marshland, the Delta experienced within historical times some profound upheavals.[43] The study of the branches of the Nile for instance prompts the realisation of the spectacular nature of displacements occurred, resulting in many territorial modifications.[44] Ancient Egyptian texts bear witness to this. Thus, the *Prophecy of Nefertiti* relates how the course of the Nile took the place of its shores.[45] In the New Kingdom (1570–1070 BC), the same theme is taken up again in different terms, by the author of *The Wisdom of Ani*: 'the Great Green was transformed into dry land, the shores became abysses.'[46] Of

42  Concerning the desert, see K. W. Butzer, *Studien zum vor- und frügeschichtlichen Landschaftswandel der Sahara*, III, 1959; *AnLex* I, 77.2998; G. Roquet, in *Mélanges offerts à Jean Vercoutter*, 1985, pp. 291-311.

43  C. Favard-Meeks, *op. cit.*, p. 42.

44  'The order of nomes often varies as a function of natural modifications. Their number increases without anyone really being able to determine whether this development occurs within the interior of any Deltaic space. The nomes situated upriver from the alignment of cities constituted by Pe, Sais, Busiris and Mendes are of quite small dimensions; on the other hand, those situated downstream, if we take into account the entire space as we find it these days, occupy vast territories. And it is within this space that the number of nomes increases. It should also be pointed out that the alignment of these cities seems to indicate a limit: the nomes of the south have their capital downstream, the nomes of the north upstream' (C. Favard-Meeks, *op. cit.*, p. 42).

45  W. Helck, *Die Prophezeiung des Nfr.tj*, 1970, pp. 24-26; pp. 24-26; and on the archaeological level, M. Bietak, *Tell El-Dabaca*, II, 1975, p. 49 *et seq.*

46  E. S. J. Suys, *La Sagesse d'Ani*, Analecta Orientalia 11, 1935, p. 80 (VIII, 8). See J. Quack, *Die Lehren des Ani*, OBO 141, 1994; P. Vernus, *Sagesses*, 2001. Passages quoted by C. Favard-Meeks, *SAK* 16, 1989, p. 42.

course, these texts offer a symbolic description of exceptional calamities suffered by Egypt, but these might after all have been observed in less brutal forms.[47]

Human geography also needs to be taken into account; 'without questioning the principle on which all space within a state is catalogued, it must be admitted, that on the margins of the metropolis of a region, where attested (the village of fisherfolk or the dispersed or seasonal habitat of papyrus gatherers, for instance), can evade all sorts of investigation for centuries, and remain forever hidden when the region in question becomes the object of a different kind of land use.'[48]

Finally, the fringes of the Delta allow us to envisage the coastal region as a constituent in the Pharaoh's dominium. This expression is one of the three constituents in the territory seized by royal power:[49]

*All the plains (t³), all the savannahs (ḫ³s.t) and the Haunebut (ḥꜥw-nb.wt) are under the feet of the king (or the god).*

This formula belongs to the Middle Kingdom (2040-1782 BC), at a time when Pharaonic power was setting up a policy in which propaganda had an important role to play.[50] To express the extent of his power, the Pharaoh found it appropriate to use these terms suggesting the range of his dominium as a whole. *Haunebut* thus represents a territory which, associated with the plain *(t³)* and the savannah *(ḫ³s.t)*, constitutes one of the three elements of the Egyptian territory and its different lifestyles, in relation to the power of the Pharaoh. They are 'three different realities that do not overlap but form an indissociable whole'.[51] *Haunebut* designates a territory lying outside the floodlands, though not the lands outside *(ḫ³s.t)*, a space without any visible frontier, but one which is always considered as inevitably comprising part of the Pharaoh's dominium, and is thus included within the territory of Egypt. The populations called *Haunebut*, living in the marshes, had as their regular dwelling place a wickerwork vessel, made waterproof by coating it with a certain substance, probably resin. These were real baskets beside or within which they spent their lives. The exact meaning of *nebut* in Egyptian was indeed 'baskets'.[52]

The *Haunebut* were originally a population living on the margins of Egypt, and thus appeared in the lists of Egypt's enemies, designated as one of the Nine Bows. With the New Kingdom, texts with a universal vocation, propping up or glorifying the royal power, became thoroughly codified. The *Haunebut* were listed among the peoples dominated by the king – and this occurred in sequences in which the other terms designated classes of Egyptians alone.[53] Each of the Nine Bows (each Bow represented a foreign people that were regarded as an enemy of the Egyptian state) received its name in this period. It is not appropriate here to analyse the motivation of the power responsible for wishing to give a name to each element of the symbolic representation comprised by the Nine Bows, but it may nonetheless be supposed that from the 18th Dynasty onwards (1570-1293 BC), 'Egypt, having emerged from its natural limits, was obliged to give a different content to the symbolic system that expressed the extent of its power'.[54] To begin with, among the Nine Bows appeared Upper and Lower Egypt, with the *Haunebut* listed first. This logically suggests that the Nine Bows were defined vis-à-vis Pharaonic power, of whatever kind that may have been, and covered the totality of the territories ruled by Pharaoh, in all their diversity. The fact that the *Haunebut* Bow should be placed first – before Upper and Lower Egypt – proves that it could not cover the Aegean, even though contacts with the latter are attested.[55]

When *Haunebut* dropped from first place in the list this marked an important change, and the use of the phrase became ambiguous. This is why it then becomes possible to situate geographically, from one period to the next, the realms under study outside Egyptian territory: 'the names applied to the traditional Egyptian territory as represented by the Nine Bows and the projection of this same system of names on to territories outside the natural limits of the Pharaoh's *dominium* coexisted. The vocabulary given by the gods was meant to allow the clergy and officials to refer, as circumstances required, to the traditional Egyptian territory and the new political realities by using the same words. So the readjustments in these lists corresponded to a need to make them coincide with the evolution of the geopolitical environment.'[56]

Both *Haunebut* and *chen-rekhyt (šn-rḫyt)* seem to describe lands situated beyond the marshlands and the lakes on the coast.[57] A whole series of geographical texts, describing the sacred waters of the nomes in the northern Delta and their hydrological system, tends to confirm a major point: when an Egyptian wished to describe the course of the Nile in its final phase, no more than the coastal fringe which the Nile had to cross was taken into account: the maritime space was never described.[58] These terms cannot designate the sea properly speaking, or the estuary: *Haunebut* and *chen-rekhyt* are in fact elements of the coastal fringe. P. Montet defines the *chen-rekhyt* as part of the Egyptian coast,[59] and J. Vercoutter sees in *Haunebut* 'a very general form of the land's overall relief' and more particularly the seashore.[60] As for *ra-haout (r³-ḥꜥ.wt)*,[61] another term sometimes associated with the coast, it is worth noting that this always related to the freshwater flora and fauna of marshlands, as attested in the texts of the offering of the lotus in particular that refer to this area.[62] Properly speaking, *ra-haout* is 'the opening of the ḥ³.wt'. This last word, although rare,[63] seems to designate a reality that links the hinterland *(pḥw)* and the waters depending on a branch of the Nile or a canal – in other words, 'prominences' between the cultivable land properly speaking and the water (other than the water of the *pḥw*).[64] They issue *(r³-*

47  B. Bell, *AJA* 75, 1971, pp. 3-26.
48  C. Favard-Meeks, *SAK* 16, 1989, p. 43 and n. 22.
49  J. Vercoutter, *BIFAO* XLVIII, 1949, p. 129 *et seq.*
50  See G. Posener, *Littérature et politique*, 1956.
51  C. Favard-Meeks, *op. cit.*, p. 42.
52  L. Basch, *CRIPEL* 4, 1976, pp. 11-51. *cf.* infra p. 56.
53  J. Vercoutter, *BIFAO* XLVIII, 1949, p. 136 *et seq.*
54  C. Favard-Meeks, *op. cit.*, p. 46.
55  *cf.* p. 33-35.
56  C. Favard-Meeks, *op. cit.*, p. 47.
57  See Edfu IV, 35; V, 24. *cf.* J. Vercoutter, *BIFAO* XLVIII, 1949, p. 182 n. 6; J. Yoyotte, *AEPHE*, 1967-1968, p. 108.
58  J. Vercoutter, *op. cit.*, pp. 181-185. pp. 181-85. See also S. Sauneron, *BIFAO* LX, 1960, pp. 11-17. But everything nonetheless rests on the equivalence of meaning between the 'Great Green' and 'sea'.
59  P. Montet, *Géographie de l'Égypte ancienne*, I, 1957, p. 73
60  J. Vercoutter, *op. cit.*, p. 191.
61  *cf.* comments of J. Yoyotte, *BIFAO* LXI, 1962, p. 100 n. 6, 104 n. 6.
62  *cf.* M. L. Ryhiner, *L'offrande du lotus*, Rites égyptiens VI, 1986, doc. 18, 45, 76.
63  *Wb* III, 24 and *AEO* I, 34*, 109; Edfu, IV, 183, 7; 196, 2; *Dendera*, IX, 135, 4.
64  Edfu, IV, 196, 3.

*ḥȝ.wt*), in any case, into the fresh water[65] used for libations – the water of the Nile – rather than into sea water.[66]

Generally speaking, *Haunebut*, a term designating the coastal region in general, eventually became confused with the terminology of confines, and so acquired a generic value. Once it was a generic term it could then, with the help of historical evolution, be applied to the Aegean world, under the Ptolemies, while continuing to designate an Egyptian area.[67]

In fact, the name of the sea in Egyptian texts may be linked with the only archaeological find so far to have a direct relation with the maritime context: the steles of the 12th Dynasty (1991-1782 BC), discovered on the Red Sea coast, attesting the existence of a port, or at least a mooring ground at the sea's edge, and apparently bearing witness to seafaring activity.[68] Although these sources are very fragmentary, they do at least attest that there is a lack of any specific tradition used to name the maritime space: the terms used are *nun (nwn)* – the primordial ocean; perhaps *chen-âa-chek (šn-ʿȝ-šk)* – a word rarely attested, but one that is also found in the Pyramid Texts and probably refers to the external aquatic space; *Wadj Wer (wȝḏ wr)* and *chen-our (šn wr)* – the 'Great Circle', which always seems to refer either to land bordering the water, or a stretch of water at the edge of the land.

One conclusion at least can be drawn: the Egyptians found it difficult to name this maritime space which they had always known but which, according to the myths, belonged to the initial chaos and thus to something lacking all organisation.

One Egyptian word is supposed to designate the sea beach from the period of Merykara onwards (?).[69] The term in question *(pds.wt n(y.)wt š)* is also ambiguous since literally speaking it would seem to designate a lakeside. Could it also have been used to refer to the sea, or does it mean the coastal lake? Unless this is further evidence of how difficult it was for the Egyptians to name the sea and its shore in texts preceding the New Kingdom.

For the Middle Kingdom, several more examples need to be quoted in which the term 'the Great Green' refers to spaces or territories which it is impossible in certain cases to locate in Egypt.[70] The literary texts quote for instance 'the islands of the Great Green' (in *The Tale of the Shipwrecked Sailor*[71] and *The Tale of Sinuhe*[72]) which several commentators translate as 'islands of the Mediterranean' or 'islands of the Red Sea'. If the example of Sinuhe does not allow this to be decided conclusively, that of *The Tale of the Shipwrecked Sailor* is more of a problem. The boat that is shipwrecked is of considerable size and corresponds very closely both in name and dimensions to the Nile boats that transported heavy materials, including obelisks.[73] The shipwrecked sailor reaches the Pharaoh's residence thanks to another Egyptian boat which, in order to return to the country, has been navigating in the north for two months. Without going into the problem of communications between the Red Sea and the Nile Valley in which all the expeditions finish, and without examining the problem of a canal that may have linked with the eastern seas of the Delta to the Red Sea,[74] it can at least be deduced that it is not the Mediterranean that is being referred to. Especially since the serpent who is the Master of the Island presents the shipwrecked sailor as he leaves with a number of gifts including giraffes' tails, elephants' tusks, guenon monkeys and baboons – and this group seems like a sample of African fauna. These contradictions, picked out from tales that were aimed as much at creating a sense of the fantastic and the

imaginary as at spreading an awareness of distant lands of which the Egyptians were only starting to become aware, perhaps go to confirm this vagueness in the maritime tradition that was still poorly integrated into the Egyptian mentality, as apparent on the steles of the Red Sea.[75]

Borrowing the term *Ym* at the time of the New Kingdom thus seems to point to an evolution. First of all, until the New Kingdom, the Egyptian word describes only the aquatic space associated with vegetation, and the sea is more particularly described with the aid of a religious vocabulary proper to the primordial ocean. Then, the aquatic space, free of any vegetation, had to be described by a term without any fundamental religious connotation; borrowing the term *Ym* in the New Kingdom, arising from the need to give a more relevant name to different spaces, occurred in a context of territorial expansion outside the limits of Egypt and within that of a different organisation of certain regions bordering on the northern Delta.

Furthermore, the civil documentation attests, as early as the second half of the 18th Dynasty, titles linked to the supervision of the river outlets called *ra-haout (rȝ-ḥȝ.wt)*[76] a word which here appears for the first time. Although, as suggested above, it is highly improbable that *ra-haout* really refers to a maritime outlet. The term *henet/hôné (ḥn.t)*, frequently attested from the 3rd millennium BC until the Roman era, in documents of everyday life as well as in the hieroglyphic texts of the temples, raises certain questions concerning the topography of the coastal fringe of the Nile Delta. In the script it is determined by hieroglyphs representing 'waters' or a 'canal' or else a 'basin', and designates a particular kind of hydrographical reality. Its ideographic form represents a hand holding water in its palm, as seen on the Stele of Naukratis.[77] The word *hôné* is employed particularly with reference to Fayum. It is not synonymous with the term *š*, literally 'the Basin', apparently applied to this province as a whole. It is also distinct from the names given to Lake Qarun, which was called *Wadj Wer* in ancient times, then *Yʿm*, preceded by the masculine article *pa*, which gave the current name of Fayum.

J. Yoyotte suggests that, according to an extract drawn from a description of the world reproduced on an inscription of the Temple of Horus at Edfu (2nd century), in recent times there were 'seven *hôné*' in the lower Delta, 'from the mountainous land of the Libyans [the Marmaric] to the great Nun of the east [Lake Sirbo or the Red Sea]'. Certain of these northern *hôné* have indeed left traces in ancient toponymy. Egyptian texts and Greek papyri mention several localities situated near the ancient outlets of the Nile; they had been given the name *T-hôné*.[78] In the region now occupied by Lake

65  Edfu, I, 329, 10.

66  C. Favard-Meeks, *SAK* 16, 1989, p. 47.

67  On this evolution, see C. Favard-Meeks, *op. cit.*, pp. 50-63.

68  Abdel Monem A. H. Sayed, *RdÉ* 29, 1977, pp. 138-178; *id.*, *CdÉ* LVIII, 115-116, 1983, pp. 23-37.

69  *cf.* W. Helck, *Die Lehre für König Merikare*, 49; see J. Quack, *Studien zur Lehre für Merikare*, GOF IV/23, 1992; P. Vernus, *Sagesses*, 2001.

70  *cf.* for example A. H. Gardiner, *Notes on The Story of Sinuhe*, 81 (210-211).

71  M. Lichtheim, *Ancient Egyptian Literature*, I, 1973, pp. 211-213.

72  *Id.*, pp. 222-235.

73  *Urk.* IV, 56, 11-15. See A. Nibbi, *GM* 58, 1982, p. 55 and 58 n. 3.

74  G. Posener, *CdÉ* XIII, n° 26, July 1938; A. Nibbi, *GM* 58, 1982, p. 55 and 58 n. 3.

75  C. Favard-Meeks, *SAK* 16, 1989, p. 56.

76  A. H. Gardiner, *AEO*\* I, 34, 109.

77  On *ḥn.t* = Thonis, on the Stele of Naukratis, and the topography of this site, see pp. 60-61.

78  J. Yoyotte, *Égypte, Afrique & Orient* 24, 2001, p. 28.

Relief on the Mastaba of Ty at Saqqara, Old Kingdom, 5ᵗʰ Dynasty, c. 2498–2345 BC. © Photo: David Fabre

Menzala there is also a reminiscence of *hôné* situated downstream towards the eastern mouths of the river, one at the extremity of the Pelusiac branch, another corresponding to the outlet of the Mendes branch. In the centre of the river route that served Diospolis downstream in the basin of the Phatmetic branch (the present Damietta branch) there was a *hôné*. There is a trace of the existence of a Thonis towards Buto, downstream on the Bolbitic branch (the present Rosetta branch). The exact meaning of the term *hôné* has been much discussed.[79] It has often been translated as 'canal', which fits the extremity of the Bahr Yussef that flows into the Fayum very well. A. H. Gardiner maintained that it designated 'a lake', perhaps Lake Moeris, in other words Lake Qarun. H. Goedicke gave his support to the translation 'branch', the number of the seven *hôné* being indeed equal to that of the seven 'mouths' identified by Greek geographers.

Many of the arguments advanced in favour of each thesis is valid, but the two equally defensible translations are obviously incompatible: the branch is a water course, its mouth is an outlet which flows into an open sea, while a lake is a closed basin that contains water within itself. J. Yoyotte thus was led to 'sketch out a theory which can explain apparently contradictory data. The common name *hôné* seems to designate specifically the lower basins

of the branches of the Nile from the place where the smaller streams breaking off laterally form at the end of the branch of the lower Delta and flow into coastal lagoons, while the only major branch flows out into the open sea.'[80] The topographical investigations of F. Goddio and satellite observations of the configuration of the whole of the lower Delta have corroborated the hypothesis according to which the Egyptian word *hôné* designates particular deltas that form at the outlet of the great branches of the Nile.

Harbour installations depend, of course, on this geography of the coastal area. The important harbours of the Delta are river ports and are located on the eastern and western branches. This can be explained by numerous factors.

For instance, the coastal fringe of the Delta offers few possibilities of establishing a port worthy of the name, except within the coastal lake. The northern swamplands constituted a sort of autonomous glacis defending Egypt. Looking northwards from the coast there are contrary winds and currents, shallows, and sandbanks that would make this coast an unpopular stretch with coasters. The

79  The most recent scholarship is presented in Abdelheid Schwab-Schlott, *Die Ausmasse Ägyptens nach altägyptischen Texten*, AÄT 3, 1981, pp. 18-20.
80  J. Yoyotte, *Égypte, Afrique & Orient*, p. 28; *id.*, *AEPHE* 73, 1964-1965, pp. 85-86.

narrow coastal cordon was also not very propitious to the approach of visitors in that it was also easy to keep under the surveillance of coastguards and shipwreckers. 'False estuaries' break up the coastal cordon of the Nile Delta. They lead the navigator into the impasse of lakes, labyrinths of floating islands and unknown channels, sedges and reeds that cut off any broader view, and muddy river bottoms on which it was easy to founder. Ships could enter the Delta only by the principal mouths of the Nile, the Pelusian and Canopic branches.[81] So it is an uncertain landscape: a wide band with limits which fluctuate in accordance with the state of the Nile, a band which is submerged for long periods and is always damp, with drainage branches and lake gulfs whose shallowness means they cannot be used by real transport boats, only by flat, narrow, fibre skiffs that have almost no draught. Low visibility over long distances is the result of the walls constituted by the forests of reeds and the great clumps of papyrus. Neither texts nor archaeological discoveries suggest the existence of any significant island towns or agricultural settlements amid the mud and the thickets before the Hellenistic era. On the other hand, hunting stations and precarious hamlets comprised the huts of fishermen and bird-hunters, and herdsmen too, were normally found there – scattered dwellings, thanks to which the many inexhaustible reserves of the great swamps could be exploited,

to be transported subsequently via the river ports of Buto, Mendes, downstream Diospolis and other townships of the nomes.[82]

Within the land, sheltered from foreign incursions, the ports were situated on the branches of the Nile that offered the most direct access to the countries that could be reached from the sea: the eastern branch for the Syro-Palestinian coast, the western branch for Cyrenaica, Crete and Greece.

Egyptian texts seem to take little account of the maritime space. While Egyptians had been practising maritime navigation and sailing up and down the Mediterranean as well as the Red Sea since remote antiquity, it seems that the content of Egyptian myths must always have comprised a barrier to any real identification of that maritime space. Then, 'external contingencies constrained the scribe to include in his accounts a foreign world which turned the data of the foundational myths upside down; within the vocabulary given by the gods it became necessary to carry out endless readjustments, so that the words eventually acquired a generic and ambiguous value.'[83]

81   J. Yoyotte, P. Chuvin, *L'Histoire* 54, 1983, p. 54.
82   *Id.*, p. 56 and map on p. 55.
83   C. Favard-Meeks, *SAK* 16, 1989, p. 62.

Relief on the Mastaba of Ty at Saqqara, Old Kingdom, 5th Dynasty, *c.* 2498–2345 BC. © Photo: David Fabre

It was the expansionist Egypt of the New Kingdom which yields precise attestations of an arrangement of river mouths that cannot be those of the coast and which introduces a term to describe the aquatic space without vegetation on its surface – though this term does not designate exclusively the sea. In the first millennium BC the Graeco-Egyptian texts were to confirm that *Wadj Wer* referred to the Mediterranean, while *Haunebut* very probably signified the Aegean from the Sais epoch onwards.[84] Furthermore, 'the Egyptian scribe, in the period of the Ptolemies, must have noted the extraordinary relevance of using these two words to designate, in the sacred texts and in royal phraseology, with no possible ambiguity, the power of the Ptolemies over the Egyptian coast and beyond it. Alexandria *ad Aegyptum*[85] would thus be an expression reflecting the attitude adopted by Egyptian civilisation towards its own shore.'[86]

---

84    *cf.* amongst others, G. Daressy, *RT* 22, 1900, pp. 1-8.

85    *cf.* G. Fowden, *The Egyptian Hermes*, 1986, p. 20 n. 40, 21.

86    C. Favard-Meeks, *SAK* 16, 1989, p. 62.

# II. The Mediterranean Sea

## II.1. The conditions of Mediterranean navigation

Winds, currents, storms and reefs… all obstacles that have to be tamed in turn by daring navigations, before it can be claimed that the maritime space has been conquered. Such too is the history and the science of the sea… Up until the appearance of the steam ship, navigation was conditioned first by the sea, 'that Mediterranean Sea which, as classical rhetoricians said, unites the continents to each other more than it separates them'.[1]

The Mediterranean, deep-set amidst the surrounding land, separates the continent of Europe from Africa and at its eastern extremity touches on the western confines of Asia. It also presents completely original geographical characteristics that almost entirely determine navigation. These characteristics stem on the one hand from general climatic conditions, on the other from local climatic conditions and the relief of the surrounding coasts.[2]

### II.1.1. Climatic conditions

It is not possible to go into the details of the Mediterranean climate here, given that a study of such magnitude would lie outside the scope of this book. It is nonetheless necessary to briefly examine its main characteristics, gleaned from the evidence of classical authors, and more informative than the Egyptian scribes' works on history and navigation, and modern *Sailing Directions*.

The Mediterranean year can be divided into two great climatic periods: these thus constitute two periods of navigation. First the winter, a season during which the Mediterranean experiences types of weather that are unfavourable to navigation of any length over the high seas: 'this situation is due to the instability of the weather and the frequent penetration into the Mediterranean basin of rapid depressions of Atlantic origin which cause bad weather in the western part of the sea. During this same period, the eastern part is subject to the opposite influences of the continental anticyclone of Siberia, and desert depressions. In consequence, while the winter period may experience fine days, these do not extend to the whole of the basin, and their length cannot be foreseen when people do not have at their disposal the modern methods of meteorology.'[3]

Then the summer, a season during which the Mediterranean experiences, as a whole, a period of set fair weather, being sheltered from the major atmospheric disturbances. 'This situation leads to navigation being heavily dependent on the weather: it establishes, on the sea's surface, a system of regular winds that makes it impossible for sailing ships to head in certain directions, especially if they do not possess – as a result of the way their sails are organised – the necessary capacity to manoeuvre to windward and to tack. Thus it is that in the eastern Mediterranean there blow the well-known etesian winds whose direction varies slightly with the region; in the Aegean, they are northern winds, while in the rest of the eastern Mediterranean, they are usually winds from the north-west. Their advantages and disadvantages meant that these winds were well-known to ancient people who, by empirical means, had managed to establish a certain number of constants defined in their works – an approximate duration of 40 days, the dates on which they began and ended, and the relative calm of these winds at night.'[4] From 10 July to 25 August, voyages from Egypt to the north-west were made difficult by the

direction of these winds. That is why, during the Roman period, major navigation in this direction occurred generally outside the period of the etesians which in turn served as the period during which return journeys could be made. Because of the frequency of winds from the western sector, frequent in the Mediterranean, Alexandrian ships bound for Italy were often obliged to head northwards first of all, towards Asia Minor, then to navigate westwards, taking advantage of the winds from the northern part of the Aegean Sea.[5]

### II.1.2. Local climatic phenomena

The contrast between the maritime mass and the continental masses surrounding it, and the configuration of the shores, means that these general atmospheric conditions are accompanied by particular local climatic conditions.

In the first place, there is a local thermal effect: land and sea breezes. In the summer, when the sea is calm and the weather fine, all sailors navigating near the coasts may observe a relatively weak wind, varying in direction over the course of the day. The appearance of this breeze is linked to thermal phenomena and to pressure differences between the surface of the continent and that of the sea. In fact, the land and the sea warm up and cool down differently under the influence of the sun's rays. During the day, the ground becomes hotter than the sea, but it cools down faster at night. The lower layers of the atmosphere undergo the same variations. As a result, at night, the air that has cooled down over the land slowly drifts seawards; this is the land breeze. During the day, the air, considerably heated on land, tends to rise by convection, and is replaced by the cooler air coming from the sea: this is the sea breeze. These land and sea breezes do not blow all day long. The land breeze 'arises two or three hours after sunset and increases in intensity until midnight; then it decreases and turns calm towards sunrise'; conversely, the sea breeze makes its appearance only after nine o'clock.[6] Furthermore, they do not blow continuously all year long and are mainly summer phenomena. The fact remains that when and where they intervene, breezes constitute vectors favourable to navigation. These alternating winds that arise at the sea coasts, but whose effects can be felt up to 20km or so from the coast, are phenomena that have been well known throughout history and have constantly been used by sailors. Breezes 'can to some degree annul the effect of dominant winds and thus enable one to sail in the

---

1    J. Rougé, *Recherches sur l'organisation du commerce en Méditerranée sous l'empire romain*, 1966. In connection with this, see too Basil of Caesarea, *Homily IV on the Hexaemeron*, 7. The subsequent section largely follows the study by J. Rougé.

2    D. Fabre, 'le *Voyage d'Ounamon* et les temps de la navigation', a paper read at the 129th National Congress of Historical and Scientific Studies, CTHS, at Besançon, from the 19–24 April 2004, on the theme of time. For an overview of the geographical conditions in the Mediterranean, see A. Philippson, *Das Mittelmeergebiet*, 1922; J. Sion, in L. Gallois, P. Vidal de la Blache (ed.), *Géographie universelle*, VII, 1934; C. Parain, *La Méditerranée : les hommes et leurs travaux*, 1936; M. Cary, *The geographical background of Greek and Roman history*, 1946; J. Rouch, *La Méditerranée*, 1946; P. Birot, J. Dresch, *La Méditerranée et le Moyen-Orient*, I, 1953; F. Braudel, *La Méditerranée et le monde méditerranéen à l'époque de Philippe II*, 1949; J. Rougé, *op. cit.*

3    J. Rougé, *Recherches sur l'organisation du commerce en Méditerranée sous l'empire romain*, 1966, p. 32. cf. M. Clerget, *Les types de temps en Méditerranée*, Annales de Géographie XLVI, 1937, pp. 225-246.

4    J. Rougé, *op. cit.*, p. 32; Aristotle, *Meteorologica*; Theophrastus, *De uentis*; Seneca, *Natureles quaestiones*, V, 10; Pliny, *Natural History*, II, 124-127 (cf. the commentary by J. Beaujeu, coll. Budé, 1950, p. 207).

5    See, for example, St Paul's itinerary: P. Pomey, A. Tchernia, in P. Pomey (ed.), *La navigation dans l'Antiquité*, 1997, pp. 10-17.

6    *Sailing Directions* quoted by J. Rouch, *La Méditerranée*, 1946, p. 53.

opposite direction to them, so long as the ship remains in their zone of influence. Another consequence, familiar to the sailors of antiquity, is the way they could use land breezes to help ships set off: often, indeed, when the wind was blowing towards the port, the ship had to wait until evening, the time when the breeze strikes up to its maximum degree, before sailing out to sea, taking advantage of the following wind.[7]

The local winds, numerous on the Mediterranean coasts, are just as important. Examples include the *cers* of Narbonne, the *bora* of the Dalmatian coast, the sirocco from North Africa, but most pertinent to this study is of course their Egyptian brother, the *khamsin*, a burning wind from the desert. The violence and speed of these winds could easily catch out a sailor who had no time to change the direction of his sails and thus found himself in a difficult position. However, insofar as they modified the overall system of the regular winds and did not bring about a storm, they were a definite aid to navigation.[8]

All these winds could be recognised and used by men thanks to their experience of the sea, and it is probable that in the Neolithic, when the first great navigations occurred, they must have been more a matter of extrapolation than of proper navigation. It was only gradually that systematic exchanges became possible.

## II.1.3. Currents

Although they did not play a major role like the winds, the surface currents were organised in such a way as to influence maritime traffic, either by making it easier or by hampering it. In the eastern Mediterranean, the current emerging from the strait of Sicily flows along the African coasts including that of Egypt, then progressively weakens until it disappears under the influence of the Nile, whose flow still has the reputation of breaking the sea's force and guaranteeing particularly safe deepwater mooring grounds. The current then heads up along the coast of Syro-Palestine, and plunges into the space separating the island of Cyprus from Asia Minor, along whose coasts it flows. The currents thus play a significant role only at certain points, such as Syrtis Major. The reluctance of ancient navigators to sail into this difficult region[9] probably finds expression in the Homeric texts. Thus it is, for instance, that Ulysses, returning to Ithaca, relates to the swineherd Eumaeus a story in which he claims he was welcomed in Egypt by a Phoenician who took him back to Phoenicia to await the return of the fine weather and then take him to Libya (Africa).[10] It was also the northern route that the Phoenician navigator had to follow, since he did not profit from his presence in Egypt, where Ulysses claims to have been welcomed so as to continue his journey westwards, towards Libya, but he brings the Greek hero back to Phoenicia, then takes a route which, following the coasts of Crete, must have had Cyprus as a first stopover.

7    J. Rougé, *op. cit.*, p. 34.

8    See the table of local winds in the Mediterranean basin in J. Rouch, *op. cit.*, pp. 224-225.

9    J. Rougé, *La marine dans l'Antiquité*, 1975, pp. 153-154. By contrast C. Picard, in H. G. Niemeyer (ed.), *Phönizier im Western*, 1982, pp. 169-171, believes that, for ships returning to Phoenicia from Spain, the winds and currents were more favourable along the coast of North Africa.

10   Homer, *Odyssey*, XIV, 285-307.

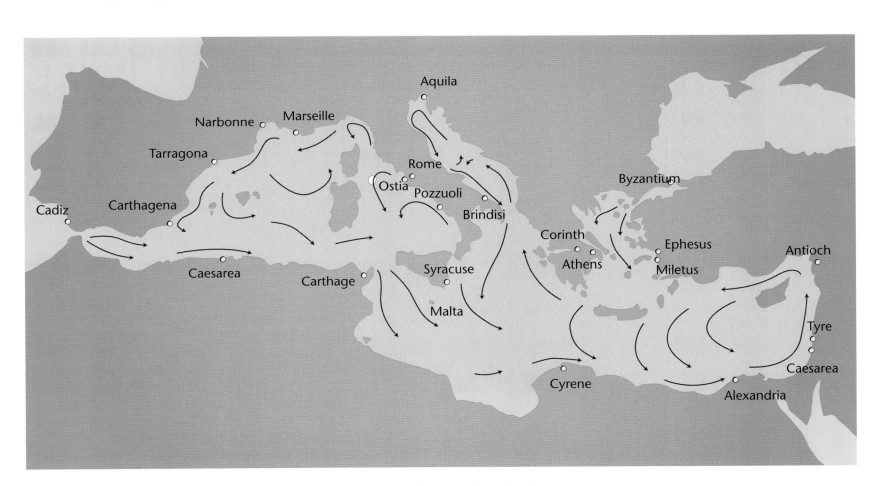

Map of the main currents in the Mediterranean, after P. Pomey (ed.), *La navigation dans l'Antiquité*, 1997, p. 27.

## II.1.4. The seasons for navigation

Navigation under sail has always depended closely on the state of the sea and weather conditions. The same was true in antiquity, especially as the Mediterranean is not the tranquil sea that its sunny aspect may lead us to believe. It is unpredictable, subject to storms and squalls that are as violent as they are sudden. Nonetheless, because of its geographical position, the Mediterranean experiences in the course of the year two great opposite atmospheric systems. In summer, it is dominated by an anticyclonic system which provides it with a long period of fine weather favourable to navigation. The winds there are generally well-established and regular. On the other hand, during the winter, it is swept by the passage of various depressions which lead to unsettled weather that is unpropitious to regular navigation. The sailors of antiquity, aware of these general conditions, distinguished between the fine season, when the sea was open to navigation, and the bad season, when it was preferable to suspend maritime activities. These two clearly distinguished periods were clearly defined by the classical authors: that in which navigation was possible, when the sea was open to 'proper navigations', following the expression of Symmachus,[11] and that in which navigation was suspended, and the sea was closed: *mare clausum*.[12] This was the bad season, characterised by unsettled weather, and the impossibility of foretelling disturbances and the violence of storms. This is also the period in which cloud cover meant it was impossible to navigate by the stars out at sea. It was not absolutely forbidden to sail in this period, but it was a custom based on experience – one which, depending on circumstances and necessities, could be transgressed.

The limits of these two seasons are so imprecise in the practice of navigation because they are imprecise in climatic reality. Indeed, 'the Mediterranean world, as a result of the latitude at which it is situated, experiences, as do all temperate lands, a climatic system of four seasons: two main seasons, winter and summer, and two intermediary seasons, spring and autumn. From the point of view of navigation these latter two really are intermediary seasons: like the winter, they do not have any set fair weather, but with the exception of the equinoctial storms of the month of September, they are much less dangerous. Furthermore, they have one advantage over the middle of summer, and one that is considerable for any navigation by sail: they have a much more varied compass card, and in consequence they allow a much greater choice of maritime routes. This is the explanation for the fact that the mariners of antiquity had two ways of reckoning the *mare clausum*, whose very dates are themselves imprecise: first of all they had a broader reckoning, which extended from the beginning of March to the middle of November – and it was this one which, in principle, was accepted by commercial navigation.'[13]

The fear of storms would have led anyone to hesitate to launch out on to the seas so early, and sailors preferred to wait for the fine weather to settle in definitively: so the start of navigation was delayed until 27 May. Likewise, navigation came to an end on 14 September. This last interpretation is recorded in the Talmud[14] and this is the one advised by Vegetius for war fleets,[15] whereas at the time the Roman empire was at its apogee, these fleets, consisting of rowing boats that strayed not far from the coasts, did not hesitate to navigate during the bad season, since they could quickly find a shelter from the storm.[16] In the 8th century BC, Hesiod tells us that the time favourable to navigation is very short – 50 days before the setting of the Pleiades, roughly speaking, from mid-July to mid-September. At this time the dangers were minimal, storms rare and the winds settled.[17] To be sure, he also tells us of a second period of navigation at the start of spring – at the time when 'the leaves on the fig tree start to grow' – but he advises against it as being too dangerous.[18] This evidence makes it clear how diverse the conditions were that determined the periods of navigation in the Mediterranean.[19]

*The Report of Wenamun* constitutes one of the most important pieces of evidence for navigation in the eastern Mediterranean in ancient times. Leaving the city of Thebes in Upper Egypt, Wenamun stops at first at Tanis (ˁn.t) in the Delta, then heading towards the eastern Mediterranean (pȝ ym ˁȝ n ȝ-rw). After a relatively long stopover at Dor (j-r) in Palestine, in the territory of the tMȝ-kȝ-r, he sails past the coastal towns of Tyre (ȝ-r) and Sidon (d-dn-nȝ) and arrives in Byblos (Kp-pw-nȝ). This town is his destination and occupies a key position in the delivery of wood from the mountain ranges of Lebanon (R-bȝ-r-nȝ). After his departure from Byblos, a violent wind and rough seas force Wenamun to put in unexpectedly at Alasia (J-r-sȝ – Cyprus). Unfortunately, the papyrus is not preserved to give an account of the later adventures of the envoy, and his return journey is unknown.

The examination of the dates mentioned in the text, the corrections needed to be applied to clarify them, together with recent studies of Pharaonic chronology, and the study of the conversion of the Egyptian calendar confirm the existence of two clearly distinguished seasons in the practice of navigation.[20] Accordingly, Wenamun embarks for Phoenicia on 8 May. A maritime navigation during this period seems conceivable, especially since this is a coasting journey in the south of the eastern Mediterranean, a region that rarely experiences storms at this time of the year. The

---

11   Symmachus, *Letters*, IV, 54.

12   See E. de Saint-Denis, *Revue des Études Latines* XXV, 1947, p. 106 et seq.; J. Rougé, *Revue des Études Latines* LIV, 1952, p. 316 et seq.; id., *Recherches sur l'organisation du commerce en Méditerranée sous l'empire romain*, 1966, pp. 32-33.

13   J. Rougé, *Recherches sur l'organisation du commerce en Méditerranée sous l'empire romain*, 1966, p. 33. By this reckoning, the opening of the sea was symbolised by a religious ceremony, the *nauigium Isidis*, which is known thanks to the description Apuleius gives of it; during this festival, a reduced scale model of the ship was launched on to the sea, bearing on its sail 'an inscription in letters of gold; these letters repeated the wish for a successful re-establishment of the maritime routes' (Apuleius, *Metamorphoses*, XI, 5 and 16).

14   *Talmud of Jerusalem*, Tractate Shabbat, II, 6.

15   Vegetius, *Epitoma rei militaris*, IV, 32.

16   J. Rougé, *Revue des Études anciennes* LV, 1953, p. 294 et seq.

17   Hesiod, *Works and Days*, V, 663-665; 678-684.

18   Likewise, Roman law could obviously not prevent anyone from sailing during the winter, but it made those who contravened the usual recommendations responsible for the consequences of their foolhardiness – in other words, in the case of shipwreck or serious damage, they could not claim that it was due to the fortunes of the sea: *Digest*, VI, 1, 36.

19   As for the identification of the toponyms (examined again below), the author agrees with the interpretation that places them in Egypt, Palestine, Phoenicia and Cyprus. So we disagree with the alternative view put forward by A. Nibbi in which the geographical framework for the journey is shifted from Palestine, Phoenicia, and Cyprus to the eastern Delta and Wadi Tumilat, which links the easternmost branches of the Nile to the Bitter Lakes and Lake Timsa, near the present-day Ismailia (A. Nibbi, *Wenamun and Alashiya Reconsidered*, 1985, pp. 9-119; id., *DE* 11, 1988, pp. 31-42. See too the objections of C. Vandersleyen, *Ouadj our*, 1999, pp. 31-42.) It is highly improbable that the whole journey happened around the Egyptian 'frontiers' and that Wenamun accomplished his mission so near his own home. For a substantial critique of his suggestion, see D. Lorto, *DE* 6, 1986, pp. 89-99. See also A. R. Schulman, reviewed in *BiOr* 43, 1986, col. 689-692; G. Vittmann, account in *WZKM* 78, 1988, pp. 224-226. A. Scheepers, in E. Lipinski (ed.), *Phoenicia and the Bible*, Studia Phoenicia XI, 1991, pp. 61-62.

20   See our study, which takes into account the maritime, meteorological, and geographical factors, but also the social, political, cultural and economic factors of the voyage of Wenamun: D. Fabre, 'le *Voyage d'Ounamon* et les temps de la navigation', communication to the 129ᵉ congrès national des sociétés historiques et scientifiques, CTHS, Besançon 19-24 April 2004, on the theme of time.

envoy of Amun sends a messenger to Egypt on 16 July, a period particularly favourable to a sailing from Phoenicia to Egypt, since it is during this period that the etesian winds blow (approximately from 10 July to 25 August), and these render southbound crossings in the eastern Mediterranean easier. The messenger returns to Phoenicia in September, after the period when the etesian winds blow – since these would have made it extremely hard to sail north – but before the season when navigation is very difficult (mid-September to early October). Finally, it should be noted that Wenamun is obliged to set out again from Phoenicia in the 3rd month of *mw* the following year, between 4 March and 12 April. This is a period that cannot be recommended for maritime navigation. On leaving Byblos, Wenamun is in any case caught in a storm which blows him off course to the coasts of Cyprus.

Among the sources that enlighten our knowledge of how long sea journeys would have taken, there exists an exceptional document. This is the palimpsest Papyrus of Elephantine (*TAD* C 3, 7), whose text (in Aramaic) consists of the register of a royal customs post of the satrapy of Egypt during the Achaemenid period (525–404, 343–332 BC): it details month-by-month the entry into and departure from Egypt of 42 ships in the course of the 11th year of an Achaemenid king, and registers the taxes levied during these passages. On the same scroll appear two fragments of a register that does not belong to year 11 and the remnants of the levies for year 10.[21]

This document provides information about the commercial vessels entering Egypt, identified in accordance with different criteria, including type of boat, then the name of its leader/captain, and finally the ethnic origin. If this customs register does not give a complete list of the boats that landed in Egypt in a certain year to trade there, the hazards of administrative organisation have meant that the register of the ships states that these came from only two regions, Asia Minor (*Yawan*) and (probably) Syro-Palestine.[22]

The arrival and departure of the ships was registered over a long period of 10 months (January and February excepted), so that the editors (followed by other commentators) think that this contradicts the usual opinion, according to which ships did not leave during the bad season. However, a passage in Demosthenes[23] already suggests that such an opinion should be qualified.[24] On this point, it is also worth noting that a papyrus from Ptolemaic Egypt shows that ships could travel from Asia Minor to Egypt during the bad season, since a certain ship arrives in Alexandria on 2 January 252 BC.[25] In fact, although the available statistics are still very incomplete, they suggest another hypothesis. It is clear that the number of ships increases throughout the year: three per month between March (or mid-February) and mid-June, four or five between mid-June and mid-August, five between mid-August and mid-September, six between mid-October and mid-December. No ship arrives in January, or in February.[26] It is known that, depending on the water level, the conditions of access of boats to the mouths of the Nile and the river itself improved from June–July onwards; conversely, in the first part of the year, it was difficult for deep-sea ships to enter (or indeed impossible in the first months).[27] So it is possible that the changing conditions of navigation in the mouths of the Nile and on the river itself explain, at least in part, the varied chronology of the arrival of boats from the sea.[28] Finally, whether trading vessels sailed and the routes they followed indubitably depended on the places where taxes were levied – on the customs ports.[29]

## II.1.5. The coast, navigation and piracy

The knowledge of the coasts followed the progress of navigation; for the needs of sea-carriers it gave birth to a whole literature of what is called *Periplus* – and which V. Bérard once compared, with some justification, to modern *Sailing Directions*. These are descriptions of the coasts with their main features, landmarks, watering places, places to put in, ports (sometimes mentioning the products that can be procured there), but also the dangerous places (reefs, mooring grounds that are exposed to the sea winds, and so on).[30] The most ancient document available dates to the 4th century BC, but they presuppose the earlier existence of numerous writings of the same kind.

From the geographical point of view, the influence of the coast, and to a lesser degree of the hinterland, on navigation should be raised and, as a consequence, the determining character of the physical conditions of the coastal region in which ports were situated should be borne in mind.[31] It is after all almost a cliché to state, as does J. Rougé, that the Mediterranean was bound to be the site of a great deal of maritime activity because the sharp outline of its shores, with their many inlets, offered numerous safe shelters for ships that were engaged in coasting. Thus, as evening fell, after his day's journey, the sailor could bring his boat into land safe from the unpredictable dangers of the sea; that is why 'the ancient concept of the disembarkation place simply cannot be compared to the way a port is imagined these days... a narrow stretch of sand on which the keel can touch a first time without incurring any great damage, a secure towpath to pull the boat aground – that is what a real port is.'[32] This practice cannot easily be verified in the case of Egyptian navigation, as the documentation is missing, and the same is true of all maritime commerce, even that of an embryonic nature, involving only small cargoes.[33] Indeed, what made it possible to pull a boat aground on a daily basis was the fact that the cargo could easily be unloaded and

---

21  B. Porten, A. Yardeni, *Textbook of Aramaic Documents from Ancient Egypt*, III, 1993; A. Yardeni, *BASOR*, 293, 1994, pp. 67-87; E. Lipinski, *OLP* 29, 1994, pp. 61-68; P. Briant, *Histoire de l'Empire perse*, 1994, p. 398, for an index of Aramaic texts, p. 1236; C. Ampolo, in *Magna Grecia, Etruschi, Fenici*, 1996, pp. 245-247; P. Briant, R. Descat, in N. Grimal, B. Menu (ed.), *Le commerce*, *BiÉtud* 121, 1998, pp. 59-104.

22  For the study of ships and their tonnages, cargoes and the names of the captains in command of the ships, and other related aspects mentioned in this register, cf. p. 126-127.

23  Demosthenes, *Against Athenodorus*, LVI, 30.

24  B. Porten, A. Yardeni, *op. cit.*, p. xx; E. Lipinski, *op. cit.*, p. 66.

25  Text and commentary in C. Orrieux, *Les papyrus de Zénon*, 1983, p. 56.

26  B. Porten, A. Yardeni, *op. cit.*, pp. 284-289; p. xx.

27  On this, see the ancient and modern texts quoted and studied by J. C. Darnell, in J. H. Johnson (ed.), *Life in a Multicultural Society*, SAOC 51, 1992, pp. 70-71.

28  Also, the 'bad season' in the eastern Mediterranean lasts from September to May (see on this subject the remarks of C. Orrieux, *op. cit.*, pp. 55-56), while it is between May–June and December that we find the greatest number of boats arriving, as registered in the papyrus.

29  On this, see the chapter concerning customs and the places where taxes were levied, to appear in *Seafaring in Ancient Egypt*, vol. 2.

30  J. Rougé, *La marine dans l'Antiquité*, 1975, pp. 23-24.

31  We will be returning to these points, p. 45 *et seq.*

32  P. Cintas, *Contribution à l'étude de l'expansion carthaginois au Maroc*, 1954, p. 11. Quoted by J. Rougé, *Recherches sur l'organisation du commerce en Méditerranée sous l'empire romain*, 1966, p. 35.

33  At the time Roman commerce was at its apogee, trading depended more on economic conditions; the great commercial port was not necessarily a natural port with a roadstead well sheltered from the storms, but often a port constructed in a place well suited to commerce, i.e. at the meeting point of a continental route (a road or a navigable river) and maritime navigation; see J. Rougé, *op. cit.*, p. 38.

Satellite image (Gemini IV) of the Nile Delta, the Gulf of Suez and part of the Sinai Peninsula. © Bettman/CORBIS

reloaded, given that the vessel could be hauled only when it was empty.[34]

If the 'Mediterranean schema' brings together elements which complement each other and facilitate both local life and relations with the outside world – a creek sheltered from the winds, with a small plain bordered by a mountainous hinterland (a schema occurring at many coastal locations of the Levant and Asia Minor) – it can also be the case that a great river (in this case the Nile) flows out to sea at a certain point which renders trade easier.

Even then it should be borne in mind that not all the Mediterranean coasts are equally favourable to maritime activities. Thus low coasts may sometimes be more dangerous, or at least more treacherous, than rocky coasts; this explains why in certain regions there was an attempt to avoid them by using routes that were a halfway house between maritime and continental routes, the routes that used ponds and pools. These routes are known above all in the case of the Egyptian coast and the lake district. Diodorus Siculus relates the difficulty of navigating between the Libyan coasts and Syria by following the Egyptian shoreline:[35]

*From Paraetonium[36] in Libya to Jaffa in hollow Syria, a voyage of some five thousand stadia,[37] there is no safe port except at Pharos. Furthermore, a sand bank extends across almost the entire breadth of Egypt and the navigators who approach it without prior experience cannot spot it. So those who think they have escaped from the perils of the sea and who, in their ignorance, joyfully set sail for land, suddenly see their vessels running aground and unexpectedly being shipwrecked. And some of them, because of the flatness of the coast, fail to see the land in time and unwittingly encounter either marshy shallows, or else desert coast.*

P. Jollois, an engineer in the French Department of Civil Engineering at the time of Napoleon, describes with great precision the sea crossing from Alexandria to the entry of the branch of the Nile at Rosetta:

*We left the lighthouse channel, sailed along the coast and dropped anchor in the middle of the French fleet, which had anchored in the bay of Aboukir. The next day we set sail for the Nile estuary. Either because the wind was blowing very violently and aroused anxieties, or because it was feared that the boghâz might not provide a sufficient depth of water, it was not felt to be a good idea to bring the sloop into the river: so we were put into a gunboat with only a small draught. As the sea was very rough, we changed vessels with the greatest of difficulty, and embarked on the gunboat cursing the sea and the voyage. Some three quarters of a league away from the Nile estuary, its waters have a very distinct green colour, and one can even make out very clearly the line of demarcation between the green and the blue colour of the sea. As one comes closer to the boghâz, the green hue changes to a yellow hue, caused by the colour of the sand which the Nile deposits at its mouth and also a muddy suspension in the river waters. The passage of the boghâz offers a spectacle that is really alarming when the sea is rough: the sand dunes bordering the river mouth are as shifting as the waves themselves; and only with the help of a seasoned pilot can one hope to avoid shipwreck. Luckily, we had a very skilful pilot, who guided us very adroitly through the perils*

*by which we were, so to speak, surrounded on all sides. When we had entered the river, he expressed the most lively joy, and all the passengers demonstrated, by giving him a few coins, how greatly they appreciated his competence and skill.[38]*

P. Jollois goes on to say that 'the word *boghâz* in Turkish means "gullet". The *boghâz* is a very narrow channel, opened up by the current in the sand banks forming a bar at the mouth of the Nile: these banks are the result of the river's deposits when it loses its speed on arriving at the sea. Nothing is more variable than this passage. The sand banks through which it cuts are continually being shifted by the sea's waves; and when the west winds and the north winds are blowing with any violence, the river waters are as it were forced back towards their source, and the currents flow wherever they find the least resistance.'

The shape of the coastline could hinder navigation substantially, but it also generated practices that were even more damaging to maritime commerce: piracy. This activity occurs in two guises, often practised by the same individuals: deliberate wrecking, and piracy properly speaking.[39]

Capes and low coasts have always tended to be the domain of wreckers who, admittedly, were merely profiting excessively from quite a widespread maritime custom according to which anything flung on to shore by the sea following a shipwreck belonged to whoever discovered it.[40] In the northern fringes of the Nile Delta, the men who raised oxen, the 'Herdsmen' (*Bucoloi*) were known for their brigandage, their armed assaults and their wrecking. Strabo explains that at the time of the Pharaohs, the inhabitants of these 'Cow prairies', the *Bucolia*, served as a kind of auxiliary police force, both coast-guards and pillagers of wrecks:[41]

*The Egyptian coast was not supplied with ports, and the port that existed at Pharos was not a way of access, but it was under the surveillance of brigand herdsmen who attacked those who put in there.*

The letters of El-Amarna refer to the dangers of piracy afflicting merchants.[42] On the coasts properly speaking, the inscription of Pepinakht, dating from the reign of Pepi II (2278-2184 BC), describes a campaign against the 'Asiatics who dwell in the sands'

---

34  The *Odyssey*, which should always be consulted when studying Mediterranean navigation, shows that when there was any reason to fear hostility from the local inhabitants, sailors would content themselves with dropping anchor without actually landing (X, 87ff). On the other hand when Odysseus leaves the island of the Phaeacians, the boat on which he is to embark is first floated, then loaded. So it must have been dragged aground while empty (XIII, 19ff).

35  Diodorus I, 31, 2-5; translation, A. Bernand, *Le Delta égyptien*, MIFAO 91, 1970, p. 22.

36  For this port, see p. 63-65.

37  Over 900km.

38  P. Jollois, in *Description de l'Égypte*, 1822, pp. 333-360; quoted by A. Bernand, *op. cit.*, pp. 497-498.

39  On piracy in general, see the studies by J.-M. Sestier, *La piraterie dans l'Antiquité*, 1880; H. A. Ormerod, *Piracy in the Ancient World*, 1924; J. Rougé, *op. cit.*, pp. 37-38; P. A. Gianfrotta, in P. Pomey (ed.), *La navigation dans l'Antiquité*, 1997, pp. 46-57.

40  We will return to this subject in *Seafaring in Ancient Egypt*, vol. 2.

41  Strabo, XVII, I, 19. On the brigandage of the herdsmen, with their long tradition of combat and rebellion, see J. Yoyotte, P. Chuvin, *L'Histoire* 54, 1983, pp. 52-62; id., *L'Histoire* 88, 1986, pp. 40-48; P. Charvet, S. Gompertz, J. Yoyotte, *Strabon*, 1997, n. 78 p. 80, pp. 114-115; J.-Y. Carrez-Maratray, *Péluse*, BiÉtud 124, 1999, pp. 407-408; E. J. Hobsbawm, *Bandits*, 1972; B. D. Shaw, *Past and Present*, 1984, pp. 3-52.

42  EA 105, 113, 114. See W. L. Moran, *Les lettres d'El-Amarna*, LAPO 13, 1987.

($^{ʿ}$m.w ḥr(y).w-šʿ), who came to attack the leader of the Ânankha expedition while he was preparing an expedition to Punt.[43] In the Mediterranean, contacts between Egypt and the Mycenaeans probably went beyond the exchanges of civilities represented on Theban tomb paintings. From the middle of the 15th century BC the first mentions of functionaries entrusted with the task of preventing and suppressing pirate attacks on the Nile Delta appear in the Pharaoh's administration. The 'chiefs of all the mouths of the sea' and the 'chiefs of the sea fortresses' are given the task of keeping the river mouths under surveillance, from the forts that controlled them. In this period, it was the Achaeans who dominated the Aegean, and much of the eastern Mediterranean thanks to the remarkable sophistication of their fleets. From Crete, each year, in the summer season, their ships came to ravage the coasts of Egypt and pillage its countryside via the branches of the Nile, sometimes penetrating deep

into the interior. A page in Homer, although from a much later period (8th century BC) contains an excellent description of these activities:[44]

---

43   This mention of Asiatics suggests that the point of departure of this expedition was on the north-western coast of the Red Sea, or, perhaps, Sinai. This aspect was suggested by A. Nibbi, *JEA* 62, 1976, pp. 45-56; however, she proposes a location for Punt which cannot be accepted for reasons explained later. See G. Posener, *CdÉ* 26, 1938, pp. 258-273: in his view, because of the location of the Egyptian capital in the course of the Old Kingdom, people naturally used a port which could be reached via Wadi Tumilat. The mention here of the $^{ʿ}$m.w ḥr(y).w-šʿ might also suggest the presence of these populations further south, along the African coasts of the Red Sea or in the eastern desert: see J. Desanges, in T. Fahd (ed.), *L'Arabie préislamique et son environnement historique et culturel*, 1989, pp. 413-429. On maritime expeditions in the Red Sea, see p. 36, 78 *et seq.*

44   Homer, *Odyssey*, XIX; translation by M. Dufour and J. Raison.

Relief of the naval battle against the Sea Peoples on the north wall of the funerary temple of Rameses III at Medinet Habu, Thebes, New Kingdom, 20th Dynasty, c. 1184–1153 BC.

*I had become an object of fear and respect among the Cretans. […] My heart impelled me to sail to Egypt. […] I rigged nine vessels, and very soon a whole people rushed up […] We embarked and, driven along by a fine north wind, that was blowing strongly, we sailed past huge Crete, easily, as if following the current of a river. […] On the fifth day we reached the Egyptos with its fine course ( = the Nile). So my vessels dropped anchor in this river (probably in its western branch) and I ordered the lookouts to keep watch. But they succumbed to their spirit of excess and following their impulses immediately started ravaging those fine fields of the Egyptians, making off with the women and the children who were deprived of reason, and killing the men. The war cry rapidly reached the town. The inhabitants, hearing the cry, came rushing up as day appeared. The whole square filled with infantry and cavalry, and with the flash of bronze. Zeus who hurls the thunderbolt threw dismal panic among my companions, and none had the courage to remain and oppose the enemy force. So they slew many of our men with their bronze points; they dragged off the survivors and forced them to work for them.*

P. Faure is certainly correct when he writes, 'ever since at least the period when men started to move between the islands and the Aegean Sea, they have always gone to see the Nile Delta. The great green archipelago embraced by the seven branches of the river is too similar to a group of islets for it to have escaped the curiosity and the cupidity of the island dwellers.'[45]

During the reigns of Amenhotep III (1386-1349 BC) and IV (1350-1334 BC), certain texts allude to pirate expeditions against the Nile Delta as well as against the island of Cyprus (*Alasia*) and the Egyptian possessions in the Levant. Some of these pirates came from the island of *Loukki*, the future Lycia, off the south-west coast of Anatolia. At the start of the 19th Dynasty (1293-1185 BC), they were continually threatening Egypt, to such an extent that, in the first two years of his reign, Rameses II (1279-1212 BC) was obliged to conduct a campaign against them, calling them 'the Shirdana with their valorous hearts […] who have come […] on their warships, across the sea.' The success of this operation is confirmed by the presence of mercenaries from their ranks in the Pharaoh's personal guard at the time of the battle of Kadesh (1275 BC). To the west of the Delta, on the shores of Marmaric [?], between Egypt and Libya, Rameses II erected a succession of fortresses that extended to a distance 300km to the west of the Nile Valley, the network of 'sea fortresses' set up by Thutmose III (1504-1450 BC). The establishment of these fortresses shows that the western part of the Delta was the first area to be targeted by the raids of pirates who followed the maritime route linking Crete to Africa. Under Merenptah (1212-1202 BC), certain 'Sea Peoples' took part in a Libyan attack on Egypt. The Libyans who attacked Egypt again in year 11 of the reign of Rameses III (1174 BC) were armed with Mycenaean weapons. It therefore seems clear that pirates first reached the area of Cyrene (the eastern part of Libya) from the Aegean Sea, where they must have established contact with the native populations, and then returned to the place of their activities by sailing along the coast where Rameses II had set up his military installations. By this time it is clear that the movements of the 'Sea Peoples', were migratory, rather than motivated by piracy, since the period is characterised by the exodus of entire peoples taking to the roads in search of new homes and resolved to conquer by force of arms, who set the eastern Mediterranean on fire at the end of the 2nd millennium BC. Naturally this represented a grave obstacle to commercial navigation.[46]

These population movements should not therefore be identified with social piracy, traditional in the Mediterranean, which in turn ought not to be confused with the large-scale piracy of the last three centuries BC, which was a veritable case of privateering, in essentially political circumstances. During the ceaseless struggles between different Hellenistic kings, pirates were used because of the swiftness of their light vessels which were a welcome complement to the royal battleships, but also because their services were free, since they were paid in booty; they were useful in blockades, in raids designed to intimidate or take reprisals, and in intercepting convoys.

### II.2. One sea or two? The divisions and maritime spaces of the Mediterranean

The eastern basin of the Mediterranean whose waters wash the shores of Egypt is, according to J. Rougé's study,[47] the part that appears most fragmentary. Since the seas overlap, it is most difficult to mark out in even an approximate fashion the limits of the different seas. To the north of Egypt, there are three big groupings: to the north, the sea of Carpathos (*mare Carpathicum*) which tends to meld into the second maritime region, the sea of Egypt (*mare Aegyptiacum*), that borders on that country; and to the west, the Libyan sea (*mare Libycum*). Finally, along the Asiatic coast from south to north, in order are: the *mare Phoenicium* or *Syriacum*, the *mare Cyprium* and the *mare Pamphylium* or *mare Lycium*.

If this nomenclature is taken from Roman onomastics, which in turn was the heir to Hellenistic onomastics, the extreme compartmentalisation of the maritime regions near the land discloses an ancient stratum of maritime knowledge; these names, which are almost all attached to islands and the countries bordering the sea, must belong to an epoch when coasting was the normal practice in the activity of navigators. It may be suggested that the more a maritime space is cut up into seas of reduced surface area, the more navigation was obliged to be active. Conversely, a coast that is not divided in the same way must have had less maritime activity. On the other hand, the vast spaces with their imprecise boundaries could have entered only belatedly into the domain of maritime life, at a period when sailors, emboldened or now having at their disposal means of navigation better adapted to long crossings, were no longer dependent on the coast.[48]

The segmentation of the eastern Mediterranean and the necessities of coastal navigation did not mean, however, that each of

45   P. Faure, *La vie quotidienne des colons grecs*, 1978, p. 135. The famous wall painting at Akrotiri could be interpreted in this way: see L. Basch, *Le Musée imaginaire de la marine*, 1987, pp. 118-119.

46   On this episode of the 'Sea Peoples', see the overview by P. Grandet in *L'Égypte ancienne, L'Histoire*, 1996, pp. 103-120; id., *Le papyrus Harris I*, BiÉtud 109, 1994, vol. 2, n. 918. See J. D. Barnett, in *CAH* II, 2, 1975; S. Deger-Jalkotzy (ed.), *Griechenland, die Aegäis und die Levante während der "Dark Ages"*, 1983; N. K. Sandars, *Les peuples de la mer*, 1981; E. Edel, in *Mélanges Gamal Eddin Mokhtar*, I, BiÉtud 97, 1985; W. F. Edgerton, J. A. Wilson, *Historical Records of Ramsès III*, 1936; G. A. Lehmann, UgForsch 11, 1979, pp. 481-494; E. D. Oren, *The Sea Peoples and Their World: A Reassessment*, 2000; J. S. Smith, BiOr LIX, 3/4, May-August 2002, pp. 399-405.

47   J. Rougé, *Recherches sur l'organisation du commerce en Méditerranée sous l'empire romain*, 1966, pp. 43-45. See also P. Pomey, in P. Pomey (ed.), *La navigation dans l'Antiquité*, 1997, pp. 20-23.

48   See J. Rougé, op. cit., p. 45.

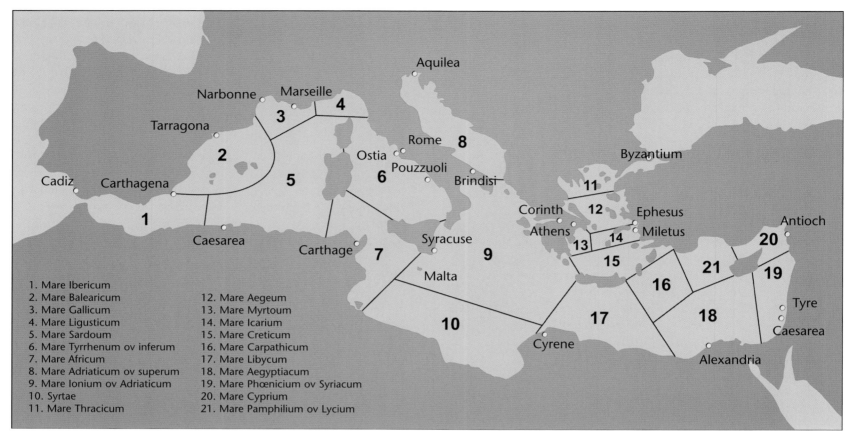

The maritime spaces of the ancient Mediterranean as defined by J. Rougé after P. Pomey (ed.), *La navigation dans l'Antiquité*, 1997, p. 23.

these 'seas' was autonomous and closed off from the others. The history of the relations between the Greeks and the East – the colonisation of Asia Minor and the Cyrene region, the establishment of warehouses in Syria, Egypt, and so on, provides evidence to the contrary. These labels which define restricted maritime areas suggest that the space so designated was quite specific, and this specific character may be interpreted in at least two ways.

The first could be the hypothesis of a 'privileged maritime zone for a community of sailors' – the zone in which they have their home ports, their habits, and the best knowledge of their surroundings; here they sail most frequently. This has nothing to do with the notion of territorial waters, which seems difficult to maintain for this period, except, perhaps, for a few cities in the middle of the 1st millennium BC.[49] In the Greek texts, institutional 'protection' seems not to go beyond the geographical approaches to the port, gulf or bay.[50] This is also what seems to emerge from Wenamun's voyage to the Syro-Palestinian coasts. As for Egypt, properly speaking, it seems that the geographical reality of the Delta does not allow the notion of territorial water to be envisaged. The ports are somewhat further in from the 'real' maritime coasts. This notion must have been applied to the fringe of the Delta bordering the Delta proper and the sea.

The other way of interpreting the specific nature of the maritime space could be that of a sort of 'preferential market' in which most exchanges were carried out; these restricted marine spaces would have been the choice sites of regional commerce.[51] Without going too deeply into the analysis of commercial exchanges and products that had crossed the Mediterranean sea, a few examples may shed light on this hypothesis.

## II.2.1. The 'Egyptian Sea'

Ancient geography describes an Egyptian sea that constitutes a coherent maritime space, whose limits Strabo enables us to trace:[52]

> *The sea of Egypt is limited on its western side by the seas of Libya and Carpathos. To the south and the east are Egypt and the coast that extends from thence to Seleucia (Pieria); to the north, Cyprus and the sea of Pamphylia. The sea of Pamphylia is for its part surrounded to the north by the capes of Cilicia Trachea, Pamphylia, Lycia as far as Rhodia (Rhodiopolis), to the west by the island of the Rhodians, to the east by that part of Cyprus that neighbours on Paphos and Cape Acamas, and to the south by the sea of Egypt.*

The Egyptian maritime space of the geographers is thus first and foremost an eastern space, and appears principally turned towards Cyprus and the coasts of Palestine, the Lebanon and Syria. But to restrict ourselves to such an analysis would mean failing to recognise the links with the Greek world.

In the 'Egyptian Sea', these links seem to have been particularly intense between the island of Cyprus and the Nile Delta, already in the 2nd millennium BC and especially in the 1st millennium BC, from the 8th century up to the seizure of Cyprus by the Ptolemies. On the

49   J. Elayi, *Pénétration grecque en Phénicie sous l'empire perse*, 1988, pp. 62-63
50   J. Velissaropoulos, *DHA*, 25, 1977, pp. 69-70.
51   J.-F. Salles, in H. Sancisi-Weerdenburg, A. Kuhrt (ed.), *Asia Minor and Egypt, AchHist* VI, 1991, p. 210.
52   Strabo, XIV, 6, 1.

basis of archaeological finds alone, the documentation available reveals a significant quantitative disproportion between the Egyptian objects discovered in very great numbers in Cyprus and the less numerous ones picked up on the Syro-Palestinian coast, at least for the 6th–4th centuries BC.[53] To attribute this state of affairs to the inadequacy of the fieldwork or the paucity of excavation reports[54] appears a facile and superficial response, especially for Cyprus and Palestine, which have been intensively explored, and the unbalanced picture that has emerged seems, on the contrary, to reflect a real difference in the circuits of navigation, and even in the exchanges of men and ideas. It has recently been pointed out how close the links were uniting Egypt to the Eteo-Cypriot city of Amathonte, in which the evidence of worship and other cultural manifestations (sculpture, architecture, and so on) bears witness to the profound influences that spread from the Nile Valley during the Archaic and Classical eras.[55] Archaeological discoveries also bear witness to sustained contact between Egypt and the Phoenician city of Kition – more, it appears, than the Nile Valley ever had with any site on the continental coast facing it. Towards the end of the 3rd century BC, for instance, the clients of a *kentro* situated near the city's port were consuming fish from the Nile.[56]

Many more examples demonstrating the closeness of relations between Cyprus and Egypt in the middle of the 1st millennium BC could be provided. However, for the period under consideration, such evidence should not lead to false interpretations, such as taking account of Egypto-Cypriot exchanges alone, to the detriment of other exchanges – Egypto-Phoenician or Cypro-Phoenician; it is merely the case that within the 'Egyptian sea', there was the existence of privileged circuits of navigation and maritime commerce, which seem to link Egypt and Cyprus in a sort of preferential market.[57]

*The Report of Wenamun* and the study of the names given to 'Cyprus' before the 1st millennium BC enable us to explain the permeable character of the commercial zones of the eastern Mediterranean. After leaving Byblos, Wenamun arrives in *J-r-s3*,[58] a toponym already known since Hatshepsut and which can be found with certainty in the cuneiform *A-la-si-ia*.[59] The location of *J-r-s3*/Alasia has in the past been the source of vehement controversies, and the fundamental question of a localisation of the toponym on the continent or on an island of the Mediterranean has split the scholarly world into two camps. An additional complication stemmed from the

uncertainty of knowing whether the object of the debate was a city with its neighbouring territory or some vaster region.[60]

Different authors have suggested a location in Asia Minor (eastern Anatolia, Cilicia) or in northern Syria for Alasia.[61] Others have opted for the island of Cyprus, following the example of W. M. Müller, whose opinion opened a long debate at the end of the 19th century.[62] The supporters of the last suggestion are however divided amongst themselves on the question of knowing whether Alasia includes the whole island or merely a part of it (east or west).[63] A text from Mari, recently published, shows that in the 18th century BC there existed a city called Alasia (*A-la-ch-ia*), from which bronze was imported and which must have been the capital of a kingdom of the same name.[64]

If the whole set of Egyptian and cuneiform texts (Akkadian, Hittite, Ugaritic) in their context are considered, the choice of Cyprus seems inevitable,[65] and in the narrative of Wenamun too.[66] Certain details of the text may perhaps implicitly suggest as much.

If Wenamun does not want to fall into the hands of the *Sakal*, it is probable that he did not use the coastal route either northward or southward. The only way out was to take to the high seas. At first view, everything seems to go wrong thanks to a storm, but the wind and the waves accompanying it drive Wenamun towards Alasia and allow him to be saved. Then it transpires that the population of Alasia does not understand the Egyptian language;[67] only an 'interpreter' is able to make the sovereign lady of Alasia understand Wenamun's words. The inhabitants of cities such as Dor and Byblos seem not have had this difficulty.[68] It can be supposed that the people of Alasia could not understand the language of the Giblite crew of Wenamun's ship, since they were clearly harbouring evil intentions towards them,[69] an attitude which is inexplicable if Alasia were to be located somewhere on the coast of northern Syria, to the north of Byblos: would they threaten their Semitic compatriots?[70] Considering that

53  In 1972 J. Leclant was already expressing the desire for a study of Egyptian objects found in Cyprus. The beginnings of a Cypriot inventory are presented in the second volume of the Kition excavations by G. Clerc, V. Karageorghis, E. Lagarce and J. Leclant, *Fouilles de Kition*, II, *Objets égyptiens et égyptisants*, 1976.

54  J. Elayi, *Pénétration grecque en Phénicie sous l'empire perse*, 1988, pp. 11-12.

55  P. Aupert, in V. Karageorghis (ed.), *Cyprus between the Orient and the Occident*, 1986, pp. 368-382. The author suggests (p. 373) a Palestino-Phoenician link in the spread of the cult of Hathor. Is this hypothesis really necessary? Archaeology does not seem to justify such a detour, but rather indicates direct relations between Egypt and Cyprus, as seems to be demonstrated, for instance, by A. Hermary, *BCH* 109, 1985, pp. 657-699.

56  *Fouilles françaises de Kition-Bamboula*, IV, *Les niveaux hellénistiques*. See also J. F. Salles, *op. cit.*, p. 210.

57  *Id.*, p.211. On the nature of the products exchanged between Egypt and Cyprus, see *Seafaring in Ancient Egypt*, vol. 2.

58  *Wenamun*, 2, 75.

59  EA 39; cf. W. Helck, in *LÄ* VI, 1986, s.v. "Zypern und Ägypten", col. 1452 and n. 2; H. Helck, *Die Beziehungen Ägyptens*, 1971, p. 538. See also the Ugaritic *'Alty*: J. Aistleitner, *Wörterbuch der Ugaritische Sprache*, 1963, p. 24.

60  cf. J. Osing, *GM* 40, 1980, p. 49. For an overview of the problem of Alasia, see for example H. W. Catling, in *CAH* II/2, 1975, pp. 188-216, particularly p. 201-205; L. Hellbing, *Studies in Mediterranean Archaeology* 57, 1979, pp. 65-78; R. S. Merrillees, *Cahiers de la Revue Biblique* 22, 1987.

61  See the old suggestions put forward by H. Gauthier: *GDG*, I, pp. 96-97; cf. the series of authors mentioned in J. Leclant, in *Salamine de Chypre*, 1980, p. 131; cf. J. Strange, *Acta Théologica Danica* 14, 1980, p. 172, 183-184; H. Helck, *Die Beziehungen Ägyptens*, *ÄgAbh* 5, 1971, p. 282-283.

62  W. M. Müller, G. Ebers, *et al.*, *Asien und Europa nach altägyptischen Denkmälern*, 1893, p. 336-337; J. Leclant, *op. cit.*, p. 131-132; W. Helck, in *LÄ* VI, 1986, *s.v.* 'Zypern und Ägypten', col. 1452 (see too n. 469 in which the author still adheres to the other opinion). What is problematic here is the fact that Cyprus is given another name, viz. *Jsj* (from the reign of Thutmose III): J. O Sing, *GM* 40, 1980, p. 45-51; W. Helck, in *LÄ* VI, 1986, *s.v.* 'Zypern und Ägypten', col. 1452. Pour *Jsj* = Alasia = Chypre: see T. Smolenski, *ASAE* XV, 1915, p. 827-828; S. A. B. Mercer, *The Tell el-Amarna Tablets*, II, 1939, p. 827-828; J. Yoyotte, *Kêmi* X, 1949, p. 73, n. 3; J. Vercoutter, *L'Égypte et le monde égéen préhellénique*, *BidÉtud* XXII, 1956; O. Masson, *Inscriptions Chypriotes syllabiques*, 1961; E. Edel, *Orientalia* 37, 1968, p. 419; J. Leclant, in *Salamine de Chypre*, 1980, p. 132-133; J. F. Quack, *ÄgLev* VI, 1996, p. 75-81.

63  For example H. Goedicke, *The Report of Wenamun*, 1975, p. 126, n. 193; M. Artzy *et al.*, *JNES* 35, 1976, p. 181. See also J. Osing, *GM* 40, 1980, p. 49.

64  D. Charpin, *RA* 84, 1990, pp. 125-127.

65  This is also the opinion of E. Lipinski; cf. L. Hellbing, *Studies in Mediterranean Archaeology* 57, 1979, p. 75 and p. 79.

66  G. Lefebvre, *Romans et contes*, 1949, p. 219 n. 82; M. Lichtheim, *Ancient Egyptian Literature*, II, 1976, p. 229, n. 22; G. Bunnens, *Revista di Studi Fenici* 6, 1978, p. 14.

67  *Wenamun*, 2, 77.

68  It should be taken into account that the Egyptian influence which will have been greater in these regions; only the upper class, or a relatively restricted group of the population knew Egyptian, such as the Prince of Byblos (*Wenamun*, 1, 50-51) and his secretary (*Wenamun*, 2, 65). However, the captain of the port of Byblos (*Wenamun*, 1, 43-45) and the sailors of the boat (*Sakal*) on which Wenamun arrives in Byblos (*Wenamun*, 1, 31-32), seem also to know a little Egyptian.

69  *Wenamun*, 2, 82-83.

70  G. Bunnens, *Revista di Studi Fenici* 6, 1978, p. 15.

most of the peoples of the Syrian coast belong to a north-western Semitic linguistic group, and thus form a unity, the Alasians must belong to an ethnic group other than the Levantines.[71] In any case, Alasia is accessible by boat and is perhaps not so far away from Byblos.[72] Wenamun's threat[73] - namely that Sakarbaal could have the sailors of Alasia slain in reprisal – may be the sign of maritime contacts between Byblos and Alasia.[74]

As for the question of whether Alasia includes the whole island of Cyprus, the text can lead to confusion. According to Wenamun, his ship heads 'towards the land of Alasia' (r p3 t3 n J-r-s3).[75] However, the toponym itself comes with the determiner meaning 'city', which could be considered as confirmation of the new factor of Mari, although the Egyptian determiner can also be used to describe a vaster region.[76] In any case, Hatiba is called 'the sovereign lady of the city' (t3 wr(.t) n p3 dmj) and the people who threaten Wenamun are 'those of the place of landing, those of the city' (n3j (n) t3 dmj.t).[77] It might be deduced, on the one hand, that 'the land of Alasia' applies to the whole island of Cyprus or at least a great part of it, while 'the city' refers to the capital of the country on which Wenamun has been cast by chance. Alasia was the name of the city and the kingdom whose capital it was, so that r p3 t3 n J-r-s3 must be understood as 'the territory of the city of Alasia'.[78]

That said, it transpires that Alasia belonged to a Mediterranean cultural, ethnic, political and commercial space that was different from that of the cities of the Levantine coast.

## II.2.2. The 'Phoenician' or 'Syrian' Sea, and 'the Great Sea of Kharu'

The 'Phoenician' or 'Syrian' Sea, which extends from the region of Al Ladhiqiyah in Syria to the Nile Delta had long been known and also seems to designate a highly specific area. Within this maritime space, the history of the kingdom of Byblos is tied up with that of Egypt. Ugaritic texts that define the stages and stopovers of navigation in this 'Phoenician/Syrian Sea' may also be cited: Byblos, Akko, Jaffa, and so on. Witness this text in Akkadian:[79]

> To the King of Ugarit… A message from the King of Tyre, your brother… the sturdy vessel that you had sent to Egypt has now itself docked; in a violent downpour it has been caught… That if your vessel anchors at Akko without loading…

These cities with which Egypt maintains intense economic relations fully belong to this maritime space. Below it is demonstrated

on the basis of solid examples, how intense the exchanges were in this marine area, in particular as far as grain, oil and wine are concerned.[80] Once more, an error has to be avoided: the archaeological and textual references do not place any question mark over the links that Egypt might have had with Cyprus or more western lands, but they do trace the limits of a privileged territory of navigation and commerce along the coast of the eastern Mediterranean and the circuits which united this same coast of the eastern Mediterranean to Egypt.[81]

Among the regions bordering on this eastern sea were Djahy, Khent-ché and perhaps Kefty. Djahy designates a space adjacent to Egypt in the north-east and extends far enough to include Syria: it is a generic term.[82] Khent-ché is an ancient name for the Lebanon[83] and Kefty could have designated part of Phoenicia.[84]

When Wenamun leaves Tanis, he sails towards Byblos on 'the great sea of Kharu' (p3 Ym '3 n 3-rw)[85] with a ship which, in the view of Sakarbaal, is manned by a crew from Kharu (js.t 3-rw).[86] The name Kharu is thus an ethnic label as well as a toponym.[87] Written syllabically,[88] it appears in Egyptian texts under the Pharaoh Thutmose III (1504-1450 BC) (Annals), first as an ethnic name, but increasingly as a toponym.[89] The territorial frontiers of Kharu remain vague and manifestly include several territories or 'countries'.[90] A passage in Papyrus Anastasi III provides some information of its extent:[91] it apparently stretches from tM3-rw (Tjaru), Sile or Tell Abu Seifa near Qantir, in the eastern Delta, to Jw-p3, the Babylonian Ube, situated in the region of Damascus or between Damascus and Kadesh.[92]

If the identification of these toponyms is accepted, as proposed by A. H. Gardiner, it may be concluded with caution that Kharu covered a territory stretching from the frontier of the eastern Delta near Sile, beyond Palestine, to the north of Phoenicia.[93] The extent of Kharu within Syria cannot be determined.

---

71 L. Hellbing, Studies in Mediterranean Archaeology 57, 1979, p. 51 and n. 8, p. 67.

72 Wenamun, 2, 74-75.

73 Wenamun, 2, 82-83.

74 H. Goedicke, The Report of Wenamun, 1975, p. 129.

75 Wenamun, 2, 75.

76 A. H. Gardiner, Egyptian Grammar, 1957, p. 498 (O 49); for example the name de Km.t = 'Egypt', P. Grandet, B. Mathieu, Cours d'Égyptien hiéroglyphique, 1997, p. 698.

77 Wenamun, 2, 75-76. Dmj(.t): 'town/port': Wb V, 456, 8-10.

78 W. Helck, in LÄ VI, 1986, s.v. "Zypern und Ägypten", col. 1454, E. Blumenthal, Atägyptische Reiseerzählungen, 1984, p. 53 (Wenamun, 2, 75); R. S. Merrillees, Cahiers de la Revue Biblique 22, 1987, pp. 67-71. In line 2, 79, Wenamun clearly distinguishes between n (= m) dmj nb 'in each city' and n (= m) p3 t3 n J-r-s3 'in the land of Alasia'. This could be the sign that the territory dependent on Alasia occupied a great part of the island. This is the argument of A. Scheepers, in E. Lipinski (ed.), Phoenicia and the Bible, Studia Phoenicia XI, 1991.

79 E. Lipinski, Syria 44, 1967, p. 283.

80 See Seafaring in Ancient Egypt, vol. 2.

81 J.-F. Salles, in H. Sancisi-Weerdenburg, A. Kuhrt (ed.), Asia Minor and Egypt, AchHist VI, 1991, p. 211.

82 C. Vandersleyen, Les guerres d'Amosis, 1971, pp. 91-102.

83 P. Grandet, Le papyrus Harris I, BiÉtud 109, 1994, vol. 2, n. 146. An expedition of Amenemhat II travelled by boat to the land of Khent-ché and brought back Asiatics ('3m.w): H. Altenmüller, A. M. Moussa, SAK 18, 1991, pp. 14-15 (§23).

84 The term designates Crete at one particular period.

85 Wenamun, 1. 1, 7, 8

86 Wenamun, 1. 1, 54, 55. In principle, the personal and plural determiners may belong to the composition js.t H3rw and not only to H3rw. Wenamun line 1, 58 gives the toponym js.t H3rw, 'in the region of J Kharu'.

87 Wb III, 232, 7-16.

88 M. Burchardt, Die alkanaanäische Fremdworte und Eigennamen im Ägyptischen, II, 1910, p. 38, nº 732.

89 H. Helck, Die Beziehungen Ägyptens, ÄgAbh 5, 1971, pp. 269-270. Note the h3rw of the theonyms '3sjtj h3rw and '3stjr h3rw, known from two egyptian inscriptions of the New Kingdom and often translated as 'Astarte (Ichtar) hurrian' or 'syrian'; bibliographical references in E. Lipinski, OLP 15, 1984, p. 111 and n. 149-150. According to this author (pp. 111-112) this was probably a homophone relating to the semitic hurru > Hor, 'an opening, a cavity'. See HAL, p. 334; Ahw I, p. 359; J. Aistleitner, Wörterbuch der Ugaritischen Sprache, 1963, p. 116. The words of the inscriptions mentioned are not accompanied by a geographic determiner: one is without a determiner, the other has the determiner of houses. The theonym on the Akkadian tablets of Ugarit and of Baniyas is also written without a geographic determiner. It is this absence which has driven the author to seek an alternative explanation. After A. Scheepers, in E. Lipinski (ed.), Phoenicia and the Bible, Studia Phoenicia XI, 1991, p. 65.

90 A. H. Gardiner, AEO I, 181*.

91 P. Anastasi III, 1, 9-10.

92 H. Helck, op. cit., 1971, pp. 266-270. A. Scheepers, op. cit., p. 65.

93 cf. C. Vandersleyen, Les guerres d'Amosis, 1971, p. 149 and n. 4.

Egyptian-style breast plate in the shape of a falcon with wings extended, Byblos, royal necropolis (tomb III), Lebanon, Middle Bronze Age, 18th century BC, gold, 10cm high, Louvre, Paris, AO 9093. © Photo RMN/Hervé Lewandowski.

That the Palestinian and Phoenician coastal zone is part of it emerges from the narrative of Wenamun.[94] He is sent to 'the great sea of Kharu';[95] since Byblos *(Kp-pw-n3)* is his final destination, he sails over the Mediterranean along the coast of Palestine and Phoenicia. It also ensues that the *kharu* sailors in the service of Smendes came from the same region.[96] Furthermore, it is the 'waves of the great sea of Kharu' which draw Wenamun's attention at the time of his first visit to Sakarbaal, the prince of Byblos,[97] and the messenger whom Wenamun sends from Byblos to Egypt returns home 'to Kharu'.[98]

Certain authors translate *Kharu* to mean 'Syria' overall,[99] as is also the case for Retenou *(R*ṯ*nw)* and Djahy *(3-hj)*. The three terms all seem to refer to geographical entities in Palestine-Phoenicia-Syria, but it seems difficult to determine how far they are synonymous designations for one and the same territory or how far they differ in their geographical extent.[100]

Various scholars[101] have related the name *Kharu* to the *Ḫurri* (Hurrites)[102] a people that settled at the beginning of the 3rd millennium BC in the region of the Upper Euphrates and Tigris (the Kingdom of Mitanni) and then spread as far as the south of Palestine towards the middle or end of the 3rd millennium BC. Hurrite onomastics reveal the great influence of other cultures and a significant geographical dispersal.[103] A. H. Gardiner supposes that the Egyptians campaigning in Palestine and Syria there came into contact with a broad swathe of the *Ḫurri* population, a name which the Egyptians then applied to the entire population of the region and later to the territory itself.[104]

Wenamun's commercial voyage on 'the great sea of Kharu' is characterised by different stopovers that are all ports on the Syro-Palestinian coast. *j-r*,[105] identified with the Biblical Dor and situated on the coast of northern Palestine, to the south of Mount Carmel and north of Caesarea, is in fact the first stopover mentioned after Wenamun's departure from Tanis. Then, *The Report of Wenamun* mentions the toponym 3-r.[106] 3-r appears in the Middle Kingdom (2040–1782 BC) and it is the Egyptian transposition of *Sōr*, the name of the commercial city of Tyre, situated south of Sidon.[107] It features

94    GDG IV, p. 151.

95    Wenamun, 1, 7-8.

96    Wenamun, 1, 55-55. W. Helck, in *LÄ* III, 1980, s.v. "Meer", col. 1277 and n. 13.

97    Wenamun, 1, 49.

98    Wenamun, 2, 39.

99    For example W. F. Albright, *The Vocalization of the Egyptian Syllabic Orthography*, 1934, p. 54; G. Lefebvre, *Romans et contes*, 1949, p. 208; M. Lichtheim, *Ancient Egyptian Literature*, II, 1976, pp. 224; R. Giveon, in *LÄ* VI, 1986, s.v. 'Syrien', col. 132.

100   H. Helck, *Die Beziehungen Ägyptens zu Vorderasien*, 1971, pp. 266-270.

101   A. H. Gardiner, *Ancient Egyptian Onomastica* I, 1947, pp. 185-186; H. Helck, *Die Beziehungen Ägyptens zu Vorderasien*, 1971, p. 270; J. A. Tvedtnes, *JNES* 40, 1981, p. 140.

102   J. Aistleitner, *Wörterbuch der Ugaritischen Sprache*, 1963, p. 117; *HAL*, p. 339.

103   I. J. Gelb, *Hurrians und Subarians*, SAOC 22, 1944, pp. 52-70; W. W. Hallo, W. K. Simpson, *The Ancient Near East. A History*, 1971, p. 109-113.

104   A. H. Gardiner, *AEO* I, 186-187.

105   Wenamun, 1, 8.

106   Wenamun, 1, 28. cf. GDG VI, p. 106; S. Ahituv, *Canaanite Toponyms in Ancient Egyptian Documents*, 1984, pp. 192-193; R. Giveon, in *LÄ* VI, 1986, s.v. 'Tyrus', col. 818.

107   A. Scheepers, op. cit., pp. 74-75; M. Burchardt, *Die alkanaanäische Fremdworte und Eigennamen im Ägyptischen*, II, 1910, p. 62, no 1227; W. Richter, *Phönizische Hafenstädte*, 1975, p. 24. For alternative spellings, see GDG, VI, pp. 106-107.

Plaquette depicting a Syrian, funerary temple of Rameses III at Medinet Habu, palace entrance, Thebes, New Kingdom, 20th Dynasty, c. 1184–1153 BC, polychrome enamelled faience work, 25cm high, 7cm wide, Egyptian Museum, Cairo, JE 36457.

© Photo: Peter A. Clayton

regularly in the El-Amarna letters, in geographical letters and several papyri. The commercial relations between Tyre and Egypt seem to have been well established from these periods onwards.[108] The ambassador of Amun then stops off at *d-dn-n³*,[109] which is none other than the Hebrew Sidon, the name of an important Phoenician harbour town, situated between Tyre and Beirut.[110] This toponym had been known since the 18th Dynasty, but it features rarely in the Egyptian sources.[111] Sidon appears as an important maritime port in the 11th century BC,[112] where its ruler maintained commercial relations with Smendes.[113] Finally Wenamun disembarks at *Kp-pw-n³*,[114] a variant form of the *Kbn* of the Middle Kingdom, which is none other than the harbour town of Byblos, situated some 30km north of Beirut.[115] It is possible that, among the variant spellings, there are several homonyms, behind which the name of the above mentioned town is not necessarily hidden.[116] However, within the present framework of Mediterranean toponyms all known to be on the Palestinian and Phoenician coast, it is suggested that the traditional identification between the *Kp-pw-n³* in question and the Hebrew *G[e]bal* (or Phoenician *Gbl*), the present-day *Gebeil* is correct.[117]

Byblos is the final destination of Wenamun's voyage, the place where he wishes to receive from the prince of the city, Sakarbaal, the wood that is destined for the construction of the barque of Amun.[118] The prince of the mountain range that supplied the famous trees is, according to the sovereign of the city, *p³ R-b³-r-n³*,[119] a variant spelling in syllabics of *Rmn*, a form attested from the 18th Dynasty (1570-1293 BC) to the 20th Dynasty (1185–1070 BC),[120] designating Lebanon.[121]

108  H. Helck, *op. cit.*, p. 303; R. Giveon, in *LÄ* VI, 1986, s.v. 'Tyrus', col. 817-818.

109  *Wenamun*, 1, 59. A. Scheepers, *op. cit.*, p. 76.

110  A. Scheepers, *op. cit.*, p. 75; W. Richter, *Phönizische Hafenstädte*, 1975, p. 11.

111  M. Burchardt, *Die alkanaanäische Fremdworte und Eigennamen im Ägyptischen*, 1909-1910, II, p. 63, n° 1247; H. Helck, *Die Beziehungen Ägyptens*, ÄgAbh 5, 1971, p. 302; R. Giveon, in *LÄ* V, 1984, s.v. 'Sidon', col. 922-923; M. Görg, *BN* 11, 1980, p. 16: this author notes a possible appearance of the name 'Sidon' in the topographical lists of Amara-west, Aksha (both dating from the reign of Rameses II) and Soleb (Amenhotep III); cf. M. Görg, *BN* 28, 1985, pp. 15-16.

112  N. Jidejian, *Sidon through the Ages*, 1977, p. 29.

113  See p. 155 *et seq.*

114  *Wenamun*, 1, 16, 29, 33, 34; 2, 82. See A. Scheepers, in E. Lipinski (ed.), *Phoenicia and the Bible*, Studia Phoenicia XI, 1991, pp. 77-78.

115  *Wb* V, 118, 2; *GDG* V, pp. 197-198; N. Jidejian, *op. cit.*, p. 1.

116  A. Nibbi, *Ancient Byblos Reconsidered*, 1985, pp. 59-72; M. Görg, *BN* 28, 1985, p. 15 thinks that he has found other examples of the name, several of them in the New Kingdom.

117  *HAL*, p. 116; A. Scheepers, *op. cit.*, n. 442 p. 77. See H. Frost, *National Museum News* 8, 1998, p. 29; D. Arnaud, *Studi Micenei et Egeo-Anatolici* XXX, 1992, pp. 179-194. For a bibliography and description of current research on Byblos, see E. Lagarce, J. Lagarce, in M. Bietak (ed.), *The Synchronisation of Civilisations in the Eastern Mediterranean in the Second Millennium BC*, 2000, pp. 143-144.

118  *Wenamun*, I. 2, 3-4.

119  *Wenamun*, 2, 25, 28. See A. Scheepers, *op. cit.*, pp. 79-80.

120  *Wb* II, 421, 5. *GDG* III, p. 120, mentions some earlier suggestions for identifications of the name.

121  *HAL*, p. 493. See A. Scheepers, *op. cit.*, n. 457 p. 79. See for example S. Moscati et al., *An Introduction to the Comparative Grammar of the Semitic Languages*, 1964, p. 25, p. 32; J. Vergote, *Phonique historique de l'Égyptien*, Bibliothèque du Muséon 19, 1945, p. 135(9) and 137(10); H. Helck, *op. cit.*, pp. 537-538.

## II.2.3. The 'Cypriot Sea'

It might seem superfluous to remember the importance of the 'Cypriot sea',[122] which unites the eastern coast of the island and those of central and northern Phoenicia, as far as the gates of Cilicia. It was, however, part of the maritime environment of the Egyptians, at least in the first millennium BC. In the Iron Age (9th-6th centuries BC) and the Achaemenid period (6th-4th centuries BC), the cartographical proposals of J. Rougé need to be modified[123] and to extend this maritime space as far as the plain of Akko, to the south. There is a superimposition of the Cypriot and Phoenician seas, which is unsurprising given the predominantly Phoenician character of Cyprus in general, and Kition in particular, until the 5th century BC at least.[124] Within this zone, commercial and cultural exchanges are extremely numerous in both directions, more significant, it would seem, than those uniting Cyprus to the coast of Palestine.[125]

In addition, P. Briant[126] insists on the political role that was played by the northern part of the 'Cypriot sea' at the time of the Achaemenid sovereigns: it acted simultaneously as an outlet for the royal road coming from Babylonia, though less (as the author correctly remarks) for merchants than for soldiers and diplomats. It was also used as a military and naval base for the forces of the great kings as they fought against the many local revolts that shook this part of the empire, in particular in Egypt, but also in Cyprus and Phoenicia. Finally, one of the particular features of the Cilician part of the 'sea of Cyprus' in this period and in more ancient times (witness numerous Greek imports to al-Mina from the 7th century BC) is that it opened more widely to the West than the 'Phoenician' or 'Egyptian Seas'. (It is not necessary to go into the details of an exact identification of this notion of the 'West': specifically the Greece of Asia Minor or continental Greece is meant). Without again referring to the maritime 'highway' cited above, it should be emphasised that it was by way of the 'sea of Cyprus' (including the island itself) that most of the contacts between the Greek world, the Near East and Egypt were established, from ancient periods onwards.

## II.2.4. The 'Carpathic' or 'Rhodian' Sea

A name such as this presupposes the existence of an Aegeo–Egyptian maritime (commercial) space, bringing together the 'Egyptian sea' and the 'Carpathic' or 'Rhodian' Sea, which brought the Aegeo–Greek world into direct contact with Egypt. Now, the Egyptian texts designating the maritime peoples of the North of Egypt are relatively few in number:[127]

- 'The islands that are in the midst of *Wadj Wer*': at the end of the 18th Dynasty and during the Ramesside period, the expression may apparently only designate the Mediterranean islands, more specifically the Aegean region or even further north;[128]
- The land of the *Keftiu*,[129] whose identification with Crete is generally accepted, though it may designate a region in Phoenicia.[130]
- The *Haunebut*: one of the oldest Egyptian geographical names, is the subject of two important articles by J. Vercoutter.[131] These are, properly speaking, 'those who are beyond the baskets'; these *nebut* are apparently forms of inhabitation half on dry land and half in marshland; applied first of all to the non-Egyptian populations of the maritime band of the Delta, the term then seems to have been extended, as Egyptian sailors spread northwards, to the inhabitants of the Aegean islands.[132]

The Egyptians integrated these newcomers into their vision of the world as best they could, enabling observers occasionally to follow their traces in the historical sources of the period. For the Egyptians to 'envisage developing their traditional vision of the cosmos in accordance with the new world order, they had first to be constrained to do so by necessity, several centuries later. The Greeks were then clearly identified in the sources, thanks to a better awareness both of the Aegean world itself and of these new interlocutors, some of them settled in Egypt as traders or colonists, others were employed by the native rulers as mercenaries.'[133]

---

122 'Sea of Cyprus' in Herodotus, I, 72.

123 J. Rougé, *Recherches sur l'organisation du commerce en Méditerranée sous l'empire romain*, 1966, p. 43.

124 M. Yon, in T. Hackens, G. Moucharte (ed.), *Numismatique et économique phéniciennes et puniques, Studia Phoenicia* IX, 1992, pp. 243-260, pls. xxv-xxxviii.

125 J.-F. Salles, in H. Sancisi-Weerdenburg, A. Kuhrt (ed.), *Asia Minor and Egypt*, AchHist VI, 1991, p. 211.

126 P. Briant, in H. Sancisi-Weerdenburg, A. Kuhrt (ed.), *op. cit.*, 1991, pp. 67-82.

127 These terms have been studied by J. Vercoutter, *L'Égypte et le monde égéen préhellénique*, BiÉtud, XXII, 1956.

128 *Id.*, pp. 125-128.

129 *Id.*, pp. 33-123; J. Strange, *Caphtor/Keftiu. A New Investigation*, 1980; W. Helck, in H. Buchholz (ed.), *Ägäische Bronzezeit*, 1987, pp. 218-226; S. Wachsman, *Aegeans in the Theban Tombs*, OLA 20, 1987, pp. 93-99; J. Osing, in *Gegengabe. Festschrift für E. Brunner-Traut*, 1992, pp. 271-280.

130 C. Vandersleyen, in E. Lipinski (ed.), *The Land of Israel*, OLA 19, 1985, pp. 46-53; J. Osing, *op. cit.*, pp. 279-280. *Kefty* appears to designate Crete up to the reign of Thutmose III (thus *Urk.* IV, 616, 1-2). Subsequently, the inhabitants of this country are clearly from the Near East. On this evolution: J. Osing, *Aspect de la culture pharaonique*, 1992, pp. 29-30. It is worth bearing in mind that the illness *r3-nt-ʿ3m.w* ('that of the Asiatics'), mentioned in a medical papyrus of the 14th century BC, is treated by a magical formula in the *Kefty* language, which is West Semitic according to a detailed analysis: R. C. Steiner, *JNES* 51, 1992, pp. 191-200. See too the remarks in A. H. Gardiner, *AEO* I, 202*-203*.

131 J. Vercoutter, *BIFAO* XLVI, 1947, pp. 125-158; *id.*, *BIFAO* XLVIII, 1949, pp. 107-209, pls. i-ii.

132 For C. Vandersleyen and A. Nibbi, the *Haunebut* were never the Aegean people: C. Vandersleyen, *Les guerres d'Amosis*, 1971, pp. 139-176; *id.*, in E. Lipinski (ed.), *The Land of Israel: Cross-Roads of Civilizations*, OLA 19, 1985, p. 44; *id.*, *GM* 103, 1988, pp. 75-80; *id.*, *DE* 12, 1988, p. 75 n. 1; A. Nibbi, *The Sea Peoples*, 1972, pp. 11-32; *id.*, *Sea Peoples and Egypt*, 1975, pp. 35-48. cf. *supra* p. 34 et seq.

133 N. Grimal, in *Entre Égypte et Grèce, Cahiers de la villa 'Kérylos'* 5, 1995, p. 11. See A. Laronde, *ibid.*, pp. 29-36; D. Mallet, *Les premiers établissements des Grecs en Égypte*, 1893; F. K. Kienitz, *Die politische Geschichte Aegyptens*, 1953; M. N. Austin, *Greece and Egypt in the Archaic Age*, 1970; J. Yoyotte, *ACF*, 1991-1992, pp. 634-635 and 1993-1994, pp. 679-692, pp. 694-698.

The list on the base of the colossus in the temple of Amenhotep III (1386-1349 BC) at Kom el-Heitan,[134] whose details are comparable with the depictions of Aegean peoples on the Theban tombs of the era of Thutmose III (1504-1450 BC), demonstrates that at the period of Amenhotep III (1386-1349 BC), routes had been established with Troy in Asia Minor and in Greece, with Mycenae, Nauplia and Messene. In Crete, the Egyptians distinguished between Amnisos, Knossos, Lyktos, Phaistos and Kydonia. They also knew of Cythera. Thanks to its organisation and its precision, this list has been interpreted as an itinerary, one that bears witness to a knowledge of the political organisation of the regions with which the Egyptians maintained state-to-state relations. This interpretation needs to be qualified, as does the idea of possible direct political relations between Greece, Crete and Egypt. The identification of the *Keftiu* is far from being unanimously agreed on by orientalists. J. Strange prefers to see the *Keftiu* as Cypriots.[135] C. Vandersleyen refuses to identify them with either Crete or Cyprus, and proposes that they should be viewed as an unidentified people of Asia Minor.[136] W. Helck identifies the *Keftiu* with Phoenicia,[137] and for A. Nibbi this is a name formed from the radical *Keftiu* and designating the populations of Syro-Palestine.[138] Opening the question up in this way is a radical move which leads its author to minimise the relations between Egypt and Crete in the 12th Dynasty (1991-1782 BC).[139]

The economic aspect of these exchanges can, however, quite easily be deduced from what the Egyptians tell us about these countries four centuries later, at the time of Thutmose III. In the tombs of Theban dignitaries of that era – essentially during the reigns of queen Hatshepsut (Senanmut) (1498-1483 BC) and Thutmose III (Pouiemrê, Antef, Useramon, Menkheperraseneb and Rekhmira, which cuts into the reign of Amenhotep II (1453-1419 BC), throughout the 15th century, between the Middle and Recent Minoan periods, the Aegeans are abundantly depicted, in the so-called 'tributes scenes'. Then they disappear, which agrees with the change from Recent Minoan IB to II and the rise of Recent Aegean II.

These data are confirmed by the concomitant presence of Aegean and Minoan pottery in the Egypt of the 18th Dynasty (1570-1293 BC). It is logical to imagine that the Egyptians preserved as a partner a state with which they had a tradition of fruitful exchanges, and whose products they valued, until the fall of this latter led them to turn to a new power, which, seen from Egypt, was quite similar to the one it was replacing. This could easily be explained by the conservatism of the modes of representation of foreign countries among the Egyptians; 'to take just one famous example, the lists of foreign lands supposed to be those of his own time that Rameses II (1279-1212 BC) features on the walls of his temple at Abu Simbel. He included in them those which Amenhotep had, long before him, engraved on the columns of the temple of Soleb. Many of the countries thus named no longer existed at the time of Rameses II, or had yielded to others.

These lists are as official a document as one could wish. If their cumulative value corresponds perfectly to the cosmological intention that presided over their creation, it is clear that it does not make the task of the modern historian any easier. As far as the Minoans are concerned, the Egyptians probably did not judge it necessary to modify the elements of the depiction that were, for them, in the final analysis equivalent, or did not present characters that needed to be distinguished. Even apart from the lack of historical distance that they must have encountered when faced with changes whose nuances they probably did not perceive, it is highly probable that, in their eyes, all that had taken place was an evolution between related tribes.'[140] It is obvious that the term *Keftiu* designated in this period the whole set of Aegean and Cretan peoples, and even those of Asia Minor.

This should be taken into account to qualify the discussion mentioned earlier on the political and historical reality covered by the name *Keftiu* in the view of the ancient Egyptians; even when nations are discussed which it could be supposed, the Egyptians could clearly identify, even if only because they had been in repeated and direct contact with them, the vagueness of the names given is astonishing. On the list of Kom al-Heitan, the supposed names of Assur and Babylon seem apparently, in fact, to be 'Canaanite toponyms', since they are mentioned elsewhere in a geographical context that can be interpreted in this way. If the study of toponymy has progressed, the keys to the depiction of space and geography that was current on the banks of the Nile are remote.

Be that as it may, during the greater part of the second millennium BC, the tenuous and scattered traces of the relations that Egypt maintained with Crete and Mycenae can be followed.[141] The difficulty comes from the sparseness of direct information, and because it is often difficult to distinguish, in the Egyptian sources, the exact geographical origin of peoples who, as often as not, are little more than some city's name on the lists – whose very organisation gives rise to numerous divergent interpretations. Nevertheless, the recent discoveries of Tell el-Dab'a, the products exchanged, the study of pottery, and of the modes of commercial diffusion, already enable observers to significantly modify the prior image of these relations, and to envisage a maritime (commercial) space between these two regions.

Finally, the discovery of frescoes dating back to the 16th century BC, at Santorini – the ancient Thera – depict magnificent ships with raised stems, moving under the already traditional square sails and with the aid of a large gang of rowers.[142] These real sea carriers refute the idea usually put forward, according to which the maritime relations between Crete and Egypt passed exclusively by way of Rhodes, Cyprus and the coast of Syro-Palestine. Similar ships cannot have had any difficulty in linking, in both directions, Crete and Egypt.[143]

---

134  E. Cline, *Orientalia* 56, 1987, pp. 1-35; L. Godart, *Le pouvoir de l'écrit*, 1990, pp. 106-111; H. Ricke, *Göttinger Vorträge*, 1964 = *NAWG* 13, 1965, pp. 199-203; id., in *Untersuchungen im Totentempel Amenophis III*, 1981, pp. 16-29; J. Leclant, *Göttinfer Vorträge*, 1964, pp. 212-216; id., *ACF* 81, 1980-1981, pp. 473-475; E. Edel, *Die Ortsnamenlisten aus dem Totentempel Amenophis III*, 1966; id., *GM* 11, 1974, pp. 19-21; J. Osing, in *Aspects de la culture pharaonique*, 1992, pp. 32-38; R. S. Merrillees, *AJA* 76, 1972, pp. 281-294.

135  J. Strange, *Acta Théologica Danica* 14, 1980, pp. 172-184.

136  C. Vandersleyen, in E. Lipinski (ed.), *The Land of Israël*, *OLA* 19, 1985, pp. 39-54.

137  W. Helck, *GGA* 221, 1969, pp. 72-86.

138  A. Nibbi, *The Sea Peoples and Egypt*, 1975; id., *Ancient Egypt and some Eastern Neighbours*, 1985; id., *Wenamun and Alashiya Reconsidered*, 1985; id., *ZÄS* 116, 1989, pp. 153-160; C. Vandersleyen, *L'Égypte et la vallée du Nil*, 1995, p. 28, p. 380.

139  C. Vandersleyen, *op. cit.*, p. 81.

140  N. Grimal, in *Entre Égypte et Grèce, Cahiers de la villa 'Kérylos'* 5, 1995, pp. 14-15.

141  Id., 11.

142  S. Marinatos, *Andrôn hèrôôn théios stolos*, 1973, pp. 289-292, pl. ii.

143  J. Rougé, *La marine dans l'Antiquité*, 1975, pp. 89-90. On Egyptian vessels and their suitability for seafaring, cf. *infra* p. 81 *et seq.*

Cretan emissaries bringing gifts, Thebes, tomb of Rekhmira (TT 100), mural painting from the transversal hall, New Kingdom, 28th Dynasty, c. 1450 BC. © 1997 Photo Scala, Florence

During the 1st millennium BC, the maritime policy of the Sais regime – alliance with Lydia, attempts at rapprochement with the Greeks of Asia, the welcoming of Greek mercenaries, the foundation of Naukratis, and so on, served, among other reasons, as a frame for Egyptian commercial circuits in the eastern Mediterranean.[144] The existence of this commercial maritime space of the 'Rhodian or Carpathic sea' is in any case confirmed in the famous Stele of Naukratis where it is a matter of taxing 'everything that comes from the *Sea of the Greeks' (m <ꜣḏ-wr Ḥꜣ.w-nb.wt)*.

Thus, even before the study of some of the products exchanged is embarked on and the proposal of some ideas about the nature of regional and inter-regional commerce is put forward, this rapid overview of the maritime spaces known to the Ancient Egyptians, which are all commercial circuits in the eastern Mediterranean, enables a major feature to be discerned and to set commercial travel back in the wider physical and cultural environment of the Mediterranean. In fact, in the Mediterranean no routes of navigation to the west are encountered (or at most only incidentally): this is not to reject or minimise the impact and the importance of distant trade with the Greek or Ionian cities, or the Phoenician and Punic west, but to set them within a different context. 'The international ( = long-range) commercial current must be conceived as a movement (or a set of movements) that is rectilinear, or at least linear: one-way and return journeys between two (or more) ports far removed from each other, regular routes, habitual circuits. It is possible to begin to glimpse, within the eastern Mediterranean, a veritable "Brownian motion" in all directions, along sinuous, complex and irregular itineraries. These two types of exchange are not mutually exclusive and it is certain that they cross over and merge together on several occasions; but one must not be neglected in favour of the other, or there is the risk of falling into excessive simplifications'.[145]

144   H. T. Wallinga, *AchHist* I, 1987, pp. *47-77*.

145   J.-F. Salles, in H. Sancisi-Weedenburg, A. Kuhrt (ed.), *Asia Minor and Egypt*, *AchHist* VI, 1991, p. 213.

# III. The Red Sea

Navigation over the Red Sea probably goes back to very ancient eras, if one could judge from the numerous rock carvings depicting boats, momentoes of expeditions to the sea, that have been discovered along the natural access routes to the coast, including Wadi Hammamat.[1] Although a more definite idea of the historical role of the Red Sea from the middle of the 3rd millennium BC is now permissible, with its first Egyptian voyages to the land of Punt, the 2nd millennium, with the celebrated expeditions to the same region that were undertaken at the behest of Queen Hatshepsut (1132-1151 BC) and Rameses III (1498-1483), yields a great deal of information about the Red Sea.[2] During the 1st millennium BC, the Red Sea, as a space of commercial navigation, seems to assume new importance. The fact that at the end of the 7th century the Phoenicians were reputed to be specialists of maritime commerce on the Red Sea[3] probably explains that the Pharaoh Nekau II (610-595 BC), who conducted a very active naval policy, ordering the construction of 'triremes, some destined for the Northern Sea, others in the Gulf of Arabia destined for the Erythrean Sea',[4] entrusted Phoenician sailors with the task of proving that Libya (Africa), was 'entirely surrounded by sea, except where it borders on Asia':[5]

> These Phoenicians, then, left the Erythrean Sea, and sailed over the Southern Sea; when autumn came, they landed and sowed the land in the part of Libya where they found themselves every year in the course of their navigation, and they awaited harvest time; once they had harvested the grain, they took to the sea, and after two years they sailed through the Pillars of Hercules and in the third year reached Egypt.

This exploit, which appears to be confirmed by the mention of the changing position of sunrise, which Herodotus, in fact, refuses to believe in,[6] says a great deal about the technical capacity and the maritime experience of the Phoenicians and the Egyptians on the Red Sea.[7]

It was the Ptolemies, in the wake of Alexander, who 'tamed' the Red Sea, insofar as it can indeed be tamed: they sent great numbers of explorers, transported elephants, and founded cities. According to the tradition, they picked up a half-drowned Indian sailor on its shores, and he was willing to reveal to the king of Egypt, Ptolemy VIII (170-163, 145-116 BC), the route back to his own country, in exchange for first aid. Thanks to this, the Egyptians were able to gain access to the most exotic and most expensive products of India.[8] The celebrated navigator Eudoxus of Cyzicus took part in the journey, which thus led to the discovery of a direct route to India using the monsoons. Credit for this was later given to the legendary Hippalos whose figure is all the more mythical in that it seems to be the very personification of the monsoon.[9] Greek and Latin texts are relatively prolix when it comes to the Red Sea, thanks to such explorations, but also because the geographers and historians of the Hellenistic period showed a particular attachment to this region: for example Agatharchides of Cnidus,[10] followed by Artemidorus, Strabo, and Diodorus Siculus, and later summarised by Photius. More 'down to earth' is the merchant who anonymously authored the *Periplus of the Erythrean Sea*, which gave details of commercial activity in the Red Sea around the middle of the 1st century AD.[11]

## III.1. General conditions of navigation in the Red Sea

> *As for this sea, its coasts present, we can make so bold as to affirm, more difficulties than the Great Ocean itself: everything contributes to these difficulties, both the direction of the winds and the lack of drinking water, the sterility of the coasts, the countless deeps, the shoals, the sand banks, the reefs, the rocks, and the islands.*

So wrote Dom Joam de Castro, on his return from the Portuguese Red Sea expedition of AD 1541, in which he participated as a captain of one of the ships.[12]

The conditions of Red Sea navigation obviously depend on its geography. The depths of the Red Sea reach 2,000m and are bordered by zones of lesser depth. The coasts are flanked by coral reefs in which are inserted the main islands, which are almost all coral too.[13] The African and Arabic coasts run in the same north-west/south-east course and have similar physical characteristics. Starting from the shore, one encounters a band of flat ground of variable size, being in general broader on the Arabian side.[14] The coast zone is bordered by a sudden area of high relief, crossed by

---

1   These depictions can be found, for instance, in J. Vandier, *Manuel d'Archéologie égyptienne*, I, 1952, pl. vii, 186, 359: for their significance, see J. Zarins, in M. Taddei, P. Callieri (ed.), *South Asian Archaeology 1987*, I, 1990, pp. 507-541; for examples of inscriptions and their meaning, see L. Bell, J. Johnson, D. Whitcomb, *JNES* 43, 1984, pp. 47-86. We will be returning in detail to these access routes to the Red Sea, p. 76.

2   For an overall view of navigation on the Red Sea, see J. Rougé, in J.-F. Salles (ed.), *L'Arabie et ses mers bordières*, I, *TMO* 16, 1988, pp. 59-74; D. Meeks, in D. Meeks, D. Garcia (ed.), *Techniques et économie antiques et médiévales*, 1997, pp. 175-194; M. Arty, *OJA* 13/2, 1994, pp. 121-147; H. Frost, *Topoi* 6, 1996, pp. 869-902.

3   This reputation could lie at the origin of the tradition that made of the Red Sea the original country of the Phoenicians: Herodotus, 1; VII, 89; cf. the essay by B. Couroyer, *RB* 80, 1973, pp. 264-276. See A. Lemaire, in E. Lipinski, *Phoenicia and the East Mediterranean*, Studia Phoenicia V, *OLA* 22, 1987, pp. 49-60; A. B. Lloyd, *JEA* 63, 1977, pp. 142-155.

4   Herodotus, II, 159.

5   Herodotus, IV, 42.

6   The historical character of this exploit has been rejected by A. B. Lloyd, *JEA* 63, 1977, pp. 142-155; however, this article brings out clearly the activity of Nekau in the Red Sea and thus presents a possible historical context for this exploit, which seems to have remained unique and for which we have some difficulty in understanding how Herodotus's source could have invented it. See below.

7   Darius I was also very active in the Red Sea. It is still difficult to claim that there existed, at this time, a maritime route joining the Gulf of Suez to the Persian Gulf. See the summary in J-F. Salles, in J.-F. Salles (ed.), *L'Arabie et ses mers bordières*, I, *TMO* 16, 1988, pp. 75-102.

8   Strabo, II, 3, 4. On the explorations of the Red Sea, the standard work is still J. Desanges, *Recherches sur l'activité des Méditerranéens aux confins de l'Afrique*, 1978. To this should be added P. Högemann, *Alexander der Grosse und Arabien*, 1985; S. Amigues, *Topoi* 6, 1996, p. 671-677. On the way the monsoon was used in navigating towards India, A. Tchernia, *Annales. Histoire, Sciences Sociales* 5, 1995, pp. 991-1009. This important contribution is reprinted (in English) with several other articles in F. de Romanis, A. Tchernia (ed.), *Crossings. Early Mediterranean Contacts with India*, 1997.

9   P. Pomey, in P. Pomey (ed.), *La navigation dans l'Antiquité*, 1997, pp. 20-23.

10  S. M. Burstein, *Agatharchides of Cnidus*, 1989.

11  L. Casson, *The Periplus Maris Erythraei*, 1989. On trade with India, see for instance P. Ballet, *Topoi* 6/2, 1996, pp. 809-840; E. Grzybek, in *Autour de Coptos*, Topoi suppl. 3, 2002, pp. 337-347. For a resume of work on 'navigation in the Erythrean Sea in Antiquity', see the excellent article by J. Rougé, in J.-F. Salles (ed.), *L'Arabie et ses mers bordières*, I, *TMO* 16, 1988, pp. 59-74.

12  After A. Kammerer, *Le routier de Dom Joam des Castro, l'exploration de la mer Rouge par les portugais en 1541*, 1936; quoted by J. Degas, *RdÉ* 46, 1995, p. 215.

13  For the Red Sea, the coral islands and the islands that are formed from them, see L. Berry, *Sudan Notes and Records 45*, 1, 1964, pp. 148-157; A. M. Ali Hakem, *et al.*, *Sudan Notes and Records* 60, 1979, pp. 97-109, particularly pp. 103-109. G. Dainelli, in *L'Africa Orientale*, 1936, pp. 69-194, particularly 99-137 and P. Meigs, *Geography of Coastal Deserts*, 1966, pp. 63-67, 75-78.

14  This coastal plain is very narrow on the African side to the north of Port Sudan (never more than 20km) but reaches 60km further south; on the Arabian side too, it is broader to the south of Jedda. See K. M. Barbour, *The Republic of the Sudan*, 1961, pp. 26-32; L. Berry, *Sudan Notes and Records 45*, 1, 1964, pp. 148-157; W. Dequin, *Arabische Republik Jemen*, 1976; P. Meigs, *op. cit.*, pp. 63-78.

Satellite image of the northern Red Sea, the Egyptian Arabian Desert, the Gulf of Suez, the Sinai Peninsula, the Gulf of Aqaba and the north-west of the Arabian peninsula.
© CORBIS

several wadis; it rarely rises more than 1,000-1,200m, except where it corresponds with the mountains of Eritrea and Yemen.[15] In these two cases, there is not a range of variable size bordering the coasts of the other regions, but the spurs of two real plateaus, with peaks that can reach a height of 3,600-4,000m and whose formation is itself very different from that of the mountains on the Red Sea.[16]

The sea is very deep: 500m on average, but over 2,000m in its central part. Its deep, clear waters, well oxygenated by the waves, are – with their raised temperatures throughout the year – highly favourable to the construction of coral, so that coral reefs are present everywhere, from north to south. These are sometimes, particularly towards the south, barrier reefs, installed on the shallows out to sea (the Farasan bank, the island of Dahlak, and so on) and comprised a multitude of elementary reefs, sometimes forming islands, but generally immersed under a shallow layer of water; sometimes they are fringing reefs which extend along the shore, faithfully following the irregularities of its outline, and penetrating into the *marsas*, with their characteristic arrangement: a clump of living coral, just breaking water at low tide, with a shallow lagoon behind them, the whole area being hundreds of metres wide.[17] The half-daily tide is insignificant (only 0.10m at Port Sudan) except in the Gulf of Suez, where it reaches 1.80m. But the variations in atmospheric pressure and, even more, the wind, can entail differences in level of between 0.60 and even 0.90m, leaving the reefs clearly exposed in summer and thus modifying the conditions of navigation.[18] While these coral reefs represented real dangers for navigation, the presence, among the coasts, of these 'corridors' protected by coral banks (and thus by very calm waters) facilitated coastal navigation and favoured the boats of antiquity, while these days this creates problems because of the deeper load-draughts of vessels.[19]

Furthermore, the mouths of most of the wadis take the form of great finger-shaped recesses, with deep waters (around 100m), whose dark blue stands out against the pale beige of the Pleistocene coral limestones that reach the surface along the shore, and that are called *marsas* – real natural ports, though difficult to access. So there are little creeks that are very well adapted to stopovers during a voyage both on the coast of Sudan, especially to the south of Port Sudan, and on the Erythrean and South Arabian coasts.[20] K. A. Kitchen has attempted to reconstruct the itinerary of the expedition fleet sent out by Hatshepsut on the basis of nautical charts. They must have progressed under sail, taking into account the currents and favourable winds on the outward journey, or using oars and a sounding line to avoid reefs. If a speed of between three and four knots and a travelling day of about eight hours is considered (travelling by daily stages of 50/60km approximately, within constant sight of the shore), the voyage out must have taken four to six weeks.[21] The return may have taken three months, if the sailors had to row against the north wind. This route presents few difficulties for a well-organised flotilla: there are plenty of mooring grounds on the coast and these make coastal sailing easier. A block discovered at Bubastis mentions a royal visit to Punt that occurred under Thutmose III (1504-1450 BC) or Amenhotep II (1453-1419 BC). The expedition, which comprised 180 men, landed each night, drew water from a well, and then took their bearings from a mountain so they could sail off. This allows a maritime voyage to be clearly envisaged.

Generally speaking, sailing conditions on the Red Sea are reputedly difficult, and have been considered so for a long time, because of the winds, the currents, and the presence of coral reefs.

Nonetheless, the numerous references in the Koran to the Red Sea – 40 or so in number – sometimes celebrate the miraculous ease of navigation there.[22] The difficulties encountered by navigators on the Red Sea are encountered both in the stories of Arthur Rimbaud or Henri de Monfreid, evidence from the beginning of the modern era,[23] and in contemporary *Sailing Directions*. What needs to be borne in mind is a high-seas navigation subject to strict seasonal constraints, and a frequently dangerous coastal navigation.[24] In the summer, the Red Sea is in thrall to a system of dominant north winds: according to Strabo and Pliny navigations would set off for India in July. The rest of the year, two systems of northern and southern winds permanently confront each other, towards the latitude of Port Sudan in general, sometimes further north towards Berenice – which would explain the way that some commentators place the site in the south.[25] Indeed, if from November until May, winds from the southern sector allowed easy navigation as far as the southern waters of the future port of Berenice, navigators there came up against an area of calm, then, as they continued, encountered almost permanent winds from the north sector. So their navigation was considerably slowed down, as they either resorted to tacking or, despite the dangers, sailed through the coastal zones using land breezes and sea breezes, or else, more simply (since these ships had mixed propulsion systems), they used oars to supplement the winds. It is also worth noting that there are numerous variable cross-winds which constitute a grave handicap when one approaches the coasts.[26] Setting sail as soon as day dawns means that sailors can take advantage of the land breeze which can carry the ship northwards for several hours; then this breeze drops and mariners need to advance under oar to continue northwards. Sea breezes, at the end of the afternoons, allow vessels to draw closer to

15    On this subject, see L. Berry, *op. cit.*, pp. 148-157; G. Dainelli, *op. cit.*, pp. 76-98; W. Dequin, *op. cit.*; P. Meigs, *op. cit.*, pp. 63-78.

16    The plateaux of Ethiopia and Yemen are indeed more recent than the other ranges bordering the Red Sea: their formation is linked to volcanic dynamics and the problem of the formation of the Rift Valley from the Oligocene onwards. For the region's geological history, K. M. Barbour, *op. cit.*, pp. 32-37; R. Bowen, *U. JUX, Afro-Arabian Geology*, 1987; W. Dequin, *op. cit.*; P. Meigs, *op. cit.*, pp. 24-29; P. A. Mohr, *The geology of Ethiopia*, 1971, pp. 3-8; R. Said, *Explanatory notes to accompany the geological map of Egypt*, 1971; A. J. Whiteman, *The Geology of the Sudan Republic*, 1971, p. 5. For a general study of the Red Sea's geology, see the overview in P. Sanlaville, in J.-F. Salles (ed.), *L'Arabie et ses mers bordières*, I, TMO 16, 1988, pp. 9-26.

17    R. Dalongeville, P. Sanlaville, *Bulletin de la Société Languedocienne de Géographie* 15, 1981, pp. 39-48; P. Sanlaville, *op. cit.*, p. 19.

18    P. Sanlaville, *op. cit.*, p. 20.

19    *cf.* Chapter III, 'The Ships'.

20    See in general P. Meigs, *Geography of Coastal Deserts*, 1966, pp. 63-67 (the Red Sea and its coasts), 67-70 (the Arabian coast), 75-78 (the coast of Sudan and Eritrea); for the coasts of Sudan, see also L. Berry, *Sudan Notes and Records* 45, 1, 1964, pp. 148-157.

21    Considering the destination to have been in the environs of Port Sudan (K. A. Kitchen, *Orientalia* 20, 1971, p. 188). For a description of the mooring grounds, capes and landmarks and an estimate of the travel times, see also J. Degas, *RdÉ* 46, 1995, pp. 215-237. We propose a locality for the Land of Punt that is further to the south (on the Erythrean coast): see *Seafaring in Ancient Egypt*, vol. 2. In this regard, the northern channel of Massua allows safe and well-sheltered navigation through the Dahlak archipelago.

22    P. Crone, *Meccan Trade and the Rise of Islam*, 1987, p. 5 and n. 7.

23    For example: W. Foster (ed.), *The Red Sea and Adjacent countries*, 1948; J. Degas, *RdÉ* 46, 1995, pp. 215-237. There are numerous modern studies: see the comments made by L. Casson on the conditions of navigation at the time of the Periplus. See also the brief but relevant resume by P. Sanlaville, *op. cit.*, pp. 9-26. The studies of the French Commission on Maritime History can also be consulted: J. Pages, A. Nied, *Itinéraires de la Mer Rouge, Études d'Histoire Maritime* 8, 1991; H. Labrousse, *Récits de la Mer Rouge et de l'Océan Indien, Études d'Histoire Maritime* 10, 1992. See also A. Gil-Artagnan, *BSFE* 73, 1975, pp. 28-43; id., *Expédition Pount*, 1994.

24    See the comments of the geographer R. Dalongeville, the author of several coastal prospecting expeditions to Sudan.

25    On Berenice, but also Mersa Gawasis and Quseir, see p. 80.

26    K. A. Kitchen, *Orientalia* 20, 1971, pp. 184-207; L. Bradbury, *JARCE XXV*, 1988, pp. 127-156, especially pp. 127-130; P. Meigs, *Geography of Coastal Deserts*, 1966, pp. 63-67.

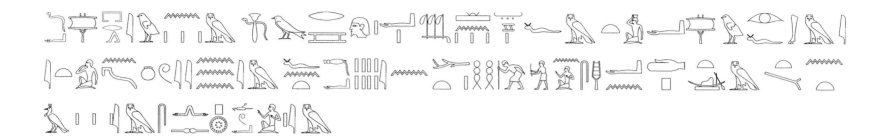

*A storm blew up while we were out at sea, before we could land; the wind arose and the tempest roared; from it there arose a wave eight cubits high that crashed onto the mast, whose presence saved me. The ship sank; none of those on board escaped…*

land to find a place to moor. Out at sea, storms are frequent. The crew in *The Tale of the Shipwrecked Sailor* has this unfortunate experience:[27]

> *A storm blew up while we were out at sea, before we could land; the wind arose and the tempest roared; from it there arose a wave eight cubits high that crashed onto the mast, whose presence saved me. The ship sank; none of those on board escaped…*

Coastal navigation has to confront the presence of fringing reefs all along the shores – the 'jagged and dense reefs that the sea covers' according to Diodorus[28] – which means that it is possible to land only in the *marsas* (big protected bays), taking every precaution, since it is sometimes difficult to find their entrance. The coast cannot be approached except with the sun quite high in the sky and behind, otherwise its dazzle makes it impossible to navigate by sight if the corals and the banks of seaweed are to be avoided. It is thus that any progress of the ships near the coast occurs in an eastward direction in the evenings, and in a westward direction in the mornings. The range and rise of the tides, very variable from one sector to another, must be taken into account. R. Dalongeville concludes: 'The exchange of cargo in antiquity and the Middle Ages would take place at points that were fixed by the points at which land routes reached the coast, and not by the greater or lesser difficulty of the landing conditions: transhipping was, and is still permitted thanks to small low-draught vessels, pushed by men walking through the lagoon water and able to cross the external crest of the fringing reef.'

Even if the obstacles to navigation were fewer than today (coral reefs), the captains of Egyptian boats could advance only with the greatest caution and had to count on the experience of pilots specially brought on board. Safety depended to a great extent on a knowledge of the route, the ability to discern dangers from the variations in water colour, and the aptitude of rowers and sailors to respond instantly to orders. This is still the advice given today by the most recent *Sailing Directions*: 'When one is forced to cross a zone of coral shallows, the best mode of navigation is by sight at a speed that permits prompt manoeuvring and, on the other hand, allows mariners to bring their ship to very quickly.'[29] Nothing seems to have changed for a long time, apart from the fact that, in bygone days, when ships had no engines, it was doubtless preferable to use oars rather than sail through difficult patches, so that one's bearings could be altered more 'promptly'.

Without going into more detail, which can be found in the modern narratives, it should be emphasised that navigation in the Red Sea was certainly more difficult and dangerous than in the Mediterranean. This doubtless implies that there were types of boat adapted to local conditions there, perhaps noticeably different from those used in the Mediterranean.

## III.2. Remarks on the seasons of navigation in the Red Sea

In 'year 8, 1st month of Shomu, in the reign of Seankhkare Montuhotep III' (1997-1991 BC), the Grand Intendant and Director of the Treasury Henu carved on the walls of Wadi Hammamat the story of his great expedition to the Red Sea where he would send *kbn.wt*-boats to Punt to fetch myrrh for the king.[30] The details of this expedition across the eastern desert (consisting of 3,000 men and which required the digging of 15 wells) are well known.[31] Nonetheless, the fact that Henu does not speak of his journey to Punt, or of any meeting with its inhabitants, suggested to J. H. Breasted[32] and A. Erman[33] that Henu did not actually go to Punt himself but returned with his army to the quarries of Wadi Hammamat once the ships had set sail. The date of Henu's inscription allows this dilemma to be resolved in part and provides firm support for an analysis of the unfolding of these events. In 2002 BC, the date

27    *The Tale of the Shipwrecked Sailor*, 33: *ḏꜥ pr(=w) jw=n m wꜣḏ wr tp-ꜥ sꜣḥ=n tꜣ fꜣt(w) ṯꜣw jr=f whmy.t nwy.t jm=f n(y).t 8 mḥ jn ḥ.t ḥḥ(w) n=j s ꜥḥꜥ~n dp.t m(w).t nt(y).w jm=s n sp wꜥ jm.*

28    Diodorus, III, 44 (trans. Bommelaer, Les Belles Lettres).

29    *Instructions nautiques, Mer Rouge et Golfe d'Aden*, 1987, p. 73.

30    J. Couyat, P. Montet, *Les inscriptions du Ouadi Hammâmât*, MIFAO XXXIV, 1912-1913, n° 114, 81-84, pl. xxxi; *PM*, VII, 331.

31    See for example R. Gunlach, in *LÄ* VI, 1985, s.v. 'Wadi Hammamat', col. 1111-1112 n. 30; K. A. Kitchen, *Orientalia* 20, 1971, p. 191; W. Schenkel, *Memphis-Herakleopolis-Theben*, 1965, pp. 253-258; J. H. Breasted, *Ancient Records of Egypt*, I, 1906, pp. 432-433; W. Hayes, in *CAH* I, 2, 1971, p. 491; R. Herzog, *Punt*, 1968; D. Dixon, *JEA* 55, 1969, pp. 55 and n. 7; T. Säve-Söderberg, *The Navy of the Eighteenth Egyptian Dynasty*, 1946, pp. 11-12; H. Winlock, *The Rise and Fall of the Middle Kingdom in Thebes*, 1947. J. Couyat, P. Montet, *op. cit.*, pp. 20-21; G. Goyon, *Nouvelles inscriptions du Ouadi Hammamat*, 1957, p. 2; G. Posener, *CdÉ* 13, 1938, p. 269; L. Bradbury, *JARCE* XXV, 1996, pp. 127-128.

32    J. H. Breasted, *op. cit.*, p. 210, n. c; *id.*, *History of Egypt*, 1905, pp. 153-154; A. Erman, *Life in Ancient Egypt*, 1894, p. 507; A. Nibbi, *GM* 17, 1975, p. 43.

33    A. Erman, *Life in Ancient Egypt*, 1894, p. 507.

'year 8, 1st month of Shomu, 3rd day' corresponds to 4 September ± 1 day.[34] August and September correspond to the ideal season in the Red Sea for anyone sailing southwards to Punt.

The sailing seasons are attested by:

- The traditions preserved by the unknown author of the *Periplus*[35] and by Pliny,[36] who both noted that the sailing season for anyone leaving Egypt and heading for the southern markets, towards the strait of Bab el-Mandeb in India, began at the start of July, but that it was reasonable to travel by sea in September.[37]

- Roman navigation which attests that from June to September, rather than in September alone, Roman ships sailed between Myos Hormos or Berenice and the Ethiopian ports of the Red Sea in relatively safe conditions.[38]

- The winds of the monsoon and the Red Sea currents which dictated the seasons of annual sailings during the Roman era and in the Pharaonic period.[39]

Consequently, it is quite unlikely that the *kbn.wt*-boats, on their return from Punt, would have sailed north (returning to Sawu and mooring at Mersa Gawasis[40]), against winds from the north-east and north-south currents – in the navigation period of the months from July to August. This would have needed to be the case if the date of 4 September of the carved inscription at Wadi Hammamat had been that of the expedition's return (bearing in mind a certain lapse of journey time to make the route from Myos Hormos to Wadi Hammamat). Remember that from November to February, winds and currents are favourable to northward navigation (current flowing northward, settled south-easterly wind sometimes blowing from the north but essentially in the Gulf of Suez[41]).

34    This is calculated on the basis of the generally accepted date for the beginning of the 12th Dynasty, 1991 BC: P. Parker, *Excursus C*. On the chronology of the Middle Kingdom, the reader will find the following of interest: W. Helck, *GM* 67, 1983, pp. 43-46; W. Ward, *AJA* 91, 1987, pp. 527-528, n. 82-84; W. Murnane, *BES* 3, 1981, pp. 73-82; W .K. Simpson, *CdÉ* 47, 1972; W. K. Simpson, in *LÄ* V, 1985, *s.v.* 'Sesostris III', col. 903-906.

35    *The Periplus Maris Erythraei*, § 6, 14, 49, 56; W. Schoff, *The Periplus of the Erythrean Sea*, 1912; L. Casson, *The Periplus Maris Erythraei*, 1989.

36    Pliny, *Natural History*, VI, 36, 104.

37    *The Periplus Maris Erythraei*, § 24, 28. See E. Ascher, *The Journal of Tropical Geography* 28, 1969, p. 1 *et seq.*; U. S. Naval Oceanographic Office, *Sailing Directions for the Red Sea and Gulf of Aden*, 1965, p. 14 *et seq.* and the map provided by L. Bradbury, *JARCE* XXV, 1996, fig. 1 p. 129; G. A. Ballard, *The Mariner's Mirror* 6, 1920, p. 149 *et seq.* and particularly p. 212. C. V. Solver, *The Mariner's Mirror* 22, 1936, p. 430ff stated that the months favourable to sailing were January for southward journeys and March for northward journeys; but his hypothesis rests on currents and winds from the coasts of southern Arabia, and does not seem to agree with the tradition of ancient navigation. He was followed by A. W. Sleeswyk, *IJNA*, 1983, pp. 279-291. Their errors have been corrected by K. A. Kitchen, *Orientalia* 20, 1971, pp. 194-195.

38    E. Ascher, *The Journal of Tropical Geography* 28, 1969, p. 1.

39    *Id.*, p. 1 and 7; G. A. Ballard, *op. cit.*, pp. 212-214; B. Landström, *The Ship*, 1961, pp. 20-21; R. Brown, *The Mariner's Mirror* 46, 1920, pp. 303-306.

40    *cf.* p. 76, 83.

41    According to E. A. Scherer, *op. cit.*, p. 5, the remarks and observations of Pliny concerning sailing to the north of the Red Sea are contemporaneous with the Roman period alone; K. A. Kitchen, *Ancient Egypt: A Cultural Topography*, 1977, pp. 194-196; I. Hofmann, *GM* 4, 1973, p. 19, relate that from October to January the southern currents end at 19°N, while from February to April they end at 17°N; G. A. Ballard, *The Mariner's Mirror* 6, 1920, p. 214 notes that north of the 21° parallel, north winds dominate throughout the year. See U.S. Naval Oceanographic Office, *Sailing Direction for the Red Sea and Gulf of Aden*, 1965, pp. 95, 107, 112-114, 135, 141, 159-160, fig. 5. It rains on the mountains of the Red Sea from November to October; fresh water is then available for replenishment. In the region of Adulis, it rains from November to February, *id.*, p. 107, 141; the same is true of the island of Dahlak: J. Bruce, *Travels to discover the Source of the Nile*, I, 1805, p. 354; D. J. Oliver, *Journal of Tropical Geography*, 1907, p. 69; L. Bradbury, *JARCE* XXV, 1996, pp. 127-130. *cf. Instructions Nautiques, Mer Rouge et Golfe d'Aden*, 1987.

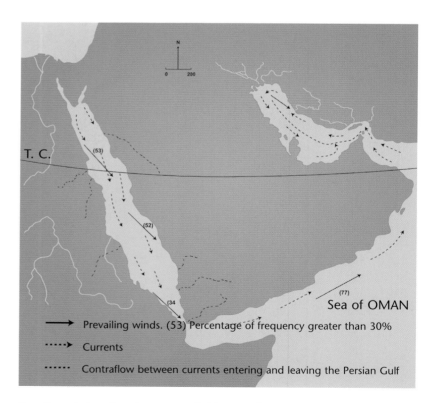

Prevailing winds and marine currents in January, according to *Sailing Directions*, after P. Sanlaville, in J.-F. Salles (ed.), *L'Arabie et ses mers bordières*, I, TMO 16, 1988, p. 21. © Travaux de la Maison de L'Orient

Prevailing winds and marine currents in July, according to *Sailing Directions*, after P. Sanlaville, in J.-F. Salles (ed.), *L'Arabie et ses mers bordières*, I, TMO 16, 1988, p. 23. © Travaux de la Maison de L'Orient

In addition, it has been pointed out that it is not only the physical conditions of the Red Sea that determine the date of navigation towards the region of Punt, but also two important aspects of the trade in 'fresh myrrh';[42]

- The period of myrrh markets in Sudan, Ethiopia, Somalia and southern Arabia[43] is strictly limited to the dry season, from mid-October and early November to April.[44]
- The myrrh and incense harvest; the purest resin is harvested at the end of the rainy season, some six to eight weeks after the trees are cut in mid-July.[45]

For both these reasons, if the ships had returned to the quayside at Sawu by the beginning of September, they would have missed the season of the myrrh harvest, implying they left the region in question in May, June or July (it is necessary to count one or two months' sailing to make a maritime link between the south of the Red Sea and Mersa Gawasis). Hence the conclusion is self-evident: the *kbn.wt*-boats weighed anchor at the end of August to go to Punt, and after 30 to 40 days' sailing they arrived there at the end of September or early October, just as the myrrh from the first harvest was being traded.

What do other documents from this period tell us? There exist inscriptions from the region of *Suw* the examination of which reveals a link between the 'Divine Land' *(#3 ntr)* and a journey whose destination is the 'Mines of Punt' *(Bj3 n Pwn.t)*. Such documents thus give more chronological evidence about navigation on the Red Sea:

- On the central block of the sanctuary of anchors is inscribed the following date: '24th (?) (Year), 1st month of Poret (?)', which was logically linked to the voyage to the Mines of Punt commemorated by the sanctuary of anchors and the stele of the vizir Antefoqer.[46] Assigned to the reign of Senusret I (1971-1926 BC), at the time of the 24th year of his reign or at the latest his 34th/35th year,[47] this seafaring event occurred some 50 years

after Henu's journey, and in the month of May.[48] Abdel Monem Sayed suggested that this was indeed the day of departure for the Mines of Punt.[49] If this hypothesis is correct, this means that the ships of Senusret I embarked at Suwa in the month of May and not in August-September like the ships of Henu or the fleet of Hatshepsut.[50] It is true that this period of the year condemned the Egyptians to travel to the mines of Sudan or Ethiopia during the rainy season and the hottest months, but navigational conditions were not too risky,[51] with a current and favourable wind that enable southbound sailing.[52] It should be borne in mind that it rains on the Red Sea mountains between November and April,[53] which implies that, from May to June, the wells, cisterns and other natural basins are full of fresh drinking water, necessary for the replenishment of any maritime expedition. A departure for the south of the Red Sea in the month of May is thus not inconceivable.[54]

It is also necessary to note that there is a difference between the objectives of the two voyages: the ships of Henu and Hatshepsut were ships bound for Punt so as to being back myrrh, incense trees and other exotic products and animals.[55] The voyage in question here, in May, was supposed to be heading for the mines – gold mines, perhaps, or mines of precious stones.[56] So there is every right to think that the ships that set sail for the mines of Punt did so as soon as the seafaring conditions on the Red Sea allowed it, while ships that were off to seek myrrh, incense and other exotic products awaited the favourable moment both from the maritime point of view and the commercial point of view. In other terms, there was a gap of four to five months between these two types of expedition.[57]

This supposition is verified in *The Tale of the Shipwrecked Sailor*:[58] the hero of the story, before being cast ashore on an island, had been given the royal command to go, together with his crew, to a mine near Punt.[59] The way that the story's episodes follow one another, set out by L. Bradbury, shows two types of navigation: a first maritime expedition to the mines, then a period of four months before a

42   L. Bradbury, *op. cit.*, pp. 130-131.

43   Depending on whether Punt is situated in one of these areas. We will be returning to the question of where Punt was located in more detail in *Seafaring in Ancient Egypt*, vol. 2.

44   Sudanese road trade from the interior to the Red Sea begins at the end of October and early November and ends in April, R. Pankhurst, *Journal of Ethiopian Studies* 2, 1964, pp. 66, 69, 71, 84, 85, 102; M. De Young, *Journal of Ethiopian Studies* 4, 1966, p. 104. At Opone, 65km from Cape Guardafui (W. Schoff, *The Periplus of the Erythrean Sea*, 1912, pp. 87, 91), the place is transformed into a real market in which 20,000 inhabitants come to trade between October and March, while it is completely deserted between April and October! At Berbera and Seylac, the annual market is held from January to March, L. Cassanelli, *The Shaping of Somali Society*, 1982, p. 48.

45   The harvesting of myrrh, incense and resin gum begins with the cutting of the trees during the rainy season when the dog star is prominent, according to Pliny, *Natural History*, XII, 32, 58; XII, 35, 66-70; and W. Schoff, *op. cit.*, part 27-30, pp. 112-114, 125-126, 218. See A. Lucas, *Ancient Egyptian Materials and Industries*, 1948 pp. 110-114; A. Lucas, *JEA* 16, 1930, pp. 41-53; G. W. Van Beek, in D. Freedman, E. Campbell (ed.), *The Biblical Archaeologist Reader* II, 1964, pp. 99-117; F. N. Hepper, *JEA* 55, 1969, pp. 66-72; A. Nibbi, *Ancient Egypt and Some Eastern Neighbours*, 1981, ch. 3.

46   Abdel Monem Sayed, *RdÉ* 29, 1977, pp. 169, 173, 176; id., *CdÉ* LVIII, fasc. 115-116, 1983, p. 29-30. H. Frost, *The Mariner's Mirror* 65, pp. 145, 154.

47   Since the vizir Antefoqer was involved in this event, year 24 is the latest evidence of his long career which began in the reign of Amenemhat I (W. K. Simpson, *AJA* 41, 1955, pp. 129-130). He was vizir when Amenemhat I launched his war against the Nubians during year 29 (Z. Zaba, *ASAE* 81, 1981, p. 41; id., *The Rock Inscriptions of Lower Nubia*, 1974, pp. 98-109, insc. 73 at El-Girgaoui). A late date during the reign of Senusret I confirms the tale told by Hecataeus of Abdera (according to Diodorus, I, 55, 1) which relates that in the 3rd century BC, the king subjugated the Ethiopians and sent his fleet out on the Red Sea (M. Malaise, *CdÉ* 41, 1966, p. 253 and n. 2). Abdel Monem Sayed, *op. cit.*, pp. 32-35 and n. 2 relates the traditional story (Diodorus, I, 55, 2) of the 400 ships of the fleet of Senusret that he sent to conquer the Red Sea, and the mention, on the sanctuary of anchors, of '400 recruits' and two fragments attesting the word '*dr*' that means 'to master, to subjugate'.

48   See L. Bradbury, *JARCE* XXV, 1996, p. 138.

49   Abdel Monem Sayed, *op. cit.*, n. a.

50   K. A. Kitchen, *Orientalia* 20, 1971, p. 202.

51   U.S. Naval Oceanographic Office, *Sailing Direction for the Red Sea and Gulf of Aden*, 1965, pp. 21, p. 141. At the latitude of Port Sudan, near Trinkitat, Haboobs, hot winds are accompanied by sandstorms between July and September. These storms are powerful, break out without warning and last for half an hour: 'vessels should not be lying to their own anchors during the occurrence' (id., p. 135, 149).

52   Id., pp. 17-23, 107.

53   See above.

54   E. Ascher, *The Journal of Tropical Geography* 28, 1969, p. 1.

55   We will be returning to these products and merchandises in detail in *Seafaring in Ancient Egypt*, vol. 2.

56   Abdel Monem Sayed, *RdÉ* 29, 1977, p. 161, in the section on the inscription on the anchor, the line X + 7 appears, a reference to the gold inspection *((j)m(y)-r(3) nbw)*; see J. Vercoutter, *KUSH* VII, 1959, pp. 145-146. This title implies that gold was one of its objectives. Nonetheless in a procession of mineral-producing regions at Luxor (*KRI* II, 617-628; W. M. Müller, *Egyptological Researches* II, 1910, p. 89, fig. 20; G. Daressy, *RT* 16, 1910, p. 51) are precious stones which relate to *T3-Ntr* and not gold; see also, under Rameses III, J. H. Breasted, *Ancient records of Egypt*, IV, 1907, p. 34. On the *T3-ntr* and the possibility that it refers to the Land of Punt, see *Seafaring in Ancient Egypt*, vol. 2.

57   L. Bradbury, *JARCE* XXV, 1996, p. 139.

58   M. Lichtheim, *Ancient Egyptian Literature*, I, 1975, pp. 211-215; G. Wainwright, *JEA* XXXII, 1946, p. 31; E. Maltzer, *GM* 22, 1976, pp. 47-49; W. Wycickl, *KUSH* V, 1957, pp. 70-72.

59   According to line 90 of the text. The two-month journey is hardly likely to have been a voyage to the mines of Sinai.

second one which went to the Land of Punt. It was in fact the navigators of this latter expedition who were to come to the aid of the poor Shipwrecked Sailor.

The table opposite envisages the historical circumstances of *The Tale of the Shipwrecked Sailor*.[60]

Although it is possible to say that this itinerary is pure speculation, the way the events and the journeys follow on from one another remains plausible.[61] It could be imagined that the two expeditions had left together, that the Shipwrecked Sailor was cast ashore on a mysterious island while the second expedition pursued its course, reached Punt and, on the return journey, rescued him. In this case, however, the island would have been an island like all others and not the whole or a part of the land of Punt. Finally, *The Tale of the Shipwrecked Sailor* suggests a certain rhythm, a periodic character to the navigations – one that cannot be definitively demonstrated by the Wadi Gawasis documents, and concerns only four or five journeys over a period of 140 years. Does the fact that the seven anchors were immediately incorporated into a coastal sanctuary indicate that in the course of the following reigns no journey was planned? It remains extremely difficult to come to a firm conclusion of the periodic character of the Red Sea expeditions. The available documentation nonetheless enables a certain regularity in the organisation of maritime commerce to be envisaged.

| Mid-May | The Shipwrecked Sailor and 120 members of his crew leave Egypt and embark near the Great Green for mines in Punt. (*Shipwrecked Sailor*, 25–30) |
|---|---|
| Late June | After a period at sea of undisclosed length, a storm breaks out. The ship is destroyed, the crew perishes at sea and the hero of the story is cast a shore on an island, in which the Sovereign of Punt tells him that in four months an Egyptian ship will come and rescue him. He goes on to explain that he will need to sail for two months to get back home. Knowing that the journey northward is slower and more difficult, it can be assumed that the Shipwrecked Man took a month or a month and a half to reach Punt.[62] (*Shipwrecked Sailor*, 31–135) |
| October | Four months later, an Egyptian ship lands in Punt and the members of its crew discover the Shipwrecked Sailor. (*Shipwrecked Sailor*, 155–57) |
| November and perhaps December | The ship is laden with myrrh, incense, giraffe tails, monkeys and precious wood (neither gold, nor precious stones are mentioned). (*Shipwrecked Sailor*, 160–67) |
| January–February | After two months' navigation,[63] the Shipwrecked Sailor reaches It-Tauy. (*Shipwrecked Sailor*, 173–175) |

60   Table after L. Bradbury, *JARCE* XXV, 1996, p. 140.

61   The dual destination of Egyptian ships was known at a later period when elephants were hunted at Ptolemais-Theron (in the Tokar delta), while commercial vessels continued to Adoulis (W. Schoff, *The Periplus of the Erythrean Sea*, 1912, p. 22-23, 60; J. W. Crowfoot, *Geographical Journal* 37, 1911, pp. 523-550; Pliny, *Natural History*, VI, 33, 171-73), counting two days under sail between Ptolemais and the trading port of Adoulis. See also Strabo, XVI, 4, 5-14.

62   C. V. Solver, *The Mariner's Mirror* 22, 1936, p. 442 informs us that it is possible to get from Suez to Berenice in a week. K. A. Kitchen, *Orientalia* 20, 1971, p. 196 worked out that it needed between one month and six weeks to make the journey from Suez to Suakim.

63   G. Wainwright, *JEA* XXXII, 1946, p. 34, quotes Herodotus, II, 8, noting that the journey from Memphis to the countries that produced spices lasted two months.

Opposite: map of ancient Egypt, after D. Valbelle and C. Bonnet (ed.), *Le Sinaï durant l'Antiquité et le Moyen Âge. 4000 ans d'histoire pour un désert*, 1998.

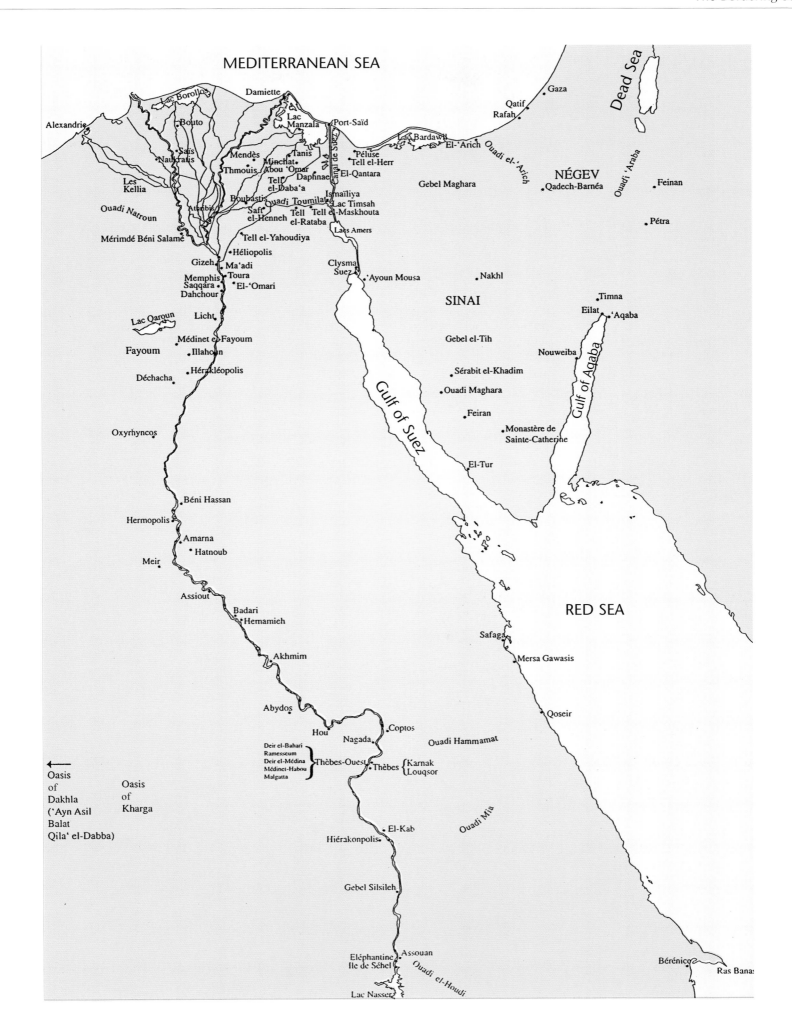

MEDITERRANEAN SEA

Dead Sea

Gaza

Lac Borollo

Damiette

Qatif

Rafah

Alexandrie

Lac Manzala

Port-Saïd

Lac Bardawil

El-'Arich

Ouadi el-'Arich

NÉGEV

Bouto

Saïs

Naukratis

Mendès

Thmouis

Tanis

Minshat

Abou 'Omar

Péluse

Tell el-Herr

El-Qantara

Gebel Maghara

Qadech-Barnéa

Ouadi 'Araba

Feinan

Les

Kellia

Tell

el-Daba'a

Daphnae

Ismaïliya

Lac Timsah

Tell el-Maskhouta

Pétra

Ouadi Natroun

Athribis

Boubastis

Saft

el-Henneh

Ouadi Toumilat

Tell

el-Rataba

Lacs Amers

Mérimdé Béni Salamé

Tell el-Yahoudiya

Héliopolis

Gizeh

Ma'adi

Toura

Clysma

Suez

Ayoun Mousa

Nakhl

SINAI

Memphis

Saqqara

Dahchour

El-'Omari

Timna

Eilat

Aqaba

Lac Qaroun

Licht

Médinet el-Fayoum

Fayoum

Illahoun

Gebel el-Tih

Nouweiba

Gulf of Aqaba

Déchacha

Hérakléopolis

Sérabit el-Khadim

Ouadi Maghara

Oxyrhyncos

Feiran

Monastère de

Sainte-Catherine

Gulf of Suez

El-Tur

Béni Hassan

Hermopolis

Amarna

Hatnoub

Meir

Assiout

Badari

Hemamieh

RED SEA

Safaga

Akhmim

Mersa Gawasis

Abydos

Qoseir

Hou

Coptos

Nagada

Ouadi Hammamat

Deir el-Bahari

Ramesseum

Deir el-Médina

Médinet-Habou

Malgatta

Thèbes-Ouest

Thèbes

Karnak

Louqsor

Oasis

of

Dakhla

('Ayn Asil

Balat

Qila' el-Dabba)

Oasis

of

Kharga

El-Kab

Hiérakonpolis

Ouadi Mia

Gebel Silsileh

Eléphantine

Ile de Séhel

Assouan

Bérénice

Ouadi el-Houdi

Ras Banas

Lac Nasser

43

# Chapter II: The Ports

## I.  Ports, moorings, quays and *emporion*

On the one hand, there was Alexandria, a vast harbour entirely focused on commercial relations, comparable, with all due allowances, to great trading ports in the modern era. On the other hand, the city ports situated on the branches of the Nile in the Delta or on the beach: big ships could not approach these and even vessels of a modest size could run aground. Any mention of the ports of Egypt immediately brings contradictory ideas to mind. There is a tendency to consider that an ancient port could, or even had to, resemble, in its size, and the depth of its waters, modern ports, or at least those of the recent past, the era of sail. As far as may be judged by the available documents, Pharaonic Egypt before the Hellenistic epoch seems not to have possessed ports of this type on its sea fronts, but at best landing stages or mooring grounds. This has, furthermore, enabled certain scholars to deny the existence of any Egyptian maritime navigation. While before the Hellenistic period there is only very variable information on the ports or moorings that could have been created by the Egyptians or used by them to any great extent, a certain number of features allows the nature of certain maritime harbour infrastructures in the Pharaonic period to be imagined.

Firstly it should be noted that the first significant harbour developments dated back to the 6th century and were the result of the maritime projects and the ambitions of the great tyrants. Over a century after the work done by Polycrates at Samos, Herodotus could still admire the two moles there, built over a depth of 35m (in reality 18m) and extending over 300m.[1] The port of Delos underwent a progressive development: pilgrims of the Archaic period disembarked in creeks to the north-west and north-east, and at the start of the 6th century the locals began to construct a wider cove, opened to the west, with a great mole 100m long to protect it from the dominant wind and flagstone quays that rose only a short way above the sea level. Over the next four centuries, a small mole to the south was constructed, and quays were deployed over a length of 1700 to 1800m; also, to the south, secondary basins were built, three of them lined by shops. The Greek method consisted of forming an artificial port or widening a natural port with the aid of jetties that provided shelter from the wind, facilitated disembarkation operations, and thus ensured the safety of the ships, frequently being curved round to form a real port. Sometimes, an islet in the roads was used as the base of a single big mole: the Heptastadium of Alexandria, that long highway pierced by two arches so the ships could pass through, which extended from the western tip of the island of the Pharos to the continent, and protected the great basin from the western currents, was the most consummate example.[2] These arrangements were enough to justify, for a Greek, the label of 'artificial port'. There were also, at least during the Hellenistic period, ports that were really dug by human hands: this was the case, at Alexandria, of the port significantly named 'The Coffer' (*kibôtos*).[3]

Generally speaking, the essential function of a commercial port is to guarantee neutrality. Permanent guarantees of security and a whole set of better conditions are necessary to make commerce possible. The guarantee of fresh provisions, the protection of life and limb and the property of foreigners needed to be ensured. A prior agreement between the interested parties was thus necessary. It was habitually based on the treaties in force. Such an agreement included, without doubt, facilities for unloading, embarkation, transport, stocking and classifying goods and fixing exchange rates under the guarantee of the authorities.[4] Merchants' quarters had to be set up around the port, with an infrastructure to make services available to them (covered markets, entrepots, markets, inns, and so on) and a special administration. Hence the existence of the Phoenician quarters at Memphis,[5] and Herodotus' statement that 'once, Naukratis alone was a port opened to trade (Εμπoριoν), and there was no other in Egypt.'[6]

The *emporion*, whose name passed into Latin in the form *emporium*, was the place of commerce, not the market where local producers came to sell directly to consumers the products of their activities, but the place to which was brought the production of an economic region vast enough to sell it with a view to exporting it to distant places: there, it would be sold to regional buyers. The *emporion* could also be a port. Nonetheless, in the *Periplus of the Erythrean Sea*, the *emporia* were always very carefully distinguished from the ports; some of them, indeed, were far from the sea, such as Coloe, described as the *emporion* for ivory.[7] This distinction between the port, as a place at which ships came to dock, and the *emporion*, as a place of commerce, explains why in the great commercial ports, the *emporion* was a clearly-defined quarter which, while being close to the port, is not to be confused with it. Such, for example, are the *emporia* of Alexandria.[8] So the *emporion* cannot be considered as part of the port unless the whole city is viewed as a port. This is how Pollux treated Naukratis.[9]

More than one tomb from the era of the Old Kingdom (2686-2181 BC) has preserved market scenes in the open air.[10] Several scenes

---

1   Herodotus, III, 60.
2   Diodorus, XVII, 52; Strabo, XVII, 1, 6.
3   See A. Bernand, *Alexandrie la Grande*, 1998; F. Goddio, *et al.*, *Alexandria, the submerged royal quarters*, 1998; A. Bernand, F. Goddio, *Sunken Egypt*, 2002.
4   R. B. Revere, in K. Polanyi, C. M. Arensberg (ed.), *Les systèmes économiques*, 1975, pp. 71-92.
5   Herodotus, II, 112.
6   Herodotus, II, 179. On Naukratis, *cf. infra* p. 60 *et seq.*
7   *Periplus Maris Erythraei*, 4, 6, 7, 8.
8   Strabo, XVII, 794.
9   Pollux, *Onomasticon*, IX, 34.
10  *LD* II, pls. 49, 96, 103; III, pl. 76a; J. Capart, *Une rue de tombeaux à Saqqarah*, 1907, pl. 31 *et seq.*; *id.*, *Recueil de monuments égyptiens*, I, 1902, pl. 13; H. Wild, *Le tombeau de Ti*, MIFAO LXV, fasc. III, 1939, pl. 174; F. W. von Bissing, *Die Mastaba des Gem-ni-kai*, I, 1905, pl. 22-23; S. B. Hassan, *ASAE* XXXVIII, 1938, pl. 96; L. Klebs, *Die Reliefs und Malereien des Neuen Reiches*, 1934, p. 230 *et seq.*; Ahmed M. Moussa, H. Altenmüller, *Das Grab des Nianchchnum und Chnumhotep*, 1977, p. 82 *et seq.*, Abb. 10; N. de G. Davies, *Two Ramesside Tombs at Thebes*, 1927, pl. 30 + 34; N. de G. Davies, R. O. Faulkner, *JEA* 33, 1947, pl. viii; A. Badawy, *The Tomb of Nyhetep-Ptah at Giza and the Tomb of Ankh'ahor at Saqqara*, 1978, p. 19 *et seq.*, figs 29-31, 32-34; H. Hodjash, O. Berlev, *AltorForsch* 7, 1980, p. 31 *et seq.*; H. Hodjash, O. Berlev, *The Egyptian Reliefs and Stelae in the Pushkin Museum Moscow*, 1982, p. 33 *et seq.*; M. Verner, *Preliminary Report on Czechoslovak Excavations in the Mastaba of Ptahshepses at Abusir*, 1976, p. 61 *et seq.*; W. Wreszinski, *Atlas zur altägyptischen Kulturgeschichte*, I, 1923, pl. 199 *et seq.*, 363, 366. Other, unpublished scenes and indicated in *LÄ* III, *s.v.* 'Markt', col. 1191 *et seq.* For some further pertinent comments, see P. Montet, *Les scènes de la vie privée*, 1925, p. 319 *et seq.*; G. Roquet, in *Mélanges H. Wild*, BSEG 9-10, 1984-1985, p. 227 *et seq.*; R. Drenkhahn, *Die Handwerker und ihre Tätigkeiten*, ÄgAbh 31, 1976, p. 10 *et seq.*; C. Eyre, in M. Powell (ed.), *Labor in the Ancient Near East*, 1987, p. 31 *et seq.*, 199 *et seq.*; R. Müller-Wollermann, *JESHO* 28, 1985, p. 138 *et seq.*; W. Helck, *Wirtschaftsgeschichte des Alten Ägypten*, 1975, p. 114 *et seq.*, 205, 259.

and texts dating from the era of the New Kingdom (1570-1070 BC) clearly show public markets being held in various different places, with market stalls set up particularly on the banks of the Nile (in the ports and on the landing stages, for instance) [11] – the best means of communication naturally being the river, always available, with a continual movement of persons and products.[12] Varied goods were also exchanged from cargo vessels transporting all kinds of harvest produce and other materials.[13] It is also certain that food and home-made goods as well as objects manufactured by artisans circulated from hand to hand between individuals. The question of the economic role of the market itself will be raised below, and the nature

of the transactions that took place in it.[14] The interest and the difficulty of these scenes reside in the nature and the status of those who trade, namely merchants and artisans who come to sell their products. This, however, goes beyond the scope of the present investigation into ports and mooring grounds. The famous scene from the tomb of Kenamun[15] shows shops on a quayside, two with men and one with a woman, spreading out clothes, sandals and other objects of uncertain identity. The men are holding a pair of scales with weights in metal (?). In this case, they are in the process of trading with foreigners. Likewise, a bas relief from the tomb of Khaemhet[16] shows a similar scene of commercial activity on a quay.

The importance of the quay as a market place should therefore be noted. The term *mry.t*, 'quay', 'landing stage',[17] was used to refer

11   For some references, see H. Römer, *SAK* 19, 1992, p. 259 *et seq.*

12   See F. Kampp, K. J. Seyfried, in *Antike Welt-Zeitschrift für Archäologie und Kulturgeschichte* 5, 1995, p. 339, Abb. 29.

13   On this topic, see P. Brooklyn 35.1453 A+B: V. Condon, *RdÉ* 35, 1984, pp. 57-82, pl. 4-7; J. J. Janssen, *VA* 1, 1985, pp. 109-112; V. Condon, *VA* 2, 1986, pp. 23-29. In addition, J. J. Janssen, *Two Ancient Egyptian Ship's Logs*, 1961, p. 105, where fabrics were probably traded from a ship, as is indicated in P. Turin, 2008 and 2016.

14   *Seafaring in Ancient Egypt*, vol. 2.

15   N. de G. Davies, R. O. Faulkner, *JEA* 33, 1947, pp. 40-46.

16   TT 57; *LD* III, 76 = W. Wreszinski, *Atlas zur altaegyptische Kulturgeschichte*, I, 1923, 199-200.

17   See W. F. Edgerton, J. A. Wilson, *Historical Records of Rameses IIII*, SAOC 12, 1936, p. 55 n 24a; J. J. Janssen, *Two Ancient Egyptian Ship's Logs*, 1961, p. 68, AnLex 77.1787, 79.1274.

Temple with obelisks, Byblos, Lebanon. © Photo: Peter A. Clayton

to the market or to commercial activity in general.[18] It reflects, once again, the fact that the river was the commercial route *par excellence*, and provides evidence of the role of navigation in commerce, as well as that of boatmen and navigators as customers and merchants.[19] The port was naturally one of the places marked out for exchanges of every kind, and in one of the reports on the pillaging of the tombs of the Theban necropolis, the accused confesses that thieves took the booty and sold it in the (river) port of Thebes.[20]

Among the maritime ports of the Delta present before the conquest of Alexander, there figures, as elaborated above, Naukratis. It is undeniable that Naukratis welcomed many ships coming from the eastern Mediterranean, in spite of the fact that it was situated not on one of the branches of the Nile but in a canal linking Sais with Naukratis. It so happens, furthermore, that one of the quarters of this city was called, in Egyptian, 'the house of the port' *(Pr-mry.t)*. The very name of this type of port *(mry.t)* implies that it was provided with a quay, which does not exclude the possibility that boats could moor there with the aid of a post.[21] The presence of quays could support the hypothesis of L. Basch, for whom such quays could have permitted the unloading of certain ships with the aid of hoisting apparatus.[22] It is interesting to note that such ports are known, through Egyptian texts, at Memphis, of course, but also at Hermopolis, Coptos or Thebes. Further investigation would doubtless show that these ports had their corresponding naval dockyards.[23] Pictorial representations together with archaeology confirm the existence of this kind of establishment.[24] It is worth bearing in mind that the port and naval dockyard of *Per-nefer*, situated near Memphis, were founded in the last years of the reign of Thutmose III (1504–1450 BC) and they prospered, from the reign of Amenhotep II (1453–1419 BC), until the very start of the 19th Dynasty (c. 1430–1295 BC). The absence of any mention of this site before and after these dates does not mean that the port and the naval dockyard of Memphis did not exist outside this period. The slow shifting of the Nile eastwards, throughout history and right up until modern times, has meant that their location followed this shift and occupied successively different sites. The royal dockyards of Memphis are known to have existed from the Old Kingdom and they are still mentioned in the Hellenistic period.[25]

In addition, the *mry.t*-ports are also attested outside Egypt, in the Mediterranean. The land of *Djahy*, which covers the coastal plain from the Egyptian frontier as far as Jaffa, at the least, possessed such ports, some of which were sometimes under Egyptian control. The best known are evidently those which were visited by Wenamun during his journey on 'the great sea of Kharu': Dor, Tyre, Sidon, and of course Byblos.

The Levantine ports of the Mediterranean coast can also be mentioned here, since they were used by the Egyptians, as is shown by Wenamun's adventure, and they provide, on the archaeological level, several elements that can contribute to a knowledge of Egyptian navigation.

Recent studies devoted to the Levantine coast of the Mediterranean and in particular the ports of the Lebanese coast bring to the fore the lack of documents on the harbour infrastructure before the Hellenistic period, and also on the necessity of carrying out more research in this particular domain of archaeology. Geomorphological prospecting, marine biologists, and palaeo-botanists, within the framework of excavations in the course of the

last few years, have highlighted – for specific regions and periods – a certain number of questions relative to ancient ports and mooring grounds. It emerges that this work in progress must rest on an overall approach to the history of the different environments: in each case, the coastal dynamic and a sedimentary analysis have been envisaged, as has the layout of the sites, in order to analyse the natural dynamic, the rhythms and the mobility of the coast and the possible eventual silting up of the harbour basins. The results show the necessity of taking into account the diversity of every site, due to the variable weight of sedimentary dynamics, the vertical mobility of the sea level and the control of the physical environment, which is directly linked to the economic and political organisation of space.[26] Furthermore, the textual documentation raises the question of a 'historical geography' which might perhaps enable us to put the ports into a hierarchy, since their impact obviously varied with the size and significance of urban development. Recent research on the Lebanese coast, especially at Tyre and Sidon, has qualified to some extent the idea that Bronze Age ports had no artificial installations. Without going into particular details, it is worth recalling that harbour protection facilities (breakwaters and dikes) have also been identified going back to the 3rd millennium before our era.[27] The Egyptians

18    J. Cerny, *A community of Workmen at Thebes*, 1973, pp. 93-97; J. J. Janssen, *De Markt op de Oever*, 1980; C. J. Eyre, *CdÉ* 67, 1992, pp. 277-281; R. Ventura, *Living in the City of the Dead*, *OBO* 69, 1986; A. Erman, H. Ranke, *Aegypten und aegyptisches Leben im Altertum*, 1923, pp. 587-591.

19    See E. W. Castle, *JESHO* 35, 1992, pp. 239-277; R. Müller-Wollermann, *JESHO* 28, 1985, pp.140-145. C. J. Eyre, in N. Grimal, B. Menu (ed.), *le commerce*, *BiÉtud* 121, 1998, p. 177.

20    P. BM 10054, rº 3, 5, T. E. Peet, *The Great Tomb-Robberies*, I, 1930, p. 62; II, pl. 6.

21    See J. Degas, *Égypte. Afrique & Orient* 1, 1996, pp. 8-12; *id.*, in B. Menu (ed.), *Les problèmes institutionnels de l'eau*, *BiÉtud* CX, 1994, pp. 141-152, figs 1-7.

22    L. Basch, *The Mariner's Mirror* 64, 1978, p. 109.23

23    The *Satire on Trades* associates naval carpenters with the *šwty.w*-merchants and the crews of *mnš*-ships that sailed to Syro-Palestine: P. Lansing, 4, 8-4, 9; A. H. Gardiner, *Late-Egyptian Miscellanies*, p. 103; R. O. Caminos, *Late-Egyptian Miscellanies*, p. 384 with notes; A. Erman, H. Lange, *Papyrus Lansing*, 1925, p. 54 *et seq.*; A. Théodoridès, *AIPHO* 15, 1960, p. 86. On the *šwty.w*-merchants, *cf.* p. 158 *et seq.*, and on *mnš*-ships see p. 94-95. See S. R. K. Glanville, *ZÄS* 66, 1930, pp. 105-121; *id. ZÄS* 68, 1932, pp. 7-41; T. Säve-Söderbergh, *The Navy*, 1946, pp. 78-79. On *wḫr.w*, 'naval dockyards', *cf.* A. H. Gardiner, *AEO* I, 215; R. A. Caminos, *Late-Egyptian Miscellanies*, 1954, p. 163; W. K. Simpson, *JEA* 59, 1973, p. 220; R. Drenkhahn, *Die Handwerker und ihre Tätigkeiten*, *ÄgAbh* 31, 1976 § 1.8.4.1.1; Abdel Monem Sayed, *RdÉ* 29 p. 170; *AnLex* 77, 1024, 78. 1077. A mention of *wḫr.t* figures already in the titles of Nymaatre I, mother of Djoser and regent (seal print from the tomb of Khasekhemwy at Abydos, Cairo CG 11106-11112): *ḥtm.t (?) wḫr.t*, 'the (feminine) chancellor (?) of the naval dockyard'.

24    B. Kemp, D. O'Connor, *IJNA* 3, 1974, pp. 104-107. On Mediterranean ports in the Pharaonic period, note the recent study by Fawzi el-Fakharani, in *Egyptology at the Dawn of the Twenty-first Century, Proceedings of the Eighth International Congress of Egyptologists*, 2000, vol. 2, 2003, pp. 203-208.

25    See S. R. K. Glanville, *ZÄS* 66, 1930, pp. 105-121; *id.*, *ZÄS* 68, 1932, pp. 7-41; T. Säve-Söderbergh, *The Navy*, 1946, pp. 78-79.

26    D. J. Blackman, *Ancient Harbours in the Mediterranean*, Part I, *IJNA* 11/2, 1982, pp. 79-104, pp. 185-211; F. Briand, A. Maldonado (ed.), *Transformations and evolution of the Mediterranean coastline*, Bulletin de l'Institut Océanographique 18, Monaco, 1997; L. Franco, *Ocean and Coastal Management* 30, 2-3, 1996, pp. 115-151; A. Raban (ed.), *Harbour archaeology, Procceedings of the first workshop 'Ancient mediterranean harbours'*, BAR IS 257, 1985; M. Provansal, *Méditerranée. Revue géographique des pays méditerranéens* 1/2, 2000, pp. 3-5.

27    H. Frost, in V. Karageorghis, D. Michaelidis (ed.), *Cyprus and the Sea, Proceedings of the International Symposium*, Nicosia, 25-26 October 1993, 1995, pp. 1-22; C. Morhange, *et al.*, in *Ports antiques et paléoenvironnements littoraux, Méditerranée. Revue géographique des pays méditerranéens* 1/2, 2000, pp. 91-100; C. Morhange, *et al.*, *Nouvelles données paléoenvironnementales sur le port antique de Sidon, proposition de datation, National Museum News* 10, 2000, pp. 42-48; C. Morhange, *et al.*, *Étude des paléoenvironnements du port de Sidon (Liban) depuis 4000 ans, Résultats préliminaires, Bulletin d'Archéologie et d'Architecture Libanaises*; C. Doumet-Serhal, in C. Doumet-Serhal (ed.), *Sidon, National Museum News* 10, 1999, pp. 40-41; P. Sanlaville, *Étude géomorphologique de la région littorale du Liban*, 1977; P. Sanlaville, R. Dalongeville, P. Bernier, J. Evin, *Journal of Coastal Research* 13/2, 1997, pp. 385-396.

Site of Byblos, Lebanon. © Paul Almasy/CORBIS

were obviously familiar with Tyre. There is, for instance, a letter from Amarna in which the king of Tyre says to Akhenaten:[28]

*the king… knows that we are si(ted) on the sea.*

As far as Byblos goes, paradoxically, while the city has been excavated,[29] the same cannot be said of the ancient ports whose exact locality, even today, is unknown, as is their spatial organisation. Recent research has cast doubt on the idea that the port of Byblos was situated on the site of the present fishing port north of the low hill, and has raised the question of the possibility of there having been two ports characteristic of Phoenician peninsula sites, including a possible open roadstead south of the promontory. H. Frost and C. Morhange have pointed out an important fact: in terms of the organisation of harbour space, the northern fishing port seems rather poorly adapted to transhipments of cedar wood in the Bronze Age. It seems much too small in size to permit the manipulation of big logs, some of them, discovered in Egypt, measuring over 25m long. Furthermore, the head of the bay, south of the Byblos promontory, has several major advantages which probably made it possible to establish an open roadstead in ancient times at the end of the El-Shkiny valley. The harbour organisation of Byblos thus reveals itself as particularly rich and promising. As for Sidon and Tyre, it is necessary to reflect on the location and use of certain ports, a small port to the north of the promontory, and a huge open roadstead probably to the south. Archaeological research in these sectors of the ancient city of Byblos would perhaps verify these hypotheses and pinpoint the site of the port in which wood from the mountains of Lebanon was loaded on to ships bound for Egypt.[30]

Merchant navigators from the Levantine coast came to Egypt to trade.[31] Depictions dating from the New Kingdom show them unloading their ships. These scenes are certainly not occurring on the Mediterranean coast.[32] Everything indicates that they penetrated into the interior via the river and moored in the nearest port, probably that of Memphis.[33] A sort of popular saying in the letters of El-Amarna compares Byblos to Memphis:[34]

*Byblos is like Memphis, for my lord ( = the king of Egypt).*

This might mean that Byblos and Memphis had, for Egypt, the same importance as far as navigation was concerned. Be that as it may, some of these foreign merchant navigators needed to cross the coastal cordon of the Nile Delta and the marshy zone before they could reach the great Egyptian river ports.

---

28    L. Moran, *Les lettres d'El-Amarna*, LAPO 13, 1987, pp. 385, 35-48. D. Meeks, in D. Meeks, D. Garcia (ed.), *Techniques et économie antiques et médiévales*, 1997, p. 193 n. 96.

29    P. Montet, *Byblos et l'Égypte*, 1928; M. Dunand, *Fouilles de Byblos*, 1937-1958; id., *Byblos, son histoire, ses ruines, ses légendes*, 1973.

30    See H. Frost, in F. Van Voorden, *et al.* (ed.), *Byblos-Lebanon*, 1999, pp. 23-26; H. Frost, C. Morhange, in *Ports antiques et paléoenvironnements littoraux, Méditerranée. Revue géographique des pays méditerranéens* 1/2, 2000, pp. 101-105; J.-F. Salles, in *Liban, l'autre rive*, 1998, pp. 66-70.

31    Ships that were not necessarily there for trade also stayed in Egypt: L. Moran, 'Les lettres d'El-Amarna', LAPO 13, 1987, p. 300 (EA 105, 14-21).

32    B. Kemp, D. O'Connor, *IJNA* 3, 1974, pp. 101-103.

33    K. Vandorpe, *Enchoria* 22, 1995, pp. 162-164.

34    L. Moran, *op. cit.*, p. 267 and n. 11, p. 367 and n. 1.

## II. The Ports of the Delta and the Mediterranean coastline

### II.1. Between land and sea

It is not the intention of this study to examine the international character of all the ports of the Nile Delta and the Mediterranean coastline, but a broad-brush picture of the structure that governed the organisation of cities and towns that were also ports shall be presented. It is enough to look at the map to realise that the political, economic and cultural contacts between Egypt and Asia, the Mediterranean and Libya inevitably passed via the roads leading to the confines of the Delta and via the branches of the Nile converging on Memphis, the crossroads of the whole kingdom. The Lower Delta nonetheless had one major disadvantage for the Egyptians: it constituted a merciless obstacle for the direct, transversal traffic travelling from one corner of the Delta to another. Already, the central section of this Delta hardly leant itself, even at low water, to a transversal crossing, from east to west. The major branches of the Nile, the canals and the muddy channels acting as natural drains often forced travellers to ford them, and from time to time to resort to ferries. In the Ptolemaic period, thanks to one of those rare 'travel journals' that has survived from Egyptian antiquity – a document of expenses – relating to a group of horsemen travelling from the north-eastern corner of the Delta to the north-western corner, from Pelusium to Alexandria, heading up as far as Bubastis, veering westwards and passing through Naukratis. They cover well over 300km *en route*, but a direct crossing of the Lower Delta would have been more difficult, more onerous and practically impossible: many water channels, bogs, pools and woody areas to circumvent or if possible avoid, and a consequent lack of safety.[1]

So there is a region of Egypt that is neither land nor sea. It cannot be understood without practising what Roger Dion called 'retrospective physical geography'. No part of the Egyptian landscape has been more greatly modified than what is called the Delta.[2]

The most significant modification was doubtless the disappearance or transformation of the branches of the Nile. This is true of the westernmost branch, what was called the 'Canopic', since it came out at Canopus, the present Aboukir. It was later called 'Herakleopolis' since a sanctuary of Herakles was to be found at its tip. The Greek historian Strabo is perfectly clear:

> *At Canopus there is first Herakleion where there is a temple of Herakles, then comes the Canopic mouth and the beginning of the Delta.*

---

1   See J. Yoyotte, P. Chuvin, *L'Histoire* 88, April 1986, pp. 40-48; J.-Y. Carrez-Maratray, *Péluse, BiÉtud* 124, 1999, n° 351 p. 178 and pp. 336-337. For a detailed study of the general configuration of the Delta, see A. Bernand, *Le Delta égyptien d'après les textes grecs, 1, Les confins libyques*, I, *MIFAO* 91, 1970, pp. 5-60.

2   The map drawn by André Bernand, map n° 74 of the *Barrington Atlas of the Greek and Roman World*, published by Richard J. A. Talbert, Princeton Press, 2002, makes clear the unusual topography of this region.

Ruins of Tanis in morning mists. © Photo: Yves Guichard

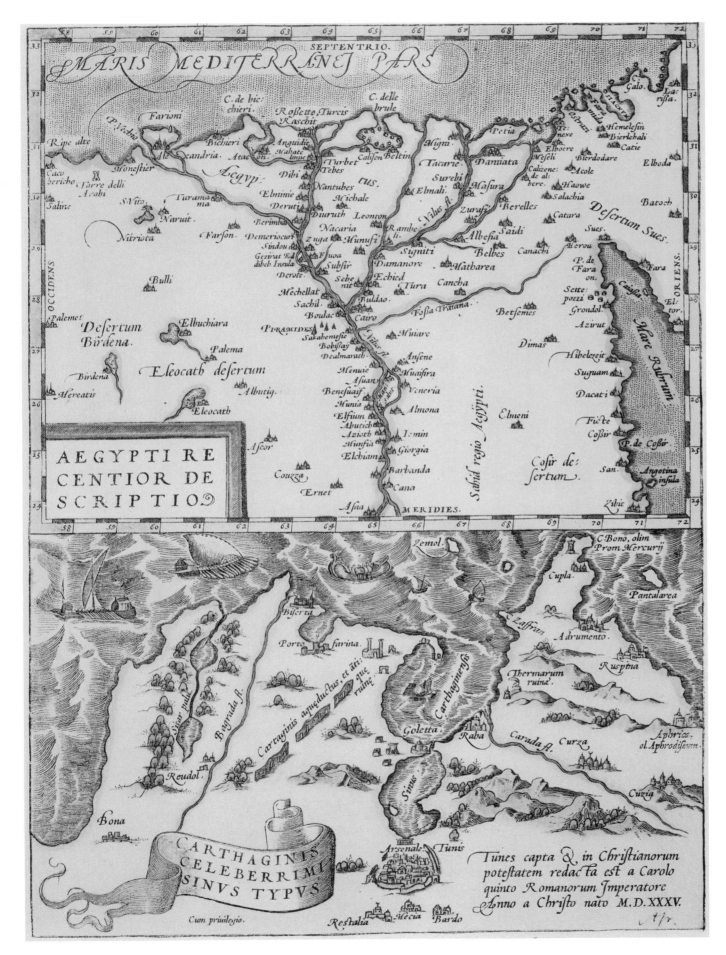

*Aegypti Recentior Descriptio* (top): the north of Egypt as depicted in Abraham Ortellius, *Theatrum Orbis Terrarum*, 1570. © AKG Images

51

Unlike the Canopic mouth which has disappeared from the landscape, the Bolbitic mouth and the branch of the same name have survived, later taking the name of the mouth and branch of Rosetta. This Bolbitic branch took its name, as in the case of the Canopic branch, from the town of Bolbitine situated at its extremity. The outline of this Bolbitic (or Bolbitine) branch hardly differed from that of the present-day Rosetta branch, but the main difference stems from the former importance of this branch, which was much smaller when the Canopic branch existed.

The disappearance of the Canopic branch led to the drying up or the notable shrinkage of the lakes extending from this region: the lake of Aboukir, Lake Maryut, the lake of Edku. These lakes used to be fed by canals leading from the Canopic branch, so that the level of these expanses of water was much higher than later. With the perennial system of irrigation, one practised all the year round, and with the appearance of the great barrage of the Delta, the lakes ceased to benefit from that massive amount of water brought to them by the floods. This spelled the end for the appearance of the Delta as described by Herodotus:

> When the Nile has flooded the land, the cities alone appear above the water, creating rather the same make as islands in the Aegean; the rest of Egypt becomes a sea, only the towns emerge. In this case, people no longer travel by boat along the river's branches, but cut right across the plain. For instance, in order to travel up from Naukratis to Memphis, they travel past the Pyramids; yet this is not the real route, which passes by the tip of the Delta and the town of Kerkasore. And if you are coming from the sea and Canopus to Naukratis, crossing the plain, you will pass near the town of Anthylla and the one called the town of Archandros.

The extent of the ancient lakes was measured by the scientists of the French Egyptian Expedition, Gratien Sr., J. G. Chabrol and M. A. Lancret, all members of the Department of Civil Engineering. They inspected these lakes both before and after the flood of 4 April to 15 June 1801 that was caused by the opening of the dikes on the Alexandria canal. It can be said that they saw these lakes in a state close to their previous appearance.

Drainage works, towards the end of the 19th century, made much of the land in the coastal province, Behera, again cultivable. Today they are great areas of plain and marshes so shallow that one hesitates to give them the name of lakes. Raised earthen mounds mark the course of the former branches of the Nile or canals, the coast being so flat that it can hardly be distinguished from the sea. Furthermore, the subsidence of the coast and this entire part of the Delta has made it a complicated matter to work out what this region must have been like in antiquity. Here too homage must be paid to the observations of the engineers of the French Egyptian Expedition, such as L. Cordier who studied the region of Tanis, or Gratien Sr. who observed the region of Lake Borollos. For his part, Saint Genis noted the lowering of the coast of Alexandria, basing his findings

The Roman mosaic in the Temple of Fortune at Praeneste, Italy, *c.* AD 80.
© Museo Archeologico Prenestino, Palestrina, Italy/The Bridgeman Art Library

53

Detail of the mosaic in the Temple of Fortune at Praeneste, depicting the shores of the Nile Delta during the flood, c. AD 80.
© Museo Archeologico Prenestino, Palestrina, Italy/The Bridgeman Art Library

mainly on the state of the aqueducts and certain tombs. As for G. Daressy, he found to the east of Alexandria, at Kom el-Giza, the site of the former Chaireon, a Nilometer whose zero point was buried about a metre below the current sea level. It was completely ensconced in a low hill and the summit of the column was approximately on the same level as the neighbouring land, which means the amount by which the ground has subsided can be calculated. Likewise, in 1909, the corps of Civil Engineers discovered between Dekkela and the tip of Agami a small submerged ancient port, 2km away from Agami. The land subsidence was measured as between 1m and 1.5m.

It must not be forgotten that the barrage established at the southern point of the Delta, near the village of Katatba, modified the entire hydrography of the province of Behera. The digging of the canal of Katatba greatly transformed the irrigation of the maritime province. Furthermore, one element of the modern landscape did not exist in antiquity: the drainage system, the canals of evacuation of the irrigation water, some in the direction of the lake of Edku, the others in the direction of Lake Mariut. These modern watercourses need to be imagined in order to gain an idea of how the landscape looked in antiquity. It is the sinuous nature of the course followed by certain canals that can best indicate the age of the watercourse. Likewise, the height with respect to the plain of the mound of earth on which a

canal is constructed can indicate its former state by calculating the mass of mud deposited, but these calculations are often hypothetical.

Walking through the marshy region of the Delta explains quite well why the measure of distance used by Strabo, the *schene*, varies considerably. Walking through boggy terrain is inevitably slower than moving over solid ground, and so this unit of distance may be perceived as a 'unit of tiredness', so to speak. This is one way of not imputing exorbitant distances to Strabo.

Two geographical considerations need to be borne in mind in order to understand the geography of the Delta: the *gezira* and the *kôm* (plural *kiman*). The *gezira* is an island formed in watercourses: it can indicate either the site of a former agglomeration or else the mere fact that the river has cut back on itself. The *kôm* is a low mound formed more often than not by debris resulting from human occupation, and producing the highly sought-after manure called *sebbakh*. Such a mound may indicate the site of an ancient city.

In the Delta, earth and water are locked in struggle or else collaborate to form a territory that is neither earth nor water. Achilles Tatius, in his novel *Leucippe and Clitophon*, described this marshy landscape, the dwelling of shepherds and herdsmen, the Greek term *poimen* designating anyone who leads a herd. Actually, they were often brigands who found a refuge in the papyrus bushes growing in these marshes. It was enough just to destroy the earthen dikes holding back the irrigation canals to drown the country and transform it into a mire in which neither men nor horses could advance any further. Achilles Tatius, relating this episode, declares:

> *It was an unprecedented disaster: so many shipwrecks and no ship! There were two extraordinary things, quite contrary to what anyone might have expected: an infantry combat in water, a shipwreck on land!*

In the modern period, during Napoleon's campaign in Egypt, the same adventure befell Vivant Denon, a member of the French Expedition, who says:

> *I take another path, and cross a dike that our enemies had broken; the water already covered the terrain we had crossed, and on all sides currents swept across it in every direction, like so many torrents.*

If fresh water could spring its surprises, sea water could also invade Lower Egypt. Indeed, the Delta, in its northern part, was bordered by a very narrow strip of land, called the *taenia* (a word used to refer to the tapeworm, long and flat). It was very difficult to take this passage, which was full of breaks, and from which it was easy to be swept away by the waves. Upstream from this coastal cordon, a zone of lakes and marshes was hardly a good site for setting up a town or city. Sailors were cautious about dropping anchor on such shifting soil. It was a kind of terrain called *barari* and even today, when you fly over it, herds of buffalo may be observed with their horns bent backwards, immersed up to their necks and tipping their heads into the water to pull up a few strands of grass from the depths of the salty marshes. They are grazing on ocean.

The particularity of the Delta, one that contributed to the role it played as a buffer between Egypt and the sea, necessitated the use of a type of boat familiar in Vietnam, but unexpected by the edge of the Mediterranean: the basket boat[3] or coracle, which must be the same as the boat used by those *Haunebut* mentioned earlier.[4] Heliodorus and Achilles Tatius refer to the lifestyle of the confines of the Delta and suggest that a whole populace had boats that served as economic, social and even family centres:

> *And this is what the lake is like; this whole region is called by the Egyptians 'the land of shepherds'; it is a natural basin, which receives part of its water from the Nile's floods and transforms itself into a lake, very deep in the middle but, at its edges, forming a marshy plain; what shores are for the sea, marshes are for the lake in question. It is here that all the brigands of Egypt have their town: one brigand finds a bit of land that emerges just a little above the water, and there he builds his hut; another lives on a barque, which serves him both as a means of transport and as a dwelling-place; it is on these barques that their wives spin wool, and on these barques that they give birth. When a child is born, first he is fed with his mother's milk then with fish caught in the lake and dried*

Tell San el-Hagar, Tanis, north-east of the Nile Delta. © Photo: David Fabre

Tell San el-Hagar, Tanis, north-east of the Nile Delta. © Photo: David Fabre

The modern Egyptian landscape, region of San el-Hagar, north-east of the Nile Delta. © Photo: Yves Guichard

---

3  L. Basch, *Le Musée imaginaire de la marine*, 1987, p. 51.

4  cf. p. 13 *et seq.*

Relief depicting men harvesting papyrus and leading oxen, Old Kingdom, c. 2700-2180 BC. © Gianni Dagli Orti/CORBIS

*in the sun. When their parents realise they want to crawl, their
ankles are tied by a cord just long enough to enable them to get as
far as the edge of the barque or the extremity of the hut…*[5]

*Around the territories that are thus inhabited by the herdsmen,
there is always a great deal of stagnant water; when all the land
is covered by the waters, lakes form there which, even when the
Nile withdraws, continue to exist and keep their water, as well as
the mud that the water has formed. And the herdsmen cross these
lakes on foot, or by boat, but only boats carrying a single person
can navigate across them; any boat from foreign parts gets bogged
down in the mud. Their boats are small and light and they need
little water to sail over; if, eventually, there is no water left at all,
the boatmen hoist their boats on to their backs and carry them
until they find more water…*[6]

The Roman mosaic of Praeneste (1st century BC), which
represents Egypt seen from the sky, shows, next to some pleasure
boats, a Roman bireme probably based at Alexandria, and some easily
recognisable papyrus barques, a coracle, situated precisely in the zone
of the Delta described by Heliodorus and Achilles Tatius. According
to L. Basch, 'we can *a priori* suspect that this vessel was of great
antiquity: already during the predynastic period, a basket worker
made a basket looking like a boat, playing on the resemblance
between them. Even more significantly, in the Amratian period (c.
3700 BC), one of the first images of Egyptian boating shows a
hippopotamus hunter mounted on a tiny boat in the shape of a
basket. Fishermen, or rather hunters of fish, perched on similar
baskets are depicted on rock paintings in South Africa (most likely

5    Heliodorus, *Aethiopica*, 5; translation by P. Grimal, *Romans grecs et latins*, 1958, p. 526.
6    Achilles Tatius, *Leucippe and Clitophon*, 12, 2; translation by P. Grimal, *op. cit.*, p. 945.

dating to the last millennium). There is no doubt that these 'fishermen' are akin to the fish harpooners of the Batla tribe, on the Mansa River, in Rhodesia. These were mounted on a kind of floating basket made of woven grass.'[7]

The geographer J. Lozach has given a good description of the strange landscape of the margins of the Nile Delta, in a book published in 1935:

*As soon as you start heading towards the lakes of Lower Egypt, you soon reach regions where life becomes rarer and even disappears; lands of solitude and wretchedness. They form a wide band extending northwards and eastwards of the cultivated region, as far as the lakes, almost as far as the sea, from which they are separated from nothing more than a few kilometres of dunes. During the flood and during the winter, this land is abundantly bathed by the waters of the Nile: we even see annexes to the lakes forming on it, and lakes and land can easily be confused. But as soon as evaporation has led to the greater part of the water disappearing, all that is left is ideally flat plains, without relief, their soil brown and white, covered by a layer of varnish which crackles under your feet and glistens in the sunlight. Saline vegetation, scrubby little shoots, dirty grey in colour – these alone*

*can survive here: there is no tree to break the monotonous circle of the horizon. From time to time a dune of middling size, sculpted by the wind, or else a longer hill, ten or twenty metres high at most, but visible from afar, can be seen: this is a kôm, a heap formed from the remains of a town that may once have been quite sizeable. Behind it the white minarets of distant villages appear like lighthouses, or rather like those landmarks that are used to set bearings by when sailing near the coast. With a little imagination, it would be easy to think that you were lost in the middle of a calm sea, but one without the slightest allure.*

*In these dreary expanses, especially mournful in winter, life seems to have fled. The plants you come across are lichens, clumps of grass that do not mind the salt, and reeds in the places where there is enough humidity – sometimes even, in privileged corners, a little greenery. Few animals, and among mammals, only the least interesting species: jackals, foxes, wolves; as for birds, there are kingfishers and kites; and, in season, quails and wild ducks; in the lakes, fish in abundance, as well as in the numerous pools that border the lakes.*

7    L. Basch, *op. cit.*, pp. 51-52.

Relief from the Mastaba of Ty at Saqqara, Old Kingdom, 5th Dynasty, *c.* 2498–2345 BC. © Photo: David Fabre

Detail of the mosaic from the Temple of Fortune at Praeneste, c. 80 BC.
© Museo Archeologico Prenestino, Palestrina, Italy/The Bridgeman Art Library

*These lands, called bararis, are certainly much sadder and much more desolate than the desert of sand or stone. In the Arabian or Libyan deserts, for lack of vegetation you at least find relief, light, and a majestic grandeur. Here, the misery is sordid, and distress frightful. In the real desert, rain is welcome, since it sometimes permits a certain cultivation in privileged spots; but here it makes everything even sadder: in the greyness of January, under a lowering sky, when the wind blows and the rain comes down in torrents, the landscape of the bararis becomes gloomy, almost funereal. How far you feel, then, from the magic of colours, from the burning light which, to the south of Cairo, turns every pebble into a precious diamond; and when you struggle along some scrubby path, where your donkey stumbles and shies at every step, where a car risks at every minute toppling into the ditch and can barely manage five kilometres an hour, despite the chains with which its wheels have been provided, you can, without any excess of imagination, believe that you have been transported far from Egypt, to some northern land.*

*Between the cultivated zone and the sterile region, the transition is not brutal as it is in the Nile Valley, on the edges of the desert; first the salt starts to make an appearance, the harvests become more mediocre, the trees rarer and more stunted; then the immense bare plain appears, criss-crossed by the rectilinear, brilliant cuttings of the drainage trenches that disappear into the lakes or the sea. And then, in the far distance, within the barari lands, the traveller has the pleasant surprise of sometimes finding a spot of greenery, some fine fields or some admirably cultivated gardens, with palm*

Rock paintings from South Africa, after L. Basch, *Le Musée imaginaire de la marine*, 1987, p. 53.

*trees whose heads sway above the lemon trees or the tangerine trees in serried ranks. But these are just oases, decors of greenery without any substance or depth, and in front of them a dreadful sterility soon resumes its sway.*

This admirable description, the product of lived experiences, cannot fail to touch all those whose area of 'fieldwork' lies in this region. It has one advantage: you hardly ever come across any tourists there.

The cause of the poverty of this region of the Northern Delta was also the cause of its importance. It was difficult to traverse it on the ground, but it was also difficult to disembark there. The sea was simultaneously menacing and protecting. As for the land, it constituted a region that was hardly ever crossed. On foot, on donkey, or on horseback, travellers made their way along the edge of the Arabian plateau on the east or the edge of the Libyan plateau on the west. This V-shaped route was the safest way of avoiding the floods brought about by the accidental or criminal breaking of dikes.

Ships took the two main branches, the Canopic or the Pelusiac. Pharaonic Egypt had become accustomed to the east-west barrier that formed the northern fringe of the country. It contented itself with a network of traffic routes arranged fan-shaped around Memphis, the head of the Delta and the gate of Upper Egypt, which had always been the urban centre of the country. The Romans later made up for this deficiency in the network of the Delta's communications. In the 2nd century AD, the astronomer Claudius Ptolemaeus (Ptolemy) placed on his map a paradoxical branch, perpendicular to the general slope of the Delta. This was the 'river of Buto' or 'Butic river', which branched out westwards on the canal leading from Alexandria to the Canopic mouth, passed near Buto (hence its name), skirted Sebennytos, Mendes-Thmouis, and Tanis, and joined the Pelusiac branch. The Roman masters were preoccupied above all by the need to drain towards the city the wheat produced by inner Egypt and the imports from the Near and Far East, which were transported down the isthmus. The river of Buto brought to the docks of Alexandria and Pelusium little more than the products of the southern provinces of the Delta: foodstuffs but also papyrus and dried fish. In fact, the 'river' cannot have been dug for purely commercial reasons. Flavius Josephus brings out the usefulness of the 'Butic river': it was a Roman route with, at first, strategic functions.[8] As such, this river facilitated in particular the intervention of the forces of law and order in a sector where public security was often precarious. Furthermore, the probable existence of a canal prior to the 'Butic' canal as early as the second half of the Ptolemaic era should be noted.[9]

The important ports of the Delta are river ports and are thus situated on the eastern and western branches. This situation has two essential reasons behind it. On the one hand, the Delta's coastal fringe offers little possibility of establishing a port worthy of the name, except within the coastal lake. On the other hand, inland, sheltered from foreign incursions, the ports are situated on the branches of the Nile that offer the most immediate access to the countries that people may wish to travel to by sea; the eastern branch for the Syro-Palestinian coast, and the western branch for Cyrenaica, Crete and Greece.

8    Flavius Josephus, IV, 11, 5.
9    J. Yoyotte, P. Chuvin, *op. cit.*, pp. 40-48.

Salt flats north of Tell el-Farama, Pelusium, north-east of the Nile Delta.
© Photo: David Fabre

Salt flats north of Tell el-Farama, Pelusium, north-east of the Nile Delta.
© Photo: David Fabre

Tell San el-Hagar, Tanis, north-east of the Nile Delta.
© Photo: David Fabre

## II.2. The western coastal fringe of Egypt

### II.2.1. Thonis and Naukratis: frontier police post and emporion

With regard to the region of the Canopic mouth, classical writers left several allusions to two waterside localities on the Mediterranean, the one bearing the Greek name of Herakleion, the other bearing the local name that they transcribe as Thonis.[10] It emerges from the contexts that both of them, situated to the east of Canopus, were near the mouth of the western branch of the Nile that were known by the names of 'Canopic mouth' and 'Herakleopolitan mouth'.[11] Now, following the phenomenon of subsidence that affected the edges of the Nile Delta, the eastern part of Canopus and the whole shore as far as this mouth were submerged. Furthermore, as shown by the surveys and excavations of the European Institute of Underwater Archaeology, the area of Canopus was not limited to the land now constituting the peninsula of Aboukir, and stretched out much further to the east, in a zone that is now underwater. It appears, in consequence, that these two cities must be sought somewhere under the waters of the vast bay extending eastward of the peninsula of Aboukir where there subsist, in a ruined state, the western part of Hellenistic and Graeco-Roman Canopus.

Diodorus writes of the site of Thonis in these terms:[12]

*It is in the place called Thonis, which was once the emporion of Egypt, that the river flows into the sea.*

So Thonis was an *emporion*, and thus a harbour and a place of commercial exchange, one that existed before the creation of Alexandria. This locality had been frequented by navigators arriving from the Hellenistic world centuries before the coming of Alexander the Great. Strabo, visiting the region of Canopus, recalled somewhat vaguely, 'It is said that, in ancient times, there was already a city there called Thonis.'[13] In the 2nd century AD, Pseudo-Scylax, bringing together all the information relative to Roman Canopus and the details he drew from an authentic itinerary of the 5th century BC, was

---

10  J. Yoyotte, *Égypte, Afrique & Orient* 24, 2001, p. 24.
11  There is a collection of Greek and Latin sources – literary, papyrological and epigraphic – relative to the region of Canopus in A. Bernand, *op. cit.*, pp. 153-258.
12  Diodorus, I, 19, 4. J. Yoyotte, *MDAIK* 16, 1958, p. 423.
13  Strabo, XVI, 1, 16.

Black-figure cup, by the Naukratis painter, c. 560 BC, Louvre, Paris, E667. © Photo RMN/Hervé Lewandowski

to speak of Thonis as a place where Menelaus, Helen and their pilot Canopus had disembarked shortly after the Trojan War.[14]

Herodotus reports a long narrative from the time when Paris eloped with Helen from Sparta and came to Egypt. 'The guardian of this river mouth was called Thonis.'[15] After telling this story, Herodotus refers to one of the passages in the *Odyssey* where mention is made of the return of Menelaus in the company of Helen whom he had now won back. Driven off course by a storm, the royal couple of Sparta landed on the shores of Egypt. It was then that Helen received, so the story goes, a precious drug to help her forget, from 'the wife of Thon, Polydamna of Egypt'.[16] Strabo referred to the same story in his turn. Hence 'it can be reasonably supposed that the frontier post and *emporion* of Thonis existed at the time when the Homeric text was fixed, in the 8th century or at the start of the 7th, which corresponds to the times when the Saite principality was being constituted – from which both the 24th (*c.* 1650 BC) and the 26th (1663-1555 BC) Dynasties were to spring.'[17] This locality commanded access to the Canopic branch. By its geographical position, it was, under the Pharaohs, the main port trading with the Greek seas and the centre from which foreign ships were kept under surveillance.[18] Under the Saites and the Persians, then under the last three native dynasties, Thonis was thus frontier, police and customs post, as well as being the *emporion* through which passed the products imported by the Greeks and destined for the warehouses they maintained in Naukratis.

In fact, in the course of the reign of Psamtek I (664-610 BC), Greek soldiers had been settled near the city that bore the Egyptian name of *Nokratj* (transcribed into Greek as *Naukratis*), on the Canopic branch of the Nile, some 100km from the river mouth. This city belonged to the nome of Sais and was only some 20km distant from the parent establishment of the 26th Dynasty and its temple of Neith, the patron goddess of the Saite monarchy. The Greek settlement soon transformed itself into an active place of trade and industry. Several city states in Ionia, Doris and Aeolis obtained concessions here, the organisation of which was formalised by Amasis (*c.* 570-526 BC).[19] The natural and regular route taken by merchandise imported by the Greeks and sent to their warehouses and factories came into Egyptian territory via the Canopic mouth and continued up the branch of the same name.[20] Herodotus writes of Naukratis in these terms:[21]

*Amasis was a friend of the Greeks and showed several of them marks of his benevolence; notably, to those who came into Egypt, he conceded as a dwelling-place the city of Naukratis; to those who did not wish to live there, but were brought there by maritime activities, he conceded sites for their gods. The greatest of these sanctuaries, the most famous and the most visited, called Hellenion, was founded in common by the following cities: the Ionian cities of Chios, Teos, Phocaea and Clazomene; the Dorian cities of Rhodes, Cnidus, Halicarnassus, Pheselis; and just one Aeolian city, that of Mytilene. These are the cities to which the sanctuary belongs, those which also provide the prefects of the market; all the other cities that claim to have a part in this do so quite without right. Independently of this sanctuary, the inhabitants of Aegina have of their own initiative founded a sanctuary to Zeus; the Samians, one to Hera; the Milesians, one to Apollo. In olden times (to palaion), Naukratis alone (mounê)*

*was an emporion, and there were no others in Egypt; if anyone penetrated another mouth of the Nile, he had to attest that he had not come there of his own volition and, having sworn that oath, set sail in his ship to the Canopic mouth; or, if contrary winds made it impossible for him to sail in that direction, he had to transport his cargo on the local barques (baris) going across the Delta until he reached Naukratis. Such were the prerogatives of Naukratis.*

The archaeological evidence shows quite clearly that Naukratis was founded long before the reign of Amasis and the text of Herodotus may be interpreted as a reference to some reform aimed at regularising the status of the concession. Archaeological remains give information about the sanctuaries, not about the entrepots, even though it has been hypothesised that each city represented had not only its own sanctuary, but also its own commercial quarter. Furthermore, Naukratis was not altogether an ordinary Greek city with its own 'citizens', comparable with the colonies of Sicily and Italy. Its existence depended on the permanence of the favour (and the self-interest) of the Egyptian king: as long as these were assured, the monopoly of these citizens over the Egyptian market was not placed in question.[22]

Naukratis, doubtless adversely affected by the period of the revolts of western Lower Egypt against the Persians, resumed its prosperous activities, duly controlled by the Pharaonic administration, under the last native dynasties, as illustrated by the Stele of Naukratis.[23] This Stele of Nekhtnebef (Nectanebo I (380-362BC)), one of the independent pharaohs of the 4th century (the stele is dated to year 2 of the pharaoh's reign – November 380), is the 'sole native source to concern the economy of the Greek *emporion*.'[24] In this 'Königsnovelle', this royal eulogy, the new pharaoh, founder of the 30th Dynasty (380-343 BC), having come to power by force, draws attention to his privileged links with the goddess Neith of Sais. To this end, the pharaoh has taken two measures: one is the transfer to the Treasury of the goddess of part of the royal taxes.[25] A tithe would henceforth be taken from the taxes regularly raised for the

14  On the texts that attest the existence of places called Thonis, see A. Calderini, *Dizionario dei nomi geografici e topografici dell'Egitto greco-romano*, vol. 2, fasc IV, p. 301.

15  Herodotus, II, 113-119.

16  Homer, *Odyssey*, IV, 228. The classical writers imagined that this Thon alias Thonis, the product of a typical transformation from place name to legendary personage, was a king. Herodotus made him an agent responsible for keeping watch over access to the Canopic mouth. This was, quite evidently, the 'official in charge of the gate of the foreign peoples at *Wadj Wer*', to use the title borne during the 26th Dynasty by the officers entrusted with the task of policing the frontiers at the river entry where the boats from Greece and its islands arrived.

17  J. Yoyotte *Égypte, Afrique & Orient* 24, 2001, p. 27.

18  *Id.*, *MDAIK* 16, 1958, p. 427.

19  J. Boardman, *The Greeks Overseas*, 1980, pp. 117-133 (= *Les Grecs outre-mer*, 1985, pp. 143-156); J. Yoyotte, *ACF*, 1991-1992, 1992-1993, 1993-1994, pp. 634-645, 679-692; A. Möller, *Naukratis*, 2000.

20  On Naukratis, the history of excavations, the recent research on the site and the difficulties of defining the way that trade and industry functioned in the city during the Pharaonic period, see J. Yoyotte, *ACF*, 1991-1992, pp. 634-644; J. Boardman, *op. cit.*, pp. 143-156; T. F. R. G. Brown, in *CAH* III /3, 1982, pp. 37-43; A. Bernard, *op. cit.*, pp. 575-863. On the subject of the products and merchandise of Naukratis, cf. *The Maritime Destiny of Ancient Egypt*, vol. 2.

21  Herodotus, II, 178-179; translation by P.-E. Legrand, Les Belles Lettres, coll. Budé.

22  On the subject of such a situation on the status of the traders of Naukratis, see p. 159.

23  Stele in greywacke, 210cm high, discovered *in situ* in 1890, preserved in the Egyptian Museum of Cairo.

24  J. Yoyotte, *ACF*, 1992-1993, pp. 679-692.

25  M. Lichtheim, *Ancient Egyptian Literature*, III, 1980, pp. 88-89; *id.*, in *Studies in Honor of G. H. Hughes*, SAOC 39, 1977, pp. 139-146.

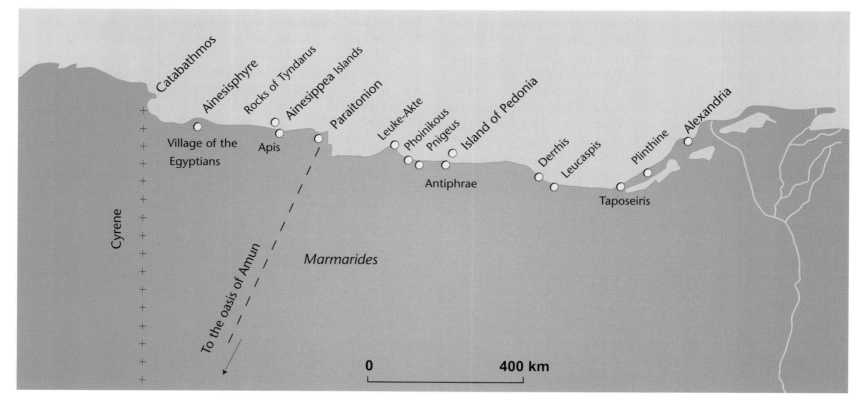

The Egyptian and Libyan coast after P. Charvet, S. Gompertz and J. Yoyotte, *Strabon, le voyage en Égypte*, 1997, p. 103.

state, partly from the goods and products of the Greeks of Naukratis, and partly from the imports that reached them from the sea via the Canopic branch.[26] So two places of taxation were planned: one at Naukratis itself where the stele had been raised, the other 'in a city called *În.t*', for 'everything coming from the Sea of the Greeks' *(m <ꜣd-wr Hꜣ. w-nb.wt)*. The research of J. Yoyotte has highlighted the etymology of Naukratis, in Egyptian *Pr-mryt*, the 'house of the port'.[27] J. Yoyotte[28] also identified the toponym transcribed and vocalised *Khenwe* by M. Lichtheim; this is the place called Thonis ( = *(T) Ḥn.t*) in several Greek authors, thus called in Egyptian because the city lay on the shores of a coastal lake *(ḥn.t)*; this was an extensive lake in antiquity situated at the entry of the Canopic branch.[29]

The topographical surveys and the soundings conducted in the Bay of Aboukir by the team under F. Goddio of the European Institute of Submarine Archaeology in cooperation with a team from the Department of Submarine Archaeology of the CSAE, led to the discovery of the site of Thonis-Herakleion. At some 6,500m from the eastern shoreline of the peninsula, on a space 1,000m by 1,200m, the plan of this site appeared to take the form of a city with its buildings; to the south the *temenos* of an important temple in the Pharaonic style; to the north and east, the basins of a vast port. The topography of the places described by J. Yoyotte applies perfectly well to the site. A central promontory where the temple and its annexes rose, surrounded by the city, with an inner lake on the western side. On the other side of the temple, the quays and a vast outport gave on to the Nile via a narrow navigable channel. The whole site was protected by a cordon of dunes on the western bank of the river. From the maritime point of view, the site was ideal: it was sheltered from the winds that dominated the north-west sector and from the south-westerly storms.[30]

In the *temenos*, the statues date for the most part from the Ptolemaic period. Soundings brought up from the ground where

debris lay scattered, various ritual utensils and bronze figurines, and pottery and calcite vases. Among these bronzes there was a classical sistrum, the base of a statue of Harpocrates and an image of Khonsu with a falcon head, all attributable to the Saito-Persian period. The dates of most of these artefacts range from the 6th century BC to the 1st century AD.[31] The most astonishing of the finds, and the most decisive, is doubtless the stele which is almost a double of the stele from year 2 of Nekhtnebef (the Naukratis stele): the same material, the same dimensions, the same quality of execution, the same double tableau, 14 columns of vertical text. There is, however, one difference between the two versions. At the end of the text, it is stated: 'His Majesty has said: be it established on the present stele…' The example from Naukratis (line 13) specifies: 'on the present stele placed in Nokratj, on the bank of the canal of the Anou'. The version from Herakleion (lines 13-14) specifies: 'on the present stele at the mouth of the Sea of the Greeks, in the city whose name is Hone of Sais'. As J. Yoyotte points out, this gives 'the full name of the original name of Herakleion, distinguished from that of the other *Thone*'s of the Lower Delta by the mention of the metropolis of which Naukratis was a dependency and which had been granted the privilege of receiving taxes raised on trade in the Canopus

---

26  These are examined in *Seafaring in Ancient Egypt*, vol. 2.

27  J. Yoyotte, *ACF*, 1991-1992, pp. 634-645.

28  *Id., MDAIK* 16, 1958, pp. 414-430.

29  On the subject of *ḥn.t*, see p. 15-16.

30  cf. the detailed bathymetric chart of the Bay of Aboukir published in *Science et Avenir* 654, 2001, p. 74.

31  A perfume burner in the form of a small Greek female sphinx is datable to the 6th century. The Greek pottery includes samples that could go back to the 5th century, among them fine Attic red-figure vases from the 4th century. The inventory of objects found at the surface includes items which are, with the exception of two small pieces of jewellery, prior to the Roman period. Large-scale monuments and votive objects are evidence of the temple's prosperity between the 5th and the 1st centuries BC; cf. J. Yoyotte, *Égypte, Afrique & Orient* 24, December 2001, pp. 28-31.

region. Finally, this provides confirmation of the hypothesis that the Thonis on which depended – according to Herodotus – a temple of Herakles and whose name and lost site were vaguely known to Hellenistic geographers was the settlement that was to become Herakleion. In addition to this, the topographical surveys of F. Goddio and observations from satellite of the configuration of the whole of the Lower Delta corroborate the hypothesis on which the Egyptian word *hôné* designated the individual deltas that were formed at the mouth of the Nile's main branches',[32] and conditioned the organisation of maritime commerce in Ancient Egypt.

## II.2.2. The Libyan coast and Mersa Mathruh

Strabo provides a clear and precise overview of the stopover ports between Cyrenaica and Alexandria, without our being able to determine with precision the significance that such mooring grounds might have had in the Pharaonic period:[33]

*From Catabathmos, the direct crossing to Paraitonion is in a straight line, nine hundred stadia long.[34] This is a city and a great port, of some forty stadia. […] In between lie, firstly, the Village of the Egyptians,[35] the promontory of Ainesisphyre (Sidi Barrani) and the Rocks of Tyndarus (the Ishaila rocks), four small islands with a port. Then come the Cape of Drepanon ('The Sickle', Ras Gargub?), the isle of Ainesippea (Ras Abu Laho?) with its port, and the Village of Apis (Zawiyet Umm el-Rakham), a hundred stadia from Paraitonion […] From Paraitonion to Alexandria,*

32   *Id.*, p. 32.
33   Strabo, XVII, 1, 14; P. Charvet, J. Yoyotte, *Strabon*, 1997, pp. 102-103. See also W. A. Daszewski, *BSFE* 132, 1995, pp. 11-29.
34   *cf. infra.*
35   Probably the memory of an advanced settlement in Libyan territory, dating back to the Pharaohs and preserving anthropological and/or archaeological traces of this origin.

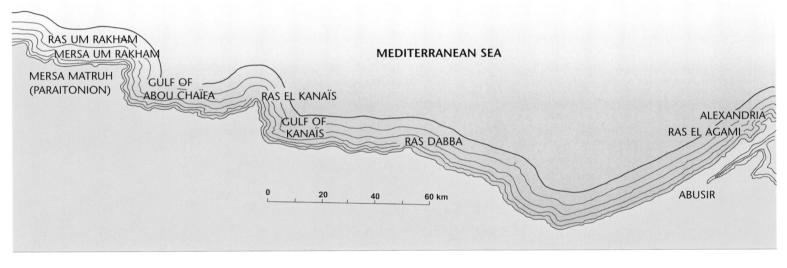

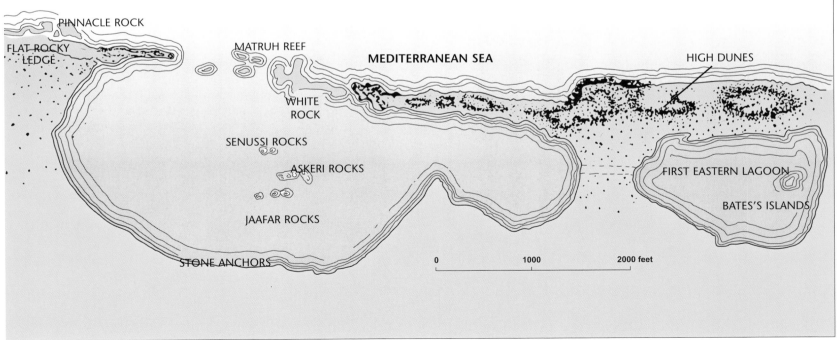

Mersa Mathruh after A. Nibbi, *SAK* 26, 1998, figs 1-2, p. 205.

*the distance is approximately three hundred stadia.*[36] *Of the places in between, the first is a promontory of white land, called Leuke-Akte ('the White Coast', Ras el-Hikma), then come the port of Phoinikous ('the territory of the Phoenicians', near Bir Musa Salih?), the village of Pnigeus ('The Stifler', Mat'an el-Qutt, near Ras el-Gharq'an), and the island of Pedonia (Samra Reef) with a port (Marsa Abu Samra). Antiphrae,*[37] *which comes next, is situated a short distance from the shore.* [...] *Then comes the port of Derrhis ('The tanned animal skin', near Ras Gibeisa), which takes its name from the proximity of a black rock that resembles a 'derrhis'* [...] *Then comes another port, Leucaspis ('White Shield', Marsa el-Hamra) which is followed by yet others. Further along there is Kynos-Sema ('The Tomb of the Bitch'), then Taposeiris (Abousir) which is not on the sea.* [...] *Then there now come Plinthine ('Construction built in bricks', near Sidi Khreir), the village of Nikias, and Cherronesos (Merabit), a fortified position, already close to Alexandria and Necropolis, at a distance of seventy stadia.*

To return to the *Paraitonion* mentioned in Strabo's text. Bates Island, at the heart of one of the lagoons of Mersa Mathruh (almost 260km west of Alexandria) has yielded to the excavators considerable evidence attesting that the sailors of the eastern Mediterranean would make a prolonged halt there during a period that extends across the 14th and 13th centuries BC.[38] The discovery of Mycenaean pottery in the Bay of Mersa Mathruh[39] and at Carthage[40] raises the question of whether *Paraitonion* was not, at this period, a sort of rallying point for sailors of the eastern Mediterranean who were voyaging along the coasts of North Africa. Egyptian pottery from those periods can be found there. The fact that these vestiges are present on the island and not on the shore bolsters the idea that the

---

36 Today, 291km by road and 280km by sea.

37 Salvage excavations at Marina el-Alamein have revealed an entire city. Without any city wall or any real unity, with its opulent dwellings and its imposing funerary structures, it was certainly the marina of wealthy landowners and merchants. Its apogee was in the 1st century BC. The site is probably that of the ancient Antiphrae. See W. A. Daszewski, *MDAIK* 46, 1990, pp. 15-36; J. Leclant, G. Clerc, *Orientalia* 95, 1995, pp. 226-228.

38 See O. Bates, *Bulletin of the Society of Biblical Archaeology*, 1915, pp. 201-207; id., *Harvard African Studies* VIII, *Varia Africana* VI, 1977, pp. 123-197; D. White, *JARCE* 23, 1986, pp. 51-84; id., *JARCE* 26, 1989, pp. 87-114; id., *JARCE Newsletter* 131, 1985, pp. 3-17; D. Cornwell, *Expedition* 29/3, 1987, pp. 25-34; L. Hulin, *JARCE* 26, 1989, pp. 115-126; Al. Nibbi, *SAK* 26, 1998, pp. 203-212.

39 On the subject of this pottery, see *Seafaring in Ancient Egypt*, vol. 2.

40 F. Rakob, *Bulletin CEDAC Carthage* 15, June 1996, p. 53.

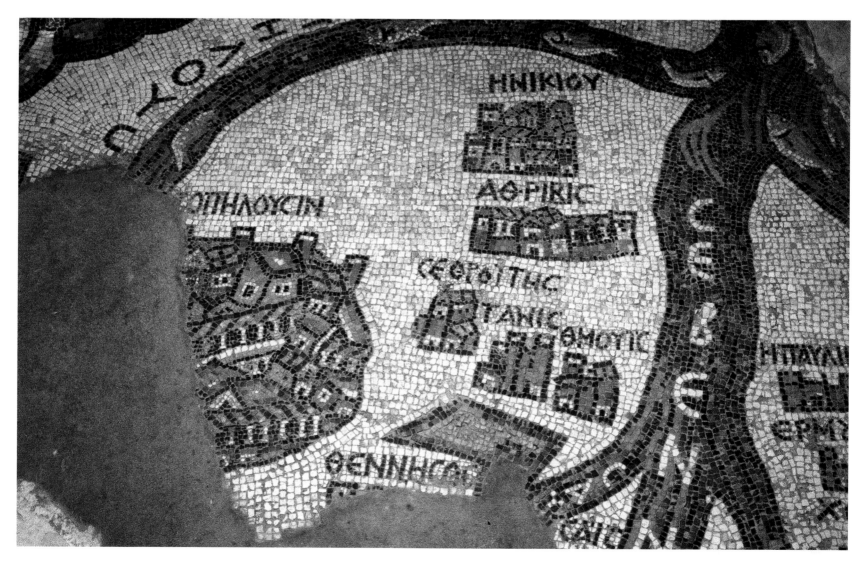

Detail of the 6th-century AD mosaic in the church of Madaba depicting the north-eastern region of the Nile Delta and mentioning *inter alia* the cities of Tanis (in the centre) and Pelusium (on the left). Photo: Z. Radovan, Jerusalem

Egyptians may have reached it by sea. But there is no decisive proof of this and only further excavations will perhaps permit the truth to be discovered. The modest scale of the lagoons, and the shallowness of their waters, must not lead us to forget that *Paraitonion* was an important port and that it could take in ships of some considerable size. It was in the western lagoon of *Paraitonion* that the fleet of Cornelius Gallus laid a trap for Mark Antony after the rout at Actium in 31 BC.[41]

## II.3. The eastern coastal fringe of Egypt

It is easy to guess what the advantages of the eastern Delta were for the sovereigns of Egypt. The eastern branch of the Nile was and is still a fundamental artery of communication between Memphis and Asia, from which various products came.[42] Generally speaking, the ports and the commercial maritime infrastructure of the eastern Delta can be related to the toponyms that begin with *r$^3$* 'mouth, outlet', and are extremely frequent in this part of Egypt. The Arabic term *Fumm–* seems to have the same meaning.[43] On the eastern fringe of the Delta, *R$^3$-$^3$ḥ.wt* 'the outlet of agricultural produce', in the environs of Tanis,[44] *R$^3$-w$^3$t.y*, 'the outlet of the two paths', somewhere at the crossing of the Pelusiac branch and the coast road that crossed Sinai towards Palestine,[45] *R$^3$-j$^3$b.t*, 'the outlet of the East', at Wadi Tumilat.[46]

Furthermore, while it is true that during the Hellenistic and Roman periods, the coastal region of North Sinai was covered with ever huger conurbations of which only a small part is known to this day, the great sites – such as Tell Abu Seifa (Sile), Tell el-Farama (Pelusium), Mohamedia (Gerrha), El-Guels, and El-Felousia (Ostracine) – even when they have been explored and excavated, would need further work on a scale that is difficult to imagine these days, if any answer to the main questions being asked by historians and archaeologists is to be obtained. Still, a sustained focus is needed on the importance of these sites at previous periods in order to reconstitute, at least sketchily, their place in commercial networks, the river routes, sea routes (and land routes too) that were followed by all

41 Dio Cassius, II, 9, 1; Orosius, VI, 12, 15.

42 On the hydrographical evolution of the Nile in the north of the eastern Delta, see M. Bietak, *Tell el-Dab'a II*, 1975 and J.-Y. Carrez-Maratray, *Péluse*, *BiÉtud* 124, 1999; B. Marcolongo, *CRIPEL* 14, 1992, pp. 23-31; R. Said, *The Geological evolution of the River Nile*, 1981; G. Sestini, in *Proceedings of the Seminar on the Delta Sedimentology*, 1976, pp. 12-24 and the contribution of H. Goedicke, B. Van Wesemael, and J. Wunderlich, in E. C. M. Van den Brink (ed.), *The Archaeology of the Nile Delta*, 1988, pp. 165-175, 125-139, 251-260.

43 H. Kees, *MDAIK* 18, 1962, p. 3.

44 J. Yoyotte, *BSFFT* 2/3, 1989, pp. 127-128; *id.*, *BSFE* 114, 1989, pp. 24-25.

45 H. Altenmüller, in *Stationen*, 1998, pp. 160-161.

46 *Urk.* II, 82, 5; Dendera, II, 131, 10.

General view of the excavations of Qantir/Piramesse (2001). © Photo: David Fabre

those who participated in trade in those bygone times, and finally the strategic centres that they had selected. It is noteworthy that the development of studies on pottery, especially imported pottery, has opened up a very rich field of investigation, which largely contributes to determining the economic circuits between east and west, but also between the Mediterranean, the Red Sea and eastern Africa, if not the Arabian peninsula.

## II.3.1. Avaris, Piramesse and Tanis: the harbour capitals of the eastern Delta

Avaris and Piramesse enjoy a remarkable strategic situation on the eastern bank of the Pelusiac branch of the Nile (the 'waters of Ra').[47] They are protected from the eastern approaches to the Delta by the great lakes of the natural drainage system of Bahr el-Baqar.[48] This latter forms with Pelusium a narrow loop giving access to the north-east of the Delta.[49] Anyone wishing to get to the Delta had to pass through the two cities.[50]

In antiquity, the settlement had concentrated on small hills and the eastern raised earth sections of the Pelusiac branch.[51] The oldest known zone of the city was situated to the east of the present-day village of Ezbet Rushdy el-Saghira, where, at the start of the 1950s, S. Adam uncovered a temple dedicated to Amenemhat I (c. 1963-1934 BC) and traces of Middle Kingdom settlements (2040-1782 BC).[52] According to a stele found in the temple, this was a royal domain of Amenemhat I, established on a site which a Herakleopolitan king had already selected as his kingdom so as to control the region and to hold off the Bedouin migrations as part of his policy of colonising the Delta.[53]

During the 13th Dynasty (1782-1650 BC), the low hill to the south-west of Ezbet Rushdy[54] was densely occupied, probably by Canaanites: soldiers, dignitaries, artisans, caravaneers, but also sailors in the service of the Egyptian crown. The city of Avaris/Tell el-Dab'a developed considerably from the Hyksos period onwards, reaching a surface area of 205km². Having been a regional centre, it rose to the rank of capital of Egypt. The stratigraphic layers and the structures of habitat relative to that period reveal how the city grew ever denser.[55]

The archaeological material of Tell el-Dab'a dating from the beginning of the New Kingdom (1570-1070 BC) shows that the end of the reign of the Hyksos was not accompanied by any cessation of relations with the eastern Mediterranean and bears witness to the vivacity of the port of the old Hyksos capital. The abundance of

foreign pottery indicates that, apart from the military function of this centre, commerce had preserved its importance. Avaris must have remained, at this period, the link between Egypt and the eastern Mediterranean. It is however strange that, given so many signs of its importance, Avaris is never mentioned during the 18th Dynasty (1570-1293 BC) relative to military campaigns and trading expeditions to Asia. Perhaps the site then bore another name. It is worth recalling a suggestion made by L. Habachi and mentioned by M. Bietak: *Prw-nfr*, the famous port and naval dockyard of the 18th Dynasty, was not actually at Memphis as is believed, but at Tell el-Dab'a. This hypothesis would explain the presence at *Prw-nfr* of Canaanite cults, that were long active in ancient Avaris,[56] but there is a lack of epigraphical and archaeological data to prove it. Nonetheless, the rich information yielded by the Memphite region and prior to the creation of Piramesse militates against such an idea.

With the 19th Dynasty (1293-1185 BC), the region of Avaris entered a new and important chapter in Egyptian history. At Qantir, north of Tell el-Dab'a, the Pharaohs Seti I (1291-1278 BC) and Rameses II (1279-1212 BC) founded a royal residence known by the name of Piramesse, most probably the Biblical city of Rameses. The region again became the capital of Egypt thanks to its strategic importance and its proximity to the Near East on which Egypt was concentrating its political interests in this period. The Pelizaeus Museum of Hildesheim is at present studying this site in close collaboration with the Austrian Archaeological Institute. The excavations directed by E. Push have disclosed barracks for chariot drivers, and stables of royal dimensions as well as arsenals from the

---

47  *P? mw n p? R?*: see, for example, A. H. Gardiner, *JEA* V, 1918, pp. 258-159; id., *AEO* II, 70*, 155*, 168*-170*; *GDG* III, 30; P. Montet, *Géographie*, I, 1957, pp. 200-201; M. Bietak, *Tell el-Dab'a* II, 1975, p. 71, n. 244, p. 119, 125, n. 512, fig. 23 p. 120; P. Grandet, *Le papyrus Harris* I, *BiÉtud* 109, 1994, vol. 2, n. 213.

48  M. Bietak, *Avaris und Piramesse*, 1997, pp. 225-296; M. Bietak, I. Hein, *et al.*, *Pharaonen und Fremde*, 1994, pp. 17-58, pp. 290-293; M. Bietak, *Avaris, The Capital of the Hyksos*, 1996. See too the bibliographical references given by this author in *L'Égypte du Delta. Les capitales du Nord, Dossiers d'Archéologie* 213, March 1996, p. 23.

49  M. Bietak, in A. Caubet (ed.), *L'acrobate au taureau*, 1999, fig. 2 p. 66.

50  Id., *Tell el-Dab'a* II, 1975.

51  Id., in A. Caubet (ed.), *op. cit.*, figs 2-3 pp. 66-67.

52  S. Adam, *ASAE* I VI, 1959, pp. 207-226.

53  M. Bietak, *op. cit.*, p. 31.

54  Id., fig. 3, p. 67.

55  M. Bietak, *op. cit.*, p. 34.

56  R. Stadelmann, *Syrisch-Palästinische Gottheiten, ProbÄg* V, 1967, pp. 146-148; W. Helck, *Die Beziehungen Ägyptens, ÄgAbh* 5, 1971, pp. 446-473.

*Until the fourth month of Shomu (the summer), I remained in Tanis, then Smendes and Tentamun made me leave with Captain Mengabot, so I set sail on the great Sea of Kharu.*

Kite photograph of part of the temenos of Amun at Tanis. © Photo: Yves Guichard

19th Dynasty.[57] The vestiges of Piramesse are spread over an area of some 10km², 5km north of the village of Fakous, on the eastern bank of a modest irrigation canal, whose course marks that of the former Pelusiac branch. The residual lake that separates Qantir from Tell el-Dab'a was a port, allowing exchanges with the Near East and the great cities of Egypt. Piramesse thus also marked the western extremity of the 'Paths of Horus', the track which led to Syro-Palestine by the Sinai Desert coast. Downstream from the conurbation, a canal that had been dug as early as the Middle Kingdom also linked the Pelusiac branch of the Nile and two great lakes bordering the isthmus of El-Qantara, permitting access by water to the fortress of Sile and the first stations on this itinerary. Piramesse thus controlled the two main communication channels, by land and sea, between Egypt and the Near East, and it had from its origins onwards a vocation at once military and commercial, depending on the friendly or hostile relations existing between Egypt and Asia.[58] At this period, Avaris thus still existed under its original name and constituted the southern part of this new residence; it was, in addition, the port of Piramesse until the 20th Dynasty (1185-1070 BC).[59]

It was at the end of the 20th Dynasty that Tanis seems to have taken over as a river and sea port. Tanis constituted the point of embarkation of Wenamun for Byblos:[60]

*Until the fourth month of Shomu (the summer), I remained in Tanis, then Smendes and Tentamon made me leave with Captain Mengabot, so I set sail on the great Sea of Kharu.*

Tanis is the Greek name of the toponym $D^{c}n.t$ in Ancient

57    E. Push, in A. Eggebrecht (ed.), *Antike Welt im Pelizaeus Museum*, 1993, pp. 126-143; J. Dorner, *Äglev* IX, 1999, pp. 77-83.

58    For an overview of Piramesse, see Ed. B. Pusch, in *L'Égypte du Delta. Les capitales du Nord*, *Dossiers d'Archéologie* 213, 1996, pp. 54-59 and P. Grandet, in *L'Égypte ancienne, L'Histoire*, 1996, pp. 73-86.

59    J. Yoyotte, *AEPHE* LXXIX, 1971-1972, p. 172; M. Bietak, *Tell el-Dab'a II*, 1975, p. 30.

60    *Wenamun*, 1, 6-8: *jw=j (hr) jr.t š³ᶜ ³bd 4 šmw jw=j m-ẖnw D̄ᶜn.t jw N(y)-sw-b³-nb-Ḏd.w T(j)-n(y).t-Jmn (hr) wḏ wj jrm ḥry-mnš Mᶜnwg³bwtj jw=j h³y r p³y m-ᶜ mw ᶜ³ n(y) Ḫ³rw.*

Ruins of the temple of Amun at Tanis. © Photo: David Fabre

Egyptian,[61] the present San el-Haggar, and is situated near the Mediterranean coast in the 29th nome of Lower Egypt (the eastern Delta).[62] In the Third Intermediate Period (1069-525 BC) the city became the residence of the kings of the 21st Dynasty (1069-945 BC), which took its name from the toponym,[63] since its founder, Smendes, there exercised an administrative function from the end of the 20th Dynasty onwards, as is clear from *The Report of Wenamun*.[64] It was also to keep this important role during the 13th Dynasty (1782-1650 BC), so that it also constituted for quite some time the northern counterweight to Thebes.[65] The Theban triad was also worshipped at Tanis.[66]

The name of the city appears for the first time in texts from the 21st and 22nd Dynasties (1069-945, 945-715 BC), such as the *Onomasticon* of Amenemope[67] and *The Report of Wenamun*, unless we attribute this latter to the end of the 20th Dynasty (1185-1070 BC), the period from which the events related date; the city probably did not acquire any importance until the end of the New Kingdom (1570-1070 BC).[68] For a long time, scholars tried to identify Tanis with the Hyksos residence of Avaris and/or the Ramesside capital Piramesse… The ubiquity of Ramesside monuments had incited P. Montet to consider the site of San el-Hagar on the basis of the equation Tanis = Piramesse, as well as being proof of the destruction of the Ramesside capital that was ruined following a victorious war waged by the Thebans against the worshippers of Seth, Semitised Egyptians. But the 21st Dynasty did not seem to usher in a period of proscription and demonisation of Seth, nor was it the result of a 'war against the impure'. In fact, the theory of the simultaneous destruction of Piramesse and the cult of Seth, based on somewhat hasty philological and historical interpretations, is impossible to maintain.[69] Geological, stratigraphical and hydrological research seem to confirm the hypothesis that the Pelusiac branch underwent modifications at the end of the Ramesside age, its upper course diverting into the Tanitic bed.[70] The change of the course of the Nile's branches, isolating the capital and making it unsuitable for commerce, is one explanation for the settling of the capital at Tanis. Natural and human factors seem to explain the dismantlement of Piramesse. It appears that the strategic and offensive function of

61  For the variant spellings and equivalent terms in other languages, see GDG, II, p. 111; A. H. Gardiner, *AEO* II, p. 199; P. Montet, *Géographie*, I, 1957, p. 192. *Sekhet Dja* appears already in the very fragmentary text *Les Plaisirs de la chasse et de la pêche*, published by R. A. Caminos, as well as in a fragmentary geographical procession of the temple of Ptah at Memphis, in the name of Rameses II.

62  For a general account of the excavations at Tanis, see P. Brissaud, C. Zivie-Coche (ed.), *Tanis, Travaux récents sur le Tell Sân el-Hagar*, 1998-2000.

63  'Tanite' Dynasty, cf. K. A. Kitchen, in *LÄ* VI, 1986, s.v. 'Tanitendynastie', col. 209.

64  *Wenamun*, 1, 3; 2, 35.

65  A. Niwinsky, *BIFAO* 95, 1995, pp. 329-360.

66  K. A. Kitchen, *The Third Intermediate Period*, 1972, § 393-397; H. Römer, in *LÄ* V, 1986, s.v. 'Tanis', col. 194-209.

67  A.H. Gardiner, *AEO* I, 199*-201*.

68  The archaeological vestiges of Tanis found *in situ* are probably not prior to the reign of the pharaoh Psusennes I (1045-994 BC). For Smendes and Tentamon, no proof has been preserved. Only *The Report of Wenamun* thus enables us to attribute to Tanis a position of relatively independent power in the Delta, cf. H. Römer, in *LÄ* VI, 1986, s.v. 'Tanis', col. 195.

69  J. Yoyotte, *AEPHE*, 5th section, vol. I XXIX, 1971; id., in *Tanis, l'or des Pharaons*, 1987. On the subject of the proscription of the god Seth: D. Fabre, *Le dieu Seth en Égypte de la fin du Nouvel Empire à l'époque gréco-romaine*, 1999; id., *Égypte, Afrique & Orient* n° 22, 2001, pp. 19-40.

70  M. Bietak, *Tell el-Dab'a II*, 1975, pp. 109, 215-217; id., in *LÄ* V, 1984, s.v. 'Ramsesstadt', col. 128-146; id., *Avaris and Piramesse*, 1979, pp. 272-279.

Piramesse was obsolete within the international context, and that the site of Tanis, raised too high and more or less surrounded by the marshes of the Lower Delta and served by the Tanitic branch, constituted a place of safety and a harbour outlet ensuring communications between Egypt and Asia.[71]

Although the archaeological evidence often dates back only to the 21st Dynasty, an initial phase starting already under the 20th Dynasty may be considered. Thus K. A. Kitchen defines Tanis as the northern outlier of Piramesse, a situation for which *The Report of Wenamun* provides implicit confirmation.[72] Smendes and Tentamon there exercise an important administrative function[73] and receive the title of 'governors whom Amun has appointed in the north of his country'.[74] It may be deduced from this that Tanis became the most important city in the Delta, since those in power in Lower Egypt reside there.[75] Thus Wenamun heads directly for Tanis, where he later has the opportunity to embark on a ship of the open seas,[76] perhaps one of the numerous ships that allowed the people of Tanis to trade with Phoenician coastal towns.[77]

## II.3.2. Tjaru

Placed at the mouth of the Pelusiac branch, Tell Hebua–Tjaru is the last base in the Delta before setting sail for the Syro-Lebanese coast or the road that follows the Mediterranean coastline towards Palestine. While the Middle Kingdom levels, which lie under those of the Second Intermediate Period (1782-1570 BC) and the New Kingdom (1570-1070 BC), are still poorly known, these latter, associated with contemporary textual allusions, already provide a good idea of Egyptian policy in this region.[78]

Excavations carried out in the region of Hebua have enabled Mohammed Abd el-Maksoud to propose with some certainty that of the city of Tjaru with the site of Hebua I. The levels can be dated precisely to the end of the Second Intermediate Period thanks to local and imported pottery. Apart from the dwelling quarters and the burial places that are rich in archaeological material, they are characterised, especially to the north of the site, by the size of the granaries and entrepots.[79]

The new sovereigns of the 18th Dynasty (1570-1293 BC) built a new fortified city on the ruins of the former Hyksos site at Tjaru (Tell Hebua).[80] A new fortification with a double enclosure was then constructed on a surface area much greater than that of the first:

600m by 300m.[81] Concomitant with this, the Pharaoahs constructed a fortress and a magnificent palace, decorated with Minoan paintings, on the vestiges of the old fortress and the old Hyksos palace that they had just destroyed at Avaris (Tell el-Dab'a).[82] To the north lay 'residential districts with huge dwellings, rectangular alignments next to a northern enclosure wall, batteries of great silos and an industrial district. In the north-west corner rose a great building that was arranged round a court yard and consisted of an administrative structure endowed with big annexes for storage. [...] Contemporary pottery at these levels clearly belongs to the very beginning of the 18th Dynasty.'[83]

Tjaru, present in the story of the first campaign of Thutmose III (1504-1450 BC), in the *Annals* that the king had engraved in the heart of the Temple of Karnak,[84] Tjaru was also, under the reign of Amenhotep II (1453-1419 BC), the northern limit of the field of action of a director of foreign countries.[85] Thutmose IV (1413-1386 BC), in his turn, entrusted one of his close courtiers with the post of 'governor of Tjaru' and the responsibility of 'royal messenger in all foreign lands'.[86] Elsewhere, the same man bears the titles of 'chief of the Medjai' and 'commander of the troops of Tjaru', two military functions that complement his administrative duties as governor. This latter title was still borne under the 18th Dynasty by a 'cavalry chief'.[87] According to Mohammed Abd el-Maksoud, 'holding these two titles at the same time, and being given the responsibility of head of the expedition to the turquoise mines of Serabit el-Khadim in year 4 of the same reign are revelatory of the importance then granted to the place of Tjaru in Egyptian foreign policy towards the East.'[88] External commerce is in particular attested, so far, by the imported pottery discovered in this zone of passage. The pottery came from the Syro-Palestinian coast and Cyprus.

The archaeological, prosopographical and literary evidence becomes even more abundant with the beginnings of the Ramesside Dynasty.[89] On the site of Hebua, the city enclosure is reinforced, to the north-west, by a wall with an indentation added to the first. Within the conurbation, towards the south, a big building with a central hall, constructed in unfired brick, with pillar bases and stone door frames, must have corresponded to a residential or administrative building of some importance.[90] The *khetem* of Tjaru 'is at once the western limit of the military intervention of Seti I (1291-1278 BC) against the *Chasou* and the frontier post where the sovereign was triumphantly greeted on his return from the campaign. The site is not configured like a fortress with one or several enclosures, but like a set of structures divided on each side by a straight canal in which crocodiles swim. The façade of these

71  J. Yoyotte, *op. cit.*, p. 56.

72  K. A. Kitchen, *The Third Intermediate Period*, 1972, § 395; J. von Beckerath, in *LÄ* V, 1984, s.v. 'Smendès', col. 991-992. Also see P. Brissaud, in *L'Égypte du Delta. Les capitales du Nord, Dossiers d'Archéologie* 213, 1996, p. 69.

73  *Wenamun*, 1, 3.

74  *Wenamun*, 2, 35.

75  A. Scheepers, in E. Lipinski (ed.), *Phoenicia and the Bible, Studia Phoenicia* XI, 1991, p. 64.

76  *Wenamun*, 1, 6 - 2.

77  *Wenamun*, 1, 58 - 2, 2.

78  According to the mathematical Rhind Papyrus (W. Helck, *Historisch-biographische Texte*, KÄT, 1975, no 113, p. 78), the capture of Avaris, capital of the Hyksos, must have occurred after the reconquest of Heliopolis and Tjaru, these two sieges lasting three months. This information clearly shows the role and strategic importance of these two last cities. If the liberator of Egypt, Kamosis, undertook military action against Tjaru before besieging Avaris, this was so as better to isolate it from its eastern rear, the Hyksos bases established on the Syro-Palestinian coast, such as Sharuhen. Indeed Tjaru, at the mouth of the Pelusiac branch of the Nile, thereby commanded access to Avaris (Mohammed Abd el-Maksoud, in D. Valbelle, C. Bonnet (ed.), *Le Sinaï*, 1998, pp. 61-65).

79  Mohammed Abd el-Maksoud, *op. cit.*, p. 61.

80  *Id.*, *Tell Héboua* I, 1992.

81  *Id.*, in D. Valbelle, C. Bonnet (ed), *Le Sinaï*, 1998, p. 61.

82  M. Bietak, *Avaris, The Capital of the Hyksos*, 1996, pp. 67-83.

83  Mohammed Abd el-Maksoud, in D. Valbelle, C. Bonnet (ed), *Le Sinaï*, 1998, p. 61.

84  *Urk.* IV, 647, 12-14 : 'Year 22, the fourth month of winter, the 25th day, (his Majesty passed the khetem of) Tjaru, during his first victorious campaign to repel those who had attacked Egypt's borders'.

85  J.-L. de Cenival, *RdÉ* 17, 1965, p. 16, fig. 3.

86  G Björkman, *JARCE* 11, 1974, pp. 43-51. For this title of 'messenger of the king in all foreign lands', see p. 175.

87  P.-M. Chevereau, *Prosopographie des cadres militaires égyptiens au Nouvel Empire*, 1994, p. 85, no 11141.

88  Mohammed Abd el-Maksoud, *op. cit.*, p. 62.

89  *Id.*, pp. 63-64.

90  *Id.*, p. 63.

Tell el-Farama, Pelusium. © Photo: David Fabre

structures is characteristic of the offices and complexes of shops reproduced on the walls of tomb chapels in the New Kingdom. The vestiges of Tell Hebua correspond perfectly to both this schematisation of the conurbation and the function of a frontier city, situated at the mouth of the Pelusiac branch that constitutes one of the main gates into Egypt in the eastern Mediterranean basin.'[91]

Thus its position on the frontier between Egypt and its eastern neighbours is confirmed by the mention of the territory opened by the authority of a messenger of the king to the Syrian princes, which begins at Tjaru.[92] It was also here that weapons were stored for the military campaigns that were to take place in the Near East.[93] Finally, Tjaru perhaps serves as a pointer to the three mountains of desert, mountainous or foreign lands.[94] This determiner alternates with that of the city which refers to the conurbation, with customs complex, sources of provisions and storehouses, that at every period constituted the main function of this site thanks to its twofold vocation: as a port and as a frontier land post with the East.[95] These same distinctions had already been brought out for the periods prior to the toponym 'The-roads-of-Horus'.[96] The name of Tjaru, pronounced Tjel/Tjele, reappeared in the Roman period in the Greek transcription Sile, designating the fortress that controlled the passage between the Mediterranean coastline of the Sinai desert and the eastern Delta.[97]

## II.3.3. Pelusium

The Saite and Persian eras were characterised by a broadening of cultural frontiers. The sites of the region of the eastern Delta of the Nile and those of North Sinai, geographically open to the Mediterranean, seem to have played a front-rank role in international commerce. Furthermore, as in the neighbouring regions, Syria or Palestine, the Persian conquest, contrary to the generally admitted opinion, seems to have given new impetus to commercial exchanges, and this was even more so with the suppression of the monopoly of Naukratis. The commercial presence of Phoenicia, Attica and the Aegean is particularly perceptible on these sites.

This commercial activity, which we can see emerging in the Persian period (5th century BC) viewed through the ceramological literature, was composed of innumerable and fragmentary aspects.

91    Mohammed Abd el-Maksoud, in D. Valbelle, C. Bonnet (ed), *Le Sinaï*, 1998, p. 64. When Rameses II went to Qadech to confront the Hittite army, he '*passed the khetem of Tjaru*' (*KRI* II, 12, 16). On the stele from the year 400, amongst varied civil, religious and in particular military titles, two successive viziers held the title of '*director of the khetem of Tjaru*' and '*director of foreign lands*': Mohammed Abd el-Maksoud, *op. cit.*, p. 64. Also see the commander of the troops at Tjaru, attested in the same period (P.-M. Chevereau, *op. cit.*, p. 85, n° 11143).

92    *Late-Egyptian Miscellanies*, 21, 6-7.

93    *Id.*, 108, 8-10.

94    *Id.*, 31, 11; 70, 7.

95    Mohammed Abd el-Maksoud, *op. cit.*, p. 64.

96    D. Valbelle, in *Hommages à Jean Leclant*, BiÉtud 106/4, 1994, pp. 379-386.

97    The identification of Sile with the ancient sites of the region of El-Qantara rests on the references to this city that occur in inscriptions on the basin of the sarcophagus of a high functionary, brought to light in a necropolis near eastern El-Qantara (G. Daressy, *BIFAO* XI, 1911, pp. 29-38). The man is in particular the 'first prophet of Horus, master of Mesen, master of Sile'. Two fortresses, one doubtless from the Ptolemaic period, the other Roman, fit the allusions of contemporary texts, especially the Antonine Itinerary. No vestige prior to these periods has hitherto been found, while the only evidence later than the New Kingdom in the site of Hebua I are the remnants of Persian encampments. If the toponym 'Tjaru/Sile' does correspond, like 'the-Roads-of-Horus', to a region as well as to the main conurbation that was sited there, a shift of several kilometres during the first millennium, brought about by a hydrological and ecological modification of this zone, does not seem improbable in this kind of environment. This is a frequently observed phenomenon, which can be seen a little further eastwards, with the toponym 'Migdol' (Mohammed Abd el-Maksoud, *op. cit.*, p. 65).

Below it will be necessary to raise the question of the itineraries of ships and merchants. Were these amphorae transported by sea, river, land, or else by a system of coastal sailing along the shores of Syro-Palestine where structures linked directly to commerce are attested from this period onwards? All means were probably used to transport perishable and non-perishable goods to Egypt. Merchandise doubtless travelled along the most important land routes of the time – especially the road that extended along the Mediterranean coastline – but also the maritime routes. According to E. Oren, structures dating from the Persian era, interpreted as entrepots, have been brought to light between Pelusium and Mohamedia.[98] This would lead to the conclusion that Pelusium, or if not Pelusium the lower Pelusiac region, assumed a commercial vocation in the Persian period, and perhaps played a role in the redistribution of products towards the interior of the country. This archaeological evidence is still, however, quite discreet, and this hypothesis awaits verification.

It appears, in addition, that the highest density of sites, where a Persian occupation is attested, is near the extreme eastern branch of the Nile. The Pelusiac branch was an important river route during the Persian era, as evidenced by the course of the river and a survey of neighbouring sites, and it enabled the region to take on a twofold vocation, both military and commercial. During the Persian period, the strategic function of this key region grew: military settlements increased in number at the best-situated sites, along the coastal cordon, which became the new route, but especially at the approaches to the Pelusiac mouth, the gateway to Egypt. This network of garrisons, which ensured the link between Egypt and the Near East while facilitating the passage of military and commercial expeditions, protected the entry to Egypt via the Pelusiac mouth.

Fieldwork (including geomorphological reconnaissance and archaeological surveys) associated with the interpretation of satellite images of the easternmost part of the Egyptian Delta, has enabled it to be demonstrated that the ancient Pelusiac branch of the Nile passed to the north of Tell el-Makhzan and that its mouth was placed 1.2km north-east of the site.[99] Elsewhere, a derivation of the branch flowed round the *tell* on the south and east, isolating it from the neighbouring zone of the el-Kanais.[100] The excavations carried out by various different missions to Pelusium bring out the variety of vestiges discovered and demonstrate the religious, cultural, economic and strategic importance of this metropolis, since at least the Saite-Persian era and up until the Islamic era.[101]

Pelusium, a place of combat under the earliest Persians, according to Herodotus,[102] had until recently revealed only a few signs of occupation prior to the Hellenistic period. Research conducted under the auspices of the Organisation of Egyptian Antiquities bore essentially on vestiges dating from the Ptolemaic and Roman periods. As for those undertaken by E. Oren,[103] within the framework of his survey, the findings of which indicated that this site was occupied under the Saite and Persian dynasties, but provide only a partial understanding. It was the excavations opened to the west of the *tell*, undertaken conjointly by J.-Y. Carrez-Maratray and the Organisation of Egyptian Antiquities in 1992 and 1993, that furnished the expected material proof.[104] From the deepest archaeological levels reached during this boring, two distinct sets of pottery were discovered. The first, issuing from the substrates immediately underlying those whose dates cover the Ptolemaic period, belongs quite probably to the period that goes from the

beginning to the third quarter of the 4th century BC, the period corresponding to that of the native dynasties (404-342 BC) and the second period of Persian domination (343-332 BC).[105] The analogies are striking, both from the point of view of form and substance, with the furnishings from Tell el-Herr extracted from the contemporary levels but also that of Tanis, situated in the eastern Delta, where the associated findings, notably of ostraca inscribed with the name of Nectanebo II (359-341 BC) clearly indicate a date of the last decades of the first half of the 4th century BC.[106] The very homogeneous material attested at these levels, composed essentially of local products – bowls, hemispherical basins, baking dishes, cupels – also includes some imports (Palestinian and Aegean amphorae; the latter seem to have been widespread mainly in the first half of the 4th century BC).[107]

The second set of items known, brought to light in the deepest level to be reached during the excavations, falls for its part into the formal repertory characteristic of the Achaemenid Persian period (5th century BC).[108] Apart from ceramics, no document supports any of the dates proposed. It is difficult to know exactly whether a fortified city existed at Pelusium in the last quarter of the 6th century BC. The existing documentation 'points in particular to a significant occupation of the site under the local dynasties; this seems to corroborate the story of Diodorus, who reports that imposing fortifications were raised in the reigns of Nectanebo I and II (378-360, 359-341 BC),[109] but no evidence presently allows scholars to trace the most ancient attestations of the site back to the start of the Persian period, or even the Saite epoch. The available data merely permit observers to deduce that Tell el-Farana, at its western extremity at least, was, for lack of any precise label (city? town? village?), an occupied place at the time of Herodotus: the most ancient occupation found on the site, in 1992, clearly dates from the Persian period, limited, *stricto sensu*, to the 5th century BC.'[110]

The commercial role of Pelusium is better known for the Ptolemaic or Roman periods. The bulk of findings of the amphorae from Tell Farama, stamped for identification, come from a huge zone situated at Pelusium, to the east of the water tower: this was without any doubt a quarter of docks and entrepots where the amphorae

98  E. D. Oren, *Le Monde de la Bible* 24, 1982, p. 18.

99  B. Marcolongo, *CRIPEL* 14, 1992, pp. 23-31; M. Chartier-Raymond, C. Traunecker, *CRIPEL* 15, 1993, pp. 45-69.

100  S. Favre, G. Nogara, *CRIPEL* 16, 1994, pp. 129-133; H. Jaritz, *et al.*, *Pelusium*, BÄBA 13, 1996, p. 24, pp. 30-31, pp. 209-210. On Tell el-Kanaïs, see J.-Y. Carrez-Maratray, G. Wagner, *CRIPEL* 15, 1993, pp. 105-110.

101  J.-Y. Carrez-Maratray, *BAGB* 2, 1995, pp. 140-151; Mohamed Abd el-Samie, J.-Y. Carrez-Maratray, in D. Valbelle, C. Bonnet (ed.), *Le Sinaï*, 1998, p. 128; E. D. Oren, *ibid.*, p. 78.

102  Herodotus, III, 11-16.

103  E. D. Oren, *Le Monde de la Bible* 24, 1982, p. 14.

104  A. El-Taba'l, J.-Y. Carrez-Maratray, *CRIPEL* 15, 1993, pp. 111-118; J.-Y. Carrez-Maratray, C. Defernez, *CRIPEL* 18, 1996, pp. 33-49.

105  J.-Y. Carrez-Maratray, C. Defernez, *op. cit.*, pp. 41 and 43, figs. 2 and 3.

106  C. Defernez, in D. Valbelle, C. Bonnet, *op. cit.*, p. 68; D. Roussel, S. Marchand, *BCE* XVIII, 1994, pp. 12-18.

107  C. Defernez, *op. cit.*, pp. 68-69, fig. 56, 4-5; fig. 56, 8-9; fig. 57, 6-7.

108  J.-Y. Carrez-Maratray, C. Defernez, *CRIPEL* 18, 1996, pp. 45 and 48, figs 4-5. It was a comparative analysis of the material with that originating from other sites in the Delta, notably Tell el-Herr, which allowed C. Defernez to establish such a chronology. The main items are bowls, cups, spherical vases, and fragments of jugs whose morphology suggests a date around the middle of the 5th century (C. Defernez, in D. Valbelle, C. Bonnet (ed.), *Le Sinaï*, 1998, p. 69, fig. 57, 3.).

109  Diodorus XV, 42, 14 and XVI, 46, 4-49, 6.

110  C. Defernez, *op. cit.*, p. 69.

coming via the Pelusiac mouth were unloaded in the city's river port; this, located to the south of the city, was served by an immense jetty which ended in a landing stage.[111]

For Greek and Latin authors, Pelusium was above all else a port. Its situation made of it a customs port for the sea and a river port where freight coming down the Pelusiac branch of the Nile landed. The first of these roles is alluded to by papyri on the import of oils,[112] fabrics[113] and wine;[114] one of the texts from the archive of Zeno gives an overview of a customs register.[115] The importance of river traffic and its link with the sea is underlined by St Jerome, Ezekiel,[116] Theodorus Lector,[117] and Theophanes.[118] Nile barges descended the river,[119] conveying people[120] and merchandise: the cattle of Middle Egypt,[121] but especially the wheat destined for export.[122] Others would have taken it back up with their cargoes.[123]

From a strictly archaeological point of view, it has been suggested that the low outcrop to the north of the site could have been the port, but it is now known, thanks to the excavations of Mohammed Abd el-Maksoud, that this part of the *tell* covers the baths. The discovery of the sites of the northern suburbs rules out any passage, at least during the final period, from the mean-water bed to the north of the site. According to G. Wagner and J.-Y. Carrez-Maratray, the abundance of specific pottery (an amphora with numerous crests) in the low zones south-east of the site, beyond the ancient water tower, would indicate a storage zone near the port. The dike on the site passes near this sector and could act as a quay. In this sector, the masonry is embellished with beds of limestone blocks. Two difficulties still remain: on the one hand, the relative dates of the vestiges of the sector of 'El-Souq' and the dike, or at least of its original course; on the other, the absence of any vestiges of the central part of the dike, a decisive element for its function. M. Chartier-Raymond and C. Traunecker have established a parallel between the dike of Pelusium and the modern dike of Assiout.[124] The latter leads from the desert to the city, crossing the bed of the flood. The mean-water bed is situated on the other side of the city, to the east. The water level is controlled by regulatory sluice gates situated at both extremities of the dike-road, at the point where the dike is at its highest. A dike of this kind serves at once as a land access transformed into an island for three months of the year, and as a regulator of the floodwaters and a means of restraint for irrigation. The dike of Pelusium has many close analogies with this: it serves as a means of access to the city and, as in the modern example, it has

111  J.-Y. Carrez-Maratray, *et al.*, *CRIPEL* 18, 1996, pp. 179-195.
112  P. Revenue, *Laws*, 93, 1-7; J.-Y. Carrez-Maratray, *Péluse*, *BiÉtud* 124, 1999, n° 344 p. 168.
113  P. Michigan Zenon, 2, 5-6; *ibid.*, n° 345 p. 168.
114  P. London VII 1930, 205-211; *ibid.*, n° 346 p. 169.
115  P. Cairo Zenon I 59012; *ibid.*, n° 347 p. 169.
116  Jerome, *Commentary on Ezechiel*, IX, 30, 1; *ibid.*, n° 119 p. 81.
117  Theodorus Lector, *Histoire Ecclésiastique*, *Épitome* 362; *ibid.*, n° 235 p. 131.
118  Theophanus, *Chronography*, 106, 33; *ibid.*, n° 236 p. 131.
119  P. Columbia Zenon II, 112, 1-3; *ibid.*, n° 352 p. 179.
120  P. Oxyrhynchos L 3576, 7-15; *ibid.*, n° 379 p. 190.
121  P. Oxyrhynchos L 3602, 1-12; *ibid.*, n° 371 p. 186.
122  P. Oxyrhynchos XL 2926, 1-7; P. Oxyrhynchos XII 1544, 1-11; *ibid.*, n° 373-334 pp. 187-188.
123  P. Oxyrhynchos XXXIV 2732, 2-11; *ibid.*, n° 383 p. 192.
124  M. Chartier-Raymond, C. Traunecker, *CRIPEL* 15, 1993, p. 65, which we have used as a source for what follows here.

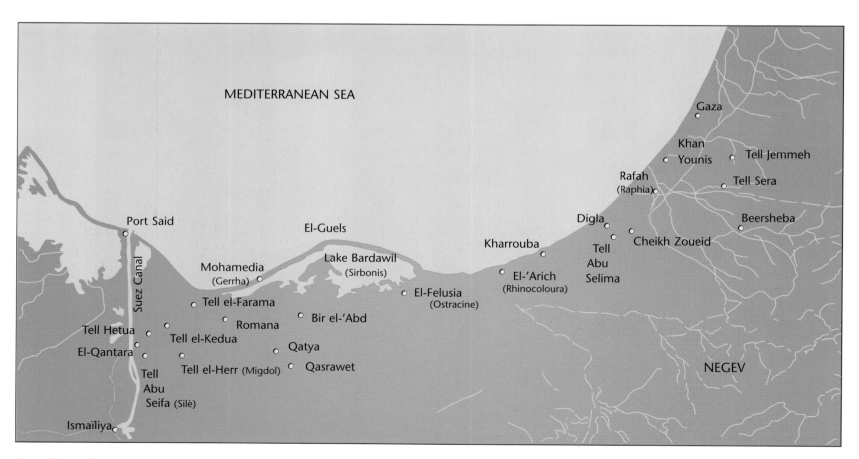

Map of North Sinai, after the drawing by M. Berti in D. Valbelle and C. Bonnet (eds), *Le Sinaï*, 1998, p. 61.

regulatory sluices/overflow channels at both its extremities. At Asyut, the main river course passes elsewhere and the dike affects only the left bank of the flood bed. To reproduce this situation it would need to be accepted that the bed passed north of Pelusium, a hypothesis that is disproved, at least for the ultimate state of the site, by the presence of the 'El-Souq' district. On the other hand, if the hypothesis of the southern passage is accepted, it would also have to be conceded that the eastern part of the dike, now vanished, was provided with an arrangement that gave free passage to the waters of the mean-water Nile, with the possibility of closing the dike. A series of sluices was doubtless enough to contain the relatively low volume of the river at this extremity of the Nile's branch. The possibility should also be borne in mind that there was a passage for ships. Perhaps there was a river port, upstream from the dike, along the segment parallel to Pelusium, and a maritime port, downstream from the dike, between the latter and the docks. The environment of Pelusium, as it appears from prospecting, is reminiscent of the text by Diodorus Siculus describing the mouths of the river:[125]

*At each mouth (of the Nile) is built a city that is divided by the river and whose two parts are separated by bridges of boats and well-sited defences.*

## II.3.4. The coastline of North Sinai

The writings of Herodotus contain valuable information on the demographic map of North Sinai and the Egyptian frontier during the Persian period. The Greek historian describes the administrative division of the fifth satrapy (*abar nahara*) at the time of Darius I (521-486 BC), and also provides evidence of the places of commerce present on the North Sinai coast. In his words:[126]

*It is only by this route that access is possible into Egypt. From Phoenicia to the confines of the town of Kadytis (Gaza), the land belongs to the Syrians who are called Syrians of Palestine; from Kadytis – a town which, it seems to me, is hardly any less big than Sardes, from this town to the town of Ienysos, the places of maritime commerce (emporia) belong to the King of the Arabs: from Ienysos onwards, you are once again on Syrian territory as far as Lake Serbonnis, near which is Mount Kasios, which extends into the sea; by Lake Serbonis, where (they say) Typhon is hidden, Egypt begins. The land between the town of Ienysos on the one side, and Mount Kasios and Lake Serbonis on the other, a land which is of no little extent but measures about three days' journey, is terribly arid.*

This description, together with another from the same book, indicates that Lake Serbonis (Lake Bardawil), and more especially the crest of the Kasios, in the middle of the sandy coastal bar, was considered as the frontier between Egypt and Syria:[127]

*Egypt properly speaking extends sixty schenes along the sea, if we fix its limits at the Gulf of Plinthine on one side, and on the other Lake Serbonis, at the foot of Mount Kasios; it is from the lake that the sixty schenes are measured.*

During the *North Sinai Survey* (1972-1982), 150 sites from the Persian period, from the 5th to the 4th centuries BC, have been discovered. The map of these settlements brings out a significant concentration of sites in the north-west of the peninsula, between Romana and the Suez Canal, on the shores of Lake Bardawil and between Wadi El-Arich[128] and Wadi Gaza. The sites involved include both urban sites and villages, as well as fortifications, commercial stages, necropolises and various encampments.[129] The material brought to light 'reveals the importance of North Sinai in the administrative and commercial organisation of the Persian Kingdom'. Archaeological discoveries considered conjointly with the few historical attestations that are known, draw attention to 'the close cooperation of Persians, Egyptians, Phoenicians, Jews, Arabs and Greeks in the commercial and administrative affairs of North Sinai', and 'the cosmopolitan character of that region'.[130]

The traditional itinerary that linked the eastern Delta to Palestine and passed to the south of the Bardawil[131] was accompanied by a new road along the Mediterranean, from Gaza to Pelusium; it followed the coastal strip of the lagoon and led to the mouth of the Pelusiac branch, in the city of Pelusium itself. This route became particularly famous during the next stages in the history of Sinai, in the Hellenistic, Roman and Byzantine periods; it is mentioned by contemporary geographers and historians, and also appears on the illustrated maps of those periods.[132] The importance of the Pelusium-Gaza itinerary is reflected in the mention made of it, from the reign of Augustus to the start of the Byzantine period, as a link of vital importance for populations in transit, the transport of goods, and administration.[133] Although a major part of this commerce may have been effected by caravans, the majority was surely carried out by the maritime route, even if the traces of shipwreck between Pelusium and Gaza are very few in number.[134] Maritime traffic along the northern coast of the Sinai was certainly important, and future submarine exploration in the region will surely yield considerable results.

The *North Sinai Survey* made it possible to bring to light the different settlements established directly on the coast and in places that were probably uninhabited in bygone days: vast habitats,

---

125  Diodorus, *Bibliotheca Historica*, I, 33, 7-8; translation by A. Bernand, *Le Delta égyptien d'après les textes grecs*, 1, *Les confins libyques*, I, MIFAO 91, 1970, p. 23.

126  Herodotus, III, 5; translation P.-E. Legrand, Les Belles Lettres, 1982.

127  Herodotus, III, 6. Also of interest is the article by J.-Y. Carrez-Maratray that retranscribes the vision that the Greeks and Romans may have had of the region of North Sinai, in D. Valbelle, C. Bonnet (ed.), *Le Sinaï*, 1998, pp. 88-92. On traffic along the Sinai coastline during the Greek and Roman periods, according to the Antonine Table, the Peutinger Table, the Map of Madaba and the Cosmography of Ravenna, see D. F. Graf, in D. Valbelle, C. Bonnet (ed.), *op. cit.*, pp. 107-113.

128  The site of El-Arich (Rhinocoroura) was probably a stopover point between Egypt and Palestine during the Pharaonic period (A. H. Gardiner, JEA VI, 1920, pp. 99-116). Nonetheless, it is essentially known only via evidence from the Greek and Roman periods: see E. D. Oren, *Bulletin of the Anglo-Israel Archaeological Society* 10, 1982-1983, n. 72 p. 18 and n. 68 p. 26; D. Baraq, IEJ 23, 1973, pp. 50-52; B. R. Rees, BJRL 51, 1968, pp. 164-183, and H. Cadell, in L. Criscuolo, G. Geraci (ed.), *Egitto e storia antica dall'Ellenismo all'età araba*, 1989, pp. 315-323; C. A. Noordegraaf, *Mnemosyne* 6, 1938, p. 273-310. For the date, E. Honigman, *Byzantion* 14, 1939, pp. 645-649; J.-Y. Carrez-Maratray, *Péluse*, BiÉtud 124, 1999, n° 77, 81, 82, 104, 178, 234, 259; id., in D. Valbelle, C. Bonnet (ed.), *op. cit.*, pp. 88-92; D. F. Graf, *op. cit.*, pp. 109-110;

129  E. D. Oren in D. Valbelle, C. Bonnet (ed.), *Le Sinaï*, 1998, p. 75.

130  *Id.*, p. 75.

131  A. H. Gardiner, JEA VI, 1920, pp. 99-116; E. D. Oren, in A. F. Rainey (ed.), *Egypt, Israel, Sinai*, 1987, pp. 69-119.

132  E.D. Oren in D. Valbelle, C. Bonnet (ed.), *Le Sinaï*, 1998, p. 75; I. Finkelstein, in Z. Meshel, I. Finkelstein (ed.), *Sinai in Antiquity*, 1980, pp. 181-198.

133  Strabo, XVI, 2, 30.

134  See A. J. Parker, *Ancient Shipwrecks of the Mediterranean*, BAR IS 580, 1992, fig. 1.

commercial centres *(emporia)*, fishing villages and mooring grounds. These newly constituted sites formed the nucleus of a dense urban fabric – towns and ports – that characterised the north coast of the peninsula in Roman and Byzantine times.[135] A network of small forts (Tell Qatifa, next to Ruqueich, on the site in the environs of Sheik Zoueid, at Ras Qasroum, on the site near Romana and at Tell el-Herr) established all along this coast road, marks the introduction of a new, more mobile strategy of defence, relying on detachments of soldiers and men policing the desert, recruited from the local Arab population. The considerable volume and the different types of Greek and Phoenician pottery, recorded on practically every site, constitutes irrefutable evidence of the central role played by the settlements and the *emporia* of North Sinai in Mediterranean trade.[136]

In summary: 'the first great unfortified coastal sites of the Persian peninsula were included within typically organised and hierarchical groups – operational bases, smaller settlements, encampments – and protected by small forts or citadels. Before the annexation of this region to the Persian empire, during for instance the Assyrian and Saite periods, the map of the settlements of North Sinai followed a completely different model: it was essentially composed of several huge centres and solidly fortified garrisons, situated at each extremity of the Sinai corridor. Unfortunately, the best candidates for this category of conurbations in the region between Gaza and Pelusium have hardly been excavated at all by archaeologists. Historical sources tell us that these towns served as central seats for regional administration and commercial trading posts, as well as communities of colonists who had settled at the gates of Egypt, especially on the Pelusiac branch of the Nile.'[137]

## II.3.5. Tell Ruqueich

Tell Ruqueich, situated near the outlet of Wadi Gaza and some 12km south of Gaza, has yielded impressive remains of a major settlement that served during the Persian period as a commercial station linked to land and sea trafficking.[138] Founded in the 8th century BC, equipped with massive fortifications and considerable storage capacities, the site seems to have played a far from negligible role as a commercial centre for the Assyrian administration in the Gaza region. E. Oren suggests that Tell Ruqueich be identified with the 'sealed *Karu* (port) of Egypt' where, according to the *Annals of Khorsabad* and the *Prism of Nimrod*, Sargon II (721-705 BC) reunited the Assyrians and the Egyptians, encouraging them to develop commercial exchanges.[139] It is the neighbouring fort situated on the small hill of Tell Qatifa which ensured the defence of Tell Ruqueich. It constituted an ideal observation post from which the coast between Gaza and Raphia could be kept under surveillance. To the south of the corner tower, on the lower limestone terrace, a granary in sun-dried bricks has been discovered in perfect condition (2.50m in circumference; preserved height around 3m). This settlement belonged to a large-scale system of supply that depended on the administration of North Sinai and Gaza. This is what is indicated by the discovery of numerous granaries of sun-dried bricks, superbly constructed and of considerable volume. For example, an impressive silo 7m in diameter, still complete with its brick pavement, has been discovered at Tell Sera, 24km to the east of Gaza, while no less than 12 others (from 4 to 7m in diameter) have been brought to light near Tell Jemmeh.[140]

The architectural vestiges of Tell Ruqueich include huge

entrepots, with industrial and harbour installations organised directly on the neighbouring coastline. The rich repertoire of pottery has parallels in the centres of the Phoenician coast. It includes storage jars of the *torpedo* type, amphorae for transport, huge jars with so-called basket-handles, thick-walled mortars, and a significant collection of Greek wine amphorae and varnished Attic pottery.[141]

The geographical position of the site and the breadth of the archaeological discoveries made there shows that 'it was a flourishing Persian trading post, one of the administrative and commercial centres situated, according to Herodotus,[142] between 'Kadytis (Gaza) and Ienysos'. The absence of comparable traces between Gaza and El-Arich certainly indicates that Tell Ruqueich was one of the 'coastal trading posts' mentioned by Herodotus. Ruqueich owed its prosperity, during the Persian era, to its top-flight commercial role on the new road as well as being the end of the *Sahar Arav*. At the end of the 4th century, the site was finally abandoned, probably because of the conquest of Alexander, and supplanted by the *polis* of Gaza, newly established.'[143]

## II.3.6. The Bardawil sites

Prospectings made by E. Oren and his team have revealed an important centre situated in the middle of the coastal strip separating Lake Bardawil from the Mediterranean: 'In the western and northern parts, a chain of dunes, whose summit (Ras Qasroun) reaches a height of 60m above sea level, bears the name of Qatib el-Guels. According to ancient sources, Kasion was known as an important station on the coast road and the crest of Ras Qasroun was almost universally identified with Mount Kasios, the site of the famous temple to Zeus-Kasios, the patron of sailors and ships. Specialists of the Biblical world attach a great importance to the site of Kasion because of the generally accepted identification of Baal-Zephon with Mount Kasios. In the Canaanite and Phoenician pantheon, Baal-Zephon, just like Zeus-Kasios, was the protector of sailors, and his name appears as that of a stage in the itinerary of the Exodus from Egypt.'[144]

135   E. D. Oren, in D. Valbelle, C. Bonnet (ed.), *Le Sinaï*, 1998, p. 75.

136   *Id.*, p. 76.

137   E. D. Oren, *op. cit.*, pp. 75-76; *cf. id., BASOR* 256, 1984, pp. 7-44; *id.*, in E. Stern (ed.), *The New Encyclopedia of Archaeological excavations in the Holy Land*, vol. 4, 1993, p. 1293-1294; H. J. Katzenstein, *Transeuphratène* I, 1989, pp. 67-86. On earlier excavations, W. J. Phytian-Adams, *PEQ*, 1923, pp. 11-36.

138   E. D. Oren in D. Valbelle, C. Bonnet (ed.), *Le Sinaï*, 1998, p. 76; *id.*, in E. Stern (ed.), *op. cit.*, 1293-1294.

139   E. D. Oren in D. Valbelle, C. Bonnet (ed.), *Le Sinaï*, 1998, p. 76. cf. H. Tadmor, *JCS* 12, 1958, p. 34; *id., BA* 29, 1966, pp. 86-102; I. Eph'al, *The Ancient Arabs*, 1982, pp. 101-105; E. D. Oren, *et al., Qadmoniot* 19, pp. 83-91; *id.*, in E. Stern (ed.), *op. cit.*, pp. 1293-1294; *id.*, in *Proceedings of the Second International Congress of Biblical Archaeology*, 1993, pp. 102-105; R. Reich, *IEJ* 34, 1984, pp. 32-38.

140   E. D. Oren, in E. Stern (ed.), *The New Encyclopedia of Archaeological excavations in the Holy Land*, vol. 4, 1993, 1334 ; W. M. F. Petrie, *Gerar, BSAE* XIII, 1928, pp. 8-10; G. Van Beek, in E. Stern (ed.), *op. cit.*, p. 673. G. Van Beek dates these granaries to the Hellenistic period, even though an attribution to the Persian period seems more appropriate given the pottery associated with them. Petrie suggests that the granaries of Tell Jemmeh should be interpreted as an element in the supply system established by the Persian administration in the region of Gaza, in view of the campaign in Egypt. By his calculations, these granaries could provide an army of at least 70,000 men with enough grain and beans for two months.

141   E. D. Oren in D. Valbelle, C. Bonnet (ed.), *Le Sinaï*, 1998, p. 76.

142   Herodotus, III, 5.

143   E. D. Oren *op. cit.*, p. 75

144   *Id.*, p. 77; *cf. Exode*, 14, 2, 9. O. Eissfeldt, *Beitr. zur Religiogeschichte des Altertums* 1, 1932, p. 30 *et seq.*; F. M. Abel, *RevBibl* 48, 1939, pp. 207-236, 530-548 ; *id., RevBibl* 49, 1940, pp. 55-75, 224-239.

The intervention of systematic salvaging in the entire zone of El-Guels, carried out by the North Sinai Expedition (1974-1976) led to the recording of 43 sites. Most of them, revealed by a few calcined remains, constituted small encampments. The western zone of the coastal strip is characterised by sites of a more permanent nature (with traces of structures in sun-dried brick). The ceramic material indicates a period from the Recent Iron Age to the Early Islamic period, but the majority of the shards belong to the Persian and Roman periods. These sites are characterised by the presence of entrepots and fireplaces in stone and clay, with hearths, stone tools and pottery. The northernmost of them, constructed directly on the limestone terrace that extends down to the sea makes it possible to envisage the existence of a mooring ground for ships of small dimensions. The site has yielded exceptional finds, such as a silver pin decorated with a cobra's head and the round lead mould of an Athenian coin from the end of the 5th century BC. The abundance of lead fishing weights indicates that this place was economically reliant on fishing.[145]

According to the discoverer's interpretation, the most significant installations in this group doubtless correspond to the peripheral dwelling-places of a significant conurbation, probably the site of Kasion that is now almost entirely buried beneath the crest of El-Guels. The great quantity of Phoenician and Greek pottery, fragments of alabaster and faience vases that were found within them, enables one to deduce the importance of these sites on the coastal strip of the Bardawil in the Persian era.[146]

The results of recent explorations on the coastal strip of the Bardawil directly concern a great number of major subjects relating to the historical geography of North Sinai. 'It is now clear that the first settlement in the region of Qatib el-Guels was constituted of a group of provisional encampments, corresponding perhaps to a staging post on the route during the recent Iron Age, at the end of the 7th century and the beginning of the 6th century BC. In the Persian period, Mount Kasios marked the frontier between Syria and Egypt, becoming an important stopover on the coast road, and also, quite probably, a place where small-sized vessels could put in. The great number of encampments, as well as the presence of several permanent settlements, over a relatively reduced area, indicates the importance that this area then assumed. It must have served as a landmark and a refuge for navigators coasting along this shore between the Delta, the land of the Philistines and Phoenicia. There too caravans could renew their provisions of food and water, and find shelter during their protracted voyage along the arid and inhospitable coastal strip of Lake Bardawil. A little later, the site of Kasion developed into a major commercial and industrial centre, provided with a significant naval dockyard and a magnificent temple to Zeus-Kasios. At the earliest, it was in the Hellenistic period that this conurbation attained its greatest extent, as confirmed by written sources.'[147] In the 5th century BC, Herodotus said nothing about any Greek temple on Mount Kasios and simply mentioned the place as a geographical landmark;[148] on the other hand, sources from Hellenistic and Roman periods – the papyri of Zeno and Oxyrhynchus, the *Antonine Itinerary*, Strabo, Flavius Josephus – speak of Kasion/Qatib el-Guels as an important place between Ostracina and Gerrha,[149] and as an industrial centre famous for its temple of Zeus-Kasios, its metals and its constructional timber, particularly well adapted to ship-building.[150]

In the south-west corner of the Bardawil, an important site has been excavated called 'Luxor' by the Bedouins of the region. Its surface area, 5 hectares, was covered by thick layers of wine amphorae and Phoenician storage vessels from the 5th-6th centuries BC, as well as the remnants of stone and clay buildings, and hearths. It is likely that this place was a centre or a depot where consignments of wine and oil were sent to Greek soldiers and merchants in the region. Such an interpretation is clearly demonstrated by the site's location, directly on the sea front of the Bardawil, where the ships bringing cargoes of amphorae could moor and unload these before they were divided up and sent into the interior. On aerial photographs, it is still possible to distinguish close by a dike of some 100m long that probably acted as a breakwater and sheltered the cargo ships in a zone that was subject, in winter, to violent storms.[151]

145 E. D. Oren *op. cit.*, p. 77; Z. Ilan, A. Yosef, *Qadmoniot* 10, 1977, pp. 77-79.

146 In addition, surface collections carried out in some of the sites of the coastal strip of the Bardawil have brought together numerous fragments of marble plaques inscribed with Greek letters, in fine craftsmanship; they must have adorned the inside walls of an important building. These fragments, too small to be read, perhaps belonged among the dedicatory inscriptions of the temple of Zeus-Kasios that stood in the environs in the Hellenistic or Roman period: E. D. Oren *op. cit.*, p. 77 ; M. Dothan, *ErIsr* 9, 1969, pp. 47-59.

147 E. D. Oren, in D. Valbelle, C. Bonnet (ed.), *Le Sinaï*, 1998, p. 77.

148 Herodotus, II, 6, 158; III, 5.

149 On these two sites, see J. Cledat, *ASAE* XVI, 1916, p. 27; E. D. Oren, *Le Monde de la Bible* 24, 1982, p. 24; J.-Y. Carrez-Maratray, *Péluse*, BiÉtud 124, 1999, n° 27, 57, 58, 64, 77, 81, 82, 234, 259, 289, 303, 372; *id.*, in D. Valbelle, C. Bonnet (ed.), *Le Sinaï*, 1998, pp. 88-92; D. F. Graf, p. 109.

150 For example Diodorus Siculus, XX, 74, 3; Pliny, *Natural History*, V, 68; Appius, *Civil War*, II, 12, 85-86; Flavius Josephus, *Jewish War*, IV, 11, 5. See E. D. Oren in D. Valbelle, C. Bonnet (ed.), *Le Sinaï*, 1998, p. 77; J.-Y. Carrez-Maratray, *Péluse*, BiÉtud 124, 1999, n° 57, 58, 64, 173, 190, 288; D. F. Graf, in D. Valbelle, C. Bonnet (ed.), *Le Sinaï*, 1998, p. 109; E. D. Oren, *Le Monde de la Bible 24*, 1982, p. 18; *id.*, *Bulletin of the Anglo-Israel Archaeological Society* 10, 1982-1983, p. 20; P. Figueras, *SCI* 8-9, 1985-1988, p. 58; J. Cledat, *ASAE* XIII, 1913, pp. 79-85; P. Chuvin, J. Yoyotte, *RevArch* I, 1986, pp. 50-51.

151 E. D. Oren in D. Valbelle, C. Bonnet (ed.), *Le Sinaï*, 1998, p. 77. It is worth noting that the site of El-Ouqsor or 'Louqsor' (Luxor) has recently been linked to the coastal stopover called Pentaschoenum in the *Antonine Itinerary* and Byzantine sources, but this hypothesis still needs confirmation by archaeological investigation.

# III. The Red Sea ports

The present archaeological data on the rim of the Red Sea are unevenly spread, and these data are in any case generally rather poor. The archaeological vestiges on the Egyptian coast are rare or, when they do exist, remain confidential before and during the Ptolemaic period; a clearer view starts to become possible only in the Roman period, around the end of the 1st century BC or the beginning of the 1st century AD. Archaeological data from the coastal sites, that could shed light on the texts of the Pharaonic period, are practically non-existent. The port of Sawu (*Suw*), in the Mersa Gawasis, some 20km south of Safaga, dating from the 12th Dynasty (1991-1782 BC),[1] raises numerous problems of interpretation, examined in greater detail below. During the Ptolemaic period, several scattered documents (coins, pottery) appear at random, depending on the excavations of sites of later date, but contemporary ruins exist only in the region of Berenice-Ras Banas.[2] A recent update has been performed for the Roman phase of the history of the coast of the Red Sea and the roads that crossed the desert to reach it. The latter are rich in settlements of every sort: mines, stopover posts, garrisons, and so on.[3] These data and a certain number of convergent elements make it possible to gain some idea of the harbour infrastructures in the Red Sea in Pharaonic times.

## III.1. Access routes to the Red Sea

The harbour infrastructures present on the coastline are inseparably linked to the access routes that lead from the Nile to the Red Sea. The system of communication in the eastern desert essentially comprised trails that leave the Valley and extend to the Red Sea coast. They were used long after the period under consideration. Inscriptions, graffiti and wells (*hydreumae*) all bear witness to the volume of traffic they bore, and make it possible to reconstruct their routes quite accurately.[4] The east-west route furthest to the north is that of Wadi Araba, which begins in the Nile Valley at the same latitude as Fayum and reaches the sea after a journey of 145km. Further south, Wadi Qena constituted the Roman road of the *Mons Porphyrites*. It crossed that of the *Mons Claudianus* and reached the coast around Disht el-Dabba and Mersa Abu Merkhaida. The path from Myos Hormos to Abu Shaar also had paths branching off it and constituted the only alternative route.[5] Further south, the trail from Qena to Philoteras, which passed through Wadi Gasus, was also very important.[6] The other well-known trail is that of Wadi Hammamat between Coptos and Leukos Limen.[7] From Coptos another trail also began which, again via Wadi Gasus, led to the coast.[8] The trail to Berenice started in the environs of Coptos but could also be joined starting from El-Kab and Aswan.[9] These latter trails doubtless played a fundamental role in the development of the mines of the eastern desert.[10] A second trail, called the *Via Hadriana* in the Roman period, led to Berenice along the shore of the Red Sea. The possibility cannot be excluded that this route continued further south.[11]

Finally, Wadi Tumilat constituted a traffic route of choice between the Nile and the Isthmus of Suez. This is a deep, steeply-sloping wadi, that runs from east to west, between the eastern side of the Upper Delta and the Lake of Timsa. This 58km strip of land, situated between Saft el-Henna (the former Pi-Sopdu) and Ismailia, is cut across by the freshwater canal and the old road joining Matariya

(Heliopolis) to the Suez Canal; but this geographical situation merely underscores a historical fact, namely that, from time immemorial, this terrain has represented a corridor of easy access between the Delta and the central and southern part of the Sinai peninsula. Egyptian occupation of Wadi Tumilat goes back to the later or archaic predynastic period, to which date rich cemeteries discovered at its eastern extremity. Old Kingdom (2686-2181 BC) texts speak of cities, situated especially to the west, where the kings of the 4th, 5th and 6th Dynasties (2613-2498, 2498-2345, 2345-2181 BC) established agricultural settlements. Certain points suggest that during the 6th Dynasty an attempt was made to fortify the region around the Bitter Lakes, doubtless to try and control the entry of the Bedouins into Sinai. On the other hand, it is difficult to state for certain that the Egyptians themselves, in the Old Kingdom, used the wadi as an access corridor to Sinai or the Negev. There is some evidence to suggest that the expeditions probably preferred to take the Pelusiac branch of the Nile leading to Palestine or to pass via Wadi Araba to reach the Gulf of Suez.[12]

Attempts to fortify the Valley go back, as elaborated above, to at least the end of the Old Kingdom. Before the 21st century, a great fortress had been constructed in the central party of the wadi some 30km away from the present-day Ismailia, near the place where, in Antiquity, the arable land began. Known today by the name of Tell el-Retaba, its original name is unknown, though it may have been associated with the fortifications of the 12th Dynasty (1991-1782 BC), known by the name of the 'Wall of the Sovereign'. In the New Kingdom (1570-1070 BC), the Tell el-Retaba was a key site in the chain of frontier forts. Equipped with maintenance and storage facilities, it was placed under the jurisdiction of a commander and served as a headquarters for desert patrols that regularly inspected the

---

1. Abdel Monem Sayed, *RdÉ* 29, 1977, pp. 138-178; id., *JEA* 64, 1978, pp. 69-71; id., *JEA* 66, 1980, pp. 154-171; id., *CdÉ* LVIII, 115-116, 1983, pp. 23-37; H. Frost, *Topoi* 6, 1996, pp. 869-902.

2. K. Sadr, in C. Bonnet (ed.), *Études Nubiennes*, 1994, pp. 7-11; S. E. Sidebotham, W. Z. Wendrich (ed.), *Berenike'94 & Berenike'95*, 1995-1996; id., *Berenike 1996*, 1998; S. E. Sidebotham, in *Autour de Coptos, Topoi* suppl. 3, 2002, pp. 199-233. See also H. Cuvigny, in *Coptos. L'Égypte antique aux portes du désert*, 2000, pp. 158-175.

3. See the contributions of J.-P. Brun, A. Bülow-Jacobsen, F. de Romanis, D. Whitcomb, S. Sidebotham, P. Ballet, in *Topoi* 6, 1996, pp. 649-941.

4. See, for example in A. Bernand, *Pan du désert*, 1977; id., *De Koptos à Kosseir*, 1972; L. A. Tregenza, *The Red Sea Mountains of Egypt*, 1955, pp. 39-46; for inscriptions that confirm the extent to which these routes were used, see Bell, J. Johnson, D. Whitcomb, *JNES* 43, 1984, pp. 47-86; J. Leclant, *Orientalia* 22, 1953, pp. 89-90; id., *Orientalia* 27, 1958, pp. 75-101; id., *Orientalia* 51, 1982, p. 90; J. Leclant, G. Clerc, *Orientalia* 60, 1991, pp. 246-247; id., *Orientalia* 61, 1992, pp. 298-300; id., *Orientalia* 62, 1993, pp. 265-267; S. Redford, D. B. Redford, *JARCE* 26, 1989, pp. 3-49; R. D. Delia, *JARCE* 30, 1993, pp. 71-91.

5. On the trails across the eastern desert, cf. L. A. Tregenza, *The Red Sea Mountains of Egypt*, 1955, pp. 1-108 (trails between Qena, Mons Claudianus and Myos Hormos), 109-239 (trails between Qena and the coast passing through Wadi Beli and Wadi Atrach); T. de Putter, *Coptos. L'Égypte antique aux portes du désert*, 2000, pp. 144-156

6. This trail has been described by Abdel Monem Sayed, *RdÉ* 29, 1977, pp. 140-178.

7. cf. D. Meredith, *JEA* 38, 1952, pp. 94-111; G. W. Murray, *JEA* XI, 1925, pp. 138-150.

8. cf. Abdel Monem Sayed, op. cit., pp. 140-178; T. de Putter, op. cit., p. 144.

9. The use of trails in the eastern desert to the east of Aswan is also confirmed by proto-dynastic remains; see G. W. Murray, *JEA* XXV, 1939, pp. 38-39, and by the rock art that may be predynastic, cf. G. W. Murray, O. H. Myers, *JEA* XIX, 1933, pp. 129-132. See also S. E. Sidebotham, in *Autour de Coptos, Topoi* suppl. 3, 2002, pp. 415-438.

10. The role of these trails in connection with mining activities has been studied by J. Vercoutter, *KUSH* VII, 1959, pp. 120-153, pls xxviii-xxxv; the same trails were used in the Roman era; see M. Reddé, T. Bauzou, in T. Fahd (ed.), *L'Arabie Préislamique*, 1989, pp. 485-498.

11. On the *Via Hadriana*, see L. A. Regenza, *The Red Sea Mountains of Egypt*, 1955, pp. 73-137.

12. D. B. Redford, in *L'Égypte du Delta. Les capitales du Nord, Dossiers d'Archéologie* 213, 1996, p. 51.

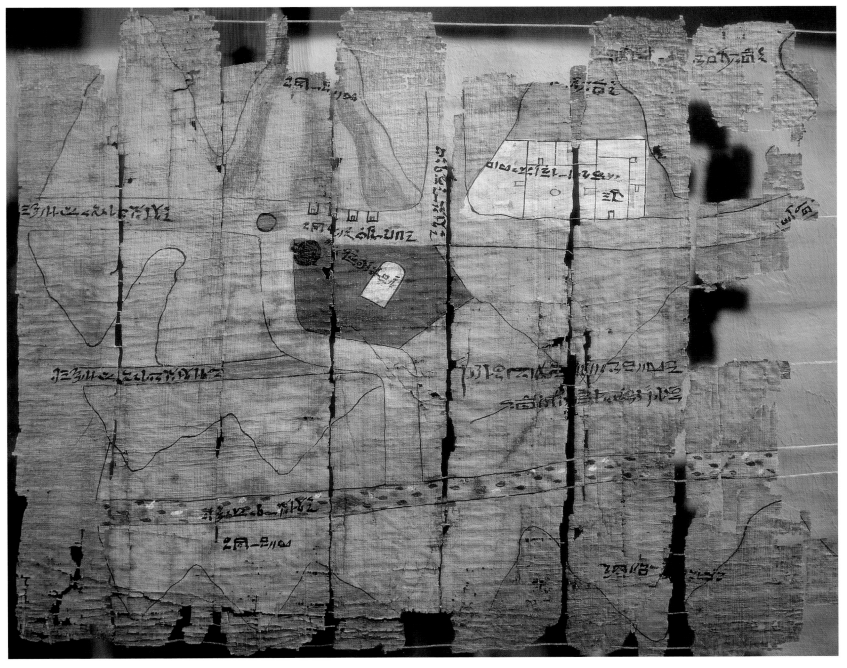

Map of the gold mines and quarries in the eastern desert: fragment of a papyrus from the Ramesside period. The names of mountains and roads are written in hieratic script. Museum of Turin. © Gianni Dagli Orti/CORBIS

Sinai. While el-Retaba continued to be occupied throughout the Third Intermediate Period (1069-525 BC), the site gradually fell into ruin at the end of the 8th century BC, and was abandoned.

Shortly before 600 BC, Pharaoh Nekau II (609-594 BC) of the 26th (Saite) Dynasty (1663-1555 BC) decided to construct a canal across Wadi Tumilat. The original aim may have been military and strategic. However, this navigable route was soon turning out to be advantageous for trade. In fact, as Herodotus explains,[13] this was a planned canal linking directly 'the northern sea to the southern sea — the same as is called the Erythrean Sea' by using the waters of the Nile. It was a gigantic task:

*One hundred and twenty thousand Egyptians perished digging it under the reign of Nekau, but Nekau stopped in the middle of*

*the cutting operations, after an oracle opposed the plan, saying that he was working in advance for the Barbarian.*

Here too, the existence of such a project speaks volumes about the economic and strategic importance, at least in the eyes of Nekau and his councillors, of maritime trade between the Red Sea and the Mediterranean. This technological exploit is confirmed by several steles in four languages discovered between the Bitter Lakes and the Gulf of Suez.[14] So this project was taken up and brought to

13    Herodotus, II, 158.

14    G. Posener, *la première domination perse*, BiÉtud, 1936, pp. 48-87, pp. 180-188. On the dating of the canal's completion, probably 513 BC, *cf.* G. C. Cameron, *JNES* 2, 1942, pp. 307-313; R. G. Kent, *Old Persian*, AOS 33, 1953, p. 111, 147.

completion about a century later by King Darius I (521–486), and Herodotus, who probably saw this canal, describes it in some detail:

> It is four days' sailing in length; it was dug wide enough for two triremes sailing in parallel to navigate it;[15] the water is brought here from the Nile, and its course leads from a point situated somewhere upstream from the city of Bubastis, passes near Patoumos (Pithom), the city of Arabia, and ends at the Erythrean Sea.

Dredged afresh and enlarged by the Persian sovereign, this 'Canal of the East', as it was called, thus left the Nile to the north of Bubastis and, after linking the navigable routes from Heliopolis, continued eastwards to Lake Timsa and then, via the Bitter Lakes, to the entrance of the Gulf of Suez, where it flowed into the Red Sea.[16] Quite recently, a systematic exploration of the region of Wadi Tumilat, undertaken by J. S. Holladay from 1977 to 1979,[17] has made it possible to grasp the importance of this region from the 7th to the 5th century BC.[18] Of particular note: the discovery, at Tell el-Maskhuta, of Phoenician wine jars from the Neo-Babylonian and Persian era, and even a Phoenician ostracon dating at least from the middle of the 5th century or thereabouts, as well as an inscribed Phoenician amphora from the end of the 7th century, including a drawing of a human head.

To replace the abandoned fort of Tell el-Retaba, several other groups of dwelling-places were founded during the 6th century BC at the eastern extremity of Wadi Tumilat, not far from modern Ismailia. A list in demotic of geographical names mentions several fortifications along the Delta, certain of which were doubtless situated at the eastern outlet of the Wadi. The most significant contribution to the demographic distribution in the Wadi is provided by the town of Pithom, situated some 15km to the west of Ismailia. Pithom was built in 600 BC by Nekau II, to be a fortress and a place of trade on the route of the 'Canal of the East'. Nekau and the kings of the 30th Dynasty (380–343 BC) decorated Pithom with monumental sculptures and *naoi* that they had taken from older buildings of the Ramesside period. Pithom comes from Per-

15 J. S. Holladay, *Qadmoniot* 12, 1979, p. 88, estimates that this width was about 40m, approximately half that of the Suez Canal.

16 On Darius and the Red Sea, *cf.* J.-F. Salles, in J.-F. Salles (ed.), *L'Arabie et ses mers bordières*, I, 1988, p. 75-102; *id.*, in T. Fahd (ed.), *L'Arabie préislamique*, 1989, p. 78; *id.*, in D. Valbelle, C. Bonnet (ed.), *Le Sinaï*, 1998, p. 96.

17 J. S. Holladay, *Qadmoniot* 12, 1979, pp. 85-89; *id.*, *Tell el-Maskhouta, Preliminary Report*, 1982.

18 *cf.* E. D. Oren, *BASOR* 256, 1984, pp. 7-44.

19 D. B. Redford, *op. cit.*, p. 52.

20 This is discussed by C. Tuplin, in H. Sancisi-Werdenburg, A. Kuhrt, *Achemenid History* VI, 1991, pp. 237-283; P. J. Sijpesteijn, *Studia Papyrologica Varia, Papyrological Lugduno-Batava* 14, 1965, pp. 106-113.

21 I. Eph'al, *The Ancient Arabs*, 1982, pp. 194-195. On the Nabateans and Tell el-Chugafiya, *cf.* R. Jones, *et al.*, *BASOR* 269, 1988, pp. 47-57, as well as the *Annual of the Department of Antiquities of Jordan* 34, 1990, pp. 239-248. The inscriptions date from the reign of Ptolemy XII Auletes (77 BC) and Cleopatra (35 BC).

22 On this Alexandrian trade in the Red Sea in the Ptolemaic period, see E. Van't Dack, H. Hauben, in H. Maehler, V. M. Strocka (ed.), *Das Ptolemaische Ägypten*, 1978, pp. 59-94, particularly pp. 63-64, 68-69, 74-75, 79-91; H. Hauben, *ZPE* 59, 1985, pp. 135-136.

23 *cf.* Diodorus Siculus, XIX 94, 4-5; also see G. Van Beek, *JAOC* 78, 1958, pp. 141-152; J. Teixidor, in D. Valbelle, C. Bonnet, *Le Sinaï*, 1998, pp. 83-87.

24 Strabo, II, 5, 12 (§ 118); *cf.* J. Aujac, *Strabon, Géographie* I, 2, Book II, 1969, p.93. On Egyptian trade with India via the Red Sea in the Roman era, see J. Pirenne, in M. Mollat (ed.), *Sociétés et compagnies de commerce en Orient et dans l'Océan Indien*, 1971, pp. 101-119; J. Teixidor, *Semitica* 34, 1984, pp. 39-45. On the importance of Clysma as an international centre of trade where goods from Arabia, East Africa and India were received, see D. F. Graf, in D. Valbelle, C. Bonnet (ed.), *Le Sinaï*, 1998, p. 109; S. E. Sidebotham, *Roman Economic Policy in the Erythra Thalassa*, 1986; R. Salomon, *JAOS* 111, 1991, pp. 731-736; P. Mayerson, *JNES* 55, 1996, pp. 119-126.1996, pp. 119-126.

Atum, 'The House of Atum'. The city was organised around the temple of this god, called 'Atum who resides at Tjeku', where he was venerated in the form of a serpent. Apart from the main temple, the site contained other sanctuaries, a cemetery and entrepots for the merchandise passing regularly along the canal. When the canal silted up, after 400 BC, Pithom declined, before finding new life around 270 BC when Ptolemy II (285-246 BC) had the canal re-dug and the temple restored,[19] and under Trajan (AD 98-117) at the apogee of the Roman Period.[20] During this time, not only was the name transformed (Heroonpolis), but the settlement became a major *emporium* and saw a fortress built, destined to keep watch over the eastern approaches to Lower

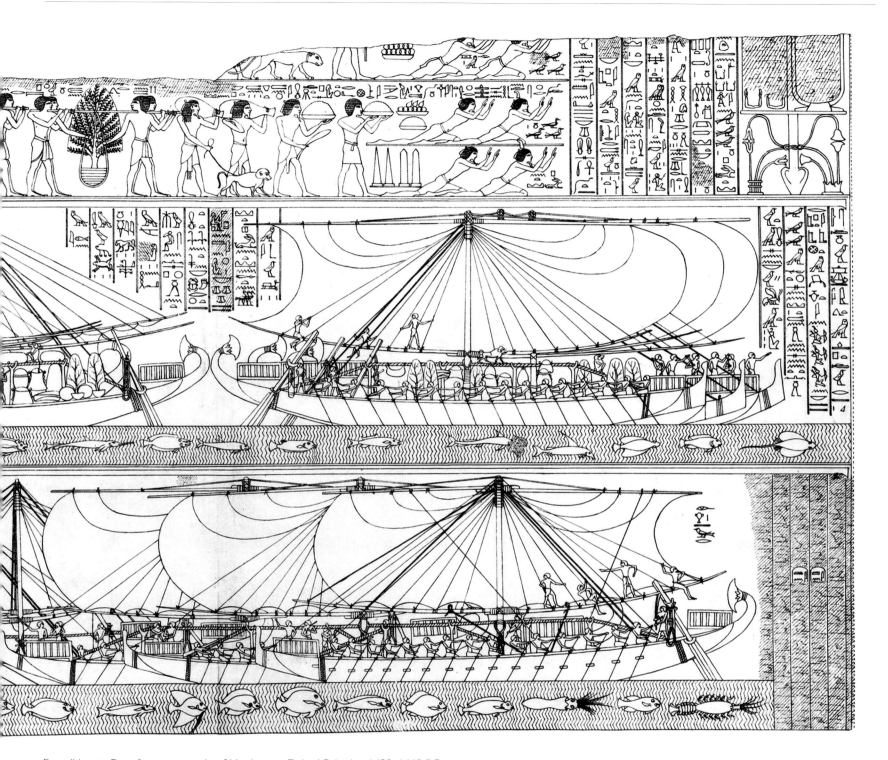

Expedition to Punt, funerary temple of Hatshepsut, Deir el-Bahari, *c.* 1490–1468 BC. © The British Library/Heritage Images

Egypt. It was obviously for this reason that Qedarite Arabs were stationed here during the Persian period: later, Nabateans are present in the environs of Tell el-Chougafiya in the Hellenistic period.[21] Heroonpolis was, in short, at the crossroads of numerous roads linking it also to the coastal towns of North Sinai and crossing the peninsula to the east towards Palestine.

This canal gradually changed the shape of international trade between the Mediterranean Sea and the Red Sea. In the Ptolemaic period, Alexandria was to play its role as a crossroads for trade between the Mediterranean and the Red Sea, a trade which extended as far as India and was facilitated by the canal being re-dug under Ptolemy II (285-246 BC).[22] Perhaps with the collaboration of

the Nabateans,[23] this trade developed even more in the Roman period. As Strabo writes:[24]

*The traffickers of Alexandria are now fitting out real floats to sail up the Nile and cross the Arabian Gulf to India… whereas previously, under the reign of the Ptolemies, very few people had been bold enough to launch their ships and trade with Indian merchandise.*

It is not known whether this canal between the Nile and the Arabian Gulf was based, at least partly, on an older canal that determined navigation and harbour settlements on the Red Sea in ancient times.

Fish depicted under the ships of the expedition to Punt, funerary temple of Hatshepsut, Deir el-Bahari, c. 1490–1468 BC. © Photo: David Fabre

## III.2. Harbour infrastructure

Three areas have preserved references to expeditions to the Red Sea extending to the land of Punt: Wadi Hammamat, Wadi Gasus and Mersa Gawasis, and finally Serabit el-Khadim in the Sinai. The inscriptions at Wadi Hammamat have been abundantly studied.[25] Depending on whether it is acknowledged that the Egyptians did or did not use the maritime route, these are interpreted differently. Those of Gawasis can be seen in the same light.[26] As they are engraved on steles and not on rocks, the adversaries of the 'navigation' hypothesis attribute their accumulation in this place to mere chance, and think that they could have been brought here from elsewhere. The Sinai inscriptions finally, dating from the 18th Dynasty (1570-1293 BC), though long judged to be secondary and treated only incidentally, have recently been re-examined by D. Meeks.[27] In one case, the mission to Serabit and the expedition to Punt are so closely associated that they may have happen in the course of the same journey, or at least used the same logistical means.[28] In another case, what subsists of the text shows that a functionary detailed the products that he had brought back from different areas of Punt, whose names he gives,[29] without, however, making the slightest allusion to the reasons for his presence in the Sinai.

Without drawing any hasty conclusions about the location of the land of Punt, it can be said, in a general way, and given the current state of documentation, that these places were linked to the access routes that led to Punt.[30]

The feeling that Coptos and Wadi Tumilat comprised two ways of reaching Punt is transcribed, in Coptos itself, in the Roman temple of el-Qala, in two neighbouring scenes of the northern sanctuary.[31] The one, on the north wall, refers to Tjeku in Wadi Tumilat, and the other, on the east wall, to Punt. This latter mention, given its direction, refers to Coptos, of which Tjeku thus appears to be the mirror site. Does this mean, however, that the one, Wadi

25  See, among others: L. Bradbury, *JARCE* XXV, 1988, pp. 127-156; C. Vandersleyen, *CdÉ* 64, 1989, pp. 148-158; D. Farout, *BIFAO* 94, 1994, pp. 143-172.

26  Abdel Monem Sayed, *RdÉ* 29, 1977, pp. 140-178; id., *CdÉ* LVIII, 115-116, 1983, pp. 23-37; A. Nibbi, *JEA* 62, 1976, pp. 45-56; L. Bradbury, *JARCE* XXV, 1988, pp. 127-156; D. Farout, *BIFAO* 94, 1994, p. 144, pl. i; C. Vandersleyen, *RdÉ* 47, 1996, pp. 107-115; H. Frost, *Topoi* 6/2, 1996, pp. 869-902.

27  D. Meeks, in *Autour de Coptos*, Topoi suppl. 3, 2002, pp. 296-303. See A. H. Gardiner, E. Peet, J. Cerny, *The Inscriptions of Sinai*, p. 165, n° 211, pl. lxvi; p. 173, n° 238, pl. lxvii; p. 213, n° 427, pl. lxxxix; W. Helck, *MIO* 2, 1954, pp. 188-193; E. Edel, *NAWG* I, 1983, pp. 176-185.

28  A. H. Gardiner, E. Peet, J. Cerny, *op. cit.*, p. 13; W. Helck, *MIO* 2, 1954, p. 207 (§ 6); compare with Abdel Monem Sayed, *CdÉ* LVIII, 115-116, 1983, p. 31.

29  E. Edel, *op. cit.*, p. 178.

30  We shall be examining the location of the land of Punt in greater detail in *Seafaring in Ancient Egypt*, vol. 2.

31  L. Pantalacci, C. Traunecker, *Le temple d'el-Qal'a*, I, 1990, n° 45 and 46, p. 10, n. 41, pp. 12-13; after D. Meeks, *op. cit.*, pp. 319-320.

Tumilat route, was purely a land route and the other, starting from Coptos, was exclusively concerned with maritime voyages? It is known that journeys by sail to Punt could start out in a region close to Sinai. This is a complex question and needs to be asked, with D. Meeks, whether the two sectors did not operate, at certain periods, in what must have been to some extent a complementary fashion.[32]

Whether a canal linking the Nile Valley to the Red Sea existed or not, the facts do not fundamentally change. The fact that ships, on return from Punt, unloaded their cargoes on the coast, in the environs of Mersa Gawasis or Quseir, cannot in any case serve as any proof of the absence of links between Wadi Tumilat and the Gulf of Suez. These disembarkation points were determined by the particular features of sailing in the Red Sea.

It is known that a channel of water came into the Nile at the latitude of Heliopolis, at least at the entry to Wadi Tumilat. That the latter was navigable in ancient times is certain: it was an old branch of the Nile. But the date at which it stopped being a water course and was replaced by a string of lakes is unknown. These lakes are mentioned in the Ramesside period,[33] which suggests that direct sailing to the Gulf of Suez was by then no longer possible. The story of Hatshepsut gives the impression that the Queen's ships left from Thebes and sailed to Punt without any transhipping, as was the case on their return. But this may just be a manner of speaking rather than the reflection of a reality. The excavations carried out at Wadi Tumilat are an attempt to provide an answer to these questions. In the current state of the remains, no definite trace of any canal prior to the Saite era has been unearthed.[34] As for the geological data that would make it possible to date the breaking of contact between Wadi Tumilat and the Bitter Lakes or even the head of the Gulf of Suez, they have not been examined recently. A zoological expedition from the University of Cambridge has explored this region:[35] it appears that the freshwater canal joining the sea existed at the start of the dynastic period. It is quite possible that it was functioning under the Old Kingdom. In addition, the Ramesside capital was situated not far from the entry to Wadi Tumilat, and during the Lower Period all the dynastic capitals were situated in the Delta.[36] Whether it was filled with water or not, Wadi Tumilat has always constituted a major access route to the head of the Gulf and Sinai.[37]

The scene depicting the expedition that Queen Hatshepsut had sent to the land of Punt shows ships sailing on water in which fish and sea creatures are living.[38] A study of these depictions by ichthyologists means that this fauna belonged to the Red Sea and not the Mediterranean, but also that certain kinds of fresh or brackish water are present in some parts of the scene.[39] The hieroglyphic text accompanying it specifies that the expedition sailed without obstacle to Punt and returned to finish its journey at Karnak (Thebes) in Upper Egypt. This detail makes it plausible to assume that there was a direct route between the Nile Valley and the Red Sea. Such a route can really only have passed via Wadi Tumilat, the Bitter Lakes and the present Gulf of Suez. The mechanism of the river flood would then have favoured the passage of ships into the Arabian Gulf; the period propitious for this journey would have been around August–September, a time that was all the more favourable in that winds from the northern sector dominate the Gulf, which meant they had less to fear from the dangers of the Gulf of Suez.[40] Thanks to these winds, ships could cover the 2,000km represented by the north-south crossing of the Gulf with a following wind, a quartering wind, or, in

cases of absolute necessity, sailing off the wind, in favourable conditions. Whether or not the hypothesis of the existence of such a navigable route in Pharaonic times is supported; two options are possible.

The first option holds that a natural navigable route probably linked the Nile to the Gulf of Suez, perhaps until the New Kingdom (*c.* 1400-1200 BC). Probably silting up, it would have been maintained and then would have ceased to be practicable, only to be cleared again by Nekau II (360-343 BC), Darius I (521-486 BC) and finally Ptolemy II (285-246 BC).[41]

The second says that the existence of such a passage is hardly possible before Nekau II or even Darius I. Thus the supporters of this option believe that ships, constructed in separate sections in the Nile Valley, were transported by caravan to the coast and there launched.[42] On the expedition's return the merchandise was taken to a halt at some place on the Red Sea coast not far from the course of the Nile and handed over to a caravan which brought it back to the valley. Here the goods were again transhipped on river transports that brought them to the capital. This hypothesis, which implies heavy and difficult operations, not without peril, finds some support in the story of an expedition to Punt that occurred in the reign of Rameses III (*c.* 1170 BC).[43] Nonetheless, it is notable that this way of doing things contrasts singularly with what may be learned from the reliefs devoted to the expedition of Hatshepsut. This is not a contradiction if it is remembered, along with the supporters of the first hypothesis, that the canal giving access to the Red Sea had ceased to be practicable before the reign of Rameses III (1182-1151 BC).[44]

The points that are still obscure thus concern the date at which the water course linking the Valley to the Gulf of Suez ceased to be naturally navigable, and the date at which maintaining it along its entire length so as to keep it navigable ceased to be possible, thus closing this direct route to the Red Sea until the reign

32   D. Meeks, *op. cit.*, pp. 320-322.

33   J. K. Winnicki, *Ancient Society* 22, 1991, p. 161, n. 40 with bibliography.

34   P. Grandet, *Le papyrus Harris I*, BiÉtud 109, 1994, vol. 2, n. 931 pp. 256-257; C. Redmount, *JNES* 54/2, 1995, p. 127-135; K. A. Kitchen, *Studi di egittologia e di antichità puniche* 18, 1998, pp. 34-35.

35   See the summary of A. Nibbi, *Ancient Egypt and Some Eastern Neighbours*, 1981, pp. 88-94.

36   For the Middle Kingdom, see L. Bradbury, *JARCE* XXV, 1988, p. 143.

37   D. Meeks, in *Autour de Coptos*, Topoi suppl. 3, 2002, p. 320.

38   E. Naville, *The Temple of Deir el-Bahari*, III, 1898, pls xlix-lxxv. See also R. Herzog, *Punt*, 1968, pl. I; A. Nibbi, *op. cit.*, p. 196: they reproduce an older and better preserved state, published by Mariette in 1877. The scenes have been freshly drawn by M. Rival in D. Meeks, D. Garcia (ed.), *Techniques et économie antiques et médiévales*, 1997, figs 2-5 pp. 181-184.

39   E. Danelius, H. Steinitz, *JEA* 53, 1967, pp. 15-24.

40   *cf.* Our remarks on seasons for sailing in the Red Sea, p. 39 *et seq.*

41   *cf.* G. Posener, *CdÉ* 13, 1938, pp. 259-273, whose minute and careful study remains the point of departure for any investigation of the subject. The same author again referred to the hypothesis of a natural waterway between the Nile and the Gulf of Suez almost 40 years after the publication of this article (*id.*, *Ägypten und Kusch*, SGKAO 13, 1977, p. 341 n. 31). For more recent studies of the existence of this canal at different periods, see A. B. Lloyd, *JEA* 63, 1977, pp. 142-155; C. A. Redmount, *JNES* 54, 1995, pp. 127-135; P. Mayerson, *GRBS* 36, 1995, pp. 17-24.

42   *cf.* the remarks of P. Lipke, in S. McGrail, E. Kentley, *Sewn Plank Boats*, 1985, p. 34: he believes, basing his view on the barque of Khufu, that stitched Egyptian ships were particularly well adapted to such an operation. In his opinion, such a conception would have permitted rapid unshipping and reshipping with a minimum of tools. For a similar view, see S. Vinson, *ZPE* 113, 1996, p. 202 n. 29.

43   P. Grandet, *Le Papyrus Harris I*, BiÉtud 109, vol. 2, 1994, n. 931 who is in agreement with K. A. Kitchen, *Orientalia* 40, 1971, pp. 189-190. But there is no text which speaks of ships being transported in separate parts (*cf.* Cl. Vandersleyen, *RdÉ* 47, 1996, p. 111), an operation which for the time being is still a matter of academic debate.

44   L. Bradbury, *JARCE* 25, 1988, p. 144 n. 87.

of Nekau II. Recent archaeological research has not shed much light on these problems of chronology.[45] It shows, among other things, that Rameses II undertook major work in Wadi Tumilat, but it is highly improbable that the canal then extended as far as the sea. It confirms that, even when it was open, the canal could probably not be navigable except at the period of highwater floods and, after a certain period, only when these floods were exceptionally high. Taking into account what was said above, it may be deduced that the expedition of Hatshepsut took advantage of particularly favourable conditions.[46] At other times, the flood being too low or the canal sanded up, it was necessary, if the maritime route was to be used, to build ships along the sea and, on returning from the expedition, disembark the merchandise and have it transported by caravan across the desert, towards the Nile Valley. This practice, which the expedition of Rameses III to Punt seems to illustrate very well, supposes the existence of moorings, if not of ports, on the Egyptian coast of the Red Sea. Even if Wadi Tumilat could no longer provide any direct access to the sea, the possibility cannot be excluded that Egyptian ships found the head of the Suez Gulf to be a convenient point of departure for their expeditions, or even a zone that was at every time propitious for the construction or assembly of vessels.[47]

If we consider the geographical situation of the different Egyptian maritime stations on the Red Sea, we find – just to mention the most important – Mersa Gawasis and Quseir to the north, quite close to each other, and Berenice to the south. The two settlements do not seem to follow the same logic. Since travellers would have wanted to head to the southernmost parts of the Red Sea, why not, after all, leave from the southernmost point to shorten the journey? And what is the justification of the ports situated further north? Berenice, in turn, poses a curious problem. It was here that the Ptolemies brought the ships on to which had been loaded the elephants captured on distant hunting expeditions. The animals were disembarked there and brought across the desert to Edfu, before heading north to Alexandria.[48] Why not disembark the animals as far north as possible, as close as possible to their destination? This difficult and dangerous journey seems to have been necessitated by the nature of the cargo, but especially by the conditions of sailing and manoeuvring at sea.

An examination of the places where, according to the texts, the ships for these voyages were built or assembled during the Pharaonic period provides an inkling of an answer to the questions raised by the location of ports and mooring grounds.

The unfortunate expedition of Anankha, in the reign of Pepi II (2278-2184 BC), was massacred by the Asiatics who were 'Sand-dwellers' while its members were in the process of assembling a *kbnt*-ship destined for Punt.[49] Thus, the place where the operations unfolded must have been both close to Egypt and to a zone more or less dominated by Asiatic nomads, perhaps in the region of the Gulf of Suez.

Henu, who led a great expedition at the time of Mentuhotep III (1997-1991 BC), left Coptos with 3,000 soldiers and an unknown number of asses.[50] After crossing the arid wastes that obliged him to dig 15 or so wells, he arrived near the *Great Green*. Here, to mark the success of this first stage of his journey, he made an offering of bovines and gazelles that may be imagined were captured *in situ*. He then constructed some *kbnyt*-boats that left for Punt. On their return, still

near the *Great Green*, he brought back to Coptos, passing via Wadi Hammamat, the valuable products with which they were laden. The outward journey was perhaps not the same as the return route, but the few toponyms included in the narrative cannot seriously be located on a map. Many hypotheses have been put forward on this question.[51] One idea is that Henu had reached the sea near Berenice, but nothing proves that this port already existed at the dawn of the Middle Kingdom (2040-1782 BC). Others have decided that he had headed for Quseir or, after the discovery of the remains of Mersa Gawasis, precisely towards that spot. C. Vandersleyen, who does not think that the Egyptians ever sailed on the sea, suggests a more original itinerary, by land and then on the Nile, towards the Deep South.[52] D. Meeks, however, thinks that it is not justifiable to send them so far south; the opposite direction may just as well been taken. The author recalls that Henu left an inscription in his tomb at Thebes, which seems to refer to the same journey.[53] In it, an armed troop is mentioned, travelling under his command to the land of the 'Sand-dwellers'.

Under Senusret I (1971-1926 BC), the stele of the vizir Antefoqer and Ameny found at Mersa Gawasis appears to describe a two-stage construction. The first, under the authority of the vizir, will have occurred in the naval dockyards of Coptos; the second, under the leadership of Ameny, on the shores of the *Great Green*.[54] In both cases, the same verb is used, *mdh* – one which applies to all sorts of construction in wood, including shipbuilding. As the inscription does not concern two expeditions but just one, it may be concluded from it that these building operations had two different aspects. What happened at Coptos was not exactly the same as what happened by the edge of the *Great Green*. It is thought, of course, that the parts of the ships were manufactured at Coptos and assembled in the second phase.[55]

As far as the first phase of shipbuilding is concerned, the role of arsenal and dockyard played by the town of Coptos needs to be examined.[56] The evidence provided by Theophrastus and Pliny suggests that the forests of the region of Coptos were reputed for their wood, perfect for shipbuilding.[57] The presence of construction wood in appreciable quantities, as used in shipbuilding, means there were doubtless arsenals in Coptos from the Middle Kingdom

45  *cf.* C.A. Redmount, *JNES* 54, 1995, pp. 127-135.

46  *cf.* G. Posener, *CdÉ* 13, 1938, pp. 261-262; C. A. Redmount, *op. cit.*, p. 134.

47  See G. Posener, *CdÉ* 13, 1938, pp. 264-265; see also K. A. Kitchen, *Orientalia* 40, 1971, p. 192 n. 32, p. 197 and n. 62; L. Bradbury, *JARCE* 25, 1988, p. 143 (§ IV A).

48  A. Bernand, *Pan du désert*, 1977, pp. 194-198; id., *Le Paneion d'El-Kanaïs*, 1972, pp. 44-46, 89-91; A. Hermary, *Cahier du Centre d'Études Chypriotes* 29, 1999, pp. 49-50, 56. On the roads between Berenice and the Nile Vallley, see S. E. Sidebotham, in *Autour de Coptos, Topoi* suppl. 3, 2002, pp. 415-438.

49  *Urk.* I, 134, 13-17. See pp. 55, 140.

50  J. Couyat, P. Montet, *Les inscriptions du Ouâdi Hammamat*, 1912, pp. 81-84, pl. xxxi.

51  B. Couroyer, *Revue Biblique* 80, 1973, p. 59-62; L. Bradbury, *op. cit.*, pp. 131-138; K. A. Kitchen, in T. Shaw, *et al.* (ed.), *The Archaeology of Africa*, 1993, pp. 589-590.

52  C. Vandersleyen, *CdÉ* 64, 1989, pp. 153-156. See D. Meeks's discussion of this hypothesis, in *Autour de Coptos, Topoi* suppl. 3, 2002, p. 322.

53  W. C. Hayes, *JEA* 35, 1949, pp. 43-49, pl. iv.

54  Abdel Monem Sayed, *RdÉ* 29, 1977, p. 170, pl. 16; id., *CdÉ* LVIII, 115-116, 1983, p. 29; D. Farout, *BIFAO* 94, 1994, p. 144; C. Vandersleyen, *RdÉ* 47, 1996, pp. 110-111.

55  K. A. Kitchen, in T. Shaw, *et al.* (ed.), *The Archaeology of Africa*, 1993, p. 591.

56  M. Gabolde, in *Autour de Coptos, Topoi* suppl. 3, 2002, pp. 137-159, to whom we owe part of what follows.

57  Theophrastus, *De historia plantarum*, vol. 2, book IV, 2, 8; Pliny, *Natural History*, XIII, 63, 19. Passages quoted pp. 108-109.

onwards, and their role in the logistics of the expeditions to Punt may be studied. The latter are mentioned on the stele of Mersa Gawasis previously mentioned:[58]

> *His Majesty has ordered the noble prince […], in charge of the town of […], the vizir […], in charge of the Six Great Courts, Antefoqer, to build this fleet[59] in the (?) naval dockyards of Coptos (so as) to undertake a voyage to the mine in Punt,[60] so as to reach it in peace and to return in peace and to look to the equipping of all his works, so it may be perfect and successful, more than all that has been done in this land previously. He (Antefoqer) has acted most excellently, in conformity with what he was commanded in the Majesty of the Palace. Then the herald, the son of Mentuhotep, Ameny, who was on the shore of Wadj Wer constructed these ships (in collaboration) with the Council of the Head of the South and of Taour (This) who was with him and the individuals who were on the shore of Wadj Wer constituting the troop accompanying the herald: 50 followers of the Lord, may he be in life, prosperity and health, an intendant of the Council, 500 persons of the fleet of the Lord, may he be in life, prosperity and health; five scribes of the Great Council, 3,200 persons of the City.*

According to the generally accepted interpretation, the ships were constructed in the arsenals of Coptos – the biggest in the south, with those of This[61] – then dismantled, transported to the desert and reassembled on the shore, which justifies the two references to shipbuilding in Antefoqer's text, once in the arsenals of Coptos and once on the shores of *Wadj Wer*.

This text means that it may be envisaged that the existence of the arsenals of Coptos was linked to the presence of abundant wood nearby.[62] The transportation of dismantled ships was well known in antiquity and later, but it has unfortunately left only a few traces in Ancient Egypt, but these cannot be ignored or denied. Such a practice is attested by various pieces of evidence:[63] Thutmose III (1504-1450 BC) is said to have had chariots transported laden with rafts to cross the Euphrates from Byblos;[64] Alexander the Great also had Phoenician vessels taken by land from the coast to Thapsacus, also on the Euphrates;[65] Baybars the Great ordered the transport of barques from Lake Kadesh to cross the Euphrates again, in year 671 of the hegira;[66] the crusaders of Renaud de Chatillon did the same, transporting their dismantled ships on the backs of animals from their fortified castles and then launching them to Aqaba.[67]

Above it was related that Anankha was 'assembling' a ship when he was killed, with his companions, by the 'Sand-dwellers'. The term employed – *sp* – is very specific and is normally applied to the assemblage of wherries of papyrus, the stems of which are bound by interwoven, tight-laced cords.[68] When applied to a *kbnt*-ship, which is made of wood, it can only designate an assemblage of pieces prepared in advance. Ancient depictions, such as the examination of the barque of Khufu, provide evidence for this practice.[69] So it can be reasonably assumed that Ameny availed himself of this operation.[70]

These textual details lead one to ask whether the places where the ships were assembled, just before their departure for Punt, were really different from one another. Certain aspects seem to suggest the embarkation point as being on the Gulf of Suez. The details provided by the great Harris Papyrus on the expedition that Rameses III

(1882-1151 BC) sent to Punt endorse the impression that the head of the Gulf offered, at every period, a point of departure propitious to distant expeditions.[71] The fact is in any case attested for the Graeco-Roman and Arab periods. This obviously has to do with the sailing conditions in the Red Sea.[72]

As demonstrated below, the rigging of the ships of antiquity allowed them to some extent to sail into the wind; those of Hatshepsut, for instance, thanks to the arrangements of their masts and their sails, could use winds that were close to being crosswinds.[73] They were all dependent on the winds and the dominant currents which, in the Red Sea, undergo a remarkable seasonal alteration. From June to September, the winds and currents carry ships southwards and favour the outward journey.[74] The *Periplus of the Erythrean Sea* recommends the month of September for departure. Winds and currents switch round between October and May. It is in January-February that the most favourable season for return journeys occurs. However, the conditions here are more complex than on the outward journey. Once they reach just below the latitude of Berenice, ships coming up from the south encounter contrary winds and currents. It is possible, by sailing along the Arabian coast, to come quite close to the entrance of the Gulf of Aqaba, but here returning to Egypt becomes a complicated matter. Winds and currents in the Gulf of Suez from the north to the south make it extremely dangerous to sail back towards the head of the Gulf.[75] However, an alternating current, helped by the wind, forces ships from the Arabian coast to the Egyptian coast and brings them into the vicinity of Mersa Gawasis and Quseir.

---

58   C. Obsomer, *Sésostris I*, 1995, pp. 385-386, 711-712.

59   'to build this fleet' : *mdh h'w pn.*

60   'Dockyards of Coptos (so as) to undertake a voyage to the mine in Punt': *whrjj.w Gbtjw (r) sbb bj3 Pwn.t.*

61   W. K. Simpson, *Papyrus Reiner II*, 1965; N. de G. Davies, *The Rock Tombs of Deir el-Gabrâwi*, 1902, pl. 10.

62   M. Gabolde, *op. cit.*, p. 143. See also B. Mathieu, *Égypte. Afrique & Orient* 11, 1998, p. 34, p. 36; J.-Cl. Garcin, *Textes arabes et études islamiques* VI, nº 4, 1976, p. 146, pp. 208-209.

63   After M. Gabolde, *op. cit.*, p. 143.

64   *Urk.* IV, 696 et seq.

65   R. Dussaud, *Topographie historique de la Syrie antique et mediévale*, BAH IV, 1927, p. 432 n. 5.

66   *Id.*, p. 107 n. 1.

67   A. Kammerer, *Pétra et la Nabatène, Texte*, 1929, p. 361.

68   A. Servin, *ASAE* XLVIII, 1948, pp. 82-88; P. E. Newberry, *JEA* 28, 1942, pp. 64-66. For the Graeco-Roman period, see C. W. Shelmerdine, *Classical Quarterly* 40, 1990, pp. 535-539; S. Vinson, *ZPE* 113, 1996, pp. 197-204.

69   L. Basch, in E. Rieth (ed.), *Concevoir et construire les navires*, 1998, pp. 22-31; P. Lipke, in S. McGrail, E. Kentley (ed.), *Sewn plank boats*, 1985, p 34.

70   This type of naval construction is reviewed in detail, p. 102 et seq.

71   See D. Meeks, in *Autour de Coptos*, Topoi suppl. 3, 2002, p. 324. See P. Grandet, *Le papyrus Harris I*, BiÉtud 109, vol. 2, 1994, n. 931 pp. 255-260. It was from here that Aelius Gallus's expedition set sail: P. Mayerson, *Greek, Roman and Byzantine Studies* 36, 1995, pp. 17-18. Also see Abdel Monem Sayed, *CdÉ* LVIII, 115-116, 1983, pp. 36-37; H. Kees, *Kulturgeschichte des Alten Orients*, 1933, p. 122.

72   cf. p. 36 et seq.

73   cf. p. 117 et seq.

74   *Periplus of the Erythrean Sea*, § 6, 3, 6-7; § 24, 8, 11-12 (L. Casson, *The Periplus Maris Erythraei*, 1989, pp. 55, 65): departures for the south of the Red Sea occurred between January and September, the latter being the most favourable month. This date allowed them to arrive at their destination (the south of the Red Sea) during the period when *antj* was being picked: L. Bradbury, *JARCE* XXV, 1988, p. 130, n. 17; S. Amigues, *Topoi* 6/2, 1996, p. 675. cf. 'Remarks on the season of navigation in the Red Sea' above pp. 39-42.

75   P. Mayerson, *JNES* 55, 1996, pp. 119-120.

The siting of maritime halts and ports can be explained as a function of the natural conditions, but also of the destinations chosen. It is indeed maritime halts that are suggested for the period under consideration; sailing across the Red Sea for a long time took place without any harbour structures. Sailors used the natural mooring grounds offered by coastal bays (*mersa*).[76] The site of Mersa Gawasis was without doubt of the greatest importance in the Middle Kingdom.[77] Several steles have been found there, an inscribed monument made of reused anchors, and hieratic ostraca, the whole collection dating from the first half of the 12th Dynasty (1991-1782 BC). The assemblage of stone anchors found on the coast bears hieroglyphic inscriptions relative to an expedition to Punt, dating from the 12th Dynasty.[78] Excavations from this site have yielded various other inscriptions that show that the site was used during the reigns of Senusret I (1971-1926 BC), Amenemhat II (1929-1895 BC) and Senusret II (1897-1898 BC) for over three quarters of a century.[79] Pieces of wood (cedarwood, according to the analyses), including one planed down with mortices as well as fragments of copper chisels, have also been brought to light, suggesting that the collection could confirm the hypothesis that ships were dismantled and reassembled.[80]

The difficulty resides in the fact that it is not known whether Mersa Gawasis served as a departure point, an arrival point or a stage post functioning on both outward and return journeys. The anchors are made out of a kind of limestone that does not exist in the immediate environs, while some of them have been left unfinished on the site.[81] The main text, already mentioned, is particularly ambiguous. It refers to 'constructing, putting together (out of wood)' a fleet (?) at Coptos, then ships on the shore of the *Great Green*.[82] The operations in both cases were led by different persons. The operation based on the shore of the *Great Green* mobilised over 3,740 persons. As the anchors were transported to Mersa Gawasis, it has been concluded that the inscriptions they bear were engraved elsewhere and have nothing to do with the site.[83] However, the inscriptions are arranged on the anchors in such a way as to be adapted to the overall structure, as it was erected at Mersa Gawasis itself.[84] They were engraved to be read at this spot. However, this is not a decisive argument for identifying the *Great Green* with the Red Sea. The ships assembled near the *Great Green* were able to sail to Punt and stop at Mersa Gawasis on their return. The analysis made by H. Frost, who shows that these assemblages of anchors were also cairns destined to direct ships to the bay, makes this port a place where ships were awaited rather than a place where they were built. The nature of the texts suggests that they were, rather, constructed on the expeditions' return rather than on their outward journey. Mersa Gawasis could mark the final point of the voyage where the boats were dismantled (?) and the anchors, of no further use, abandoned. And indeed, there are many problems in sailing back up to the head of the Gulf of Suez.[85] The assembling of the ships is more likely to have occurred in a place where it was easier to obtain supplies, especially of drinking water,[86] and where there was wood nearby.

The aridity and isolation of the region of Quseir – Mersa Gawasis means that an abundant troop of men staying there cannot easily be imagined, in the way that has been described, to assemble ships, with all the requirements for drinking water and food that this presupposes. The 3,000 men (and more) of these expeditions could not all go to Punt. The ship or ships must have had just the right

number of men in the crew to allow them both to load the necessary quantity of food and water and, on their return, a sufficiently impressive volume of merchandise for the journey to be economically viable. The bulk of the troops could have made only a short stopover at the chosen spot, just enough time to assemble the ship or ships. Only a small number remained at Mersa Gawasis, in a bivouac, awaiting the return of the expedition. This at least is what can be deduced from the finds made on site.

The choice of Mersa Gawasis, as later that of Quseir or even Berenice, thus seems justified by the particularities of Red Sea navigation. At whatever period, and whatever the point of departure, it was a matter of facilitating the outward journey but especially, on the return, of allowing the ships to get to Egyptian soil without running any excessive risks while disembarking the products they had brought back.

The archaeological and textual data mentioned earlier can easily be compared with the description given by Rameses III (1182-1151 BC), in Papyrus Harris I, of the expedition he sent to Punt. In the King's *Speech* to his subjects, there is indeed mention of an expedition to the land of Punt (before year 22?):[87]

> *Expedition to the land of Punt (before year 22?).*
> *I have constructed great mnš.w-ships (destined to be?) preceded by br.w-ships,*[88] *and they have been provided with innumerable crewmen and servants of (every) sort. Among the latter were the chiefs of the troops of the mnš-ships, directed by controllers and assisted by under-officers*

76  K. A. Kitchen, *Orientalia* 20, 1971, p. 193; A. W. Sleewyk, *IJNA* 12/4, 1983, p. 287; J. Degas, *RdÉ* 46, 1995, pp. 222-227.

77  Abdel Monem Sayed, *RdÉ* 29, 1977, pp. 140-178; id., *JEA* 64, 1978, pp.69-71; id., *JEA* 66, 1980, pp. 154-157; id., *CdÉ* LVIII, 115-116, 1983, pp. 23-37; H. Frost, *Topoi* 6/2, 1996, pp. 869-902.

78  Abdel Monem Sayed, *RdÉ* 29, 1977, pp. 138-178. id., *CdÉ* LVIII, 115-116, 1983, pp. 23-37.

79  On this site and the problems it raises, see the recent work by H. Frost, *Topoi* 6, 1996, pp. 869-902.

80  H. Frost, *Topoi* 6, 1996, pp. 882-883.

81  Id., pp. 878-879, pp. 882-883.

82  The text employs the same word twice, in the singular then the plural, to designate ships, hence certain modern translations: 'the fleet' (in the case of Antefoqer, at Coptos), 'the ships' (in the case of Ameny, on the shore of the 'Great Green'). cf. D. Farout, *BIFAO* 84, 1994, p. 144; C. Vandersleyen, *RdÉ* 47, 1996, pp. 110-111.

83  C. Vandersleyen, *op. cit.*, pp. 107-115.

84  H. Frost, *op. cit.*, pp. 878-879, pp. 888-889. Note that the original shape of certain anchors was altered when the whole thing was erected, so as to make the stones contiguous.

85  P. Mayerson, *JNES* 55, 1996, pp. 119-120. D. Meeks, in D. Meeks, D. Garcia (ed.), *Techniques et économie antiques et mediévales*, 1997, p. 194 n. 112.

86  See the remarks of P. Mayerson, *Greek Roman and Byzantine Studies* 36, 1995, p. 19 on the construction of the fleet of Cornelius Gallus at Cleopatris. cf. D. Meeks, in *Autour de Coptos*, *Topoi* suppl. 3, 2002, p. 325, responding to C. Vandersleyen, *RdÉ* 47, 1996, pp. 107-115.

87  P. Harris I, 77, 8 - 78, 1. Mdh=j mnš.w ʿȝ.w br.w r-ḥȝ.t=sn (...). Nȝy=sn hry.w-pd.wt n mnš jm=sn hr rwḏ.w hwty.w r sdbh=w. ȝtpw m ḥ.t Km.t nn rȝ-ʿ=sn jw=w m tnw nb mj ḏbʿ.w. Wḏ(w) m pȝ Ym ʿȝ n Mw-qd st sprw r ḥȝs.t n(y.)t Pwn.t nn ḥʿm st ḏw wḏȝw ḥr hry.t. ȝtpw nȝ mnš.w br.w m ḥ.t Tȝ.wy-nṯr m bjȝy.t nb(.t) ȝtȝ.t n(y.)t ḥȝs.t=sn ʿntyw qnw nt Pwn.t. ȝtpw mj ḏbʿ.w nn rȝ-ʿ=sn. Nȝy=sn ms.w-wr.w nt Tȝ.wy-nṯr jw(w) r-ḥȝ.t=sn m hr=w r Km.t. St spr(w) jw=w swdȝw r ḥȝs.t Gbtyw (...). St ȝtp(w) m hrty hr ʿȝ.w hr rmṯ ȝtpw r ʿhʿ.w hr jtrw mry.t Gbtyw. Ms(w) m jnw m-bȝh=j mj bjȝy.t. Nʿy=sn ms.w-wr.w m jȝw.t n hr(=j) (hr) sn-tȝ (hr) hbrbr n hf.t-hr(=j). Dj=j st n psd.t nb.w tȝ pn r shtp ḥȝwty=w tp-dwȝ.t. cf. P. Grandet, *Le papyrus Harris I*, *BiÉtud* 109, 1994, vol. 1, p. 338. Apart from the present passage, some indirect allusions to this expedition may be found in Egyptian sources dating from the reign of Rameses III: hȝq=j (= the king) n=k (= Amun) Pwn.t (Reliefs and Inscriptions at Karnak I, 23, 19 = *KRI* V, 225, 1); stȝ=j (= the king) n=k (= Amun) Pwn.t m ʿntyw (P. Harris I, 7, 7; P. Grandet, *op. cit.*; vol. 2, n. 152); sn=j (= Amun) n=k (= the king) mtn.w nw Pwn.t m ʿntyw sntr (Medinet Habu II, 101, 13-14 = *KRI* V, 93, 5-6); shwy=j (Amun) n=k (= the king) hȝs.t nb.t n(y).t Pwn.t jnw=sn m qmy ʿntyw špsy sty hȝs.t nb ndm (Medinet Habu II, 102, 15 = *KRI* v, 97, 8-9); after P. Grandet, *op. cit.*; vol. 2, n. 931.

88  On the subject of mnš.w-ships and br.w-ships, cf. pp. 94-96.

*Having been laden with goods from Kemet without limit and of every kind, in their tens of thousands, and (then) sent on the Great Sea of Mw-qd, they ( = the boats) landed at Gebel in Punt, without (anything) untoward afflicting them and having been preserved from fear.*

*Mnš.w-ships and br.w-ships were (then) laden with goods from the Double-Land-of-the-God: with all the mysterious marvels of their ( = the Puntites') gebel, and with much myrrh from Punt. (Thus) laden with tens of thousands (of articles) without limit, the (literally: their) children of the princes of the Double-Land-of-the-God, at the head of their presents, came upon them to Kemet. They landed, safe and sound, at the Gebel of Coptos and moored in peace, laden with the presents they had brought back. These were laden on to caravans, on the backs of asses and men, (then) transhipped on to ʿhʿ.w-ships on the river, at the landing stage of Coptos. Having been sent on them northwards, having landed in festivity (at the residence), having been brought as presents [89] before (me) like marvels – the children of princes who accompanied them bowing in adoration before (my) face, sniffing the ground and creeping before (me), – I gave them ( = the presents) to the Ennead of the Lords of this land, to appease the face of each of them at dawn.*

The story can be divided into four episodes:[90]

1. Outfitting of the expedition, setting sail of its ships; their journey on the Red Sea.
2. Arrival at Punt, acquisition of local products.
3. Return of the expedition to Egypt, accompanied by children of the Puntite princes; arrival at the 'Gebel of Coptos', transhipping on land of the products brought back by the expedition, from the Red Sea to Coptos, where they are loaded on to river ships.
4. Descent of the Nile from Coptos to the royal residence; presentation to Rameses III of the children of Puntite princes and the products brought back from the expedition; the gift of these products by the king to the divinities of Egypt.

The king does not indicate where exactly the ships were built. Likewise, the point of departure of the maritime part of the expedition is not specified. Its departure point, as well as its ultimate destination, were probably the residence of Rameses III at Piramesse. It can be easily imagined that the place of maritime embarkation was either at the same spot as the one where the expedition landed in Egypt on its return from Punt, a point on the coast of the Red Sea at the level of Coptos, or some point on the Red Sea in the Gulf of Suez.[91] Various considerations (of a climatic nature in particular) seem to indicate that the second hypothesis is the most likely.

According to the reconstruction of the voyage to Punt by P. Grandet,[92] the expedition personnel, the materials used on the construction of its ships and the goods necessary to fit out the latter[93] were probably conducted *in situ* to the Suez region from Piramesse through the whole of Wadi Tumilat, then along the western shore of the Bitter Lakes. The small temple of Rameses II at 'Serapeum', and the one dedicated to Horus and Hathor at Gebel Abu Hassa (founded in the 18th Dynasty and still in service under the reign of Rameses II) still perhaps formed under Rameses III the centre of the conurbation that served as a staging post on this itinerary.[94]

From its point of departure in the Suez region, the expedition of Rameses III set sail towards Punt, crossing the 'Great Sea of Mouqed'. It was elaborated above that the information relative to Mouqed takes one to Sinai, Mou-qed designating one or more of its coastal zones.[95]

The constraints of sailing in the Red Sea justify well the itinerary of the Rameses II expedition to Punt, as described in the Papyrus Harris I. Provided that the periodicity of the winds was respected, the Red Sea offered, in the direction of Punt, better conditions of propulsion for Egyptian ships than the Nile. On the return journey, however, it was desirable to abandon as soon as possible the maritime route in order to take the river route, whose current naturally led northwards. All things being considered, to the north of Souakin, the conditions in the Red Sea, as indicated, were never entirely favourable to sailing from south to north. Hence the practice of transferring by land, between the Red Sea and Coptos, the personnel and goods brought back by the expedition, and then of loading these on river boats. In fact the Papyrus Harris I describes with a certain degree of precision the expedition's return to Egypt, accompanied by a delegation of *ms.w-wr.w* from Punt – an embassy. It refers explicitly to the mooring of Egyptian ships on the coasts of the Red Sea at the latitude of Coptos and the transferal by land of the goods they were bringing back to this town to load them on to river vessels.[96] The existence of graffiti representing Rameses III at the wadis Atolla and Saki, provided that they in fact commemorate this event, has been drawn on by K. A. Kitchen to suggest that this land convoy must first have taken, as it travelled between the Red Sea and Fawachir, Wadis Gasus, Saki and Atolla, then, between this locality and Coptos, Wadi Hammamat.[97] It is thus possible to deduce on the basis of this that the expedition of Rameses III to Punt landed at the site of Mersa Gawasis.[98]

So Coptos combined two advantages. Firstly, the well-known merit of being situated at a point where the Nile Valley is at its closest to the Red Sea coast, but also, that of leading on this coast to the place where ships were almost naturally constrained to land on the

---

89  The term used is *jnw*.
90  P. Harris I, 77, 8-10; 77, 10-11; 77, 11-13; 77, 13 - 78, 1.
91  Probably excluding the locality of Suez itself, since no trace of the 20th Dynasty has been discovered there: B. Bruyère, *Fouilles de Clysma-Qolzoum (Suez)*, FIFAO XXVII, 1966; M. Alliot, *RdÉ* 7, 1950, p. 146.
92  P. Grandet, *Le papyrus Harris I*, BiÉtud 109, 1994, vol. 2, n. 931, from which we have taken the following details.
93  The *h.t Km.t* mentioned in the text (77, 9) and among which there were probably included products destined for commerce with the Puntites.
94  J. Cledat, *BIFAO* XVI, 1917, pp. 208-212; *KRI* II, 406, PM IV, 53; B. Bruyère, *Bulletin de la Société d'études historiques et géographiques de l'Isthme de Suez III*, 1949-1950, p. 37. P. Grandet believes that the expeditions sent by Rameses III to the mines of Sinai and Timna probably took a route that was partly identical. Furthermore, he considers that at the time of the three expeditions of Rameses III, part of the personnel, goods, and materials came from the urban zone of Heliopolis and Memphis, in particular from the arsenals of that locality, and were taken to the Suez region via the future Darbel-Hagg: P. P. Grandet, *op. cit.*, vol. 2, n. 931.
95  cf. p. 13.
96  K. A. Kitchen, *Orientalia* 20, 1971, pp. 189-190; *id.*, *JEA* 64, 1978, p. 170.
97  K. A. Kitchen, *Orientalia* 20, 1971, pp. 189-190; *KRI* V, 272, 11; P. Grandet, *Le papyrus Harris I*, BiÉtud 109, 1994, vol. 2, n. 931. See also D. Meredith, *JEA* 38, 1952, p. 95, fig. 1; *LÄ* VI, s.v. 'Wadi el-Fawachir', col. 1096-1097; s.v. 'Wadi Gawasis', col. 1097-1099; s.v. 'Wadi Hammamat', col. 1099-1100.
98  In the itinerary suggested by K. A. Kitchen mentioned above, we probably need to substitute Wadi Gawasis for Wadi Gasus, since the mooring ground situated at the extremity of the latter, Mersa Gasus, has not yielded any Pharaonic remains: K. K. Zibelius, *Afrikanische Orts- und Völkernamen*, 1972, s.v. 'Sw'; Abdel Monem Sayed, *RdÉ* 29, 1977, pp. 146, 175-176; *id.*, *JEA* 64, 1978, pp. 69-71; *id.*, *JEA* 66, 1980, pp. 154-171; *id.*, *CdÉ* LVIII, 115-116, 1983, pp. 23-37.

return from their trip. The very age of Coptos and its wealth in the 4th millennium BC demands the question of whether this prosperity was not linked, already, to contacts with distant places – something to which its position made it suitable.[99] As a destination, from the origins of Pharaonic civilisation onwards, of all the trails, that were later converted (under Ptolemy II Philadelphus and the Roman emperors) into 'rapid' routes that were under military surveillance, the natural position of the Coptite city had facilitated its major function as a 'gateway' to the African East as well as to the Arabian peninsula. A little more than 200km to the east of its walls lay the Red Sea and access to all the landing places – Myos Hormos, Berenice, Philotera – that were so precious on this dangerous, sheer coast; and close, on its western flank, to the Nile and its huge volume of river traffic heading north. Through Coptos, from time immemorial, flowed gold, galena and malachite from the kohls, spices and perfumed resins, myrrh or frankincense, ostrich eggs and feathers, the shells of sea turtles, the skins of mottled felines and giraffe tails, ebony and ivory. Hence, for Strabo among others the city was the most famous *emporion* in Africa, 'a city inhabited in common by Egyptians and Arabs',[100] where, at the beginning of Roman domination over Egypt, were registered and received, to be sent on to Alexandria and the west, all the exotic and precious merchandise of Ethiopia and Arabia.[101]

The abandonment of the Red Sea sites were surely the consequence of phenomena that affected the ancient mooring grounds and ports, silting up and the invasion of coral reefs. The Pharaonic expeditions were too widely separated in time, and so no attempt was made, as in the case of ports in the Graeco-Roman period, to clear them periodically.

Finally, it must be pointed out that an Egyptian port of the New Kingdom seems to have been identified in the Gulf of Suez, on the coast of the Sinai Desert, at Merka, a little to the north of the routes leading to the temple of Serabit el-Khadim.[102] Unfortunately the (rapid) surveys carried out by the discoverers of the site, in 1948, have not been published and these remains seem essentially to have disappeared during the construction of a road and a railway line. However, the existence of an Egyptian port might be postulated on the basis of an inscription of Serabit el-Khadim[103] – dating from the reign of Hatshepsut – relating the offerings of a scribe who had come with the expedition and was presenting to 'Hathor the Lady of Turquoise', the sovereign lady of this place, to thank her for having reached port *(mry.t)* without accident.

The island of Geziret Faraoun ('the island of the pharaoh') at the head of the Gulf of Eilat seems from its name to have preserved the memory of Egyptian expeditions to the mines of Timna in the Negev.[104] The research carried out there has not revealed any architectural traces older than the Old Kingdom (2686-2181 BC).[105] It has however made it possible to bring out the qualities of a particularly well-sheltered mooring ground and the existence of a real port with jetty, in a small lagoon. Silting, and the invasion of coral reefs, explain to a great extent the paucity of the most ancient remains. The latter are essentially limited to non-Egyptian pottery datable to the 14th-12th centuries BC.[106]

---

99    See H. S. Smith, in *The Followers of Horus*, 1992, pp. 235-246; P. B. Adamson, *Aula Orientalis* 10, 1992, pp. 175-179.

100   Strabo, I, 44-45.

101   See the contributions of G. Galliano, M. Gabolde, J.-C. Goyon, T. de Putter, H. Cuvigny, P. Ballet et al., in *Coptos. L'Égypte antique aux portes du désert*, 2000, pp. 10-11, 12-14, 18-24, 144-156, 158-175, 176-187.

102   W. F. Albright, *BASOR* 109, 1948, 10 fig. 2 and pp. 13-15.

103   Inscription of Sinai n° 181, pointed out by W. Helck, *MIO* 2, 1954, p. 207.

104   cf. P. Grandet, *Le papyrus Harris I*, BiÉtud 109, 1994, vol. 2, n. 943.

105   Flinder, *IJNA* 19, 1990, pp. 135-139, who proposes that we identify this island with the fortified port of Ezion Geber used at the time of Solomon for expeditions to the land of Ophir (I Kings 9: 26). On these expeditions, see A. B. Lloyd, *JEA* 63, 1977, p. 147.

106   A. Flinder, *IJNA* 19, 1990, p. 136.

# Chapter III: The Ships

*Perhaps it is because, of all man's creations, this is the one which is most akin, thanks to its appearance as an autonomous, complex and mobile machine, to a creature? Is not the ship the only object to which the English language grants a sex – the feminine? This feeling is not modern: from antiquity onwards, ships have borne names that bear witness to the affection of which they were the object, names that make us dream, such as those of 'Amun's Beloved', on the Nile, or Kallixena, 'the Lovely Foreign Lady', an Athenian Trireme.*

*But this sentimental aspect is not the most important: the ship has been, in all civilisations, the biggest and most complicated machine that men have conceived and used.*

(L. Basch, *Le Musée imaginaire de la marine*, 1987, p. 17)

The Egyptians knew, or perhaps even invented, the sail at the end of the predynastic period, around 3100 BC.[1] But it was during the Old Kingdom (*c.* 2700 BC) that a phenomenon of great importance in Egyptian naval architecture occurs: the importing of cedars and pines from the Syro-Lebanese region, which provided long planks, made it necessary to set up expeditions which only the Pharaoh had the political and technical means to organise and make use of, especially in the form of big ships. From the start of the 3rd millennium BC, the development of a properly Pharaonic naval architecture occurs, distinct from that of his subjects.

For the reign of Snefru (*c.* 2630-2609), the *Stone of Palermo* mentions in particular 'the year when the ship called *Praise-of-the-Two-Lands* was constructed', 100 cubits long, some 52m (as long as some of the vessels of Louis XIV). This was no idle boast, since the boat discovered at the foot of the Pyramid of Khufu, son of Snefru, is 43.63m long, some 83 cubits. This wooden structure, whose weight has been estimated at 380.5 tonnes, was created with the aid of a complex set of ligatures, mortice and tenon joints, and is evidence of the great antiquity and quality of Egyptian naval construction.[2]

The experience of the Egyptians in the field of naval architecture and sailing is thus very ancient. Certain reliefs showing detailed depictions of ships, permit the recognition of the existence of sea vessels from the Old Kingdom onwards.[3] The presence on the ships of Sahure (*c.* 2500 BC), as well as on those of Hatshepsut (*c.* 1470 BC), of a tension cable 'pulled out in the shape of a bow above the full length (…) and destined to prevent, in heavy seas, the breaking of stem and stern',[4] in fact made them seaworthy. This latter detail has been underlined many times, and justifiably so, by the historians of ancient navigation, as being characteristic of the use to which these ships were to be put.[5] Another important element, the rudder oars, offered a significant submersible surface area so as to ensure the boat's stability, either because their blades were very big (Hatshepsut), or because their number was multiplied so as to increase the surface area (Sahure).[6] Without any keel, these ships could navigate as well on the Nile as on the sea, and pass from the latter into the river to land somewhere upstream, in the Delta, at Memphis or even further south.[7]

Terracotta vase depicting a boat with oars, a mast and a sail, Predynastic period, *c.* 4000 BC.

© Werner Forman Archive/Otago Museum, Dunedin, New Zealand.

1  C. Boreux, *Études de nautique égyptienne, MIFAO* I, 1925, pp. 65-66 and fig. 23; L. Casson, *The Ancient Mariners*, 1991, pl. 1; E. Black, D. Samuel, *The Mariner's Mirror 77*, 1991, pp. 217-226. See also K. C. Seele, *JNES* 33, 1974, pp. 37, figs 21-22, pp. 38-39; N. Dürring, *Materialien zum Schiffbau im Alten Ägypten*, 1995, p. 134 (a); B. Williams, in T. Celenko, *Egypt and Africa*, 1996, pp. 95-96; D. Meeks, in D. Meeks, D. Garcia (ed.), *Techniques et économie antiques et médiévales*, 1997, n. 2 p. 191. On the ships of the predynastic era, also of interest is the article by Farid El-Yahky, *BIFAO* 85, 1985, pp. 187-195, pls xxxii-xxxiv.

2  See R. Partridge, *Transport in Ancient Egypt*, 1996, pp. 23-32.

3  See B. Landström, *Ships of the Pharaohs*, 1970, pp. 64-65 and pp. 122-123.

4  C. Boreux, *Études de nautique égyptienne, MIFAO* I, 1925, p. 474 ff, where the function of this cable is clearly explained. The author also insists on the fact that his tension cable must not be confused with the swifting cable which served to preserve the curves of Nile vessels. See the depictions published by N. Dürring, *Materialien zum Schiffbau im Alten Ägypten*, 1995, p. 121. On this tension cable, *cf. infra*, p. 110-111.

5  R. O. Faulkner, *JEA* 26, 1940, pp. 4-5; B. Landström, *op. cit.*, p. 64; L. Basch, *The Mariner's Mirror 71*, 1985, p. 455; L. Casson, *The Ancient Mariners*, 1991, p. 14.

6  See the remarks of L. Basch, *IJNA* 23, 1994, p. 226 n. 2.

7  L. Basch, *op. cit.*, pp. 219-227. L. Bradbury, *JARCE* 33, 1996, pp. 37-60 postulates the existence of keels on certain Egyptian sea vessels on the basis of somewhat dubious graphic representations and lexical arguments that cannot be credited. For the latter compare with D. Jones, *A Glossary of Ancient Egyptian Nautical Titles and Terms*, 1988, p. 192 n° 174. See D. Meeks, in D. Meeks, D. Garcia (ed.), *Techniques et économie antiques et médiévales*, 1997, p. 192 n. 8.

Funerary barque of Khufu at Giza, Old Kingdom, 4<sup>th</sup> Dynasty, c. 2575–2465 BC. © Photo: Peter A. Clayton

# I. The Egyptian navy

Wall paintings on the rocks and wadis of Upper Egypt and Nubia, dating from the 4th millennium BC, show a whole panoply of ships. A dozen types of boats have been identified as papyrus barques or wooden vessels.[8] In the Gerzean period (3600-3100 BC), Egyptian potters seemed to adopt the boat as one of the favoured decorative subjects for their vessels. These images of hundreds of ships from the Predynastic period present an overview of the intense river activity of that period: 'it is highly unlikely that in the earliest period, before the unification of the country – of the various small kingdoms that composed Egypt – the ships of Upper Egypt would have had access to the sea. On the other hand, the ships of Lower Egypt did have this possibility, which does not mean that they made any use of it'.[9] It is in any case difficult to distinguish the ships from the towns and cities of the Delta on the one hand from those of Upper Egypt on the other. As this type of 'boomerang boat' of the Gerzean boats is also found in numerous rock engravings as far as Nubia, it can be supposed that, in the 4th millennium BC, it was able to sail along the Nile. But nothing proves that it originated in the Delta and even less that it ever took to sea, even if there is a tendency to see in the Lower Egypt of the predynastic era a vast uninhabitable swamp. This is, however, in the process of being reversed in view of archaeological research being carried out in the Nile Delta. The importance of the role of this region in the general economy of predynastic Egypt and as a major place of exchange, especially by sea with the East, is starting to become apparent. It is certain that wood from the Levant

Knife from Gebel el-Araq, ivory and flint, Predynastic period, *c.* 3400 BC, Louvre, Paris. © Photo: Peter A. Clayton

---

8    R. Engelmayer, *Die Felsgravierungen im Distrikt Sayala-Nubien*, 1965.
9    L. Basch, *Le Musée imaginaire de la marine*, 1987, p. 43.

Detail of fresco decorating a tomb, perhaps a royal tomb, from the end of the Gerzean period, (*c.* 3100 BC) Hierakonpolis, after L. Basch, *Le Musée imaginaire de la marine*, 1987, p. 59.

Boats painted on Gerzean vases, after L. Basch, *Le Musée imaginaire de la marine*, 1987, p. 59.

is their crew in the service of the Egyptians, or else are they Egyptian ships employing Asiatics? For M. Bietak, the fact that sea ships are known from the Old Kingdom (2686-2181 BC) onwards by the name of *kbn.wt/kpn.wt*, usually translated as 'ships of Byblos'[14] would argue in favour of the hypothesis that sees the ships of Sahure as '*Asiatic*' ships in the service of the Egyptians. It may be contended, with D. Meeks, that such 'ships of Byblos' were constructed by the Egyptians themselves in the Old Kingdom, if certain texts are to be believed.[15] These *kpn.wt*-ships are more frequently mentioned in relation to Egyptian sea voyages to Punt, on the Red Sea, than in connection with Mediterranean expeditions.[16] The fleet of Hatshepsut which sailed to Punt was composed of *kpn.wt*-boats.[17] But the last mention of *kpn.wt*-boats, before the Late Period,[18] dates from the reign of Thutmose III (1504-1450 BC), 25 years after the expedition to Punt; the king collected different logs, beams, masts and trees that were transported by *kpn.wt*-boats, *sk.wt*-boats and *kftj.w*-boats to his port at Djahy.[19]

was imported from the 4th millennium BC onwards,[10] and it is practically impossible that it could have reached Egypt any other way than by sea. It cannot, however, be determined for certain whether the ships which habitually transported this wood were Levantine or Egyptian.

Their masts lowered, their rowing and rudder oars out of the water, the ships on the reliefs of Sahure are represented as stationary, in Egypt.[11] Standing in the ships, members of the crew acclaim the pharaoh. The majority of these characters are 'Asiatics'. Some of the Egyptians are designated as being 'interpreters'. M. Bietak thinks that these Asiatics are neither slaves nor prisoners brought back to Egypt; the way in which they are represented, the presence of some of them near the rudder oar, make them the equal of the Egyptians.[12] They are part of the ship's crew.[13] This being so, are these Asiatic ships, and

10    G. Brunton, G. Caton-Thompson, *Badarian civilisation*, pp. 62-63.

11    J. Vandier, *Manuel d'archéologie égyptienne*, V, 1969, pp. 875-886, figs 331-334.

12    M. Bietak, in *Pyramid Studies and others Essays* presented to I.E.S. Edwards, 1988, pp. 35-40.

13    Nonetheless, the presence of women and children is difficult to explain.

14    *Wb*. V, 118-119. A. Nibbi, *The Mariner's Mirror* 65, 1979, pp. 205-206 denies that the ships have any link at all with Byblos. Nonetheless, the El-Amarna letters speak of Egyptian ships present at Gubla ( = Byblos). This way of designating the ships has made a great deal of ink flow: see H. Frankfort, *JEA* XII, 1926, p. 83 n. 3; R. O. Faulkner, *JEA* XXVI, 1941, pp. 3-9; *id.*, *JEA* XXVII, 1942, p. 158; D. B. Redford, *JARCE* XXIII, 1986, p. 127, n. 26; L. Bradbury, *JARCE* XXXIII, 1996, p. 37 n. 2.

15    D. Meeks, in D. Meeks, D. Garcia (ed.), *Techniques et économie antiques et médiévales*, 1997, p. 178.

16    K. A. Kitchen, *Orientalia* 40, 1971, p. 191 and n. 29. Among the references to these ships, cited by D. Jones, *A Glossary of Ancient Egyptian Nautical Titles and Terms*, 1988, pp. 148-149, the following relate to Punt or the Red Sea: the inscription of Pepinakht (Punt, 6th Dynasty, c. 2220 BC); Wadi Hammamat inscription no. 114 (Punt, 9th Dynasty, c. 2000 BC); expedition of Hatshepsut (Punt, 18th Dynasty, c. 1470 BC); steles from the Red Sea canal (Darius I, c. 500 BC); Stele of Pithom (Red Sea, Ptolemy II, 264 BC). To these can doubtless be added *Urk*. IV, 1452, 16 (Punt, 18th Dynasty, c. 1430 BC). This term is only exceptionally applied to the ships of the Mediterranean, before the Saite era (7th century BC). For these ships from the later period, see the recent work by J. C. Darnell, in J. H. Johnson, *Life in a Multi-Cultural Society. Egypt from Cambyses to Constantine*, 1992, pp. 67-89. L. Bradbury, *JARCE* 33, 1996, pp. 47-48 believes that in every case the reference is to ships 'in the style of Byblos', he thinks, sewn ships. This is an idea worth considering, even if there is no proof.

17    *Urk*. IV, 323, 2, n. b.

18    *cf. infra*: *kbn.wt*-boats seem to designate war galleys (A. B. Lloyd, *JEA* 58, 1972, pp. 268-279). The funerary-boats *kbn.wt* of the 22nd Dynasty, without sail, are certainly designated in this way by reference to the Old and Middle Kingdoms, and thus by 'archaism', and also perhaps by reference to the history of Isis and Osiris; see L. Bradbury, *JARCE* XXXIII, 1996, p. 50.

19    *Urk*. IV, 706.

Sea ship from the relief in the temple of Sahure, Old Kingdom, 5th Dynasty, c. 2400 BC, drawing after L. Borchardt, *Das Grabdenkmal des Königs Sahure II*, 1981, pl. 12; S. Vinson, *Egyptian Boats and Ships*, 1994, p. 23.

Reconstruction of a boat from the expedition to Punt, Museo della Scienza e della Tecnica, Milan. © 1990, Photo Scala, Florence

From the earliest signs of the existence of an Egyptian fleet (however sporadic and circumstantial in ancient times), the inhabitants of the Nile Valley resorted to the services of their Mediterranean neighbours. The ships depicted in the funerary temple of Unas (*c.* 2460 BC) also include characteristics which make them sea ships.[20] It may be deduced from this that the Egyptian navy was a fixed feature in the half-century concerned. However, errors in the way the ships have been drawn do not allow us to grant these reliefs all the credit they require.[21] The elements at our disposal 'are too inexplicit to say whether this Egyptian navy had a permanent existence in the Old Kingdom, whether or not it was built by Asiatic experts or whether it was, for example, the fruit of shared experiences'.[22]

The ships used for expeditions to Punt were mixed ships, with oars and sails. The rigging is constituted by a big sail, more wide than tall, stretched between two horizontal yards balanced by numerous lifts. Noteworthy are the analogies between the Puntite boats of Queen Hatshepsut (*c.* 1500 BC) and the Cretan ships depicted on a fresco, discovered in 1972 at Akrotiri on the island of Thera (Santorini), dating from around 1600 BC: the ships in the procession have central-mast rigging, but most of them are nonetheless propelled by paddlers whilst at the stern a man, sometimes two men, steers the boat with an oar held vertically on the side. This latter particularity is different from the ships of Deir el-Bahari, provided as they are with a steering apparatus comprising two blades. Furthermore, the Cretan ships are characterised by a hull in the shape

of a half-moon whose stem extends into a slender pole bearing decorations.[23] It is difficult to know if the occasional resemblances between Cretan and Egyptian ships are the result of contacts that will have influenced naval architecture. Likewise, it is extremely difficult to know what type of boats the *keftiu*-ships were (Cretan boats? Boats inspired by Cretan models? Crewed by Cretans? Sailing between Crete and Egypt?).[24]

By way of comparison, the voyage of King Zimri-Lim to Ugarit as recounted by the archives of Mari is instructive:[25] around 1765 BC, the last king of Mari, Zimri-Lim, undertook, with part of his court and the palace administration, a long journey which led him from the Middle Euphrates to Ugarit, on the North Syrian

20  M. Bietak, in *Pyramid Studies and others Essays presented to S. Edwards*, 1988, pp. 35-40 studies the ships depicted in the funerary temple of Unas from a historical perspective, as compared with those of Sahure.

21  L. Basch, *The Mariner's Mirror* 71, 1985, pp. 455-456 remarks, among other things, that the engraver has given the tension cable an improbable appearance. A tiny fragment of the relief from the reception temple of Unas seems also to have depicted a ship with a tension cable supported by a prop: A. Labrousse, A. M. Moussa, *Le temple d'accueil du complexe funéraire du roi Ounas*, 1996, p. 80, doc. 28.

22  D. Meeks, *op. cit.*, p. 178.

23  P. Pomey, in P. Pomey (ed.), *La navigation dans l'Antiquité*, 1997, p. 62.

24  See, for example, *Urk.* IV, 706; S. R. K. Glanville, *ZÄS* 66, 1930, pp. 105-121; *id.*, *ZÄS* 68, 1932, pp. 7-41; T. Säve-Söderbergh, *The Navy*, 1946, p. 49; J. Vercoutter, *L'Égypte et le monde égéen préhellénique*, 1956, p. 53.

25  P. Villard, *UgForsch* 18, 1986, pp. 387-412; J. M. Durand, in A. Caubet (ed.), *L'acrobate au taureau*, 1999, p. 155.

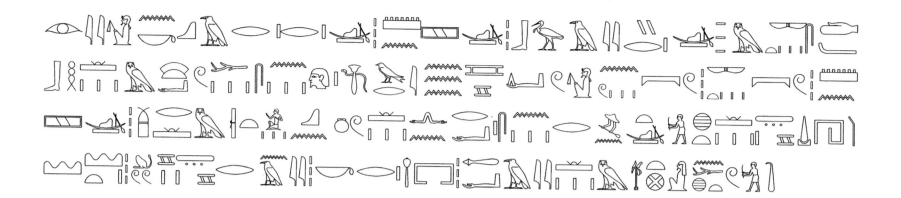

*I have made for you krr-ships, mnš-ships and br-ships, with equipped troops, for the sea. On it I have placed chiefs of troops and captain of mnš-ships, provided with numerous crews, so as to bring back goods from the land of Djahy and the ends of the earth to your great treasuries in Thebes-the-Victorious.*

coast. At Ugarit, he made contact with Cretans who taught him a new way of shipbuilding, Cretan-style – a way that could be copied on the banks of the Euphrates.[26]

As L. Basch has shown, the other Egyptian sea-ships at the Ramesside period, the *mnš*, were in fact copied from ships of the Levant and characterised by the presence of side hurdles, designed to protect cargoes from big waves.[27] The presence of this hurdle then made it impossible to use the oars. These 'real' sailing ships were probably used by the merchant navigators of the Levantine coast who came to Egypt to trade. It was perhaps to a ship of this kind that belongs the 14th-century BC wreck, the *Ulu Burun*, recently discovered near Kas, on the present Turkish coast.[28] The *mnš*-boat, attested from the 19th Dynasty (399-380 BC), was used for commercial purposes or in time of war, both on the Nile and at sea, if we are to believe the Harris Papyrus.[29] Rameses III (1182-1151 BC) boasts that he built a whole fleet of them:[30]

*I have made for you krr-ships,[31] mnš-ships and br-ships,[32] with equipped troops, for the sea. On it I have placed chiefs of troops and captain of mnš-ships, provided with numerous crews, so as to*

*bring back goods from the land of Djahy and the ends of the earth to your great treasuries in Thebes-the-Victorious.*

Before him, Seti I (1291-1278 BC) and then Rameses II (1279-1212 BC) had also undertaken to construct a fleet of *mnš*-boats.[33]

The word *mnš* is perhaps of Semitic origin.[34] This origin is suggested by, among other things, the fact that the determining hieroglyph for the ship[35] has some resemblance with the depiction of

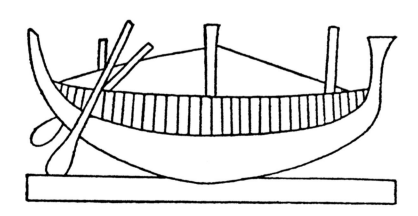

Determiner of the *mnš*-ship (the battle of Kadesh, version in the temple of Abydos, Rameses II, 19th Dynasty), drawing after L. Basch, *Le Musée imaginaire de la marine*, 1987, p. 65.

26  *Id.*, p. 162.

27  L. Basch, *The Mariner's Mirror* 64, 1978, pp. 99-109. On hurdles, see J. Rougé, *Aechaeonautica* 2, 1978, pp. 277-278. On the term *mnš*, see *Wb* II, 89, 7-10.

28  For a bibliography on the wreck of Ulu Burun, see *Seafaring in Ancient Egypt*, vol. 2.

29  W. F. Edgerton, J. A. Wilson, *Historical Records of Rameses III*, SAOC 12, 1936, p. 54 and n. 20a. On the likelihood that *mnš*-ships could sail the Nile, cf. see for example Y. Kœnig, in *Hommages à S. Sauneron*, I, BiÉtud 81, 1979, p. 217.

30  P. Harris I, 7, 8: *jry=j n=k qrr.w mnš.w br.w m pd.wt sdbhw m h3.w=sn tp w3d wr dw=j n(y).w hry.w-pd.wt hry.w-mnš ʿpr.w m js.wt qn.wt nn r-ʿ=sn r hn.t h.t d3hj h3s.wt phw.w t3 r n3y=k r3.w-hd ʿ3.w m w3s.t nht.t.* cf. P. Grandet, *Le papyrus Harris I*, BiÉtud 109, 1994, vol. 1, p. 230; vol. 2, p. 40 and pl. 7. Transcription: W. Erichsen, *Papyrus Harris I, Bibliotheca Aegyptiaca* V, 1933, p. 9, l. 2-5). See also P. Harris I, 48, 6 and Medinet Habu V, 229-235, 2nd court, north wall, lower level.

31  Ships whose function is only vaguely known; it may have involved cargoes of grain, inasmuch as their name could link them to *qr*-ships; the term is possibly of foreign origin: see *Wb* VII, 1261; V, 61, 7; *AnLex* 77.4563; *KRI* I, 2, 49, 15; C. Boreux, *Études de nautique égyptienne*, MIFAO L, 1925, p. 432 n. 7; F. L. Griffith, *JEA* XIII, 1927, pl. 40, 24-25; T. Säve-Söderbergh, *The Navy*, 1946, p. 53 n. 1; J. Barns, *JEA* 34, 1948, p. 39; R. A. Caminos, *Late-Egyptian Miscellanies*, 1954, p. 10; E. F. Wente, *Late Ramesside Letters*, SAOC 33, 1967, p. 74 (s); D. Jones, *A Glossary of Ancient Egyptian Nautical Titles and Terms*, 1988, no 77, pp. 147-148.

32  On *br*-ships, 'barge', which appeared at the beginning of the 19th Dynasty, possibly of foreign origin, and transcribed in Greek as βαριΩ, see *Wb* I, 465, 8-9; II, 403; V, 423; *AnLex* 77.1275; 79.0910; W. F. Edgerton, J. A. Wilson, *Historical Records of Ramsès III*, SAOC 12, 1936, p. 54, n. 20b; T. Säve-Söderbergh, *The Navy*, 1946, p. 50, 60, n. 5; A. Alt, *Archiv für Orientforschung* 15, 1945-1951, pp. 70-71; R. A. Caminos, *Late-Egyptian Miscellanies*, p. 156; E. F. Wente, *Late Ramesside Letters*, SAOC 33, 1967, p. 74 (x); L. A. Christophe, *ASAE* LV, 1958, p. 21; W. Helck, *Bie Beziehungen Ägyptens*, ÄgAbh 5, 1971, p. 511; S. Vinson, *JARCE* XXX, 1993, pp. 146-147; D. Jones, *A Glossary of Ancient Egyptian Nautical Titles and Terms*, 1988, no 30, pp. 136-137.

33  Decree of Nauri, 23-24 (cf. C. E. Sander-Hansen, *Historische Inschriften der 19. Dynastie*, I, *Bibliotheca Aegyptiaca* 4, 1933, pp. 16, 18); Abydos, Temple of Seti I, dedicatory Inscription (PM VI, 3, 34-37; *KRI* II, 332, 15-333); H. Gauthier, BiÉtud IV, 1912; C. Vandersleyen, *Ouadj our*, 1999, no 8, p. 178); P. Leiden I 350, 4-12 (cf. A. H. Gardiner, *ZÄS* 42, 1905, p. 14; J. Zandee, *De Hymnen aan Amon van Papyrus Leiden I 350*, OMRO XXVIII, 1947, p. 5; C. Favard-Meeks, *SAK* 16, 1989, p. 58 and n. 74).

34  J. M. Sasson, *JAOS* 86, 1966, p. 131; E. Martin-Pardey, in *LÄ* V, 1984, s.v. 'Schiff', col. 609 and n. 50-51; A. Raban, in M. Heltzer, E. Lipinski (ed.), *Society and Economy in the Eastern Mediterranean*, OLA 23, 1988, pp. 264-265: a similarly angular shape is also seen in the hulls of boats of the Sea Peoples and it may be of Aegean origin: cf. *infra*.

35  T. Säve-Söderbergh, *The Navy*, 1946, p. 58, fig. 12.

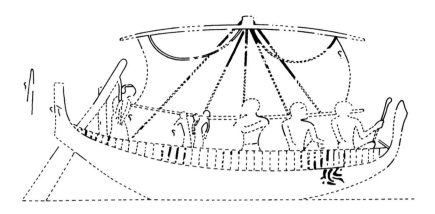

Syro-Palestinian ship, tomb of Nebamun, New Kingdom, 18th Dynasty, *c.* 1450 BC, drawing after L. Basch, *Le Musée imaginaire de la marine*, 1987, p. 63.

Anastasi VIII contains a long letter concerning numerous boats of different sorts including the *mnš*-ships circulating in the eastern Delta, between Memphis, Heliopolis, and Piramesse, notably in the 'Water of Ra', the Pelusiac branch of the Nile.[40]

The precise Semitic equivalent of the term *mnš* is not known. J. M. Sasson relates the term with the unattested form *munʿššu*:[41] this would be a participial derivation of the duplicated form of the radical *nʿšu* 'to raise, to be high', known in Hebrew, in Phoenician (*nšʾ*)[42] and in other Semitic languages; the word seems to refer to the main mast in the middle of the ship and, subsequently, to designate the whole boat (*pars pro toto*). Rather than seeing the term as derived from a Semitic origin, as previously suggested, H. Goedicke considers the word to come from the Egyptian *mnš* 'royal cartouche',[43] assuming that the *mnš*-ships transported goods especially under the royal flag, on the king's orders – to commercial ends – without

the Syrian ships of the tomb of Nebamun and Kenamun,[36] as with the *mnš*-ships on the reliefs of the Battle of Kadesh.[37]

The depiction of the tomb of Kenamun (18th Dynasty, 404–399 BC) shows the Syrian crew in the process of unloading a ship. These scenes certainly do not happen on the Mediterranean shore.[38] Everything indicates that such ships made it possible to sail inland by way of the river and moor in the nearest port, probably that of Memphis.[39] Some of them must even have pushed on further south, as far as Thebes. The interest that such boats, able to navigate on sea and river, could arouse in the eyes of the Egyptians is clear. Papyrus

36  *PM* I/L, pp. 275-276 (TT 162); N. de G. Davies, R. O. Faulkner, *JEA* 33, 1947, pl. viii.
37  M. C. Kuentz, *La bataille de Qadech*, MIFAO LV, 1928, I, p. 248 (nº 107), II, pls III and VI (7). R. de Spens, in N. Grimal, B. Menu (ed), *Le commerce*, BiÉtud 121, 1998, p. 111.
38  B. Kemp, D. O'Connor, *IJNA* 3, 1974, pp. 101-103.
39  K. Vandorpe, *Enchoria* 22, 1995, pp. 162-164. cf. infra.
40  P. Anastasi VIII, vº III, 1. 4; S. I. Groll, *Jerusalem Studies in Egyptology* = ÄuAT 40, 1995, pp. 173-192.
41  J. M. Sasson, *JAOS* 86, 1966, pp. 131-132.
42  *HAL*, pp. 683-686; R. S. Tomback, *A Comparative Semitic Lexicon of the Phoenician and Punic Languages*, 1978, pp. 221-222.
43  *Wb* II, 89, 2.

*mnš*-ship from Syro-Palestine, tomb of Kenamun (TT 162), New Kingdom, 18th Dynasty, *c.* 1450 BC, drawing after L. Basch, *Le Musée imaginaire de la marine*, 1987, p. 64.

constituting any real piece of royal property.[44] It is possible that the hurdle that extended completely round the ship whose deck was thus enclosed as in an *mnš*-cartouche could have led to this type of ship being given this name?

Whatever the truth of the matter, it was on an *mnš*-ship that Wenamun travelled to make the journey between the Egyptian coast and Byblos. Their captains, the *ḥry.w-mnš*, were often foreigners, and this suggests that they sometimes had contractual links with the Egyptian state.[45] Finally, the Prince of Byblos indicated to Wenamun the significant number of *mnš*-vessels travelling to and from Tanis.[46]

Some evidence thus suggests that close relations in the domain of a maritime fleet and naval architecture existed between Egypt and the Syro-Lebanese coast.[47]

In view of the documents, this navy seems to have been under the command of the royal power from the earliest times; it was a State navy. It will be elaborated that some evidence contributes to the idea that external commerce was not completely in thrall to the state and its various different institutions.[48] It remains extremely difficult to grasp what logistical means were deployed by this 'private' maritime commerce, however tiny it may have been.

According to Diodorus,[49] it was Sesoosis who, in Egypt, was the first to construct long vessels (vessels of war). This legendary king amalgamates in his person several conquering sovereigns: Senusret III (1878-1841 BC), Thutmose III (1504-1450 BC) and Rameses II (1279-1212 BC). The extent of his conquests, as attributed to him by Diodorus, are in fact magnified to grant the character a stature superior to that of Alexander the Great himself. Also, 'the historicity of the creation of a war navy by one of the kings named above should be treated with caution'.[50]

At the start of the 5th century BC the Egyptian ships and their crews, in the service of the Persian navy, had distinguished themselves at the battles of Artemisium and Salamis (480 BC).[51] The Saite pharaohs, anxious to play a role in the eastern Mediterranean, had built a fleet capable of fulfilling the commercial and military objectives they had set before themselves. The number of Egyptians involved in these engagements, and their capabilities – acknowledged and feared – shed light on the durable consequences of a maritime policy that can be imagined to have been inherited from a more distant past. There is some considerable evidence of the quality and reputation of the Egyptian navy in the Pharaonic epoch.[52]

A tablet discovered at Ugarit contains a letter addressed to Amenophis III (1386-1349 BC) by the king of Alasia.[53] The latter was interested in the purchase of ships from Egypt, 'which would tend to prove that, in this period, Egyptian ships were sufficiently highly esteemed for a foreign sovereign to be inclined to acquire them'.[54] Another tablet, found at Amarna, seems to reveal the presence of Egyptian ships at Beirut.[55] It is true that in the same correspondence, Canaanite cities suggested repeatedly to the Pharaoh that they could place their ships at the service of his armies.[56] Under the reign of Merenptah (1212-1202 BC), a letter from the Egyptian chancellery and sent to the king of Ugarit was the reply to a communication that has not survived: while refusing the request for a sculptor to be sent, it announces the arrival of joiners and carpenters for the sovereign of Ugarit to use as he sees fit.[57] Were these naval carpenters? The text does not allow this to be confirmed.

D. Meeks also points out that there is 'an exceptional document' dating from the New Kingdom (1570-1070 BC), and belonging to

the Hittite archives of Boghazköy.[58] This is a letter sent by Rameses II (1279-1212 BC) to the Hittite king and concerning the construction of ships. In spite of the fragmentary state of the text, the reconstitution of the terms, and their meanings, are certain, so that it is possible to understand the overall meaning: basically, the Egyptian king warns the Hittite king that an Egyptian ship is arriving. The Hittite carpenters will need to execute a drawing or a plan of this ship so they can make a copy of it. Rameses II also recommends that they proceed to caulk it with the aid of mineral pitch or bitumen so that the ship will not sink at sea. The crucial point of the text resides evidently in the mention of a drawing or 'plan' of the ship taking material form probably on a tablet. The terms here employed (the verb 'to draw' and the substantive 'drawing') are well attested in Akkadian. They are used when it is a question of reliefs, decorations on the walls of a house, the plans of buildings, and so on. It can only be speculated that the exact nature of this 'drawing', 'the fact remains that it is something made on the basis of a pre-existing ship and enables a copy to be constructed. This is, it seems, the most ancient attestation known, at present, of this kind of practice, although its origin cannot be precisely fixed. The barque of Khufu bore, on its central line, repeated motifs, serving as markers, that enabled the builders to ensure that the hull was properly symmetrical'.[59] These motifs could have been put in place by using the help of a plumb line or other means of measurement.[60] These painted or incised signs exist on almost all the 'pieces of the jigsaw': there are 650 different ones, most of them repeated; in total, their number reaches 1131. There was also the exceptional discovery, on one of the two Punic shipwrecks (from the 3rd century BC) of Marsala, in Sicily, of carpenters' marks painted on the different pieces of the hull to guide its assembly, which adds interesting details about this type of construction. These marks show that the different stages of construction were carefully prepared

44  H. Goedicke, *The Report of Wenamun*, 1975, p. 25.

45  cf. p. 151-152.

46  *Wenamun*, L, 52-2, 2. Text cited p. 155. In the report of Amun's envoy, *mnš* is sometimes replaced by *b-pȝ-jr(.t)*; L. H. Lesko (ed), *A Dictionary of Late Egyptian* I, 1982, p. 157. The *b-pȝ-jr(.t)* boat is generally designed for travel and the transportation of merchandise on the Nile, cf. R. A. Caminos, *Late Egyptian Miscellanies*, 1954, p. 156, and W. F. Edgerton, J. A. Wilson, *Historical Records of Rameses III*, SAOC 12, 1936, p. 54 n. 20b.

47  On this subject, see the presence of Syrian naval carpenters in the dockyard of Peru-Nefer, p. 140.

48  The activity of Egyptian merchants of the New Kingdom who traded in the Mediterranean was placed under the control of the State institutions. But see E. W. Castle, *JESHO* 35, 1992, pp. 249-250, pp. 253-256 and E. Lipinski, in J. D. Hawkins (ed.), *Trade in the Ancient Near East*, 1977, pp. 213-217. cf. our chapter p. 158 *et seq.*

49  Diodorus, *Bibliotheca historica*, I, 15, 2.

50  D. Meeks, in D. Meeks, D. Garcia (ed), *Techniques et économie antiques et médiévales*, 1997, p. 179

51  A. Deman, *CdÉ* 60, 1985, pp. 56-74.

52  After the study by D. Meeks, in D. Meeks, D. Garcia (ed), *Techniques et économies antiques et médiévales*, 1997, pp. 179-180: it is from him that we take the following remarks.

53  E. Lipinski, *op. cit.*, pp. 213-217. For other sea contacts between Alasia and Egypt, see also L. Moran, *Les lettres d'El-Amarna*, LAPO 13, 1987, p. 197 n. 4, p. 208 (*EA* 39), p. 209 (*EA* 40), and compare with E. W. Castle, *JESHO* 35, 1992, pp. 255-256.

54  D. Meeks, *op. cit.*, p. 179.

55  L. Moran, *op. cit.*, p. 373 (*EA* 143); 257 (*EA* 77) and p. 345 (*EA* 129) where the king of Byblos asks for an Egyptian ship to be sent. The Egyptians may then have had warships: p. 310 (*EA* 110).

56  *Id.*, p. 388 (*EA* 153), p. 391 (*EA* 155), p. 398 (*EA* 161).

57  S. Lackenbacher, in *Les relations internationales*, 1995, pp. 107-118.

58  Re-examined in E. Edel, *Die ägyptisch-hethitische Korrespondenz aus Boghazköi in babylonischer und hethitischer Sprache*, 1994. See D. Meeks, *op. cit.*, pp. 179-180.

59  D. Meeks, in D. Meeks, D. Garcia (ed), *Techniques et économie antiques et médiévales*, 1997, p. 179.

60  P. Lipke, in S. McGrail, E. Kentley, *Sewn Plank Boats*, 1985, p. 25.

Above left: relief of the naval battle against the Sea Peoples on the north wall of the funerary temple of Rameses III at Medinet Habu, Thebes, New Kingdom, 20th Dynasty, c. 1184–1153 BC. © AKG Images. Photo: Erich Lessing Right: diagram of a fighting ship of Rameses III, 20th Dynasty, Medinet Habu, drawing after J. Degas, *Égypte, Afrique & Orient* 1, 1996, p. 18. Below: detail of the battle against the Sea Peoples. © AKG Images. Photo: Erich Lessing

in advance. From their position, it can even be deduced that the installation of certain pieces was planned right from the start of construction, long before their eventual placing, and that a certain form of preparation, not to say prefabrication, of the work was practised.[61]

This text shows that there was a navy under Rameses II and that his ships could serve as models for the Hittites. It may be concluded that the statement by Diodorus had at least a grain of truth.

It was after the second half of the 2nd millennium BC that the trading ship seems gradually to have been distinguished from the war ship. Until then, the two activities were not distinct, and naval understanding was not yet such as to allow this difference to be expressed. Furthermore, it is Egypt which provides the first depictions of ships specially conceived for combat, with reliefs from the temple at Medinet Abu. These record the memory of the first great naval battle of antiquity, which, around 1190, set the fleet of Rameses III (1182–1151 BC) against that of the Sea Peoples. These

depict light ships equipped with tops and combat platforms, and with strongly arched keels. It is all the more probable that these Egyptian ships were purely military in that their prows, in an extension of the keel, ended in the shape of a lion's head that must have acted like a battering ram.[62]

61  P. Pomey (ed.), *La navigation dans l'Antiquité*, 1997, pp. 93-94.
62  cf. P. Grandet, *Ramsès III*, 1993; id., in *L'Égypte ancienne, L'Histoire*, 1996, pp. 87-101; P. Pomey, in P. Pomey (ed.), *op. cit.*, p. 64; E. Marx, *The Mariner's Mirror 32*, 1946, pp. 242-251; id., *The Mariner's Mirror 34*, 1948, pp. 118-119; B. Landström, *Ships of the Pharaohs*, 1970, p. 112 and n. 24; id., *The Ship*, 1961, p. 33; Y. Yadin, *The Art of Warfare in Biblical Lands*, 1963, p. 253 and p. 342. See too the Mycenean trading ships, symmetrical in shape and equipped with a hold big enough for men to stand upright in it. The contrast between the bellying shape of the latter and the sleek lines of the warships clearly illustrates the distinction that was made throughout Greek and Roman antiquity between the 'round ships' of trade and the 'long ships' of combat: P. Pomey, *op. cit.*, p. 64; J. Rougé, *La marine dans l'Antiquité*, 1975, p. 156; L. Casson, *Ships and Seamanship*, 1971, pls 78, 57-58, 92. See too J. Morrison, R. Williams, *Greek oared Ships 900-322 B.C.*, 1968, pp. 7-11, 37, pls 1-2; A.B. Lloyd, *JHS* 95, 1975, p. 55; L. Basch, *The Mariner's Mirror 55*, 1969, p. 142 and n. 3; id., *IJNA 4/2*, 1975, p. 201; id., *The Mariner's Mirror 55*, 1983, pp. 129-142.

Phoenician warship on a bas-relief from the palace of Sennacherib at Nineveh, Iraq, 7th century BC, British Museum, London. © The British Museum/Heritage Images

The so-called 'pendant of Nekau', a fragment of Egyptian gold necklace, Saite period, Louvre, Paris. © Gianni Dagli Orti/CORBIS.

According to Herodotus, it was Nekau II (594-588 BC) who restored, or created, a real fleet in the Mediterranean and the Red Sea:[63]

*When he had finished cutting the canal, Nekos turned to military expeditions; he ordered the construction of triremes, some of them for the southern sea, the others in the Arabian Gulf for the Erythrean Sea – these with holds that are still very evident.*

Were the triremes meant for Mediterranean navigation Greek or Phoenician? Trusting the legend of the invention of the trireme at Corinth in 704 BC, certain scholars believed that Nekau had a war fleet built by the Corinthians. 'Such a conclusion,' according to L. Basch, 'might appear normal and even inevitable if there had existed only a single type of galley with three banks of oars, but there were in fact two. The Greek trireme, if it existed at the time of Nekau II – which is not absolutely certain – must have remained at the experimental stage. Why would Nekau have turned to Corinth to obtain what he practically had already, at a period when the Greeks themselves hardly used the trireme – if it existed?[64] Especially since he sent Phoenicians round Africa, and had at his disposal the dockyards of Peru-nefer and his district of Phoenician carpenters, and whose New Kingdom predecessors had regularly appealed to the shipbuilders of the Levant.

In any case, Egypt has yielded, at Ermant, the model of a trireme of Phoenician type. Nekau's successors obviously preserved and

perhaps even developed this fleet of triremes. In 587 BC, the Pharaoah Apries, following the revolt of Zedekiah, King of Judah, against Babylon, intervened in Phoenicia. Sidon submitted, but Tyre resisted. The Tyrian naval forces, reinforced by Cypriot contingents, confronted Apries and were defeated.[65] Cyprus was conquered by Apries' successor, Amasis.[66] So it is proven that 'Egypt enjoyed, during the first quarter of the 6th century BC, a hegemony in the eastern Mediterranean, acquired thanks to her supremacy over the Phoenician squadrons'.[67] The ostracon of Saqqara as well as the fragment of the necklace called 'Nekau's' are both two fine examples that can be compared with Phoenician coins.[68] Finally, the Egyptians sent a contingent of triremes to fight at the sides of the Phoenicians at Salamis; 'so there are no better judges than the Greeks themselves when it comes to deciding on whether, at the beginning of the 5th century BC, the Egyptians were using a trireme of Phoenician type or, on the contrary, a type similar to their own'.[69]

63    Herodotus, II, 159, trans. P.-E. Legrand, Les Belles Lettes.
64    L. Basch, *Le Musée imaginaire de la marine*, 1987, p. 334.
65    Diodorus, *Bibliotheca historica*, I, 68.
66    Herodotus, II, 182.
67    L. Basch, *op. cit.*
68    Ostracon of Saqqara, Fitzwilliam Museum, Cambridge; fragment of the so-called 'pendant of Nekau', in the Louvre.
69    *Id.*, p. 335.

As far as the Red Sea is concerned, the construction of triremes here would indicate that, 'unlike his predecessors – Sahure and Hatshepsut – he had military objectives'.[70] This brief reference raises several problems, that are far from resolved. The first is that of the opening (partly aborted, since it was Darius who, later on, resumed digging it) of a 'canal' from the Nile to the Red Sea via Wadi Tumilat.[71] Another problem is that of the nature of the warships that sailed up and down the Red Sea in the 6th century BC.[72] Were the triremes mentioned by Herodotus Greek[73] or Phoenician?[74] It is very difficult to say; however, the historic context makes the second solution more likely. Most commentators agree that the 'long' ships cited by the Greek sources were a recent modification of the Egyptian boats designed previously as *kepenet*, cargo vessels for the high seas: the designation of trireme is widely accepted.[75]

Without getting involved in a difficult technical debate, one question nonetheless needs to be raised: how could a trireme 40m long travel in the *marsas* mentioned above, on the crests of fringing reefs only at certain hours of the day? It needs to be borne in mind that the 'mistake' attributed by Strabo to Aelius Gallus – that of having built 'long' boats for his expedition against Leuke Kome: 80 biremes and triremes. Changing his mind, Aelius Gallus then embarked on a 130 cargo ships better adapted to sailing in the Red Sea, although several of his vessels sank before reaching Leuke Kome, not for any reasons of war but only because of the difficulties of sailing. Strabo's text intimates that the troops were unable to adapt to local sailing conditions.[76] Policing the Red Sea on triremes of a Greek or Phoenician type seems difficult to square with what is known of sailing conditions in the region. One part of the answer might come from the non–existent description of the naval installations mentioned by Herodotus although, unlike certain commentators, the Greek historian never says that he saw them himself.[77] The term *holkos* designates an arrangement designed to pull the boats out of the water during the period when they were not sailing – surely a military installation:[78] when triremes are being mentioned, it is the term *neoria* that is habitually used – at Athens, Thassos, Kition, and so on. It would surely be wrong to claim that the difference between *holkos* and *neoria* was merely a matter of the ship's size,[79] but it might be argued that the terminology used by

Herodotus does not fit, in the case of the Red Sea, the contemporary terminology used for triremes.[80] Finally, as far as the hypothetical expedition around Africa is concerned, if it really did take place, there is little chance that it was undertaken by triremes, but rather by cargo ships, even if the wider Phoenician trireme could hold the seas better than the Greek trireme; furthermore, since whenever Herodotus talks of the war fleets of Nekau he uses the precise term 'trireme', would he then use the imprecise term of *ploion*, without qualification, if he meant war ships?

Another question is this: why would there have been a military fleet in the Red Sea in the 6th century BC? The argument most frequently put forward is that of commerce with the East and/or the land of Punt – Ethiopia, Southern Arabia? – , without the slightest archaeological or historical proof, except for proof by analogy: what happened at the time of Hatshepsut or Solomon was repeated by

---

70  E. Van't Dack, H. Hauben, in H. Maelher, V. M. Strocka (eds), *Das ptolemäische Ägypten*, 1978, p. 65.

71  cf. p. 78 *et seq.*

72  On these two problems, see A. B. Lloyd, *JEA* 63, 1977, pp. 142-155; id., *Herodotus, Book II*, 1988, pp. 149-160; J.-F. Salles, in J.-F. Salles (ed.), *L'Arabie et ses mers bordières*, I, 1988, pp. 75-102; C. Tuplin, in H. Sancisi-Weerdenburg, A. Kuhrt (ed), *AchHist VI*, 1991, pp. 237-283; P. Briant, *Histoire de l'Empire perse*, 1996, ch. IX, p. 369 *et seq.*, pp. 395-396; D. Meeks, in D. Meeks, D. Garcia (ed), *Techniques et économie antiques et médiévales*, 1997, pp. 175-194.

73  A. B. Lloyd, *JEA* 58, 1972, pp. 268-279; id., *JHS* 95, 1975, pp. 45-61.

74  L. Basch, *The Mariner's Mirror* 55, 1969, pp. 139-162; id., *JHS* 97, 1977, pp. 1-10; L. C. Casson, *Ships and Seamanship*, 1971, p. 81 n. 19.

75  L. Bradbury, *JARCE* 33, 1996, pp. 37-60. H. T. Wallinga, *AchHist* I, 1987, pp. 47-78, rejects this hypothesis on convincing linguistic and historical grounds. It is the term *kbnw* which appears on the Stele of Pithom (Tell el-Maskhuta, CGC 22183) and refers to the ships that Ptolemy II Philadelphus ordered to be built to sail on *Wadj Wer*: See *Urk*. II, 86, 10; E. Naville, *The store-city of Pithom*, 1903, p. 19; G. Roeder, *Die ägyptische Götterwelt*, 1959, pp. 117-118.

76  Strabo, XVI, 4, 2. See J.-F. Salles, in D. Valbelle, C. Bonnet, *Le Sinaï*, 1998, p. 94.

77  Herodotus, II, 154 referring to the Carian installations in Caria which he might have seen for himself, and II, 159, on the constructions that could be seen in the Red Sea (second-hand information).

78  H. T. Wallinga, *AchHist* I, 1987, pp. 47-78, recalls that such installations needed to be 'guarded', with all that this implies for the deployment of an Achaemenid military force.

79  P. Chantraine, *Dictionnaire étymologique de la langue grecque*, 1968: he suggests, instead, variations in the overall shape of the complex (number and size of ships drawn up, organisation of the wet dock, and so on.). He translates *neoria* by 'arsenal'. See also the term *neolkoi*, cf. J.-F. Salles, *op. cit.*, p. 95 and n. 22.

80  Id., p. 95.

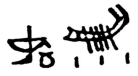

Hieroglyphs from the Ptolemaic period designating the *kbnw*-ships, drawing after L. Basch, *The Mariner's Mirror* 64, 1978, fig. 3b, p. 101.

Nekau and his Achaemenid successors, and the best demonstration resides in the description in the *Periplus of the Erythrean Sea*. Reference is also made to the need to combat piracy, as is shown by the texts of Strabo and Pliny, several centuries later, when they discuss Nabatean pirates.[81] In both cases, 'the amalgamation of sources from very different dates constitutes a fragile argument, despite the justification of historical plausibility'.[82]

A. B. Lloyd proposes an interesting hypothesis: the desire of the Saite Pharoah to fight off commercial and military competition from the Edomite kingdom with its great port in the Gulf of Aqaba, Ezion Geber.[83] On the other hand, the idea that Nekau would have wished to defend a southern front threatened by the growing power of Babylon in the Persian Gulf seems implausible: no neo-Assyrian or neo-Babylonian expedition to the Red Sea ever took place, and in any case the 1500km of unknown coasts between the Ras Musandam at the exit from the Persian Gulf and the Bab el-Mandeb at the entry to the Red Sea protected the Egyptian sovereigns from any maritime invasion from the east.[84]

To shed light on Nekau's policy, it is still necessary to know the maritime history of the South Arabian kingdoms, in full expansion on the high plateaux of the Yemen from the 7th century BC: they could indeed have menaced Egyptian supremacy in the Red Sea: but the historians of South Arabia continue to place the emphasis on the notion of 'caravan kingdoms',[85] without any real maritime vocation.

Before the Persian era, there is no more information about any Egyptian military fleet in the Red Sea before the middle of the 2nd century BC, when the strategos of Thebes found himself in charge '*of boats*' – more probably those of the Red Sea than those of the Nile, and then at the start of the 1st century BC, when the strategy of the Erythrean Sea was created;[86] no detail is known about this military force, except perhaps the ships laden with archers cited by Pliny,[87] and designed for protection against the pirates infesting the Erythrean Sea, or the 'special' ship built by the Egyptians for their trade with India referred to by the author of the *Life of Apollonius of Tyana*[88] – but do these enigmatic references have any relation to the Ptolemaic strategy of the Erythrean Sea? Still, there is proof that Egyptian boats did sail along the African coasts of the Red Sea in the 3rd and 2nd centuries BC: those of the exploratory expeditions sent out by the Ptolemies – Stayros, Strato, Demetrius (?), Conon (?) under Ptolemy II Philadelphus, in 270 BC, though it is not known how far these expeditions might have travelled; and the ships of the 'elephant hunts'

(*elephantegoi*) with their escorts, which sailed from the ports founded by Ptolemy II.[89] What kind of ships were these?

Finally, for these periods, there is also the problem of naval construction on the Red Sea coasts, a *sine qua non* for maritime traffic in the region. Above, the transporting of dismounted ships from the Nile to the Red Sea was mentioned; such an argument, which can be applied to distant expeditions, is unconvincing in the framework of the maintenance of a permanent Red Sea fleet, or that of regular international trade with India. The problem, often cited in written sources but very unclear on the archaeological level, of the canal between the Nile and the Red Sea, still underlies any better interpretation of sailing in the Red Sea.[90] Without going into further detail about the absence of local resources, it should be noted that 'no text refers to imports of construction wood to the Red Sea, while such mentions are numerous for the Persian Gulf and Babylonia where the raw material is just as rare'.[91] Without calling into question the reality of 'Mediterranean' navigation in the Red Sea – using boats built in accordance with the norms of the eastern Mediterranean – it may be asked in accordance with J.-F. Salles and H. P. Ray, whether the ships that crossed the Bab el-Mandeb as mentioned by Strabo and Pliny, and referred to in the *Periplus of the Eryhthrean Sea*, were Roman (in the broadest sense, Egyptian and Mediterranean), Arabic, Persian, Indian, or African?[92]

---

81 Strabo, XVI, 4, 18; Pliny, *Natural History*, VII, 52, 206

82 J.-F. Salles, op. cit., p. 95.

83 E. Stern, et al., *The New Encyclopedia of Archaeological Excavations in the Holy Land*, 1994, vol. 2, pp. 867-870. See too F. Briquel-Chatonnet, *Les relations entre les cités de la côte phénicienne et les royaumes d'Israël et de Juda*, OIA 46, 1992, pp. 271-287.

84 J.-F. Salles, op. cit., p. 95

85 Y. Calvet, C. Robin (ed.), *Arabie heureuse, Arabie déserte*, 1997, especially pp. 28-31 and bibliography; C. A. Nallino, BIFAO XXX, 1930, pp. 465-475. See also the pertinent observations of J.-F. Salles, op. cit., pp. 95-96.

86 J. D. Thomas, The epistrategos in Ptolemaic and Roman Egypt, I, Papyrologica Coloniensia VI, 1975, pp. 71-72 and pp. 106-107. The existence of a Ptolemaic fleet in the Red Sea is clearly indicated for the period of the battles fought against Nabatean pirates (Strabo, XVI, 4, 8) at an indeterminate era but one prior to Strabo himself (1st century BC).

87 Pliny, *Natural History*, VI, 26, 101.

88 Text quoted by J. Rougé, in J.-F. Salles (ed.), *L'Arabie et ses mers bordières*, I, 1988, p. 69-70.

89 S. M. Burstein, *Agatharchides of Cnidus*, 1989, p. 141 n. 3; S. M. Burstein, *Topoi* 6, 1996, pp. 799-807.

90 On the existence of this canal in the Ptolemaic and Roman periods, *cf.* p. 80-81.

91 J.-F Salles, in D. Valbelle, C. Bonnet (ed.), *Le Sinaï*, 1998, p. 96.

92 H. P. Ray, *The Winds of Change*, 1994, pp. 62-86; H. P. Ray, J.-F. Salles (ed.), *Tradition and Archaeology. Early Maritime Contacts Indian Ocean*, 1996; J.-F. Salles, op. cit., p. 96.

## II. Egyptian naval architecture

*I can see the ship of that observer who has greeted our suppliant throng. It is easily distinguished: nothing escapes my notice, neither the arrangement of the sails, nor the vessel's bulwarks, nor its prow which, with her own eyes, surveys the route ahead of her, docile to the rudder that guides her at the stern — too obedient, indeed, in the eyes of those for whom she does not come as a friend. I can make out the sailors, with their black limbs emerging from their white tunics; and now, here are the other ships and the whole army coming into view. The leading vessel, as it approaches the shore, has taken in its sails and is advancing to the great noise of its oars.*

(King Danaos on spotting the vessel of the pursuing Egyptians in Aeschylus, *The Suppliant Women*)

The study of naval architecture is now dependent on submarine archaeology which has filled in the gaps left by traditional documents, and opened the way to a new investigation into the methods of shipbuilding and the way they evolved over time. The study of innovations in transport makes it possible to tackle problems that ultimately affect historiography and the history of technology in general. The concept of the ancient system of technology as something primitive and blocked has been subjected to revision. Recent research has renewed the whole problem of ancient transport. It brings out the diversity and wealth of modes of transport, the originality of certain techniques, and an efficiency and technical accomplishment that render obsolete the traditional ideas about low yield and inadequate returns.

## II. 1. The hulls

In the 4th century BC, wood was widely used in naval construction on the banks of the Nile: without the use of this material, the shape of many predynastic ships, known to us from similar sequences of rock engravings, would be inexplicable. This implies several problems, a solution to which can only be hypothetical: in the first place, that of the material itself, Egypt always having been extremely poor in wood suitable for shipbuilding, especially long wood; in the second place, that of the equipment available at such a remote epoch to fashion and assemble this wood.

However, the investigation of wooden ships that were still observable on the Upper Nile, in Chad and Niger – territories even poorer in wood that Egypt – at the beginning of the 20th century, leaves no doubt: short pieces of wood (acacia, for instance – very common in Egypt) could easily be sided thanks to the use of instruments made of hard stone; they could then be assembled by a complex system of splicing and wads of caulking. Ships 15 to 20m long, propelled by 12 or 15 paddlers, could be constructed by this means without difficulty, which can, in view of its very distant origins, be labelled 'African'. An Old Kingdom (2686-2181 BC) relief, dating back two millennia before the description of Herodotus, illustrates well the assembling of short irregular planks 'in the manner of bricks'. As for archaeology, in 1894, six barques, dating from *c.* 1650 BC, were discovered near the pyramid of Senusret III (1878-1841 BC) at Dashur. Some 10m long, they are made of short pieces of wood assembled in mortice and tenon fashion, as well as sometimes being spliced together. There is no rib: these are shells. A 'specialist', 'Pharaonic' influence cannot be excluded, but a development of the 'African method', already two millennia old by the time of the Middle

Sea ships, monumental avenue of Unas, Saqqara, Old Kingdom, 5th Dynasty, *c.* 2465-2323 BC. © Photo: David Fabre

Kingdom (2040–1782 BC), seems more probable.[1] The development is marked above by a more frequent use of tenons instead of splices. It would be quite wrong to consider such vessels as 'primitive': they were perfectly well adapted to their environment, as shown by the fact that such barques, without ribs, were still sailing on the Upper Nile until the middle of the 20th century; the only difference was that the short planks were held together by nails.

The unification of Egypt, around 3200–3100 BC, had a far from negligible consequence for Egyptian naval architecture: as a result of the very centralised manner in which it took place, the sovereign – and he alone – benefited from an increase in his means that was as sudden as it was considerable. Already at the end of the predynastic period, cedar wood from the Syro-Lebanese coast had arrived in Egypt. These importations of cedar wood became increasingly significant throughout the Old Kingdom, on the one hand being used in the architecture of great royal constructions, and on the other in the construction of great ships, which could not be built on the 'African method'.

## II.1.1. The skeleton

'The hull of a ship is formed from two parts closely united: the carcass and the siding, the external covering of the carcass; to this is often added the inner planking on the inside of the carcass. In theory, this latter is formed of a number of pieces that are found in most ancient ships.'[2]

The hulls of the ships of Sahure are more or less symmetrical, the stern being hardly any higher than the stem, and the latter being a little thicker than the stern. The two extremities are slightly curved. In these boats, what is especially striking is the importance given to the part under water: this detail is no doubt to be explained by the need to give seagoing ships a greater stability.[3] It should be noted that Egyptian ships were not necessarily equipped with a keel.[4] A typical case is that of the royal funerary barque of Khufu (2589–2566 BC), designed for the Nile, and discovered practically intact. Its carcass is composed of four groups of elements:

- Following the shape of the planking, a series of continuous pieces that play the part simultaneously of frames and floor frames, but not rising to the top of the planking.
- Linking the sides to each other, a series of beams more numerous than the frames.
- The beams are linked together in their middle and at their extremities: in their middle by a long piece of wood placed beneath them in which they are set, and at their extremities by two sets of pieces of wood placed above them and running parallel to the sides.

Funerary barque of Khufu at Giza, Old Kingdom, 4th Dynasty, *c.* 2575–2465 BC.
© Photo: Peter A. Clayton

- The central piece of wood rests on vertical pillars that are supported by the frames at the bottom of the barque.

The discovery of the barques of Khufu and the reconstruction of one of them has thus made it possible to study the way they were built. These were, of course, barques designed for river sailing alone. Furthermore, such barques could not sail by themselves and needed to be tugged by one or more oar-propelled boats.[5] This way of sailing ceremonial boats is in any case attested by the sacred barque of Amun.[6] An attentive examination reveals that the assembling of the

1   L. Basch, *Égypte. Afrique & Orient* 1, 1996, p. 6.
2   J. Rougé, *La marine dans l'Antiquité*, 1975, p. 38.
3   C. Boreux, *Études de nautique égyptienne*, MIFAO L, 1925, p. 470.
4   The term *tp-ḥ.t* supposed to designate the 'keel' in any case raises problems of interpretation. It appears in the New Kingdom where it is mentioned in the registers relating to use of wood: S. R. K. Glanville, *ZÄS* 66, 1930, P. BM 10056, v° col. 6, 12-15; col. 8, 6 and 9-10; id., *ZÄS* 68, 1932, pp. 27, 32, 36. Glanville compares the term *tp-ḥ.t* to the term used in *The Report of Wenamun*: *tpy-ḥ.t*, generally translated as 'keel'. E. Wente, 1973, p. 151; M. Lichtheim, *The Literature of Ancient Egypt*, II, 227; J. Wilson, in *ANET*, p. 28; A. Gardiner, *Egypt of the Pharaohs*, 1976, p. 310; H. Goedicke, *The Report of Wenamun*, 1975, p. 95. cf. *Wb* V, 294, 3; V, 294, 6. This term could equally well refer, for a Nile vessel, the 'first part in wood', the first piece of the planking on which are fixed (by splices and mortice and tenon joints) the other parts of the planking. On the construction of the planking, see p. 106 *et seq.*

5   P. Lipke, in S. McGrail, E. Kentley, *Sewn Plank Boats*, 1985, p. 34.
6   J. Wiercinska, *Études et Travaux* 14, 1990, pp. 72-85 and p. 81 n. 29; N. Dürring, *Materialien zum Schiffbau*, 1995, pl. 12.

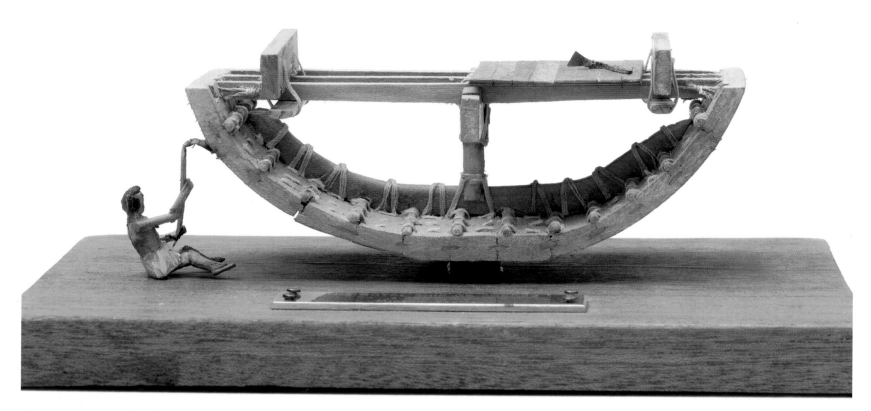

Cross-section model of the funerary boat of Khufu. © Science Museum

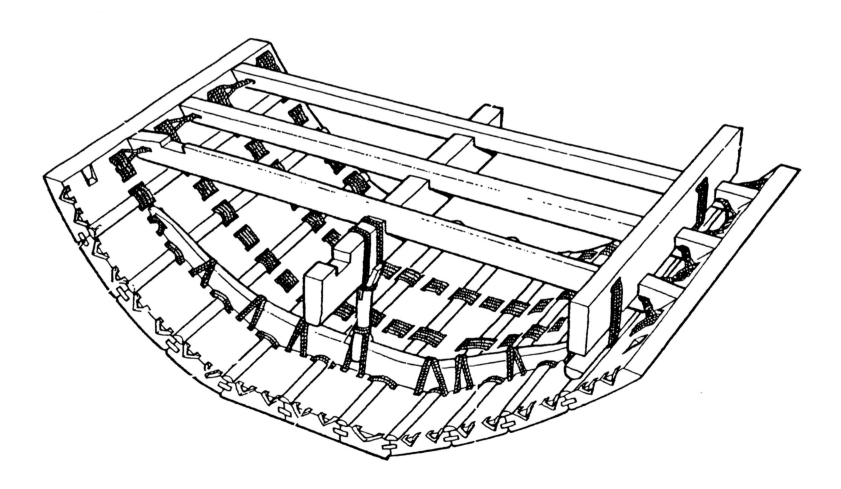

The planking is assembled by splices and tenons. Drawing after P. Pomey (ed.), *La Navigation dans l'Antiquité*, 1997, p. 90. © P. Pomey

timbers of Khufu's barque was achieved both by splices and by mortice and tenon joints.[7] The barques of Licht (reign of Senusret I, *c*. 1950 BC) and Dashur (reign of Senusret III, *c*. 1850 BC), confirm this practice, even if the systems of splices are slightly different in each case.[8]

The waterproofing of the construction was ensured by pulling the papyrus bonds very tight together, as is shown by the barque of Licht which confirms, on this point, the evidence of Herodotus.[9] The tension of the ropes was increased to a maximum when sailing by wetting them.[10] This method was still being used in the Nile Valley in the Hellenistic period.[11] The technique is attested in Egypt, by archaeological and textual evidence, only for river boats. It is known, however, that it was used elsewhere in antiquity for seagoing ships.[12] From at least the reign of Khufu, the Egyptians were aware of techniques useful in the construction of this type of boat. It is possible that these techniques were introduced, at this period or later, by Levantine carpenters. The fact that sea ships are often described as 'ships of Byblos' in Egyptian texts, from the earliest times, might indicate that the techniques used by Levantine carpenters complemented and improved those known by the Egyptians.[13] There is, however, no evidence to prove this, and the barques of Khufu seem rather to be the product of a purely local expertise, as the written documents suggest. In the Hellenistic and Roman periods, the barques and the other constructions of the carpenters of Kasion were reputed for the quality of their assemblage, which relied on interwoven knots.[14] In the New Kingdom, as demonstrated below, sea ships were doubtless caulked with bitumen.

In Egypt – even if the real influence of Egyptian naval shipbuilding on Mediterranean construction remains a topic for debate[15] – it is interesting to note that the two principles of assemblage coexisted in the 3rd and 2nd millennia BC on the ship of Khufu, and on the boats of Licht and Dashur. As repeatedly emphasised, these were Nile vessels where the systems of assemblage, with mortice and tenon joints as well as splices, stemmed from technical methods that were different from those in use in the Mediterranean.[16]

In the Mediterranean, the technique of creating the joints by

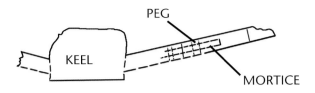

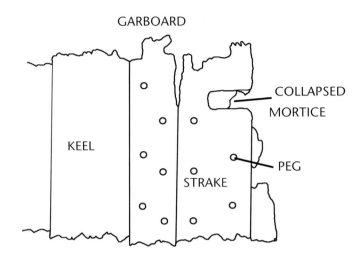

Wreck of Ulu Burun (14th century BC). The assembly of the planking and the keel is constructed by tenon and mortice joints. After C. Pulak, reproduced in P. Pomey (ed.), *La navigation dans l'Antiquité*, 1997, p. 91.

tenons plugged into mortices has recently been brought to light on the wreck, probably of Syro–Palestinian origin, of Ulu Burun (Turkey, *c*. 1320 BC),[17] but the very fragmentary state of the remains makes it difficult to know whether it was used exclusively or not, or even to know the architectural system of the ship. This technique was also apparently attested by Homer.[18] According to the interpretation of L. Casson, it was with tenons plugged into mortices that Odysseus assembled the boat on which he would leave the island of Calypso to sail back to his native land.[19] Finally, and quite recently, the Phoenician wreck of *Mazarron* (Carthagena, 7th century BC) provided evidence of mortice and tenon joints for the planking and assemblage by splicing for the frame.[20] In this case, it is difficult for the moment to say whether this is a tradition that practised mixed assemblage right from the start, or whether this was already a later phase of evolution.[21]

In short, it may be deduced that the two techniques of assemblage coexisted for a long time in the Mediterranean, either independently or in combination.[22] However, it is difficult, given the

7   P. Lipke, in S. McGrail, E. Kentley, *Sewn Plank Boats*, 1985, p. 26 and fig. 3; C. Haldane, in *Tropis* IV, 1996, pp. 235-236.

8   C. Haldane, in *Tropis* IV, 1996, pp. 236-241.

9   C. Haldane, *IJNA* 19, 1990, pp. 135-137.

10  B. Landström, *Ships of the Pharaohs*, 1970, p. 28; J. Rougé, *La marine dans l'Antiquité*, 1975, pp. 39-41.

11  S. Vinson, *ZPE* 113, 1996, pp. 197-204, announcing the study he has made of an Egyptian text of the Ramesside period (c. 1200 BC) alluding to this method. In spite of the different pieces of evidence brought together by the authors who have just been quoted, A. Nibbi, *RdE* 44, 1993, pp. 81-101 thinks that the Nile ships were caulked, on their submerged parts, with the aid of pieces of sewn leather, whatever the material from which this hull was built.

12  P. Pomey, in D. Meeks, D. Garcia (ed.), *Techniques et économie antiques et médiévales*, 1997, pp. 195-203; *id.*, in P. Pomey (ed.), *La navigation dans l'Antiquité*, 1997, pp. 90-93.

13  L. Basch, *The Mariner's Mirror* 64, 1978, p. 99 he considers that the technique of sewn frameworks is an Egyptian invention.

14  P. Chuvin, J. Yoyotte, *RevArch* I, 1986, pp. 50-51, who considers that the practise of sewing planks together is an Egyptian invention.

15  L. Basch, *Le Musée imaginaire de la marine antique*, 1987, pp. 42-54; D. Meeks, in D. Meeks, D. Garcia (ed.), *Techniques et économie antiques et médiévales*, 1997, pp. 175-194.

16  See J. R. Steffy, *Wooden ship building and the interpretation of shipwrecks*, 1994, pp. 23-36 and C. Haldane, in *Tropis* IV, 1996, pp. 235-244. According to C. Haldane, most of the joints in the boats of Dashur were remade in the modern period and the splices, today very residual, were doubtless more numerous at the time. C. Haldane also points out the recent discovery, at Mataria, near Cairo, of a 5th-century BC boat, Egyptian in type but with its planking joined together by tenons plugged into mortices, according to the Mediterranean technique.

17  C. Pulak, *AJA*. 92/1, 1988, pp. 1-37; J. R. Steffy, *op. cit.*, pp. 36-37.

18  Homer, *Odyssey*, V, 244-245.

19  L. Casson, *AJP* 85, 1964, pp. 61-64.

20  I. Neguervela, *et al.*, *IJNA* 24/3, 1995, pp. 189-197.

21  P. Pomey (ed.), *La navigation dans l'Antiquité*, 1997, pp. 89-93.

22  The method of assemblage by splices in naval construction is well attested, long after the method of mortice and tenon joints was mastered. Thus, a ship from the Augustan age, found on the Adriatic coast, raises the problem of the survival of certain techniques that should have been supplanted by others: M.-B. Carre, in D. Meeks, D. Garcia (ed.), *Techniques et économie antiques et médiévales*, 1997, pp. 204-205.

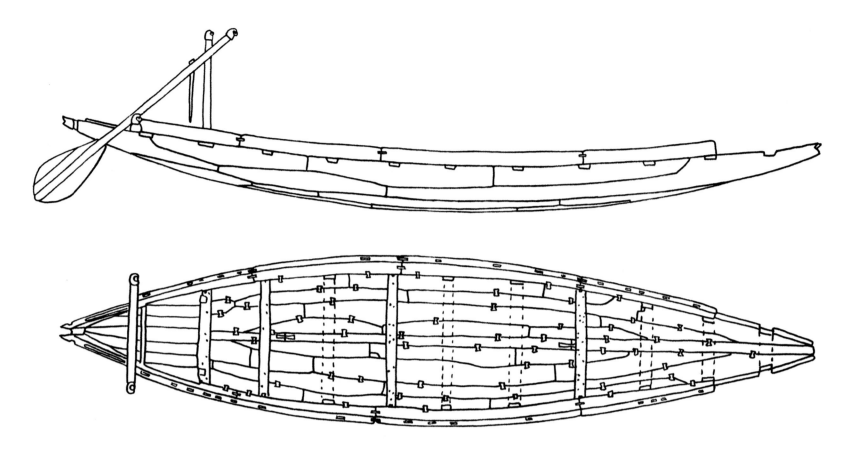

Plan of the barque of Dashur, Middle Kingdom, Museum of Cairo. Without keel or ribs, reinforced solely by transversal beams, these Nile barques were assembled by tenons and splices. Drawing after P. Pomey (ed.), *La navigation dans l'Antiquité*, 1997, p. 90, and R. Partridge, *Transport in Ancient Egypt*, 1996, p. 49.

data currently available, to specify the area of development of each of these two techniques. Nonetheless, it is known that assemblage by splices was less common in the 6th century BC, whereas the most ancient testimony of mortice and tenon assembly refers rather to a pre-Phoenician and Phoenician context. It would be tempting, as a hypothesis, to see this as indicating the extent of development of these two techniques. In favour of this hypothesis, the testimony of Cato[23] may be cited who refers to mortice and tenon assemblage as *coagmenta punicana*.[24] In the light of such a hypothesis, it is likely that the adoption of mortice and tenon assemblage in the milieu that traditionally practised assemblage by splices or by splices and mortice and tenon together could have taken place under Punic influence.

It is easier to ascertain some of the reasons that would have motivated the adoption of mortice and tenon joints to the detriment of assemblage by splices. Taking into account the fragility of assemblage by splices, and their short lifespan, mortice and tenon assemblage comes with definite advantages. In the first place, it frees the need to remake the splices on a regular basis, as their short lifespan makes necessary.[25] In the second place, it is more solid, a matter of some significance once the network of tenons has become even denser.[26] This last quality enabled ships to increase in size, and thus tonnage, and it is doubtless significant that mortice and tenon assemblage was, as observed, adopted on the biggest wrecks of the ships that were designed for trade.[27]

## II.1.2. The planking

Herodotus stated that, not having trees that would yield big planks, the Egyptians used cargo boats made of acacia wood, one of the few trees to be found in relative abundance in the country, which they 'saw into planks two cubits long, which they then assemble like bricks'; to give the ship the desired shape, 'they fix these planks together with long pegs very close together'.[28] In fact, a tomb painting (*c.* 2000 BC) found at Beni Hassan and often reproduced shows a hull under construction,[29] made of a real patchwork of small planks. This painting was corroborated by the discovery in 1893 of several ships built in accordance with this procedure. The only difference lies in the fact that, contrary to what Herodotus says, the timber of the planking is not of uniform size. Likewise, the description he gives of the way they are linked together does not exactly correspond to reality, unless the word he uses, *pyknos*, and whose meaning is not really known, had a more specific sense. In fact, the timbers are joined by numerous mortices carefully fitted together.[30]

23  Cato, *On agriculture*, XXI, 18, 9.

24  A. W. Sleeswyk, *IJNA* 9/3, 1980, pp. 243-244; L. Basch, *The Mariner's Mirror* 67/3, 1981, pp. 245-250 had deduced from this that the Romans had adopted the technique of mortice and tenon assemblage of Punic origin via the Etruscans.

25  J. Hornell, *Water Transport*, 1946, p. 236; L. Varadarajan, *Sewn boats of Lakshadweep*, 1994.

26  J. R. Steffy, in *Tropis* III, 1995, pp. 417-428.

27  P. Pomey, in D. Meeks, D. Garcia (ed.), *op. cit.*, p. 201.

28  Herodotus, II, 96.

29  L. Casson, *Ships and Seamanship*, 1971, figs 11 and 13.

30  J. Rougé, *La marine dans l'Antiquité*, 1975, p. 42.

After this particular case, which should not be applied to all Egyptian ships, it is worth bearing in mind that there are normally two main types of planking: what is called carvel built and clinker built.

- Carvel built: the planking is placed adjacently, with the planks sometimes right next to each other; the wood is shaped so that each piece fits into the next.
- Clinker built: the upper plank overlaps the lower plank.

The ancients, at least in the Mediterranean, seem to have used exclusively carvel built planking, but the real problem is that of the assemblage between the planks and the strakes (horizontal lines of planks). Numerous texts mention sewn ships (*nauis sutilis* in Latin): what does this mean? The expression needs to be understood literally. Even if this type of boat seems to have disappeared from the Mediterranean world by the time Virgil speaks of them,[31] it persisted elsewhere. The best example of this technique is, once again, that of the funerary barque of Khufu. The planks are maintained with the aid of tenons that fit into mortices hollowed out on both sides in the full thickness of the plank, and the whole assembly is kept in place by ropes passing inside V-shaped holes made in the inner part of the planks. In the Graeco-Roman period, the normal form of assemblage consisted of using mortice and tenon joints – very numerous and often arranged in a quincunx within the planking – which are then held firmly in place by nails of copper and, later, iron. Only a few rare ships, constructed with their carcass forward, have their planking nailed directly on to it.[32]

Once the carcass and the planking had been joined together, it became necessary to set up the wales designed to reinforce the cohesion and strength of the ship. These appear very clearly on most depictions from the Graeco-Roman period onwards; they were

reinforcements of certain upper strakes that formed sallies on the surface of the hull, and their number varied from ship to ship. One curious feature is that certain Egyptian depictions, such as those of the ships of Sahure, seem to have a supplementary seam in the guise of the wale, and this seam reinforces the yoking of the upper strakes. It is also at this point that, when there is one – which is the case for all big cargo ships – the inner planking is constructed within the carcass: this inner planking protects the cargo from water seeping in, and the water can thus gather in the bilge without getting into the inside of the ship. Then, once the inner planking is complete, the decks are constructed.

Egyptian ships always have decks, if one can call a 'deck' what, after all, is merely a floor. Indeed, as a consequence of the shallowness and reduced dimensions of the carcass, there was no question of embarking merchandise, or even men, inside Egyptian ships. So, on the numerous beams, which also served as rowing benches, a floor was put down covering the entire length of the ship or leaving free a more or less broad strip on each side to enable the rowers to sit down.

## II.1.3. The materials and the sheathing

Over and above the obvious interest of dendrochronology, the anatomical study (and the study of the morphological characteristics of the construction elements) is correctly seen these days as equally fundamental for research into maritime carpentry as it has developed within the framework of studies in naval archaeology, and as a good way of gaining a better understanding of the selection criteria and modes of use of wood in naval architecture, from the choice of

---

31    Virgil, *The Aeneid*, VI, 413-414.
32    J. Rougé, *La marine dans l'Antiquité*, 1975, p. 42.

Assemblage of a barque by means of short pieces of wood, tomb of Khnumhotep, Beni Hassan, Middle Kingdom. After L. Basch, *Égypte, Afrique & Orient 1*, 1996, p. 3. © L. Basch

species with an eye to their eventual use, to their setting in place, via their sawing, shaping and assembling. Dendrochronological and dendromorphological observations of the wood of several ancient wrecks found in the Mediterranean concern both the choice of species and their use in view of the position of the pieces of the frame within the overall structure of the hull. Macroscopic analyses bear on the morphology and sawing of the pieces of the frame and lead to the recognition of the way in which the management of the supply of curved, cross-grained, or straight pieces of wood was effected.

They also permit the reconstruction, via the transformation of raw material into worked pieces, of the skills of maritime carpenters. This recent research allows several elements of analysis.[33] Thus, for instance, there is the small number of species that were used in the building of the same ship – this appears as a factor making for homogeneity and often, when noble species were used, as a guarantee of quality. However, diversity of species is not necessarily, *a priori*, a criterion of quality. It can be a reflection of the heterogeneity of structures, problems in the supply or the rational use of the wood available, as well as resulting from phenomena of repair which did not affect the homogeneity of the essential parts of the structure. In response to the mechanical demands of any given piece, the maritime carpenters of antiquity could select species whose characteristics as wood (an intrinsic factor) were mechanically speaking the best adapted.

Next to that was the choice of anatomical characteristics conferred by the conditions in which the trees had grown (extrinsic factors). The macroscopic observation of the wood (morphology and sawing of the pieces) has led researchers to note an optimization in the use of the raw wood as fashioned by ancient carpenters. Two reasons may be advanced to explain this optimization of the wood used as raw material. On the one hand, economic reasons linked to problems in the availability of the material, delays in transporting it, and, probably, its cost. On the other hand, mechanical reasons related to the fact that differences in shrinkage and variation in size from one type of sawing to another may have an effect on the upkeep of the joints, if eventual deformations are to be avoided and the arrangement kept watertight. Maritime carpenters, visibly aware of the very limited character of local resources in wood that was usable for shipbuilding, seem to have given great importance to the varying availability of supply, to recycling, to the use of cross-grained wood and, if necessary, pre-formed wood, when the shape of the pieces required it. The type of sawing used also took into account the management of wooded areas and the economic imperatives linked to delays in construction and the need for rapid delivery.

Despite the difficulties inherent in the sources (problems in identification, the non-existence of any wreck of an Egyptian sea ship, and so on), it has been possible to draw up a picture of the resources of vegetable origin in the Nile Valley[34] and their use in naval construction. Big trees, especially those capable of providing beams and long straight-lined planks, are rare in Egypt. This paucity of wood of a certain quality has often been underlined, as has its consequence: the need to import this wood either from Lebanon[35] or from Nubia, at the dawn of Pharaonic history. However, this fact does not for all that imply, as there has sometimes been a tendency to believe, that the Nile Valley was always lacking in trees worthy of the name. Without going as far as to constitute a real forest gallery, the natural risings running parallel to the river were wooded; likewise, in the Neolithic

subpluvial period, from the 5th to the 3rd millennium BC, numerous trees grew along the rivers flowing into the Nile that were then active, as well as in the savannas that encircled the alluvial valley. The trees that originated in the Nile Valley and the surrounding steppes were widely used at every period; they included the acacia, the sycamore and the tamaris, together with three varieties of palm tree, the jujube, the persea and the willow.[36] Their use in Egypt is attested from the Predynastic period onwards, and sometimes even from the end of the Paleolithic. There are several species of acacia in the Nile Valley. Its very hard wood is difficult to work, but it is used in shipbuilding (and in carpentry). The Egyptians used the wood of the acacia that grew in abundance in their country; they also used the wood of the sycamore for the same reason. P. Vernus has shown that the term designating wooded expanses (*št3.w*) was applied to the areas where wood was grown and cut, especially in Middle Egypt.[37] These wooded zones, used to obtain wood for building, are mentioned by Theophrastus and by Pliny the Elder:

> *The acacia owes its name 'spiny' to the fact that the tree is covered all over with spines, apart from the trunk; there are spines on the branches, the young shoots and the leaves. It is a large tree, which is sawn into scantlings of twelve cubits' length. There are two varieties: 'the "white" and the "black". (The wood of) the "white" has no resistance and rots easily; (that of the "black") is solider and rots less easily; thus it is used in naval constructions for the frames. [...] It is a common species, which in the nome of Thebes forms a great wood where there also grow the oak, the persea in abundance, and the olive.'[38]*

> *Of no less repute among them is the spiny acacia, at least the black sort, since it never deteriorates in water, and thus is frequently employed to construct the flanks of ships; as for the white sort, it rots easily. It is found in the environs of Thebes, in the company of the oak, the persea and the olive, 300 stadia from the Nile, but in a wooded region, watered by its own sources.[39]*

Upper Egypt and especially the region of Coptos was famous for its forests in close proximity to the naval dockyards.[40] The jujube tree (*Ziziphus spina Christi*), an African tree, is also very hard; in carpentry it is used especially to make pegs for assemblages. The tenons on the barque of Khufu are made of jujube wood. Three varieties of palm tree are known from earliest times. The date palm

33　See F. Guibal, P. Pomey, in É. Rieth (ed.), *Méditerranée antique*, 1998, pp. 159-175.

34　L. Keimer, *Die Gartenpflanzen im Alten Ägypten*, 1924; V. L. Täckolm, M. Drar, *Flora of Egypt*, 1950-1954; *LÄ, s.v.* 'Flora', 'Holz', 'Holzbau'; J. Vercoutter, *L'Égypte et la vallée du Nil*, 1992, pp. 44-52.

35　In particular, cedar, cypress and pine (A. Lucas, J. R. Harris, *Ancient Egyptian Materials and Industries*, 1962, pp. 429-439). However, we need to note that the lack of information on the ancient flora of the Delta allows a question mark to hang over the possible presence of these trees even in Egypt, during the humid climatic phases of the prehistoric period (A. Nibbi, in L. Krzyzaniak, M. Kousiewicz (ed.), *Origin and early Development of Food-producing Cultures in North-Eastern Africa*, 1984, pp. 287-293).

36　A. Lucas, J. R. Harris, *op. cit.*, pp. 428-455.

37　P. Vernus, *RdÉ* 29, 1977, pp. 179-193.

38　Theophrastus, *De Historia Plantarum*, vol. II, book IV, 2, 8; translation by S. Amigues, Les Belles Lettres, 1989

39　Pliny, *Natural History*, XIII, 63, 19; trans. A. Ermout, Les Belles Lettres, 1956.

40　On this role of Coptos, see p. 76 *et seq.*

(*phoenix dactylifera*) had a wild variety (*phoenix silvestris*) that grew in the Kharga oasis in the Upper Paleolithic. It seems that it was only from the Middle Kingdom onwards (2040-1782 BC), at the end of the 3rd millennium BC, that the Egyptians managed to master the techniques to make it bear fruit (pollination). Already before then, the palm date was used as wood for carpentry. The doum palm, with its characteristic bifurcated trunk, is found only in Upper Egypt, in Nubia and in the oases. Its very hard, non-fibrous wood, is also used in construction. The persea (*mimusops schimperi*), of Nubian origin, grew in the Egyptian Nile valley as early as predynastic times; it was one of the trees of the ancient Egyptian landscape. Its wood was hard and sometimes used. The willow (*salix sasaf*), whether native or not to the Nile Valley, was known there in very ancient times for its very resistant wood. The sycamore (*ficus sycomorus L.*) is a fig tree and has nothing in common with the sycamore of cold climates which is a maple. It was acclimatised in Egypt from the Neolithic, and its wood has been used ever since that period.

In addition to the species that have just been enumerated and that form the essential part of the arboreal flora of Egypt to be used for their wood, there was also the carob tree (*ceratonia siliqua*), acclimatised in Egypt from the 1st Dynasty (3050-2890 BC) for its fruit and its hard wood. The trees native to the Nile Valley were amply sufficient for the needs of a nascent civilisation, with a low population density. However, these resources in wood and in products derived from trees rapidly became insufficient. This relative penury resulted partly from the increasing dryness of the climate that entailed the disappearance of trees from the savanna and the banks of the Nile tributaries, and partly from the wood clearances effected so as to cultivate the alluvial valley; and partly, too, from the sudden demographic upsurge that increased the country's needs from the Thinite era onwards. These various different causes explain the way that the Egyptians resorted to an appreciable level of importation either of wood or of trees for transplanting, brought from Syria and Nubia.

Nubia provided Egypt with ebony and acacia, the latter supplementing local production. The biography of Weni, governor of the whole of Upper Egypt in the time of Pepi I (2332-2283 BC), refers to trees being cut down in Nubia.[41]

From Syro-Palestine came, in succession,[42] in the Predynastic period, and during the first dynasties, the conifers, the cedar of Lebanon, the cypress and pine of Aleppo, and the juniper; in the Old Kingdom the fir tree, and the yew in the Middle Kingdom.[43] In the 18th Dynasty (1570-1293 BC), following deep penetration into Asia Minor, the import of wood intensified and new species of trees were introduced into the Egyptian Valley: the oak, the maple, the ash, the liquidambar, the elm, the almond, the pomegranate, the olive tree. More often than not the wood was imported, but the trees themselves were also transplanted into Egypt, where they became acclimatised.

In the customs register of the satrapy of Egypt,[44] as on the Stele of Naukratis,[45] a distinction is drawn, with reference to the cargoes of wood imported into Egypt, between the wood for construction (the raw material) and the pieces of wood already worked. As for the use of different kinds of wood in Egyptian naval construction in the Achaemenid era, the reader should be referred to the famous papyrus detailing the repair of a boat at Elephantine.[46]

The ancient reputation enjoyed by Phoenician wood persisted into the Achaemenid period, since it was cedars of Lebanon that were delivered to Jerusalem for the building of the Temple, but also used for the roofs of the Temple of Apollo at Utica and Herakles at Cadiz.[47] The cypresses of Cyprus and the forests of the island were just as highly reputed, and their wood used in naval construction: deliveries of Cypriot wood to Egypt are mentioned from the period of the El-Amarna letters, and Strabo refers to the fact that the forests were cleared for all those who desired to use the wood for shipbuilding.[48]

Wood that is in permanent contact with water allows it to slowly seep in, especially along the seams, however tightly fitted they are; in addition, the wood is sooner or later attacked by ship worms and other crustaceans. To guard against these dangers, two remedies were used in antiquity, as in later periods. The first was, of course, the caulking of the joints. This process can use various materials of vegetable origin whether or not they lend themselves to being turned into tow. The Egyptians sometimes used papyrus leaves to caulk their ships. Once the caulking was complete, the quick works were given a coating of bitumen or liquid pitch.[49] An interesting detail from the letter dating from the New Kingdom that belongs to the Hittite archives of Boghazköy[50] concerns caulking with the aid of bitumen, a practice which the archaeological or textual evidence of Egypt has not brought to light, at least for the Pharaonic period.[51] The fact that it was the Pharaoh who advised the Hittite king to caulk his ship with bitumen suggests that the technique was known in Egypt in this period. It seems that it was a particularity proper to sea ships since the waterproofing of Nile vessels was generally achieved by pulling the mesh of the papyrus fibres that bound the different parts of the hull together very tightly.[52]

41    J. H. Breasted, *Ancient Records of Egypt*, I, 1907, § 324; J. Vercoutter, *L'Égypte et la vallée du Nil*, 1992, p. 330.

42    A. Lucas, J. R. Harris, *Ancient Egyptian Materials and Industries*, 1962, pp. 429-434.

43    The term *ˁš* designates the Cilician fir (*Abies cilicica Carr.*): R. Germer, *Flora des Pharaonischen Ägyptischen*, 1985, pp. 7-8, 92; A. H. Gardiner, *AEO* I, 8-9, n. L; R. A. Caminos, *Late-Egyptian Miscellanies*, 1954, p. 29; W. Helck, *Materialien zur Wirtschaftsgeschichte des Neuen Reiches*, v, 1964, pp. 874, 905; *LÄ* VI, s.v. 'Tanne', col. 210; G. Charpentier, *Recueil de matériaux épigraphiques relatifs à la botanique*, 1986, pp. 176-181; P. Grandet, *Le papyrus Harris I, BiÉtud* 109, 1994, vol. 2, n. 146. The term *mry* probably designated the cedar of Lebanon to the Egyptians (*Cedrus libani Loud.*): R. A. Caminos, *op. cit.*, p. 122; J. J. Janssen, *Commodity Prices*, 1975, p. 205; G. Charpentier, *op. cit.*, 1986, pp. 342-343; R. Germer, *Flora des Pharaonischen Agypten*, 1985, pp. 6-7; *LÄ* VI, s.v. 'Zeder', col. 1357-1358; *AnLex* 79.1272; P. Grandet, *op. cit.*, n. 558. The terms *ḥntš* and *tp-ḥntš* designated the forests of Lebanon: W. F. Edgerton, J. A. Wilson, *Historical Records of Ramsès III, SAOC* 12, 1936, p. 116 and n. 1, 6; R. Givéon, *Les bédouins Shosou*, 1971, p. 189 (12); P. Vernus, *RdÉ* 29, 1977, p. 187, n. 77; *LÄ* III, s.v. 'Libanon', col. 1013-1014; P. Grandet, *op. cit.*, n. 146.

44    B. Porten, A. Yardeni, *Textbook of Aramaic Documents from Ancient Egypt*, III, 1993; P. Briant, R. Descat, in N. Grimal, B. Menu (ed.), *Le commerce, BiÉtud* 121, 1998, pp. 59-104. For this text and a complete bibliography, see pp. 420-432.

45    For the Stele of Naukratis see, M. Lichtheim, *Ancient Egyptian Litterature*, III, 1980, p. 88.

46    A. Cowley, *Aramaic Papyri of the Fifth Century B.C.*, 1923, n° 26 (AP 26); P. Grelot, *Documents araméens d'Égypte*, 1972, pp. 283-295 (DAE 61); id., *Semitica* 20, 1970, p. 23-31; D. Whitehead, *Early Aramaic Epistolography*, 1974, pp. 119-154; B. Porten (ed.), *The Elephantine Papyri in English*, 1996, pp. 115-122, particularly n. 26-36). Also of interest are the articles by J. Elayi and C. Zaccagnini concerning the importation of food in Mesopotamia: J. Elayi, *JESHO* 31, 1988, pp. 14-41 and C. Zaccagnini, in E. Acquaro (ed.), *Il Mediterraneo tra tradizione e ihnovazione*, I, 1996, pp. 451-466.

47    M. Gras, P. Rouillard, J. Teixidor, *L'univers phénicien*, 1979, p. 104.

48    Strabo, XIV, 6, 5; Pliny, *Natural History*, XVI, 203.

49    J. Rougé, *La marine dans l'Antiquité*, 1975, p. 46.

50    Reexamined by E. Edel, *Die ägyptisch-hethitische Korrespondenz aus Boghazköi in babylonischer und hethitischer Sprache*, 1994. See D. Meeks, in D. Meeks, D. Garcia (ed.), *Techniques et économie antiques et médiévales*, 1997, pp. 179-180.

51    For the Roman era and regarding the barque of Isis at Philae: S. Vinson, *ZPE* 113, 1996, p. 200 n. 18.

52    D. Jones, *A Glossary of Ancient Egyptian Nautical Titles and Terms*, 1988, p. 208 n° 1 mentions a term meaning 'to smooth or level' (a surface) and that is also used in relation to river boats. This may be some kind of caulking.

## II.1.4. The berthing

Once the ship has a deck, it becomes vital to place a protective barrier around it. This barrier is usually formed by the upper part of the planking, or more exactly by a bulwark which rests on the last strake, the gunwale, and can be extended, if necessary (in the case of bad weather, for instance) by moveable wash strakes. On the depictions of Syro-Palestinian *mnš*-ships from the tomb of Kenamun, above the gunwale, a vertical fence acts like wash strakes and protects the cargo from the sea's assaults.[53]

Finally it is on the gunwale, towards the prow, that are found the bridges of planks necessary to the loading and unloading of the cargo.

Only some Nile ships bore in their middle section a chamber or tent on the deck serving to accommodate the persons of quality who sailed on the river. It seems that not until the Hellenistic period, on the Mediterranean, merchant ships sailed equipped with a chamber at the rear of the ship above the deck: this was the *thalamus* of the Greeks, the *diaeta* of the Romans. This chamber, whose roof acted as a command bridge and a post for the helmsman, was in principle meant for the captain and the economic services of the ship; it could be placed at the disposal of passengers of note, whenever there were any such on board. On normal ships, there were surely no other chambers at the disposal of passengers; the latter would have to travel on deck, as is demonstrated in practically all the tales of maritime voyages that have been preserved. The *thalamegos* ships with multiple chambers are Egyptian luxury ships that seem not to have sailed anywhere other than the Nile. Nonetheless, one of the texts concerning them described a luxury boat, a sort of floating

town, designed to sail from Egypt to the Troad. But the fact that it foundered confirms its unsuitability for seafaring voyages.[54]

## II.2. Rigging and outfitting

### II.2.1. The girdles

Technical limitations probably meant that perfect coordination between the hull and the frame could not be ensured. To reinforce this cohesion, therefore, a whole system of tension or tightening cables was used, which formed veritable girdles around the ship.

The ships of Sahure have a 'decorated strip' in a broken line along the upper level of the hull, all along the ship's length. It is approximately two-thirds up the side, and this cannot be the rails. E. Assmann thinks that it is a beam-shelf, an inside strake, solidly spliced, in which the beams rested.[55] The beam-shelf was placed inside the hull, but to maintain it in position, the planking had to be pierced with several holes through which a rope passed. This was wrapped round the beam-shelf and the planking successively, and thus made it possible to fix the inner strake firmly to the wall. In addition to the horizontal band there are vertical bands placed fore and aft, either between the bottom of the hull and the lengthwise band, or between the latter and the upper planking, and analogous

---

53    N. de G. Davies, R. O. Faulkner, *JEA* 33, 1947, pl. viii.

54    Maximus of Tyre, *Dissertations*, I, 3. cf. J. Rougé, *La marine dans l'antiquité*, 1975, p. 48.

55    E. Assmann, in L. Borchardt, *Das Grabdenkmal des Königs Sahure*, II, 1913, p. 138.

Reconstruction of a ship of Sahure. © Science Museum

bands along the raised part of the stem and the stern. C. Boreux supposes that these vertical bands constituted so many splices which, by bringing together the sides of the ships where their surfaces intersected, at the fore and aft of the barques, protected the stem and the stern against the repercussions that would have been entailed by the effort of a tension cable that would, in stormy weather, have acted on the extremities with sudden powerful jolts.[56]

The ships of Sahure also have two girdles fore and aft, composed of strong cables; they end in carefully spliced eyes (one at each extremity) within which a spar passes. This spar also passes through the eye of a long axial cable that joins the forward girdle to the aft girdle and which, to keep the deck clear, rests on a series of stanchions. The whole is kept under tension by a small spar passed between the fibres of the axial cable in its middle and which is blocked on the central stanchion when the desired tension is reached.

This procedure is depicted on the ships of the New Kingdom, those of Queen Hatshepsut (1498-1483 BC), but with some interesting modifications. The fore and aft girdles have now become complete belts of rope that penetrate the ship's deck by hawse holes; in addition, the forward girdle, the aft girdle, and the axial cable seem to be the same cable. Furthermore, it is possible that the system for maintaining tension was no longer the same; according to some authors, the tension was now obtained by raising the ropes more or less high up the mast with the aid of an annex rope enabling the whole to be kept in position once the desired tension had been obtained.[57] Such a system, which is hardly ever seen outside ships

Papyrus fragment on which is drawn a barque with oars, necropolis of El-Gebelein, Predynastic period, early 4th millennium BC, Museum of Turin.
© The Art Archive/Egyptian Museum, Turin/Dagli Orti

designed for long voyages, equipped with a maximum sized carcass, must have had a twofold purpose: to ensure the cohesion of the hull and the carcass, but also to ensure the cohesion of fore and aft as in certain types of Chinese boat.[58]

It is to be noted that the argument by which the tension cable was invented to make up for the only drawback of a type of construction that was good only for river navigation needs to be seriously qualified. In the first place, it does not take into account the fact that there exists at least one image of an Egyptian ship designed for river sailing, and this is also equipped with a tension cable: the

56   C. Boreux, *Études de nautique égyptienne, MIFAO* I, 1925, p. 478.

57   J. Vandier, *Manuel d'archéologie égyptienne*, V, 1969, pp. 883 and 933.

58   J. Poujade, *La route des Indes et ses navires*, 1946, p. 288.

Nile barque, Saqqara, Middle Kingdom, 6th Dynasty, c. 2323–2150 BC. © Photo: Gianni Dagli Orti/CORBIS

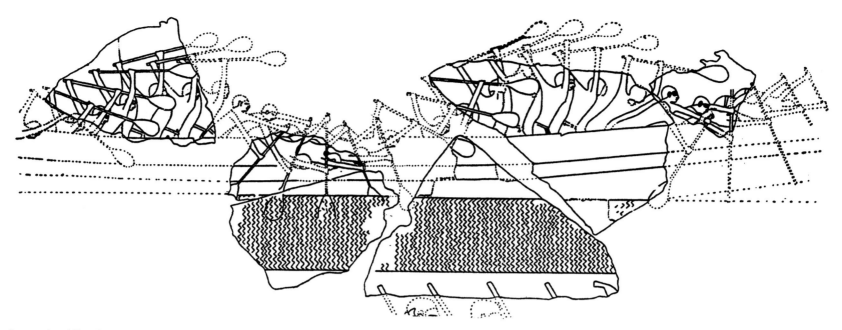

Scene of paddling, funerary temple of Userkaf, after L. Basch, *Le Musée imaginaire de la marine*, 1987, p. 125. © L. Basch

obelisk-carrier of Hatshepsut at Deir el-Bahari.[59] In reality, the presence of a tension cable on an Egyptian boat does not necessarily mean that it was conceived for sea navigation, but only that once a certain size has been reached, this type of reinforcement became indispensable to make up for the structural weaknesses of boats whose ribbing probably included floor frames. On the other hand, as emphasised by L. Basch, 'the fact that cables were used to ensure the strength of the hull is not unique to Ancient Egypt. This method was reinvented in the 19th century to equip the great paddle steamers of the American rivers. These were still river boats, but the Greeks and the Romans used tension cables for their sea ships: *hypozomata* for the former and *tormenta* for the latter. Their function was barely different from that of their Egyptian equivalents, but they were arranged differently; probably inside the hull, since no surviving depiction of them has been found'.[60]

## II.2.2.  The means of propulsion

### The oar

Often associated with the sail, the oar is the common means of propulsion for small and medium-sized boats but also for bigger boats with a significant coefficient of elongation (length-to-breadth ratio). Egyptian paintings and bas-reliefs show a difference between the way a paddle was handled and the way an oar was handled.

The paddle was handled facing forward in the ship; in relation to the paddler, the movement of the blade in the water is effected from fore to aft. The movement of the rower, on the other hand, means that he is normally with his back to the fore of the boat and, in relation to him, the active movement of the blade goes from aft to fore. Furthermore, the paddle is free, while the oar is a lever whose fixed point is situated on the side of the ship on a special fitting permanently installed there.[61]

Egyptian rowing was a curious affair. 'First of all, the oar was nothing other than a paddle fixed on the gunwale, doubtless by a grommet, and its blade was not rectangular, but in the shape of a spearhead, and its point of attachment was located very close to the blade, hence the abnormal length of the handle. The rower had his feet on the bottom of the vessel, and the beams served as thwarts. The length of the handle explains the different successive postures of the rower: first, while standing, he pulled the blade as far as possible backwards to attack the water; then, as it passed through the water, he sat down and pulled his body strongly backwards; finally, as the blade emerged, he stood up again and, leaning forwards, pulled the oar back into attack position. This mode of navigation could not have been very suitable for seafaring, since rolling and pitching would have considerably hampered the rower in his movements. This is probably why it is found only in Egypt and for sailing on the Nile'.[62]

On the depictions of sea ships, the rowers were installed on the deck and their oars were fixed to the base of the bulwark and equipped with thole pins and grommets.

The oar has one advantage over the sail: it is not dependent on the wind. The use of the oar made it possible to bring the boat up to the quay, always a delicate operation, or to allow it to move out to sea and pick up the wind, but also to bring it up a river or even make it move forward in a dead calm.

### The sail

The sail is the mode of propulsion *par excellence* of sea vessels, for 'true' sailing ships and mixed coasting vessels when the winds are favourable. The sail is to be understood as a real complex, including the mast, the yard, the sail properly speaking and the ropes that serve to keep them in place and manoeuvre them. This is acceptable usage for the definitive form of the system of sails. For the wealth of predynastic iconography enables judgement to be made of the first tentative steps in the quest for a mode of propulsion that could use the strength of the wind. Foliage of various shapes garnishing the

59   B. Landström, *Ships of the Pharaohs*, ,1970, pp. 128-133.
60   L. Basch, *Le Musée imaginaire de la marine*, 1987, p. 47.
61   J. Rougé, *op. cit.*, pp. 53-54.
62   *Id.*, p. 54. *cf.* C. Boreux, *Études de nautique égyptienne*, MIFAO I, 1925, pp. 319-331.

Terracotta vase decorated with a boat, Predynastic period, *c.* 3500-3100 BC. © Photo: Peter A. Clayton

prows of all the barques painted on Gerzean vases proves that palm fronds were used as 'sails'.[63] A similar method is used in Central Africa and in an estuary of the Cameroon.[64] The use of branches as rigging seems to have undergone a development at the end of the Gerzean period: behind the subsisting leafy branches is a kind of rectangular shield probably comprising a matting of woven vegetable material, fixed to a pole.[65] There is 'only this one example of this kind of rigging, which seems to indicate that it soon disappeared, probably a victim of its own success. Indeed, the crucial invention, that can be captured as it comes into being, and which was to enjoy a great future, is the mast. On the other hand, what constituted the sail could be advantageously replaced by a bigger surface area. For this, it was necessary to abandon the matting and replace it by a sail hung between two rods, to invent the sail hung between two yards. It is this kind of sail that suddenly emerges on a vase from the end of the predynastic period, on a Nubian rock painting that is probably contemporary with it, and on an incised Nubian limestone fragment probably contemporary with the first Egyptian dynasty. Thus to the time of the 32nd century BC, in Egypt, may be attributed the significant invention of a form of rigging including the mast, the yard and the sail'.[66] This Egyptian rigging underwent various adaptations in the course of its long history.

Most of the paintings and bas-reliefs of the Old Kingdom (2686-2181 BC) present a system of masting of an altogether original kind: the derrick mast, a designation derived from the hoisting machinery of the same name. This mast is formed of two uprights that are widely separated at the base and come together at the summit with the aid of a certain number of pieces comparable to the

Different types of prow shapes on barques painted on Gerzean vases, after L. Basch, *Le Musée imaginaire de la marine*, 1987, p. 49. © L. Basch

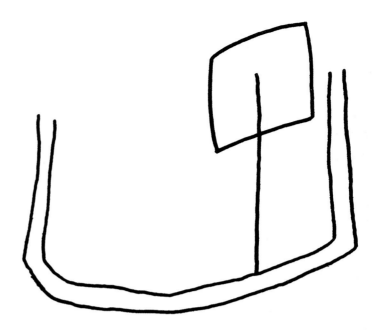

Rock painting at Gebel Sheikh Yacoub, Sudan, after L. Basch, *Le Musée imaginaire de la marine*, 1987, p. 50. © L. Basch

rungs of a ladder. Its form seems to stem from the necessity, for the original papyrus barques, of not bringing all the weight of the mast to bear on a single point.

Sometimes the mast ends in a pawl-head that forms a projection pointing backwards and must have been designed to ensure the position of the yard. 'When the mast was raised, the uprights were engaged in holes made within the floor, and the solidity of this implantation reinforced by ropes that bound it to the gunwale. This type of mast was that of the ships of Sahure; it is true that in this case it is not actually seen in service, but half-laid on the deck, its head resting on a support formed by two spars yoked by a non-taut cable. Derrick masts were not merely solidly fixed at their bases but also strongly braced. They had a bent mast-head stay that tied them to the fore, and a whole series of braces passing through holes made in the uprights of the mast and tying them to the aft.

The Old Kingdom was also acquainted with the single mast in the shape of a vertical pole fixed into the deck and one of the beams, as is seen on scale models; its base was, furthermore, consolidated by a solid spar which seems to have come from the bottom of the ship and to which it was solidly spliced. These masts seem to have been very high; they were situated very far forward on the ship. Subsequently, in the Middle Kingdom (2040-1782 BC), there were merely single masts which, although maintaining the same system of steps, were less tall and closer to the centre of the ship'.[67]

The single mast was that of the New Kingdom (1570-1070 BC) navy. According to the depictions, it seems to have been made of one piece. According to the studies of ships from the Roman period, this

63    cf. J. de Morgan, *La préhistoire orientale*, II, 1926, p. 268 fig. 296; *id.*, *Recherches sur les origines de l'Égypte*, I, 1897, p. 92 figs 240-246.
64    See L. Basch, *Le Musée imaginaire de la marine*, p. 49 and fig. 77, with bibliography.
65    Vase in the British Museum n° 36326 A.
66    L. Basch, *Le Musée imaginaire de la marine*, 1987, p. 49 and figs 79-81.
67    J. Rougé, *op. cit.*, p. 56-57; *cf.* J. Vandier, *Manuel d'archéologie égyptienne*, V, 1969, p. 881.

Relief from the Mastaba of Ty at Saqqara, Old Kingdom, 5ᵗʰ Dynasty, c. 2498-2345 BC. © Photo: David Fabre

single mast passed inside a beam or into a strong strake fixed on the keelson which attached it to a beam, and its base was lodged in a step solidly fixed on a keelson. This step was formed of a big block of wood in which a cavity had been dug to lodge the foot of the mast which was chocked by small planks. On trading ships the vessel was dismasted only in cases of absolute necessity. These masts were solidly braced both fore and aft, but also on the sides.

The square sail was used in Egypt throughout the Pharaonic period. Its basic principle remained the same, though that did not prevent it from undergoing a certain evolution, so that the sail of the Old Kingdom was different from that of the New Kingdom. Egyptian sails were characterised by the presence of a lower yard: the sail of the Old Kingdom was very high in comparison with its width and came quite down close to the deck, while the sail of the New Kingdom was, on the contrary, very broad and narrow and its lower yard was, in its normal position, very high above the deck.[68] The rigging of Syro-Palestinian *mnš*-ships, as represented in the tomb of Kenamun, was, by the proportions of the sail and its two yards balanced by numerous lifts, analogous in numerous respects to

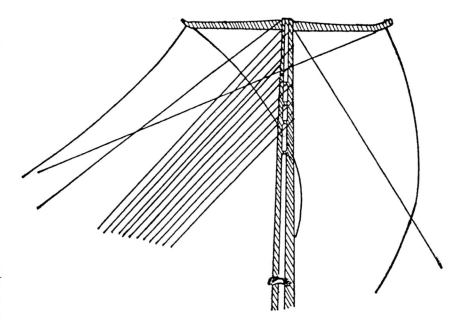

---

68    J. Rougé, *La Marine dans l'Antiquité*, 1975, pp. 59-60.

Crane mast from the Old Kingdom, after J. Rougé, *La Marine dans l'Antiquité*, p. 56.

Model of a Nile boat from the Middle Kingdom, necropolis of Beni Hassan, 12th Dynasty, *c.* 2000 BC, wood with stucco, painted. © Science Museum/Heritage Images

Egyptian rigging. It was, however, distinguishable in the way it was manoeuvred, since here the lower yard in its rest position joined the upper yard that remained stowed, and not the other way around.[69]

The sail was supported by a yard generally made of two spars firmly kept in place by a woolding, a narrow diameter rope system forming a series of half-hitches tightened close together. This yard was hoisted or lowered with the aid of a halyard that passed over a pulley or a masthead block and tackle; more often than not, this pulley was located in a mast-head dug into the mast itself (it is possible that in the Egyptian derrick mast the pulley was fixed to the pawl-head described above). Some scholars even think that there was, on several ships, a double halyard that would facilitate the manoeuvring of the yard and lessen the effort needed from the sailors.[70]

This yard was kept against the mast by a parrel. On several depictions are ropes linking the yard to the mast head: these ropes were what are called lifts. They appear on certain Egyptian ships from the Middle Kingdom, though the first ships did not possess any. The

Creto-Mycenaean ships also had them, to judge from preserved depictions. These lifts seem to have linked the yard to the mast head; they enabled the upper yard to be balanced and inclined.[71] However, not everybody agrees that they were in fact lifts. To resolve this problem, it is necessary to examine the sail itself and the way in which the sails were shortened, which these days is done by taking in reefs.

The complex of sail and yard was manoeuvred by at least two and perhaps three sorts of ropes in pairs. The yard was oriented and laid apeak depending on the wind, with the help of arms that extended from its ends. The sail, which followed the movement, was maintained at its base by sheets made fast at the lower corners (the

69  N. de G. Davies, R. O. Faulkner, *JEA* 33, 1947, pl. viii.

70  L. Casson, *Ships and Seamanship* 1971, pp. 259-263. J. Rougé, *La marine dans l'Antiquité*, 1975, p. 60.

71  This was particularly the case on Roman trading ships of the 1st century BC: see P. Pomey, in P. Pomey (ed.), *La navigation dans l'Antiquité*, 1997, p. 86.

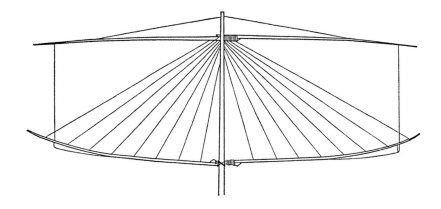

Egyptian sail from the New Kingdom, after J. Rougé, *La Marine dans l'Antiquité*, p. 60.

points); but, unlike modern sails, the sheets did not also have tacks. Finally, certain authors think that there were bowlines, ropes made fast to leech ropes, at their mid-point, which enabled the sail to stiffen better in the wind.

When thinking about the nautical qualities of ancient ships, the ship's capacity to sail upwind has to be borne in mind, essential for the regularity of the traffic. In the fine season, when the traffic is at its most intense, the different basins of the Mediterranean are subject to dominant wind systems, favourable on certain journeys but contrary on others. Sailing upwind and tacking require the ship to combine a certain number of qualities when it comes to its steering

apparatus, its sails and its bottom. It shall be observed that the double lateral rudder was a good device, not at all incompatible, in principle, with the practice of such manoeuvres.

Square rigging, however, has never been very suitable for sailing upwind. Nonetheless, the great flexibility of the square sail, and the advanced position of the centre of the sails (as the mast was always situated fore of the ship's centre), were very favourable to this tactic. This was all the more so in that the improvement in manoeuvres, and in particular the possible use of the bowline (that rope which allows the windward side of a sail to be opened and made taut, so as better to sail upwind) clearly show the care taken by sailors to improve the qualities of their rigging.

Several ancient texts indeed give a description of the manoeuvres that had to be made by a ship with one mast when, encountering a contrary wind, the captain still wanted to pursue his course by tacking.[72] The yard was first of all braced to be lowered into the position closest to the axis of the ship, then the sail was taken in at its rearward part so as to leave just a triangle at the front.

The *deliberate* peaking of a yard and its sail is not without its advantages at certain speeds: on ancient ships rigged with a square sail, 'it was sufficient to peak it to bring the centre of the sails to the aft of the centre of drift so that the ship would carry a weather helm and easily sail upwind'.[73] F. Beaudouin has demonstrated that from the

---

72   For the most recent description see: J. Rougé, *Archeonautica* 2, 1978, pp. 265-280.
73   N. Fourquin, in *Medieval Ships and the Birth of Technological Societies*, II, 1991, p. 431.

Reconstruction of a processional Nile barque from the New Kingdom. © Science Museum

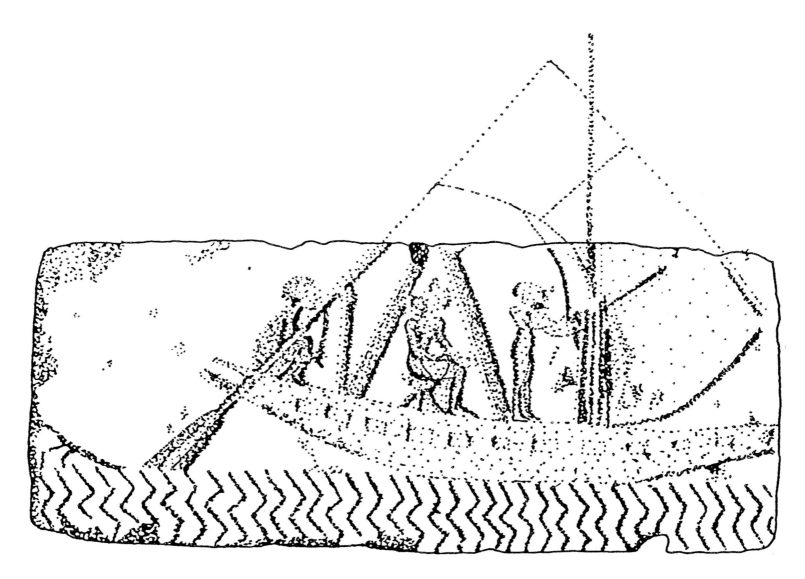

*Talatat* from the Amarna period, Hermopolis, New Kingdom, 18th Dynasty, *c.* 1364–1347, collection of Stéphane Cattaoui, drawing by H. Dinkel in S. Vinson, *Egyptian Boats and Ships*, 1994, p. 42.

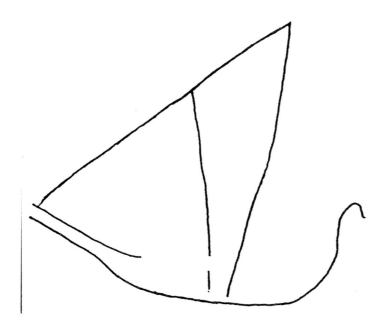

*Dipinto* depicting a small vessel with a lateen sail, Hypogeum no. 2, Anfouchy, Alexandria, probably 1st century BC, drawing after L. Basch, in D. Meeks, D. Garcia (ed.), *Techniques et économie antiques et médiévales*, 1997, fig. 1, p. 221.

18th Dynasty (1570-1293 BC) at the latest, the peaking of the yards must have been practised on the ships of Hatshepsut depicted in her funerary temple at Deir el-Bahari: the aim of this practice was to bring the centre of the sails aft (to sail upwind). The same author proposed a reconstruction of the rigging of a boat belonging to the flotilla of Tutankhamun with the yards inclined at 45°;[74] this theoretical suggestion was brilliantly confirmed by the discovery in the Stéphane Cattaui collection of a *talatat* from the Amarnean period, originally from Hermopolis and depicting a single barque peaked at 45°.[75]

This technique of sailing under peaking probably led to the conception of the lateen sail whose origin seems to lie in the first centuries AD. In hypogeum no. 2 of Anfouchy, in Alexandria, dating probably from the 3rd century BC, there is a series of graffiti, or rather *dipinti*, since the drawings were not incised but traced in charcoal, probably in the 1st century BC.

Among these *dipinti* two ships are depicted with a three-bladed

74   F. Beaudouin, *L'Ethnographie*, n.s., 60-61, 1966-1967, pp. 53-54, fig. 5.
75   S. Vinson, *JARCE* 30, 1993, p. 135, fig. 2; *id.*, *Egyptian Boats and Ships*, 1994, p. 42, fig. 29.

cutwater, characteristic of the Hellenistic period. A third *dipinto*, drawn in the same way, shows a barque equipped with a 'pure'[76] lateen sail; if it is contemporary with the first two, as the drawing technique seems to suggest, this would be the first representation of a lateen sail.[77]

Again in Alexandria, a *dipinto* dating probably from the 6th century BC, drawn on the wall of a house, shows a ship whose sail is most probably lateen: the yard is very peaked, but the design of the lower extremity of the sail is not altogether clear.[78] The painting of the ship decorating the monastic cell of the Kellia, some 80km from Alexandria, dating from AD 600-630, shows the depiction of a lateen sail[79] and is thus situated at the end of what was a very long process of evolution in Egypt, where there is no lack of chronological landmarks. Should we conclude from this that it was at Alexandria that the lateen sail came into being? Such a question goes far beyond the scope of this study. Nonetheless, it is certain that the great port of Alexandria was the ideal place to constitute a laboratory for new naval experiments.

Nonetheless, sailing by the bowsprit, in order to be profitable, also presupposes that the ship's keel possesses a significant drift surface (the lower part of the keel, which enables a course to be kept despite a contrary wind or current). Egyptian ships were very badly provided for from this point of view. However, the absence of a keel was certainly largely compensated for by the action of the tension cable.

To bring this chapter to a close, it is necessary to discuss the materials, usually of vegetable origin, that were used to make the sails and the ropes. The sails are generally made out of linen which means they can be both light and resistant. Linen (*Linum usitatissinum*) was used in Egypt from the Neolithic to make fabrics.[80] The thread, extracted from the fibre after a long and delicate process, constituted the textile *par excellence* of Pharaonic Egypt.[81] Papyrus stems were used to make ropes.[82] The same is true of the fibre of the date palm (*lif*, in Egyptian Arabic), which builds up between the trunk and the base of palms. Egyptian ropemakers and weavers used, from the Neolithic and ancient Predynastic periods, numerous vegetable materials, all of them native: a type of alfa (*desmotachya bipinatta*), a composite (*caruana pratensis*), hemp (*hibiscus cannabinus*) and the rush (*joncus arabicum*).[83]

## II.2.3. The steering mechanism

J. Rougé has described the Egyptian rudder thus: 'Originally, it seems to have been formed from several oars, hardly bigger than the sailing oars, manoeuvred at the stern by several helmsmen. Although in general they all appear on the same side, it is possible that this is an artistic convention and that they were also arranged on either side. Quite soon there appeared a real rudder formed of one, or two, oars whose blade was much bigger than that of a rowing oar. Placed at the aft, it rested on the gunwale, or passed through a hole made for this purpose at the summit of the planking; its very long handle was often supported on a small mast to which it must have been linked by a grommet. At its extremity there was a vertical helm that descended to the deck; it was this helm that was manoeuvred by the helmsman sitting behind it; in other words, the helmsman acted by rotating the blade around its axis, since the two points of support prevented it from being moved laterally. In the case where there were two oars on the same side, they were more often that not coupled by a horizontal spar equipped in its middle with a helm that made it possible to give

the two oars the same movement. These rudders are known above all through small and medium-sized Nile vessels.

As far as big ships are concerned, the steering mechanism of the vessels sent by Queen Hatshepsut (1498-1483) to the land of Punt provides a good example. This was formed by two enormous oars situated either side of the stern and each of them apparently handled by a helmsman; their handle passed into a grommet that held it against the gunwale, then rose above the deck slightly leaning forward, so that the blade, without being absolutely vertical, was nonetheless quite close to the vertical. Each handle rested on the fork of a small mast to which it was firmly attached by a rope; then, at its end, there was a vertical helm manoeuvred by the helmsman. Consequently, these oar-rudders could have been propelled by one movement alone: rotation.'[84]

Nonetheless, this type of rudder had several advantages over the stern rudder that succeeded it: it was much more sensitive and easier to manoeuvre. In fact, the blade of the rudder turned on its own axis and not on one of its edges, and the water's action was shared more or less equally over the surfaces on either side of the axis, diminishing by the same amount the pressure exerted by the speed of the vessel on the blade, so that the effort required from the helmsman was relatively small. This, then, is the principle of the balanced rudder.[85] In addition, while in this type of rudder the helmsman could not push the blade away from the edge to settle the ship better on the wave, he nonetheless preserved the possibility of doing it to a certain degree by acting simultaneously on the two helms.[86]

Apart from the efficiency of the steering oar, it could be shifted along the planking; thus, by combining the regulation of the boat's disposition with that of the position of the oars, it must have been possible to keep the boat perfectly balanced and enable it to head upwind in spite of its rudimentary rigging.[87]

The reliefs from the temple of Deir el-Bahari show certain differences in the manoeuvrability of the steering mechanism combined with the action of tension cables in accordance with the

76  L. Basch, *Le Musée imaginaire de la marine*, 1987, p. 480, fig. 1084; id., *The Mariner's Mirror* 75, 1989, p. 331, fig. 8.

77  L. Basch, in D. Meeks, D. Garcia (ed.), *Techniques et économie antiques et médiévales*, 1997, p. 221 fig. 11.

78  M. Rodziewicz, *Les habitations romaines tardives d'Alexandrie*, 1984, p. 221, fig. 250; L. Basch, *Graeco-Arabica* V, 1993, p. 51, fig. 23.

79  L. Basch, in D. Meeks, D. Garcia (ed.), *op. cit.*, p. 215 fig. 1; P. Pomey, in P. Pomey (ed.), *La navigation dans l'Antiquité*, 1997, p. 86.

80  However, up until now, toadflax (Linum bienne or angustifolium) has not been found in the Nile Valley. Does this mean that its cultivation originated in the east, where it is attested in more ancient times? Taking into account the complexity of the operations indispensable for the utilisation of its fibre (extraction, retting, crushing, swingling, weaving), linen must have become acclimatised in Egypt at the very start of the Neolithic (c. 5500 BC) and even before that.

81  For the meaning of *mhʿw*, 'linen', see J. J. Janssen, *Commodity Prices*, 1975; id., SAK 3, 1975, p. 151; W. Helck, *Materialien zur Wirtschaftsgeschichte des Neuen Reiches*, V, 1964, pp. 810-811; *LÄ* II, col. 256-257; AnLex 77.1812, 78.1815, 79.1299; G. Charpentier, *Recueil de matériaux épigraphiques relatifs à la botanique*, 1986, pp. 354-355; R. Germer, *Flora des Pharaonischen Agypten*, 1985, pp. 100-102. cf. J. Yoyotte, in *Dictionnaire de la civilisation égyptienne*, 1992, s.v. 'linen', pp. 149-150.

82  J. Yoyotte, in *Dictionnaire de la civilisation égyptienne*, Paris, 1992, s.v. 'papyrus', p. 212.

83  J. Vercoutter, *L'Égypte et la vallée du Nil*, 1992, p. 51. cf. J. Rougé, *La marine dans l'Antiquité*, 1975, p. 75.

84  J. Rougé, *op. cit.*, pp. 66-68. cf. C. Boreux, *Études de nautique égyptienne*, MIFAO L, 1925, pp. 387-403; J. Vandier, *Manuel d'archéologie égyptienne*, V, 1969, pp 741-748; P. Pomey, *op. cit.*, p. 87.

85  Cdt Guilleux de la Roerie, *Annales d'histoire économique et sociale*, 1935, pp. 564-583.

86  J. Rougé, *op. cit.*, p. 71.

87  A. Guillerm, *la marine dans l'Antiquité*, 1995, p. 9.

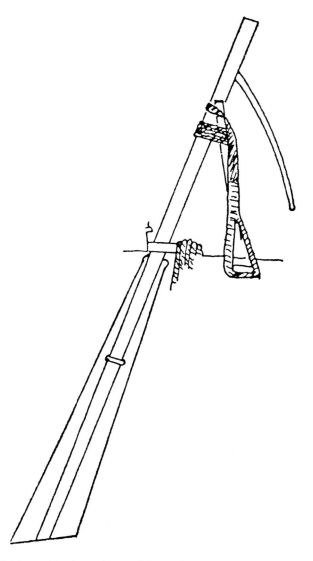

sailing conditions. On the lower register, in a scene on the right,[88] three ships have hoisted their sails.

The rowers are in action. On the ship to the far right each of the rudder oars is manoeuvred by a distinct person. The manoeuvring cables that enable a greater or lesser degree of freedom of movement to these oars are not taut; the torsion bars that serve to tighten them are absent.[89] In the situation described, the oars can easily be manoeuvred independently of one another. The slack manoeuvring cables enable one, as need be, to lay them flat against the sides of the ship or, on the contrary, to pull them free of them. Should it be concluded from this that this arrangement was designed to facilitate navigation in calm waters? The fact that the prows of the ships are turned towards the land leads to the supposition that this is a manoeuvre of the flotilla coming from Thebes: the boats are landing at a point where they can take in fresh supplies before leaving for Punt. The sequence of marine animals depicted on the ships along this lower register makes such a hypothesis uncertain. At the extreme right of the register a squid and a lobster are depicted, and perhaps several freshwater or brackish-water fish.[90] It is possible that this scene principally represents the last taking on of supplies at the borders of Egypt, then a navigation that progresses from freshwater to saltwater, with, perhaps, an intermediate passage in brackish waters.

On the second register, the scene on the left,[91] the land of Punt is shown. The ships are stationary and have 'touched land', their sails lowered, some distance from the beach, though they have not run aground. Nothing indicates that they have moored or dropped

Rudder of ships on Hatshepsut's expedition to Punt, drawing after J. Rougé, *La Marine dans l'Antiquité*, p. 67.

---

88  E. Naville, *The Temple of Deir el-Bahari*, III, 1898, pl. lxiii; D. Meeks, in D. Meeks, D. Garcia (ed.), *Techniques et économie antiques et médiévales*, 1997, fig. 3 p. 182 (drawing by M. Rival).

89  cf. R. O. Faulkner, *JEA* 26, 1940, p. 8; B. Landström, *Ships of the Pharaohs*, 1970, p. 127 (380).

90  E. Danelius, H. Steinitz, *JEA* 53, 1967, pp. 22-23.

91  E. Naville, *The Temple of Deir el-Bahari*, III, 1898, pl. lxxiv; D. Meeks, op. cit., fig. 4, p. 183 (drawing by M. Rival).

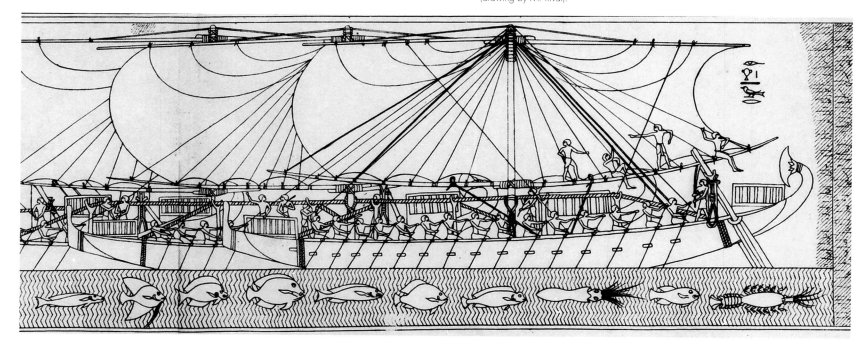

Expedition to Punt, funerary temple of Hatshepsut, Deir el-Bahari, c. 1490–1468 BC; departure manoeuvres and first part of the journey. Drawing after M. Rival, in D. Meeks, D. Garcia (ed.), *Techniques et économie antiques et médiévales*, 1997, p. 182. © Heritage Images

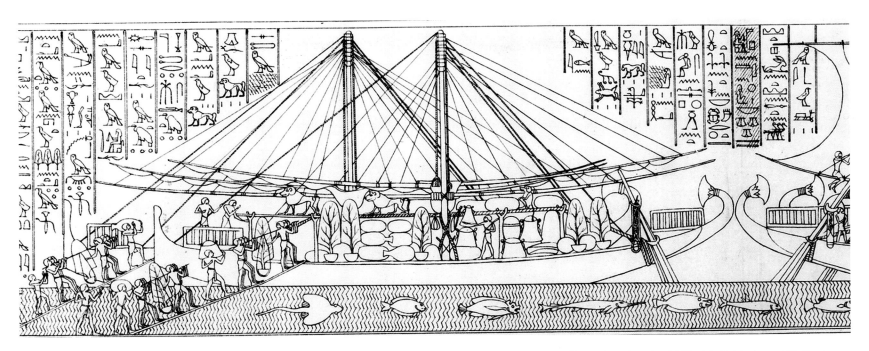

Expedition to Punt, funerary temple of Hatshepsut, Deir el-Bahari, *c.* 1490–1468 BC; loading of the ships in the land of Punt. Drawing after M. Rival, in D. Meeks and D. Garcia (eds), *Techniques et économie antiques et médiévales*, 1997, p. 183. © Heritage Images

anchor. Only a footbridge links the ships to the land. The manoeuvre cables of the rudder oars are taut; a torsion bar can be seen in the midst of the cables.

One feature, leading from the middle of the oar's blade to the cables that girdle the poop, might represent a stopping cable designed to completely immobilise the rudder oar. These waters are less calm than at the start or, at least, are moving as an effect of the undertow.

Finally, on the second register, right-hand scene,[92] the ships that have returned from Punt are setting sail for Egypt. The two steering oars are now manoeuvred simultaneously by a single person. The manoeuvring cables are taut and can leave only a limited freedom of movement.

In short, it may be concluded that boats without a keel were perfectly able to sail at sea.[93] The problem faced by flat-bottomed boats is that they drift: this can be counteracted by a very broad poop rudder stretching deep into the water, combined with the action of the tension cable. The ships of Sahure and Unas possess three steering oars on each side; the total surface of six rudder–oars and that of all the oars together meant that the boat would not drift. The steering mechanism of Hatshepsut's ships, of large dimensions, presented a significant submersible surface so as to ensure the boat's stability.

## II.2.4. The anchors

One of the most reliable criteria for distinguishing Nile ships from sea ships is the presence, at the prow, of a large stone anchor that definitely indicates a sea ship. 'Indeed, these anchors only worked thanks to their weight, which made it possible to fix the boat over a rocky or sandy bottom; on the Nile, a stone anchor would have been sucked down into the mud, which would never have let it go: the only way the boat could have been set free would have been by cutting the anchor cable. This solution is obviously absurd, so it seems that the Nile boats never had an anchor, as it would have been superfluous: if the boat came to a halt, the boat was attached to the river bank by a mooring rope attached to a stake.'[94] Chapter 99 of

the *Book of the Dead,* which contains the formula to be pronounced by the dead person to summon the ferry that will take him or her to the Land of the Dead, enumerates the names of the different parts of the boat. It is remarkable that it does not mention the anchor but designates very clearly the name of the mooring rope, the stake to which it was tied and even that of the mallet that was used to drive the latter into the river bank.[95]

The anchor depicted on Egyptian monuments takes the form of an elongated cone; the mooring cable is simply attached to its summit and kept in place by a groove dug into the stone rather than by a hole. When dropped into the sea, these anchors would end up vertical or be laid down on the bottom, depending on their form and their weight. Ships generally took numerous anchors of different sizes that were arranged fore and aft, or kept in reserve on the deck.[96]

The anchors discovered at Mersa Gawasis that bear hieroglyphic inscriptions relating to an expedition to Punt, dating back to the 12th Dynasty (1991-1782 BC),[97] have opened a debate on the question whether stone anchors, found in Egypt, had been used only on the river or also at sea. The Mersa Gawasis anchors are made out of a form of limestone that does not exist in the immediate environment, while some of them have been left unfinished on the site.[98] Since the anchors were transported to Mersa Gawasis, it has been claimed by some that the inscriptions they bear were engraved elsewhere and

---

92 E. Naville, *op. cit.,* pl. lxv; D. Meeks, *op. cit.,* fig. 5 p. 184 (drawing by M. Rival).

93 At the end of the 19th century, the flat-bottomed Thames barge shuttled between Ireland, France, Belgium, the Netherlands, Germany and Portugal (G. G. Carr, *Sailing Barges,* 1951, pp. 78-79). It is also worth remembering the flat-bottomed bragozzi boats that sailed in the Adriatic Sea between Chioggia, Fiume, Pola and Rimini (M. Marzari, *Il Bragozzo,* 1982).

94 L. Basch, *Le Musée imaginaire de la marine,* 1987, p. 47.

95 For an overview of this question see L. Basch, *The Mariner's Mirror* 71, 1985, pp. 453-467.

96 P. Pomey, in P. Pomey (ed.), *La navigation dans l'Antiquité,* 1997, pp. 87-88; *id., Archeologia Subacquea, storia, tecniche, scorperte e relitti,* 1981; P. A. Gianfrotta, P. Pomey, *L'archéologie sous la mer,* 1981.

97 Abdel Monem Sayed, *RdÉ* 29, 1977, pp. 138-178; *id., CdÉ* LVIII, 115-116, 1983, pp. 23-37.

98 H. Frost, *Topoi* 6, 1996, pp. 878-879, pp. 882-883.

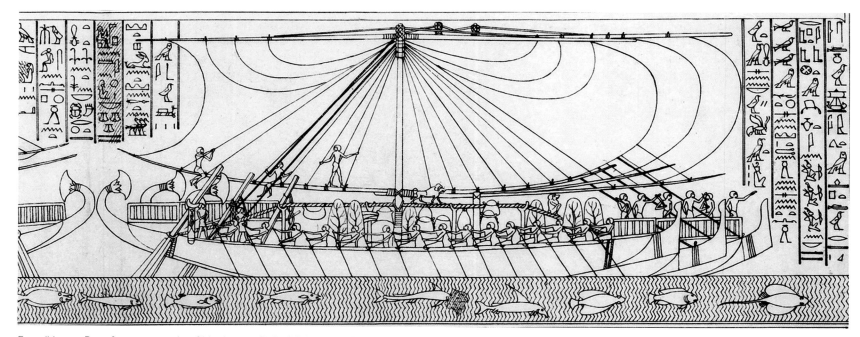

Expedition to Punt, funerary temple of Hatshepsut, Deir el-Bahari, c. 1490–1468 BC; sailing home to Egypt. Drawing after M. Rival, in D. Meeks and D. Garcia (eds), *Techniques et économie antiques et médiévales*, 1997, p. 184. © Heritage Images

have nothing at all to do with the site.[99] However, the inscriptions are arranged on the anchors in such a way that they fit the overall structure as it was erected at Mersa Gawasis itself.[100] They were engraved so as to be read at this very site. The analysis carried out by H. Frost has shown that these assemblages of anchors were also cairns designed to guide ships towards the bay.[101] The relatively great number of anchors found at Mersa Gawasis (16 are known at present) leads one to doubt whether they could have been designed exclusively for river use. It is difficult to imagine a caravan transporting to the shores of the Red Sea such heavy objects (up to 250kg), in some cases unfinished, without any other use being found for them than to pile them up or scatter them about near the shore.

The existence of stone anchors in the eastern Mediterranean, their typology and different uses, has been progressively established by different studies.[102] The anchors found in the Nile Valley properly speaking may raise a problem. It has been shown that some of them were being recycled, while others were votive deposits.[103] The votive nature of the anchors is amply demonstrated by the leaden anchors from the Hellenistic period dedicated to Zeus Kasios.[104] The offering of anchors in temples, during ancient times, is easy to imagine.[105]

Among the anchors found in Egypt are those from Bubastis in the Delta. These three stones are trapezoidal and rectangular in shape; they all have unpolished surfaces and are pierced by a single hole in their upper parts. They weigh in, respectively, at 41.5, 45, and 10.5kg. While the weight of this last stone seems particularly inadequate to anchor a boat, the description of the two preceding ones might indeed mean that this artefact was not an anchor since not every pierced stone was used to anchor boats. The anchors discovered at Bubastis, to the east of the Delta, are particularly interesting and it would be well worth reinvestigating the circumstances in which they were discovered. According to certain texts, the city of Bubastis was more or less directly linked to *Wadj Wer*.[106] This *Wadj Wer* appears as a zone of passage to the land of Punt, but also to the Mediterranean coasts of the Levant. This might well accord with L. Basch that these anchors are evidence of the existence here of a port that was the

destination of sea ships.[107] To the west of Bubastis, on another branch of the Nile, at the heart of the Delta, Athribis doubtless represented another departure point for sailings.[108] One would like to think that the mention of the god of this city, Khentiketi, on one of the Mersa Gawasis inscriptions, is not due to mere chance.

The depictions of pierced stones on the deck, at the front of the ships of Sahure and Unas, correspond typologically to the Mersa Gawasis anchors and their type: of this there is little doubt.[109] L. Basch has convincingly shown that the triangular objects represented at the stem of Pharaonic river ships are of a different kind

99  C. Vandersleyen, *RdÉ 47*, 1996, pp. 107-115.

100  H. Frost, *Topoi 6*, 1996, pp. 878-879, pp. 888-889. Note that the original shape of certain anchors was refurbished at the time the whole assembly was erected to make the stones fit together: *id.*, pp. 878-879, p. 886, fig. 2a n° 7-8.

101  See p. 84.

102  See L. Basch, *The Mariner's Mirror 71*, 1985, pp. 453-467.

103  For a Bibliography on this problem, see C. Vandersleyen, *RdÉ 47*, 1996, p. 112 n. 18.

104  P. Chuvin, J. Yoyotte, *RevArch I*, 1986, pp. 59-61

105  On the subject of votive deposits of anchors in these sanctuaries in the western Mediterranean, see H. Frost *Mariner's Mirror 56*, 1970, pp. 377-394; *id.*, *Report of the Department of Antiquities*, 1970, pp. 14-23; V. Karageorghis, *Kition, Mycenaean and Phoenician discoveries in Cyprus*, 1976, p. 60; *id.*, *Bulletin de correspondance hellénique 100*, 1976, p. 878; L. Basch, *The Mariner's Mirror 64*, 1978, pp. 118-123.

106  On *Wadj Wer*, see pp. 12-13.

107  L. Basch, *The Mariner's Mirror 71*, 1985, p. 464; *id.*, *IJNA 23*, 1994, pp. 219-227; L. Habachi, *Tell Basta*, 1957, pp. 2-3. On Bubastis, see too J. Yoyotte, Mohammed Ibrahim Bakr, in *L'Égypte du Delta. Les capitales du Nord, Dossiers d'Archéologie 213*, 1996, p. 45; A. El-Sawi, *Excavations at Tell Basta, Report of Seasons, 1967-1971*, 1979; Mohammed Ibrahim Bakr, *Tell Basta I*, 1995; *id.*, *DE*, special number I, 1989, pp. 39-49; *id.*, in *L'Égyptologie en 1979. Axes pioritaires de recherche*, 1982, pp. 154-167. The canal from the Nile to the Red Sea started at Bubastis: G. Posener, *CdÉ 13*, 1938, p. 259; see pp. 121-124. On the position of the Egyptian Mediterranean ports situated inland from the coastal strip, see p. 40 and 94 *et seq.*

108  G. Scandone Matthiae, *Studi epigrafici e linguistici sul Vicino oriente antico 7*, 1990, pp. 39-42.

109  See the photographs published by M. Bietak, in *Pyramid Studies and others Essays presented to I.E.S. Edwards*, 1988, pl. 5 and 8. See too S. Hassan, *ZÄS 80*, 1955, pp. 136-139; G. Goyon, *BIFAO 69*, 1971, pp. 11-41. Compare these forms to those of the anchors of Mersa Gawasis published by H. Frost, *Topoi 6*, 1996, p. 886 and see the comments of L. Basch, *The Mariner's Mirror 71*, 1985, pp. 454-456.

and are not anchors.[110] An altogether similar anchor has been discovered at Byblos in an Old Kingdom (2686-2181 BC) context. It bore a hieroglyph meant to bring good luck.[111]

Finally, the existence of 'floating anchors' on ancient ships should be mentioned, designed to slow down and better control the ship's course when it was being driven before a storm. This mechanism, constituted of floating bodies (spars, wooden panels, and so on) that were allowed to drag windward of the ship, meant that its course could be slowed down while maintaining it in the eye of the wind.[112]

## II.3. Ballast, stowage and tonnage

Ballast, stowage and tonnage certainly constitute 'the most complicated and most controversial questions in naval history, not only in ancient navies, but in all navies'.[113] So, far from presenting a general and definitive study, the examination below will merely raise some of the problematic items.

### II.3.1. Ballast

Equipped with insignificant keels and being flat-bottomed, the ships must have loaded ballast to ensure they could keep their balance and stay upright at sea.[114] This ballast was most often composed of blocks of stone, in different shapes and sizes, piled on to the floor of the bilge. In the wreck found off Cape Gelydonia, in the south of Asia Minor, submarine excavations have brought to light 116kg of stones that constituted a part or the entirety of the ship's ballast.[115] This ballast could also have been formed from part of the cargo, which presupposes that once it was disembarked, it needed to be replaced.[116] It must have been tightly stowed in the bilge to prevent it from shifting, otherwise it would have risked making the ship capsize or else might have smashed its sides.

### II.3.2. Stowage

A distinction needs to be made between two types of cargo stowage: stowage on deck and stowage in the hold. As elaborated, most Egyptian ships apparently had no hold, so only the ballast can have been present under the floor deck; thus, as attested on the monuments – such as the depiction of the ships of Queen Hatshepsut returning from the land of Punt – all the merchandise embarked was piled on deck. It must have been firmly stowed there by ropes, even

if they cannot be discerned on the reliefs. This cargo does not cover the whole surface of the deck, and leaves free spaces all along the sides, as fore and aft for the manoeuvres, in particular for rowing when the ship was under oar. It is this practice of stowing on deck which must explain the shape of the sail on the ships of the New Kingdom, which left a large space between the lower yard and the deck.[117]

Cereals were probably transported in baskets, leather bags or great earthenware vases with wide mouths. Perhaps they were stocked in bulk in big containers, or, at more recent periods, in the hold. As for the pottery pieces, whether containers or not, they must have been positioned belly to belly, or piled up, packed with straw to prevent them knocking into one another and limiting the risks of breakage. They could have been packed into crates or baskets. These two procedures were in fact used for all small, fragile objects that needed to be transported: statuettes, lamps, and so on. The fabrics were packed in cubic bundles that were easily piled up and the same was true of the goods sent by individuals comprising various objects.

Archaeologist examining the keel and planking of the wreck of Ulu Burun; the latter is concealed behind two stone anchors. © Institute of Nautical Archaeology

110  L. Basch, *IJNA* 23, 1994, p. 221-223, figs 1a and 1b p. 222; E. Assmann, in L. Borchardt, *Das Grabdenkmal des Königs Sahure*, II, 1913, p. 165, fig. 24; M. Mogensen, *Le mastaba égyptien de la Glyptothèque Ny Carlsberg*, 1921, p. 18, fig. 11. The Stele of Abydos, of course, pierced by three holes, has been interpreted as a counterweight to the *saqiyeh* and not as an anchor: R. A. Farag, *MDAIK* 36, 1980, pp. 77-79, pl. 26. Likewise, the hypothesis that sees the holed stones discovered at Mirgissa as anchors (A. Nibbi, *IJNA* 21, 1992, p. 265) needs to be reconsidered; this may have been material used either in the construction of shields, or in the raising of oxen (a pierced stone enabling the oxen to be gathered): see L. Basch, *op. cit.*, pp. 223-226.

111  H. Frost, in *Mélanges de l'Université de SaintJoseph*, 1969, pl. V.

112  P. Pomey, in P. Pomey (ed.), *La navigation dans l'Antiquité*, 1997, pp. 13-14.

113  J. Rougé, *op. cit.*, p. 76.

114  J. Rougé, *La marine dans l'Antiquité*, 1975, p. 76.

115  G. F. Bass, *Transaction of the American Philosophical Society*, 57, 1967, p. 48.

116  For a cargo being used as ballast, see the Ulu Burun wreck (numerous copper ingots, and so on): S. McGrail, in N. H. Gale (ed.), *Bronze Age Trade in the Mediterranean*, 1991, pp. 83-86; id., *OJA* 8, 1989, pp. 353-358.

117  J. Rougé, *op. cit.*, pp. 77-78.

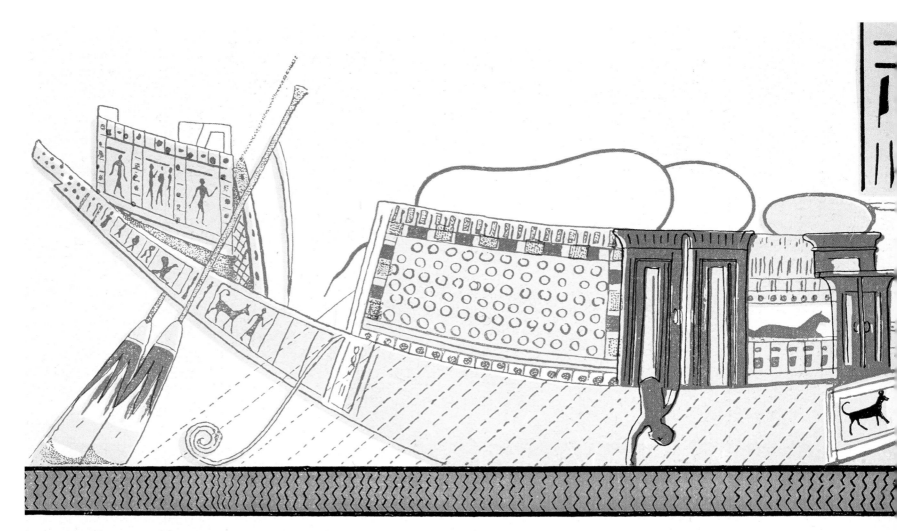

Mooring a Nile boat with the help of a stake. © AKG Images

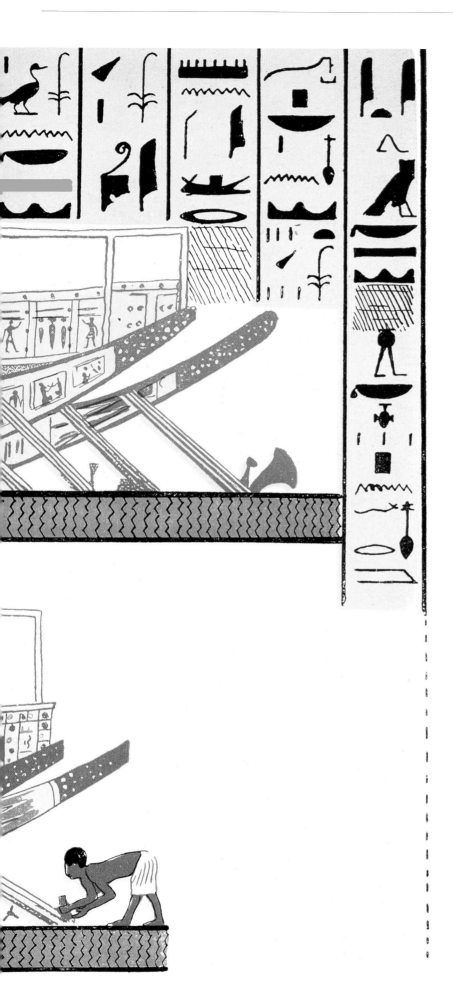

These were sometimes enclosed in baskets, then covered with canvas and carefully tied up. Liquids as well as certain foodstuffs were transported in amphorae. The shape of these recipients varied considerably from period to period and country to country, and also depended on the nature of the goods.

Stowing the cargo raises the problem of the methods used for the embarkation and disembarkation of merchandise. Firstly it should be noted that the footbridges and ladders enabling people to come aboard were situated at the front of the ship, and when the ship drew up to a quayside, it did so, in principle, three quarters ahead. Then, the most usual method for loading and unloading merchandise was manpower. Thus several monuments show dockers loading and unloading the ships.[118]

On the lower register of the depictions of Hatshepsut's expedition to Punt,[119] the first two ships have not hoisted their sails; they are still moored with the aid of cables wound around the trunks of trees growing on the river bank, and the rowers are resting. Near the first ship there is a small boat with a single rudder oar passing through a slot. This particularity is familiar from certain Nile vessels.[120] The sacks and the amphorae they contain look very much like revictualling goods needing to be moved on to the ships before sailing. The barque is accompanied by a legend that is generally translated as 'unloading the kepenout ships'. But the normal meaning of the verb translated by 'to unload' is, in fact, 'to give air (to someone suffocating)' and, in the figurative sense, 'to relieve, to save (the poor by giving them their means of subsistence)'. Applied to ships that sailed from Thebes, and which still had a long journey ahead of them, the sense of 'revictualling' fits well.[121] As well as revictualling, the ships must also have embarked merchandise to exchange it with that of the Puntites.

As far as the transport of wood is concerned, something which gave a definite rhythm to journeys between Egypt and the Lebanese coast, a few details will permit an understanding of how such a cargo was loaded. After the trees had been cut down, the logs were dragged or rolled along the slope:[122]

> *He (the Prince) prepared three hundred men and three hundred oxen, and at their head placed foremen to make them cut down the trees. They cut them down and the trees spent the season of germination lying where they were. In the third month of the harvest, they were dragged to the coast.*

At the coast, the logs were probably assembled into rafts. The transportation of wood by sea is well attested and even represented on Assyrians reliefs.[123] In several Biblical texts, the wood of Lebanon

118   On stevedores, *cf.* p. 135.
119   E. Naville, *The Temple of Deir el-Bahari*, III, 1898, pls Lxxii-Lxiii; D. Meeks, in D. Meeks, D. Garcia (ed.), *Techniques et économie antiques et médiévales*, 1997, fig. 2, p. 181 (drawing by M. Rival).
120   N. Dürring, *Materialien zum Schiffbau*, 1995, p. 135 fig. 61g. Note that the manoeuvering cable of the rudder oar differs from that which is known from the Nile (illustration in *idem*, p. 80 fig. 41) but greatly resembles that of the ships it is revictualling.
121   According to the interpretation of D. Meeks, *op. cit.*, p. 185 and n. 57 p. 193
122   See *Wenamun*, 2, 43-44.
123   E. Pottier, *Catalogue des antiquités assyriennes*, 1924; A. Parrot, *Sumer* 6, 1950, pp. 115-117. See the depiction in stone from the palace of Sargon II at Khorsabad (last quarter of the 8th century BC), this is the celebrated 'maritime scene' where barques are shown with great beams, probably squared trunks of cedar: P. E. Botta, E. Flandin, *Monuments de Ninive* I, 1849, pl. 32, 33; A. Parrot, *Assur*, 1961, pp. 115-117 and fig. 48; W. Stevenson Smith, *Interconnections in the Ancient Near East*, 1965, pp. 121-122 and figs 155-156.

*He (the Prince) prepared three hundred men and three hundred oxen, and at their head placed foremen to make them cut down the trees. They cut them down and the trees spent the season of germination lying where they were. In the third month of the harvest, they were dragged to the coast.*

is transported to Jaffa, under Solomon, by floating it. Thus King Hiram addresses Solomon in these terms:[124]

*I have considered the things which thou sentest to me for: and I will do all thy desire concerning timber of cedar, and concerning timber of fir. My servants shall bring them down from Lebanon unto the sea: and I will convey them by sea in floats unto the place that thou shalt appoint me, and will cause them to be discharged there, and thou shalt receive them.*

The logs could also be transported on rafts. Huram, King of Tyre, replies to Solomon's request in these terms:[125]

*And we will cut wood out of Lebanon, as much as thou shalt need: and we will bring it to thee in floats by sea to Joppa; and thou shalt carry it up to Jerusalem.*

This type of transport was again used at the time of the reconstruction of the Temple, under Cyrus:[126]

*They gave money also unto the masons, and to the carpenters; and meat, and drink, and oil, unto them of Zidon, and to them of Tyre, to bring cedar trees from Lebanon to the sea of Joppa, according to the grant that they had of Cyrus king of Persia.*

It was certainly, given the technical conditions of the period, the most convenient means of transport. It is probable that the wood was transported in this way to the closest possible point to its destination, so as to reduce to a minimum the distance to be covered by terrestrial means of transport.

## II.3.3. Tonnage

Calculating the tonnage of ships encounters many difficulties which render the question insoluble. Firstly, the non-existence of any wreck of an Egyptian ship; then, the imprecision, in the text, of the descriptions of cargoes (weight and volume).[127]

The palimpsest Papyrus of Elephantine (*TAD* C 3, 7) which includes a customs register for the satrapy of Egypt in the Achaemenid period is a choice document since it contains references both to certain types of foreign ships that penetrated Egypt to trade there, and also indicates what cargoes they carried and allows us to estimate their tonnage.[128] The ships are identified in accordance with three criteria which are presented thus in the order of the text: first the type of boat (there are four different types), then the name of the leader/captain, and finally place of origin. Without going into the details of the origins of the boats,[129] it is sufficient to say that the hazards of administrative organisation have meant that the register of the boats that came from only two regions: Asia Minor (*ywny*-boats) and Syro-Palestine (*ksr*-boats).

These *ksr*-boats are called '*dwgy qnd/r* '. They are also classified by size, since (in Aramaic transcription) two demotic words meaning big (*tˁt*) and little (*tšyry*) may be distinguished.[130]

The study of the cargoes[131] suggests that the capacity when fully laden of the 'big' *ksr*-boats was around at least 60 tonnes, and that of the 'little' ones around 40 tonnes — and these figures can be

---

124  1 Kings, 5, 22-23
125  2 Chronicles, 2, 15.
126  Esdras, 3, 7.

127  On the tonnage of ancient ships in general, see P.-M.-J. de Bonnefoux, Fr.-Ed. Pâris, *Dictionnaire de marine à voiles*, 1999 (1st ed. 1859), s.v. 'Tonnage', 'Tonne', 'Tonneau', p. 618; L. Casson, in *Studi in onore di A. Calderini e R. Paribeni*, Milan, 1956, pp. 231-238; *id.*, *Ships and Seamanship*, 1971, pp. 164, 166, 183-200; H. T. Wallinga, *Mnemosyne* XVII, 1964, pp. 1-40; J. Rougé, *la Marine dans l'Antiquité*, 1975, pp. 83-87; A. Tchernia, P. Pomey, A. Hesnard, *L'Épave romaine de la Madrague de Giens* (Var), *Gallia* 34th suppl., 1978, pp. 101-107; P. Pomey, A. Tchernia, *Archeonautica* 2, 1978, pp. 233-251; J. Rougé, *la Marine dans l'Antiquité*, 1975, pp. 83-84.
128  B. Porten, A. Yardeni, *Textbook of Aramaic Documents from Ancient Egypt*, III, 1993; A. Yardeni, *BASOR*, 293, 1994, pp. 67-87; E. Lipinski, *OLP* 29, 1994, pp. 61-68; P. Briant, *Histoire de l'empire perse*, 1994, p. 398, and an index of Aramaic terms, p. 1236; C. Ampolo, in *Magna Grecia, Etruschi, Fenici, Taranto 8-13 Oct. 1993*, 1996, pp. 245-247; P. Briant, R. Descat, in N. Grimal, B. Menu (ed.), *Le commerce, BiÉtud* 121, 1998, pp. 59-104.
129  See the problems that such a study causes, and consult the excellent discussion by P. Briant and R. Descat, *op. cit.*, pp. 62-63.
130  E. Lipinski, *op. cit.*, p. 65.
131  R. Descat, in N. Grimal, B. Menu (ed.), *Le commerce, BiÉtud* 121, 1998, pp. 66-69.

viewed as tending to underestimate the reality somewhat, but they fall well within the average tonnage of ships in the eastern Mediterranean in the classical era.[132]

By way of comparison, there is the *Kyrenia* wreck, that of a small Greek coaster from the 4th century BC, with a loading capacity of 20 tonnes when fully laden for a length of 14m and a width of 4.20m.[133] The texts and inscriptions of the 4th and 3rd centuries BC show that the trading ships of the period could reach much bigger weights. In fact they mention tonnages of 100 to 120, which seem quite common, but also ships of 165 tonnes or even 330 tonnes fully laden, a substantial weight for the time. From an inscription from the 3rd century in the port of Thassos, dividing ships up between different basins depending on their tonnage, three categories can be deduced: boats less than 80 tonnes, those from 80 to 130 tonnes and finally those of more than 130 tonnes. These tonnages can be considered as defining the categories of small, medium and big ships at that period.[134] The grain ships of imperial Rome, according to juridical texts, possessed a tonnage corresponding to a fully laden weight of 90 and 450 metric tonnes,[135] but these are ships with single cargoes; this was rarely the case in the Mediterranean navy in the periods in question. Fortunately, the volume is known of the cargo transported on the return from India of the merchant ship of the Papyrus of Mouzinis (the *Hermapollon*). The merchandise was weighed, valued, taxed and sealed in the Red Sea port where it arrived (Berenice or Myos Hormos). If the recent calculations of D. Rathbone are taken into account,[136] this consisted of 60 crates of nard (whose weight is not given), 3314 tonnes of whole elephant tusks and 553kg of broken

132   For tonnage capacities, see most recently (with cross-references to earlier work) P. Pomey, A. Tchernia, *Archeonautica* 2, 1978, pp. 233-251; J. Vélissaropoulos, *Les Nauclères grecs*, 1980, p. 62; J. P. Stronk, *Talanta* 24-25, 1992-1993, pp. 130-135. In a preliminary publication, the ship discovered not far from Dor in Palestine and dating back to the end of the 5th century is estimated at 25 tonnes, which leaves little room for freight, as E. Linder remarks, *New Encyclopaedia of Archaeological Excavations in the Holy Land III*, 1993, pp. 918-919. See P. Briant, R. Descat, *op. cit.*, pp. 68-69.

133   P. Pomey, in P. Pomey (ed.), *La navigation dans l'Antiquité*, 1997, pp. 168-169; J. R. Steffy, *AJA*, 1985, pp. 71-101.

134   P. Pomey, *op. cit.*, pp. 82-83.

135   See P. Pomey, *L'Histoire* 36, 1981, pp. 96-101; *id.*, in *3000 ans sur la mer*, *Les collections de L'Histoire* 8, 2000, pp. 24-27.

136   D. Rathbone, in *Alexandrian Studies II in Honour of Mostafa el Abbadi*, BSAA 46, 2000, p. 46; F. Burkhalter, in *Autour de Coptos*, Topoi suppl. 3, 2002, p. 204.

Transport of wood. Stone representation from the palace of Sargon II at Khorsabad, c. 710 BC: barques are transporting heavy beams, probably squared trunks of cedar, Louvre, Paris, AO 19889. © Photo: Peter A. Clayton

tusks, 100 pairs of complete tusks and 17 other pairs of broken tusks; five tonnes of a product (spices and sweet-smelling substances?) divided into 167 units; and 135 tonnes of a merchandise that may have been ebony or teak.

The tonnage just defined is in general conformity with the average tonnages of sailing ships of the 18th century; but, as then, apart from the average tonnages there must have been big tonnages. Among these types of ship, the one that has made the most impression is the *Lady of Syracuse*, a ship presented to Ptolemy (doubtless Ptolemy III Euergetes I, 246-222 BC) by Hiero II (*c.* 265-215 BC) of Syracuse. This was a gigantic ship for the period, and a good idea of its cargo is known; it must have had a capacity of around 2000 metric tonnes. However, this was a ship out of all proportion to the harbours and the economic possibilities of the time, and it made only one journey, from Syracuse to Alexandria where it slowly rotted away in port.[137] One of the war ships that marked the final stage of the Ptolemaic monsters was certainly the *tettarakontere* of Ptolemy IV Philopator (222-205 BC) which admittedly must have remained no more than an object of curiosity. This is easy to imagine if it is remembered that it measured 120m long and 15m wide, its maximum height above the water line was 21m, and it had a crew of 4000 oarsmen.[138]

This demands the question: did tonnages evolve (change) with time? The Hellenistic and Roman periods demonstrate that, from the technical point of view, there was not necessarily an evolution: the Hellenistic shipbuilders as well as their Roman successors were perfectly capable of building big tonnages, and did so. If, however, there was an economic evolution, this was to be found on the economic level: big tonnages need to be used rationally; 'only the appearance of the huge Roman market and the need to revictual it in a rather short sailing time gave the big tonnages any economic value and they were then much bigger than they had been previously'.[139]

## II.4. The naming of ships

'Aa-kheperu-Ra is enduring', 'Aa-kheperu-Ra reinforces the Two-lands', 'Isesi is powerful', 'Me-kheperu-Ra ravages the land of Khor'… In each case, the name is based on that of the sovereign and confirms the royal character of the commercial and military expeditions.[140] One example studied by D. Meeks is extremely interesting and allows this state of affairs to be qualified.[141] It was the discovery made on the site of Mersa Gawasis that enabled him to make certain deductions. The excavations made on the site have revealed, *inter alia*, a series of hieratic ostraca dating from the 12th Dynasty, a period during which the site was in service (*c.* 1920-1840 BC). Two of them bear, as their only mention, '*Our-djeded-baou* is vigorous'.[142] This proper name is extremely rare; it is known only for the chancellor of Isesi,[143] a character who, according to the narrative of Kerkhuf, brought back a dwarf from his peregrinations to Punt.[144] So it must be the same character in both cases.

What is the meaning of the text of these ostraca? In its structure, 'it seems irresistibly to refer to the name given to a ship'.[145] Such a name gives a particular importance to *Our-djeded-baou*. 'Given current scholarly information, it is not known whether the expression '*Our-djeded-baou* is vigorous' was followed by a determiner for ships, which would have removed any doubt. However, a stone

fragment on which a list including the fragmentary names of three ships, this time with the expected determiner, includes one ship that was called 'Senusret is long-lived'. If '*Our-djeded-baou* is vigorous'[146] really does designate a ship, a reason may be imagined, at least, why it was given the name of a traveller who had lived nearly six centuries previously. *Our-djeded-baou* would be the first, if not in historical reality at least in collective memory, to have successfully led a maritime expedition to Punt and back. It may be understood why the sailors, renewing his exploit and drawing on his attainments, would have sought to pay homage to his memory'.[147]

This study reveals certain number characters, such as the son of a 'chief boatman of Maat' (*ḥry nfw n M3ˁt*) who was himself 'boatman of Ptah',[148] as well as a ship's boatman named 'Mery-Amun'.[149] Now, if the name of divinities doubtless refers to the domain to which the boatman was attached, it might define the real 'personality' of the ship, like a boat of the Hellenistic and Roman period, more often than not named with the aid of divine names that ensured it has the protection of the divinity who protects it. A certain number of ancient trading vessels are known bearing the name of Isis, the protective goddess of navigation *par excellence*, at that period; her great festival opened, with the ceremony of the *nauigium Isidis*, the sea routes to trading sailors.[150] Two such ships are well known to historians: the *Isis* of Lucian's dialogue *The Ship*, the celebrated *Isis Germiniania*, a woodcutting ship of the Tiber;[151] and the *Isopharia*, the Isis of Pharos which is known through an inscription found in Crete.[152] The name and emblem of the ship are the permanent elements that enable the ship to be designated; next to them are a certain number of other elements that can be subject to variation, such as the names of the owner (person or institution) or the captain; this seems to be the case with the boat moored at Piramesse whose owner seems to have been the *sm*-priest of Ptah of Memphis, Khaemwaset.[153] In the customs register of the Persian epoch, the ships mentioned above are identified by three criteria that are presented in this way in the order of the text: first the type of the boat, then the name of the leader/captain, finally the place of origin.[154]

---

137 Athenaeus, *Deipnosophistes*, V, 206d-209; L. Casson, *Ships and Seamanship*, 1971, pp. 184-186. On the Hellenistic navy, see the summary of A. Guillerm, *La marine dans l'Antiquité*, 1995, pp. 38-43.

138 Plutarch, *Life of Demetrius*, 43; J. Rougé, *La marine dans l'Antiquité*, 1975, pp. 104-105.

139 J. Rougé, *op. cit.*, p. 87. On the tonnage of Roman ships, see also P. Pomey, in P. Pomey (ed.), *La navigation dans l'Antiquité*, 1997, pp. 88-89.

140 See the numerous examples quoted by D. Jones, *A Glossary of Ancient Egyptian Nautical Titles and Terms*, 1988, p. 231-233.

141 D. Meeks, in *Autour de Coptos, Topoi* suppl. 3, 2002, pp. 313-314.

142 Abdel Monem Sayed, *CdÉ* 58, 1983, p. 27.

143 H. Ranke, *Die ägyptischen Personennamen*, I, 1935, 82, 6.

144 *Urk.* I, 128, 17-129, 1.

145 D. Meeks, in *Autour de Coptos, Topoi*, suppl. 3, 2002, p. 314.

146 Abdel Monem Sayed, *RdÉ* 29, 1977, p. 150 and pl. 12b.

147 D. Meeks, *op. cit.*, p. 314.

148 G. A. Gaballa, *SAK* 7, 1979, pp. 42-44, Stele of Cairo JE 8781. *cf.* p. 151.

149 A. P. Zivie, *RdÉ* 31, 1979, pp. 135-151; S. Bickel, in N. Grimal, B. Menu (ed.), 'le commerce', *BiÉtud* 121, 1998, p. 160. See p. 151.

150 Apuleius, *Metamorphoses*, XI, 16.

151 Lucien, *The Ship*, 5.

152 J. Rougé, *Recherches sur l'organisation du commerce en Méditerranée sous l'empire romain*, 1966, p. 327.

153 P. Leyde I 350, vº; J. J. Janssen, *Two Ancient Egyptian Ship's Logs*, 1961, pp. 1-52. *cf.* p. 135.

154 *cf.* p. 152.

Finally, the papyrological sources of the Ptolemaic and Roman periods relating to the professional traders provides much food for thought when it is considered how the ships were used, who was responsible in case of loss, and how the property of the ship was transferred and delegated.[155] This identity of the ship naturally leads to the quest of all those who embarked on a sea voyage.

---

[155]   *cf.* p. 166-173.

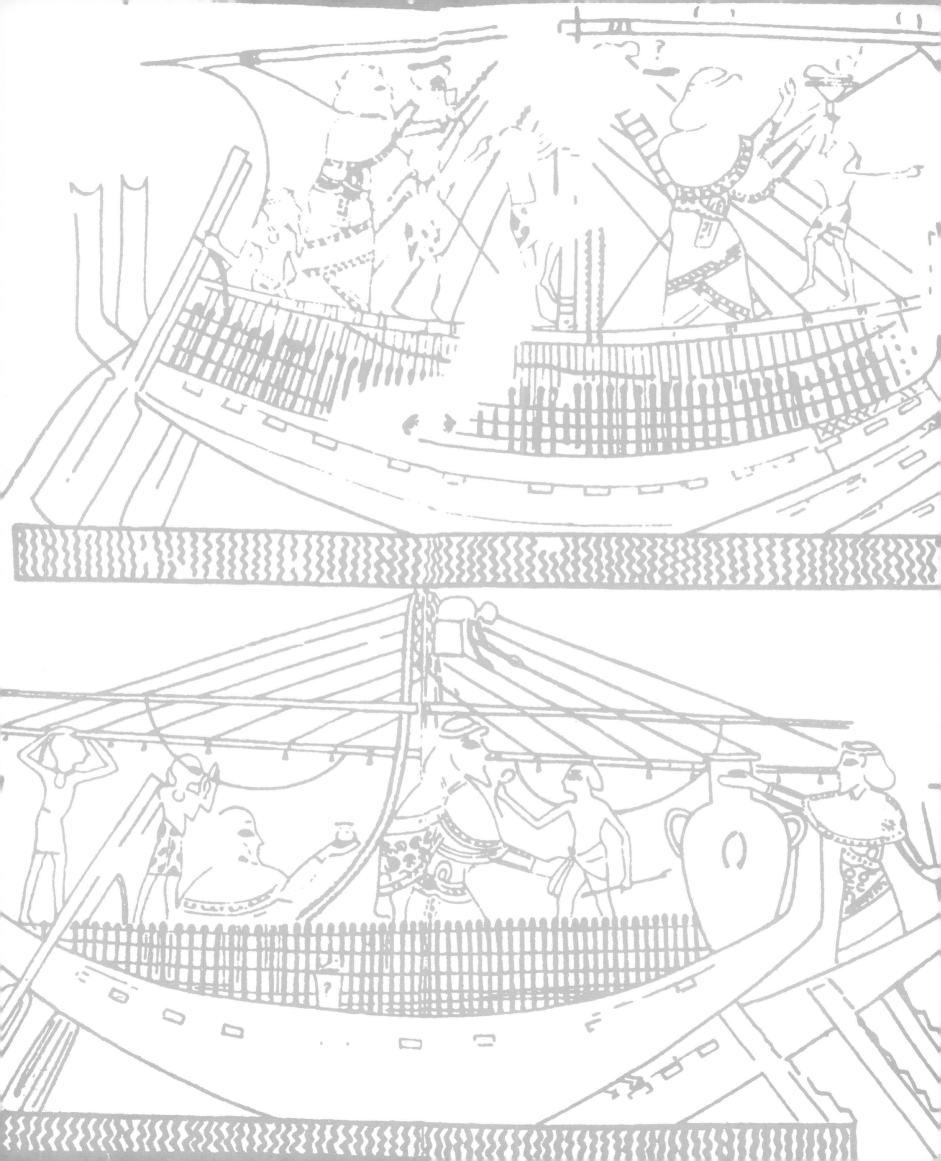

# 2

# THE PROFESSIONALS OF MARITIME VOYAGING

## The personnel of ports and ships, outfitters and ships' owners, traders, traffickers and merchants

*I ask myself in amazement how, yes how, as all alone he listened to the waves breaking all around him, he put up with a life that consisted entirely of tears?*
(Sophocles, *Philoctetes*)

During periods of internal stability, and especially in the New Kingdom (1570-1070 BC), in tandem with local trade between individuals of the same village or district who exchanged goods for their immediate needs (exchanging vegetables for pottery, cereals for sandals, and so on), there existed in Egypt a larger-scale trade. This type of trade depended essentially on the great institutions of the country, namely the temples and their domains, the royal palace, and sometimes a few wealthy big-property owners. On this scale, the exchange of goods generally involved significant quantities, thus considerable sums of money, and they could bring into play very distant partners. So they had to resort to intermediaries, to different types of specialists: transporters, mainly boatmen, wholesale traders, and several types of overseers. Different professions were led to cooperate in commercial exchanges; they thus formed a professional and social group that was more or less homogenous and they also rubbed shoulders in private life.[1] The sources reveal several aspects of the daily life of these people, their activities, their deeds and sometimes their misdeeds, the milieu in which they moved, their lifestyles and their living standards.

This social group, this corporation, did not belong to the elite. Although a certain margin for private manoeuvre remained possible,

there hardly existed in Egypt any merchant lords, or any great fortunes that had been created by commerce. To understand this state of affairs and to grasp the world in which these professionals of commercial travel lived, it is necessary to dwell again on the conception of the Egyptian economy, and to underline the difficulty of writing a real history of the Egyptian economy: if the theoretician wishes to try and make up for the enforced silence of Egyptology, he/she risks going against the documents and ultimately misunderstanding the proper characteristics of the Pharaonic regime. J. Yoyotte warns against such theories: 'Thus the thesis explaining the good times in Egypt by the predominance of imaginary liberal "bourgeois classes" from the Delta, traders and seafarers, and the unhappy intermediate periods by the upsurge of "feudal" groups from the South, continental, agrarian and despotic in nature, is the result of an arbitrary extrapolation of certain data of our medieval history'.[2] In the normal conditions of international commerce, granaries and entrepots, great fisheries, fleets with their carpenters and their mariners, and works of general interest (irrigation, navigation, architecture, and so on) were organised and minutely controlled by functionaries dependent on the sovereign, either directly ('The King's House') or indirectly ('The Houses of the

1  S. Bickel, in N. Grimal, B. Menu (ed.), *Le commerce, BiÉtud* 121, 1998, pp. 157-172, figs 1-5. p. 157.

2  J. Yoyotte, in *Dictionnaire de la civilisation égyptienne*, 1992, s.v. 'Économie', p. 92.

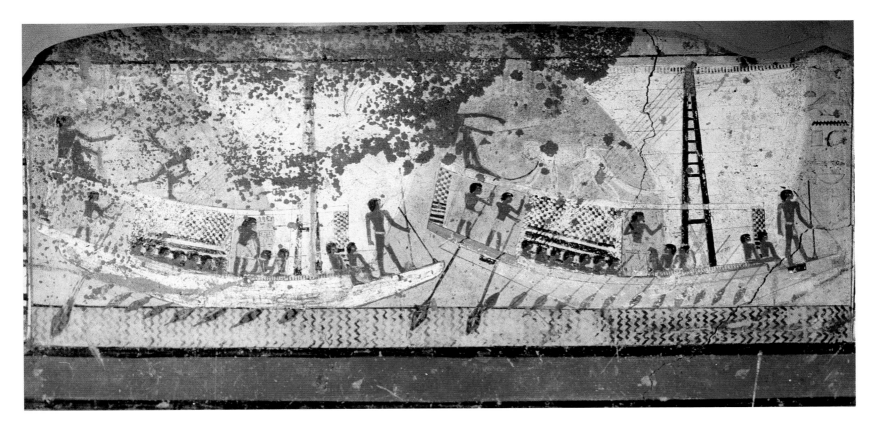

Painting from the tomb of In-Snefru-Ishtef at Dashur, Old Kingdom, 5th–6th Dynasties, c. 2500–2000 BC, Egyptian Museum, Cairo. © Werner Forman Archive/Egyptian Museum, Cairo

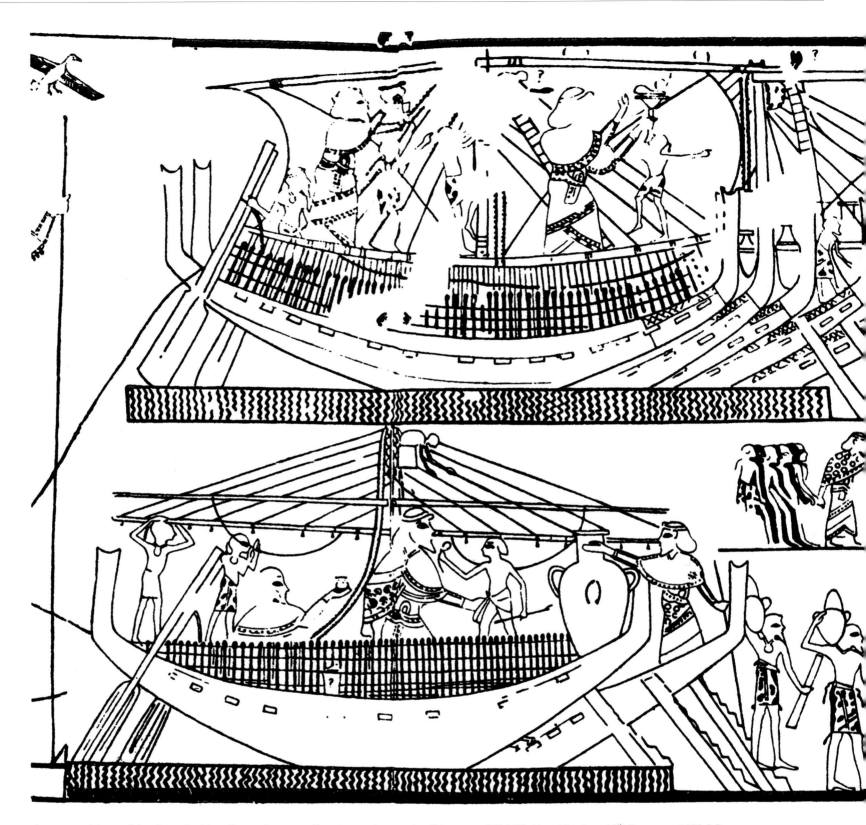

A commercial expedition from the Near East arrives at an Egyptian market, tomb of Kenamun (TT 162), New Kingdom, 18th Dynasty, c. 1450 BC, drawing after L. Basch, *Le Musée imaginaire de la marine*, 1987, p. 64. © L. Basch

gods...'). The land, in principle the shared property of the gods and Pharaoh, was placed under the immediate administration of royal agents and entrusted to perpetual beneficiaries, the temples; or they were attributed to functionaries who looked after their management and gathered its revenue as a lifetime salary. Farming enterprises – their soil, buildings, equipment, men and beasts – were also dependent on the king or his higher delegates (temple

administrators, civil beneficiaries). In spite of everything, far from undergoing 'state socialism', Egypt in fact was acquainted with a sort of private property, hallowed by custom. Apart from land, and salaries in nature that came with their function, the notables could count on considerable 'personal holdings' from ancient times onwards: fallow land transformed by them into domains that bore their names, buildings and movables given as gifts by the king, herds built up and

principle a 'statist' economy and private property, like individual enterprise, while occupying a notable place on the local scale, played only a minor role in comparison with the direct (royal) domain or the indirect (divine) domain of the State, the service of the pharaoh, work that was supervised and salaried, and the division of the means of production and consumer goods by the administration. So the status and lifestyle of the professionals of trade was intrinsic to this conception of the Egyptian economy. Furthermore, Egyptian society conserved a rather archaic economy, essentially based on the annual production and the immediate consumption of foodstuffs. A high dignitary could stockpile clothes, jewels, and plate for his own usage both present and posthumous as well as that of the members of his household, but otherwise the bulk of his wealth comprised the harvests from lands he administered in payment, the harvests from the lands in his personal domain, and the revenue in food paid by the temples of which he was the priest, more or less fictively.

This mass of perishable goods enabled him to recruit a private clientele, and hence to have a political influence, but his wealth could not constitute an 'active capital'. If small trade and loans were certainly intense on the local scale, it does not seem that any real merchant class with power based on commercial gain ever came into being. The literary image of wealth, J. Yoyotte tells us, was not treasure; it was always the well-stocked granary, the fine herd, the marsh full of game.[3] The fundamental economic circulation was that of the cargo-ships, carrying grain levied as tax to the silos of the king; it was the convoy headed to the neighbouring nome that was affected by penury.

The professionals of trade were principally those who carried out the orders of the institution to which they were attached. These institutions, responsible for significant parts of the population and some of them holding large domains across the whole country, were the real engines of the economy.[4] They possessed their own transport fleets, and they sent the appropriate teams to proceed to the necessary exchanges. Two ships' logs paint a picture of the different professions that were involved in this kind of commercial expedition: 'navigators' (*nfw.w*), 'man in charge of the ship' (*ḥry wsḫ*), 'overseers' (*sꜣw.w*) and 'escorts' (*mškb.w*), different subalterns and a whole series of persons designated by the general term of 'personnel of the temple', among whom were probably specialists of transactions, the *šwty.w*. These rare and precious documents bring out the multiplicity of the personnel of ports and ships.

---

3  *Id.*, p. 94.

4  P. Leyde I 350, vᵒ; P. Turin 2008 + 2016: J. J. Janssen, *Two Ancient Egyptian Ship's Logs*, 1961 pp. 1-52, 53-95; S. Bickel, *op. cit.*, pp. 157-158.

increased by them, and also 'goods coming from the paternal house', all things which they could transmit to their children. Furthermore, the pharaoh himself, who often conferred the heredity of offices and benefices, contributed to the setting up of a 'possessing class'. At certain periods of weakness, clerical collectivities or even highly-placed personages appropriated for themselves a large share of the king's gifts. The fact remains that the Egyptian economy was in

# Chapter 1: The Personnel of Ports and Ships

*Is it true that, to the roar of the waves as they are beaten twice over, their oars of fir and their sails swollen by the breeze have made their marine chariot sail over the waters of the sea to increase the wealth of their houses? Men cherish, alas for them, an insatiable hope that drives them to seek weighty riches by wandering across the waves and sailing to barbarian cities, the playthings of the same illusion. But some of them never make their fortune, while others succeed in getting their hands on it.*
(Euripides, *Iphigenia in Tauris*)

## I. The port personnel

This is the name that shall be given to all those who by their functions are led to busy themselves with harbour activity without thereby being directly engaged in maritime voyaging: in other words, stevedores and shipbuilders are considered, as well as harbour officials.

## 1.1. Stevedores and allied professions

The mural paintings in Egyptian tombs bring before our eyes a whole series of personages loading and unloading ships, but it is not known whether they were crew members or a real social group that was specialised in this activity. This is true of the fine representations in the tomb of Ipuy (TT 217),[1] and on the bas–reliefs of the tomb of Kenamun (TT 162), it is the Syrian crew which busies itself with unloading the merchandise.[2] Several texts mention people called *qwr.w*, and these might be a sort of stevedore or carrier,[3] obviously related to the word *qwr/qr* that designates a transport ship.[4] *Qwr.w* are also attested as carriers in mining expeditions;[5] ever since the Old Kingdom (2686-2181 BC) there had been a close link between the modes of organisation of the fleet, that of the expeditions and the organisation of work in the mines and quarries.[6]

The functions carried out by these stevedores consisted not merely in the loading and unloading of ships, which is the function most frequently represented, but also, quite certainly, in the transport of merchandise and products from the quays or the river bank to the entrepots and from their entrepots to the places of distribution or exchange.

On several depictions moored boats are clearly represented destined to transport freight. There are men who, under the surveillance of overseers, are busy loading and unloading objects. As emphasised above, it seems that as a general rule there were no specialised dockers. Once the sailors arrived in port, they transformed themselves into stevedores and the quartermasters into overseers. To facilitate the comings and goings of the men, an inclined plane was placed against the stem of the boat.[7] In the ships from Hatshepsut's expedition to Punt,[8] the *proreutes* filled the role of overseers; placed behind their parapets, and was thus able to look down on the activities around them, they were all designated, it seems, to fulfil this important function, but they were helped by a colleague, probably a quartermaster, who oversaw the best arrangement of the freight on the deck: the man is holding out his right arm horizontally, his hand open and holding in his left hand, placed on his chest, a baton that rests on his shoulder.

In one of the Asiatic boats from the tomb of Kenamun, an Egyptian has climbed on board, either to take delivery of the cargo, or to direct its disembarkation; he is holding a baton in his left hand, which is lowered, and a banner in his right hand, which is held out and raised to face height.[9] On a relief representing the loading of a Nile barge, the chief is on the ground: his left hand, open, and obviously being used by him as a loudspeaker, is placed in front of his mouth, and his right hand, held out and raised to shoulder level, is holding a baton. The overseers, in the boats of the tomb of Khaemhat (TT 57)[10] are raising one hand, some armed with a baton, and lowering their free arms thus controlling the unloading of the boats.

As for the stevedores, they are represented in full action in the boats of Hatshepsut. The men are transporting incense trees; six men are necessary for this task, divided into two groups of three. They are using rods that they are carrying on their shoulders; from every rod hangs a rope that passes round a big receptacle in which the incense tree has been potted. The other objects being transported are packed or placed in sacks or baskets; only the big vases are either carried on shoulders or held in the hand. The packets, always voluminous, are placed on shoulders and the stevedores hold them, like the big vases, either with one hand or two. The sacks are also carried on shoulders and held with one hand. It is baskets that are most often used; they are generally provided with two upper corners. The men place the baskets on their shoulders and hold them either with both hands or with a single hand.[11]

A Theban tomb of Khaemwaset (TT 261) shows two Egyptians unloading a wine jar with the aid of a pole resting on their shoulders.[12] Their means of transport is particularly cunning since the rod does not pass through the handles of the amphora, but the latter is held in a net attached by two ropes to the rod. This limits the risk of breakage. It is desirable to place this depiction in tandem with the representations in the Roman period of *phalangarii* or *falancarii*. These harbour workers constituted a real professional

1     N. de G. Davies, *Two Ramesside Tombs at Thebes*, 1927, pl. xxx; C. J. Eyre, in N. Grimal, B. Menu (ed.), *Le commerce, BiÉtud* 121, 1998, p. fig. 2, p. 191.

2     N. de G. Davies, A. H. Gardiner, *JEA* 33, 1947, pl. viii.

3     O. Berlin, P. 11292 (for the photo, *cf.* Endesfelder, *ForshBer* 8, pl. 22, erroneous transcription; refer to that in *Hier. Pap. Berlin* III, pl. xxxa); P. Lansing 12, 6 (A. H. Gardiner, *Late-Egyptian Miscellanies*, 1937, 111, 8; R. A. Caminos, *Late-Egyptian Miscellanies*, 1954, 413 and 417).

4     *Wb* V, 21, 12-13.

5     Y. Kœnig, in *Hommages à S. Sauneron, BiÉtud* 81/1, 1979, pp. 185-220, pl. xxx-xxxviia.

6     *LÄ* I, col. 371; II, col. 65.

7     E. Naville, *The Temple of Deir el-Bahari*, III, 1898, pls lxxi, lxxiv; E. Mackey, *JEA* III, 1916, pl. xiv = M. Baud, *RdÉ* 19, 1968, pl. 2 (TT 261 of Khaemwaset); N. de G. Davies, R. O. Faulkner, *JEA* 33, 1947, pl. viii (TT 162 of Kenamun); *LD* III, pl. 76a (TT 57 of Khaemhat); N. de G. Davies, A. H. Gardiner, *The Tomb of Huy*, 1926, pl. xxxi (TT 40 of Huy). See J. Vandier, *Manuel d'archéologie égyptienne*, V, 1969, p. 1012, figs 126, 128, 129, 348, 351, 363.

8     E. Naville, *op. cit.*, pls lxxi, lxxiv.

9     N. de G. Davies, R. O. Faulkner, *op. cit.*, pl. viii (TT 162 of Kenamun).

10     *LD* III, pl. 76a (TT. 57 of Khaemhat).

11     E. Naville, *op. cit.*, pls lxxi-lxxiv; E. Mackey, *op. cit.*, pl. xiv = M. Baud, *op. cit.*, pl. 2 (TT 261 of Khaemwaset); *LD* III, pl. 76a (TT. 57 of Khaemhat). See the examples given by J. Vandier, *op. cit.*, p. 1014 and figs 137, 348, 428; 351, 362.

12     E. Mackey, *op. cit.*, pl. xiv.

Transporting of cereals, tomb of Paheri, Elkab, New Kingdom, 18th Dynasty (reign of Thutmose III), c. 1450 BC. On the upper register, bags of cereals are being brought aboard several barges. © AKG Images. Photo: Andrea Jemolo

group of stevedores who carried their loads hanging from *phalangae*, rods resting on their shoulders. Paintings and sculptures sometimes show *phalangarii* hard at work transporting amphorae or barrels, or even other kinds of burden.[13] Nonetheless, while in the harbour complex of the Tiber the stevedores formed well-organised professional groups, in most other Roman ports they belonged to a wretched group of the populace that lived on the seasonal work that commercial navigation could procure for them; thus in every port there was a crowd of anonymous labourers whom the winter and the period of *mare clausum* reduced to unemployment and beggary. This was a 'floating population, whose social condition is unknown and which represents a workforce of unskilled labourers, taken on as and when required, without any doubt badly paid and by this very fact representing, in the great ports, where there existed organised colleges of stevedores, a clandestine workforce that was shunned by the real professionals who demanded a monopoly over the loading and unloading of ships'.[14] While the ways of loading and unloading the boats were the same and the techniques age–old,

the condition of the men who practised these activities was not always identical at different times and in different places.

## 1.2. Measurers and weighers

The painting in the tomb of Kenamun (TT 162) that shows the arrival of Syro-Palestinian ships at a quayside on the Nile, depicts a scene in which Asiatic merchandise (wine or oil) is exchanged with manufactured Egyptian objects (clothes, fabrics, sandals, and so on).[15] In the first and third registers, two seated Egyptian men are busy weighing the products exchanged. This scene suggests that there was a whole series of people appointed to the service of

13   J. Rougé, *Revue des études ancienes* LIX, 1957, pp. 320-328.
14   Id., *Recherches sur l'organisation du commerce en Méditerranée sous l'empire romain*, 1966, p. 179.
15   N. de G. Davies, A. H. Gardiner, *JEA* 33, 1947, pl. ix.

weights and measures. They were necessary for the control of merchandise transported in bulk and for that of solid heavy goods.[16] As for liquids, they must have played an insignificant part given that the volume of the receptacles was probably known. They measured cargoes when these had been ordered in advance or were subject to customs taxes.

Were these men specialised for particular types of merchandise? Did they constitute a specific professional group like the *mensores machinarii*, the Roman measurers equipped with their double-pan scales, a sort of elite that was handsomely paid?[17] Let us just say that the men who performed this function at disembarkation or during the exchange of merchandise, measured everything there was to measure.[18]

## I.3. Shipbuilders

Apart from the construction of the most primitive forms of ships, it is evident that shipbuilding requires a certain specialisation[19] on the part of those who practise it. From the most ancient times, there

were naval dockyards, but their condition and organisation are practically unknown until the Roman period. To be sure, the depictions on Egyptian paintings and bas-reliefs often show them at

16  Refer to the articles by H. Ducros dedicated to the weighing scales of the Pharaonic period: scales set on a foot and hand-held scales: H. Ducros, *ASAE* IX, 1908, pp. 32-53; *id.*, *ASAE* X, 1910, pp. 240-253 The first article contains 49 illustrations; they are in general extracted from scenes of the weighing of the heart, but about ten of them show the heart being weighed. On one of the pans of the scales we find one or two weights, in the shape of oxen, and on the other pan are piled up golden rings. On the weighing of monetary metallic units as coins, see *Seafaring in Ancient Egypt*, vol. 2.

17  For theses *mensores*, see J. Rougé, *op. cit.*, pp. 186-187.

18  For Egyptian scales in general, see *LÄ* VI, *s.v.* 'Waage', col. 1081-1086. For concrete representations of the weighing of goods presented to temples or their workshops, see, for example, the depiction in Medinet Habu (weighing of goods offered by Rameses III to Amun: Medinet Habu V, 320; *KRI* V, 318, 2-10), but also the weighing scene *b3k(w) n3 n mrwt pr Jmn* in the tomb (TT 178) of Neferrebpet, or Kel (W. Wreszinski, *Atlas zur alt äegyptischen Kulturgeschichte*, I, 1915, pl. 74a; S. Schott, *GM* 29, 1978, pp. 127-132; *KRI* III, 330, 14-15); likewise the weighing scene *jnw n pr-ḥd* in the tomb (TT 343) of Benia, or Paheqamen (H. Guksch, *Das Grab des Benja*, ArchVer 7, 1978, pl. 9, p. 18; *id.*, *MDAIK* 38, 1982, p. 31, pls 31-35); for examples of similar scenes, see W. Wreszinski, *op. cit.*, 1915, pls 50, 59a, 78a ; N. de G., Davies, *The Tomb of Rekh-mi-re'*, II, 1943, pl. xxxi. The term *jry-mḥ3.t* concretely designated the person entrusted with control of the weighings (*Wb* I, 104, 5; *KRI* III, 330, 11).

19  On the naval architecture of sea ships, *cf.* p. 102 *et seq.*

*Mensor machinarius*, mosaic from Susa. On a beach, not far from the ship at anchor, a mensor is weighing the ingots that are being unloaded (Late Roman Period).
© 1996 Photo Scala, Florence. Bardo Museum, Tunis

work, which means their tools can at least be studied; but this is more or less all that can be done, or, at least, all that has been attempted thus far.[20]

The *Satire on Trades* acquaints us with the conditions of life of naval carpenters.[21] The latter were associated with the *šwty.w*-merchants and the crew of the *mmnš*-boats who travelled to Syro-Palestine. There exists valuable information on the activity of the naval dockyard of Peru-nefer, probably near Memphis, under the New Kingdom (1570-1070 BC), thanks to Papyrus 10056 of the British Museum. Here there appear, under Thutmose III (1504-1450 BC) and Thutmose IV (1419-1386 BC), the names of Syrian naval carpenters, a highly qualified personnel, not a servile workforce. And these names appear in places other than Peru-nefer; a Syrian constructs divine barques for the whole of Egypt. Under the reign of Amenophis II (1453-1419 BC), offerings were made to an oriental god, the 'Baal of Peru-nefer' and there existed, at the time of Akhenaten, a priest with a Hurrite name, serving in particular in the worship of a certain 'Astarte of Peru-nefer'. The presence in Peru-nefer, the main Egyptian naval dockyard, of a couple of Canaanite gods, both of them protectors of navigation, can be explained by the existence of an immigrant Canaanite or Syrian population in Egypt, one having a relation to sailing: sailors, perhaps, and shipbuilders certainly. So W. Helck is quite right to say: 'doubtless the Egyptians built their (sea) ships in their own dockyards, but under the technical direction of Syrian carpenters, just as in the Middle Ages Dutch carpenters built the Hanseatic ships'.[22] In several texts celebrating his victories in Asia, engraved on the walls of temples at Karnak, Luxor and Abydos, Rameses II glories in having sent *mnš*-ships to sea, so as to bring back, for the god Amun, tribute from foreign lands. It was observed above that the *mnš*-ship was Syrian in type.[23]

Everything leads us to suppose that there were dockyards for building ships, and also for repairing and maintaining them. To these dockyards there belonged different groups of workers. The classical sources indicate four big groups of shipbuilders who provide evidence of the division of tasks: the *architecti nauales*, the *fabri nauales*, and the *stuppatores*, often together with the *unctores* and the *saburrarii*.[24] While Pharaonic Egypt did not perhaps go in for this specialisation of labour, this documentation is evidence of the particular competence required in naval construction.

The distinction between the architects of naval construction and the constructors properly speaking is easy to imagine. For if it is easy for a naval carpenter to construct a barque corresponding to a definite type, one he is used to, he cannot by himself construct a big ship; he needs to work under the control of an architect who has calculated and designed the plans for the ship. The architect who is then responsible for the construction does not work alone, he is to some extent at the head of a practice, in modern parlance. Unfortunately not much is known about these naval architects: were they specifically attached to the war fleets or the civil fleets?

Different depictions show naval carpenters at work, under the direct control of the architects.[25] It was they who fashioned and assembled the different pieces of wood that were to form the ship. In order to do this, their main tool was the adze, which enabled them to shape the curves of the floor frames and the timbers as well as of the planking. On certain depictions, carpenters also use the axe (which is used for large-scale carpentry, rough-planing and squaring), the saw (with which the squared trees are cut into planks), the chisel

and mallet (used to dig mortices), but also the rammer (a sort of heavy mass equipped with two handles, used to drive in either the tenons into the mortices, or the boards, shaped on demand, into the place they are to occupy between two elements already in place). On a scene of the Mastaba of Ty, on the deck of a boat, there are three men digging a mortice, another is planing the bulwarks with an adze, and two workers are busy, one sawing a plank, and the other dressing a cleft post with an adze.[26]

It is obvious that not all those bearing the name of naval carpenters were in the same position: among them there were probably bosses, entrepreneurs of naval construction, mere workers or apprentices, and so on.

Caulking and protecting the hull must have necessitated specialised hands and particular skills.[27] Once the ship was complete, one last operation still needed to be carried out: ballasting it. This was a delicate operation since the ship's stability at sea depended on it. The ballast was probably formed from stone blocks placed at the bottom of the hold, which had to be carefully arranged and secured to balance the ship and prevent any shifting. Nothing entitles us to conclude that there were specialists in ballasting in Pharaonic Egypt; some naval carpenter or experienced sailor must have taken on this task.[28]

Finally, it should be stressed that there is little information on the manufacture of ropes and sails. Nonetheless, in later periods, it is possible that in the regions that were great producers of raw materials there were specialised corps of manufacturers.[29] As far as the sails are concerned, there must have existed specialised weavers in this type of work.

20 J. Vandier, *Manuel d'archéologie égyptienne*, V, 1969, pp. 660-686.

21 P. Lansing, 4, 8-4, 9; A. H. Gardiner, *Late-Egyptian Miscellanies*, 1937, p. 103; R. A. Caminos, *Late-Egyptian Miscellanies*, 1954, p. 384 with notes; A. Erman, H. Lange, *Papyrus Lansing*, 1925, p. 54 *et seq.*; A. Théodoridès, *AIPHO* 15, 1960, p. 86. There is a bibliography on *The Satire on Trades* in B. Mathieu, *Grafma newsletter* 2, 1998, pp. 37-40.

22 W. Helck, *Die Beziehungen Ägyptens*, 1962, p. 544.

23 *cf.* p. 94-95.

24 M. C. Bottigelli, *Ricerce epigrafiche sulla marineria nell'Italia romana*, IV, 1942 p. 150 *et seq.*; F. Moll, *Der Schiffbauer in der bildenden Kunst*, 1930; J. Rougé, *Recherches sur l'organisation du commerce en Méditerranée sous l'empire romain*, 1966, p. 190; L. Casson, *Ships and Seamanship*, 1971. Naval carpenters were to form powerful corporations in the Roman ports. The *Edict of Diocletian* gives us the daily wage of these *fabric nauales*; this wage is, indeed, quite instructive since it shows us that these were well-paid specialists; a naval carpenter, working on the construction of a sea ship, earned 60 *denarii* per day, and only the more artistic workers earned more – the marble workers, painters and sculptors (*Edict of Diocletian*, VII, 13). See J. Rougé, *op. cit.*, p. 190.

25 On the relief of the Mastaba of Ty (5th Dynasty, Saqqara), the carpenters are busy working under the surveillance of a man (the naval architect?): H. Wild, *Le tombeau de Ti*, III, MIFAO LXV, 1939, pls xcvi-xcvii; J. Vandier, *Manuel d'Archéologie égyptienne*, V, 1969, p. 669. See the photograph published in A. Gros de Beler, *Vivre en Égypte au temps de Pharaon*, 2001, n° 126 p. 107.

26 H. Wild, *op. cit.*, pls xcvi-xcvii. See the numerous depictions of naval carpenters studied by, J. Vandier, *op. cit.*, pp. 659-686.

27 In the Latin documentation, the *stuppatores*, the caulkers, ensured that the hull was waterproof by applying tow to the seams between the strakes of the planking, as well as the scarfs, the abutments, and the cracks (on the caulking of Egyptian ships, see p. 109-110). As for the *unctores*, they were entrusted with applying wax to the ships' hulls; we doubtless need to see in this a measure designed to protect the wood against the action of the seawater, similar to that which, these days, still consists of coating the fishing barques with coal tar. On these two professional bodies and the sources that refer to them, see J. Rougé, *op. cit.*, p. 190.

28 For comparison, see the specialists in ballasting, the *saburrarii*, who are known to us only through the ports of the Tiber: J. Rougé, *op. cit.*, p. 192.

29 Pliny the Elder, *Natural History*, XIII, 72; *cf.* N. Lewis, *l'industrie du papyrus dans l'Égypte gréco-romaine*, 1934, pp. 6, 30-31.

Naval carpenters, relief of the Mastaba of Ty at Saqqara, Old Kingdom, 5th Dynasty, c. 2498–2345 BC. © Archivo Iconographico, S.A./CORBIS

## I.4. The port 'officials'

This review of the port personnel will conclude by investigating those whom could be called the 'officials' of the port. This category will include people of origins and functions, as different as scribes, harbour masters, customs officers, the guardians of ships and entrepots, and so on. These were people whom can be linked with the services performed by the harbour master's office. Unfortunately, if the existence of the latter is a consequence of the great importance of maritime commerce and thus the activity of ports, it has to be recognised that its organisation is not well known and the same study will have to include people who did not necessarily have a great deal in common, apart from the fact that they belonged to the harbour administration.

Scribes were omnipresent in all these transactions, as authorities and as overseers. They were not part of the crew, did not travel, did not live on the ships and did not receive any ration as members of the crew.[30] Was this because of their more elevated social rank? Whether this was so or not, these bureaucrats seem to have been established *in situ*, in offices situated either in the ports or in adjacent towns, where they kept the registers of all operations on behalf of the institutions to which they were attached.

An on-board register dating from the reign of Rameses II (1279–1212 BC) concerns a boat moored at Piramesse.[31] The owner

seems to have been the *sm*-priest of Ptah of Memphis, Khaemwaset, probably the well-known son of Rameses II, with whom the crew was in almost daily correspondence by the intermediary of several *šms.w*-envoys. Every day, transactions (coming in or going out) of foodstuffs were registered under the supervision of a scribe.

The Turin papyri 2008 and 2016,[32] dating from the 10th Dynasty (*c.* 2160–2040 BC), mention a voyage that set out from Thebes, probably on behalf of the domain of Amun. Two months later, the ship left Heliopolis and went to Memphis. Here, after a few days' wait, and changing its mooring place several times over, the crew waited for the scribe of the Treasure to come and draw up a list of the cargo. As an example, over a week after their delivery, between 3,000 and 5,000 fish were still on board: the rest must have been part of a transaction which is not known.[33] The cargo also included oil, wine, seed, papyrus scrolls, salt, rushes and the heads of poultry. Rushes and ropes (four coils of 1,000 cubits, and 27 of 500 cubits

---

30    These scribes are to be distinguished from the 'scribes of the crew': see below.

31    P. Leyde I 350, v°; J. J. Janssen, *Two Ancient Egyptian Ship's Logs*, 1961, pp. 1-52; S. Bickel, in N. Grimal, B. Menu (ed.), 'le commerce', *BiEtud* 121, 1998, p. 157.

32    P. Turin 2008 and 2016. J. J. Janssen, *op. cit.*, p. 53-95; S. Bickel, *op. cit.*, p. 157.

33    S. Bickel, *op. cit.*, pp. 157-158.

long) were delivered a little later by the 'crew's boatman' (*nfw n rmt js.t*), again under the authority of a scribe.[34]

There is little information on the financial and economic agents who exercised their activities in the ports. Nevertheless, the control and surveillance of the arrivals, the collection of taxes, the protection of ships and their occupants, and even the settling of court cases, must have kept a certain number of people busy.[35]

Egyptian sources provide a glimpse, however general and vague it may be, of these people who were in charge of harbour administration.[36] There must without any doubt have been a police force, watchmen and so on, in charge not only of preventing fires and accidents that might affect the ships anchored in port, but also a harbour master's office, whose main role was the regulation of ships coming alongside the wharfs. Every port required officials to oversee the maintenance work on harbour installations (quays, entrepots, and so on), to check out river and sea navigation, to collect harbour dues and taxes, and different characters to look after relations with pilgrim merchants. Generally speaking, this harbour personnel participated in the good functioning of the harbour activities. The role of these functionaries must have been an important one if the text detailing the taking of Memphis by Assarhaddon (680-669 BC) in 671 BC is to be believed:[37]

> *I besieged Mempi, its (Taharqa) royal residence, and took it in half a day by means of saps, breaches and assault ladders. His queen, the women in his palace, Ouchanahourou, his heir apparent, his other children, his possessions, his countless horses, his cattle small and large — all of them I carried off as spoils to Assyria. All the Kushites I deported out of Egypt, leaving not one to pay me homage. Everywhere in Egypt I appointed other kings, governors, officers, harbour controllers, functionaries, and administrative personnel.*

Documents from the Roman period provide more detailed information about this harbour administration. Thus there were functionaries of the State corn supply entrusted with the task of overseeing everything that had to do with the administration, and one of their main functions was the payment of transport indemnities to those entitled to them. Furthermore, several procurators are known, some of whom had, or may have had, a role in harbour administration. This is certainly true of the procurator of the lighthouse, an imperial emancipated slave, who definitely had the task of presiding over the upkeep of that monument that was indispensable to the activity of the great port, but whose function could extend as far as constituting a real harbour master's office.[38]

This is less sure, but not impossible, for the equestrian procurators who bore just the title *procurator Alexandreae*. The most interesting case is that of *procurator Alexandreae Pelusi et P...*, an ancient post; the procurator went on to administer the Tiber ports. Whatever the interpretation may be given to a third term (*phari, philiacae, potamophyliacae, Paraetoni*), it is undeniable that this was a function relating to harbour activities.[39] Outside Egypt, imperial functionaries placed directly at the head of a harbour organisation are not known.

To the study of the purely administrative harbour functions, those fulfilled by the limenarch, known to us from a papyrus[40] should be added. The limenarch can be viewed as an inspector of the ports of the Nile controlling the corn expeditions and their embarkation to the granaries of Neapolis, in the Alexandrian suburb. Mentions of this function in the *corpus iuris ciuilis* enable us to conclude, as does J. Rougé, that the limenarch was not a local functionary, since he was clearly distinguished from the *magistratus municipales* and his appointment depended on high imperial functionaries, without our being able to know exactly which ones. The limenarch had police powers and as such he had authority over certain prisons. Finally, he was closely linked to harbour navigation: he was the guardian of the ships. All of this, when added to the etymology of the word ('the person at the head of the port'), might lead us to see him as the harbour master. However, J. Rougé rejects this hypothesis, since it seems from the juridical texts that they were merely representatives of the State police in the ports and they did not intervene in the technical problems of the administration of the latter; they were rather police commissioners than harbour masters.[41]

As for the *custodes litorum*, their name evokes their function. They were the ancestors of modern customs officers, charged with coastal surveillance rather than being maritime guards, but they also had a police role.[42]

34    *Id.*, p. 158.

35    'Those appointed to the gates' and the collection of customs dues are examined in more detail in *Seafaring in Ancient Egypt*, vol. 2.

36    Kenamun (TT 162, 18th Dynasty) occupied several extremely high positions simultaneously, including that of the administrator of *Pr-nfr*, the royal domain near Memphis that was equipped with a port; cf. p. 47.

37    J. B. Pritchard, *ANET*, 293.

38    J. Rougé, *Recherches sur l'organisation du commerce en Méditerranée sous l'empire romain*, 1966, p. 208.

39    *Id.*, p. 209.

40    Gissen Papyrus, 10 (dating from AD 118).

41    J. Rougé, *Recherches sur l'organisation du commerce en Méditerranée sous l'empire romain*, 1966, p. 210.

42    *Id.*, p. 211.

## II. The sailing personnel

*I was going to* Wadj Wer *on board a ship 120 cubits long and 40 cubits wide. One hundred sailors manned it, from the elite of Egypt; whether they surveyed the sky, or whether they surveyed the earth, their heart was braver than (that) of lions; they predicted a tempest before it had blown up, and a storm before it had arrived. (The Tale of the Shipwrecked Sailor, 25–32)*[43]

*Look at the crew of this ship, do you see how some are embarked on tugs and have taken the oars, others have hoisted the anchors and are making them fast, others are setting the sails to the winds, others remain in observation at the poop and the prow? If a single member of the crew abandoned his particular and unique task, or accomplished it contrary to the art of sailing, everyone would endure a bad crossing and they themselves would be their own tempest. But if they compete with one another and if everyone endeavours to appear just as skilful as his fellow, then this ship will reach a good port, it will everywhere encounter fine weather and a successful navigation, and their prudence towards themselves will be the equivalent for them of the intervention of Poseidon, the dispenser of security.*

(Philostratus, *Life of Apollonius*, IV, 9)[44]

These two texts from different times and places 'embark on' a description of sailors' activities on board their ships, and express the pride and the anxieties of seafarers. Since, on water, any mistake is unforgivable and quickly punished, every crew member must fulfil his own task and keep to the position that has been allotted him at the moment of departure. This rigour stands out against the traditional description presented by certain classical moralists who see these sailors as out-and-out scoundrels, a gang of more or less shifty characters, drunken and debauched, braggarts and spongers. In short, a minuscule and separate world of its own, in which everyone is employed in accordance with his own competences, and everything is working at full blast.

It is necessary to find out the names and exact functions of the crew members, that 'ship's populace' to use the expression of Philostratus. Nonetheless, this sailing personnel will only be briefly referred to.[45]

### II.1. The crew

A certain number of Egyptian terms are used to describe the members of the crew of an Egyptian ship. This profusion sometimes reveals a certain degree of specialisation on the part of the people who embarked. *Js.t* is the first term that comes to mind when it is a question of the ship's 'crew'. In a document dating from the reign of Rameses II,[46] a ship moored at Piramesse carried a crew (*js.t*) of 35-38 persons. The term seems to designate all the people present on the ship, both the sailors and the captain, without any distinction of rank and function. The word '*pr*' is applied to 'people who are teamed together in the same work', sailors when the navy is mentioned in the text.[47] The word '*mš*', 'the (armed) troop' can also designate the members of the ship's crew.[48] *Pd.t* refers to any human collectivity, civil or military, organised for a precise task, either permanent or exceptional, equipped with a chief, such as those *ḥry.w pd.wt n mnš*, 'heads of the troops of *mnš*-ships',[49] who participated in the expedition to Punt organised in the reign of Rameses III.[50]

*Sqd.w* designates the sailors, whose essential task was probably to manoeuvre the sail and the gear, but it is practically impossible for us to know what particular names were borne, included within the function *sqd*, by the various different specialities that were visible in different nautical depictions, in accordance with the usages of the navy under sail. How was continuous service effected? Was there a system for sharing the work time? There are few scenes that indicate how the sail was manoeuvred. One of the Asiatic ships from the tomb of Kenamun[51] has preserved an example, albeit one that is difficult to interpret. The ships have just arrived in port; those on the lower register, to the right, are already at anchor, and the yards have been either lowered (the upper yard) or hoisted; thanks to this manoeuvre

43  *Hꜣ=kw r Wꜣd-wr m dp.t n(y).t 120 mh m ꜣw=s 40 mh m šhw=s 120 sqd.w jm=s m Km.t mꜣ=sn p.t mꜣ=sn tꜣ mꜥkꜣ jb=sn r mꜣ(j).w sr=sn dꜥ pr dꜥ n jjt(=f) nšny n ḫprt=f.*

44  Translated from the Greek by P. Grimal, *Romans grecs et latins*, p. 1144.

45  See the numerous references both documentary and bibliographical given in D. Jones, *A Glossary of Ancient Egyptian Nautical Titles and Terms*, 1988.

46  P. Leyde I 350, v°; J. J. Janssen, *Two Ancient Egyptian Ship's Logs*, 1961, pp. 1-52.

47  D. Meeks, *RdÉ* 24, 1974, p. 57 n. 8. For the '*pr.w n n(y)-sw(.t) wjꜣ* 'the crews of the royal barques', see for example, in the chapel of Hathor at Deir el-Bahari: *Urk.*, IV, 304, 17; 307, 15.

48  See for example *The Tale of the Shipwrecked Sailor*, 170-171.

49  P. Grandet, *Le papyrus Harris I, BiÉtud* 109, 1994, vol. 2, n. 159, 929, 933. See too T. Säve-Söderbergh, *The Navy*, 1946, p. 83; A. H. Gardiner, *AEO* I, 113*; R. O. Faulkner, *JEA* 39, 1953, p. 45; R. O. Caminos, *Late-Egyptian Miscellanies*, 1954, p. 111; L. A. Christophe, *ASAE* LV, 1958, p. 20.

50  P. Harris I, 77, 9; passage cited p. 86-87. On the subject of *ḥry.w pd.wt n mnš*, cf. infra. p. 148.

51  N. de G. Davies, R. O. Faulkner, *JEA* 33, 1947, pl. viii.

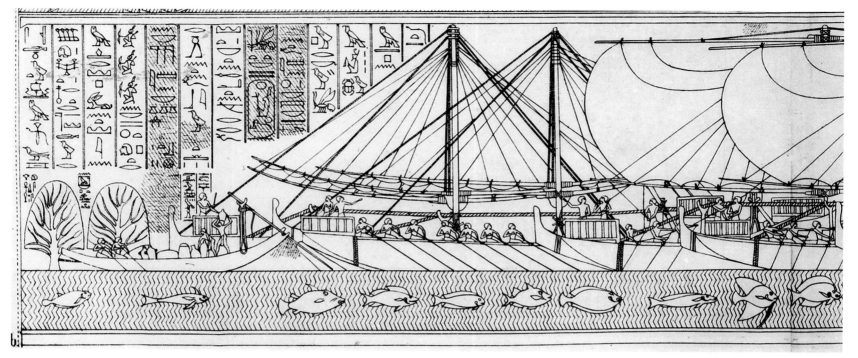

Expedition to Punt, funerary temple of Hatshepsut, Deir el-Bahari, *c.* 1490–1468 BC; supplying the ships about to leave. Drawing after M. Rival, in D. Meeks and D. Garcia (eds), *Techniques et économie antiques et médiévales*, 1997, p. 181. © Heritage Images

the two yards are placed one after the other, approximately a third of the way up the mast. The sail is clumsily depicted; in any case it has not been unbent, nor does it seem that it has been furled. For a halt of short duration it was doubtless enough to bring the two yards together without touching the sail. On the left the start of the operation is perhaps depicted: the two yards are still in place and the sail is still swollen by the wind. Two men are occupied with the manoeuvre of the halyards. These halyards, in the register on the right, are clearly visible and seem to have been attached to the lower yard. Two sailors are busy handling the halyards while two others are endeavouring to reach the summit of the mast, one using the mast, the other the halyards. In one of the ships on the left a sailor is leaning forward in such a way that his torso is horizontal: with his arms lowered, he is holding a rope in both his hands, probably a lift. His companion on the right is perhaps standing at the awning rope and turning round, doubtless to transmit the orders being transmitted to him by the *proreutes* who is standing on the stem. In one of the boats on the right, in the upper register, three men are again standing on the lower yard, two at each extremity, and the third near the mast; the latter is doubtless getting ready to climb up. Two additional sailors are busy around the yards, though it is not clear exactly what they are doing. Finally, on the lower register, a sailor standing upright on the deck is lifting his two arms and placing his hands on his head, as if he wished to hold up the lower yard. In reality he must be making a gesture of greeting, addressed to the Egyptians who are standing on the shore and who have come to take delivery of the cargo.

In the ships of Queen Hatshepsut that were sent to the land of Punt, certain sailors are represented standing on the lower yard. It was doubtless their role to use their weight to increase the stability of the sail in its given orientation, and their presence perhaps explains the great number of lifts that are holding up the lower yard. It is possible that these men also had the task of setting the sail in a certain direction following the indications of the head of navigation. Their

postures are quite varied but there is no point in describing them in detail. The men are sitting, standing or lying on the yard near the preventer lifts or the halyards.[52] All these depictions, as stated above, are difficult to explain and the few details present do not allow us to describe the complexity of the sail's manoeuvres in any detail.

The word *ny.t* designates 'the rowers'. The oars, in sea ships, were reserved for the secondary manoeuvres of navigation, for example when they were leaving the shore or when they were preparing to land.[53] In one of the boats of Sahure that took part in an expedition to Syro-Palestine, seven sailors can be found on the port side; they have short hair and are wearing belts from which are hanging segments of fabric that form 'aprons'. They are standing on the deck; their legs are apart, one foot is forward and placed flat, the other is on tiptoe. Their bodies are leaning forward; the left arm is held extended forwards, slightly above the horizontal, and the right arm is held out lowered, with the hands thus holding the oar in two points quite far removed. The oars are being held at an angle, the blades behind the rowers (and so towards the prow), and they are attached to the side of the boat by means of grommets.[54]

In the depictions of the ships of Sahure, 'Asiatics' were to be found on board and apparently comprised part of the crew of rowers and sailors. The expedition of Hatshepsut included five ships with 210 men on board (42 men per ship), counting 30 rowers per boat, to which should be added the crew entrusted with manoeuvres, a small armed troop, and the officers.

52   E. Naville, *The Temple of Deir el-Bahari*, III, 1898; see depictions in M. Rival, in D. Meeks, D. Garcia (ed.), *Techniques et économie antiques et médiévales*, 1997, pp. 181-184.
53   See C. Boreux, *Études de nautique égyptienne*, MIFAO I, 1925, p. 482.
54   L. Borchardt, *Das Grandenkmal des König, S3hure'*, II, 1910, pl. 11; J. Vandier, *Manuel d'archéologie égyptienne*, V, 1969, p. 876, fig. 331.

The Lansing Papyrus, a New Kingdom version of the *Satire on Trades*, describes the activity of the crews of the merchant navy; the text presents sea voyages as being dangerous enough for the sailors to fear that they will never see their lands again:[55]

*The crew of the mnš-ships of each domain (pr) has received its load and is ready to leave Egypt for Djahy. The god of each man is with him. Not one among them dares to say, 'We will see Egypt again'.*

There is every justification in proceeding by comparison, since an extract from the Chester Beatty Papyrus shows us the kind of life that awaits the crews of Nile vessels. The traditional cliché of the crocodiles is not spared:[56]

*As for the sailor, it is said that crocodiles have taken up their positions (to spy on him), while the ship, his town, is (in a fine predicament?). For the sailor is exhausted, while the oar is in his hand, and the lash on his back; his stomach is empty of nourishment.*

## II.2. The ship's guardian

Among the characters endowed with a certain authority on the boat was the *s³w*–guardian, who must have been responsible for the cargo and was thereby present at every transaction.[57]

This term/function can be related to a profession that was known by Greek and Latin texts, which is not directly linked to the ship's staff, and does not have any relation to manoeuvring the ship, namely the *custodes nauium*, a Latin translation of the Greek

ναυφυλακες.[58] These terms define precisely the functions of those to whom it applies: the ships' guardians, but in spite of this apparent ease of interpretation, this term presents a certain number of difficulties. Are the guardians ordinary sailors placed in charge of overseeing access to the ship when it is in port or is moored? The text of the *Digest* clearly distinguishes them from the rest of the crew – especially since they have been proposed as such by the outfitter and that is why they can, to some extent, make a contract with the passengers and the loaders, thus engaging the outfitter's responsibility. So if they have been given a clearly defined mission of surveillance, this must not be extended merely to the ship in port, but also during its crossing. In other words, this is a veritable police corps entrusted with overseeing good order on the ship, avoiding conflicts between crew members, and between the crew and the passengers, and finally between the passengers themselves, but they must also oversee the cargo to prevent thefts and criminal damage and make sure that no act of a nature prejudicial to the good functioning of the ship is committed on board.[59]

---

55  *P. Lansing*, 4, 8-4, 9.

56  *Chester Beatty* V, r°, 6, 4-5 (= A. H. Gardiner, *Hieratic Papyri in the British Museum, Third Series*, 1935, I, p. 47; II, pl. 25); cf. B. Van de Walle, *CdÉ XXII/43*, 1947, p. 62.

57  P. Leyde I 350, v°; P. Turin 2008 + 2016: J. J. Janssen, *Two Ancient Egyptian Ship's Logs*, 1961 pp. 1-52, 53-95; S. Bickel; in N. Grimal, B. Menu (ed.), *Le commerce*, BiÉtud 121, 1998, pp. 157-158.

58  J. Rougé, *Recherches sur l'organisation du commerce en Méditerranée sous l'empire romain*, p. 218.

59  *Digest*, XLVII, 5. On the 'guardians' of trading ships in the Hellenistic era, see J. Vélissaropoulos, *Les nauclères grecs*, 1980, pp. 85-86.

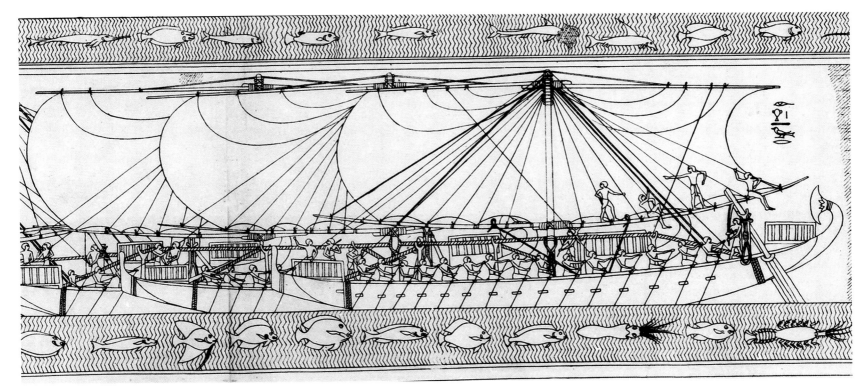

Expedition to Punt, funerary temple of Hatshepsut, Deir el-Bahari, c. 1490–1468 BC; departure manoeuvres and first part of the journey. Drawing after M. Rival, in D. Meeks and D. Garcia (eds), *Techniques et économie antiques et médiévales*, 1997, p. 182. © Heritage Images

## II.3. The 'officers of transport'

A category of official that is more difficult to define is that of the *mškb.w*. They form a troop under the orders of a *ḥry mškb.w*-chief. They are found engaged on three types of activity: that of chariots and horses, tax collecting, and transport vessels. In this last domain their function consisted probably of ensuring the security of the ships: they might have constituted a sort of escort.[60] They can be compared to the *s3.w pr.w* on land, a sort of security force with the task of cleansing the trails of brigands who could menace the smooth journey of a caravan, joined to the *nw.w*, the corps of dog trainers, one of whose main functions was to ensure the safety of police missions in the desert.[61]

There is some evidence for the role of the *mškb.w* and the *ḥry.w mškb.w*.[62] One document tells us that an *mškb* could have under his authority ships transporting construction stones.[63] Another *mškb* worked on a ship which carried pigs and he had been granted one of these beasts,[64] either as a salary or as a tip. Two chief *mškb.w*[65] and two ordinary *mškb.w* are known from funerary steles.[66] This profession is also attested in the entourage of the people of Deir el-Medina: one of the sons of Neferhotep (TT 6) is 'first *mškb* of His Majesty'.[67]

A passage in Harris Papyrus I, speaks of the *mškb.w* in these terms:[68]

> *I have made for you (crews of) rowers and (of) mškb(y).w, composed of people I have trained, so as to collect the contributions on the production of the Double Land (b3kw T3.wy), the allowances (ḥtr) and the taxes (š3y.t) (then) to transport these by ship to your treasury in the domain of Ra, so as to increase your divine offering millions of times over.*

The exact function of the *mškb.w* is thus still imperfectly known. This term seems to designate the people entrusted with tasks that have not been properly elucidated, in respect of things as diverse as ships, horses, transport, the collecting of products and the departure into the countryside. They seem to have been organised militarily and J. H. Breasted sees them as 'tax officials', J. J. Janssen as 'haulers' of ships, subsequently (and secondarily) charged with looking after the horses. It is usually translated, following A. H. Gardiner, as 'officers of transport'. The passage of Papyrus Harris I previously mentioned suggests this designated soldiers or police entrusted with providing, for obvious security reasons, the escort for the collectors of products that were, for various reasons, owed to the temple treasuries.[69]

There is nothing surprising in the fact that an escort is present on the ships; in the papyrological documentation, the Nile trading ships were accompanied by supercargoes and police who were there to oversee the cargo; in addition, the Nile was patrolled not only by the ships of the river police, but by detached units of the war fleet placed at the disposal of the *dioecetes* of Egypt to protect cargoes against rebel and pirate attacks and to keep open the communication channels with the capital.

The discovery of weapons on board peaceful merchant ships clearly indicates, however, that there was a defensive intention here, thanks to the presence of armed men — either robust crew members or elements who had embarked essentially to serve as an escort and face the threat of acts of piracy.[70] Such a measure of precaution, close in many respects to the organisation of security guards engaged these

days, in many European countries, to protect the transport of funds or the persons at risk of kidnap, comes as no surprise, since this must have been a common practice in the ancient world, one which cannot have failed to produce results. Underwater discoveries provide us with numerous examples of the types of weapons used: light armour for self-defence (helmet, breastplate) as well as swords and knives for use against the enemy should he board the ship, or else short-range projectiles (bows, slings, catapults, javelins, and so on). However, it is possible that in certain cases, more significant weapons may have been brought into play — more efficient ones, designed to strike at greater distances and preventing the assailants from coming up to the vessel, perhaps by inflicting on them losses that would dissuade them from acting. In short, ships with more sophisticated weaponry, and with weapons making long-range firing possible, necessitated the presence of specialised personnel. An extract from Xenophon seems perhaps to hint as much, with his allusion to a Phoenician merchant ship equipped with war machines destined to ward off the enemy assaults.[71] An old underwater archaeological discovery endorses this view, thanks to new analyses of the wreck of *Mahdia* in Tunisia, dating from the start of the 1st century BC and found in 1907. On its discovery, the ship yielded a load of marble and bronze sculptures as well as some 70 columns with their bases and capitals; the other materials — various objects in bronze that were recovered in bulk — at that time escaped attention. Now, a recent re-examination of this equipment has enabled us to recognise in it metallic pieces coming from a catapult. A projectile made to inspire respect, then, clearly carried on a cargo vessel to serve for defence, at a time, precisely, when piracy was at its height in the Mediterranean.[72]

60  P. Leyde I 350, v°; P. Turin 2008 + 2016: J. J. Janssen, *Two Ancient Egyptian Ship's Logs*, 1961 pp. 1-52, 53-95; S. Bickel, in N. Grimal, B. Menu (ed.), 'le commerce', *BiÉtud* 121, 1998, pp. 157-158. For the various attestations and functions cf. J. E. Hoch, *Semitic Words in Egyptian Texts*, 1994, pp. 160-163; A. R. Schulmann, *Military Rank, Title and Organization*, MÄS 6, 1964, p. 48; id., *ZÄS* 93, 1966, pp. 123-132. On a *ḥry mškb.w* of the crew of the ship Merenptah which is also *wpwty r ḫ3s.t nb.t*, see H. El-Saady, *MDAIK* 55, 1999, pp. 419, 425 n° 27.

61  For example, Henu describes the advance of the expedition sent by Montuhotep to the Red Sea coasts in these terms: `s3.w pr.w` clear the roads before me and overthrow every man who is a rebel to the king' (*s3.w pr.w ḥr ḏsr w3.wt ḥr-ḥ3.t(=j) ḥr sḫr.t sb ḥr n(y)-sw.t*): Hamm. 114, 11-12 (J. Couyat, P. Montet, *Les inscriptions du Ouadi Hammâmât*, MIFAO XXXIV, 1912-1913, p. 83, pl. 31). On the *s3.w pr.w*, see the study by J. Yoyotte, *RdÉ* 9, 1952, pp. 139-151.

62  After the documentation mentioned by S. Bickel, in N. Grimal, B. Menu (ed.), 'le commerce', *BiÉtud* 121, 1998, n. 5-10 p. 159

63  H. Frankfort, A. de Buck, B. Gunn, *The Cenotaph of Seti I at Abydos*, 1933, I, p. 94, l. 5; II, pls 90, 92.

64  W. Spiegelberg, *RT* 15, 1893, pp. 142-143: P. Boulaq XII, r° 6-7.

65  Ashmolean Stele 1947.294 of the *ḥry mškb.w* Djehutihotep, *KRI* V, 396, 2-12; Stele of Amenemuia (BM 1183) who was '*ḥry mškb.w* of the fleet of Rameses III beloved of Sekhmet' (*ḥry mškb.w n ḥn.t R°-mss-Ḥq3 Jwnw mry Sḥm.t*).

66  A. R. Schulmann, *ZÄS* 93, 1966, pl. 8-9, fig. 1, Stele of Pentaur, Philadephia 61-13-1 (the same character is also figured on Stele BM290, see, id., pls 8-9, fig. 2; S. Bickel, *op. cit.*, p. 159 and fig. 2 p. 165); also see the Stele of Pakharu, Budapest 51.2145 mentioned by A. R. Schulmann, *op. cit.*, pls 8-9, fig. 3).

67  H. Wild, *La tombe de Neferhotep (I) et Neb-nefer*, MIFAO 103/2, 1979, pls 6 and 20; S. Bickel, *op. cit.*, p. 159.

68  P. Harris I, 28, 5 (things performed by Rameses III in favour of the gods of Heliopolis): translation by P. Grandet, *Le papyrus Harris I*, BidÉtud 109, vol. 1, p. 261.

69  J. H. Breasted, *Ancient Records of Egypt*, IV, 1906, § 266 and p. 146 n. f; L. A. Christophe, *ASAE* LV, 1958, pp. 20-21; W. F. Edgerton, J. A. Wilson, *Historical Records of Ramsès III*, SAOC 12, 1936, p. 8, n. 16a; R. O. Faulkner, *JEA* 39, 1953, pp. 32-47; A. H. Gardiner, *AEO*, I, 92*; P. Grandet, *op. cit.*, vol. 2, n. 506 p. 121A; J. J. Janssen, *op. cit.*, pp. 34-35; R. Schulmann, *Military Rank, Title and Organization*, MÄS 6, 1964, p. 48; M. Valloggia, *Recherche sur les «Messagers» (Wpwtyw)*, 1976, p. 161, n° 117(a); Anlex 78.1882, 79.1378.

70  On piracy, see p. 25-27.

71  Xenophon, *Oeconomicus*, VIII, 11.

72  P. A. Gianfrotta, in P. Pomey (ed.), *La navigation dans l'Antiquité*, 1997, p. 57.

## II.4. The officials of the crew

'Director of the crew of oarsmen' ((*j*)*m*(*y*)-*r*(*ꜣ*) *js.t ẖnw.w*), 'director of rowers' ((*j*)*m*(*y*)-*r*(*ꜣ*) *ẖnw.w*), 'chief of the galley-slaves' (*ḥry ẖny.t*).[73] With these terms, we take up the theme of the officers corps. The *ḥry ẖny.t* is the chief of the galley slaves, for whom he beats time (sometimes with a lash of the whip).[74] On the depictions of the ships of Sahure one of them, his right hand held out in front of his mouth, extends his left arm horizontally forwards, with his hand holding a rod of office. The signal must be addressed to the helmsmen, but it is possible that the man is at the same time directing by voice the rhythm of the rowing.[75] The ships of Hatshepsut are under sail, but a team of oarsmen is at work, certainly at the moment when the ships leave the port to reach the open sea. In the only two boats that appear in their entirety on the reliefs of Deir el-Bahari, a chief of the oarsmen is placed behind his men, on the deck; he is holding a rod in his right hand, held out and raised to face level.[76] The *ḥry ẖny.t* is thus responsible for carrying out the manoeuvre when the ship makes the use of oars necessary. He can be compared to the Greek *keleustes*.[77]

A certain number of officers in charge of the crews are present in Egyptian lists: 'director of the crews' ((*j*)*m*(*y*)-*r*(*ꜣ*) *js.wt*),[78] 'director of the crews (of the ship)' ((*j*)*m*(*y*)-*r*(*ꜣ*) *ꜥpr.w*),[79] 'manager of the crew of *ks.w*-barques' (*ꜥḥꜥ ꜥpr ks.w*),[80] and 'manager of the crew of recruits' (*ꜥḥꜥ ꜥpr nfr.w*).[81]

The famous inscription of Weni refers to an *ꜥpr wjꜣ*.[82] C. Boreux, taking up the argument advanced by K. Sethe, considered that *ꜥpr wjꜣ* did not refer to sailors but rather to 'the man who fits out a boat'.[83] In a more literal sense, *ꜥpr wjꜣ* would correspond, following the suggestion made by J. Yoyotte, to the definition of the 'fitter-out of a royal ship'.[84] A very similar reading also figures on a graffito of Hatnub; in it, the author refers to the work carried out by an expedition and states that he has prepared the ships necessary for the transport of stones, in concert with the team of *ꜥpr wjꜣ*.[85] The

existence of the title *ꜥpr wjꜣ* is attested by several private monuments and rock inscriptions.[86] His rank and the fact that he belonged to the corps of the navy are confirmed by the inscriptions of Wadi el-Gidami, which preserves the traces of the combined post of *ꜥpr wjꜣ* with that of 'man in charge of ten' ((*j*)*m*(*y*)-*r*(*ꜣ*) *mḏ*)[87] and 'manager of the crew of the royal barque' ((*j*)*m*(*y*)-*r*(*ꜣ*) *ꜥpr wjꜣ*).[88] Two private funerary monuments mention two deceased bearing the title *ꜥpr wjꜣ*, of which one is also a 'scribe of the team' (*sš js.t*) while the other is a 'scribe of the crew' (*sš ꜥpr*).[89] The few indications furnished by these lists of titles 'suggest that these persons were thus actively employed, in the navy, not in performing specific sailing tasks but rather in managing and directing crews of sailors; these were probably the prerogatives that entitled these fitters-out of the royal barque to participate and to aid those in charge in their technical expeditions'.[90]

The *jmy-jrty* was also a naval officer who took part in the management of the crew on expeditions.[91] The authors of the *Wörterbuch* had suggested translating this term by 'pilot' or 'ship's captain'.[92] A. Erman had proposed a literal translation of the title, as meaning 'he who has the eyes', he who exercises surveillance and not 'he who is in the eyes'.[93] C. Boreux preferred the second suggestion, proposing that the title be related to the frequent depiction of two eyes painted on the prow of the barques.[94] He acknowledged, however, that the exceptional scene[95] showing a *jmy-jrty* at the stern of the boat did not mean that this personage could be seen as having the role of *proreutes*. The legend in this context must have applied to the ship's captain. The analysis of H. Junker is identical: the *jmy-jrty* is an officer of the foredeck, whose name was originally linked to the presence of the decoration on the prow and was later used to designate the captain. Nonetheless, following M. Valloggia, an investigation of this scene of navigation engraved on a wall of the Mastaba of Senedjemid Inty (5th Dynasty, 2498-2345 BC) at Giza suggests a different interpretation; this depiction is not an episode from a funerary procession, but it illustrates the journey of a sarcophagus and its lid from its place of extraction to the tomb of the dead man.[96] The role of the *jmy-jrty*, represented behind the coffin, can no longer be linked to the funeral procession or even to the manoeuvring of the barge. His effigy which presents him as armed with his sceptre[97] more probably reveals dockyard activity, associated

73 H. Junker, *Giza*, IX, fig. 15; *PM*, III, index k, n° 421; *AnLex* III, 79.0332; D. Jones, *A Glossary of Ancient Egyptian Nautical Titles and Terms*, 1988, p. 51, 91-92; T. Säve-Söderbergh, *The Navy*, 1946, p. 78-79; W. A. Ward, *Index of Egyptian Administrative and Religious Title*, 1986, n° 310.

74 See the magnificent depiction in the Tomb of Payri on which two men installed on the roof of the cabin seem to be beating time with a whip (TT 139, 18th Dynasty, Sheikh Abd el-Gourna; photographs in A. Gros de Beler, *op. cit.*, n° 128 p. 109). See the numerous scenes of Nile sailing described by J. Vandier, *Manuel d'Archéologie égyptienne*, V, 1969, pp. 658-1014.

75 L. Borchardt, *Das Grandenkmal des König S3hure'*, II, 1910, pl. 11; J. Vandier, *op. cit.*, pp. 878-879.

76 E. Naville, *The Temple of Deir el-Bahari*, III, 1898, pls lxxi, lxxiv.

77 See J. Rougé, *Recherches sur l'organisation du commerce en Méditerranée sous l'empire romain*, 1966, p. 220.

78 W. A. Ward, *op. cit.*, n° 46; T. G. Allen, *Egyptian Stelae in the Field Museum of Natural History*, 1936, n° 31694; *LD*, II, pl. 62; A. M. Blackman, M. R. Apted, *The Rock Tombs of Meir*, V, 1953, pls xlii, xliii; Ahmed M. Moussa, H. Altenmüller, *Das Grab des Nianchchnum und Chnumhotep*, 1977, fig. 9; L. Epron, F. Daumas, H. Wild, *Le tombeau de Ti*, MIFAO 65, fasc. 1, 1939, pls xix, xxvi; P. Duell, *The Mastaba of Mereruka*, 1938, vol. 2, pl. 134; D. Jones, *op. cit.*, p. 51. Note that in the Ptolemaic period there was the title of (*j*)*m*(*y*)-*r*(*ꜣ*) *js.wt n*(*y*)-*sw*(*.t*) 'director of the crew of the king's boat': references in D. Jones, *op. cit.*, p. 51.

79 For example A. H. Gardiner, E. Peet, J. Cerny, *The Inscriptions of Sinai*, 1952-1955, n° 47. See W. A. Ward, *op. cit.*, n° 64; D. Jones, *op. cit.*, p. 51, points out the title, from the Saite period, borne by a certain Sema-Tawy-TefNakht: (*j*)*m*(*y*)-*r*(*ꜣ*) *ꜥpr*(*.w*) (*n*) *ꜥẖ'w n*(*y*)-*sw*(*.t*) 'Director of the crews of the royal fleet' (*Wb* I, 181, 10; A. Mariette, *Monuments divers recueillis en Égypte et en Nubie*, 1872-1882, pl. 34; P. M. Chevereau, *Prosopographie des cadres militaires*, 1985, doc. 107; P. Vernus, *Athribis*, BiÉtud LXXIV, 1978, p. 92.

80 H. Junker, *Giza*, V, 1941, p. 15.

81 A. H. Gardiner, E. Peet, J. Cerny, *op. cit.*, n° 13 and 17.

82 *Urk.* I, 99, 13.

83 C. Boreux, *Études de nautique égyptienne*, MIFAO I, 1925, p. 127, 139; repeating the argument of K. Sethe, in L. Borchardt, *Das Grandenkmal des König S3hure'*, II, 1913, p. 85, n. 11.

84 J. Yoyotte, *BSFE* 73, 1975, p. 48.

85 R. Anthes, *Die Felseninschriften von Hatnub*, 1928, Gr. 3, 4, 20, pl. 10; M. Valloggia, in F. Geus, F. Thill (ed.), *Mélanges offerts à Jean Vercoutter*, 1985, p. 357.

86 See the examples given by M. Valloggia, *op. cit.*, p. 357.

87 On this title, see D. Jones, *op. cit.*, p. 58-59.

88 See M. Valloggia, *op. cit.*, p. 357 and inscriptions n°s 3-4.

89 T. G. H. James, *Corpus of Hieroglyphic Inscriptions in the Brooklyn Museum*, I, 1974, p. 31, n° 74, pl. 29; L. Borchardt, *Denkmäler des Alten Reiches*, II, CGC, 1964, 1690b. Under Senusret I, the stele of the vizir Antefoqer and Ameny found at Mersa Gawasis indicates the presence of '5 scribes of the Great Council' at the time of the expedition to Punt, but it is not known whether they all took part in the maritime voyage. (See A. M. Sayed, *RdE* 29, 1977, p. 170, pl. 16; id., *CdÉ* 58, 1983, p. 29; D. Farout, *BIFAO* 94, 1994, p. 144; C. Vandersleyen, *RdE* 47, 1996, pp. 110-111. Stele cited on p. 129).

90 M. Valloggia, *op. cit.*, p. 357.

91 D. Jones, *A Glossary of Ancient Egyptian Nautical Titles and Terms*, 1988, pp. 47-48.

92 *Wb* I, 72, 22; 106, 17.

93 A. Erman, *ZÄS* 52, 1915, p. 107.

94 C. Boreux, *op. cit.*, p. 433 n. 6.

95 *LD* II, 76th. C. Boreux, *op. cit.*, p. 490.

96 See the arguments of M. Valloggia, *op. cit.*, p. 358-359.

97 On this insignia, see H. G. Fischer, *MMJ* 13, 1978, p. 16-17.

with the work performed on expeditions sent outside the Nile Valley. The attestations of this title as taken from the itineraries of mines and quarries confirm as much.[98] It appears that the activities of the *jmy-jrty* are essentially those of a person who manages and directs subordinates. Sometimes attached to the navy, he appears especially as the head of a team or an overseer of works. This is probably what justifies the insertion of this title among the laudatory epithets of the vizir.[99]

Finally, the combined epithet of the two preceding titles *ꜥpr wjꜣ jmy-jrty*[100] obliges us to envisage the existence of a title with two components, characteristic of a rank higher up in the hierarchy than that of the *ꜥpr wjꜣ* and the *jmy-jrty* alone. Stone inscriptions indeed show that the *ꜥpr wjꜣ jmy-jrty* sometimes assumed the direction of a mission to Sinai[101] or Wadi Hammamat,[102] in this case leading the 400 members of his expedition there. On other occasions, he is the close assistant of the head of the expedition.[103] This qualification is sometimes also embellished, on funerary monuments, by the title of 'head of an expedition' (*(j)m(y)-r(ꜣ) mšꜥ*)[104] or a promotion to the rank of 'chancellor of the god (in the two royal barques)' (*nṯr ḥtm, vꜥr. nṯr ḥtm m wjꜣ.y ꜥꜣ*). This category of documents emphasises the closeness of relations between the *ꜥpr wjꜣ jmy-jrty* and the regions at the edge of the Nile Valley.[105] The conspicuous presence of the navy in certain title-holders may also be underlined: thus on the table of the offering of Kasnebef (late 5th Dynasty, c. 2345 BC)[106] there appear his titles as 'head of the Six (sailors?) of the royal barque' (*(j)m(y)-r(ꜣ) srsw wjꜣ*), 'Head of ten men on the royal barque' (*(j)m(y)-r(ꜣ) mḏ wjꜣ*), 'manager of the crew of recruits' (*ꜥḥꜥ ꜥpr nfr.w*), and 'inspector of the royal barque' (*sḥḏ n wjꜣ*). The *ꜥpr wjꜣ jmy-jrty* thus combined the functions of ship's fitter-out and those of chief (or the teams) in the expeditions to mines and quarries. He thus appears to have been a naval officer whose priority was to lead technical missions to the fringes of the Nile Valley. In this respect, his prerogatives were not those of a 'captain' but rather those of an 'admiral', the commander in chief of a mission sent to Sinai.[107]

Among the chiefs of the crews should be mentioned the presence in the expedition to Punt launched by Rameses III (1182–1151 BC)[108] of 'heads of troops of *mnš*-ships' (*ḥry.w-pḏt n mnš*),[109] commanded by 'controllers' (*rwḏ.w*)[110] and assisted by 'under-officers' (*ḥwty.w*).[111]

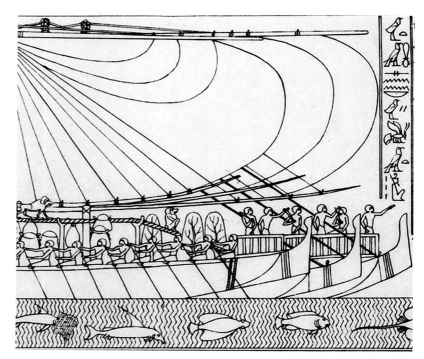

Expedition to Punt, funerary temple of Hatshepsut, detail of the ships' prows. Drawing after A. Mariette, *Deir el Bahari*, 1877, pl. vi. © Heritage Images

## II.5. 'The man at the prow' or *proreutes*

This term from Greek onamastics is taken to designate the man of the prow (*jry ḥꜣ.t*) who, on Nile vessels, had the job of sounding the riverbed with rods, while on the sea ships he had to keep an eye on the waves and survey the stars to indicate the route to be followed at night time. Both by day and by night he observed the direction of the winds and as far as possible studied the outlines of the coast that could be seen in the distance and identified its landmarks. So he was an officer of navigation whose role was essentially a role of observation rather than command.[112]

The importance of the functions of the *proreutes* is particularly evident in classical sources. Following the increase in the size of ships, the *proreutes* became the man who commanded at the front of the ship.[113] This definition suggests a very clear distinction between the fore and aft of the ship, a distinction that can be explained from the fact that when the mainsail was established, especially when sailing under a quartering wind, these two parts of the ship had a certain independence from one another. The sail, lowered almost to the

---

98 M. Valloggia, *op. cit.*, p. 359 gives numerous examples.

99 *Id.*, p. 361.

100 On the reading of this title, its interpretation, and documentary and bibliographical references, *id.*, p. 361-364; *id.*, BIFAO 85, 1985, pp. 259-266, pls xlii-xliii.

101 A. H. Gardiner, T. Peet, J. Cerny, *The Inscriptions of Sinai*, 1952-1955, p. 60-61, no 13, pl. 7.

102 J. Couyat, P. Montet, *Les inscriptions du Ouadi Hammâmât*, MIFAO XXXIV, 1912-1913, p. 94, no 169.

103 R. Anthes, *Die Felseninschriften von Hatnub*, 1928, Gr. 2, 3, 19, pl. 9; J. Couyat, P. Montet, *Les inscriptions du Ouadi Hammâmât*, MIFAO XXXIV, 1912-1913, p. 72, no 103; A. H. Gardiner, T. Peet, J. Cerny, *op. cit.*, pp. 62-63, no 16, pl. 8

104 According to the interpretation of J. Cerny, in A. H. Gardiner, T. Peet, and J. Cerny, *op. cit.*, p. 14.

105 Other examples are given by M. Valloggia, *op. cit.*, no 38, 42, 43, p. 364.

106 G. T. Martin, *The Tomb of Hetepka*, 1979, p. 32, no 74.

107 J. Cerny, in A. H. Gardiner, T. Peet, J. Cerny, *op. cit.*, p. 14. See M. Valloggia, *op. cit.*, p. 362: 'At Balat, the attestations of this title probably do not translate anything other than the survival of a memory linked to the colonisation of the region. On the other hand, its primacy and its persistence on monuments are evidence, if not of the influence that the directors of the Oasis ascribed to him, at least of the hierarchical importance of his rank'.

108 P. Harris I, 77, 9; P. Grandet, *Le papyrus Harris I*, BiÉtud 109, 1994, vol. 1, p. 338. Passage cited p. 86-87.

109 P. Grandet, *op. cit.*, vol. 2, n. 159, 929, 933. Also see T. Säve-Söderbergh, *The Navy*, 1946, p. 83; A. H. Gardiner, AEO I, 113*; R.O. Faulkner, JEA 39, 1953, p. 45; R. O. Caminos, *Late-Egyptian Miscellanies*, 1954, p. 111; L. A. Christophe, ASAE LV, 1958, p. 20.

110 The term *rwḏ.w* (whatever translation we adopt: 'agents', 'inspectors', 'controllers', and so on) seems to have designated functionaries attached to an administration, and managing or controlling, in its name, property that belonged to it but was situated at some distance from its seat. They may end up administering religious or secular institutions, herds, and also participate, as here, in directing an expedition to Punt; see P. Grandet, *Le papyrus Harris I*, BiÉtud 109, 1994, vol. 2, n. 144; A. H. Gardiner, JEA 27, 1941, p. 48 and n. 1; *id.*, *The Wilbour Papyrus*, II, 1948, p. 21, 83; A. H. Gardiner, JEA 38, 1952, p. 28; R. O. Caminos, *Late-Egyptian Miscellanies*, 1954, p. 159; L. A. Christophe, ASAE LV, 1958, p. 21; J. Cerny, *A Community of Workmen*, BiÉtud 50, 1973, p. 257; J.-M. Kruchten, *State and Temple*, II, p. 517; AnLex 77.2388, 79.1737.

111 For the *ḥwty.w/ḥty.w*, a term akin to (and perhaps merely representing a variant of) *ḥꜣwty.w*, 'chiefs', cf. P. Grandet, *op. cit.*, n. 933; J. Cerny, *op. cit.*, pp. 241-242 (at Deir el-Medina, it designated the three or four principal persons in a village. In the text of the Harris Papyrus I, it manifestly designates the associates of the *ḥry.w-pḏt n mnš* (J. H. Breasted, *Ancient Records of Egypt*, 1906, § 409: 'petty officers'; A. M. Blackman, JEA 27, 1941, p. 87 [15]: 'sergeants'; R. O. Caminos, *Late-Egyptian Miscellanies*, I, 1954, pp. 252-253; J. J. Janssen, *Commodity Prices*, 1975, p. 461.

112 See the innumerable representations on bas reliefs and paintings depicting the *proreutes*, as described by J. Vandier, *Manuel d'Archéologie égyptienne*, V, 1969, pp. 658-1014.

113 Xenophon, *Anabasis*, V, 8, 20; Philostratus, *Life of Apollonios*, III, 35.

deck, prevented the ship's pilot and captain, who were on the raised platform at the aft, from seeing what was happening at the prow. Their only link with it was the *proreutes* who signalled with his voice what was happening at the front and thus gave the indications necessary for the safe pursuit of the journey.

Many Egyptian depictions and paintings provide evidence of the task of the *proreutes*.[114] Classical sources seem to indicate that in the naval hierarchy the *proreutes* was always a subordinate, an intermediary between the crew and the captain of the ship.[115] His functions were thus first and foremost those of a navigator, but eventually, through his position in the on-board hierarchy, he was first mate; and was one of those crew members who could be called on to treat with the passengers and the loaders. It may be asked whether, as in the case of modern first mates, it was he who presided over the operations of loading and unloading ships?[116] No text proves this, but there is every possibility that this was indeed his function, since — as represented — these operations were conducted from the front of the ship, in the zone placed under the permanent authority of the *proreutes*. He is also the figure in the depictions of Deir el-Bahari showing the expedition to Punt in the reign of Hatshepsut, and illustrating the revictualling of ships about to set sail or the loading of ships bound for the land of Punt.[117]

## II.6. 'The man at the poop'

To the rear of the ships was found 'he who is at the poop' (*jrw ḥmy*), in charge of the rudder: he appears on almost all depictions of ships.[118] When there were no helmsmen at the aft of ships,[119] their absence can logically be explained either as the result of a lacuna, or by circumstances that keep the ships in port. Generally speaking, the helmsman is standing, with his torso upright or leaning forwards; his legs are generally apart, and his feet placed flat. He does not always occupy the same place on the quarter deck. In the ships of the Syrian expedition of Sahure, there are three helmsmen and they use, respectively, the simple rudder oar.[120] In the depictions of ships on Queen Hatshepsut's expedition to Punt, the helmsman is standing between the helm and the small mast, and turning his back on the latter.[121] On the bas-reliefs of the tomb of Nebamun, he is situated at the level of the helm with his back turned to the small mast and the oar rudder.[122] In the Asiatic ships of the tomb of Kenamun, the oar rudders are equipped with a helm. In two of the four examples, the helmsman is at his post. He is in front of the helm, looking forward, and holding out his right arm to the back, so that his hand can grasp the helm. In the two other examples, the helmsman has left his post, either to take part in the manoeuvre of the halyards, or to salute, by raising his arms, the Egyptians who have come to shore to greet the foreign ships.[123]

Those two specialists of navigation, 'the man at the prow' and 'the man at the poop' are associated with the *nfw*-boatman in lists that bring together the known components of the universe so as 'to instruct the ignorant and know all that exists', which may be designated by the term *Onomastica*.[124]

'The man at the poop', tomb of Sennefer (TT 96), Sheikh Abd el-Gourna, Thebes-West, New Kingdom, 18th Dynasty, c. 1550–1300 BC.

© AKG Images. Photo: Suzanne Held

114 See the example of the tomb of Niankhkhnum and Khnumhotep (Saqqara, 5th Dynasty; Ahmed M. Moussa, H. Altenmüller, *Das Grab des Nianchchnum und Chnumhotep*, ArchVer 21, 1977, pl. 24, 10; C. J. Eyre, in N. Grimal, B. Menu (ed.), *Le commerce*, BiÉtud 121, 1998, p. fig. 1, p. 190); The tomb of Payri (TT 139, 18th Dynasty, Cheikh Abd el-Gourna; photography in A. Gros de Beler, *Vivre en Égypte*, 2001, n° 128 p. 109); the tomb of Menna (TT 69, 18th Dynasty, Cheikh Abd el-Gourna; photography in *id.*, n° 127 p. 108); the tomb of Rekhmira (TT 100, 18th Dynasty, Cheikh Abd el-Gourna; photography in *id.*, n° 130 p. 110); the tomb of Sennefer (TT 96, 18th Dynasty, Cheikh Abd el-Gourna; photography in *id.*, n° 132 p. 112).

115 Aristophanes, *Cavaliers*, 541-543; Plutarch, *Agis and Cleomenes*, 1; Pollux, *Onomasticon*, I, 95; VII, 139 and 190; Jerome, *Commentary on Ezechiel*, IX, 27, 29. See J. Rougé, *op. cit.*, 1966, p. 221. See also J. Vélissaropoulos, *Les Nauclères grecs*, 1980, pp. 77-78.

116 J. Merrien, *Dictionnaire de la mer*, p. 552.

117 E. Naville, *The Temple of Deir el-Bahari*, III, 1898; see the representations of M. Rival in D. Meeks, D. Garcia (ed.), *Techniques et économie antiques et médiévales*, 1997, p. 181-184 (for the 'normal function' of the *proreute*); L. Casson, *Ships and Seafaring*, 1994, p. 24; St. Vinson, *Egyptian Boats and Ships*, 1994, p. 40, and so on. See also the depictions of the unloading of jars of wine in the Theban tomb TT 261 (E. Mackey, *JEA* III, 1916, pl. xiv).

118 See the examples cited above concerning the *proreutes*.

119 E. Naville, *op. cit.*, pls lxxi, lxxiv; *LD* III, pl. 76a (TT. 57 de Khaemhet). See the numerous examples of Nile navigation given by J. Vandier, *op. cit.*, p. 658-1014.

120 L. Borchardt, *Das Grandenkmal des König S3hure'*, II, 1910, pl. 11; J. Vandier, *op. cit.*, p. 877.

121 E. Naville, *op. cit.*, pls lxxi, lxxiv.

122 T. Säve-Söderbergh, *The Navy*, 1946, pl. xxiii (TT 17 of Nebamun); J. Vandier, *op. cit.*, fig. 320.

123 N. de G. Davies, R. O. Faulkner, *JEA* 33, 1947, pl. viii.

124 A. H. Gardiner, *AEO* I, 2*; 90*-96*, pl. ix, l. 8-12, n° 206 and 207.

125 T. Säve-Söderbergh, *The Navy*, p. 86.

Expedition to Punt, funerary temple of Hatshepsut, Deir el-Bahari, c. 1490–1468 BC. Detail of the poop of the ship. After A. Mariette, *Deir el Bahari*, 1877, pl. vi.

© Heritage Images

'The man at the prow', tomb of Sennefer (TT 96), Sheikh Abd el-Gourna, Western Thebes, New Kingdom, 18th Dynasty, c. 1550–1300 BC.

© AKG Images. Photo: Suzanne Held

## II.7. The navigator

The status of *nfw.w*-navigators was certainly quite high. The tomb of the vizir Rekhmira gives us a definition of them: they were veritable pilots, the technicians of navigation.[125] Rekhmira declares, by metaphor:[126]

> *I am his (the king's) nfw, and I do not know sleep by day or night. My attention is fixed on the rope of the prow and on the rope of the poop…*

From these words it may be possible to specify the sense of this term/function. In navigation by sail, the essential element is the wind and its direction; for the navigator, wind direction is the sole constant, and he must refer to it as an immutable axis. Hence the importance of the sail and rigging ropes. The *nfw* seems to be the man who unfurls and refurls the sail and positions it depending on the winds and the route to be followed, or is at least the man who gives the orders to do this. This might explain the presence of several navigators[127] and a 'chief navigator' (*ḥry nfw*)[128] on board the ships. Some fine depictions indicate these characters hard at work manipulating the ropes that activate the mainsail.[129] This hypothesis is confirmed by the way the word is written, thanks to the sign of the sail swollen by the wind highlighted by a man striking with his rod, which refers to his elevated status in the ship's hierarchy and his role of command.

The reality and the relevance of this professional group are confirmed by the *Onomastica*. In these lists, the navigator is followed by two 'specialists', *viz.* 'the man at the prow' (no. 206, *jry ḥ3t*) and 'the man at the poop' (no. 207, *jrw ḥmy*).[130]

Like the other professions already referred to, the navigators could be attached to a god and his temple or to an individual. Senmut for example, the steward of Hatshepsut, had his *nfw*.[131] In the case of several navigators of the high-priest of Amun,[132] it is difficult to know whether they were in his service on a personal basis or whether the high priest was the representative of the institution of the temple of Amun.[133]

Several funerary objects that belonged to navigators are known, in particular a pectoral that includes chapter 30b of the *Book of the Dead*[134] and a whole series of steles.[135] One of these is particularly

---

126 *Urk.* IV, 1076, 17-1077, 2.

127 P. Leyde I 350, v°; P. Turin 2008 + 2016: J. J. Janssen, *Two Ancient Egyptian Ships' Logs*, 1961, pp. 1-52, 53-95.

128 *cf. infra.*

129 See for example, the tomb of Niankhkhnum et Khnumhotep (Saqqara, 5th Dynasty; Ahmed M. Moussa, H. Altenmüller, *Das Grab des Nianchchnum und Chnumhotep*, ArchVer 21, 1977, pl. 24, 10; C. J. Eyre, *op. cit.*, fig. 1, p. 190); the Mastaba of Kaiemankh (Giza, 6th Dynasty; depictions in J. Yoyotte, in *Dictionnaire de la civilisation égyptienne*, 1992, *s.v.* 'Économie', p. 184; L. Casson, Ships and Seafaring, 1994, p. 33); the tomb of Inti, Dechacha, 5th Dynasty; W. M. F. Petrie, *Deshasheh*, 1898, p. 24, pl. VI.

130 A. H. Gardiner, *AEO* I, 90*-96*, pl. IX, l. 8-12. On these two characters, *cf. supra*, p. 147-148.

131 T. Säve-Söderbergh, *The Navy*, 1946, p. 87 n. 2.

132 D. Jones, *A Glossary of Ancient Egyptian Nautical Titles and Terms*, 1988, pp. 77-80, no 117, 124, 131.

133 S. Bickel, in N. Grimal, B. Menu (ed.), *Le commerce*, BiÉtud 121, 1998, p. 160.

134 G. Kueny, J. Yoyotte, *Grenoble, Musée des Beaux-Arts*, 1979, pp. 123-124.

135 H. M. Stewart, *Egyptian Stelae, Reliefs and Paintings*, II, 1979, pl. 32, 2, *nfw n pr-ḥḏ Ḫnmw*; pl. 30, 2, the two steles dating from the Middle Kingdom; P. Ramond, *Les stèles égyptiennes du musée Labit à Toulouse*, BiÉtud 62, 1977, pp. 23-25, pl. 6 (Stele of Tjeremty, end of the Second Intermediate Period, with an appeal to the departing). In the Late Period, an *nfw* attached to the domain of Amun had a sarcophagus made for him, with high quality decoration, G. Kueny, J. Yoyotte, *Grenoble, Musée des Beaux-Arts*, 1979, p. 102 no 123. After S. Bickel, *op. cit.*, p. 160.

Painted relief from the tomb of Ankhmahor at Saqqara, Middle Kingdom, 6th Dynasty, c. 2323–2150 BC. © Werner Forman Archive

interesting because it teaches us that the son of a 'navigator in chief of Maat' (*ḥry nfw n Mȝˁt*) was himself a 'navigator of Ptah' (*nfw n Ptḥ*). So the profession was passed down from father to son, both of them working within the framework of neighbouring Memphite institutions. On the same stele, with an indeterminate link of kinship, there also appears a scribe.[136] A certain Rech (*Rš*), perhaps a foreigner, who combined functions at the court, in the army and the navy, where he was, among others, 'the navigator of a ship called Mery-Amun', had a small tomb at Saqqara.[137]

## II.8. The captain or the 'head of the ship'

Boatmen included the sailors, 'those who are in the (wide) ship' (*jmy.w wsḫ*) and their superior: the 'head of the (wide) ship' (*ḥry wsḫ*). The profession appears in the entourage of Deir el-Medina: the father-in-law of Pached is 'head of the ship of Amun' (*ḥry wsḫ n Jmn*), a title that seemed to indicate that he worked for the merchant fleet of the temple of Amun.[138] There were also both the 'head of the *mnš*-ship' (*ḥry mnš*) and the sailors, 'those who are in the *mnš*-ship' (*jmy.w mnš*). While the sailors were certainly subalterns, their chief

probably had a more respectable status. He was doubtless the head of the hierarchy and probably in charge of the ship himself – superstructure, sails, oars and their functioning: he was the man who determined the route to be followed and gave the orders in consequence. It goes without saying that all these functions could not be performed by one pair of hands; and they were indeed divided up between the different naval officers or sailors. It is contended that the *ḥry wsḫ* or the *ḥry mnš* was the real ship's captain, the ship's commander, a commander who, in principle, possessed no more than technical responsibilities, leaving the commercial responsibilities to others.[139]

In Egypt, a country in which 'being without a ship' meant a state of absolute impoverishment, Herodotus does not fail to specify that the pilots were part of the seven hereditary classes:[140]

---

136  G. A. Gaballa, *SAK* 7, 1979, p. 42-44, Cairo Stele JE 8781.

137  A. P. Zivie, *RdÉ* 31, 1979, p. 135-151; S. Bickel, *op. cit.*, p. 160.

138  A.-P. Zivie, *La tombe de Pached à Deir el-Medineh*, MIFAO 99, 1979, p. 65, 128, n. 4, pl. 24.

139  cf. *infra* p. 155 *et seq.*

140  Herodotus, II, 164.

*There are seven classes of Egyptians, called priests, warriors, oxherds, swineherds, merchants, interpreters and pilots (κυβερνηται).*

The role of Egyptian boatmen is well attested in Aramaic documents, especially concerning the revictualling of the garrison of Elephantine,[141] but also in the delivery of post[142] and in trading exchanges between Upper and Lower Egypt.[143]

In Papyrus Harris I, Rameses III (1182-1151 BC) boasts that he has built a fleet of *mnš*-ships[144] and has designated their captains (*ḥry.w mnš*).[145] His captains were often foreigners, unless it was Egyptians with foreign names. For example there is a certain Benanat on ostracon Louvre 2262, dating back to year 42 of Rameses II;[146] but also Kener (or Kel) of Papyrus Bologna 1086;[147] Paalsa on a stele of Abydos that is now in Liverpool.[148] The first document is very interesting; it tells us that Benanat, the captain of the *mnš*-ship, had a son-in-law, Prince Samontu, the 23rd son of Rameses II (1279-1212 BC). This shows that the social position of a captain could be considerable.

Mengabot (*Mˁ-n-gꜣ-bw-tj*) was the *ḥr(y)-mnš* captain who was ordered by Smendes and Tentamun to take Wenamun from Tanis to the 'great sea of Kharu'. He carried the envoy of Amun as far as Dor.[149] Later on, Sakarbaal, the Prince of Byblos, characterised him clearly as the 'captain of a foreign ship' (*ḥr(y)-mnš ḏrjḏrj*).[150]

These captains of foreign nationality suggest that they were sometimes part of a system of contractual links with the Egyptian State, as were later the *naucleroi* of Greek sources.[151]

The *Customs register of the satrapy of Egypt* of the Achaemenid period provides us with information about foreign merchant expeditions which were welcomed to Egyptian ports.[152] One of the criteria of identification of the ships is the name of the master/captain of the ship. For every ship entering Egypt, there is a list of the names and patronyms of the captains of Ionian vessels. For ships from Asia Minor, as far as can be judged from the current state of our readings, the most readable anthroponyms are those of Ionian captains, but several of them are still difficult to read. A series of common Greek names (transcribed from the Aramaic) may be recognised, such as Somenos son of Simonides, Timotheos, Moskhos, Pantaleon, Timokedes, and so on.[153] There are names that are more difficult to derive from Greek such as *Mrggś* or less probable such as *Ywny* or *Spytk*. Overall, the dominance of Greek names is quite real, but not exclusive, which corresponds well to the image that may have been formed of the merchant population of a port of Asia Minor. As far as the names of the people of Syro-Palestine are concerned, the only discernable name can be read as *šm(p)rwn* and transcribed *Sumpheron* – a Hellenised Greek name, a sign of the influence or presence of Greeks on the coasts of Phoenicia and Palestine.[154] It is impossible to specify the juridical link between the personage cited and the ship. Let us note, to end this chapter, that in the papyri of the customs of Pelusium of the era of Ptolemy II Philadelphus (285-246 BC), each ship is designated by the name of its captain.[155]

---

141  DAE 54: P. Grelot, *Documents araméens d'Égypte*, LAPO 5, 1972, pp. 267-271.

142  DAE 14 and 17: P. Grelot, *op. cit.*, pp. 125-128, 130-133.

143  DAE 26 and 109: P. Grelot, *op. cit.*, pp. 154-157, 504-505.

144  On this type of ship, *cf.* p. 94-95.

145  P. Harris I, 7, 8. P. Grandet, *Le papyrus Harris I*, BiÉtud 109, 1994, vol. 2, pl. 7. Transcription: W. Erichsen, *Papyrus Harris I, Bibliotheca Aegyptiaca* V, 1933, pp. 9, l. 2-5. Passage cited p. 96. For the occurrences of the term in the sources, see D. Jones, *A Glossary of Ancient Egyptian Nautical Titles and Terms*, 1988, p. 88, § 168. *cf.* also A. Scheepers, in E. Lipinski (ed.), *Phoenicia and the Bible*, OLA 44, 1994, 1991, pp. 37-38.

146  *KRI* II, 907, 370.

147  *KRI* IV, 80, 2.

148  *KRI* IV, 445, 16

149  *Wenamun*, 1, 6-8.

150  *Wenamun*, 1, 55-57. G. Lefèbvre and M. Lichtheim consider him to be a Phoenician or Syrian (G. Lefebvre, *Romans et contes*, 1949, p. 208, n. 5; M. Lichtheim, *Ancient Egyptian Literature*, II, 1976, p. 230 n. 4. His name is considered by M. Burchardt, *Die alkanaanäische Fremdworte und Eigennamen im Ägyptischen*, 1910, II, p. 24, n° 456). W. F. Albright thinks he was a Syrian and he identifies **Mngbt** to Manqabt, the equivalent of the Hebrew *maqqebet*, 'hammer' (HAL, p. 591) because of the fact that Egyptian *g* corresponds to the Semitic *q* (W. Helck, *Die Beziehungen Ägyptens*, ÄgyAbh 5, 1971, p. 538), without assimilation of the *n*. But this assimilation is usual in the Semitic dialects of the north-west (S. Moscati, *et al.*, *An Introduction to the Comparative Grammar of the Semitic Languages*, 1964, p. 57; J. P. Lettinga, *Grammatica van het Bijbels Hebreeuws*, 1976 (8th ed.), p. 31). Seeing that such a name is not attested in any Semitic language, H. Goedicke (*The Report of Wenamun*, 1975, p. 25) seeks another explanation and suggests we derive it from a toponym: the individual in question would then be called after his place of origin, *min Gibton*, 'from Gibton'. Gibton or Gibbeton is the present Tell el-Melat, situated to the west of Geser in Palestine, and it belonged to the Israelite tribe of Dan or to Philistine territory (F. M. Abel, *Géographie de la Palestine II*, 1938, p. 53; Z. Kallai, *Historical Geography of the Bible*, 1986, pp. 81-82 (and map n°. 1). Finally, E. Lipinski suggest that we see in it the name Munnabittu, 'Fugitive', frequent in Middle Assyrian and Neo-Assyrian, where the double *nn* has been dissimilated as an *ng* (*Mungabit). See A. Scheepers, *op. cit.*, pp. 36-37.

151  *cf.* p. 169 *et seq.*

152  See B. Porten, A. Yardeni, *Textbook of Aramaic Documents from Ancient Egypt*, III, 1993; A. Yardeni, *BASOR*, 293, 1994, pp. 67-87; E. Lipinski, *OLP* 29, 1994, pp. 61-68; P. Briant, *Histoire de l'empire perse*, 1994, p. 398, and index of Aramaic texts, p. 1236; P. Briant, R. Descat, in N. Grimal, B. Menu (ed.), *le commerce*, BiÉtud 121, 1998, pp. 59-104. For a summary of the customs dues applied to these ships that came into Egyptian territory: *Seafaring in Ancient Egypt*, vol. 2.

153  After P. Briant, R. Descat, in N. Grimal, B. Menu (ed.), *le commerce*, BiÉtud 121, 1998, pp. 62-63.

154  See the remarks of J. Elayi, *REG* 105, 1992, pp. 305-327; R. Avner, E. Eshel, *Transeuphratène* 12, 1996, pp. 59-6 and P. Briant, R. Descat, *op. cit.*, p. 65.

155  P. Cairo Zenon 59012 (259); C. C. Edgar, *ASAE* XXIII, 1923, pp. 73-84; U. Wilcken, *Archiv* 7, 1924, pp. 293-294; A. Andréadès, in *Mélanges Glotz*, I, 1932, p. 7-48; C. Préaux, *L'économie royale des Lagides*, 1939, pp. 372-374.

# Chapter 2: The Traders

*You run, indefatigable merchant, to the ends of the earth*
*To flee from poverty, you cross sea, rocky terrain and extreme heat*
(Horace, *Epistula*, I, line 46)

If the crew and staff of the ship were strictly kept to the technical operations of navigation, it should be asked who was responsible for trading operations both on board and at sea? It has been observed that in most cases the ships, crew and commercial agents depended on Pharaonic and religious institutions. Nevertheless, if the documentation available is examined, this description of the social universe of the traders can be qualified to some extent.

## I. Ship's operators and commercial associations

The fact that captains of foreign nationality were active in the Egyptian fleet suggests that they sometimes had contractual links with the Egyptian State.[1] This hypothesis is supported by the *Report of Wenamun*. The tale of the envoy of Amun presents a ship and a crew in the service of Smendes. Received by Sakarabaal, the Prince of Byblos, he was told by the latter of the number of vessels that were in communication with Tanis (see below).[2]

These ships were probably not the property of Smendes, but they sailed under his name and on his behalf.[3] Urkatil, mentioned in the text, appears to be a man who kept up commercial relations with Sidon and probably with Smendes. The controversial point, as discussed by Wenamun and Sakarbaal, concerns the maritime power of Smendes and his possible dependence on foreign ships. While Wenamun claims that the vessels sailing for Smendes are Egyptian and manned by Egyptian sailors,[4] Sakarbaal contradicts him and quotes in support of his own view some undeniable figures: 20 ships from his own port of Byblos trade with Smendes and some 50 or so ships of Sidon; on the orders of Urkatil they transport merchandise

to Smendes.[5] Wenamun probably means that a ship's crew, whatever its nationality, has to be considered as Egyptian as soon as it starts sailing under an Egyptian flag.[6] This clearly shows that Smendes was appealing to foreign ships and crews to conduct his commercial relations overseas.[7]

Certain scholars have attributed to Urkatil the profession of outfitter: the name of his 'enterprise' seems to be found in a 2nd-century BC document, the *Testament of Naphtali*.[8] This refers to the seizure of a ship that was drifting, abandoned at sea, without a crew, and whose mast bore the inscription 'belonging to the son of Barak-El'. Barak-El can be compared to Urkatil; this would then have been a well-known seafaring business, known by the name of the father (founder?) and his sons, and not by that of the later directors. This would explain why the name Barak-El survived until the 2nd century

---

1   *cf. supra.*

2   *Wenamun*, 1, 58 - 2, 2. See G. Lefebvre, *Romans et contes*, 1949, pp. 212-213; R. de Spens, in N. Grimal, B. Menu (ed.), *le commerce*, BiÉtud 121, 1998, p. 112.

3   E. Blumenthal, *Atägyptische Reiseerzählungen*, 1984, pp. 50-51 (2, 2). This is the opposite of A. Erman, *Die Literatur der Ägypter*, 1923, p. 230 n. 3.

4   *Wenamun*, 1, 58-59

5   *Wenamun*, 1, 58-2, 2; literally *r pȝj=f pr*, 'towards his house'; according to the viewpoint of A. Scheepers, the third person masculine pronoun suffix = *f* refers to Smendes, because it is a question of knowing whether Smendes is appealing to foreign sailors. In principle, it is also possible that the pronoun suffix refers to Urkatil: Sidonian ships would then transport merchandise 'to his house', it being understood that the load was ultimately destined for Smendes. In that case, Urkatil would be a Phoenician trader residing at Tanis. *Pr* is the 'house of trade' or simply 'the domain'; see for instance W. Helck, *Die Beziehungen Ägyptens*, ÄgAbh 5, 1971, p. 431, n. 9 and G. Bunnens, *L'expansion phénicienne en Méditerranée*, 1979, p. 366. On the interpretation of the reading of the name Urkatil, see A. Scheepers, in E. Lipinski (ed.), *Phoenicia and the Bible*, Studia Phoenicia XI, 1991, p. 46.

6   G. Lefebvre, *Romans et contes*, 1949, p. 213 and n. 333; M. Lichtheim, *Ancient Egyptian Literature*, II, 1976, p. 230 n. 11.

7   As in line 1, 5 where it is a question of the foreign captain Mengabet (see. p. 152). *cf.* W. Helck, in *LÄ* III, 1980, *s.v.* 'Meer', col 1277.

8   R. Eisler, *ZDMG* 78, 1924, pp. 61-63; G. Lefebvre, *op. cit.*, p. 213 n. 34.

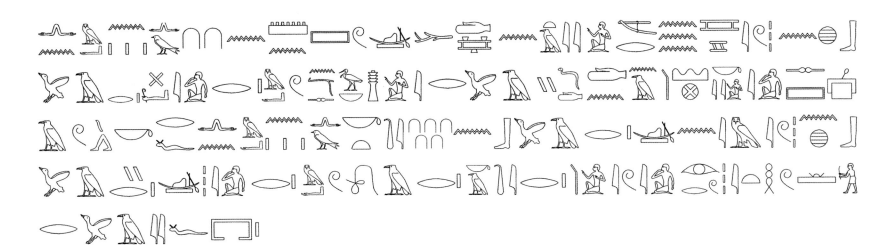

*Are there not 20 mnš-ships here, in my port, that are in commercial association (ḥbpȝr) with Smendes? And Sidon, the other place through which you have passed — are there not 50 other boats there in commercial association (ḥbpȝr) with Urkatil, and that have sailed to his domain?*

BC, but it is not clear that the business was still going at that time. In this respect, it is worth noting that the meaning of *hubur (ḫbpꜣr)* is 'society, association', and in particular a commercial society. Only the context can indicate whether this was an outfitting company.[9] In addition, there is a small difference between W/Birkatel, with the substantive *bᵉraka*, 'blessing'[10] and Barak-El, formed on the verb *berak*, 'to bless'.[11] Furthermore, it does not seem probable that the name of an outfitting company from the 11th century BC was still known in the 2nd century BC.[12]

Be that as it may, Urkatil was in relation with Smendes within a commercial association *hubur*, a Semitic term with the original sense of 'friend', 'confederate'[13] and a way of describing the juridical link between the captains of *mnš*-ships and the authorities. Within our context is thus an 'association' of persons, and also their business relations.[14] It probably underlies a veritable commercial status, an institution common in the ancient Near East defined by customary rules that were internationally respected.[15] The root is attested in the Bible with the sense of 'commercial associations'[16] The word *hubur* would then designate a mercantile association directed by a prince, a group of merchants united to set up a risky commerce with a distant land, necessitating significant capital.[17] These companies would thus have had a function that was both financial and commercial. In the *Report of Wenamun*[18] the elements necessary to define its content and value are not present, so it cannot be established whether it was simply a regular commerce or whether it covered a veritable large-scale association.[19]

In this text the trace of *societies of sailors,* more or less informal in kind, based on national origin can be detected. No less than 11 Sakal[20] ships blockaded Byblos to prevent Wenamun from leaving, believing that he had committed a misdemeanor against one of them.

## Another time, another sea

The data concerning the role of the Phoenicians in international commerce between the Mediterranean and Red Seas, although sporadic and of diverse origins, and sometimes difficult to make use of, reveal quite clearly that from the 10th to the 4th centuries BC the Phoenicians and more particularly the Tyrians played a capital role thanks to their technical ability to construct and sail high–seas ships. These lucrative but risky enterprises were rarely carried out by the Phoenicians alone; they generally indulged in this practice in association, even in a sort of mixed liability company, with the leaders of the countries they had to cross, whether it was the kingdom of Egypt, or Jerusalem, Samaria or Edom. At the end of the 7th century BC, it was to the Phoenicians, reputed as specialists of maritime commerce on the Red Sea,[21] that Pharaoh Nekau II (610-595 BC) turned with the aim of conducting a very active naval campaign, asking them 'to construct triremes,[22] some bound for the Northern Sea, others in the Arabian Gulf bound for the Erythrean Sea',[23] and entrusted them with the mission of proving that Libya (Africa) was 'completely surrounded by the sea, except insofar as where it borders with Asia'.[24]

That raises a new problem: the role devolved to traders in any eventual commercial policy, a question that cannot be broached, for lack of documentation, until the Ptolemaic period and afterwards. It is a lesson that is constantly learnt from the historians of the Ptolemaic period: while navigation was free, maritime commerce was monopolistic, with the State purchasing every cargo at whatever price it desired and reselling it in the same way.[25] At the same time, following the loss of Syria and thus of the land routes for spices at the beginning of the 2nd century BC, the Ptolemies carried out an intensive exploration of the southern coasts of the Arabian Gulf and crossed the strait of Bab el-Mandeb, as Agatharcides[26] shows; so they would have tried to oppose Arab preponderance and to suppress their intermediary. While the second point is possible and indeed probable, what about the first? In fact, in these conditions, how would it have benefited the maritime traders sailing from Egypt to take part in a commerce from which they would have derived no profit since they would not have been free to sell their cargo? They did derive advantage from it however, otherwise it would be impossible to understand a contract that is unfortunately very mutilated, hence the numerous discussions it has raised. In this contract several maritime traders form an association to contract a cartel with a view to an expedition to the land of spices. It is also interesting to see that among the various witnesses a Lacedaemonian is present and a Thessalonican, who may be descended from Greeks who settled in Egypt following the conquest, but also a Carthaginian and a

9    G. Bunnens, *L'expansion phénicienne en Méditerranée*, 1979, pp. 49-50.

10   *HAL*, p. 154: the authors do not mention any anthroponym formed on the construct state of this substantive; but see F. L. Benz, *Personal Names in the Phoenician and Punic Inscriptions*, StudPohl 8, 1972, p. 291.

11   *HAL*, p. 154: the anthroponym Barak-El ('El/God has blessed') is attested, *cf.* M. Noth, *Die israelitischen Personennemen, Beiträge zur Wissenschaft vom Alten und Neuen Testament* 46, 1928, p. 183; *cf.* F. L. Benz, *op. cit.*, pp. 291-292.

12   W. F. Albright, in G. Mylonas (ed.), *Studies Presented to D.M. Robinson I*, 1951, p. 228, n. 21.

13   The word *hubur* derives from a root signifying 'to link', 'to join' (Z. S. Harris, *A Grammar of the Phoenician Language*, 1936, p. 100; F. Brown, S. R. Driver, C. A. Briggs, *An Hebrew and English Lexikon of the Old Testament*, 1976, pp. 287-288; C. F. Jean, J. Hoftijzer, *Dictionnaire des inscriptions sémitiques de l'Ouest*, 1965, p. 82). The word sometimes refers to the members of a social and religious association. See W. F. Albright, in G. Mylonas (ed.), *Studies presented to D. M. Robinson*, 1951, pp. 229-230; J. E. Hoch, *Semitic Words in Egyptian Texts*, 1994, p. 240, n. 333 and A. Scheepers, *op. cit.*, p. 47.

14   See H. Goedicke, *The Report of Wenamun*, 1975, pp. 66-75 and H. J. Katzenstein, in *Atti del I Congresso Internazionale di Studi Fenici e Punici*, 1983, pp. 598-602.

15   *cf. Seafaring in Ancient Egypt*, vol. 2.

16   W. F. Albright, in G. E. Mylonas (ed.), *Studies presented to D.M. Robinson*, I, 1951, pp. 223-231.

17   H. J. Katzenstein, *The History of Tyre*, 1973, p. 70; M. O'Connor, *JANES* 18, 1986, pp. 67-80.

18   H. Goedicke, *The Report of Wenamun*, 1975, p. 66.

19   H. J. Katzenstein, *op. cit.*, p. 70; F. Briquel-Chatonnet, *Les relations entre les cités de la côte phénicienne et les royaumes d'Israël et de Juda*, Studia Phoenicia XII, OLA 46, 1992, pp. 285-286.

20   On the transcription 'Sakal', and on this Middle-Eastern people in general, see A. Scheepers, *op. cit.*, pp. 70-74.

21   This reputation could be at the origin of the tradition that made of the Red Sea the land of origin of the Phoenicians: *cf.* Herodotus, I, 1; VII, 89; also see the essay by B. Couroyer, *RB* 80, 1973, pp. 264-276 and A. Lemaire, in E. Lipinski, *Phoenicia and the East Mediterranean*, Studia Phoenicia V, OLA 22, 1987, pp. 49-60.

22   Were these triremes Greek? (*cf.* A. B. Lloyd, *JEA* 58, 1972, pp. 268-279; *id.*, *JHS* 95, 1975, pp. 45-61) or Phoenician? (*cf.* L. Basch, *The Mariner's Mirror* 55, 1969, pp. 139-162; *id.*, *JHS* 97, 1977, pp. 1-10; L. C. Casson, *Ships and Seamanship*, 1971, p. 81 n. 19). It is difficult to tell; however, the historical context makes the second solution more likely. *cf.* p. 99 *et seq.*

23   Herodotus, II, 159.

24   Herodotus, IV, 42. See A. Lemaire, *op. cit.*, pp. 59-60.

25   C. Préaux, *L'économie royale des Lagides*, 1939, pp. 366-371; M. Rostovtzeff, *The Social and Economic History of the Hellenistic World*, I, 1941, p. 389.

26   Agatharchides, 108.

Massaliot, which shows the cosmopolitan character of this trade.[27] It was a desire to break the Arab stranglehold that doubtless explains the adventures of Eudoxus of Cyzicus, as related by Strabo, who did not believe them.[28] Indeed, in the reign of Ptolemy VIII Euergetes II (170-163, 145-116 BC), *c.* 145 BC, a Greek from Cyzicus in Propontis, Eudoxus, is said to have encountered in Egypt an Indian pilot whose ship, blown off course by tempests, had foundered on the Egyptian coast of the gulf. After talking with him, he took him into his service and suggested to the king that he set up an association for a direct voyage to India. Despite the contract, when Eudoxus returned with a rich cargo, he was dispossessed of it by the sovereign. In spite of this first setback, he carried out a new expedition, after the death of Ptolemy VIII, in association with his widow Queen Cleopatra. On the return voyage he was blown off course and landed on the coast of Africa beyond Ethiopia from whence he returned to Egypt by sailing along the coast. Once again he was dispossessed, the new sovereign not considering himself as bound by agreements made before his own reign. These voyages may be interpreted as being carried out by an association, with the sovereign as financial backer and Eudoxus as maritime trader, an association based on the principle that was to become, in Roman law, the *societas unius negotiationis* and that should have been concluded by a sharing of the profits.[29]

It was during the Roman period that the commercial structures organised on the scale of the entire known world took concrete shape. With the development of the very large-scale commerce necessitated by huge conurbations and, first and foremost, by the existence of the enormous Roman market, structures started to appear that were more differentiated than the old ones. Great business enterprises, often specialised, were set up, those of the *negotiatores*: *negotiatores frumentarii*, corn wholesalers, and *negotiatores uinarii*, wholesale wine sellers. In tandem with this commerce there developed a significant maritime transport business – the *nauiculares*, the word now becoming detached from that of *naucleres*. These *nauiculares* possessed ships that they operated via the intermediary of a whole world of dependents; they had representatives in the ports; were not specialised in particular forms of transport, and they loaded their ships with everything that was proposed to them.[30]

---

27  P. Berlin 5883-5853; J. Vélissaropoulos, *Les nauclères grecs*, 1980, pp. 356-357.

28  Strabo, II, 3, 4; J. Desanges, *Recherches sur l'activité des Méditerraens aux confins de l'Afrique*, 1978, chap. 10.

29  J. Rougé, in J. H. D'Arms, E. C. Kopff (ed.), *The Seaborne Commerce of Ancient Rome*, 1980, pp. 291-303.

30  J. Rougé, *La marine dans l'Antiquité*, 1975, pp. 196-197. On the status of merchants and traders during the Hellenistic and Roman periods (with a bibliography) see below, p. 168 *et seq.*

## II. Brokers, merchants, traders, traffickers

### II.1. Trade as a profession?

The *šwt.y* are generally known to have been members of the personnel of different institutions, 'brokers' or economic intermediaries between institutional producers and consumers, with the role of establishing a direct economic relation, in the sense of 'offer' as well as that of 'demand' – both of them being fixed administratively - between the institution on which they depended and other institutions, and/or, from the New Kingdom (1570-1070 BC) onwards, between the latter and private persons. In this administrative framework that was *a priori* rigid,[1] could these *šwty.w*, in certain contexts and at particular periods, possess a minimum of freedom of initiative or economic independence? Two questions will then guide our thoughts: were there real merchants who practised trade as a profession? What share fell to merchants and private initiative in this sector?

Given the almost total silence of documentation from the epochs prior to the New Kingdom, one is reduced to tackling – although this exceeds the framework of our study – the huge literary composition called *The Tale of the Oasis Dweller*.[2] This work is one of the longest of all the Egyptian literary texts that have come down to us. Despite certain obscure passages, this text is particularly interesting for anyone investigating the history of society and law. This story indicates quite unequivocally that commerce – if only on a modest scale – was practised by people who gave themselves over to it and made it a profession in the full sense of the word.

The protagonist of this tale is designated by the term *sḥty* which literally means 'peasant'. Nothing proves that this oasis dweller was a peasant however; he was a dweller in the oasis of Salt (*sḥ.t-ḥmȝ.t*, today's Wadi el-Natron?). Taking the route to the capital, which was then in Middle Egypt, he came down with his 'private cargo' into the Nile Valley. Various products had been previously loaded on the backs of asses. They comprised all sorts of plants and wood as well as skins and furs, natron and salt, pigeons and birds, semi-precious stones and seeds of every kind. In short, a huge 'quantity of products of every kind from the oasis of Salt'.

The products brought by the oasis dweller were doubtless not of his own manufacture and certainly did not come from his house. He had probably obtained them and stored them – and probably bought them too – with the aim of transporting them to the valley and selling them there at an advantageous price, or at least exchanging them in return for subsistence goods. This is perfectly clear from the words of the oasis dweller just before he leaves his family. Just before his departure, he says to his wife, 'Ha, you there, I will go down into Egypt to bring back food for my children'. This literary composition reflects some episodes of social life in general, so it is probably not wrong to deduce from it the existence of 'traders' at this period, around the start of the 2nd millennium BC.[3]

In spite of everything, the literary composition known as the *Satire on Trades*, whose most ancient version goes back to the Middle Kingdom (2040-1782 BC), makes not the slightest mention of merchants. The author of this work, a certain Khety, glorifies the studies and the profession of the bureaucrat-scribe. He then reviews the different professions to bring out their disadvantages and to conclude how superior the scribe-functionary is whose security and prestige are obvious attractions. Saying that bureaucracy is the best

profession in existence, the author compares the career of the scribe and its advantages to the most varied professions: potter, weaver, barber, sculptor, and so on.[4]

The absence of the profession of merchant in this composition, the fact that there is no tomb that can be irrefutably attributed to a merchant, nor any inscription that describes an appropriate activity, has led many Egyptologists to posit as a principle that economic life in ancient Egypt, essentially agricultural, excluded all activity of a commercial nature.[5] For these scholars, texts and images referring to this subject could only be the sign of small-scale commerce, enough to keep local bazaars busy; this system of exchange would be of minor importance, not having the character of commerce *strictu sensu*. Furthermore, they acknowledge the full importance of Egypt's mercantile relations with its neighbours, for the acquisition of raw materials and the other products that it lacked. But they are more willing to see this as the mark of crown organisation,[6] the king being considered as the master of all property and the supreme landowner in the country. The description habitually made of the Egyptian economy has been summarised in these terms by É. Drioton: 'Pharaoh, master of the land and its fruits, of all people and their work, had from early antiquity been the sole patron of industrial production, and he alone could distribute or exchange its products. He was, and would remain throughout the Pharaonic monarchy, the sole industrialist and sole recognised merchant in Egypt. There were in Egypt only employees who handed over the fruits of their labour, and functionaries who dispensed to them, in the name of the king, the food and everything that was necessary for life'.[7]

This way of looking at things seems all the more fragile in that *The Tale of the Oasis Dweller* provides us with certain evidence of the existence of merchants as such, though without any specific designation. This is the case for other professions. On the subject of the term 'purveyors of dates' *(bnry.w)* on Papyrus E 3226 in the Louvre, and Papyrus Brooklyn 35.1453 A and B, it may be observed that these two documents might be referring to certain traders

---

1   This issue shall be examined in detail in *Seafaring in Ancient Egypt*, vol. 2.

2   G. Lefebvre, *Romans et contes*, 1949, p. 47 *et seq.*

3   It will be relevant to recall in passing two personalities of high social rank, if we are to judge from the architecture of their tombs: Si-Amun from the oasis of Siwa (from a pre-Ptolemaic date) and Djedimeniouef-ankh from the oasis of Bahariya (26th Dynasty). With no title to indicate any administrative or priestly function, both of them may have practised commerce on a large scale. For Si-Amun, see A. Fakhry, *Recent Excavations in the Oases of the Western Desert*, 1942, p. 159 *et seq.*; id., *Siwa Oasis*, 1944, p. 134; for the date see K. Kuhlmann, *Das Ammoneion*, ArchVer 75, 1988, p. 85. For Djedimeniouef-ankh, see A. Fakhry, *Bahria Oasis*, I, 1942, p. 50. The hypothesis is formulated by S. Allam, in N. Grimal, B. Menu (ed.), *Le commerce*, BiÉtud 121, 1998, p. 149.

4   For a presentation of the *Satire on Trades*, see for example G. Posener, *Littérature et politique*, 1956, pp. 5-7. For a complete bibliography, see B. Mathieu, *Grafma Newsletter* 2, 1998, pp. 37-40

5   Is the argument that deduces, from the absence of 'merchants' in the *Satire on Trades*, that commercial activities were also absent a valid argument? We might as well claim that in the Nile Valley, before the Ramesside era, there were no priests, bakers and soldiers.

6   See for example H. H. Kees, *Aegypten, Kulturgeschichte des Alten Orients*, 1933, p. 102: 'Grundzüge der Wirtschaftspolitik'; W. Helck, E. Otto, *Kleines Wörterbuch der Aegptologie*, 1956, pp. 135-136 ; J. A. Wilson, *The Burden of Egypt*, 1957 (3rd ed.), p. 81: 'Foreign commerce was probably a royal monopoly, although our evidence is slight and comes from texts which express attachment to the King'.

7   É. Drioton, *L'organisation économique de l'Égypte ancienne*, in *Cahiers d'histoire égyptienne* III, fasc. 3 March 1951, p. 197 and p. 201; note too, concerning the same problem, this explanation on p. 200: 'Both of them (worker and peasant) were attached in the same way to the earth and the workshop; the fruit of their labour belonged by the same right to their master, who, in exchange, fed them and saw to their needs. This master himself was simply a delegate of the king, to whom he transmitted the revenues of the domain, agricultural or industrial, which he managed. The whole of Egypt thus worked on behalf of Pharaoh.' These questions will be discussed in *Seafaring in Ancient Egypt*, vol. 2.

engaged in the operations recorded, but without using the designation *šwty*.[8] According to another papyrus (P. Turin 2008 + 2016), it might be suggested that the trading of fabrics was performed from the ship[9] and the possibility cannot be excluded either that the proprietors of several ships could be real traders.[10] Finally, the passage from the *Satire on Trades* concerning the basket maker (*btty*) is particularly eloquent:[11]

> *The basket-maker goes down the river to the marshes to procure profit for himself;*[12] *he has worked more than his arms (permit); the flies have massacred him, the sand flies have butchered him too.*

The economy at this moment in Egyptian history thus incontestably admitted the existence of private wealth, with the acquisition of gain, the mobility of property and the freedom for individuals to move from place to place. Clearly, these characteristics are not those of a completely closed and state–controlled economy, as it has often been defined. However, it cannot be concluded just from the *Satire* that there were traders as such. The text presents us with artisans who sell their own products, but it does not reveal the presence of traders, whose role would have been that of selling off merchandise that they themselves had not made, and who earned a living by serving as intermediaries; but nor does it offer anything that goes completely against this possibility.

With time, the theme of the *Satire on Trades* evolved, and the edition that dates from the Middle Kingdom was expanded.[13] Indeed, Papyrus Anastasi II provides some new ideas about other trades and professions – priests, soldiers, and even bakers.[14] As for the *šwty.w*, who can be defined as commercial agents, it is in the Lansing Papyrus that they are satirised.[15] Totally absent from the Middle Kingdom version, they make an appearance only at the end of the New Kingdom in the last version of this text. Here is the passage dedicated to them:[16]

*The šwty.w go up and down the river,*[17] *and trade with copper;*[18] *they transport merchandise from one city to another so as to provide him who lacks (something); while the (tax) collectors carry off the gold,*[19] *the most precious of all minerals.*

From this descriptive extract, it may be gathered that the *šwty.w* formed at the time of the New Kingdom a separate category of professionals,[20] who did not make products that had to be sold off;[21] and they had, it appears, to pay dues to the state tax collectors (or contributions in metal in which gold had a predominant role).[22] This does not however mean that the profession of these men did not exist before. What is new is merely the term *šwty/šwtj*, which our dictionary attests only from the New Kingdom.[23]

In addition, in the *Onomastica*, the term *šwty* figures, followed by two words, *mḥr* and *mkrj*; these words, which respectively designate 'buyer' and 'seller' seem to be of Semitic origin.[24] To claim on this basis that the term *šwty* is of the same origin would be erroroneous, since this verb can be built on the verb *šwj* attested with the precise meaning of 'unloading (a ship)',[25] which is altogether compatible with the profession of *šwty.w*. It would also be an evident mistake to believe that the Egyptians were merely awaiting the arrival of foreigners among them – the peoples of the North and the Sea Peoples – to learn from them the practices proper to trade. Certain scholars have proposed, for the etymology of *šwty*, making it a nisbé of *šw(.t)*, 'lack, penury'; the *šwty* would then literally be 'the man of lack', a sort of purveyor of goods, as it were, able to meet the needs of everyone.[26]

It is appropriate now to turn to the activities of the *šwty.w* as they can be read out of the evidence that is now available. The sources, both literary and documentary, mention the *šwty.w* quite frequently, but no text adequately depicts their role on the specifically commercial terrain.

8    M. Römer, *SAK* 19, 1992, p. 274, n. 77; M. Megally, *Recherches sur l'économie, l'administration et la comptabilité*, BiÉtud LXXI, 1977, p. 267.

9    J. J. Janssen, *Two Ancient Egyptian Ship's Logs*, 1961, p. 105.

10   E.W. Castle, *JESHO* 35, 1992, p. 250. See S. Allam, *op. cit.*, pp. 149-150.

11   P. Sallier II, 5,5-6: *btty ḥd=f r jdhw r jtt n=f swnw jr~n=f m ḥʿw n(.y)w ʿ.wy=fy ḥr jr.t smₐ~n sw ḥnms.w ḥmy.w sftn sw m sn.t*. On the translation of *btty* as 'basket maker, rush-mat maker', see the demonstration in A. Théodoridès, *AIPHO* XV, 1960, pp. 60-67. On this passage, see for example H. Brunner, *Die Lehre des Cheti*, 1944, pp. 120-121.

12   Litterally, 'what will make a profit for him' (*r jtt n=f swnw*); *swn* signifies 'to do trade' (*Wb* IV, 68, 'handel treiben'; see for example the translation given by G. Posener, *ZÄS* LXXXIII, 1958, p. 40, of the document Semnah Dispatches: '*Nḥs(y).w* [(number?)] arrived in the year] III, 4ᵗʰ month of *pr.t*, day 7, in the evening, to trade. What [they] brought was eventually traded… this trade (?)…)' *cf.* P. Smither, *JEA* XXXI, 1945, pls i-vii, p. 3-10, pl. ii and p. 6) and *swt.n* subsumes any commercial transaction, with the special meanings, depending on the case, of 'sale', 'purchase', 'price', 'payment', 'profit'… (A. Théodoridès, *RIDA*, VI, pp.126-127 and n. 80-83); in the context envisaged, we probably have a case, more precisely, of 'gain'. Either way, the literal translation would give: the 'basket maker' goes into the marshes 'so as to take for himself *swn(w)*', i.e. enough for him to trade with or, more generally, enough for him to procure gain for himself, which comes down to the idea of him earning a living.

13   A. Théodoridès, *RIDA*, 3ʳᵈ series, VI, 1959, p. 84 *et seq.*

14   A. H. Gardiner, *Late-Egyptian Miscellanies*, 1937, p. 16 *et seq.*; R. A. Caminos, *Late-Egyptian Miscellanies*, 1954, p. 50 *et seq.*

15   For the spellings of the term *šwty.w*, see W. Reineke, *AltorForsch* 6, 1979, p. 11 n. 38; M. Römer, *SAK* 19, 1992, p. 269 *et seq.*

16   P. Lansing, 4, 8-4, 9; A. Erman, H. Lange, *op. cit.*, p. 54 *et seq.*; A. H. Gardiner, *Late-Egyptian Miscellanies*, 1937, p. 103; R. O. Caminos, *Late-Egyptian Miscellanies*, 1954, p. 384 with notes; A. Théodoridès, *op. cit.*, p. 86; S. Allam, *op. cit.*, p. 150.

17   In BM Papyrus 10053 rᵒ 7, 18, we read of a ship that belonged to a certain *šwty*; see below on the subject of the Brooklyn Papyrus 35.1453 A + B and the Turin Papyrus 2008 + 2016.

18   E. Castle, *JESHO* 35, 1992, p. 257 translates: 'as they do business with copper, carrying goods…'

19   The expression *fₐj nbw* has been interpreted in different ways. There is certainly a relation – in the form of a pun – between the *fₐj* of the traders who 'carry' their merchandise from one town to another, and that of the tax collectors who 'carry off' the gold; but the exact meaning of the passage must surely be understood – as A. De Buck clearly grasped – by setting up an antithesis between the demand for gold on the part of the public powers, which the merchants cannot evade, and the payment facilities that they sometimes have to grant to their customers (A. De Buck, *JEOL* V, 1937-1938, p. 295 and n. 4).

20   Given the title *ḥry šwty.w*, 'chief of commercial agents'; see the examples given by W. Reineke, *AltorForsch* 6, 1979, p. 9, p. 11. The stele of the Cairo Museum JE 36861 (from the Ethiopian period) mentions chiefs of commercial agents; D. Meeks, in *Hommages à S. Sauneron*, BiÉtud 81/2, 1979, pp. 249-250. Another example is in M. Malinine, G. Posener, J. Vercoutter, *Catalogue des stèles du Sérapéum de Memphis*, I, 1968, nᵒ 7. See too A. Mariette, *Catalogue général des monuments d'Abydos*, 1880, p. 410, nᵒ 1115; *id.*, *Monuments divers recueillis en Égypte et en Nubie*, 1889, pl. 56; R. Navailles, F. Neveu, *GM* 103, 1988, p. 55, n. 1.

21   See below, the Lansing Papyrus, 4, 8-9; the essential activity of merchants was to transport the 'things' (merchandise), and not their own things, 'from one town to the other'.

22   A. Théodoridès, *RIDA*, 3ʳᵈ series, V, 1958, p. 96; E. Castle, *JESHO* 35, 1992, p. 250, p. 257.

23   *Wb* IV, 484, 1-4, 5-6, 9-13. See *AnLex* I, 78.4070; II, 77.4126; III, 79.2951; *KRI* II, 333, 1; 800, 7; 801, 7; 802, 5; D. Meeks, *op. cit.*, p. 249 n. 56; W. F. Reinecke, *AltorForsch* 6, 1979, pp. 5-14; A. Nibbi, *JEA* 64, 1978, p. 62; Mounir Megally, *Recherches sur l'économie, l'administration et la comptabilité*, BiÉtud LXXI, 1977, pp. 254-256; G. A. Gaballa, *The Memphite Tomb Chapel of Mose*, 1977, pl. xv.

24   A. H. Gardiner, *AEO* I, 1947, 95* and pl. 9, 12. For *mkrj*, see E. Castle, *op. cit.*, p. 256. *cf. infra*, p. 166.

25   *cf. Wb* IV, 428, 1; M. Römer, *SAK* 19, 1992, p. 270.

26   B. Menu, in N. Grimal, B. Menu (ed.), *Le commerce*, BiÉtud 121, 1998, p. 199. Note that the Greek term *chrematistike*, usually translated as 'the art of earning money', has the literal meaning 'art of providing the goods necessary to life', 'art of supplying you' with indispensable goods. This meaning corresponds to an economy based on the postulate of self-sufficiency of a community in which commerce serves to restore autonomy (as opposed to lucrative commerce). See K. Polanyi, in K. Polanyi, C. M. Arensberg (ed.), *Les systèmes économiques*, 1975, p. 116.

## II.2. Traders and internal trade

The *Satire on Trades* of the Lansing Papyrus refers to the mobility of goods in Egypt in the Ramesside period as well as attesting to the fact that travel and change of place were inherent to the professional activity of the *šwty.w*.

The *šwty.w* constituted a professional category which, together with navigators, guards, escorts and so on, participated in commercial expeditions along the Nile Valley. They were commercial agents, probably responsible for the organisation and management of transactions. They were certainly specialists in the evaluation of a commodity, and in the virtual conversion of a given commodity into an equivalent sum in precious metal: but they were not really independent entrepreneurs, but generally the employees of an institution, even of an individual. They functioned as brokers, playing the role of intermediaries between institutional producers and consumers. It is difficult to define their way of working, of selecting the commodities for exchange, of dealing and even negotiating with other traders.[27]

## II.3. Traders and external trade

The *šwty.w* could be involved in the organisation of external commerce. A Memphite scribe thus suggested to one of his chiefs, the Scribe of the Treasury, that he send for the *šwty* to see whether the latter had returned from Kharu (Syro-Palestine).[28] It is probable that at least one *šwty* accompanied the ships that set out regularly for the different ports in the Near East to exchange Egyptian products for other merchandise.

Apart from the official emissaries, a sort of commercial diplomat, it is known that in the Near East there were permanent settlements of foreign merchants. The Biblical texts provide us with an example: this is the negotiation over the establishment of 'streets', granted by Ben-Hadad, the King of Aram, to a king of Israel who is doubtless Joas.[29] It is generally agreed that these were merchant streets, 'bazaars' or 'souks'. There are two points worth focusing on in this text: the foreign merchants could settle permanently in the capitals of the countries where they carried out their commerce and this necessitated an agreement on the part of the sovereign of the host country, negotiated between states.[30] Nothing excludes the presence of Egyptian merchants. It may be extrapolated that there must have been Egyptian bazaars in the *emporia* of Syro-Palestine, but the latter would probably have had to be negotiated with the town's authorities. Commercial exchange was entirely organised and negotiated between states. So there must also have been private merchants who sold the products of artisans in other countries. Even if it does not concern Egypt, the journey of Elijah to Sarepta,[31] in the kingdom of Tyre and Sidon, shows that it was relatively easy to travel and to settle in the territory of another kingdom. Without generalising hastily from such limited data, it should be noted, all the same, that outside state and official commerce, the exchanges carried out by merchants in a system of private commerce were especially intense between border regions.[32]

In more recent times, Egyptians or Phoenician families originally from Egypt had probably left their countries while maintaining close relations with their homelands and their host countries. One family of Egyptian immigrants into Carthage has been discovered that, in the 4th century BC, could be attested for over 17 generations: this was the family of the suffete of Carthage, whose name Panoufe *(Pnp')* (< Egyptian *P3-nfr* 'the Good') suggests Egyptian origins. The names of certain ancestors named *Mśry*, 'the Egyptian' or 'Abdr'a, 'Servant of Ra',[33] even *R'amlk* 'Ra is prince',[34] a transposition into Phoenician of Egyptian or mixed names, makes this proposition indubitable.[35] The frequency in Punic onomastics of names connoting Egypt, of the kind *Mśry*, *Mśrt*, 'the Egyptian man or woman', is unequalled if not by the multiplicity of Egyptian deities worshipped at Carthage itself.[36] Furthermore, the permanence of an Egyptian family (or a family originally from Egypt) over more than 17 generations is sufficiently remarkable in the city's elite to conclude that there was a significant settlement there, especially when it is taken into account that the suffetes were the supreme magistrates in the city.[37] Although some of the Egyptian-sounding names were probably borne by the 'ancestors of Phoenicians originally from Egypt',[38] the fact remains that they were not all in the same situation. At the very least, the desire to preserve Egyptian names shows that they had familiarised themselves not only with the language of Egypt[39] but with its customs as well, not forgetting the fact that their business could lead them to return from time to time to the Nile Valley. The situation was extremely paradoxical: while Egypt was present through its cults in Carthage, there was no Carthaginian cult that has been attested in Egypt, and very few examples referring to any Carthaginian presence in Egypt.[40] This is one more argument for imagining that the Egyptians left their own land for commercial reasons at a time when they could be useful for the development of relations between Phoenicia, Carthage and Egypt.

In short, there is a lack of knowledge about the personal networks or the networks of merchants' customers overseas, as well as the existence of community centres (for communities based on profession, culture, religion, and so on) or entrepots where traders in transit could have sheltered their cargoes.

27   S. Bickel, in N. Grimal, B. Menu (ed.), *Le commerce*, BiÉtud 121, 1998, pp. 161-162; P. Grandet, *le papyrus Harris I*, BiÉtud 109, vol. 2, 1994, p. 168.

28   P. Bologna 1094, 5, 5: R. O. Caminos, *Late-Egyptian Miscellanies*, 1954, pp. 16-17; S. Bickel, *op. cit.*, p. 162.

29   I Kings XX, 34

30   F. Briquel-Chatonnet, *Les relations entre les cités de la côte phénicienne et les royaumes d'Israël et de Juda*, Studia Phoenicia XII, OLA 46, 1992, pp. 265-268.

31   I Kings XVII, 8-24.

32   For an example of Phoenician merchants settled abroad, see E. Lipinski, RSF 3, 1975, pp. 1-6.

33   E. Lipinski (ed.), *Dictionnaire de la civilisation phénicienne et punique*, 1992, pp. 26, 342.

34   Id., p. 26.

35   S. Aufrère, in N. Grimal, B. Menu (ed.), *Le commerce*, BiÉtud 121, 1998, pp. 34-35.

36   J. Leclant, in *Actes du IIIe congrès international des études phéniciennes et puniques*, 1995, p. 47.

37   E. Lipinski (ed.), *op. cit.*, p. 429.

38   Id., p. 26.

39   See *Wenamun* who, on his arrival in Cyprus (Alasia), asks, 'Is there not someone here who understands the language of Egypt?', whereupon someone replies, Yes, I do': G. Lefebvre, *Romans et contes*, 1948, p. 220.

40   The only known attestations, dating fron the 2nd century BC, are to be found on a sphinx in the Serapeum of Memphis.

## II.4. Foreign traders in Egypt

Several documents refer to foreign *šwty.w*. Thus the letter from a woman addressed to a *šmsw*-servant mentions a *šwty* whose name – Aper-Baal – might betray an Asiatic origin.[41] The *Decree of Nauri* orders the protection of 'traders from abroad' (*šwty.w n ḫ3s.t*) who in Nubia practised their trade thanks to a foundation of Seti I (1291-1278 BC).[42] If there is some trace of foreigners working as traders in Egypt, 'we nonetheless have to underline the fact that the great majority of *šwty.w* bore purely Egyptian names and that their activity as often as not occurred within the country'.[43]

Egypt would occasionally welcome into its great ports merchant expeditions that came from outside. The scene from the tomb of Kenamun depicts this type of event.[44]

In the corpus of the Amarnian correspondence, the King of Cyprus (*Alasia*), in a letter addressed to Akhenaten, asks for protection and tax exemption for his merchants and their ship during their passage to Egypt:[45]

> *My brother, let my messengers go… These men are my merchants… Let no one approach my merchants or my ship to require anything in your name.*

In order to understand this situation, it should be remembered that in Cyprus large-scale trade was a royal privilege; only central power was authorised to sell off the surplus of national production. In the king's entourage there was a category of merchants that had been attested for a long time previously. Around the middle of the 1st millennium BC, in fact, there were perhaps merchants, together with mercenaries, who signed over 40 graffiti in the Cypriot syllabary language on the walls of the temple of Seti I, at Abydos, where there was an oracle of Isis.[46]

*A priori*, Naukratis could provide an excellent observation post for the study of the role of foreign (Greek) traders in Egypt, at least from the 7th century BC. Nonetheless, it is not easy to work out with any precision how trade developed through this *emporion*. The archaeological remains provide information about the sanctuaries, not about the entrepots, although it has been hypothesised that each city represented had not only its own sanctuary, but also its own commercial district. The great 'independent' sanctuaries founded by Samos and Miletus – and also, apparently, by Chios and Aegina – probably belonged to the most ancient phase of the city; and the diversity of origin of the dedications and those making them that these sanctuaries have yielded clearly shows that they were not separate 'national' places of worship, but were open to the whole of the Greek community. The Hellenion, built perhaps in the reign of Amasis (1201-1199 BC), constituted a bigger sacred area for other buildings, some of them doubtless erected by the cities involved in trade at Naukratis, others by the Greek community of the residents.

In addition, Naukratis was not altogether an ordinary Greek city with its own 'citizens', comparable to the colonies of Sicily and Italy. Its existence depended on the permanence of the favour (and the interest) of the Egyptian king, which would ensure that their monopoly on the Egyptian market remained unchallenged. This implied a certain understanding between them, not necessarily at the level of the metropolises, but rather among the diverse categories of merchants residing at Naukratis itself. It was from among them that the *prostatai* mentioned by Herodotus[47] must have been designated –

these were magistrates responsible for the management of the *emporion*, even if the historian seems to suggest between the lines that this appointment was made by the metropolises. It is clear, too, that the founders of the Hellenion and promoters of the independent sanctuaries were associated in the commercial and more general organisation of urban life. The *prostatai* must have simultaneously played the role of magistrates of the city and 'consuls' for the families and merchants of their respective metropolises.[48] The life of this huge, rich Greek community, kept within strict limits of activity and settlement, must have presented a strange and varied appearance. It was different from all that the Greeks had experienced elsewhere. It was neither a colony - an independent, self-sufficient city - that had reached an understanding with the local population, nor was it a simple trading post, like Al-Mina (in Syria), where to begin with there cannot have been any real civic life organised in the Greek style, with sanctuaries and other structures of the same kind. Naukratis attracted the most enterprising of the merchants of eastern Greece and their colleagues from Aegina, masters of trade with central Greece – but also poets, artists, men of state and historians, and in periods of danger it was able to offer a refuge to the professionals of eastern Greece, desirous of resuming their activity. It is probable that when the Greeks arrived, there was already an Egyptian city or village on this site. It is certain that the Egyptians still lived at Naukratis alongside the Greeks, doubtless in a native district, providing the necessary workforce; but the foundations, in unfired bricks that have been excavated in a damp zone, provide us with barely any useful information about these houses, either Greek or Egyptian.

According to Herodotus, certain Levantine traders had their own reserved district in Memphis, the 'camp of the Tyrians'.[49] The texts describing the Asiatic milieu of Egypt under Achaemenid domination, familiar through the Jewish and Aramean communities of Elephantine,[50] provide a particularly interesting glimpse of the life of merchants and dealers present in Egypt as well as allowing us to investigate the role the Persians might have played in the organisation of commerce. The problem is not to imagine the (apparently rather insignificant) share that might have been comprised by commercial profits in the formation of tribute: this was a station that depended on the tribute-payers themselves in which the power of the satrap had no need to intervene as long as the royal granaries were full and the tribute paid. It may, however, be envisaged that Persian intermediaries infiltrated the systems of organisation of commerce on an individual basis or more officially to control a part or all of them, or at least to derive some profit from them.

41  A. H. Gardiner, *Late-Egyptian Miscellanies*, 1937, p. 9, P. Bologna 1094, 10, 3.

42  *Decree of Nauri*, I. 40, F. L. Griffith, *JEA* XIII, 1927, p. 201, pl. 41.

43  S. Bickel, *op. cit.*, p. 163.

44  Tomb of Kenamun (TT 162): N. de G. Davies; A. H. Gardiner, *JEA* 33, 1947, pl. 8; S. Bickel, *op. cit.*, and fig. 1, p. 162.

45  *EA*, 39, 10-20: W. L. Moran, *Les lettres d'El-Amarna*, LAPO 13, 1987, p. 208, EA 39, 14-20; E. W. Castle, *JESHO* 35, 1992, p. 245; cf. on the same subject letter 40, W. L. Moran, *op. cit.*, pp. 209-210. See also E. Lipinski, in J. D. Hawkins (ed.), *Trade in the Ancient Near East*, 1977, pp. 213-217. On the identification of Alashiya/Alasia with Cyprus, see p. 29.

46  O. Masson, *Les inscriptions chypriotes syllabiques*, 1961; I. Nicolau, in *Cyprus between the Orient and the Occident*, 1986, p. 425.

47  Herodotus, II, 179-180, passage cited p. 61.

48  J. Boardman, *Les Grecs outre-mer*, 1985, pp. 158-159; A. Möller, *Naukratis*, 2000.

49  Herodotus, II, 112.

50  P. Grelot, *Documents araméens d'Égypte*, LAPO 5, 1972.

In the Aramaic texts of Egypt, the rare passages that present or relate commercial, local or more distant exchanges mention only private individuals; trade seems not to have been one of the satrap's functions. His economic responsibility consisted of ensuring that the royal warehouses were filled and the rations distributed to the garrisons,[51] and that dues and tributes reached the central power.[52] On the other hand, a 'business letter' relative to the payment of a grain transport on the Nile mentions a dispatcher and a sleeping partner who have Iranian names, and mariners with Egyptian names who are addressed in the letter:[53]

(Recto:)[1] *To my brothers Iori and PetemeHu, your brother Spentadata. May all the gods at all times grant prosperity to my brothers! And now,[2] I have a ship, shared between myself and its master, (which is) in your hands. For me, see to it that Armantidata tells you[3] to entrust him, and what he wants, he will do (it) for him (?). Furthermore, my share in the hiring of the boat [...] you should give into his own hands. There is a sum[4] of eight s(hekels) (that) I have given to X... for him to give it in exchange for corn to be brought to my house; and there is a sum of one karch that I have given you myself to[5] buy corn for Yatma. Total: a sum of one karch eight s(hekels). If you buy (with) them corn and (if) you take (it)[6] to our houses, that is fine! If not, give the money back into the disposal of Armantidata; it is he who will bring it to us. And if much corn[7] remains at your disposal, inform Armantidata and give it into his own hands. May PetemeHu remain*

(Verso:)[8] *with you on the boat: let him not leave you until he has come too my house.*

(Address:)[9] *To my brothers Iori son of X... and PetemeHu, your brother Spentadata son of Fravartipata.*

The commentator suggests that the Iranians belong either to the administration or the corps of officers.[54] This is perhaps an example of Persian participation in local commerce, outside any intervention on the part of the satrap.

## II.5. The juridical and institutional status of traders

Various studies devoted to the *šwty.w* insist on the institutional side of their activity and the absence of what these days would be called free trade in the pursuit of profit.[55] It must, however, be remembered that in Ancient Egypt very few people seem to have worked in a manner entirely independent of, or outside, the state system and the temples. Everyone or almost everyone – peasants, artisans, functionaries – was attached to an institution. Should this exclude all possibility of private initiative?

On the basis of this varied and singularly disparate information, may the personality of a *šwty* on the institutional and juridical level be sketched out?

The corpus of sources relative to the pillaging of tombs from the end of the Ramesside era tells us something about the role played by the *šwty.w*-traders in this unhappy business. One of the lists enumerates no less than 60 *šwty.w* involved in the thefts.[56] Their origin shows once again the mobility of this category of people. The

great number of *šwty.w* compromised in the crime can doubtless be explained by their very profession, and illustrates their margins for manoeuvre. Their institutional and official activity easily gave them an opportunity to sell off merchandise, and, in the present case, to 'launder' the spoils of their pillages and evidently to derive profit from them; and a good profit at that. This would then imply the 'existence of a free market, in which it was habitual to see *šwty.w*-merchants, and in which everyone was able to exchange in their own manner not only the products of everyday consumption but also luxury items'.[57]

The trial report of the BM Papyrus 10053 ro designates 19 *šwty.w*; at least 15 of them are accused of receiving and concealing, since many stolen objects were found among them (their value sometimes estimated in terms of gold or copper). Nine of these *šwty.w* came from a locality called *Mr-wr*, probably the region of Fayum.[58] Furthermore, one of these *šwty.w* came, in all probability, from Aswan, since he was a dependent of the temple of Khnum at Elephantine. Given these facts, it is possible that these *šwty.w*, the majority of whom came from very far away, arrived on the scene with the intent to collaborate, one way or another, with the robbers.[59]

The verse of the BM Papyrus 10068 provides, *inter alia*, a census of the conurbation of Thebes-West, from the temple of Seti I to a certain hamlet;[60] it is worth pointing out in passing that the workers' colony of Deir el-Medina is not included, whether or not it was actually deserted at that time. This census is presented in topographic form for 179 private dwellings. It is strange that no *šwty* is found in this conurbation. And yet, several *šwty.w* were involved in the inquiries into the pillages committed in the neighbouring necropolis.[61]

The report of one of these investigations provides details of the various individuals who profited from the booty of the pillagers: women, scribes, priests, and also several *šwty.w*. The latter, 14 of them, are mentioned separately, before the other beneficiaries who are named pell-mell. It is not known why the robbers gave these *šwty.w* objects that were for the main part in gold. Were the latter receivers of stolen goods? Had they offered other objects in exchange? Or else, had they accepted the stolen gold and silver as a kind of deposit?[62] E. W. Castle has made a judicious comparison between the price of gold in Egypt and that in Syria.[63] In Ugarit (in

51   *DAE* 60, 54, 55. P. Grelot, *op. cit.*, n° 60 pp. 280-283; n° 54 and 55 pp. 266-275.
52   *DAE* 71-72. See P. Grelot, *op. cit.*, pp. 320-323. Although no text expressly mentions how dues were brought from Egypt to Babylon or Susa, the commentator refers to the caravans and excludes any circumnavigation of Arabia (J.-F. Salles, in J.-F. Salles (ed.), *L'Arabie et ses mers bordières I*, TMO 16, 1988, pp. 75-102).
53   *DAE* 109. See P. Grelot, *op. cit.*, pp. 503-505.
54   P. Grelot, *Documents araméens d'Égypte*, LAPO 5, 1972, p. 505.
55   This position is defended in the extreme by W. F. Reineke, *AltorForsch* 6, 1979, pp. 5-14 ; M. Römer, *SAK* 19, 1992, pp. 268-284; the opinion of E. W. Castle, *JESHO* 35, 1992, pp. 256-257 is more nuanced.
56   P. BM 10053; E. Peet, *The Great Tomb-Robberies*, 1930, I, pp. 104-109.
57   S. Bickel, in N. Grimal, B. Menu (ed.), *le commerce*, BiÉtud 121, 1998, p. 167.
58   For another *šwty* from Fayum and implicated in the inquiries by one of the accused, P. BM 10052, ro 5, 1 + 5, 11-12: E. Peet, *op. cit.*, I, p. 147.
59   S. Allam, in N. Grimal, B. Menu (ed.), *le commerce*, BiÉtud 121, 1998, p. 154. Some of these accomplices seem to have been free men, and not subject to a master or any institution.
60   E. Peet, *op. cit.*, I, p. 93, II pl. 14 *et seq.*; D. Valbelle, *CRIPEL 7*, 1985, p. 86.
61   S. Allam, *op. cit.*, p. 153.
62   A. Théodoridès, *RIDA*, 3rd series, V, 1958, pp. 94-95.
63   E. W. Castle, *op. cit.*, p. 253.

the 14<sup>th</sup>-13<sup>th</sup> centuries BC) a shekel of gold was worth three or four shekels of silver, while in Egypt (at the end of the 12<sup>th</sup> century BC) it cost only two shekels of silver, if a passage in the BM Papyrus 10068 ro 4, 14 is to be believed. Was this price of gold in Egypt perhaps one of the motives that drove the *šwty.w* to procure so much gold for themselves, so that they could then sell it off in Syro-Palestine? Be that as it may, at their homes, the public authorities succeeded in discovering five *deben* + 1/2 *kite* of gold as well as 32 *deben* of silver, and some fabrics of superior quality, while from the thieves they recovered objects of a much higher value and in higher quantities.

The rubric referring to the *šwty.w* mentioned in the account of the trial speaks volumes:[64]

*(What was) received in the year 17, 2nd month of winter, day 21 in the temple of Maat in the City (consisting of) the gold and silver recovered from the homes of the worker-thieves (belonging to the institution) of the (royal) Tomb, and (some of which, as it) was discovered, the (pillagers had) given to the šwty.w of diverse domains (n pr nb).*

The expression *n pr nb* ('of every domain', 'of each domain', 'of diverse domains') is identical with the one given by the Lansing Papyrus in connection with sailors.[65] The word *pr* must certainly not be translated as 'house of commerce' or 'firm'.[66] These 'domains' *(pr.w)* can designate different 'houses' and 'institutions', including temples. The list of the BM Papyrus 10068 contains 14 names of these *šwty.w n pr nb* each of them with the determiner of his place of attachment. The text mentions in particular two *šwty.w* working under the authority of a priest who depended on the temple of Sobek at Crocodilopolis:[67]

*The trader Khonsoudja, son of Katjay, in (the service of the) Temple (pr) of Sobek (of Crocodilopolis), under the authority of the Prophet Nekhemhatef: 2 deben of silver.*

It is clear that *pr* in reality designates the 'domain' of a particular god, or quite simply the 'temple' as a whole.[68] A third *šwty* was subject to the authority of a *sm*-priest of the temple of Ptah.[69] The *Dedicatory Inscription of Abydos* alludes to the *šwty-w*-merchants and confirms the close relation that they could have with the temples. Rameses II theoretically addresses Osiris, the lord of Abydos, in these terms:[70]

*I have enriched your treasury so that it is filled with all that your heart desires, which I have granted with your taxes.[71]*

*I have given a mnš-ship with its cargo on Wadj Wer, which transports for you (the great treasures) of the Divine Land; merchants (do) business with it[72] and their revenues will consist of gold, silver and copper. [...]*

The Pharaoh not only makes positive donations to the temple, but he also grants it *atelia*: the domain of Osiris will no longer have to pay taxes to the central power.[73] In addition, the king grants him a ship for long-distance voyages (*mnš*-ships). This favour increases even more the material advantages enjoyed by the temple, since the merchants seem to be in the service of the temple – though it cannot

be ascertained if they already were, or whether the king made them such, by giving them at the same time the 'ship' which, *ipso facto*, would have been given along with a maritime personnel and a trading personnel.[74] This suggests that the merchants 'engage in commerce' (*jry šwt*[75]) and trade the cargo in the name of the temple in question. In other words, the merchants 'sell off' the exotic products that the temple crew has brought back from the 'Divine Land', and the revenue from which (*b3kw*) issuing from the sale of this merchandise, in gold, silver and copper, is paid back into the temple treasury. Should the term *b3kw* be translated as 'taxes' paid by the traders to the temple in question?[76] Should it be assumed that the traders paid the temple a sum in gold, silver and copper, after selling the cargo of the *Mnš*-ship in question, a sum equivalent or proportional to the profits derived from the deal?

In the account of the pillaging of the tombs, not all of the traders accused worked uniquely for the domain of the temples. Nine of the *šwty.w* involved were employed by three commanders of military troops; for example, the 'trader Nessobek, son of Seniry, of the general (*n(j)m(y)-r(3) mš*ᶜ), leader of the foreign troop, Amenhefer':[77] in other words, Seniry was in the service of the 'domain' of the general named.

The Turin Papyrus 1887 tells us that after the death of the captain of the ship attached to the temple of Khnum, a 'trader' was made 'captain'. His essential task was to transport to Elephantine the

---

64    P. BM 10068, ro 4, 1-21. T. E. Peet, *The Great Tomb-Robberies*, 1930, I, p. 90; II, pl. xi.

65    P. Lansing, 4, 10: 'The crew of *mnš*-ships of every domain (*n pr nb*) has received its load, so as to leave Egypt for Djahy'.

66    'Commercial house' or 'firm' are the suggestions, respectively, of T. E. Peet, *op. cit.*, p. 100, n. 18 and A. De Buck, *JEOL* V, 1937-1938, p. 295. See R. A. Caminos, *Late-Egyptian Miscellanies*, 1954, p. 387. In the same sense, Al. Moret, *CRAIBL*, 1915, p. 371.

67    P. BM 10068, ro, 14. A. Théodoridès, *op. cit.*, p. 100.

68    See for example A. H. Gardiner, The Wilbour Papyrus, II, 1948, p 83, on the subject of scribes: 'There are a few temple-scribes, one of them, who is often named (...) being described just in that way (*sš ḥw.t-nṯr*), while others are said to belong to the House (*n pr*) of such and such a god [...]'

69    In the Berlin Papyrus 10460 (S. Allam, *Hieratische Ostraka und Papyri, Urkunden zum Rechtsleben im alten Ägypten* I, 1993, p. 276) there appear several *šwty.w* dependant on the temple of Ra.

70    *Dedicatory Inscription of Abydos*: PM VI, 3 (34-37); KRI II, 332, 15-333, 1; J. H. Breasted, *Ancient records of Egypt*, III, 1907, § 274; H. Gauthier, *La grande inscription dédicatoire d'Abydos*, BiÉtud IV, 1912, p. 18; id., *ZÄS* XLVIII, 1911, p. 63; A. Théodoridès, RIDA, 3<sup>rd</sup> series, V, 1958, p. 94. transliteration of this text: *špss~n=j pr-ḥd=k mḥ m ḥ.t m ḥr.t jb rdy=j n=k ḥnᶜ ḥtr.w=k dw=j n=k mnšw ḥr sbt.w tp w3d wr st3 n=k [...] n t3 nṯr šwty.w ḥr jr.t šwt ḥr ḥn.wt=sn b3kw=sn jry m nbw ḥd ḥmty.*

71    *htr.w*: Wb III, 202, 2-3; AnLex I, 77.2912;

72    Literally, 'merchants make commerce with it under their orders'.

73    On the immunity of the temples of the New Kingdom, see for example A. H. Gardiner, *The Wilbour Papyrus*, II, 1948, p. 202; J. Pirenne, AHDO and RIDA I, 1952, p. 23; J.A. Wilson, *The Burden of Egypt*, p. 271-272.

74    It is not stipulated in the text that they are 'foreign merchants', as H. Kees, *Kulturgeschichte des Alten Orients*, 1933, p. 104 n. 1; as did W. Helck, E. Otto, *Kleines Wörterbuch*, 1956, p. 137, n. 16, in comparison with the decree of Seti I at Nauri, l. 40 (= W. F. Edgerton, *JNES* VI, 1947, p. 222).

75    We find the same expression, *jrj šwt*, 'engage in commerce', 'undertake trade', in the Mayer Papyrus A, 3, 5, where the wife of one of the pillagers from the royal necropolis declares: 'he took away copper that belonged to this tomb'; *jw=n...* 'we traded it and we ate the proceeds' (= we converted it into foodstuff)'; W.W. Spiegelberg, *Rechnungen aus der Zeit Setis* I, I, 1896, p. 61; See also P. BM 10052, 3, 19 (= T. E. Peet, *The Great Tomb-Robberies*, 1930, I, p. 146; II, pl. xxvii); and cf. on the expression G. H. Hughes, in *Festschrift zum 70. Geburtstag von Professor Dr H. Kees*, MDAIK 14, 1956, pp. 82-83. In the language of the Middle Kingdom, the transitive verb *swn* is used with the same meaning (P. Smither, *JEA* XXXI, 1945, pl. ii and p. 7; A. H. Gardiner, *Egyptian Grammar*, p. 340, n. 21) See also AnLex III, 79.2951; KRI II, 333, L; 800, 7; 801, 7; 802, 5; D. Meeks, in *Hommages à S. Sauneron, Égypte pharaonique*, BiÉtud 81/1, 1979, p. 249 n. 56; W. F. Reinecke, *AltorForsch* 6, 1979, pp. 5-14; cf. *supra*, p. 231.

76    This is the interpretation of A. Théodoridès, RIDA, 3<sup>rd</sup> series, V, 1958, pp. 94-95. On the term *b3kw*, see Wb I, 427, 13-428, 15; AnLex I, 77.1188; cf. p. 252.

77    P. BM 10068, ro, 4, 4.

product of the land which the Temple possessed in Ancient Egypt; but he embezzled numerous sacks of corn, with the complicity of 'scribes, controllers (*rwḏw*) and farmers of the temple of Khnum'. It is not stated that the merchant in question already belonged to the temple of Khnum.[78] The temple may have attached him to its service just when it had become necessary to appoint a captain. If a little later in the text the same merchant really appears as 'captain of the ship of the temple of Khnum', it was after the appointment.[79]

BM Papyrus 10068, states that the 'trader Nesptah, of [80] the musician of Sobek, Isis, the daughter of Hori, who was a general'.[81] This merchant was attached to the property of the said singing woman and he was not the only one, since the 'merchant Hori', quoted in line 17, had exactly the same role.

It follows unequivocally that the '*šwty.w* mentioned in the report were exercising their activities as agents under the control of a master, possibly in the interests of some house or other; either a temple or another institution – a lord's domain being quite possible'.[82] In fact, at least seven of these *šwty.w* were working for the same officer named Amunnefer (commander of foreign troops). Since he had access to foreign 'markets', it may thus be envisaged that this officer was actively involved in large-scale commerce that went beyond the borders of Egypt.

As a result, the *pr.w*, in whose service the merchants were, as well as the merchants of the Lansing Papyrus, cannot have comprised exclusively a 'commercial firm', but a 'house' in the more general sense, a 'property' or 'domain', or even 'institution' (or 'foundation') belonging to individuals, members of the laity as well as religious collectives. Thus the merchant Hempayka was in the service of Payounedjem, 'Chief of the Archers of the Temple of Ra'[83] and not, properly speaking, in the service of the *pr* of Ra himself, understood as a socio-economic entity.

In the BM Papyrus 10068, in addition to a trader from the domain of Sobek at Crocodilopolis; and the domain of Khnum at Elephantine, other *šwty.w* work under the authority of, or in the service of a master, but in several places in the documents relating to the pillage of the royal necropolis mention is made of a 'trader of *Mr-wr*', from 'Lake Moeris', or rather from Fayum in general.[84] Since no other information about them exists, it may be deduced that they were not attached to 'domains' and that they were working for themselves. As perhaps was the trader who appears in the judicial case in the Cairo Papyrus 65.739.[85]

It seems, indeed, that some *šwty.w* were, by all appearances, free men.[86] Furthermore, two *šwty.w* who each seem to possess a servant (*ḥm*)[87] and one who might be subject to the authority of another *šwty*[88] are also encountered. Moreover, from a judicial case some *šwty.w* justified their haggling before a municipal council (*qnbt sḏm.yw*, here acting as a tribunal) on the subject, it appears, of a dispute concerning several servants.[89]

Some documents seem to have preserved a trace of dealings performed outside one's official activity. The Lansing Papyrus describes the wretchedness of the peasants by referring to the case of a particularly unfortunate farmer; the snakes had eaten his grain and he was obliged to re-sow his fields with borrowed seed. As neither he nor his wife were able to reimburse the loan, his wife 'fell prey to the merchants'.[90] So the latter were probably the creditors.[91] Although the passage is difficult to interpret, it seems that this is a tentative example of a private operation from which the traders took the

direct profit. Since they probably picked up the greater part of their wages in corn, they could try to make any surplus bear fruit. As they were regularly in charge of the great corn cargoes, they could certainly also recover, over and above the official tally, small quantities and dispose of them to make a profit. Such practices must have been fully part of the system, and hardly judged to be forms of abuse and corruption.[92]

A juridical document from Thebes reports that a *šwty* sold a Syro-Palestinian servant woman (*ḫ³rw*) to a lady of high rank in exchange for several sorts of fabrics, metal containers and a jar of honey, to the total value of four *deben*, one *qedet* of silver.[93] This transaction 'seems not to have taken place within any institutional framework [...]; it could be that the trader acquired this servant on one of his official travels to the Near East before selling it to her at a profit'.[94] This is not the opinion of certain scholars, who have claimed that if the sale, which was apparently concluded between two private persons, was in fact realised, it was in the name of one institution and to the profit of another or the same institution, probably the temple and the necropolis of Thebes.[95] Be that as it may, such transactions necessitate a certain number of more specific details on the exchange of persons and must be set within the general framework of the status of such workers. It should also be emphasised that the variety of juridical frameworks for exchanges whose object

---

78  P. Turin 1887, v°, 2, 9-11 (= A. H. Gardiner, *Ramesside Administrative Documents*, 1948, p. 89; *id.*, *JEA* XXVII, 1941, p. 61); cf J. A. Wilson, *The Burden of Egypt*, pp. 279-280.

79  P. Turin 1887, v°, 2, 9-11 (A. H. Gardiner, *Ramesside Administrative Documents*, 1948, p. 81; *id.*, *JEA* XXVII, 1941, p. 62).

80  'In the service of'.

81  P. BM 10068, r°, 4, 13.

82  S. Allam, in N. Grimal, B. Menu (ed.), *Le commerce*, BiÉtud 121, 1998, p. 154.

83  P. BM 10068, r° 4, 11. We have here taken the syllable *ḥm* to form the first element of the proper name Hempayka, unlike T. E. Peet, *The Great Tomb-Robberies*, 1930, I, p. 90, who translates as 'the trader and the slave Paiika...'

84  T. E. Peet, *The Great Tomb-Robberies*, 1930, I, p. 110, n. 7; on Lake Moeris: A. H. Gardiner, AEO II, 115*-116*; A. Théodoridès, *op. cit.*, p. 102.

85  P. Cairo 65.739, 3: A. H. Gardiner, *JEA* XXI, 1935, pp. 140-146, pls xiii-xvi; J. Pirenne, B. Van de Walle, *Documents juridiques égyptiens* I, AHDO I, 1937, p. 36; Abd el-Mohsen Bakir, *Slavery in Pharaonic Egypt*, ASAE suppl. 18, 1952, p. 70); cf. W. Helck, E. Otto, *Kleines Wörterbuch*, 1956, p. 339.

86  P. BM 10053. cf. J. J. Janssen, *Two Ancient Egyptian Ship's logs*, 1961, p. 102.

87  P. BM 10053 r° 4, 10 + P. BM 10052 r° 8, 2 : E. Peet, *The Great Tomb-Robberies*, 1930, I, p. 106, p. 150. The last servant who was examined by the authorities is mentioned several times over in our dossier. He is described as *ḥm/bἰk* or even ³ˁˁ ('foreigner'), but always dependent on the same *šwty*, cf. P. Abbott Docket, 9 and B, 10 (E. Peet, *op. cit.*, p. 132 et seq.) and P. Mayer A 12, 24 (E. Peet, *The Mayer Papyri A & B*, 1920, p. 17).

88  P. BM 10053, r° 3, 1; however E. Peet, *The Great Tomb-Robberies*, 1930, I, p. 105 translates this passage differently.

89  P. Berlin 10460: S. Allam, *Hieratische Ostraka und Papyri, Urkunden zum Rechtsleben im alten Ägypten* I, 1993, p. 276. Furthermore, Cairo P. 65739 and Bankes P. I where three *šwty.w* were engaged in haggling over several servants: I. E. S. Edwards, *JEA* 68, 1982, pp. 126-133; R. Navailles, F. Neveu, *GM* 103, 1988, pp. 51-60; H. Satzinger, in B. M. Bryan, D. Lorton (ed.), *Essays in Egyptology in Honor of H. Goedicke*, 1994, pp. 233-242; J. Winand, RdÉ 46, 1995, pp. 197-202. See Sc. Allam, in N. Grimal, B. Menu (ed.), *le commerce*, BiÉtud 121, 1998, p. 153.

90  P. Lansing 7, 1; A. H. Gardiner, *Late-Egyptian Miscellanies*, 1937, p. 105.

91  S. Bickel, *op. cit.*, p. 164.

92  *Id.*, p. 164.

93  P. Cairo 65739, A. H. Gardiner, *JEA* 21, 1935, pp. 140-146.

94  S. Bickel, *op. cit.*, p. 166.

95  See the study of the text in the article by B. Menu, in N. Grimal, B. Menu (ed.), *op. cit.*, p. 199.

96  A refinement in our juridical notions leads us to consider that 'slavery' does not play the role generally ascribed to it. 'It constitutes, on the level of numbers brought in and their enrolment, a stage prior to their being found various temporary or durable jobs, being inserted into a juridical system whose fundamental mechanism [...], does not imply the loss of liberty. Furthermore, on the institutional level, the presumed role of slavery, i.e. providing, gratis, an abundant workforce, is filled by a system of forced labour required periodically from every level of the working population, whether they be pure-blooded Egyptians or displaced foreigners': B. Menu, in N. Grimal, B. Menu (ed.), *le commerce*, BiÉtud 121, 1998, p. 206.

was the labour of another person implies the existence of a great diversity of social status and degrees of responsibility.[96]

All in all, a picture is painted of some *šwty.w* at least as managing the business of a master (an institution, an establishment or a lord's domain) by virtue of a certain mandate; in general, they had to move from one locality to another to sell off their master's merchandise. Concretely, they would have had the power to bargain to the fullest extent, as they carried out their boss's orders. In other words, the independence that they could have was a function of the freedom they enjoyed to strike a deal with this or that domain. It remains to be known what profit they could derive from it.

Taking account of these characteristics, a *šwty* was a businessman and manager,[97] but his position cannot have been that of a deputy, since ancient Egyptian law did not recognise such an institution with its juridical consequences, as far as is known. In short, a *šwty* would appear to us, these days, as something like an attorney or trustee manager.[98] It could be mentioned, for the purposes of comparison, the role of a *Samallum* ( = broker) in relation to his master *tamkarum* ( = trader) in Mesopotamia.[99] There were certainly real businessmen; such as the example just mentioned of an officer who had at least seven *šwty.w* in his service. Being a member of the army, the administration, or an institution such as a temple was not incompatible, it seems, with economic and commercial activity on the part of an individual; but the man who engaged in this was not himself a *šwty*. Doubtless such a businessman was in a position to indulge in dealings on a grand scale – wholesale and for his own profit.

In this context it is still necessary to review the content of the Boulaq Papyrus XI.[100] This is a piece of accounting relating the work of two parallel teams, one of them at least composed of three *šwty.w*. It also includes a record of different consignments – especially of bread, wine and meat – that these men received in enormous quantities in the space of a fortnight. They probably received them so they could trade them, given that they had to pay in return a price calculated on the Saty standard, sometimes in gold, sometimes in silver. It is noteworthy that these *šwty.w* sometimes appear here as independent, not being subject to the control of any master, but it is not known whether the transportation and sale of products constituted their sole task. Had they been working for themselves? The report, although carefully elaborated, does not reveal the identity of the purveyor-wholesaler. Was this a temple, an institution or a lord's house? And what were the links that attached such *šwty.w* to the producers of merchandise? Perhaps we will never know. Whatever the facts of the matter, it is improbable that it was a royal establishment, given that our sources do not reveal any *šwty.w* in the service of the sovereign.[101]

Nonetheless, the Cairo Stele JE 36861 can be mentioned, in which Taharqa makes donations to the temple of Amun in the region of Memphis: he hands over measures of oil 'that come from the port of Memphis, via the intermediary of the merchant leaders' *(... m-dr n³ ḥry.w šwty.w)*. The document speaks only of 'merchant leaders' (or 'chief-merchants', 'merchants-in-chief') since in the eyes of the king, and administratively speaking, it was most likely they who incurred the responsibility for the deliveries made by their subordinates. Were they 'chief-merchants' of the Temple or functionaries with the same title attached to the port of Memphis or the royal palace, specially appointed to the service of imports? This is not known, but it was

certainly thanks to the intermediary of the *šwty.w* (with *ḥry.w šwty.w* at their head) that the objects actually did reach the temples. It could also be asked, if every possibility is considered, whether the *ḥry.w šwty.w* had not reserved the biggest orders for themselves. In practical terms the problem would still be the same, since for the orders of lesser importance the *šwty.w* would have depended on them.[102]

## II.6. The way of life and social status of traders

Some of the *šwty.w* possessed the financial means necessary to build up for themselves the basic elements of funerary equipment, though no tomb of theirs is known.[103] S. Bickel refers to a stele from Saqqara that belonged to a 'trader in chief from the domain of Aten' *(ḥry šwty.w n t³ ḥwt p³ Jtn)* called Huy. He is represented standing erect, followed by his wife and a boy in front of a seated couple, probably his parents, of whom the man is also a leading trader.[104] Another *ḥry šwty.w* from the temple of Min is known through a stele from Abydos.[105] The exact rank of a *ḥry šwty.w* in relation to a mere Swty is not known. Was this an honorific designation or a real specific responsibility? Two *šwty.w* were also in a position to acquire a copy of the *Book of the Dead*.[106] In the Cairo Papyrus 65739 a *šwty* exchanges a servant for a tomb, which again brings out how this professional category was seeking to acquire a final dwelling-place and to build up a set of funerary furnishings for itself.[107]

Their status and their financial means allowed certain *šwty.w*-traders to possess their own servant. The servant of a *šwty* is designated as a foreigner *ʿ³mw*[108] and a fragmentary passage in a list of personnel mentions a servant woman who belonged to a *ḥry šwty.w*.[109]

According to the texts and the documentation, the *šwty.w*-traders appear more often than not to have been linked to navigation; these professionals of river and sea journeys were members of the crew and must have experienced long periods of sailing on the ships.

97  On this subject see the contents of the Bankes Papyrus I (I.E.S. Edwards, *JEA* 68, 1982, pp. 126-133; R. Navailles, F. Neveu, *GM* 103, 1988, pp. 51-60; H. Satzinger, in B. M. Bryan, D. Lorton (ed.), *Essays in Egyptology in Honor of H. Goedicke*, 1994, pp. 233-242; J. Winand, *RdÉ* 46, 1995, pp. 197-202), as well as P. BM 10383, 3, 1-7 (E. Peet, *The Great Tomb-Robberies*, 1930, I, p. 125).

98  M. Römer, *SAK* 19, 1992, p. 277 speaks of the deputy merchants (*Zwischenhändler*).

99  For some relevant observations based on the code of Hammurabi, see R. Haase, *Keilschrift-rechtliche Marginalien*, 1996, p. 45 et seq., cf. infra, p. 291.

100  T. E. Peet, in *Mélanges Maspéro* I/1, MIFAO 66/1, 1934, pp. 188-191; Mounir Megally, *BIFAO* 74, 1974, pp. 161-169, pls xxi-xxii; id., *BIFAO* 75, 1975, pp. 165-181, pl. xxviii.

101  See J. J. Janssen, *Two Ancient Egyptian Ship's Logs*, 1961, p. 103 and following; id., *SAK* 3, 1975, p. 163, n. 162; S. Allam, op. cit., p. 156.

102  See D. Meeks, in *Hommages à S. Sauneron*, BiÉtud 81/1, 1979, pp. 249-250; A. Théodoridès, *RIDA*, 3rd series, V, 1958, pp. 114-115.

103  S. Bickel, in N. Grimal, B. Menu (ed.), *Le commerce*, BiÉtud 121, 1998, p. 164.

104  CGC 34182; P. Lacau, *Stèles du Nouvel Empire*, CGC nᵒ 34065-34186, 1926, p. 222, pl. 69; S. Bickel, op. cit., p. 164 and fig 3 p. 165.

105  A. Mariette, *Catalogue général des monuments d'Abydos*, 1880, p. 410, nᵒ 1115.

106  A fine papyrus from Thebes and dating back to the end of the 18th Dynasty belonged to a *šwty* whose father had the same profession: E. Naville, *Das Aegyptische Todtenbuch*, 1886, p. 91 *(Qnn³*, 18th/19th Dynasty, Leyde), p. 87 *(Hnsw*, 19th Dynasty, Naples); M. J. Raven, *De dodenkultus van het Oude Egypte*, 1992, p. 37; S. Bickel, op. cit., p. 164 and fig. 4, p. 165.

107  P. Cairo 65739, A. H. Gardiner, *JEA* 21, 1935, pp. 140-146. On this type of transaction, see below.

108  E. Peet, *The Great Tomb Robberies*, 1930, I, pp. 132-133, II, pl. 23; P. Abbott Dockets, B, 10: *ʿ³mw šḫ3-ḥ3ty-Jmn b3k n šwtj P3-s-m-w³s.t*, the same servant is mentioned in A, 9: *ḥm šḫ3-ḥ3ty-Jmn n šwtj P3-s-m-w3s.t*. Another servant belonging to a *šwty* is mentioned in P. BM 10053, 4, 10.

109  W. Spiegelberg, *Rechnungen aus der Zeit Setis* I, 1896, pl. 10; *KRI* I, 271, 4, 15.

Their profession placed them in permanent contact with the different boatmen and policemen who also lived in big ships. BM Papyrus 10053 indicates that a *šwty* could, for some reason or another, live on the ship of another *šwty*.[110] Their skill could have been sufficient for them to be entitled to take over the command of a ship.[111]

The boatmen, guards and traders seem to have formed a homogeneous professional group that shared its different competences and responsibilities to carry out major trading missions, that maintained social or even friendly relations with each other, and which, should the case arise, come together in complicity to commit the misdemeanours whose trace has been preserved thanks to their trial.[112]

The reality and relevance of such a professional group has been well illustrated by S. Bickel, in particular through the lists of the *Onomastica*.[113] In one of the categories of these components of the universe, there is in succession:[114] the *s³w*-guard (no. 1994), the *mškb* (no. 199), a policeman, a bearer of arms and a guardian of the harvest. Then come the boatmen: the *nfw*, followed by two other specialists of navigation, *viz.* 'the man at the prow'[115] (no. 206, *jry ḥ't*), and 'the man at the poop' (no. 207, *jrw ḥmy*). Enumerated next is the bird-catcher (no. 208), the fisherman (no. 209) and the *šwty*-trader (no. 210).[116] The mention of the *šwty* is followed in the *Onomastica* by two designations that cover partial aspects of his activity, the buyer (no. 211, *mḫr*) and the seller (no. 212, *mkrj*).[117] In the use of these terms of Semitic-Asiatic origin, the close relation is again observable between the profession of trader and the region of the Near East.[118] The *Onomastica* go on to enumerate the singers, musicians and dancers who are probably included in this category of society by virtue of the fact that they were probably also itinerant professions – strolling players, so to speak. At the end of this section the *šmsw*-envoys are mentioned.[119]

This section of the *Onomastica* 'brings together exactly the professions of different branches that participated in merchant expeditions and rubbed shoulders in private life. It was a relatively clearly defined social group that was obviously lower than the elite. Their lifestyle included many journeys especially within the country, but also on the borders of Egypt and abroad, a life led in common, far from their families, on ships and in ports. They must have been men to trust since they were given the responsibility for significant quantities of diverse commodities'.[120] The cases of theft repeatedly mentioned by the sources (the scandals at Elephantine, the pillage of tombs, Wenamun, and so on) 'should not lead us to think that this was a particularly corrupt group, since the particular events of this kind, more easily recorded, have a greater chance of coming down to us than normal operations, even those on a bigger scale. Nonetheless, these misdemeanours illustrate the temptations to which these men could be exposed, being permanently in contact with raw materials, money, markets and sometimes foreigners'.[121]

The *šwty.w*-traders and their colleagues 'were the members of a middle class, situated hierarchically and socially just below the first professions that belonged to the literate elite, in particular below the class of small scribes with whom they were in frequent contact when the transactions were recorded. […] If the sons of traders also became traders, more than one father must have nursed the ambition to send his son to a school of scribes to push him into the upper class, that was more respected and free of the harsh conditions of life on board ship'.[122]

For the scribe of the Lansing Papyrus, the most disagreeable aspect of the profession of *šwty* was the obligation to often travel long distances. The dangers of the voyage must have aroused a certain aversion for such distant journeys. The difficulties and irritations of long peregrinations could be of a linguistic order.[123] The person 'from outside' was by definition 'suspect and despised'. In the exercise of their activity, 'traders and boatmen were more often than not outsiders. Conversely, by dint of frequenting foreign lands and people, were they too not considered as coming from the outside, since for long periods they were not part of the fabric of local social life?'[124]

The *Instructions of the Insinger Papyrus'* (from the Ptolemaic period[125]) provide evidence that travel inspired fear, since it exposed one to every fatigue, every uncertainty, every accident – to countless unknown dangers, and even to death. *Instruction XXII* is entirely devoted to these themes and it entitled *Do not abandon the place where you live*:[126]

> *A little job with a little salary are better than prosperity abroad*
> *The man who goes away saying "I will return" will return only*
> *if God gives him a hand*
> *The man who is far and whose prayer is far, his God is far*
> *from him*
> *Everywhere the foreigner is the slave of an inferior man*
> *When a wise man is abroad, his heart sighs for his town.*

As for the Dua-Khety the *Satire on Trades,* much older (early Middle Kingdom, *c.* 2000 BC?), it already describes, admittedly with some exaggeration, so as to bring out the excellence of the scribe's profession, the paltry conditions of that professional traveller, the messenger:

> *The messenger wanders through the desert, abandoning his property to his children; fearing lions and Bedouins, he knows himself again only when he returns to Egypt. When he returns to his home, night and travel have exhausted him; whether his house be of canvas or bricks, his return is without joy.*

110  P. BM 10053, r° 7, 18, E. Peet, *The Great Tomb-Robberies*, 1930, I, p. 109; S. Bickel, *op. cit.*, p. 163.

111  P. Turin 1887, vol. 1, 8-11, which relates various thefts committed in Elephantine, tells us that every year a ship brought 700 khar of corn to the granary of Khnum. After the death of the captain of the ship (*ḥry wsḥ*), the priest of the temple of Khnum asked a *šwty*-trader to replace him, to go and fetch corn in the North district and to bring it back by ship. The partly fragmentary continuation of the story seems to accuse this *šwty* of a major embezzling of corn (to the value of some 7 deben of gold): A. H. Gardiner, *Ramesside Administrative Documents*, 1948, p. 79; translation, T. E. Peet, *JEA* X, 1924, p. 123; *cf.* S. Bickel, *op. cit.*, p. 164.

112  S. Bickel, in N. Grimal, B. Menu (ed.), *Le commerce*, BiÉtud 121, 1998, p. 167.

113  S. Bickel, *op. cit.*, p. 168, our following remarks are based on this work.

114  A. H. Gardiner, *AEO* I, 90*-96*, pl. ix, L. 8-12. See S. Bickel, *op. cit.*, p. 168.

115  *cf. supra*, p. 147-148.

116  Their professional relationship can be explained by the fact that the fishermen were sometimes the owners of ships which could, in certain cases, be used as and when required to transport corn: E. W. Castle, *JESHO* 35, 1992, pp. 248-249.

117  These two terms are rare and of Semitic origin; there does not seem to be any precise Egyptian equivalent; see J. E. Hoch, *Semitic Words in Egyptian Texts*, 1994, pp. 150-151, p. 169.

118  S. Bickel, *op. cit.*, p. 168.

119  On the role of couriers and postmen played by the *šmsw*, see M. Valloggia, *Recherche sur les "Messagers" (wpwtyw)*, 1976, pp. 215-216.

120  S. Bickel, in N. Grimal, B. Menu (ed.), *Le commerce*, BiÉtud 121, 1998, p. 168.

121  *Id.*, p. 168.

122  *Id.*, p. 169.

123  *Id.*, p. 171.

124  *Id.*, p. 170.

125  The papyrus dates from the 1st century AD, but the work must have been composed in the later Ptolemaic period, according to M. Lichtheim, *Late Egyptian Wisdom Literature*, OBO 52, 1983.

126  F. Lexa, *Papyrus Insinger*, 1926.

Whether it is a life experience or a school of danger, travel bears fruit only if it is nourished by a certain ethic. It is easy to understand in these conditions how 'travel and the state of "separation" that it entails might have been felt to be a means of rejecting the world, society, and religion itself. The traveller then becomes a vagrant and wandering is turned into rebellion…'[127]

Nonetheless, the mission of a functionary on the move could thus be perceived as positive and affirmative. 'Thanks to the status and responsibility granted to the senior functionary, travel could have an honorific aspect. This is also intimated by certain autobiographies written by professional messengers. But these travels are described as a duty towards the king, one that the functionaries perform with dignity, and not as a pleasure or a life-enhancing experience'.[128] Setting out on a journey of your own free will, out of curiosity, was considered to be a form of 'social deviance'; 'for people obliged to leave their homes and their towns for purely professional reasons, without any glory being attached to this, this visceral fear and this repugnance towards travel must have weighed extremely heavily'.[129] In the letter addressed by a father to his son Pay-iri, a bad boy from Deir el-Medina known through the lawsuits brought against him for adultery and theft, the desperate father seeks to bring him back after he has run away:[130]

*Your desire to travel is like that of a swallow with its young, you reached the Delta after a long journey, you have mixed with Asiatics, you have eaten bread with your blood.*

In this context it is of interest to glance at one last literary text, a piece of wisdom literature from the Hellenistic period. This is the *Instruction of Ankhchechonqi*, preserved in demotic.[131] This instruction contains, among others, some important precepts on our subject. In one of these precepts, Ankhchechonqi gives this advice:[132]

*Do not (even) drink water in the house of a šwty; he would (then) overwhelm you, demanding money from you.*

Another maxim is as follows:[133]

*If a thousand servants are found in the house of a šwty, (the latter) is merely one of them.*

And in yet another aphorism, Ankhchechonqi states openly:[134]

*Do not take a šwty for a friend; (it is because he) lives (only) to carry off his share.*

This unfavourable image of the *šwty*, as reproduced in the literary texts, visibly reflects nothing other than the attitude of men of letters.[135] In their view, the *šwty* was a kind of pariah and his profession was obviously undesirable and even contemptible.

The temptation cannot be resisted to compare this description of the *šwty.w* with the rarely flattering image of the Phoenician merchant as he is depicted in Greek texts: this apparently tenacious image is one of a hawker and mountebank, a seller of trash.[136] The Athenian moralists of the Classical Age express a generally rather unfavourable image of the *emporoi* and *naucleroi*;[137] Phoenician sailors, outfitters, brokers, merchants and bankers are mocked in the theatre

as examples of the *palinkapelos* – 'the intermediary' – and appear repeatedly in the speeches of orators.[138] Over and above types of behaviour that might have been found irritating, it can be surmised that the way trade was organised in the wider framework of the eastern Mediterranean imposes a different vision that underlines the role that foreign traders and outfitters owed it to themselves to play in the development of a city. The archives of Zeno (as well as certain Athenian honorific decrees or even the writings of Xenophon[139]), bring out the large-scale activities undertaken by family groups, within the framework of the city's institutions.[140]

The nature of these commercial agents has been addressed, these *šwty.w*, and thus also the question of the different categories of traders encountered at the start of the 2nd millennium BC and their place in society: a sort of middle class sometimes compared with strolling players, less than functionaries, sometimes even pariahs, but ones who brought in wealth, especially as they worked both for themselves and the State. They constituted one of the cogs essential to the good functioning of the institutions of Egypt. It was, furthermore, thanks to the shifting and handling of money (in the widest sense of the word) that they managed to have a different place in society. As for the penal aspect, above it was elaborated how the *šwty.w* were implicated in the pillage of the Theban necropolis and it was suggested that in certain cases they were involved in real money-laundering operations; there is nothing surprising in that, since the *šwty.w* obviously had the power, though not the capacity, to cream off for their own use certain property over which they enjoyed a delegated authority. The link between the agents and the legal rules thus appears incredibly complex. C. Eyre speaks of the 'hybrid status'[141] that many of these merchants had. Perhaps, but the fact remains that the *šwty.w* were managed by scribes, and thus by the State. It is necessary to be cautious on this point: in a system of domanial economy such as that of Egypt the notion was perhaps not relevant. It was in fact within the domanial economy that production

127  C. Cannuyer, in C. Cannuyer, J. Ries, A. Van Tongerloo (ed.), *Les voyages dans les civilisations orientales, Acta Orientalia Belgica* XI, 1998, pp. 6-7.

128  *Id.,* p. 171. *cf. infra,* p 175 *et seq.,* on royal messengers and ambassadors.

129  S. Bickel, *op. cit.,* pp. 171-172.

130  *tw=k m nꜣ swtwt n tꜣ mn.t hnꜥ nꜣy=s tꜣy.w ph=k tꜣ-mhw m phr.t ꜥꜣ.t bnw=k hnꜥ ꜣmw wnm=k ꜥq hr snf=k*): W. Guglielmi, *WeltOr* 14, 1983, p. 147-166; L. Foster, *JSSEA* 14, 1984, p. 88-98; J. J. Janssen, in *Gleanings from Deir el-Medina,* 1982, p. 116-123.

131  P. BM 10508: *LÄ* III, col. 974; M. Lichtheim, *Ancient Egyptian Literature,* III, 1980, p. 159 *et seq.;* H. J. Thissen, in O. Kaiser (ed.), *Texte aus der Umwelt des Alten Testaments* III, 1991, p. 251. For a special study, see S. R. K. Glanville, *Catalogue of Demotic Papyri in the British Museum,* II, 1, 1955; H.J. Thissen, *Die Lehre des Anchscheschonqi,* 1984.

132  *Instruction of Ankhchechonqi,* 16, 5.

133  *Instruction of Ankhchechonqi,* 19, 18.

134  *Instruction of Ankhchechonqi,* 28, 4.

135  For the existence of *šwty.w* through documentary texts in Demotic, see R. H. Pierce, *Three Demotic Papyri in the Brooklyn Museum,* 1972, p. 38, § 29. We also find mentioned here *šwty.w* who were specialised in the commerce of a precise product (wine, as it happens). For the marriage contracts entered into by certain *šwty.w,* see E. Lüddeckens, *Ägyptische Eheverträge,* 1960, p. 234 *et seq.*

136  As Herodotus describes it (M. Gras, P. Rouillard, J. Teixidor, *L'univers phénicien,* 1979, pp. 106-108); the textual tradition probably goes back to Homer: see for example P. Wathelet, in E. Gubel, E. Lipinski, B. Servais-Soyez, *Histoire phénicienne/Fenicische Geschiedenis, Studia Phoenicia* II, *OLA* 15, 1983, pp. 235-243.

137  J. Velissaropoulos, *Le monde de l'emporion,* 1977, p. 70.

138  M.-F. Baslez, in E. Lipinski (ed.), *Phoenicia and the East Mediterranean, Studia Phoenicia* 5, 1987, pp. 271-273.

139  Xenophon, *Poroi,* 3.

140  J. Velissaropoulos, *Le monde de l'emporion,* 1977, p. 71; M.-F. Baslez, *op. cit.,* p. 275.

141  C. Eyre, cited by J. Bouineau, in N. Grimal, B. Menu (ed.), *Le commerce, BiÉtud* 121, 1998, pp. 291-292.

occurred, even if the administration kept control of it and even if the diminishing of Pharaonic power in the intermediary epochs inevitably entailed a relative 'privatisation'. All the same, the *šwty.w*-traders were not exactly traders in the sense understood today – people who earned a living by buying and selling, picking up a profit on the price differences in the course of a transaction. They had the status of traders, probably by virtue of a right of succession or an early apprenticeship and perhaps in certain cases by appointment. Part of their revenue must have come from the circulation of merchandise that could give rise to such a commission. This was certainly the origin of all 'profit', of that stock of merchandise, including money, that the members of the commercial society ended up sharing amongst themselves.

## II.7. By way of comparison: *Emporoi, Kapeloi, Naucleroi* and other merchants

### II.7.1. Emporoi *and* Kapeloi

The Demotic texts mention two terms to designate the merchant – *šwt(y)* and *šbty*[142] – that should not be confused. The term Sbty that was translated into Greek by μεταβολος ('retailer')[143] and the *Revenue Laws* of Ptolemy Philadelphus give clear indications of the differences that existed between different categories of merchants:[144]

> *The proxy of the economos and the antigraphos (it prescribes) will make a list of local merchants (the* kapeloi, ψαπελοι, *who are 'in every town'), and the retailers (the* μεταβολοι*), and in agreement with the farm managers, he will agree with them on the quantity of oil and sesame and castor oil that they need to receive for their daily sale. In Alexandria, they will make a compact with the great merchants and they will write down each of these compacts in a contract, with the merchants of the flatlands, every month, with those of Alexandria…*[145]

It is understood that these *kapeloi* of the 'towns' were the equivalents of the *šwty.w* whose activity is described by the Lansing Papyrus. It is worth remembering in this connection that Herodotus makes of the *kapeloi* a class of Egyptians:[146]

> *There are seven classes of Egyptians, called priests, warriors, oxherds, swineherds, merchants (*emporoi, ψαπηλοι*), interpreters, and pilots.*

And he distinguishes them from the 'market people' (αγοραιοι ανθρφποι):[147]

> *Trusting in what he had seen and heard in a dream, Sethos took with him the Egyptians who were willing to accompany him, and*

camped at Pelusium (as that is the way one enters Egypt); he had with him no man of the warrior class, but shopkeepers, artisans, and market traders (αγοραιοι ανθρφποι).

The Greek tradition confirms that the *šwty.w* should not be seen as shopkeepers or retailers, but suppliers who – as is suggested by an etymological hypothesis – 'empty' (*šwj*) the cargo ships of their merchandise so as to sell it off in the country.[148]

Later sources shed more light on the commercial role of the *kapelos* and thus to understand that of the *šwty*-merchant better. The activity of the *kapelos*, namely *kapeleia*, is always being contrasted with that of the *naucleroi* and the *emporoi*, namely the *naucleria* and the *emporia*; the one related to small retail commerce, thus a commerce essentially sedentary in nature, and the others related to large-scale commerce – especially maritime commerce.[149] These documents are indeed rare, and for the purposes of this research, three are selected, but they are of such a quality, and overlap to an extent, that it is absolutely impossible to cast doubt on their reliability, and they cannot be ignored, in spite of the fact that they belong to documentation that dates to the Roman era.[150]

The first of these texts in the work of Philo of Alexandria, is towards the beginning of our era. In his *De Migratione Abraham*, considering the lack of care that he takes of his reason and the excessive care he takes of everything else, he writes:[151]

> *In any case, it is put about as an improbable fact that* emporoi *and* kapeloi *cross the seas in search of filthy lucre and sail all around the inhabited world…*

As evident, this is another theme from classical rhetoric; but what is important is the fact that, while in all comparisons of this kind, *emporoi* are mentioned, here Philo associates them with the *kapeloi*, showing the latter as involved, like the others, in enterprises of maritime commerce. Philo cannot be accused of having made a mistake here and of having mixed up his words, given that never, in literary and epigraphic usage, are *emporoi* and *kapeloi* associated: on the contrary, they are opposed. So he wrote *kapeloi* deliberately, so for him there were indeed *kapeloi* who sailed the seas.

Two centuries later, Lucian, in the *Toxaris*, after making one of the interlocutors in the dialogue boast of the maritime exploits of the Argonauts, has one of his characters retort:[152]

> *So tell me what else they did that was venerable and divine. If it is their navigation and their voyage that you admire, I can quote many other men who were more divine then they were, for example the Phoenicians… You think that they are to be regarded as gods, although they are not* kapeloi *and salt-provision merchants for the most part.*

142 In Neo-Egyptian there is the expression *rdj m šbt* meaning 'to sell': *Wb* IV, 436, 16.

143 *cf.* W. Erichsen, *Demotisches Glossar*, 1954, p. 498, and U. Wilcken, *Urkunden der Ptolemäerzeit*, II, 1935, nº 180a, p. 151, and p. 169, note to col. 5/2.

144 Col. 47, 10-18 (= A. S. Hunt, C. C. Edgar, *Select Papyri*, 1956, pp. 22-23).

145 Translation of C. Préaux, *l'économie royale des Lagides*, 1939, p. 81.

146 Herodotus, II, 164.

147 Herodotus, II, 141; *cf. id.*, I, 93.

148 W. Spiegelberg, *Rechnungen aus der Zeit Setis' I*, 1896, I, p. 61.

149 M. I. Finkelstein, *Class. Philology* XXX, 1935, pp. 320-336; G. Humbert, in C. Daremberg, E. Saglio, E. Pottier, *Dictionnaire des Antiquités grecques et romaines*, 1877-1918, s.v. 'negotiator'.

150 On the texts, see J. Rougé, *Recherches sur l'organisation du commerce en Méditerranée sous l'empire romain*, 1966, pp. 270-271.

151 Philo of Alexandria, *De migratione Abraham*, 217; translation by R. Cadiou, *Sources chrétiennes* 47, 1957.

152 Lucian, *Toxaris*, 4; translation by Chambry, vol. II, p. 282.

It might be objected that Lucian, to lower those of whom he speaks, deliberately uses an inadequate and pejorative term; but to his mind, the term of *emporoi* would have been just as negative. So his testimony cannot be denied, and we are obliged to accept that for him, the *kapeloi* were also maritime traders and that they were numerous among the traders from Phoenicia.

The last of these texts transports us to the 4th century AD. Libanius in one of his discourses reports that a certain Heliodorus, a *kapelos* of garum, was led by his commercial activities to sail the seas.[153] The text of Libanius is all the more interesting in that he juxtaposes in the same sentence the two traditionally antithetical terms when he describes Heliodorus as a *kapelos* and his activities as *emporia*. In consequence he states that the *kapelos* Heliodorus was not a retailer, a small shopkeeper whose activity can be described as *kapeleia*, but as fairly and squarely a maritime trader.

The comparison of these three texts is instructive. There seem to have been *kapeloi* who were great maritime traders, but why did they bear this name, which seems in contradiction of their activities? Perhaps the last two texts offer us the beginnings of a solution. Lucian associated the activity of these *kapeloi* with that of salt-provision merchants, a general term which includes the trade in salted fish as well as that of that fish-based condiment, garum and its sub-varieties,[154] and it is indeed a trader of garum who is described as a *kapelos* by Libanius. Thus, it is observable that concentrated into the hands of these *kapeloi* was a luxury and semi-luxury trade that was small in volume but very profitable. Perhaps this is the solution? If this hypothesis is correct, the maritime trader known as *kapelos* was at the head of a luxury trade: he went to buy, on external markets, the product on which he lived, and whose commercialised quantities were not sufficient for him to merit the description of *emporos*; he brought this product back home where it was sold to the consumer either via the intermediary of his family members or his associates, or else via middlemen. In these conditions, one of these *kapeloi* may be considered, a certain Italian merchant whose funerary inscription tells us that he was a 'merchant of products from overseas'.[155]

## II. 7. 2. Naucleroi

The *šwty*, master of trading operations, and in charge of the merchandise embarked on board ship, had the task, not of indicating his route to the captain, but of fixing the ports to which he was to sail the ship, leaving him master on board. To understand the relations between merchant and ship's captain, as well as the exact functions played by everyone on board, it is proposed once again that the chronological limits are exceeded and observe what the Egyptian *naucleroi* ('convoying officers') of the Hellenistic and Roman periods did. The papyrological evidence gives little information on maritime navigation, even of a commercial sort,[156] but on the other hand, it is extremely rich in everything to do with navigation on the Nile, both in the Ptolemaic and the Roman periods. So it is interesting to see, by way of comparison, what meaning the papyri allow us to give to the term *naucleros* frequently encountered there.[157] The *naucleros* was the man on board the Nile vessels who was charged with the transport of corn to the official granaries, in particular those of Neapolis in Alexandria, signed the transportation contracts and the receipt for the cargo with the local authorities. It was he who made *inter alia* the well-known

commitment to transport the cargo to its place of destination without its suffering any damage on the journey. In general, this *naucleros* does not appear to have been the owner of his ship, but he is described as the *naucleros* of different craft, even as the *naucleros* of this administration or that collectivity.[158] When he was the owner of his ship, as happened, this was clearly specified by the document.[159] It does not seem, given that the *naucleroi* seem to have accompanied the cargoes they received in deposit, that they can be described as great contractors of transportation;[160] anyway, it seems difficult to accept that the contractors were not at the same time the owners of the ships that they ran.[161] As well as the *naucleroi*, the papyri also show that there was a navigational captain present, who sometimes substituted for the *naucleroi* in the signing of documents; like them, these captains were not the ships' owners, but dependent on individuals or administrations.[162] The difficulty in defining the functions of the people responsible for commercial operations (a difficulty encountered in defining the *šwty*) comes precisely from the way these functions could always potentially be combined. Thus it is that in the work of Plautus, the *naucleros* is also a merchant (*nauclerus mercator*, ναυκληροσ εμπορος).[163]

Be that as it may, if it is wished that the Nile *naucleroi* are the heirs of 'our' *šwty.w*, it is still necessary to place ourselves in the context of Hellenistic Greece. The wealth of the latter and in consequence the power of the Ptolemies were to a great extent based on the abundance of cereals produced by the country.[164] So as to exploit these resources to the maximum, 'the Ptolemies had developed an efficient but crushing tax system, one which tended to levy on the harvests, as fast as possible, the largest possible share. Thus there was established an intense network of road and (especially) river transportation, by means of which vast quantities of corn were sent to the royal warehouses of Alexandria, where they were destined to replenish the city and be exported to the Aegean world. It goes without saying that in such circumstances merchant ships played an essential role. They must have shuttled in their hundreds between the

153   Libanius, *Discourse*, LXII, 46.

154   See P. Grimal, T. Monod, *Revue des Études anciennes* LIV, 1952, pp. 27-52; C. Jardin, *Revue des Études ligures*, 1961, pp. 70-96.

155   *CIL* IX, 4680. J. Rougé, *op. cit.*, p. 271.

156   See for example P. Oxyrynchos 87 or the contract of a maritime loan concluded between συνναυχληροι and two money lenders via and Egyptian bank (*Papyrus Vindobonensis* 19.792)

157   F. Preisigke, *Wörterbuch der griechischen Papyrusurkunden* II, p. 124. In the extensive bibliography relative to naucleroi, see for example J. Gachet, *CRIPEL* 12, 1990, pp. 101-129; M. Merzagora, *Aegyptus* 10, 1929, p. 111; C. Préaux, *L'économie royale des Lagides*, 1939, p. 160, 345; A. Swiderek, *JJP* 7-8, 1954, p. 245; id., *JJP* 9-10, 1956, p. 385; J. Hengstl, *Private Arbeitverhältnisse freier Personen in den hellenistischen Papyris bis Diokletian*, 1972, p. 106; J. Scherer, *BASP* 15, 1978, pp. 95-101; J. Vélissaropoulos, *Les nauclères grecs*, 1980; C. Orrieux, *Les papyrus de Zénon*, 1983; id., *Zénon de Caunos*, 1985; T. Reekmans, in *Proceedings of the International Colloquium*, 1983, pp. 325-350; H. Hauben, *CdÉ* LVIII, 1983, pp. 237-247.

158   P. Oxyrynchos 1229, 1259, 1260, 2125; P. London 256a, 948.

159   P. London 948 = P. M. Meyer, *Juristische Papyri*, 1920, no 43.

160   F. Oertel, *Die Liturgie : Studien zur ptolemaischen und kaiserlichen Verwaltung Ägyptens*, 1917, p. 121.

161   J. Rougé, *op. cit.*, p. 232.

162   P. Oxyrynchos 1260.

163   Plautus, *The Swaggering Soldier*, 1109-1110 and 1175-1182. See J. Rougé, *op. cit.*, 233.

164   See for example, C. Préaux, *L'économie royale des Lagides*, 1939, pp. 117-152; M. Rostovtzeff, *The Social and Economic History of the Hellenistic World*, I, 1941, pp. 359-362, 392-393. cf. the reflections of E. Will, *Histoire politique du monde hellénistique*, I, 1979, pp. 168-200.

capital and the ports situated all along the Nile and the adjacent canals'.[165]

These ships in the service of the state were sometimes the property of the king or queen,[166] but more often than not of private individuals, generally Greeks,[167] both men and women, a good number of whom seem to have belonged to high society.[168] The pilots or captains, on the other hand, bore Egyptian names. Finally there was the *naucleros* (ναθκληρος) who must be clearly distinguished from the owner (κυριος) and the pilot (κυβερνητης).[169]

He was the contractor with responsibility for the transport. Often, he was also the pilot of his ship, but this was not the rule. Exceptionally speaking, at least in Ptolemaic Egypt, he could also be its owner. Most of the *naucleroi*, who evidently must have had at their disposal certain financial reserves, were Greeks. Some of them, all the same, had Egyptian nationality.[170]

From the last third of the 3rd century BC onwards, there is a tendency among the *naucleroi* of the Nile to form groups,[171] but the first corporation to be attested within this milieu with any certainty, and the only one from the Ptolemaic period, dates only from 63 BC.[172] These were the '*naucleroi* of the hippodrome of Memphis': 'οι απο Μεμφεφς ναυκληροι Ιπποδρομιται.[173]

The corporation appears in the three papyri from the nome of Herakleopolis.[174] It emerges from them that the corporation had taken over the transport of state corn from this nome to Alexandria.[175]

The name 'Hippodromitai' was derived from the hippodrome of Memphis, the site either of the meeting-place for its members, or of the place where they loaded their boats.[176] The port of Memphis

was doubtless the main one for the interior of Egypt,[177] controlled to the north and the south and perhaps also in the centre by significant guard posts.[178] The city was the place of origin of two Egyptian captains who are known through papyrological documentation.[179]

It goes without saying that the description of *naucleros* could be applied to all the members of the association. At least two of them piloted their ships in person and it is possible that they were also their owners.[180] It is indeed quite possible that the three functions generally involved in the river transport of state corn were here, each time, united in the same person.[181] This fact, as well as the low tonnage of their ships[182] implies that they were people of a relatively modest status:[183] the great *naucleroi* employed third persons as captains and the property-owners of high society did not occupy themselves with enterprises of this kind and, above all, did not pilot their ships in person.[184]

This situation partially explains why certain *naucleroi* had formed an association; together, they felt better able to face and thus to share the risks of their enterprises.[185]

The climate of insecurity and instability into which the Egypt of Ptolemy XII Auletes (80-58, 55-51 BC) was plunged also needs to be taken into consideration. Not only were the ships of the Hippodromites accompanied by supercargoes and police who were there to keep an eye on the cargo,[186] but, in addition to the ships of the river police, the Nile was patrolled by units detached from the war fleet and placed at the disposal of the *dioecetes* of Egypt to protect the cargo vessels against rebel and pirate attacks and to keep open the communication channels with the capital.[187] While in this context the need to form an association was becoming more and more urgent, it was no less convenient for the central administration to deal, rather than with individual contractors, with corporations that could take on the transport for an entire nome: this is why it might be supposed that the State would have favoured their establishment.

It is necessary to take into account the influence that must have been enjoyed by the many associations of traders, *naucleroi* and warehousemen in Attica, at Delos and in Alexandria. These

165  H. Hauben, in T. Hackens, G. Moucharte (ed.), *Numismatique et économique phéniciennes et puniques*, Studia Phoenicia IX, Numismatica Lovaniensia 9, 1992, p. 321. For this entire system, see the literature cited in H. Hauben, in *Actes du XVe Congrès International de Papyrologie* IV, Papyrologica Bruxellensia 19, 1979, pp. 68-77, particularly p. 69 n. 1; N. Hohlwein, *Le blé d'Égypte, Étude de Papyrologie* 4, 1938, pp. 33-120, particularly pp. 90-102; A. J. M. Meyer-Termeer, *Die Haftung der Schiffer im griechischen und römischen Recht*, 1978, pp. 3-52; J. Frösen, *Annali della Facoltà di Lettere e Filosofia, Università degli Studi di Perugia* 18, n.s. 4, 1, Studi Classici, 1980-1981, p. 161-176; D. Thompson, in P. Garnsey, K. Hopkins, C. R. Whittaker (ed.), *Trade in the Ancient Economy*, 1983, pp. 64-75, 190-192.

166  H. Hauben, op. cit., pp. 68-77; id., ZPE 66, 1986, p. 148.

167  D. Thompson, op. cit., pp. 67-68. A notable exception was the Jew Dositheos, but this exception is only apparent, since he was a completely Hellenised character, assimilated into the ruling class: see H. Hauben, Ancient Society 10, 1979, pp. 167-170.

168  H. Hauben, op. cit., pp. 167-170; W. Clarysse, CdÉ LVI, 1981, pp. 347-349.

169  H. Hauben, in T. Hackens and G. Moucharte (ed.), op. cit., p. 321.

170  For the Nilotic *naucleroi* of the Ptolemaic period, H. Hauben, ZPE 8, 1971, pp. 259-275; id., ZPE 28, 1978, pp. 99-107; id., CdÉ 58, 1983, pp. 237-247; J. Velissaropoulos, *Les naucléres grecs*, 1980.

171  H. Hauben, ZPE 8, 1971, pp. 272-275; id., CdÉ 58, 1983, p. 245; A. J. M. Meyer-Termeer, *Die Haftung der Schiffer im griechischen und römischen Recht*, 1978, p. 11; J. Velissaropoulos, op. cit., p. 111 n. 121.

172  J. Velissaropoulos, op. cit., pp. 110-121, passim; H. Hauben, CdÉ 58, 1983, p. 241.

173  On this, see W. Kunkel, APF 8, 1927, pp. 169-215, particularly pp. 185-186; F. Heichelheim, *Wirtschafts-geschichte des Altertums*, I, 1938, pp. 511-512; E. Broerner, *Der staatliche Korntransport im griechisch-römischen Ägyptens*, 1939, pp. 42-43; C. Brecht, *Zur Haftung der Schiffer im antiken Recht*, 1962, pp. 26-28, 33, 133; H. Hauben, ZPE 8, 1971, pp. 269-272; id., ZPE 28, 1978, p. 101, no 34-38; id., CdÉ 58, 1983, pp. 240-241; P. M. Fraser, *Ptolemaic Alexandria*, 1972, I, pp. 187-188; II, p. 322 n. 437-439; A. J. M. Meyer-Termeer, op. cit., pp. 11-12, 41 n. 151, p. 39 n. 140 and 142, pp. 41-42 n. 152; J. Velissaropoulos, op. cit., pp. 113-115; D. Thompson, op. cit., pp. 69-70, 191 n. 19-28; id., in *Alessandria e il mundo ellenistico-romano*, 1983, pp. 16-24, particularly p. 21. cf. W. Peremans, E. Van't Dack, *Prosopographia Ptolemaica* V, Studia Hellenistica 13, 1963, no 14016, 14026, 14032, 14057, 14079.

174  cf. H. Hauben, in T. Hackens, G. Moucharte (ed.), op. cit., n. 10 p. 322.

175  H. Hauben, ZPE 8, 1971, pp. 270-271 n. 60; W. Kunkel, APF 8, 1927, p. 186; E. Broerner, op. cit., 1939, p. 43; C. Brecht, op. cit., pp. 26-28, 133; J. Velissaropoulos, op. cit., pp. 296-297; H. Hauben, in T. Hackens and G. Moucharte (ed.), op. cit., p. 322.

176  J. Velissaropoulos, op. cit., pp. 113-114 and n. 131; D. Thompson, op. cit., p. 21 and n. 57.

177  H. Wild, BIFAO 56, 1957, pp. 229-230; A. Calderini, D. Daris, *Dizionario dei nomi geografici e topografici dell'Egitto greco-Romano*, III, 1978, pp. 258-262; C. Zivie-Coche, in LÄ IV, 1982, s.v. 'Memphis', col. 24-41, particularly col. 28; D. Thompson, op. cit., p. 21; J. B. Segal, *Aramaic Texts from North Saqqâra*, 1983, p. 6 (with references) and p. 42.

178  cf. H. Hauben, ZPE 60, 1985, pp. 183-187; F. de Cénival, BIFAO 71, 1972, pp. 33, 54 n. 19, 56 n. 20 (197 BC).

179  cf. H. Hauben, in T. Hackens, G. Moucharte (ed.), op. cit., n. 16 p. 323.

180  H. Hauben, ZPE 8, 1971, pp. 269-270 and n. 55; J. Velissaropoulos, op. cit., p. 114.

181  J. Velissaropoulos, op. cit., p. 114: 'It is probable that the *naucleroi Hippodromitai* were both the users and owners of the ships which, following a contract established with the tax authority, carried out the transport of corn from the chora to Alexandria.'

182  One *skaphe* with a capacity of 1200 *artabes* (BGU, VIII, 1741, l. 9; 1742, l. 9) and the other measuring 1800 *artabes* (BGU, VIII, 1743, l. 7).

183  W. Kunkel, APF 8, 1927, p. 186; E. Broerner, op. cit., p. 43; D. Thompson, op. cit., p. 69.

184  On these hypotheses, see H. Hauben, in T. Hackens, G. Moucharte (ed.), op. cit., p. 323.

185  W. Kunkel, op. cit., p. 186; E. Broerner, op. cit., p. 43; A. J. M. Meyer-Termeer, op. cit., p. 12 ('Man arbeitete vermutlich in der Absicht zusammen, größere Mengen verschiffen und das Transportrisiko streuen zu können') and pp. 41-42 n. 151-152; D. Thompson, op. cit., p. 69.

186  BGU, VIII, 1742, l. 12-14, 17; 1743, l. 9-10, 13-14. W. Kunkel, op. cit., pp. 184-185; H. Zilliacus, Aegyptus 19, 1939, pp. 59-76, particularly pp. 66-68; J. Frösen, in Arctos, Acta Philologica Fennica 12, 1978, pp. 5-17; id., in *Fifty Oxyrhynchus Papyri*, 1979, pp. 54-55, 61-63; J. Velissaropoulos, op. cit., p. 70, 191 ns. 26-28.

187  See first and foremost M. Rostovtzeff, in *Études dédiées à la mémoire d'A. M. Andréadès*, 1940, pp. 367-376; H. Hauben, in *Miscellanea in honorem J. Vergote*, OLP, 6/7, 1975-1976, pp. 267-271, particularly p. 269 n. 6; E. Van't Dack, H. Hauben, in H. Maehler and V. M. Strocka (ed.), *Das Ptolemäische Ägypten*, 1978, p. 59-94, especially pp. 61, 80-81, p. 89. See also M-T. Lenger, *Corpus des ordonnances des Ptolémées*, 1980, pp. 204-207, 382, no 73.

188  D. Thompson, op. cit., p. 69.

organisations, engaged in international commerce, appeared towards the end of the 4th century BC, but only started to spread from the 2nd century BC. Their existence must have contributed to the formation of corporations of Nile *naucleroi*.[188] In any case, it is striking that they were often constituted on an ethnic basis and composed of sea peoples from abroad.[189] The principal corporations of sea peoples, the most dynamic and best organised, were formed by the Phoenicians,[190] whose traditional propensity for naval affairs is well known: especially the Poseidoniasts of Beirut and the Heracleists of Tyre, associations that were established at Delos in the 2nd century BC. Equipped, so to speak, with an individual personality, they had a character that was simultaneously professional, religious and cultural.[191]

Lastly, and importantly, the final reason for which the *naucleroi* might have been associated should be considered. As elaborated below, the corporation of Memphis was composed, at least in part, by people who belonged to an ethnic minority. More than Greeks or natives, these people must have been inclined to form groups.[192]

Ever since the 18th Dynasty (1570–1293 BC) the city had been cosmopolitan in character.[193] Over the centuries it had been settled not only by Greeks and Carians, but also by Semites of every kind: Phoenicians, Syrians, Arameans, Judeans and (from the Hellenistic period) Idumeans.[194] In the eastern part of the nome of Memphis, on the other side of the Nile, there were also, in the Hellenistic and Roman period, Arab tribes.[195] Living in their own districts and keeping their own forms of worship, several ethnic groups had managed to hang on to their national identity.[196]

It was doubtless in the Semitic milieu, that was more or less mixed but apparently markedly Phoenician in character, more or less Hellenised, but nonetheless attached to its own traditions, that the Hippodromites of Memphis should be placed. Within the corporation, Eudemos, a Greek if not by birth at least by culture, to judge from his name, the most Hellenistic of the group, took on the job of secretary.[197] Was it a matter of chance that he had been chosen

– he who was to maintain contacts and written correspondence with the Ptolemaic administration which, for its part, had remained fundamentally Greek?[198]

The papyrological studies linked to the status of traders bring us right into the countless administrative and financial complications relative to the price of transport, whether this concerns the price of the complete freighting of a ship or the price of transport for one part of the cargo. The word ναυλον, *naulum*, as well as the verb ναυλοω is often found in the papyri.[199] The verb means 'to charter and load', referring to the contract that brings together the loader and the ship, so it is used both to designate the way one hires out one's ship or, on the other hand, the way one hires a ship oneself to transport a cargo that belongs to an individual'.[200] As for the word ναυλον, it is of more varied usage. It often designates the price of passage on to a ship. It may refer to the price of transporting a consignment of merchandise or even the price of loading up a small ship completely for a quick crossing.[201] In the Roman period no distinction seems to have been drawn between private and state transportations: at best those who agreed to work for the state corn market received a certain number of advantages of a juridical or economic kind, doubtless because by so doing they gave up transportation enterprises that might have been more fruitful for them. It is, however, clear that the appearance of requisitioning raises, as far as payment for maritime transport is concerned, a certain number of problems that all normally fall within the sphere of the problem of the *naulum*. In Roman Egypt, for small–scale transportation from the place of production to local granaries, transportation that was effected by barques or on the canals, there was no problem with the *naulum*: it was a kind of forced labour imposed on producers who had to deliver their grain *in situ*. However, when it was a matter of transporting the products levied in kind from local granaries to the central granaries of the chief cities in the provinces, or the granaries of the administration of the state corn market in the Alexandrinian suburb of Neapolis, the administration must have resorted to organised transport. So this must have been remunerated. Very often, this *naulum* was divided into two: on the one hand, remuneration in silver, on the other, a certain percentage of the cargo embarked, a percentage proportional to the ship's tonnage and the distance that needed to be travelled.[202] Thus, at least in part, the responsibility for the payment of transport rested on the taxpayer and this was the case until the 4th century BC; from then on, the introduction of the money tax on the *naulum*, destined to pay money part of the transport costs for the state cargoes, made the taxpayer fully responsible for paying for the transport.[203]

This demands the question: what were the problems relating to the responsibility of the ship's people vis–à–vis the traders. Only the papyrological documents of the Hellenistic and Roman epochs

189 J. Velissaropoulos, *op. cit.*, pp. 91-124; H. Hauben, *CdÉ* 58, 1983, pp. 240-241. See too M.F. Baslez, *Recherche sur les conditions de pénétrations et de diffusion des réligions orientales à Délos*, 1967, *passim*; id., *Studia Phoenicia* IV, 1986, pp. 289-305.

190 J. Velissaropoulos, *op. cit.*, pp. 106-110

191 M.-F. Baslez, *op. cit.*, pp. 206-208; id., in E. Lipinski (ed.), *Phoenicia and the East Mediterranean, Studia Phoenicia* v, 1987, pp. 267-285.

192 H. Hauben, in T. Hackens and G. Moucharte (ed.), *op. cit.*, p. 323.

193 On the cosmopolitan character of Memphis in general, see W. M. F. Petrie, *Memphis*, I, 1909, pp. 3-4; H. S. Smith, *A Visit to Ancient Egypt*, 1974, p. 12; A. Calderini and D. Daris, *Dizionario dei nomi geografici e topografici dell'Egitto greco-Romano*, III, 1978, pp. 260-261; W. Clarysse, in *Studies on Ptolemaic Memphis, Studia Hellenistica* 24, 1980, pp. 101-103; C. Zivie-Coche, in *LÄ* IV, 1982, *s.v.* 'Memphis', col. 28, 30, 31; J. B. Segal, *Aramaic Texts from North Saqqara*, 1983, pp. 8-10, 42; D. Thompson, in *Alessandria e il mundo ellenistico-romano, Studi in onore di Achille Adriani*, 1983, pp. 18-20; A. Kasher, *The Jews in Hellenistic and Roman Egypt*, 1985, pp. 184-185; C. Orrieux, *Zénon de Caunos*, 1985, p. 107.

194 As regards the Hellenomemphites, see A. Swiderek, *Eos* 51, 1961, pp. 55-63; P. M. Fraser, *Ptolemaic Alexandria*, 1972, I, p. 137; A. Swiderek, in J. Bingen, G. Cambier and G. Masson (ed.), *Le monde grec, Hommage à Claire Préaux*, 1975, pp. 670-675; For the Carians (6th century BC), see O. Masson, *Carian Inscriptions from North Saqqara and Buhen*, 1978, pp. 6-7, 68. For the Semitic populations in Memphis, see, apart from the studies mentioned under the preceding note, H. Schaefer, *ZÄS* 40, 1902-1903, p. 31-35; W. Spiegelberg, *Kêmi* 2, 1929, pp. 107-112; J. Élayi, *JANES* 12, 1980, pp. 13-28, especially p. 15; E. Lipinski, in S. Scheers (ed.), *Studia Paulo Naster oblata, I, Numismatica antiqua*, 1982, pp. 23-33, especially pp. 27-28; E. Bresciani, in *Egitto e società antica*, 1985, pp. 93-104. For the Idumean colony in particular, see U. Rappaport, *RPh* 43, 1969, pp. 73-82; D. Thompson in *Atti del XVII Congresso Internazionale di Papyrologia*, 1984, pp. 1069-1075, especially pp. 1071-1072.

195 U. Wilcken, *Urkunden der Ptolemäerzeit* I, 1927, pp. 341-342; W. H. M. Liesker, A. M. Tromp, *ZPE* 66, 1986, pp. 85-89 (with bibliography).

196 See for example D. Thompson, *op. cit.*, p. 18; H. Hauben, in T. Hackens and G. Moucharte (ed.), *op. cit.*, p. 329.

197 For the tasks and responsibilities of the grammateus, see M. San Nicolò, *Ägyptisches Vereinswesen zur Zeit der Ptolemäer und Römer*, II, 1, 1915, pp. 73-75.

198 H. Hauben, *op. cit.*, p. 331.

199 F. Preisigke, *Wörterbuch der griechischen Papyrusurkunden* II, 1927.

200 P. London 948, 1. See J. Rougé, *Recherches sur l'organisation du commerce en Méditerranée sous l'empire romain*, 1966, p. 361.

201 See the examples given by J. Rougé, *op. cit.*, p. 362.

202 *cf.* A. C. Johnson, in T. Franck, *Economic Survey*, 1936, II, p. 400 *et seq.*, the papyri cited often give a *naulum* in terms of money, or as a percentage of the cargo, or both.

203 J. Rougé, *op. cit.*, p. 362.

make it possible to mention the reports that found concrete form in a number of types of contracts entailing certain actions, some of them more specially devoted to questions of a maritime order, the others more general – application to maritime law was but one of their many aspects. The content of these contracts and these actions, their origins, their aims and their developments form problems which are far from having been solved definitively. It is not practical to detail all of these within the scope of the present study, especially as this would again overstep our chronological limits. Discussion will therefore be confined to what appears essential. It is necessary to make a rapid overview of the papyrological documentation on contracts concerned with river navigation, since no contract on maritime navigation has survived. These contracts were either between a carrier, represented by the captain or the *naucleros* of the ship, and a loader, since transactions exclusively dealt with the transportation of merchandise; or they were contracts between a carrier and the public service of the state corn system for the transport of the cereals levied in taxation to the great public granaries. In the latter case, is a document through which the carrier acknowledges that he has received his orders to embark and commits himself to fulfilling his commission. These documents begin by listing those party to the contract, or, if they are State contracts, naming the carrier and the magistrate overseeing the transport, as well as a mention of the ship which is the object of the contract. This reference to the ship is, in principle, accompanied by its name, sometimes even by its other distinctive signs, and its capacity. Then comes the object of the contract itself, a specification of the cargo, the place to which it is to be taken, and the *naulum* that is to be paid to the carrier. At the end of the contract and before the clauses are annexed, when such there are, occurs a formula which does not seem to be obligatory, since it is not encountered in all documents of this genre, specifying clearly what the carrier is committing himself to:[204]

> *I will deliver this merchandise safe and sound and free of all naval fraud.*

What exactly did this clause mean? What guarantees did it add to the contract for the benefit of the loader? And what responsibility, conversely, did it impose on the carrier? It is generally agreed that this represents an increase in the conditions imposed on the loader, who is thus made responsible for any damage that might befall the cargo during carriage. What is difficult to explain is that this clause is not found on all contracts of this kind, though it cannot be certain whether it appeared at one moment and disappeared at another: contracts from the same period can appear with or without the clause in question. So this is a very particular type of contract, distinct from the ordinary contract, in which the carrier engages to deliver the merchandise that is laden whatever may happen on the sailing, or to bear the economic consequences. It is a contract that is wholly to the advantage of the loader who in return must have been obliged to guarantee a certain number of advantages to the carrier. At present, those who study this type of contract in its Graeco-Egyptian context have suggested that this can only be a contract of the Hellenistic type.[205]

This kind of documentation allows us to map out the extent of the problem, and the developments of the juridical and administrative

management of maritime and river commerce, at the same time as it makes it necessary to set the problem of exchange back within the definition of the status of professionals of maritime commerce and more broadly that of the economy of Egypt. Such a development in terminology explains the need to specify the functions of each of the professionals of commercial trade at the same time as it seems to testify to the manifold character of trade, and the increasing complexity of exchange, in the Hellenistic and Roman periods.

*Emporoi, naucleroi, kapeloi*: the terminology is sometimes so tangled that it becomes too uncertain to use it to define the respective functions of traders involved in large-scale Hellenistic trade, but at least one thing is certain: trade and conveyance constitute the two complementary aspects of the same activity, if not of a unique individual, at least of a single society or a single family. Furthermore, the collaboration of different professional categories within these associations is observable, as well as the appearance of a new activity, that of *endocheus*. This is a category dedicated to large-scale maritime commerce, and it seems to correspond to a well-defined profession, but it is not easy to specify its function in the import-export chain. Given that it is a profession unknown to the Greeks, attested solely in Egypt and by two inscriptions in Delos (the only descriptions of this activity come from the Papyrus of Zeno), it is a category of person who held foreign money, like the *emporoi* and passing foreigners.[206] Ptolemy, in the 2nd century AD, classified this activity among those of luxury commerce (perfumes, food, jewellery) – the *kapeleia*,[207] and a 3rd-century papyrus mentions the *endocheis* as executive agents;[208] so it has been suggested that the *endocheis* of Egypt are either 'innkeepers' – which is incompatible with Ptolemy's text – or 'brokers' or 'shippers' linked to maritime commerce.[209] The interpretations based on the inscriptions at Delos are quite different. Certain scholars, basing their conclusions on the etymology of the verb *ekdechomai* ('to receive from the hands of someone'), have inferred that they were 'intermediaries'.[210] French historiography, sensitive to the transit function of the port at Delos and the apparent 'go downs' possessed by the Berytos establishment discovered on the island (exchange, entrepots, hostelry), has seen these *endocheis* as 'warehousemen', fulfilling a new economic role, that of carrying out the transit of merchandise.[211] Furthermore, as M. Rostovtzeff emphasised,[212] these warehousemen could also have played the role of intermediaries; so it might well have been imagined that the increase in the volume of traffic meant an expansion and

204  P. London 948; J. Rougé, *op. cit.*, p. 382.

205  See for example J. Gachet, *CRIPEL* 12, 1990, pp. 101-129; M. Merzagora, *Aegyptus* 10, 1929, p. 111; C. Préaux, *L'économie royale des Lagides*, 1939, p. 160, 345; A. Swiderek, *JJP* 7-8, 1954, p. 245; id., *JJP* 9-10, 1956, p. 385; J. Hengstl, *Private Arbeitverhältnisse freier Personen in den hellenistischen Papyri bis Diokletian*, 1972, p. 106; J. Scherer, *BASP* 15, 1978, pp. 95-101; J. Vélissaropoulos, *Les nauclères grecs*, 1980; C. Orrieux, *Les papyrus de Zénon*, 1983; id., *Zénon de Caunos*, 1985; T. Reekmans, in *Proceedings of the International Colloquium*, 1983, pp. 325-350; H. Hauben, *CdÉ* LVIII, 1983, pp. 237-247.

206  P. Cairo Zenon 59021: a letter relative to the conversion of foreign gold and *trichrysa* into the new currency. C. Préaux, *op. cit.*, p. 271, translates it as 'courtiers'.

207  Ptolemy, *Tetrabiblos*, IV, 4.

208  P. Oxyrhynchos 1669.

209  C. Préaux, *op. cit.*, p. 271; F. Cumont, *L'Égypte des Astrologues*, 1937, p. 110.

210  OGI 140 (inscription of the warehousemen of Alexandria), cf. C. Préaux, *op. cit.*, p. 271.

211  P. Roussel, *Délos, colonie athénienne*, 1916, p. 91; F. Durrbach, *Choix d'inscriptions de Délos*, 1921, p. 143 n. 1; C. Picard, *BCH* 44, 1920, pp. 263-311; L. Robert, *ACF* 73, 1972-1973, pp. 473-479. See too P. M. Fraser, *Ptolemaic Alexandria*, 1971, II, pp. 319-320; J. Vélissaropoulos, *op. cit.*, pp. 107-108.

212  M. Rostovtzeff, *Journal of Economic and Business History* 4, 1932, p. 762 and particularly n. 9.

diversification in the role of the broker. According to M.-F. Baslez, this hypothesis is acceptable only for the Poseidoniast Berytians of Delos who had their seat on the island.[213] This was not the case with the *endocheis* of Alexandria. Their name indicates that they were in residence in their city of origin. So they could not have had the specific function of acting as intermediaries in a place of transit, of depositing merchandise there for a certain time and managing the entrepots. On the contrary, the *endocheis* should be situated at the origin of maritime trafficking, in Alexandria, and the functions they occupied there need to be made explicit. These should include the exporters mentioned by Demosthenes in the Egypt of Cleomenes: unlike the *emporoi*, these exporters did not embark with their merchandise, but handed it over to *naucleroi* who carried out their sales orders; if they were involved in the trafficking of Greek ports, it was indirectly, acting in concert with the conveying officers and the merchants who sold off the merchandise *in situ*.[214] F. Cumont was not so far from this hypothesis when he interpreted the *endocheis* of Egypt as '*shippers*',[215] a translation that has the advantage that it fits all the situations described, whatever the character and the volume of traffic, and which means it is not necessary to fall back on a semantic development that had been hitherto judged necessary.[216]

---

213  M.-F. Baslez, in E. Lipinski (ed.), *Phoenicia and the East Mediterranean, Studia Phoenicia* V, 1987, p. 277.

214  Demosthenes, *Against Dionysodoros*, 8.

215  F. Cumont, *L'Égypte des Astrologues*, 1937, p. 110.

216  See M.-F. Baslez, *op. cit.*, p. 277.

# III. Messengers, ambassadors, diplomats and wholesalers

## III. 1. *Bidalu* and *tamkaru*: the 'businessmen' in the Ancient Near East

Sources that go well beyond the limits of Egyptology provide an opportunity to establish a transition between the 'trader' properly speaking, as defined above, and the 'messengers', the 'ambassadors' and the 'diplomats' who could play a commercial role.

Many of the exchanges were the result of royal orders. They concerned principally the economy of the palace and, in particular, prestige constructions.[1] Certain evidence from the Bible confirms this dual function performed by royal envoys. The servants of Hiram in 1 Kings, 5:15 bring a congratulatory message to Solomon, and in his response, doubtless carried by the same persons or by his own servants, Solomon simultaneously replies to the diplomatic message and asks for the first consignments of wood.[2] A new example of the association of these two functions may be seen from another biblical story that places in tandem the 'merchantmen' and the 'traffickers'.[3] These were probably royal emissaries who travelled round the country in the sovereign's name and performed a mission that was diplomatic as well as commercial. This dual role was particularly clear in the case of the envoys of the King of Cyprus in Egypt in a letter from El-Amarna: the King of Alasia says that his messengers (*mar Sipri-ia*) were also merchants (*tamkari-ia*).[4] These emissaries could be of either nationality and acted as the representatives of the country abroad.[5] This royal commerce has been seen as an exchange in the shape of gifts and reciprocal gifts, and informal and spontaneous organisation that regulated relations between sovereigns.[6] Nonetheless, the exchanges also involved everyday goods, without any prestige value, and they were characterised by their regularity.[7]

For commerce, as for international relations as a whole, a structure of remarkable homogeneity seems to have been already established shortly after the middle of the 2nd millennium BC in the Near East. Given the documentation at present available, the period most rich in evidence is centred on the 14th century BC; it also included to some extent the end of the 15th century and the first half of the 13th. Useful sources come from the archives of Bogazköy, El-Amarna and especially Ras-Shamra.

In the Near East in the middle of the 2nd millennium BC, it is necessary to distinguish between commercial exchanges, characterised by the spirit of lucre, and official exchanges, characterised by the principle of generosity and to which is attached the Akkadian term *Sulmanu*, 'gift of courtesy'.[8] This distinction is just as evident at the level of the status of the person responsible for the dealings: his character could be rather 'hybrid' at times. In documents from this period, the person who assumes the function relative to commercial exchanges bears the Akkadian title *tamkaru* and the Ugaritic title *bidalu*, 'merchant, businessman'.[9] Among the internal distinctions within this socio-professional group, the texts refer to two: the *tamkaru Sa giri-su*, of whom practically nothing is known;[10] the *tamkaru Sa mandatti*, 'the businessman who is an active partner, the buyer', a term which seems to designate the person charged with buying for one or more other people.[11]

The businessman may see himself invested with an ordinary diplomatic task,[12] especially that of an envoy or that of consul.[13] In tandem, the functionary of the public sector of transportation also constituted a base for ordinary diplomacy.[14] This is very clear in the Pharaonic administration:[15] out of 30 envoys, eight are high dignitaries and involved in extraordinary diplomacy, seven are known in no other way than as envoys, and the 15 others, the only certain practitioners of ordinary diplomacy, are all functionaries of the public system of transports – either chariot drivers, or cavalry officers.[16] The same is true in the Syro–Anatolian administration of the period; the *qardabbu*, 'cavalry officer' may have been involved in diplomatic relations;[17] the *sa rechi*, 'charioteer',[18] sometimes placed under the responsibility of a cavalry officer,[19] could also be an envoy.[20] The Akkadian term *aširu* should also be added since this functionary seems to have been involved in the organisation of royal dispatches[21] and worked in parallel with the commercial sector.[22]

In addition, the permeability between commerce and transport is evident in the texts under consideration here. A cavalry officer may play the role of a public buyer – a broker.[23] A cavalry officer and a charioteer intervene in commercial disputes together with businessmen. Conversely, a businessman who is part of the public administration enters the category of charioteers. Finally, the permeability between diplomacy and commerce seems just as evident in the texts: an envoy can play the role of a commercial clerk.[24]

1  *Seafaring in Ancient Egypt*, vol. 2.
2  I Kings V, 15.
3  I Kings X, 15. *cf.* M. Elat, in *World History of Jewish People*, IV, 2, 1979, p. 178.
4  *EA* 39. For an overall view of the men mandated by the king to organize commerce, see K. Polanyi, in J. A. Sabloff, G. C. Lamberg-Karlovski (ed.), *Ancient Civilization and Trade*, 1975, p. 137; *id.*, in K. Polanyi, C. M. Arensberg (ed.), *Les systèmes économiques*, 1975, pp. 51-62; W. W. Hallo, in D. Charpin, F. Joannès (ed.), *La circulation des biens, des personnes et des idées*, 1992, pp. 351-356; B. Lafont, in D. Charpin, F. Joannès (ed.), *Marchands, Diplomates et Empereurs*, 1991, pp. 275-282.
5  E. Lipiński, *Studia Phoenicia* III, 1983, pp. 213-220.
6  G. Bunnens, *JESHO* 19, 1976, pp. 1-31.
7  These types of commerce are reviewed in detail in *Seafaring in Ancient Egypt*, vol. 2.
8  See C. Zaccagnini, *Lo scambio dei doni nel vicino Oriente*, 1973, pp. 117-124; G. Kestemont, *Diplomatique et droit international en Asie occidentale*, 1974, p. 590.
9  *PRU* III, 236.
10  *RS* 17. 424.
11  G. Kestemont, *op. cit.*, p. 572; *id.*, in J. D. Hawkins (ed.), *Trade in the Ancient Near East*, 1977, p. 191.
12  *EA* 7, 77-80; *RS* 15.109, 54.
13  *RS* 17.383; *RS* 17.422; *RS* 20.184.
14  Extraordinary diplomacy is assured by the highest state officials.
15  W. Helck, *Die Beziehungen Ägyptens*, 1962, pp. 472-474.
16  Cavalry and chariots are a regular feature of this period; *cf. RS* 17. 289.
17  *RS* 15.19, vol. 2; *RS* 17.137, vol. 5.
18  *RS* 17.144 and certainly *EA* 125, 35.
19  *RS* 17.112, 4.
20  *cf.* G. Kestemont, *op. cit.*, no 20 p. 192.
21  *EA* 287, 54
22  *RS* 16.257; *RS* 17.131, 14). *cf.* A. F. Rainey, *JNES* 26, 1967, pp. 296-301.
23  *cf.* The officiers and cavalry of Hanja in *EA* 369, Tahmaja in *EA* 265, Sunailu in *RS* 17.244, 5.
24  See G. Kestemont, *op. cit.*, p. 192.

## II.2. 'Messengers' and 'explorers'

*If you are a man of trust whom a Great man sends to (another)*
*Great man, be perfectly precise when he sends you. Accomplish the*
*mission as he has said.*
(*Maxim of Ptahotep*, 8)[25]

The designation in Ancient Egypt *wpwty* (or *jwpwty*) used to refer to the 'messenger' derives from a verbal root, *wpj*, 'to open, divide, separate', from which stem *wpw.t*, 'the mission, the commission', 'the work', and *wpwty*, the name of the passive equivalent: 'he who is separated, he who is detached' – the 'envoy' or the 'messenger'.

This general interpretation of the word 'messenger' can cover, depending on the context, a simple notion of 'postman' or more specifically that of 'attorney' in the sense of proxy. Or even of 'ambassador', when it is a matter, for example, of an Egyptian delegation, sent by Rameses II to Hattusa to broker a diplomatic marriage with a Hittite princess.[26] In Sinai, the inscriptions left by these figures sent on missions extend from the 18th to the 19th Dynasty (1570-1293, 1293-1185 BC). Two categories of 'royal messengers' left traces of their passage there: they include heads of expedition and couriers.[27]

In his study of the administration of Syro-Palestine during the New Kingdom (1570–1070 BC), A. K. Muhammad devotes a paragraph to the royal delegates and draws up a catalogue of their responsibilities, as they appear in Amarnean diplomatic correspondence.[28] It emerges from these letters that these envoys were given the most varied tasks; as well as transmitting the mail, they were occasionally charged with levying tribute from the natives, accompanying important personages on their travels, escorting precious materials or gifts, entering negotiations and maintaining good relations between Asiatic vassals. The missives preserved in the archives of El-Amarna include numerous references to Egyptian or foreign messengers and it is evident that the use of this material enables us to establish to some degree the status and functions of these royal emissaries. Certain authors have deduced that the title of 'royal messenger to every foreign land' (*wpwty nsw r ḫ₃s.t nb.t*) could bear other foreign titles, such as *rabisu*.[29] W. F. Albright has suggested that the reference to the *wpwty* should be recognised as an 'envoy' and a 'commissioner' that may be compared to that of *rabisu*.[30] The equivalent Egyptian form was that of 'man of trust' (*mḥ-jb*),[31] whose attributes included, it may be imagined, a group of diplomatic functions rather than a simple conveying of messages.

Then there was the title of 'director of missions' (*(j)m(y)-r(₃) wp.wt*) conferred on certain categories of functionaries. From the 4th Dynasty (2613-2498 BC) onwards it was included in the titles of heads of military expeditions, and was accompanied by more specific titles such as 'general in chief' (*(j)m(y)-r(₃) mš*).[32] In this context, the missions assumed the appearance of military campaigns and the title would then have been one of those regularly awarded in the army. In the same period, it was also associated with the servicing of the fortifications.[33] In the civil domain, still linked with operations, the title was borne by Kaemib[34] who, as a *(j)m(y)-r(₃) wp.wt n ʿš* 'chief of the cedar expeditions' probably participated in a journey to the northern marches in quest of construction materials. More generally, an examination of the texts does not allow us to decide on the concrete functions associated with the title *(j)m(y)-r(₃) wp.wt*;

nonetheless, the juxtaposition of the categories enumerated brings out one element common to all the groups: the title designates a hierarchical rank rather than a specific occupation. Except for the examples selected from the titles of viziers and nomarchs, the other attestations probably give the names of stewards, in the case of expedition leaders, and inspectors or sorts of foremen, in the other references. The way the title is combined is revealing: it does not distinguish a subject from a corporation, but entitles its holder to control the activities of subordinates and to be in charge of them'.[35] Furthermore, the presence of the substantive *wpw.t* implies notions of time and place. The mission that covers tasks that are diverse in number and importance nonetheless preserves a temporary character. Furthermore, a mandate is frequently associated with changes of place – as witness, for instance, the autobiographical clichés. It thus appears that this title was borne by people who moved from place to place and were entrusted with the execution of a particular project. Even this passing distinction justified its insertion in the list of titles of the man who had worked at any moment of his career as an executive agent.

The hierarchic rank of these *wpwty.w* was associated with considerable prerogatives; for instance, the respect shown them by the nomarchs;[36] but their transport rights should also be mentioned, as set down in royal decrees of the Old Kingdom (2686–2181 BC),[37] and especially their ability to impose the costs of their personal maintenance on the local administrations and clergy that were not exempt.[38] Nonetheless, this privilege was not always exclusively reserved to dignitaries and functionaries; in the later part of the instructions that Pepi II addressed to Herkhuf, the sovereign drew the attention of his explorer to the powers that were conferred on him:[39]

*Orders have been brought to the governor of the new towns, the*
*friend and director of the prophets, with the aim of ordering that*
*food be levied by his intervention in any rural depot and in any*
*temple that has not been exempted.*

25  P. Prisse 7, 3; Z. Zaba, *Les maximes de Ptahotep*, 1956, n° 148.

26  Note that this ambassador was later promoted as viceroy of Nubia: M. Valloggia, *Recherche sur les 'Messagers' (Wpwtyw)*, 1976, p. 128.

27  *Id.*, p. 244-256, p. 263-271; *id.*, in D. Valbelle, C. Bonnet (ed.), *Le Sinaï*, 1998, pp. 39-43; *id.*, in *LÄ* IV, col. 289; E. Otto, in *LÄ* I, col. 846. See too H. El-Saady, *MDAIK* 55, 1999, pp. 411-425.

28  A. K. Muhammad, *ASAE* LXVI, 1959, pp. 119-122. See too W. Helck, *Die Beziehungen Ägyptens*, 1962.

29  A. K. Muhammad, *ASAE* LXVI, 1959, p. 120.

30  W. F. Albright, in I. E. S. Edwards, *et al.* (ed.), *History of the Middle East and the Aegean Region, CAH* II, 2, 1975, p. 7

31  W. F. Albright, *JEA* XXIII, 1937, p. 200 and n° 4.

32  See the examples given by M. Valloggia (with bibliography) in M. Valloggia, *Recherche sur les 'Messagers' (Wpwtyw)*, 1976, p. 31.

33  *(j)m(y)-r(₃) wp.wt mnn.w*, 'Head of fortifications' (Mastaba of Nefer-nesout: H. Junker, *Giza*, III, 1938, 163-187; H. G. Fischer, *JAOS* 74, 1954, pp. 26-34).

34  On a table of offerings currently in the Pelizaeusmuseum (Hildesheim inv. n° 2406), see H. Junker, *Giza*, III, 1938, Abb. 62.

35  M. Valloggia, *op. cit.*, p. 32.

36  Architrave in the tomb of the Ameny at Beni-Hassan: 'The prince, a valued helper, one who is highly praised at the palace, he who folds his arms before messengers'. cf. *Urk.*, VII, 19, 14; M. Valloggia, *op. cit.*, n° 18 p. 81, p. 222 and n° 8 p. 226.

37  Decree of Pepi I in favour of the pyramid towns of Snefru (Berlin 17500): *Urk.* I, 210, 7-11; H. Goedicke, *Königliche Dokumente aus dem Alten Reich, ÄgAbh* 14, 1967, p. 47 n° 8, p. 55; L. Borchardt, *ZÄS* 42, 1906, p. 6; M. Valloggia, *op. cit.*, n° 3 p. 68; Decree of Pepi I in favour of the chapel of his mother, Queen Iput (Cairo JE 41890): *Urk.*, I, 214, 12-13; H. Goedicke, *op. cit.*, p. 41; M. Valloggia, *op. cit.*, n° 4 p. 69.

38  See the examples given by M. Valloggia, *op. cit.*, n° 6, 7, 8 pp. 71-72.

39  *Urk.* I, 131, 4-7. After M. Valloggia, *op. cit.*, p. 71.

These privileges granted to certain functionaries on the move are a well-known feature of every period and in several civilisations. For instance there were the satrapic authorisations in the period of Persian domination in Egypt. The Achaemenid royal routes 'cross inhabited and safe areas', to use an expression employed by Herodotus in his description of the road from Sardes to Susa[40] – which means that there was no risk of running into famine or ambush on it. For military historians these were also roads where the armies could also find victuals easily, but in order to take these roads one needed to obtain official authorisation in advance; this was called *halmi* (a sealed document). This is precisely the content of the letter entrusted by Archama to his steward Nehtihor on his way to Egypt, in an Aramaic document:[41]

*From Archama to Marduk the steward (peqid) of x (toponym), Nabuladani the steward of La'ir; Zatuvahya the steward of Arzuhin; Upastabara the steward of Arbeles, Halsu and Mat-am-Ubach; Bagafarna, the steward of Sa'lam; Fradafarna and Gawzina the stewards of Damascus. And now, behold the said Nehtihor, my steward (peqid) is going to Egypt. Do you give him rations (ptp) on my House (beth) in your provinces: each day, in white flour, two handfuls (1.7 litres); in grey flour, three handfuls; in wine and beer, two pints (1.7 litres); and for his servants, i.e. 10 men, to each of them per day, a handful of flour (0.9 litres); in hay, as his team of animals requires. Give also rations to two Cilicians and one artisan, all three of them my servants, who are going with him to Egypt: per man and per day, in flour, one handful. Give them these rations, steward to steward, following the route that (goes) from province to province (medinah) until Nehtihor reaches Egypt. And, if he is in any place for more than a day, do not give them any more rations. Bagasaru is responsible for this order. Rachta the scribe.*

The interest of this letter lies in the way it brings back to life exactly the administrative process. Every leader of an official caravan had to be provided with a sealed document, both a safe conduct and a travel permit, which included the number of travellers, the amount of their ration, and the route followed. The Persian royal roads were dotted with stopover places, staging posts, and stores. The storekeepers could hand over merchandise only when they were shown the satrap's authorisation. On arrival at the stopover place, the leader of the caravan had to produce this document, without fail, as it allowed him in particular to obtain rations for the journey, to an amount that was indicated exactly on the document that he was bearing. The letter of Archama specifies that even if the travellers were confronted with an unforeseen difficulty, or if they dallied on their road, they would not have any right to supplementary rations. It also confirms that the halting posts and the places for revictualling were generally a day's journey from one another.[42]

As for the administration of the Pharaoh's residence, varied information proves that the corporation of 'messengers' pursued its mobile activities. The report of Henu at Wadi Hammamat (year 8 of the reign of Montuhotep III (2060-2010 BC), 11th Dynasty (2134-1991 BC) states that distant expeditions, such as those that led to the land of Punt, maintained, throughout the territory of Egypt at least, contacts with the Court through the intermediary of its representatives. The inscription, engraved on the return from a trip to the land of Punt, sets out the aims of the enterprise. At the start of the narrative, this Henu describes the way the expedition functioned:[43]

*All the members of His Majesty's office were under my direction; they announced the messengers (to me) as to the sole commander who is obeyed by millions.*

This type of 'messenger' were probably travelling agents, entrusted with missions of coordination. Furthermore, these envoys left traces of their passage, both in the South on the road to the fortresses of Nubia[44] and in the North, in Syria, where Sinuhe undertook to control their movements and thus to obtain news of his native land.[45]

*The messenger who was heading north or coming back south to Court would stop with me, since I made everyone halt.*

This literary contribution, confirmed by the data of archaeology, attests to diplomatic relations that were developing in these regions from the start of the 12th Dynasty (1991-1782 BC). Unfortunately, the text does not allow us to know if these couriers reached the court of local kinglets or whether they were expected in the Egyptian embassies directed by permanent representatives such as Senusret-Ankh in the reign of Amenemhat III (1842-1797 BC).[46]

Depending as they did on local or central authorities, the *wpwty.w* carried out functions that were always of a peripatetic nature. Missions of coordination led these functionaries to move from the Residence to the nomes and vice versa. Others kept up the links between the advanced posts of Nubia[47] or in the North, but the tasks with which they were sometimes entrusted seem to have had some relation with justice. From the Old Kingdom onwards, their office was attached to the tribunals: bailiffs, ushers for the vizir, or assessors in local courts.[48]

Since the affairs of the sovereign were identical to those of the State, royal missions must have been entrusted to more experienced subjects. They were probably found from among the king's suite and more especially among those who composed his immediate entourage. The function of *wpwty n(y)-sw(.t)*, 'royal messenger', was

40    Herodotus, V, 52.

41    *DAE* 67: P. Grelot, *Documents araméens d'Égypte*, LAPO 5, 1972, pp. 67-68.

42    On this document and its interpretation, see P. Briant, *Histoire de l'Empire perse*, 1996, p. 381. For more details on letters of recommendation, *Seafaring in Ancient Egypt*, vol. 2.

43    J. Couyat and P. Montet, *Les inscriptions du Ouâdi Hammâmât*, MIFAO XXXIV, 1912, n° 114, p. 83; W. Schenkel, *Memphis, Hierakonpolis, Theben*, ÄgAbh 12, 1965, n° 426, p. 256; M. Valloggia, *op. cit.*, n° 12 pp. 77-78.

44    Graffito of Akhty-hetep at Kumna: LD II, 139 g; D. Dunham, J. M. A. Janssen, *Second Cataract Forts*, I, 1960, r.i.k. 118, pl. 102 f, p. 165; M. Valloggia, *op. cit.*, n° 22 p. 84.

45    *Sinuhe*, B 94.

46    This personage is known by a statue discovered at Ras Shamra and a stele (Stele Florence 2579). On the role of *Snwsr.t-'nh* at Ugarit, C. Schaefer, *Ugaritica* I, 1939, p. 22; W. A. Ward, *Orientalia* 30, 1961, p. 131. Concerning the monuments and their dating, cf. M. Valloggia, BIFAO 74, 1974, pp. 131-132.

47    For example, see P. Genève D. 407, vols. 5-9 (end of the 20th Dynasty); cf. E. F. Wente, *Late Ramesside Letters*, SAOC 33, 1967, pp. 33-37.

48    M. Valloggia, *op. cit.*, pp. 225-226.

Expedition to Punt, funerary temple of Hatshepsut, Deir el-Bahari, c. 1490–1468 BC. © Photo: David Fabre

dependent on the supreme authority and crowned the merits of a high-ranking noble.[49]

While an examination of the documents does not permit us to retrace the successive stages in the career of a functionary promoted to this position, M. Valloggia has nonetheless made it possible to make a comparison with certain generic norms. The attachment of the 'royal messenger' to the nobility is habitually marked by the insertion, in the lost of titles, of the sequence ('prince') (($j$)$r$($y$) $p^ct$), 'governor' ($ḥ3ty$-$^c$), 'unique friend' (zmr waty), 'dignitary' ($s3b$). The most frequent professional appellations of the 'messenger' are those of a man of letters: he is a 'scribe' (sš), even a 'royal scribe' (sš $n$($y$)-sw(.$t$)). The personal aptitudes of the title holder sometimes require him to embrace an administrative career; he is then dependent on the Treasury and inscriptions describe him as 'chancellor of the king of Lower Egypt' (ḫtmt($y$)-bjty).[50] At other times he was attached to building activities and then bore the title of 'architect' or 'director of the works' (($j$)$m$($y$)-$r$($3$) $k3$.wt).[51] Towards the end of the 18th Dynasty (1570–1293 BC), certain 'messengers' showed a real interest for the profession of arms. Stationed in the Delta when they were 'directors of all the mouths of *Wadj Wer*' (($j$)$m$($y$)-$r$($3$) $r$($3$)-$ḥ3w$.t nb.t $n$($y$).t w3ḏ-wr),[52] they were also posted to other garrisons as 'commanders of troops' (ḥry pḏ.t)[53] or 'officers of horses' (($j$)$m$($y$)-$r$($3$) ssm.wt).[54]

The episodic mention of 'royal messenger' (wpwty $n$($y$)-sw(.$t$)) in the *cursus honorum* could well mark 'a transitional stage or a particular distinction in a career rather than a hierarchical grade'. In these conditions this distinction should not be viewed as a title of rank; it would more probably be right to recognise it as 'an indication of function'. Furthermore, this low frequency in the number of attestations, found in a tomb or on a series of private monuments,

49  See the language used by the scribe Nekhet in an inscription he left in Sinai; the text relates the royal choice that led him to direct the expeditions to the mines. 'The Horus himself sent me to accomplish what his *ka* desired. He promoted me and I found myself placed at the head of thousands of men, having been chosen from among hundreds of thousands. He appointed me royal attorney, being (thus) distinguished among the courtiers' (A. H. Gardiner, T. E. Peet, J. Cerny, *The Inscriptions of Sinaï*, 1952-1955, 181, 1; 3-6; cf. M. Valloggia, *op. cit.*, n° 33 p. 91).

50  Graffito of Ty at Sehel (reign of Hatshepsut; L. Habachi, *JNES* 16, 1957, pp. 99-101); Stele of Sinai (year 25 of the reign of Thutmose III; *Urk.* IV, 886-888; A. H. Gardiner, T. E. Peet and J. Cerny, *op. cit.*, 196, 15-16, pl. 64, pp. 159-160). See M. Valloggia, *op. cit.*, n° 32 pp. 90-91, n° 34 p. 92, n° 47, p. 105.

51  M. Valloggia, *op. cit.*, p. 243 and n° 17.

52  Stele of Sinai, year 25 of the reign of Thutmose III: *Urk.* IV, 886-888; A. H. Gardiner, T. E. Peet, J. Cerny, *op. cit.*; M. Valloggia, *op. cit.*, n° 34 p. 92; statue of Paramessu from Karnak, reign of Horemheb: *Urk.* IV, 2175, 7-16; M. Valloggia, *op. cit.*, n° 54, pp. 112-113.

53  M. Valloggia, *op. cit.*, n° 47 pp. 105-106; n° 54, pp. 112-113.

54  *Id*, n° 49, p. 107; n° 54, pp. 112-113

could also be explained by 'the temporary character of the royal mission that covered a precise action'.[55]

The missions entrusted to the 'royal messenger', missions that were sometimes circumscribed to the region, for the most part had an international character. Civilian and military in nature, they were essentially oriented towards economic and diplomatic objectives. It is with this in mind that the study of the documents relative to the 'royal messengers' engaged on expeditions to the land of Punt should be envisaged. These journeys to Punt often took on the character of commercial embassies sent abroad. At Deir el-Bahari, the Egyptian troop, represented as being under the conduct of a 'royal messenger', greeted the Puntite dignitaries very considerately. Here are the texts mentioning the 'royal messenger' that relate to this famous expedition:[56]

- Scene of the arrival of the Egyptians in the land of Punt:[57]

  [A] *Arrival of the royal messenger on divine land, with his accompanying army, before the Great of Punt, sent with all the good things of the palace, l.h.s for Hathor, mistress of Punt.*

- Setting up the camp:[58]

  [B] *Prepare the camp of the royal messenger, with his army, on the incense hills of Punt near* Wadj Wer *to receive the great of this (foreign) land.*

- Reception of the products from Punt:[59]
  (Legend before the royal emissary)

  [C] *Reception of the gifts of the King of Punt by the royal messenger*

55 *Id.,* p. 243.
56 *PM* II, 345 (10); *Wb* I, 269, 14; E. Naville, *The Temple of Deir el-Bahari,* III, 1898, 69. See, for alternative translations, C. Vandersleyen, *Ouadj our,* 1999, n° 59-60 p. 203; M. Valloggia, *op. cit.,* n° 31 pp. 89-90.
57 *spr wpwty n(y)-sw(.t) r tꜣ nṯr hnꜤ mšꜤ nty m-ḫt=f tp-m wr.w n Pwn.t sb(=w) m ḫt nb.t nfr.t m stp-sꜣ Ꜥnḫ wḏꜣ snb n Ḥw.t-ḥr nb.t Pwn.t :* Urk. IV, 323-324, L.
58 *ḥr jmꜣ n wpwty n(y)-sw(.t) hnꜤ mšꜤ=f ḥtyw Ꜥntyw n(y.)w Pwn.t ḥr-gs wꜣḏ-wr r šsp wr.w n(y).w ḫꜣs.t tn:* Urk. IV, 325, 12-14.
59 *šsp jn.w n(y) wr n(y) Pwn.t jn wpwty n(y)-sw(.t):* Urk. IV, 326, 2-3.

A

*Arrival of the royal messenger on divine land, with his accompanying army, before the Great of Punt, sent with all the good things of the palace, l.h.ś for Hathor, mistress of Punt.*

B

*Prepare the camp of the royal messenger, with his army, on the incense hills of Punt near* Wadj Wer *to receive the great of this (foreign) land.*

C

*Reception of the gifts of the King of Punt by the royal messenger.*

D

*Arrival of the Great Chief of Punt laden with his gifts by the shore of* Wadj Wer *before the royal envoy.*

(Legend above the Puntites):[60]

[D] *Arrival of the Great Chief of Punt laden with his gifts by the shore of* Wadj Wer *before the royal envoy.*

In these extracts it is possible to detect the traces of the complex commerce of reciprocity at work; from this point of view, the 'royal messenger' is acting temporarily in the manner of an ambassador to the Puntites. Nonetheless, his mandate as a negotiator rapidly disappears and gives way to that of an escort of merchandise, entrusted with the task of overseeing the safe delivery of the cargoes in his care. This function might find a parallel in the participation of the 'royal messenger' within the army. On this subject, G. Maspero[61] noted in connection with the Hood Papyrus: 'The place that it (the title of 'royal messenger in any foreign country' (*wpwty n(y)-sw(.t) nb.t ḫȝs.t*) occupies on our list and the circumstances in which it is mentioned on the monuments show the nature of the functions it designated. The booty captured during war, the taxes imposed on the vanquished, the tributes levied regularly on the subjugated cities, belonged to the king who distributed part of them to the soldiers, and kept the rest to allocate part of it to the temples or to deposit it in his treasury. Each army must then have been accompanied by employees whose task it was to take possession of the booty and the taxes, to record them, to regulate the way they were divided up, and to dispatch them in the name of the king. These were the functions of the royal delegate in any foreign country; he was seen as one of the agents of the state tax and placed beside the directors of the double house of gold and silver, the directors of oxen, the directors of horses…'

Documents have now confirmed the hypotheses of G. Maspero, and certain analogies with the civil activities of the 'royal messengers' occupied with regulating the transmission of the royal donations suggest that these functionaries, often attached to the Treasury,[62] were able to carry out accountancy tasks in the army. The Zizinia relief, though incompletely preserved, relates a mission led by the 'royal messenger' Horemheb in Nubia.[63] On return from the expedition, the inscription relates that His Majesty appeared, in the company of Horemheb, under the 'dais of the bringing of tribute'. There is no question here of a real military campaign in the south, but more probably a tour of inspection during which tribute from the natives was levied. On this occasion Horemheb does not bear – at least not on the fragment that has come down to us – any military title; his sole functions are those of *wpwty n(y)-sw(.t)*, which cover the mandate of an expedition leader, but also that of a tax collector. The 'royal messenger' was thus led to represent the Treasury in the army and to carry out the role of a tax agent. According to the documents of the 18th Dynasty the missions of the royal messengers concerned two domains which were interlinked: diplomacy and economy, which took on a supranational character, if it is taken into account that the contributions were from the provinces and further afield.

The conjunction of these elements explains on the one hand the new importance of the 'royal messengers' within the administration, and on the other hand the development of the formula 'royal messenger in any foreign country'.

These elements allow us to draw a parallel between the function of *smntj* known from some 30 graffiti on the cliffs that border the valley and especially in the eastern desert,[64] as well as two funerary steles of Edfu[65] and certain inscriptions from the Middle and New Kingdom.[66] The determiners of desert mountains in certain variants of the word and the places themselves, where scattered signatures of the *smntj.w* on the rocks are found, tell us that the latter operated in the areas outside the Egyptian valley. It is clearly the same word within the engraved legend of Deir el-Bahari, where the god Amun speaks to Queen Hatshepsut of the land of Punt, the road to which the Egyptians had forgotten under their previous kings:[67]

*The marvels that were brought back from there were transmitted from hand to hand and at the price of numerous exchanges and no one reached it except for your* smntjw.

A picture of the tomb of Pouyemre illustrates the official texts of Hatshepsut, and uses the term '*smntj* of the king' for the personage supervising the registering by the accountants of the products being brought back from the land of Punt. Furthermore, at Deir el-Bahari, the old sign of 'the man with the money bag' is replaced by a determiner showing a traveller *en route*, his scrip at the end of a rod that he is carrying on his shoulder, a figure which determines the words 'nomad' and 'shepherd' and corresponds to the image of travellers returning from Punt, via the Arabian trails.[68] So under Hatshepsut 'the corporation of the *smntj.w* survived only as a literary reminiscence; it emerged from the old texts that, in bygone days, agents designated as such explored for the kings the routes leading to Punt'.[69] Indeed, this corps in the Old Kingdom was evidently organised in a hierarchical manner. The titles that developed ('directors of the *smntj.w*' *(j)m(y)-r(ȝ) zmntj.w*') attest to the way these people combined several responsibilities of military chiefs that qualified them for the exercise of high command in zones outsides Egypt. Some of them were called 'chancellor of the god' (*ḫtmt(y) nṯr*), a specific designation of the admirals delegated by the pharaoh to direct far-flung economic expeditions.[70] Some assumed, on occasion, the title of any military or para-military head of a mission, 'general in chief, director of the troop' (*(j)m(y)-r(ȝ) mšʿ*).[71] One of these 'chancellors of the god' glorified himself as being 'one who spreads the terror of Horus in foreign lands', akin

60    *jj(t) jn wr n(y) Pwn.t ḥr jn.w=f r gs wȝd-wr tp-m [wpwty] n(y)-sw(.t)*: Urk. IV, 326, 5-6.

61    G. Maspero, *Études égyptiennes* II, 1888, pp. 38-39.

62    See the examples provided by M. Valloggia, *op. cit.*, pp. 246-247.

63    Relief Zizinia–Alexandrie (col. 2-3) (reign of Tutankhamun; *Urk.* IV, 2087; R. Hari, *Horemheb et la reine Moutnedjemet*, 1964, pp. 64-68, pl. 11, fig 13.

64    A. Weigall, *Travels in the Upper Egyptian Deserts*, 1909, pl. 7, 1; J. Couyat, P. Montet, *Les inscriptions du Ouadi Hammâmât, MIFAO XXXIV*, 1912-1913, 35, 69, 151 pl. 34, 156 pl. 33, 74 pls 18, 163, 166, 167, 169, 170, 211; G. Goyon, *Nouvelles inscriptions rupestres du Wadi Hammamat*, 1957, n⁰ 2, 10, 12, 23, 32, 40, 43, 48, 49; Green, *PSBA* 31, 321 pl. 53 n⁰ 31, 320, pls 53 n⁰ 25 and 27, 321 pls 54 n⁰ 32, 34 and 37; M. J. De Bruyn, *JEA* 44, p. 97, pl. 14 (1); A. H. Sayce, *PSBA* 17, 40-41; A. Weigall, *A Report on the Antiquities of Lower Nubia*, 1907, 2-3, pl. 57, pls 58, 19 and 24; J. Lopez, *Las inscripciones rupestres faraonicas entre Korosko y Kasr Ibrim*, 1966, n⁰ 25, pl. 15, 1 = *RdÉ* 19, p. 53 and fig. 5.

65    M. Alliot, *FIFAO* 10, p. 29, pl. 14, 3-4; *id.*, *BIFAO* XXVII, 1937, pp. 99-101.

66    *Sinai* 112, eastern face, col. 3; *Urk.* IV, 344, 16. See also the cylinder-seals; imprints on clay stoppers: P. Kaplony, *Die Inschriften der ägyptischen Frühzeit*, III, 1963-1964, pl. 98 fig. 404; pl. 126 fig. 755; W. B. Emery, *Kush* 11, 1963, p. 119, fig. 2. See the study by J. Yoyotte, *BSFE* 73, 1975, pp. 44-55.

67    *Urk.* IV, 344, 16. J. Yoyotte, *op. cit.*, p. 46.

68    J. Yoyotte, *op. cit.*, p. 47.

69    *Id.*, p. 47.

70    J. Couyat, P. Montet, *Les inscriptions du Ouadi Hammâmât, MIFAO XXXIV*, 1912-1913, 35, 69.

71    J. Couyat, P. Montet, *op. cit.*, 35, 69, 170; J. Lopez, *op. cit.*, n⁰ 25, pl. 15, 1 = *RdÉ* 19, p. 53 and fig. 5.

'The great men of Punt': Parekhoou and his wife *Itj*. Expedition to Punt, funerary temple of Hatshepsut, Deir el-Bahari, *c.* 1490–1468 BC.
© Photo: Peter A. Clayton

*I have followed my master into this land ( = Sinai) and I have seized the occasion (?) when he gave me the order (?). I left by the shores of Wadj Wer to announce the marvels of Punt (sr bjȝy.t n Pwn.t) and to receive the sweet-smelling gum brought by the princes with their ships-of-eight (?), the tributes from lands that were unknown. And then I returned after having crossed the land of that goddess and I directed the working of the turquoise.*

to other specialists in foreign affairs.[72] Like several expedition commanders in the Old Kingdom, a 'director of the *smntj.w*' was 'inspector, lieutenant of a vessel' (*shd wjȝ*), then 'admiral' (*ʿpr wjȝ jmy jrty*).[73] Some of the *mntj.w* were at the same time *jʿȝ.w*, a word generally translated as 'interpreters', and in whom 'head of foreign troops'[74] is discernible. It turns out that 'the *smntj.w* comprised a corporation comparable to those famous expeditionary troops that frequented Byblos, Sinai, and Punt, the routes of the two deserts and the Nubian riverbanks to bring back exotic products: their signatures are sometimes found on the rocks next to those of the "men with the money bag". The economic aim of the missions carried out by the latter in any case springs from the description "he who brings back the royal adornment from foreign lands" with which some of their directors honoured themselves, as did other expedition leaders. The phrase "royal adornment" seems in fact to have designated the luxury goods that served for the manufacture of golden jewellery and beauty products, substances whose use was originally or theoretically reserved to the sovereign alone'.[75]

The dedication of Senusret I (1971-1926 BC) at Tod tells us that a portion of the metals and semi-precious stones used to make the sacred vases of the temples had been procured by travelling *smntj.w*:[76]

*They presented sacred vessels (made of) silver, gold, copper... (decorated) with lapis, turquoise and all sorts of hard stones brought together. It was more abundant and more precious than everything that had been seen in this land previously, being the contribution of foreign peoples and smntj.w who travel from land to land.*

This testimony raises the question of whether the *smntj.w* were not specialised in the importation of precious minerals. Depictions from the New Kingdom show that money bags (*ʿrf*) of the same type as that of the *smntj* were used to transport and conserve the gold yielded by the tribute from Nubia, Sudan, and Punt, or brought from the mines in the eastern desert'.[77]

At once prospectors, miners and escorts, enjoying an elevated status and resources,[78] the *smntj.w* took part in huge military and economic operations in the Old Kingdom.[79] Their role explains their presence in the text relative to the expedition to the land of Punt under the reign of queen Hatshepsut (1498-1493 BC). Just like the

*wpwty.w* they were thus involved in the organisation of military, mining and commercial voyages.[80]

The texts concerning certain expeditions to Punt have much to say about the function of a certain category of persons who were entrusted with prospecting, exploration, and making contact with the local populations so as to establish relations of exchange. Thus, after the account of a mission sent to Sinai in year 36 of Amenhotep III (1386-1349 BC), the scribe of the expedition, a certain May, set down a few phrases to commemorate his personal exploits:[81]

*I have followed my master into this land ( = Sinai) and I have seized the occasion (?) when he gave me the order (?). I left by the shores of* Wadj Wer *to announce the marvels of Punt (sr bjȝy.t n Pwn.t) and to receive the sweet-smelling gum brought by the princes with their ships-of-eight (?), the tributes from lands that were unknown. And then I returned after having crossed the land of that goddess and I directed the working of the turquoise.*

For J. Yoyotte, the expression 'the marvels of Punt' (*sr bjȝy.t n Pwn.t*) used to define the aim of the journey there and back accomplished by many along the Red Sea between Sinai and the mysterious land of Punt is certainly the origin of the epithet *sr-bjȝ*

72  J. Yoyotte, *op. cit.*, p. 48; E. Edel, *ZÄS* 97, pp. 55, 57.
73  J. Sainte Fare Garnot, *Tell Edfu*, 1937, p. 50, pl. 14, 2. On the title *ʿpr wjȝ jmy jrty*, admiral, see M. Valloggia, *BIFAO* 85, 1985, p. 262-263; *id.*, in F. Geus, F. Thill (ed.), *Mélanges offerts à J. Vercoutter*, 1985, pp. 355-364; L. Pantalacci, *BIFAO* 85, 1985, nº 9. cf. *supra*, p. 147 et seq.
74  See D. Camus, *CRIPEL* 12, 1990, pp. 13-15; B. Bell, *Interpreters and egyptianized Nubians*, 1976; Z. Zaba, *The rock inscriptions of Lower Nubia*, 1974, 142 pp. 155-156; A. Roccati, *La littérature historique*, LAPO 11, 1982, 200-207; E. Edel, *ZÄS* 97, 1971, pp. 53-59.
75  J. Yoyotte, *op. cit.*, pp. 48-49.
76  Translation of J. Yoyotte, *op. cit.*, p. 49.
77  The contributions of the nomes and those of the vassals of Asia were presented in the form of rings or ingots.
78  See the references given by J. Yoyotte, *op. cit.*, p. 52.
79  Under the 4th Dynasty, they participated in the vast operations that ransomed and depopulated Lower Nubia: J. Lopez, *op. cit.*, nº 25-26, pl. 15, 1-2 = *RdÉ* 19, pp. 52-53, fig. 4-5.
80  On this difficult problem of war and commerce, see *Seafaring in Ancient Egypt*, vol. 2.
81  *Sinai* 211: *jw šms~n=j nb=j hr hȝs.t tn dr~n=j sp rd=f m hr=j pr~n=j hr gs.wy wȝd wr r sr bjȝy.t n(y.t) Pwn.t r šsp tȝ qmy.t n s.t jn(w) m wr.w m hnmwty.w m bȝkt hȝs.wt nn rh rmt js.t wj jj=k(w) gr.t hnd~n=j hȝs.t ntr tn hrp~n=j kȝ.wt n(y.w)t mfk.t.* PM VII, 350; *Urk.* IV, 14; A. Gardiner, E. Peet, J. Cerny, *The Inscriptions of Sinai*, I, 1952, pl. 66; Leed, *JEA* 8, p. 3; T. Säve-Söderbergh, *The Navy*, 1946, p. 25; J. Yoyotte, *RdÉ* 9, 1952, pp. 133-134.

in the Ptolemaic texts that are found for example in this text from the temple of Edfu:[82]

> *I come to you, sr-bj₃ of Punt, good medjai of the eastern desert,*
> *I bring you gathered aromatic fragrances, prepared with sweet-smelling substances to make up the divine substance of your ka.*

Without dwelling particularly on the sense of the word *sr*, and basing our views on the rest of the narrative, it may be asked whether the Sinai inscription does not allude to this type of mission, which consisted of reaching the Red Sea shores to take delivery of the commodities brought by the inhabitants of Punt.[83] Finally, the meaning of 'marvels of Punt' is not very different from that of the expressions 'bring back the marvels of Punt' (*jn bj₃.w n Pwn.t*) or 'to receive the marvels of Punt' (*šsp bj₃.w n Pwn.t*) attested by other texts. The man who 'revealed (to the king) the marvels of Punt' seems to have been none other than an explorer entrusted with the task of reconnoitring the economic resources of distant lands.

All of these designations as a whole correspond to what is represented in the scenes where Puntites are encountered: armed men setting off on an expedition, with a caravan of asses, hunters and dogs. Indeed, two scenes, the one engraved, the other painted, in two tombs from the 18th Dynasty (1570-1293 BC), show the Egyptians and the Puntites meeting in a place difficult to identify.[84] The fact that the Egyptians are bearing arms and led by an officer on a chariot with a team of horses, while the troop uses dogs in one case, and asses as beasts of burden in the other, indicates that this is one of those units specialised in expeditions to the deserts bordering Egypt or more distant lands. In both cases, the Puntites are bringing many products that they lay down before the Egyptians. In any case, nothing here recalls the passage and the environment of the scenes of Hatshepsut. This time it is the Egyptians who welcome the Puntites. One of the depictions shows the latter on fragile boats, rafts or coracles (this cannot be certain, as the drawing is not precise enough).[85] Their rigging is very simple; a triangular sail and a sheet of sail to manoeuvre it with; a single oar that could be used to steer with.[86] On one of the registers, the Puntites are represented arriving, and on the other, leaving. In the text accompanying the name of the place to which the Egyptians are returning is in great part destroyed and its restoration remains, unfortunately, hypothetical.

So the evidence points to corps of military or paramilitary professionals who sometimes took part in the organisation of commercial expeditions. If the 'messengers' (*wpwty.w*) are once again examined it becomes apparent that they were recruited from among the soldiery when they were dependent on the relay post or had the task of making contact with the exterior. However, the 'royal

*Scale* 2:13

82    *Edfu* II, 202, 13-14 = *Edfu* XII, pl. 390, 6. Text cited by; J. Yoyotte, *RdÉ* 9, 1952, p. 134.

83    T. Säve-Söderbergh, *op. cit.*, pp. 22-25.

84    Reproduced by K. A. Kitchen, in T. Shaw, *et al.* (ed.), *The Archaeology of Africa*, 1993, pp. 587-608; L. Bradbury, *JARCE* XXXIII, 1996, pp. 40, 57.

85    K. A. Kitchen, in T. Shaw, *et al.* (ed.), *The Archaeology of Africa*, 1993, p. 599, fig. 35.7; L. Bradbury, *JARCE* XXXIII, 1996, p. 40 fig. 2. For what remains from the texts that accompany these scenes, see *Urk.* IV, 1472-1473.

86    Such rafts were frequently used in the Red Sea, both on the African and Arabian sides: L. Bradbury, *op. cit.*, pp. 43-44; L. Casson, *The Periplus Maris Erythaei*, 1989, pp. 117-118. They were used for commerce as well as for piracy, as classical authors from the 3rd century BC tell us: J.-F. Salles, in D. Valbelle, C. Bonnet (ed.), *Le Sinai*, 1998, pp. 97-98.

Reception and transporting of products from Punt, Theban Tomb 189, New Kingdom 18th Dynasty, c. 1450 BC. Drawing after N. de G. Davis, *JEA XXVI*, 1940, pl. xxv; T. Säve-Söderbergh, *The Navy of the Eighteenth Egyptian Dynasty*, 1946, fig. 5, p. 25. © The Egypt Exploration Society

Reception of an expedition from Punt,, Theban Tomb 143, New Kingdom, 18th Dynasty, c. 1450 BC. Drawing after T. Säve-Söderbergh, *The Navy of the Eighteenth Egyptian Dynasty*, 1946, p. 24, fig. 6.

messengers' (*wpwty.w n(y)-sw(.t)*) were also chosen from the corps of functionaries, when economic and/or diplomatic factors required. It is within this perspective that the particular case of the plenipotentiary Wenamun should be examined.

### III.3. Wenamun: 'messenger, ambassador' and 'keeper of the porch of the temple of Amun'

Entrusted with the task of going to fetch wood from Byblos so as to rebuild the great river barque of Amun, Wenamun leaves Upper Egypt, and goes first to Tanis, the new capital of Lower Egypt, whence he is sent on a ship to the Levant. During a stopover in the port of Dor, Wenamun is robbed of some of the property that had been given him for safekeeping by one of the crew members. Arriving finally in Byblos, amid many vicissitudes, he strikes up commercial negotiations that conclude in a sale. Setting off again with his load, he is cast ashore by a storm on the coasts of Alasia (Cyprus). The text breaks off just as Wenamun is bargaining with the authorities of Alasia so as not to fall victim to the right of shipwreck.[87]

So the most important aspect of the text concerning Wenamun's expedition has to do with the practice of international commerce. This enables us to understand in part the administrative, institutional, and juridical status of Wenamun who is travelling to engage in trade (*jrj šwt*).[88]

In the very first line of the report, acquaintance is made with the protagonist of the story who is 'Wenamun, keeper of the porch of the temple of Amun, master of the thrones of the two lands' (*Wn-Jmn smsm-ḥȝj(.t) n pr Jmn nb-ns.wt-tȝ.wj*). His name appears a second time, in this case accompanied by an apposition that reflects his function in the text: 'Wenamun, his (= Amun's) human ambassador' (*Wn-Jmn pȝj=f jwpwtj rmṯ*).[89] So he is ambassador of the god Amun whose title confers on him a particular status. He is enjoined to leave Byblos by the Giblite dynast, and is getting ready to return to Egypt, when Amun, through the intermediary of an ecstatic, sways the prince's resolution:[90]

*Bring the god on high, bring the messenger responsible for him; it is Amun who has sent him, it is he who made him come.*

87  For a bibliography on *The Report of Wenamun*, see p. 1.

88  W. F. Albright, in G. Mylonas (ed.), *Studies presented to D.M. Robinson*, 1951, p. 223; H. Goedicke, *The Report of Wenamun*, 1975 (with bibliography pp. 10-11); G. Bunnens, *Revista di Studi Fenici* 6, 1978, pp. 1-16; M. Green, *ZÄS* 106, 1979, pp. 116-120; J. Osing, *Nubia et Oriens Christianus*, 1988, pp. 37-39; S. N. Morschauer, *SAK* 18, 1991, pp. 317-330; M. Liverani, *Prestige und Interest*, 1990, pp. 247-254; A. Egberts, *JEA* 77, 1991, pp. 57-67, J. Winand, *GM* 139, 1994, pp. 95-108; A. Scheepers, in E. Lipinski (ed.), *Phoenicia and the Bible*, OLA 44, 1994, 1991, pp. 17-83; *id.*, in *Amosiadès, Mélanges offerts au Professeur C. Vandersleyen*, 1992, pp. 355-363; C. Eyre, in J. Assmann, E. Blumenthal, *Literatur und Politik*, BiÉtud 127, 1999; J. Pirenne, *Bulletin de la classe des lettres et des sciences morales et politiques de l'Académie royale de Belgique*, 5th series, 41, 1955, pp. 604-609; *id.*, *Histoire de la civilisation de l'Égypte ancienne*, 1962, p. 502-505; *id.*, in *Les grandes escales*, I, *Recueil Jean Bodin* XXXII, 1974, pp. 43-50; R. de Spens, in N. Grimal, B. Menu (ed.), *Le commerce*, BiÉtud 121, 1998, pp. 105-126.

89  As ambassador in the court of Amun, he is mentioned again in lines 1, 39-40 and 2, 73. On the term *ji/wpw.tj*, cf. *supra*.

90  *Wenamun*, 1, 39-40

Once the negotiations are over, the Giblite prince presses Wenamun to leave his country in these terms:[91]

> *In truth, I did not do to you what was done to the messengers of Khaemwaset, when they spent seventeen years in this country; they died where they were [...]. (Wenamun's reply:) As for Khaemwaset, they are men whom he had sent to you as messengers, and he too was a man. You do not have (today, in your presence) one of his messengers, and yet you say "Go and see your colleagues". Why should you not rather rejoice and make a stele for yourself, on which you would say "Amunrasonther sent me (the statue of) Amun-of-the-Way (as) his messenger, life, health, strength, with Wenamun (as) his human messenger, to find wood for the great and magnificent barque of Amunrasonther". [...] "If some day in the future, there comes from the land of Egypt a messenger who knows the writing and reads your name on this stele, (you will receve a libation in Amenti like the gods who dwell there)".*

Subsequently the Prince of Byblos takes up the defence of Wenamun when he is threatened by the grim designs of the Sakal:[92]

> *He says to them: "I cannot stop the messenger of Amun in my country".*

Finally managing to return to Cyprus, Wenamun encounters the hostility of the islanders; then he resorts to the help of the conciliatory lady sovereign of the island:[93]

> *Will you permit them to receive me only to kill me, I who am the messenger of Amun?*

So Wenamun is attached to the temple of Amun in Karnak. It can be deduced from the text that he was in the service of the temple; Herihor, the great priest of Amun at Karnak, is presented as his master *(p3j=j nb)*.[94] When, through the intermediary of an oracle (?) Amun gave Herihor the order to send Wenamun, the latter was entrusted with the mission of setting off with the statue of the Amun-of-the-Way with the aim of fetching wood from Byblos to build a new barque for Amun or repair the old one (1, 2-3). So he intervened as the ambassador and the delegate of Amun, and he would go on to negotiate with Sakarbaal over the cargo of wood.

He meets with every kind of difficulty on his way: the theft of his money at Dor, the negative attitude of Sakarbaal when he arrives at Byblos, embarrassing questions on the occasion of his first visit to the prince. Wenamun persists, however, and thanks to his volubility,

he expresses all sorts of consideration and comes out with all kinds of attractive promises to incite Sakarbaal to act:[95] thus his reminder of the task of Sakarbaal's ancestors, who set an example with their noble lifestyle, and the statement that everything belongs to Amun, Lebanon included; the 'spiritual' gifts of Amun, together with a warning; the material gifts of Smendes and Tanetamun.[96]

Even after the delivery of his wood, he does his best to keep Sakarbaal in a good mood; note for example the proposition of the stele which appeals to the ambition of Sakarbaal, or the foreseeable reply of Herihor.[97] While the arrival of the *Sakal* makes him somewhat melancholy, he gathers his strength at Alasia and by enchantment he again demonstrates his eloquence in front of Hatiba, the princess of the land: for example, he glorifies the justice in this land and warns her of the reprisals that will follow his murder or that of the Giblite crew.[98] In addition, as an ambassador, he also seems to be *au fait* with the juridical rules or customs that may help him out in case of need, although his knowledge does not always seem to be up to date.[99]

The title *smsm-h3j(.t)*, borne by Wenamun, means 'the keeper of the porch'[100] and designates a functionary of the palace or temple, since Wenamun belongs to the temple of Amun.[101] The title is well attested for the Old and Middle Kingdoms, when those persons were also attached to the palace, while it appears less frequently in the New Kingdom and then designates persons who are mainly in the service of the temple.[102]

A. H. Gardiner suggests that they perhaps fulfilled the same role at the entrance to the palace as the *(j)m(j)-r(3)* did within it, in the reception halls: they led in the nobles of Egypt, reported on events in the country, and gave instructions to courtiers and others.[103] Nothing, however, proves the veracity of these hypotheses. Still, it is easy to agree with D. Meeks when he proposes that the 'keepers of the porch' exercised a function as doorkeepers both in the palace and

---

91  *Wenamun*, 2, 51-56; 58-59.
92  *Wenamun*, 2, 73.
93  *Wenamun*, 2, 81.
94  *Wenamun*, 1, 15.
95  H. Goedicke, *The Report of Wenamun*, 1975, p. 9.
96  *Wenamun*, 2, 4-5; 2, 31-32; 2, 23-24; 2, 32-34; 2, 35-36.
97  *Wenamun*, 2, 55; 2, 60-62.
98  *Wenamun*, 2, 75-83.
99  On the juridicial aspect of *The Report of Wenamun*, and the knowledge of customs that it shows, *Seafaring in Ancient Egypt*, vol. 2.
100  G. Lefebvre, *Romans et contes*, 1949, p. 208.
101  *Wb* II, 476, 8-9.
102  W. Helck, *Zur Verwaltung des Mittleren und Neuen Reiches*, PÄ 3, 1958, p. 280.
103  A. H. Gardiner, *ZÄS* 60, 1925, p. 64.

*Bring the god on high, bring the messenger responsible for him; it is Amun who has sent him, it is he who made him come.*

*In truth, I did not do to you what was done to the messengers of Khaemwaset, when they spent seventeen years in this country; they died where they were […]. (Wenamun's reply:) As for Khaemwaset, they are men whom he had sent to you as messengers, and he too was a man. You do not have (today, in your presence) one of his messengers, and yet you say "Go and see your colleagues". Why should you not rather rejoice and make a stele for yourself, on which you would say "Amunrasonther sent me (the statue of) Amun-of-the-Way (as) his messenger, life, health, strength, with Wenamun (as) his human messenger, to find wood for the great and magnificent barque of Amunrasonther". […] "If some day in the future, there comes from the land of Egypt a messenger who knows the writing and reads your name on this stele, (you will receve a libation in Amenti like the gods who dwell there)".*

*He says to them: "I cannot stop the messenger of Amun in my country".*

*Will you permit them to receive me only to kill me, I who am the messenger of Amun?*

in the temple, just as they belonged to the service of the guard. Their titles suggest that the control of this service also fell to them and conferred on them all sorts of responsibilities, such as the overseeing of the corn granaries and the measuring of corn. In short, whenever any activity occurred near the gates of the temples, they must have had responsibilities to fulfil there – surveillance, judicial functions, relations with traders, control of the entry of offerings and other revenues.[104] The last occupations quoted imply that they probably also fulfilled a sort of administrative function when they were receiving persons or goods.[105]

In the light of the preceding explanations, it may be understood why Wenamun was assigned such an important mission: as 'keeper of the porch', he was regularly in contact with all sorts of people, negotiated with merchants, and was familiar with the development of affairs in the administration of the domain of Amun.[106] All this enabled him to bring his trip abroad to a successful conclusion.

A passage from the biography of the vizir Rekhmira does however provide information on the functions of the 'keeper of the porch':[107]

*When I reached the door of the palace, the courtiers bowed their backs. I found the keeper of the porch who opened the way to me…*

The keeper of the porch played for Rekhmira the role of an usher. This ascription may have a much more direct link than it would seem with the expedition of Wenamun.[108] In the *Attributions of the Vizir*, the ushers are 'messengers' (*wpty.w*):[109]

*Concerning all that enters and all that leaves the zone of the Residence: on entering and leaving, it is a messenger (of the vizir) who makes you enter and leave…*

It is as a 'messenger of Amun' (*wpwty n Jmn*) that Wenamun accomplished his mission.[110] The title 'keeper of the porch' might thus point to a dignity within the category of 'messengers'. On this hypothesis, the keeper of the porch could be the messenger to whom falls the honour of instructing important personages. As seen above, the 'messengers', apart from their minor role as beadles, were specifically used as couriers. However, Wenamun, like all other 'messengers' of high rank, did not merely carry letters, but also had to negotiate a transaction. So he really was an extraordinary ambassador of the domain of Amun. His direct superior was none other than the high priest of Amun, Herihor, with considerable administrative and political powers, but he could not manage without the administration of Lower Egypt and had to resort to the mediation of Smendes and Tentamun to gain access to Mediterranean commerce.

When Wenamun reached Tanis where Smendes and Tentamun were, he gave them the letters from Amun (*wḥ³*). These constituted the indispensable diplomatic instrument to show that the mission was of public interest and thus to encourage them to cooperate:[111] Smendes and Tentumon did what Amun said, not what the high priest said. They thus recognised the legitimacy of Wenamun's mission, without thereby placing themselves under the authority of Herihor. On the contrary, Wenamun, having left the domain of Amun, was now dependent on the administration of Tanis.[112] While

Wenamun was at Byblos, he remained under their responsibility and received bounty from them.[113] Thus, without losing his administrative status as a messenger of Amun, Wenamun was mandated by the whole of Egypt, because of the public interest of his mission.

Finally *The Report of Wenamun* provides information on the status of a foreigner and that of the functionary involved on a mission, on the customs relating to individual travel, and on international relations. Thus in the great and cosmopolitan city of Byblos, the authorities were proud and scrupulous. Wenamun, however much he belonged to a great power, learned to his cost that he too had to respect international customs when it came to embassies. The prince was furious that Wenamun did not present him with any accreditation.[114] Nonetheless, as an ambassador and a messenger, Wenamun was the object of a particular interest and care on the part of the authorities of the cities in which he stayed.[115]

104  D. Meeks, in E. Lipinski (ed.), *State and Temple economy*, II, OLA 6, 1979, pp. 605-687 (see p. 648, n⁰ 195). As far as the function of the doorkeeper is concerned, see the graffito of a *smsm-h³j(.t)* on the 8ᵗʰ pylon of the temple of Amun at Karnak (G. Lefebvre, *Inscriptions concernant les grands prêtres d'Amon Romê-Roy et Amenhotep*, 1929, p. 40, n⁰ 18).

105  G. Lefebvre, *Romans et contes*, 1949, p. 208, n⁰ 3. We are unable to agree with H. Goedicke *The Report of Wenamun*, 1975, pp. 18-19 when he states that *h³j(.t)* means 'administrative chambers', situated just outside the king's private rooms, even though the *h³j(.t)* could potentially fulfil such functions in a restricted sense: A. Scheepers, in E. Lipinski (ed.), *Phoenicia and the Bible, Studia Phoenicia* XI, 1991, pp. 31-32.

106  H. Goedicke, *op. cit.*, p. 19; the author considers *smsm-h³j(.t)* to be a rank rather than a real function and translates it as 'senior administrator'.

107  N. de G. Davies, *The Tomb of Rekh-mi-re*, 1943, pl. xi, 5-6 (= *Urk.* IV, 1073, 3-6).

108  R. de Spens, in N. Grimal, B. Menu (ed.), *Le commerce*, BiÉtud 121, 1998, p. 106.

109  N. de G. Davies, *The Tomb of Rekh-mi-re*, 1943, pl. xxvi, 4. cf. G. P. F. Van den Boorn, *The Duties of the Vizir*, 1988, pp. 42-53.

110  On messengers in Egypt and the Near East, M. Valloggia, *Recherche sur les « Messagers » (wpwtyw)*, 1976; see also the review of this work by B. Menu, *Revue de l'historique du droit français et étranger* 55, 1977, p. 413 *et seq.*; M. Abdul-Kader Mohammad, *ASAE* LVI, 1959, pp. 119-122) and in the Near East; see also the references quoted by G. Bunnens, *Revista di Studi Fenici* 6, 1978, p. 3, n⁰ 14.

111  Wenamun, 1, 4-6.

112  Wenamun, 1, 6-7.

113  Wenamun, 2, 41-42.

114  Wenamun, 1, 51-52.

115  Wenamun, 1, 9-10.

## IV. 'Market women'[1] and neighbourhood trade

It is necessary to recognise that up until now, the world of the professionals of commercial travel might appear just a little phallocratic. Is it possible to discern a masculine and elitist domination at work here? Such a recognition leads us to investigate the role of women in commercial transactions and travels. After all, Herodotus affirmed:[2]

> *In general, the Egyptians have customs and laws contrary to those of the rest of the world. Among them, women go to the market and carry out commerce, the men stay at home and weave.*

This passage, that was certainly written with a rhetorical aim in mind, is partly erroneous, since it still allows us to imagine that women played an institutional, juridical or social role in the economy, or more specifically in commercial exchanges.

The feminine production of goods destined to be sold or exchanged on a market played a structural role in local commerce. In addition, the activity of women in the market place represented an extension of feminine activity within the household and the family. In this context this is a social and economic contribution and participation that gives the family an economic structure.[3] Women seem to have played a far from negligible role in neighbourhood commercial transactions and they participated in exchanges involving traders or merchandise that had been transported by sea and landed on the banks of the Nile.

So it is necessary to examine the economic role of the market itself, the nature of the transactions that took place there, and the role played by women in this respect. This raises the question of a contrast between 'professional' commerce, which was domanial, controlled by the temple officials or those of the conceded domain, and performed across the whole territory by specialised agents (merchants and boatmen) involving great quantities of specific products, and a neighbourhood commerce that concerned individual exchanges and in which, as demonstrated below, women were significantly involved. The first was often distinguished by major investment and accumulation of capital, while the second – small-scale trade, often opportunistic – was defined by buying, selling and the different mechanisms of exchange that were fully part of a subsistence economy[4]

It first seems necessary to explain the role of women in the market place, and the exact nature of their activity; but this turns out to be a perilous procedure since it is difficult to perceive the activity of women, and historical and archaeological evidence of local markets is rare. However, quite a lot is known of the Deir el-Medina community in the Ramesside period. The documentation mentions transactions of different goods and products occurring between the inhabitants: funerary and construction equipment, animals (asses and oxen) and sometimes luxury objects; but the site of this trade remains problematic. In spite of the fact that the local market and the booths were not a great source of inspiration for tomb decoration, a few isolated scenes and rare funerary depictions furnish proof of the existence and nature of a local commerce of goods of everyday consumption,[5] and concern the circulation of merchandise.

The scene of the tomb of the two brothers Nankh-khnum and Khnumhotep at Saqqara,[6] royal manicurists of a king of the 5th Dynasty (2498-2345 BC), shows ships sailing on the Western Canal.[7]

Above, probably on the banks of this canal, certainly near Memphis, a series of registers depicting commercial activities is discernible. If, as a whole, the merchandise is not easy to identify, the same foodstuffs may be observed all the same, vegetables, fruits and fish (fresh and dried), clothes, and small pieces of pottery (?). Cereal grain and copper are used in exchanges. Two women appear among the traders: one of them seems to be carrying small pots, the other is pouring out a liquid – beer, perhaps. Furthermore, among the customers, there is a woman, carrying a small boy, buying sycamore figs.

The interest and the difficulty of these scenes resides in the nature and status of those who were trading – merchants, artisans who had come to sell their products, and especially women. Were artisans specialised in trading, 'free' markets in which men or women could sell their products in a completely 'free' manner? It is known that artisans and artisanal production depended on institutional structures (temples, king, senior functionaries). Does this idea *per se* exclude any idea of a private market? It is very difficult to answer this question, but certain depictions from the New Kingdom (1570-1070 BC) allow us to sketch out the beginnings of an answer. In the tomb of Ipuy at Deir el-Medina, a scene represents men on barges in the middle of trading with women on the shore.[8] The men are bearing sacks of cereals and emptying them into the baskets of the women.[9] Women are holding cobs of bread (?), fish and fruits (?); one of them is sitting in front of a small hut in which there are jars of beer and wine on a jar-shelf. This would seem to be food and drink for the boatmen, paid for in grain by the latter. Log books contain references to transactions in small quantities of provisions and victuals embarked.[10] This food was, it seems, prepared by the women on the quaysides.[11]

One of the scenes from the tomb of Kenamun shows a Syro-Palestinian expedition landing at a quay with several shops.[12] In one of them, a woman is spreading out clothes, sandals and other objects of uncertain identity. The men are holding scales with metal (?) weights. In this case, however, they are trading with foreigners.[13]

1   The term is borrowed from C. J. Eyre, in N. Grimal, B. Menu (ed.), *Le commerce*, BiÉtud 121, 1998, pp. 173-191. This article constitutes the basis for our views on the role of women in transactions and commercial travel.

2   Herodotus, II, 35: translated by A. Barguet, *Hérodote*, 1985, p. 176; cf. A. B. Lloyd, *Herodotus Book II, Introduction*, EPRO 43, 1975, pp. 141-142, pp. 151-152; *Commentary*, 1976, pp. 147-148.

3   C. J. Eyre, op. cit., p. 173. See too H. L. Moore, *Feminism and Anthropology*, 1988; J. Tucker, *Women in Nineteenth-Century Egypt*, 1985; D. Sweeney, JEA 80, 1994, pp. 208-212.

4   cf. J. J. Janssen, *Commodity Prices*, 1975, pp. 539-550, pp. 556-558; B. J. Kemp, JEA 65, 1979, pp. 184-187; B. J. Kemp, *Ancient Egypt*, 1989, pp. 248-260.

5   H. Altenmüller, in *LÄ* III, s.v. 'Market', cols. 1191-1194; S. I. Hodjash and O. D. Berlev, AltorForsch 7, 1980, pp. 31-49; C. J. Eyre, in M A. Powell (ed.), *Labor in the Ancient Near East*, 1987, pp. 34-35; R. Müller-Wollermann, JESHO 28, 1985, pp. 121-168; M. Römer, SAK 19, 1992, pp. 257-284. C. J. Eyre, op. cit., p. 174.

6   Ahmed M. Moussa, H. Altenmüller, *Das Grab des Nianchchnum und Chnumhotep*, ArchVer 21, 1977, Abb. 10, Tafel 24, pp. 79-85.

7   C. J. Eyre, op. cit., p. 175 and fig. 1, p. 190.

8   N. de G. Davies, *Two Ramesside Tombs at Thebes*, 1927, pls xxx and xxxiv.

9   C. J. Eyre, op. cit., p. 176 and fig. 2, p. 176. On the problem of the cereal trade: C. J. Eyre, in A. Bowman, E. Rogan (ed.), *Agriculture in Egypt: from Pharaonic to modern times*.

10   cf. P. Turin Taxation 3, 16; 4, 3; 4, 5 = RAD 39, 16-40, 11; A. H. Gardiner, JEA 27, 1941, pp. 30-32; J. J. Janssen, BSEG 18, 1994, pp. 41-47.

11   F. de Cenival, *Cautionnements démotiques du début de l'époque ptolémaique*, 1973, pp. 16-17 (P. Lille 6); pp. 34-39 (P. Lille 41); pp. 54-55 (P. Lille 52). Also see J. J. Janssen, *Commodity Prices*, 1975, pp. 346-348.

12   N. de G. Davies and R. O. Faulkner, JEA 33, 1947, pp. 40-46.

13   See also the tomb of Khaemhat (TT 57; LD III, 76 = W. Wreszinski, *Atlas zur altaegyptische Kulturgeschichte*, I, 1923, 199-200) in which a similar scene is depicted of commercial activity on a quay, but seems to include only men as traders.

It may be noted and justifiably emphasised anew the importance of the quay as a market place. The term *mry.t*, 'river bank', is used to designate the market or commercial activity in general.[14] It reflects the fact that the river was the commercial route *par excellence*, testifies to the role of navigation in commerce, indicates the role of boatmen and navigators as customers and merchants, and reveals the importance of fish as merchandise[15]

In addition, women seem to play a determining role in the making and exchange of clothes and garments and thereby in the household economy.[16] In transactions, clothes have an important function, perhaps, indeed, more important than metal.[17] The existence of 'institutional' workshops in which there worked both men and women[18] shows that certain weaving or spinning techniques could have been 'industrialised' or 'centralised'; but it is probable that there was a network of independent or semi-independent producers, like the household of Hekanakht, or a system of working at home, with the raw materials being distributed for production by the household.[19]

Certain scholars believe that these women retailed clothes and honey, probably for the temples.[20] Perhaps they were themselves producers or local agents of the home workers, spinning, weaving, and practising beekeeping at home?[21]

Local transactions frequently involved clothes amid the merchandise, used as a means of payment.[22] In addition, there is an interesting contrast between the Brooklyn Papyrus, which seems to mention merchandise such as clothes and honey – local products – in Upper Egypt, and the Ship's Log of Turin,[23] which seems to attest to the activity of a ship (or a fleet of ships) of the temple of Amun at Karnak, selling clothes from Upper Egypt at Heliopolis and Memphis in exchange for products from the Delta and the marches of Egypt.[24] Very provisionally, it may be wondered whether these two texts did not comprise part of the commercial activities of an 'intermediary', a real commerce of wholesale and distribution and not the retail sale of neighbourhood trade, in short the sector of trade in close association, in the New Kingdom, with the temples. There is an indication that the ships' captains and the *šwty.w*-traders sailed on the Nile to engage in buying and selling, but this commercial navigation seems to have been highly structured; while local products and the goods that issued from domestic artisanal work could be sold within the system of neighbourhood trade, their distribution was carried out by the intermediary of agents.[25]

Should it be concluded from this that the commercial activity of women was limited by travel and the need to move from place to place, and gain access to places further away than local markets and immediate social and family circles? Be that as it may, the role of women on the level of local transactions and neighbourhood trade, and more widely in the economic system of Ancient Egypt, was far from negligible.[26]

25   C. J. Eyre, *op. cit.*, p. 183.

26   *Id.*, p. 189. See also D. C. Snell, *JESHO 34*, 1991, pp. 129-141; D. A. Warburton, *State and Economy*, 1997.

14   J. Cerny, *A community of Workmen at Thebes*, 1973, pp. 93-97; J. J. Janssen, *De Markt op de Oever*, 1980; C. J. Eyre, *CdÉ 67*, 1992, pp. 277-281, R. Ventura, *Living in the City of the Dead*, OBO 69, 1986; A. Erman, H. Ranke, *Aegypten und aegyptisches Leben im Altertum*, 1923, pp. 587-591. See p. 88.

15   See E. W. Castle, *JESHO 35*, 1992, pp. 239-277; R. Müller-Wollermann, *JESHO 28*, 1985, pp. 140-145. C. J. Eyre, N. Grimal, B. Menu (ed.), *le commerce*, BiÉtud 121, 1998, p. 177.

16   N. de G. Davies, *Metropolitan Museum Studies I*, 2, 1928-1929, pp. 232-240; F. Doyen, in *Seventh International Congress of Egyptologists, Abstracts*, 1995, pp. 52-53.

17   C. J. Eyre, *op. cit.*, p. 180; P. Posener-Kriêger, in M. Görg, E. Push (ed.), *Festschrift E. Edel*, 1979, pp. 318-331; B. Menu, in *Mélanges offerts à J. Vercoutter*, 1985, pp.249-262.

18   For clothes in general, E. D'Amicone, in *LÄ VI*, s.v. 'Stoffe und Webarten', cols. 57-63; W. Barta, in *LÄ IV*, s.v. 'Opferliste', col. 587; R. Hall, *Egyptian Textiles*, 1986, chap. 3; and bibliography given by C. J. Eyre, *op. cit.*, p. 180, no 37.

19   C. J. Eyre, *op. cit.*, p. 181.

20   See E. W. Castle, *JESHO 35*, 1992, p. 251.

21   Information on beekeeping and the production of honey is sparse and concerns mainly the temples, but the maintenance and conservancy of the hives could be considered a domestic activity; the transaction in P. Cairo 65739 includes a great jar of honey of considerable value (1 *jʿr-mn.t* de 1 *ḥqȝ.t* de 5 *qd.t* of silver), acquired by *Jry-nfr*, ouab-priest. In general honey was considered as a monopoly of the temples, but did not exclude the production outside these institutions. See : J. Leclant, in *LÄ I*, s.v. 'Biene', col. 786-789; W. Helck, in *LÄ III*, s.v. 'Imker', col. 151; J. J. Janssen, *Commodity Prices*, 1975, pp. 352-353; P. Posener-Kriêger, *JEA 64*, 1978, p. 86, no (g); E. V. Pischilova, *GM 139*, 1994, pp. 74-77; H. Chouliara-Raïos, *L'abeille et le miel en Égypte d'après les papyrus grecs*, 1989; A. Singer, *Palestinian Peasants and Ottoman Officials*, 1994, pp. 49, 51.

22   C. J. Eyre, *op. cit.*, p. 183.

23   J. J. Janssen, *Two Ancient Egyptian Ships' Logs*, 1961, particularly pp. 98-104. For a general commentary on the ships involved in this commerce: J. J. Janssen, *Commodity Prices*, 1975, pp. 161-164.

24   Use of the term *šmȝ* for linen leaves no doubt as to the origin of this product.

# Chapter III: Religion and Beliefs

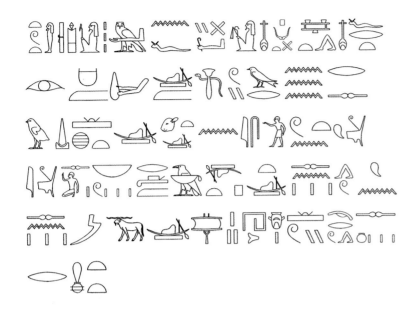

*You are the pillar god, the chief of the two pillars,*
*The good protector of those who travel the right way;*
*He who pilots (ships) on Wadj Wer, so as to preserve those who*
*sail to the north and to the south;*
*Let a man call on him, if he fears to see his ship capsize, and he*
*comes to him, in the form of a serene breeze, so that he will reach*
*the port.*
(Hymn to Khnum, *Esna* III, 378, 20-21)[1]

## I. Superstitions, beliefs and religion

Although sources have allowed us to sketch a picture, however approximate, of the status and social environment of the crews of commercial vessels, it remains difficult to apprehend their mental universe. Their preoccupation with life after death has been touched upon above, but how did they experience everyday life? What were their beliefs and their spiritual protectors during their trips? How could a man with an Egyptian mentality react to the problems that the need to travel imposed on him?[2]

Because the world of the professional maritime merchants seems to have formed a society apart, with its own statutes, its own juridical customs and organisation, there is a justification in asking about its religion and its beliefs – especially as the sailor was, at least according to the tradition, both the most immoral of men and the most religious. This religiosity may be explained by the dangers he had constantly to face, dangers for which he often had no recourse other than a god or goddess. This is why he was also said to be the most superstitious of men. Any attempt to gain access to the mental world of professional travellers leads us inevitably to envisage this problem in terms of the dichotomy between popular beliefs and official religion. In other terms, did a commercial expedition depend on any religious organisation? Yes, if it is accepted how important Amun was — as instigator — in the expedition to the land of Punt under the reign of Queen Hatshepsut (1498-1483 BC), or for the voyage of Wenamun. The beneficiaries of these journeys were the gods. In one case, it was the incense traded on the shores of the Red Sea that was burned in

the temples to satisfy the gods; in the other, it was the wood purchased at Byblos that made it possible for the divine barque to be built. More generally, the comings and goings on land and sea naturally fell under the aegis of specialised divine forces who could instigate or protect those voyages.[3] In tandem with the official documentation, it is difficult to apprehend the fears and hopes of 'our' travellers, since this is a maritime universe that is in its very nature irrational, a world made of poetry, of the superstitions and beliefs of sailors.

Among these superstitions there was one that concerned the fear of dying abroad and the happiness of benefiting from a funeral on Egyptian soil. The lamentations and the sorrow of Sinuhe are the very exemplar of the feelings of an Egyptian who was forced into exile:[4]

> *O god, whichever you may be, you who have predestined this*
> *flight, be merciful, bring me back to the court. Perhaps you will*
> *grant me to see again the place where my heart has never ceased*
> *to be. What could be more important for me than to be buried in*
> *Egypt, given that I was born there?*

The sailor's life was not always compatible with a happy old age. The numerous epitaphs of shipwrecked sailors from the *Palatine Anthology* remind us of the anxiety of sailors and the frequency of wrecks: "At sea, numerous are the journeys that lead to grief and tears".[5] The harshness of the sailor's life and the dangers of the sea are themes that are often dealt with. The old age and death of sailors are also referred to on the Graeco-Roman epitaphs of Egypt. Addressing the passer-by in a well-known convention of epigraphy, the dead man describes the circumstances surrounding his death and burial:[6]

> *My name is Menelaus, passer-by, that of my father is Doros. I was*
> *a sailor, but I was enjoying a happy old age when I departed for*
> *Hades. I was buried by the cherished hands of my children, and I*
> *gave thanks for this to the Sun, since I was granted his sweet*
> *marks of gratitude.*

*The Tale of the Shipwrecked Sailor* says the same thing, when the divine serpent of the island on which the hero of the tale was shipwrecked predicts a happy end to his (mis)adventures:[7]

1   *twt jwn ḥry jwn.w mnfy nfr wp wꜣ.t nfr.t jr ḥmw m wꜣḏ wr r swḏꜣ ḫt ḫnd njs.tw n=f jn s nb r tm kꜣ dp.t=sn jw=f n=sn m ṯꜣw ḥr-jb spr=sn r mjtt;* PM VI, 112, 17; S. Sauneron, *Les fêtes religieuses,* Esna V, 1962, p. 216. See also p. 163 § 8: 'Fear Him who is at the head of Nun (Khnum), you who are *Wadj Wer*, wind that remains [...], for it is he who is the good pilot of the man who has set him in his heart; all who exalt him reach the port safe and sound!' (*snḏ n ḫnt nnw ny nt(y) m wꜣḏ wr ṯꜣw wn r [...] ntf jrty m ḫn nfr n dj sw m jb=f spr sw ꜣ š=f nb 'ḏ wḏꜣ):* Esna III, 277, 23-24.
2   See S. Bickel in N. Grimal, B. Menu (ed.), *Le commerce, BiÉtud* 121, 1998, p. 169.
3   This was also the case for mining expeditions: see S. Aufrère, *Archéo-Nil* 7, 1997, pp. 116-121.
4   *Sinuhe,* B, 156-160; translation by G. Lefebvre, *Romans et contes,* 1949, p. 15. See also the letters addressed by the expatriates to their original cities, Thebes or Memphis: J. Assmann, *Ägyptische Hymnen und Gebete,* 1975, n° 183-185; B. Mathieu, *la poésie amoureuse, BidÉtud* 115, 1996, pp. 234-235, n° 796; S. Bickel, *op. cit.,* p. 170.
5   *Anthologie palatine,* XI, 480-538. See A. Tchernia, in P. Pomey (ed.), *la navigation dans l'Antiquité,* 1997, p. 39.
6   É. Bernand, *Inscriptions métriques de l'Égypte gréco-romaine,* 1969, n° 1, pp. 43-45; B. Boyaval, *CRIPEL* 19, 1998, pp. 57-58.
7   *Tale of the Shipwrecked Sailor,* 119-124 and 134-135. *Mk tw r jr.t ꜣbd ḥr ꜣbd 'r km.t ꜣbd 4 m ḥnw n(y) jw pn jw dp.t r jj.t m ḥnw sḏdw jm=s rḫ n=k šm=k ḥn'=sn r ḥnw m(w).t=k m njw.t=k rš.wy sdd dp.t~n=f sn ḥ.t mr(.t) (...) jr ꜣn=k rwḏ jb=k mḥ=k ꜣnj=k m ẖrd.w=k sn=k ḥm.t=k mꜣꜣ=k pr=k nfr s.t r ḥ.t nb.t pḥ=k ḥnw wn=k jm=f m-q ꜣb n(y) sn.w=k.*

*See, you will be here for month after month, until you have completed four months on this island. A ship will come from your country, with sailors on board whom you know, and it is with them that you will return home! You will die in your own city! Happy the man who relates what he has experienced, once the evil times are over!* [...]

*If you are valiant, master your heart. You will hold your children in your arms! You will embrace your wife! You will see your home (again)! That is more wonderful than anything else! You will reach the land in which you were amidst your brothers.*

A passage from the *Satire of Trades* on the Lansing Papyrus which relates that "the *šwty.w*-traders sail up and down the Nile…" continues to hold forth about their alleged misery, and their fear that they will never see Egypt again:[8]

*The crew of every domain has received its load so as to leave Egypt for Djahy. The god of each man is with him. Not a single one from among them dares say, "We will see Egypt again".*

The *šwty.w* and their colleagues sent on a commercial mission were obliged to leave behind them not only their family environment, but also that of their gods and their temples that were the centre of all social and civic life. Yet there does not seem to have been in Egypt any specific divinity, any patron saint of travelling such as the St Christopher of western travellers. Although there is one reference to a divinity who protected voyagers in the *Report of*

*Wenamun*: the man sent out on a mission took with him a statue of 'Amun of the road' (*Jmn tꜣ mtn*),[9] a hypostasis of the great god. This epithet is unique, so it is not known whether it is a rare form, maybe even one created for the needs of the narrative, or whether this aspect of Amun was more generally venerated by all those who happened to be travelling.[10] Certain hymns celebrate him as 'Amun the helmsman' (*Jmn pꜣ ḥmy*) or as 'the pilot who knows the waters' (*ḥꜣty rḫ mw*), and thus probably attribute to him a role as guardian of sailors.[11] His name is invoked on '*Wadj Wer* in fury', whereupon the sailors can land in peace. In the mammisi of Dendera (30th Dynasty, 380–343 BC), reign of Nectanebo I (380–362 BC), it is said:[12]

*He has invoked your name on* Wadj Wer *in fury; he has reached firm land in peace.*

8    P. Lansing 4, 10-5, 2; A. H. Gardiner, *Late-Egyptian Miscellanies*, 1937, p. 103.

9    M. A Korostovtsev, *Puteschestvie Un-amuna v Bibl.*, 1960, p. 122, l. 3, 12.

10   M. Lichtheim, *Ancient Egyptian Literature*, II, 1976, p. 208, n. 8.

11   For example Ostracon BM 5656a, J. Cerny and A. H. Gardiner, *Hieratic Ostraca* I, 1957, pl. 89, l. 10.

12   Dendera, Mammisi, 28, 2f, Hymn to Amun: *kꜣ~n=f n kꜣ=t ḥꜣw wꜣḏ wr khbtj sꜣh~n=f dmj.t m ḥtp*. F. Daumas, *Les mammisis des temples égyptiens*, 1958, pp. 431-434; id., *Les mammisis de Dendera*, 1959, 27-28; A. Barucq and F. Daumas, *Hymnes et prières*, 1952, 27-28. A similar text can be found in the mammisi of Edfu, Chapel C, west wall: Edfu, Mammisi, 47, 20: '*He who has invoked your ka on* Wadj Wer *in fury, he reaches firm land in peace*' (*kꜣ~n=f kꜣ=k <m->ḥꜣw wꜣḏ wr khbtj sꜣh~n=f r dmj.t m ḥtp*). See PM VI, 173, 74; É. Chassinat, *Le mammisi d'Edfou*, MIFAO XVI, 1939, 47, 20; F. Daumas, *Les mammisis des temples égyptiens*, 1958, pp. 431-434; H. Te Velde, *Seth, God of confusion*, 1967, pp. 22-23. Amun is also invoked on *Wadj Wer*, in the temple of Opet at Karnak: see PM II, 248, 27; 250, 39; C. De Wit, *Les inscriptions du temple d'Opet*, BiAeg 11, 1958, I, 123; I, 166; C. Vandersleyen, *Ouadj-our*, 1999, no 168-169 p. 265.

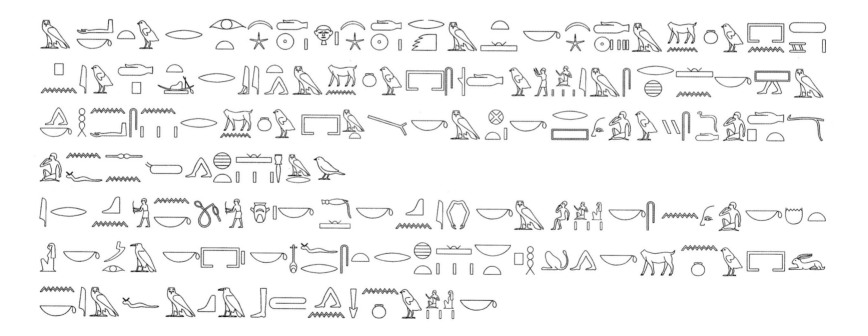

*See, you will be here for month after month, until you have completed four months on this island. A ship will come from your country, with sailors on board whom you know, and it is with them that you will return home! You will die in your own city! Happy the man who relates what he has experienced, once the evil times are over!* [...]

*If you are valiant, master your heart. You will hold your children in your arms! You will embrace your wife! You will see your home (again)! That is more wonderful than anything else! You will reach the land in which you were amidst your brothers.*

*He has invoked your name on* Wadj Wer *in fury; he has reached firm land in peace.*

More often than not, the travellers invoked as a protector the god to whom they were attached at home; their 'personal god' travelled with them. So a letter addressed to functionaries of the temple of Amun who had been sent on a desert mission mentions 'Amun-Ra, the king of gods… your good lord who spends his time acting as your pilot (*ḥȝty*)'.[13] It is probable that 'every traveller tried to take his favourite god with him, the local or eponymous god, in the form of an amulet or statuette. This is doubtless what the text of the *Satire* is referring when it affirms that the 'god of each man is with him'.[14]

Certain gods, the virtual guardians of East and West, guided the professions of people who dwelt in the mining lands. As allegorical representations of those regions, they wore the ethnic features of the tribes who were used to moving from place to place; those of benevolent nomads who adhered to the interests of Egypt. Sopdu thus appears in the guise of a bearded Asiatic Bedouin travelling through these lands. In this latter figure – analogous to Shu in the texts on the tribulations of Geb[15] – the populations that bordered eastern Egypt recognised the paragon of the divine trader entrusted with commercial and diplomatic transactions between Egyptians and Asiatics.[16]

The association of a god with an enterprise such as commercial expeditions to foreign lands to acquire exotic products or to work mineral seams is commonplace. When, in the *Report of Wenamun*, the Giblite sovereign abrogates to himself all authority over the stocks of wood from Lebanon[17] and declares that at his command 'heaven may open', the Egyptian ambassador Wenamun reacts against this in a violent speech aimed at defending Amun and his authority over Lebanon,[18] in which the mountain is called 'the habitat'[19] of the barque of Amun,[20] in the sense that wood from Lebanon is the main material used in the construction of the barque. Amun's rights over the mountain range of Lebanon may have had their roots in the early New Kingdom (1570–1070 BC), when Phoenicia was part of the Egyptian zone of influence.[21] Sennefer, the leader of the expedition sent by

Thutmose III (1504–1450 BC), did not dare however to cut down the trees before imploring the local goddess with all sorts of offerings.[22]

The divinities represented respectively the category of the regions concerned, the routes that led there – or the sanctuary of the town at the end of these routes – the mineral deposits that were the object of the expedition and in some cases the principal god of the town from which the expedition set out.[23] Thus in the eastern desert, Min was the god most popularly invoked, next to Amun who at certain periods benefited from the working of the gold mines of Wadi Hammamat; there was also Horus of the deserts and, on certain mining sites, Hathor.

Ithyphallic statuette of Amun-Min in bronze, Late Period (525-332 BC), Louvre, Paris. © Photo RMN/Hervé Lewandowski

13    W. Helck, *JARCE* 6, pp. 135-136, *pȝy=tn nb nfr nty jrr=f nw ˁš n=tn ḥȝty*.
14    S. Bickel, in N. Grimal and B. Menu (ed.), *Le commerce*, BiÉtud 121, 1998, p. 169. On the 'personal god' see É. Suys, in *Miscellanea Biblica*, II, 1934, pp. 6-9; É. Drioton, in M. Brillant, R. Aigrain, *L'Histoire des Religion*, 1955, pp. 35-36.
15    G. Goyon, *Kêmi* VI, 1936, pp. 1-42 (part. p. 23, l. 10).
16    S. Aufrère, *L'univers minéral*, BiÉtud CV, 1991, vol. 2, pp. 118-122, 751-769; id., *Archéo-Nil* 7, 1997, p. 116.
17    *Wenamun*, 2, 14-24.
18    For example, the line 2, 28 where Amun is called *pȝj=f pr*, 'his master'
19    *Wenamun*, 2, 25.
20    For example, G. Lefebvre, *Romans et contes*, 1949, p. 215; M. Lichtheim, *Ancient Egyptian Literature*, II, 1976, p. 227.
21    R. Giveon, in *LÄ* III, 1980, s.v. 'Libanon', col. 1013.
22    K. Sethe, *Urkunden der 18. Dynastie*, IV, 1927, p. 535; H. Helck, *Die Beziehungen Ägyptens*, ÄgAbh 5, 1971, p. 375.
23    See for example 'the pantheon of Wadi Hammamat' studied by C. Traunecker, in *Autour de Coptos, Topoi*, suppl. 3, 2002, pp. 355-381.

Min was the god of Coptos, the departure point for several routes that served the mining centres of the Arabian desert and led to the Red Sea. He became the patron and prototype of travellers who imported ore from eastern regions[24] or went to seek exotic products in the distant land of Punt.[25] The term *n'y*, 'traveller'[26] used to describe Min[27] could be the prototype of the epithet ο ενοδοσ θεοσ applied to Min-Pan in the inscriptions of Akhmin. This epithet, in which ενοδοσ is generally understood as meaning 'favourable (to voyages)' can also signify 'the god who has a good journey' (*n'y nfr*).[28]

Horus and Hathor were habitués of the frontier regions. Horus was the god *par excellence* – whether as Horus the Elder, creator of the Egyptian State, or Horus son of Osiris, the last divine link in the chain before the transmission of royalty to humans – assimilated to Ra and Atum, and the prototype of the king of Egypt, but in various guises he was also the god of several localities, in Egypt as in the bordering countries. Hathor was the goddess who presided over the mining sites of the deserts around the Nile Valley – the eastern Egyptian desert, Sinai, certain sites in Nubia – and over ore and hard stones (gold, turquoise, lapis lazuli, amethyst, galena, and so on) and over the foreign lands where the Egyptians procured the precious products that they lacked: the land of Punt, the 'Land of the God', Byblos, Timna, and so on. It was, of course, as mistress of turquoise that she appeared at Wadi Maghara and especially on the plateau of Serabit el-Khadim from the 12th Dynasty (1991-1782 BC) onwards.[29] As the 'Lady of Punt', Hathor was the natural owner of all the products of this region.[30] It is in a chapel dedicated to Hathor, at Deir el-Bahari, that the famous voyage to Punt is evoked. From the start of the 6th Dynasty (*c.* 2300 BC), Punt was sufficiently integrated into the Egyptian economic environment to be personified by a little goddess. She was represented, on an alabaster vase, facing the list of titles of King Teti, bringing incense.[31]

Generally speaking, the divinities who acted as the patrons of the land of Punt were those who participated in the protection of the access routes between the Nile Valley and the coasts of the Red Sea, embarkation points to the distant land. This is the case of Hathor and Min in particular, but also, depending on those divine functions that it is necessary to attempt to understand, the fact that Punt was placed under the patronage of Egyptian divinities who were *a priori* very 'distant' from the spice lands. Thus, Shesmetet, the lion goddess, close to Sekhmet and closely linked to the eastern Delta,[32] is known as sovereign or lady of Punt from the 18th Dynasty (1570-1293 BC) onwards, in a text that apparently dates from Hatshepsut (1498-1483 BC) and possibly from Deir el-Bahari.[33] Her name is etymologically linked to that of the territory Shesmetet designating part of Sinai, that of the mineral *shesmet* that is found there (probably malachite), and that of the *shesmet* apron worn by certain Bedouins of the region.[34] Sopdu,[35] also linked to the Shesmetet region, was the patron of the caravan trails, and is depicted with the features of someone from the Near East, reigning over Sinai and protecting Egypt against invaders from the Levant. It is doubtless by virtue of his function as intermediary between Egypt (the Nile Valley) and the land of Punt that he is depicted on the stele erected by Senusret II (1897-1878 BC) at Wadi Gasus, to the north of Quseir, on one of the points of passage used by the maritime expeditions to Punt.

The case of the god Ptah is particularly instructive.[36] The great nephew of Nectanebo I (380-362 BC), also named Nectanebo, who had placed himself at the service of the Ptolemaic dynasty, fulfilled

important functions. He bore the titles of generalissimo, prince in Tjaru, Nebecheh and Sebennytos, governor of the land of the East and priest of Ptah of Punt.[37] His administrative and military activities thus brought him into close contact with the eastern marches of the Delta and made him responsible for the communication channels between Egypt and the north-east of the country. So the priesthood of Ptah of Punt needs to be included within a geographical and administrative logic: Ptah was considered as the 'refiner' of the aromatic spices from Punt.[38] Holding the priesthood must have had economic implications and 'it can be imagined that it enabled Nectanebo to control, on behalf of the State, trade with Punt, and to tax the products destined to enter Egypt'.[39]

It was doubtless the presence of embarkation or disembarkation points in the Gulf of Suez and access routes between the Nile and the Red Sea (Wadi Tumilat)[40] that explains in part the Puntite functions of certain gods who were the protectors of the eastern border areas of Egypt.[41]

Khentikheti, the god of Athribis is not mentioned in direct relation with the land of Punt, and yet Ankhu, in the story he tells of his voyage to that land on his monument at Mersa Gawasis, places Senusret I (1971-1926 BC) under his protection.[42] Among the members of the expedition to Sinai and Punt, a far from negligible number of them bear a name formed on that of the god, suggesting that they originated from Athribis.[43] From the Middle Kingdom (2040–1782 BC) onwards, Athribis appears to have been one of the points of departure for seafaring expeditions.[44] Khentikheti was, from the New Kingdom onwards, one of the gods who held the helm of the

24   S. Aufrère, *L'univers minéral*, BiÉtud CV, 1991; id., *Archéo-Nil* n° 7, October 1997, p. 128; VI. Vikentiev, ASAE LIV, 1956, pp. 179-189.

25   M. Gabolde, in *Coptos. L'Égypte antique aux portes du désert*, 2000, p. 80.

26   *Wb* II, 206.

27   *Edfu* V, 109, 15; VII, 106, 7.

28   See J. Yoyotte, RdÉ 9, 1952, n° 6, p. 133. On Pan, see A. Bernand, *Pan du désert*, 1977.

29   D. Valbelle, in D. Valbelle and C. Bonnet (ed.), *Le Sinaï*, 1998, pp. 50-51; id., *Le sanctuaire d'Hathor*, 1996, p. 118.

30   S. Aufrère, *L'univers minéral*, BiÉtud CV, 1991, vol. 2, p. 174.

31   A. B. Elsasser and V.-M. Fredrickson, *Ancient Egypt*, 1966, p. 44 (inv. 11551a,b); J. Leclant, *Annales d'Éthiopie* 11, 1978, p. 70.

32   P. Derchain, *Elkab* I, 1971, pp. 14-32.

33   P. Vernus, RdÉ 33, 1981, p. 92, 97 n° (v), 118 (8).

34   A. H. Gardiner, JEA V, 1918, pp. 218-223; J. Yoyotte, BSFE 114, 1989, p. 37.

35   I. W. Schumacher, *Der Gott Sopdu der Herr der Fremdländer*, 1988; J. Yoyotte, BSFE 114, 1989, pp. 28-58.

36   After D. Meeks, in *Autour de Coptos*, Topoi, suppl. 3, 2002, p. 293.

37   *Urk.* II, 24, 6-7; 25, 3-6; 26, 1-2; P.-M. Chevereau, *Prosopographie des cadres militaires égyptiens de la Basse Époque*, 1985, p. 156.

38   N. de G. Davies, A. H. Gardiner, *The Tomb of Antefoker*, 1920, pl. x.

39   D. Meeks, in *Autour de Coptos*, Topoi, suppl. 3, 2002, p. 293. This author points out that the 'treasury' of the temple of Ptah in Memphis acted as a sort of central bank, from at least the Persian period onwards: id., p. 293 and n. 149 p. 293-294 (bibliography).

40   cf. pp. 76 et seq.

41   We disagree with the interpretation of D. Meeks (in *Autour de Coptos*, Topoi, suppl. 3, 2002, pp. 291-295). In his view, these divinities linked to the east of the Delta and to Sinai are a proof that the land of Punt was situated on the Arabian peninsula. The products and merchandise of Punt will be examined at length in *Seafaring in Ancient Egypt*, vol. 2, and will demonstrate that Punt, in the Pharaonic period, was an African land. In later times a certain number of goddesses bore the title of 'lady' or 'sovereign of Punt', more often than not because they were identified with a particular aspect of Hathor (F.R. Herbin, RdÉ 35, 1984, p. 118, n. 43). In addition, they were also often linked to the east of the Delta; this is the case of Hatmehyt of Mendes (Dendera V, 30, 12) and Nebet-hetepet of Ro-nefer, today Tell Tebilleh, 20km to the east of Mansurah (Edfu VII, 258, 10-11).

42   A. M. Sayed, RdÉ 29, 1977, p. 159.

43   A. H. Gardiner, T. E. Peet, J. Cerny, *The Inscriptions of Sinai*, 1952, p. 227; A. M. Sayed, RdÉ 29, 1977, p. 141, pl. 8b.

44   G. Scandone Matthiae, *Studi epigrafici e linguistici sul Vicino Oriente antico* 7, 1990, pp. 39-42. In fact, a ship can determine the name of a god: P. Vernus, *Athribis*, BiÉtud LXXIV, 1978, p. 371.

solar ship.[45] Finally, Athribis is the only Egyptian site in which archaeologists have discovered one of those slabs dedicated to Arsinoe Philadelpha, identified with the Marine Aphrodite, that were part of the little altars of sand and brick that sailors dedicated to the goddess.[46]

## II. Ceremonies and thank-offerings

As the regular ceremonies relative to maritime voyages are concerned, it is necessary to distinguish between those of departure and those of arrival. The text on the Stele of Khentikhetiour, from year 28 of Amenemhat III (1386-1349 BC), discovered on the shores of the Red Coast (Wadi Gasus) emphasises in a clear and concise style the story of how an expedition to Punt returned, and the expression of the thank-offering to the gods for having made a safe and sound return possible:[47]

> *Adore the god, give thanks to Haroeris and Gebytou, through the prince and governor, chancellor of the king of Lower Egypt in the audience chamber, Khentikhetiour, after he had returned in peace from Punt, his expeditionary corps being safe and sound with him, his ships having landed at the port of Sawu (Mersa Gawasis), in the year 28 of the reign.*

*The Tale of the Shipwrecked Sailor* explains the thank-offering that was given to the god on the ship's arrival:[48]

> *See, we have reached our native land; the mallet has been seized, the mooring peg struck home; the prow is now moored to the land; a thank-offering has been made, and the god adored.*

This is the rite of mooring that celebrates the final moment of the sailing. The god is thanked for having allowed good sailing and the return of the crew, safe and sound. It is a matter of tying the ship

to the *mnj.t*-mooring peg and fixing it firmly to the shore. The term is often used in the metaphorical sense of 'dying', with the reassuring notion of 'arriving at a good port' in the world of the dead.[49]

Likewise, at the moment of departure, the hero of the tale and his rescuers give thanks to the god of the mysterious island:[50]

> *Then I came on to the shore near this ship. I started to hail the group of people in this ship. I made a thank-offering on the shore to the master of this island; those who were on board (did) the same. Then we set off northwards to the residence of the Sovereign.*

This 'thank-offering' may be compared with what is known of the ceremonials of arrival and departure of ships in the Graeco-Roman era. On departure, quite often, those who were about to embark began by carrying out a pilgrimage to a neighbouring temple to place themselves under divine protection. Then, once on board, a ceremony took place not in the port when the ship had just weighed anchor, but as soon as it reached the open sea. Likewise, when the ship was about to arrive in port a new ceremony of thank-offering took place. When the departure or arrival of a military squadron or a convoy of state corn was concerned, sacrifice was performed on board the flagship or on board the trading vessel that

---

45   See P. Vernus, *op. cit.*, pp. 286-288 (doc. 247-251).

46   L. Robert, in *Essays in honor of C. Bradford Welles*, 1966, pp. 201-208.

47   See Abdel Monem Sayed, *RdÉ* 29, 1977, p. 139, pl. 8b; C. Obsomer, *Sesostris I*, 1995, pp. 386-387; M. Gabolde, in *Coptos. L'Égypte antique aux portes du désert*, 2000, p. 149. On Mersa Gawasis, see p. 82 *et seq.*

48   *Tale of the Shipwrecked Sailor*, 2-3: *Mk ph~n=n ḥnw šsp ḥrpw ḥw mnj.t ḥȝt.t rd.t ḥr tȝ rd ḥknw dwȝ nṯr.*

49   H. Grapow, *Die bildlichen Ausdrücke des Ägyptischen*, 1924, p. 152; J. Zandee, *Death as an Enemy*, 1960, p. 53.

50   *Tale of the Shipwrecked Sailor*, 170-174: *ꜥḥ~n ḥȝ=kw r mry.t m-ḥȝw dp.t tn ꜥḥꜥ~n=j ḥr jȝš n mšꜥ nty m dp.t tn rd~n=j ḥknw ḥr mry.t n nb n(y) jw pn nty.w jm=s r mjt.t jry nꜥ.t pw jr~n=n m ḥd r ḥnw n(y) jty.*

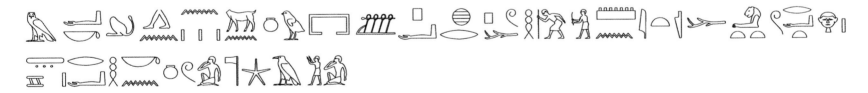

*See, we have reached our native land; the mallet has been seized, the mooring peg struck home; the prow is now moored to the land; a thank-offering has been made, and the god adored.*

*Then I came on to the shore near this ship. I started to hail the group of people in this ship. I made a thank-offering on the shore to the master of this island; those who were on board (did) the same. Then we set off northwards to the residence of the Sovereign.*

was the first to arrive in port. Thus for the convoys of Egyptian corn the sacrifice took place when the first ship in the convoy passed before the island of Cyprus, and this sacrifice occurred in the form of a libation of wine in honour of Minerva.[51] During the journey, other sacrifices took place when the ships passed a particularly famous sanctuary, or when the sailors found themselves confronting a danger that required that they resort to the gods. One problem arises in connection with these ceremonies of the cult of navigation: when they were on board, who officiated? In other words, who was the ship's priest? It seems that this role must have belonged to the captain, since the successful progress of the journey depended on the respect given to the gods.[52]

## III. Egyptian religion and the beliefs of the Phoenician traders

The religious environment of the traders and navigators is perhaps easier to see at later periods, thanks to the diffusion of certain myths in the Mediterranean basin. This investigation of the way the myths spread through the bordering lands leads us to study a whole set of religious markers spread by the commercial and cultural exchanges on the periphery of the Valley of the Nile.[53] This problem then leads us to tackle the relation between the mythological strands and ancient culture – more specifically what has been called 'merchant culture'. Then it is not a matter of studying the whole range of Egyptian material or material influenced by Egyptian culture but rather of bringing out, with the help of certain documents, the religious trends which impelled the 'spirituality' of those who crossed and re-crossed the Mediterranean to trade certain economic resources.

It is for the first millennium BC, within the Egyptian and Phoenician-Punic spheres of influence, and thanks to the privileged relations between Egypt and Phoenicia (and its warehouses), that it is relatively easy to determine, or at least to gain some inkling of this merchant 'religiosity'.

Generally speaking, the different beliefs current in the Mediterranean were nourished by the most diverse mythological currents. The *interpretatio*, the mythology, the economic links, the spread of Egyptian concepts through the Mediterranean thanks to the spread of objects of piety made in Egypt, all constitute the elements that enable us to approach certain aspects of ancient culture.[54] In the ancient world, mythology – in its original form, or a mythology that had undergone the influence of the most diverse trends of thought – transmitted concepts that could be shared by a great number of individuals.[55] *Interpretatio* was based on syncretism, and put into operation by ancient cultures to enable a reciprocal identification on the part of superhuman beings who were venerated in the respective religions. So this procedure gives us the possibility of facilitating human relations between social groups of different

origins.[56] These relations are expressed by hospitality and acculturation;[57] they thereby simplify the integration of external elements and facilitate the mixed nature of these groups, hence the sometimes obvious syncretisms between divine forces that present identical aspects – but these hybrids can also be ambiguous.[58] The study of these religious and mythological contacts between the Phoenicians, a merchant people *par excellence*, and the Egyptians, comprises a particularly interesting perspective from which to observe the modes of life and thought, and the beliefs and spiritual protectors of the traders. Economic and religious life is often astonishingly closely linked.

In a quite special and yet natural way, religious trends follow the broad outlines of economic activity since merchants, who are superstitious because they are the professionals of chancy and risky activities, attribute the success of their activity to specialised divine forces that govern sea winds and currents or protect the production of raw materials (metals and precious minerals). This protection is activated by aetiological legends that establish a direct relation between a divine force and the desired object.[59] The multiple exchanges made of the Mediterranean the place of an intense syncretistic movement.[60] The more economic links intensified, the more the centres of culture influenced one another and the more complex myths and divinities became.

Phoenicia was subjected to the powerful Egyptian influence on the one side, from the start of the 1st millennium BC, and also turned to other places of colonisation and various 'points of implantation' in the Mediterranean.[61] During the 6th century BC, it was 'obliged' to turn towards Egypt, so as to escape from its powerful neighbour, Assyria.[62] While Nebuchadnezzar II (604–562 BC) made sure of an outlet to the sea with the capture of Sidon, Tyre escaped him thanks to Apries who kept the city supplied between 585 and 573 BC.

Several recent studies have brought out the dispersion of this culture and its different staging posts through the Mediterranean basin.[63] It has attracted all the more attention since it contributed to draining a great degree of Egyptian influence beyond the natural frontiers of Egypt. It is necessary to distinguish between two sets of documents. First, the Egyptian objects of the Levant: this is the series known about the longest.[64] The discovery of Egyptian objects in the region of the Levant has been frequently studied and the results summarised.[65] Then come the objects of an Egyptian kind from the western Mediterranean; this series comprises Egyptian (and then

51   Stace, *Silves*, III, 2, 21-24.

52   J. Rougé, *La marine dans l'Antiquité*, 1975, pp. 206-210, which refers to D. Wachsmuth, *Pompimos ho daimôn, Untersuchungen zu den antiken Sakralhandlungen bei Seereisen*, 1967.

53   S. Aufrère, in N. Grimal and B. Menu (ed.), *Le commerce*, BiÉtud 121, 1998, p. 19

54   *Id.*, p. 19.

55   M. Gras, *La Méditerranée archaïque*, 1995, pp. 70-74.

56   On this concept, see, for example, J. G. Griffith, in *LÄ* III, col. 164-172, s.v. 'Interpretatio graeca'; E. Lipinski, *Dictionnaire de la civilisation phénicienne et punique*, 1992, p. 230.

57   M. Gras, *op. cit.*, pp. 115-116, pp. 123-125.

58   W. Schenkel, in *LÄ* II, 1976, s.v. 'Götterverschmelzung', col. 720-725.

59   J. Spiegel, in *LÄ* I, col. 80-83, s.v. 'Ätiologie. Ätiologische Mythen'; S. Aufrère, *op. cit.*, p. 20.

60   Generally speaking, on Egypto-Phoenician commercial relations, see J. Padró, in N. Grimal and B. Menu (ed.), *Le commerce*, BiÉtud 121, 1998, pp. 41-58, fig. 1-10; *Seafaring in Ancient Egypt*, vol. 2.

61   M. Gras, *op. cit.*, p. 29-31; S. Aufrère, *op. cit.*, p. 20.

62   É. Drioton and J. Vandier, *L'Égypte*, 1984, p. 551; J. Padró, *ASAE* LXXXI, 1987, pp. 213-222.

63   S. Moscati (ed.), *The Phoenicians*, 1988; E. Lipinski, *op. cit.*

64   For instance, A. Rowe, *A Catalogue of Egyptian Scarabs, Scaraboids, Seals and Amulets in the Palestine Archaeological Museum*, 1936. To those objects from the Levant can certainly be added those from the island of Cyprus: see, for example, G. Clerc, 'La Nécropole d'Amathonte, Tombes 110-385', *ÉtudChypr* XIII, 1991, pp. 1-157.

65   J. Leclant, in W. Ward (ed.), *The Role of the Phoenicians*, 1968, pp. 9-31, pl. viii-xii; *id.*, in *Atti del II Congresso Internazionale di Studi Fenici e Punici*, I, 1991, pp. 7-17.

Egyptian-style griffon discovered in Nimrud, 8<sup>th</sup> century BC, 19cm high, 15cm wide, Iraq Museum, Baghdad. © AKG Images. Photo: Erich Lessing

pseudo-Egyptian and Egyptian-style[66] objects found in Sicily,[67] Sardinia,[68] North Africa,[69] Ibiza[70] and the Iberian Peninsula.[71] This series has also been known for a long time, but it was not really given due importance until the excavations at Almunecar (the ancient Sexi, in Andalusia), during which archaeologists found, in a Phoenician necropolis, numerous Egyptian stone vases, some of them with hieroglyphic inscriptions.[72]

The fact that Egyptian pieces exported from Egypt (first generation of prototypes) were copied in their turn – Egyptian-style objects (second generation) from Phoenician and Punic workshops – immediately giving rise to many local pseudo-Egyptian avatars (third generation),[73] shows a priori the importance that their users ascribed to them.

Were these objects that were adopted, as well as spread by the Phoenicians, in themselves the reflection of a simple commercial curiosity, or, via the intermediary of an interpretatio punica, did they take on a particular meaning? To what extent was this a fashion, very evident in clothes and hairstyles, or was it a more profound adherence to the beliefs of the Nile? Is the diffusion of Egyptian

material a sign of the beliefs of merchants and traders (Egyptian or Phoenician)? Is the Egyptian object in itself an indicator of beliefs?

If such products appear to some extent as entirely commercial objects, the presence of Egyptian amulets in the Phoenician and Punic world and the choice presiding over their selection do not always seem innocent. In other terms, there were, over and above the everyday Egyptian knick-knacks, markers of belief that were perhaps more pronounced. 'Though one cannot go so far as to admit that their users had any precise idea of their meaning, they can be credited with at least a second-hand knowledge of Egypt. However, in a world so inclined to myths and beliefs, it barely seems possible to imagine that these objects were used for no particular reason, since the person who wears them or places them in his/her tomb certainly expects something else from them than an action ascribed to mere phylacteries whose very effectiveness was not known; so they must have had some specific meaning attached to them'.[74]

The Egyptian material scattered along the shores of the Mediterranean is significant in all the Phoenician and Punic sites, in particular those in the south of Spain[75] and the western part of Sardinia.[76] In Malta, known for the Egyptian influences it underwent, an amulet bearer in bronze has been discovered containing a papyrus with a silhouette of Isis accompanied by a Phoenician inscription.[77] Several cases for amulet bearers in gold have been discovered at Tharros and Carthage, decorated with protoma in the shape of lions, falcons or boars.[78] Some of these cases have gold, silver or lead plates inside them, on which scenes of Egyptian magic were engraved.

Did divinities such as Sekhmet, Isis, Horus, Bastet, Bes, Ptah-Pataicus, and so on, that are found in the form of amulets in Phoenician and Punic centres, have the power to seduce Phoenician traders, and if so, why?

Floral capital supporting a mask inspired by the goddess Hathor, limestone, Cyprus, second half of the 6th century BC, Louvre, Paris, AM 93.

© Photo RMN/Musée du Louvre

66   In connection with this classification of the documents of an Egyptian kind, J. Padró, Egyptian Type Documents, I, EPRO 65, 1980, pp. 52-62. J. Padró understands by Egyptian material the objects indisputably made in Egypt; the pseudo-Egyptian material is constituted of objects that, morphologically, have an Egyptian appearance and, at first sight, can be taken to be Egyptian, while some features in them allows us to say that they were not really made in Egypt; the Egyptian-style objects are manifestly not Egyptian, though they have decorative details that are of Egyptian inspiration.

67   G. Matthiae Scandone, OrAnt X, 1971, pp. 21-46, fig. 5 and pl. v.

68   Id., Scarabei e Scaraboidi Egiziani ed Egittizzanti del Museo Nazionale di Cagliari, 1975; A. Acquaro, Amuleti Egiziani ed Egittizzanti del Museo Nazionale di Cagliari, 1977.

69   J. Vercoutter, Les objets égyptiens et égyptisants du mobilier funéraire carthaginois, 1945; P. Cintas, Amulettes puniques, 1946.

70   L. Baqués, Ampurias 36-37, 1974-1975, pp. 87-146; I. Gamer-Wallert, Ägyptische und ägyptisierende Funde von der iberischen Halbinsel, 1978, pp. 127-175; J. H. Fernández, J. Padró, Escarabeos del Museo Arqueológico de Ibiza, 1982; id., Amuletos de tipo egipcio del Museo Arqueológico de Ibiza, 1986; J. Boardman, Escarabeos de piedra procendetes de Ibiza, 1984.

71   I. Gamer-Wallert, op. cit., pp. 127-175; J. Padró, Egyptian Type Documents, I-III, 1980-1995; M. A. García Martínez, Documentos preromanos, OrMonsp XIII, 2001.

72   M. Pellicer Catalán, Excavationes en la necrópolis púnica 'Laurita', 1963.

73   I. Gamer-Wallert, op. cit.; J. Padró, Egyptian Type Documents, I-II, 1980-1983; id., in Atti del I Congresso Internazionale di Studi Fenici e Punici, I, 1983; M. A. García Martínez, op. cit.

74   S. Aufrère, op. cit., p. 24.

75   I. Gamer-Wallert, op. cit.; J. Padró, Egyptian Type Documents, I-III, 1980-1995; id., La Religión Romana en Hispania, 1981, pp. 337-352; id., Cuadernos de Prehistoria y Arqueología y Castellonenses 9, 1982-1983, pp. 149-191; id., dans Atti del I Congresso Internazionale di Studi Fenici e Punici, I, 1983; id., ASAE LXXI, 1987, pp. 213-222; M. A. García Martínez, Documentos preromanos, OrMonsp XIII, 2001; S. Moscati (ed.), The Phoenicians, 1988, pp. 226, 729-731.

76   S. Moscati (ed.), op. cit., pp. 668-669, 678, 697-792; E. Lipinski, op. cit., pp. 393-395.

77   T. Gouder, B. Rocco, Studi Magrebini 7, 1975, pp. 1-18.

78   S. Moscati (ed.), op. cit., pp. 371, 388; J. Leclant, in Actes du IIIe congrès international des études phéniciennes et puniques, I, 1995, pp. 41-50.

Kohl pot in the shape of the god Bes, polychromatic faience work, New Kingdom, 18th Dynasty (reign of Amenophis III), c. 1402-1364 BC, Louvre, Paris, N 4469.
© Photo RMN/Daniel Lébée

Bes, Mammisi of Dendera, Upper Egypt, Roman period. © Photo: David Fabre

Bes is a divine figure of grotesque or frightening appearance, with multiple names and functions, reputed in particular to protect against serpents and scorpions, to favour love, fecundity, and birth; he is a dancer and musician, and attached to the circle of Hathor. From the Middle Kingdom (2040-1782 BC) onwards, Bes is shown, normally frontally, as a lion-shaped god with a grimacing face, wearing the coat of a wild animal whose tail appears between his parted legs; he is bearded, and wears a crown of feathers or palms. This image appears in Syria and Phoenicia and in Cyprus during the Later Bronze Age on cylinder seals, faience vases and ivories, notably at Megiddo. These objects show that the image and functions of the Egyptian god were well known outside Egypt.

The example of the spread of his depictions as well as the figures of Ptah-Pataicus enables us to study in a rather special way this relation between Egyptian religion and the beliefs of Phoenician merchants. In the western basin of the Mediterranean, the god Bes had places where he was strongly implanted, in particular Ibiza[79] and Cyprus.[80] In the sanctuaries of Kition, and more especially Amathus,

the Egyptian goddess Hathor is adored side by side with other eastern divinities such as the god Bes. Hathoric capitals, dating from the 6th and early 5th century BC which constitute in themselves little monuments erected in the courtyards of the sanctuaries, have been found in Amathus, where they are also depicted on vases.[81] At Kition, several miniature plates in terracotta bearing depictions of Hathor have also been found. While it is superfluous to dwell on the extraordinary diffusion of the mask of this divinity in the Mediterranean world, the great number of Egyptian amulets of Bes in the necropolis of Puig des Molins in Ibiza may be cited, where pseudo-Egyptian imitations are also found.[82] Casts with images of Bes demonstrate the local manufacture of statuettes in terracotta of this god.[83] Again in Ibiza there are various Egyptian-style objects, but

79    J. Padró, *Ampurias* 41-42, 1979-1980, pp. 386-388.

80    V. Wilson, *Levant* VII, 1975.

81    A. Hermary, *BCH* CIX, 1985, pp. 657-701; V. Karageorghis, 'Entre Égypte et Grèce', p. 113.

82    J. H. Fernández, J. Padró, *Amuletos de tipo egipcio del Museo Arqueológico de Ibiza*, 1986; id., pp. 30-33, pl. v.

83    M. J. Almagro Gorbea, *Corpus de las Terracotas de Ibiza*, 1980, pp. 273-274, pl. cciii.

what draws the most attention is the coinage with the image of Bes[84] and the Punic inscription of the name of the island: 'island of Bes'.[85] It is remarkable that the image of Bes represented on the coins of Ibiza is identical with the statues of Bes found in several places on the island of Sardinia, such as Bitia, Cagliari or Maracalagonis. These are cult images sculpted in stone. It can thus be deduced that the image reproduced on the coins of Ibiza must also have belonged to some cult statue from somewhere on the island. If it is found on the coins, it is because the god gave his name to the island that was dedicated to him by its Punic inhabitants.

It would be surprising if the Phoenicians had been seduced by Bes, a grotesque divinity, if he had not connoted some major concept. Bes was an oracular deity. In his lion form, he was considered to be the guardian of the eastern frontier of the Delta, a function that led him naturally to be assimilated to Sopdu and Hormerty, who traditionally fulfilled this role.[86] Furthermore, the god with bandy legs had a link with the Pataici, misshapen and achondroplastic characters that the Phoenicians, as Herodotus relates, 'carry on the prows of their warships'.[87] There is every chance, in view of the successful spread of the image of Bes in Phoenician and Punic colonies,[88] that the latter had a close link with the Cabiri to whom was ascribed the building of the first Phoenician ship.[89] After all, Herodotus reminds us that the Cabiri were the sons of Ptah, a function that they shared with the little images called Ptah-Pataici.[90] It is no chance if these silhouettes of a dwarfish Ptah were also spread throughout the Mediterranean basin by the Phoenicians, not only on the basis of an existing similarity with those graceless figurines of Ptah, reminiscent of the lame god Hephaistos, and the Pataici that decorated the prows of ships, but also because the Phoenicians, metallurgists and goldsmiths of repute,[91] indubitably placed themselves under the protection of Ptah of Memphis, patron of artisans and goldsmiths who, by tradition, were often dwarves.[92] Memphis was by tradition the place of the Egyptian arsenals, until a late date.[93] It should be remembered that the god Khusor, considered at Ugarit to be an artisan-god and architect, was also regarded as a blacksmith and armour-maker.[94] Khusor was also known in Egypt, if the stele of a stonecutter is to be believed (Usersutekh), on which he

can be recognised by the set-square he holds.[95] Thus, thanks to the links between these more or less kindred geniuses, the Phoenicians, having chosen to dwell at Memphis, knew Bes and recognised in this dwarfish divine figure a travelling god who would favour trade. Likewise they generally considered that he chased away the carriers of diseases, kept thieves away, and brought back laughter and *joie de vivre* as well as prosperity. All of these were positive elements that were desired when a ship set sail and people hoped to see it return.

On the basis of numerous reciprocal exchanges between Phoenicians and Egyptians, there are thus a few elements that bear witness that certain divinities with a Mediterranean vocation existed, under whose protection traders would place themselves and place the cargoes of their ships.

The Ptolemies, and then Rome, inherited these concepts that were part and parcel of economic activity, with divine cycles that brought in divinities who protected the transport of wealth in the Mediterranean basin. Agathodaimon and Agathe Tyche kept watch over Alexandrine commerce, while Serapis and Isis like the Dioscuri protected shipping convoys transporting the state corn from Alexandria to Ostia.

Indeed, Isis became the goddess who protected seafaring people. While it is very difficult to explain this ascription from an Egyptological point of view, there were festivals that marked the beginning of the sailing season: at the start of the month of March the *nauigidium isidis* took place, the feast of the ship of Isis, which is described at length at the end of the 2nd century AD by Apuleius. On this occasion a ship, or rather a scale model according to the depictions of the ceremony, with its sails embroidered with good wishes for the success of the sailing, loaded with offerings and lights, was launched on to the sea where it followed its course and opened the way to proper sailings.[96] The 'good mother' of the port of Pelusium was called Isis ορμιστρια, 'Our Lady of the Harbour', she who brings the traveller to a good port; but as Avienus says, it was the whole coast of Pelusium that was placed under the protection of Isis when the sea was full of perils.[97] The Isidion of the Sethroite where she was venerated under the epiclesis of 'salvation of men' must have been by the sea. And the texts by Plutarch[98] and Athenagoras[99] show that her gaze, like that of the sailors of Pelusium, was particularly turned to the East. In Pelusium itself and along the coast she had a rival: Zeus-Kasios.[100] He was not a newcomer in these places since his presence goes back to the Third Intermediate Period (1069-525 BC), when he gave his name, Egyptianised to Amun, to the city of Pelusium; and in the Persian period at Daphnae, his form is of Baal

---

84  J. Padró, in N. Grimal and B. Menu (ed.), *Le commerce*, BiÉtud 121, 1998, fig. 8b, p. 57.

85  See A. Hermany, in E. Lipinski, *Dictionnaire de la civilisation phénicienne et punique*, 1992, p. 69, s.v. 'Bès ' and fig. 257, 6.

86  See the bibliography given by S. Aufrère, op. cit., p. 26.

87  Herodotus, III, 37.

88  J. Padró, in *Acts of the First International Congress of Egyptology*, Cairo, 1976, SGKAO 14, 1979, pp. 507-514; id., in *Atti del I Congresso Internazionale di Studi Fenici e Punici*, I, 1983.

89  E. Lipinski, *Dictionnaire de la civilisation phénicienne et punique*, 1992, p. 86.

90  Herodotus, III, 37. cf. D. Meeks, in *Génies, anges et démons*, Sources Orientales 8, 1971, p. 55.

91  S. Morenz, in *Festschrift F. Zucker*, 1954, pp. 275-290 = *Religion und Geschichte des alten Ägypten*, 1975, pp. 496-509; J. Berlandini, RdÉ 46, 1995, pp. 19-46; E. Lipinski, op. cit., pp. 332-334, 343-346.

92  S. Aufrère, op. cit., p. 27.

93  S. Sauneron, *Villes et légendes d'Égypte*, BiÉtud XC, 1983, pp. 44-90; id., BIFAO LIV, 1954, pp. 7-12. Regarding the links between Ptah and the artisans: J. Vercoutter, CdE LXVIII, n° 135-136, 1993, pp. 70-83. In the Ptolemaic era, Memphis was still a metallurgical site; cf. G. Gagsteiger, *Die ptolemäischen Waffenmodelle aus Memphis*, HÄB 36, 1993. On the level of beliefs, Ptah was the one who manufactured the weapons of Horus when he was making ready to combat Seth; cf. É. Drioton, *Le texte dramatique d'Edfu*, CASAE 11, 1948, p. 60; M. Alliot, *Le culte d'Horus à Edfu au temps des Ptolémées*, BiÉtud XX, 1954, vol. 2, p. 777; S. Aufrère op. cit., n. 9 p. 27.

94  E. Lipinski, op. cit., p. 105.

95  J. Leibovitch, ASAE XLVIII, 1948, pp. 435-444. For a study devoted to Hathor, whose myths accompanied the metal trade in the Mediterranean from the first half of the 1st millennium BC, see the long discussion by S. Aufrère, In *Égypte & Provence. Civilisation, survivances et « Cabinets des curiosités »*, 1985, pp. 146-169, and especially p. 149.

96  Apuleius, *Metamorphoses*, XI, 16.

97  Avienus, *Aratea phaenomena*, 282: 'La déesse du rivage de Péluse'; text and translation by J. Soubiran, Coll. des Univ. de France, 1981; J.-Y. Carrez-Maratray, *Péluse*, BiÉtud 124, 1999, n° 254 p. 137.

98  Plutarch, *Isis and Osiris*, 17, 357 E: 'The city (Pelusium) that the goddess founded'; ed. C. Froidefond, Coll. des Univ. de France, *Œuvres Morales*, 1988; J.-Y. Carrez-Maratray, op. cit., n° 256 p. 138.

99  Athenagoras, *Embassy*, 22, 8: J.-Y. Carrez-Maratray, op. cit., n° 253 p. 137.

100  A. Salac, BCH 46, 1922, pp. 160-189; J. Yoyotte, RevArch, 1986, pp. 41-63; C. Bonnet, OLA 22, 1987, pp. 125-132.

Head of a statue of Serapis in marble, wearing a *calathos*. © Photo: Peter A. Clayton

Saphon, known since the New Kingdom. In the Greek and Roman periods Baal Saphon thus became Zeus Kasios, while still preserving foreign characteristics that made him a god who corresponded to the main canons of eastern cults.[101] He was first and foremost a 'god of salvation' and a protector of voyagers and in particular sailors; the heroes of Achilles Tatius, after their shipwreck, came to give him thanks for their rescue and prayed to him for their lost comrades.[102] He was seen in the Hellenistic period on the solarium of Mount Kasion, associated with Hermes, 'herald of good luck, noble and attentive', like all those Egyptian gods who were interpreted as Horos, son of Horos, from Kasion, in the Serapeion A of Delos.[103]

As for Serapis, that 'divine creature' of the first Ptolemy, he too became one of the great gods of navigation. This explains why his cult is well represented in more or less all the great ports of the Atlantic as well as the eastern shores of the Mediterranean and why certain associations of sailors placed themselves under his protection, such as the college of Serapis in the Dalmatian port of Salona. There is also evidence for the role of this god in certain Egyptian papyri where the author of the letter asks his addressee to offer on his behalf a sacrifice to the Lord Serapis in thanks for the good crossing he has just made.

---

[101] R. Turcan, *Les cultes orientaux dans le monde romain*, 1989, p. 168 *et seq*. See also J. Teixidor, *The Pagan god*, 1977, pp. 30-34, pp. 43-44; J. Ebach, in *LÄ* III, s.v. 'Kasion', 1980, col. 354; G. Del Olmo Lete, *Seafarer* 51, 1991, pp. 99-114.

[102] Achilles Tatius, *Leucippus and Clitophon*, III, 5-6; see J.-Y. Carrez-Maratray, *op. cit.*, no 272 p. 143 and pp. 218-220, 246-247.

[103] P. Roussel, *Les cultes égyptiens de Délos du IIIᵉ au Iᵉʳ siècle av. J.-C.*, 1916, pp. 94-97; F. Dunand, *Le culte d'Isis dans le bassin oriental de la Méditerranée*, EPRO 26, vol. 2, 1973, p. 102.

# Conclusion

*In the depth of bottomless abysses may I be swallowed up, or let a god give me wings and place me among the bands of flying creatures! If only I could hover over the sea's waves, there where, in the dark swells of their father, unhappy girls weep over Phaethon, distilling the golden amber of their tears! I would like to arrive at the coast of apples in the land of the Hesperides, who sing where the king of the dark sea offers no further route to sailors, since it is there that he encounters the sacred frontier of the sky that Atlas holds up; there, the sources of ambrosia flow in front of the nuptial chamber of Zeus, into the divine earth which gives life and increases the happiness of the gods.*
(Euripides, *Hippolytos*)

This is how the choir of the women of Troezen dream of confronting the perils of the sea. The Greek tragedians also emphasised, as did the Egyptians, the misfortune, the dangers, the griefs for which the sea is responsible, but also the happiness of a successful crossing and the fortunate return of the exile. What a wonderful shared maritime destiny, that of Egypt and Greece. So we can rejoice! For we have reached the end of our first voyage on the seas of Egypt. But the

multiple, truncated, deformed sources and the abundance of modern literature on this or that point of detail have made it impossible to present the ports, the ships and the men who embarked on them exhaustively. It is hoped that, in spite of everything, leafing through the pages of this book will have constituted an agreeable 'periplus' through the fantastic and fascinating universe of the navy in the Pharaonic period of Egypt. It is for everyone to follow the efforts made by people to overcome the fear inspired in them by the infinite expanse of the sea and to launch off on voyages that take mariners ever further while ceaselessly improving their means of navigation. This tableau, fragmentary and incomplete though it may be, seems nonetheless to present, in its various different aspects, two apparently contradictory aspects: permanence and evolution.

The permanence results above all from the very conditions of maritime sailing. It does not seem, indeed, that this has changed much in the course of the history of Pharaonic Egypt. The routes conditioned by the winds could obviously not change since there were no means of propulsion known for ships of heavy tonnage other than sails, and so long as these routes were not forbidden by new political conditions they continued to be used. Likewise the

Roman mosaic of Medusa, Graeco-Roman Museum, Alexandria. © Photo: David Fabre

meteorological organisation of the Mediterranean and the Red Sea has always imposed precise seasons of navigation, an imperative laid down by nature which people dare to disobey only on occasion. Evolution is nonetheless manifest in the designation of types of ships, in the development of the ship and the increase in its ocean-going capacities, and in a certain number of technical improvements.

Permanence, too, of the great expeditions in quest of spices that headed to the south of the Red Sea, but in a sea that seems not to have been tamed until the Ptolemaic period by the founding of ports and the use of the monsoon system. Alexandria, by virtue of its huge population and its activities, was to drain towards itself a major part of Mediterranean and Erythrean commerce following the enlargement of the maritime world that began in the middle of the 1st millennium BC. Well equipped with its harbour basins, its quays, its entrepots, and its watering places, Alexandria would be the headquarters of eastern navigation in the Hellenistic period, with its trade benefiting from the state organisation of the Ptolemaic economy. It was from here that Egyptian corn left – corn that was used by the sovereigns as a veritable political weapon.

There is also a permanence found in men who indulge in maritime voyages. Their methods and their characteristic ways of behaving, as well as their functions, are often the same through the ages. From the earliest times, small expeditions travelled by land and sea, reached the land of Punt, Nubia or Byblos and there procured for themselves exotic wares from the natives. The key products that Egypt lacked (wood, spices, and so on) – when they were not seized as booty or levied as tribute – were traded by proxies on behalf of the sovereign or the temples that possessed their own commercial fleet.

Commissioners also went to the shores of the Red Sea or to the far south to trade with coasters or boatmen from Punt, or sailed to the land themselves. Others such as Wenamun traded in the ports of the Levant.

Innovation is found in the specialisation of certain professions and the appearance of others. This was especially the case with the commercial agent *šwty*, who appears in the sources in the New Kingdom, a broker or economic intermediary between institutional producers and consumers. Their role was to establish a direct economic relationship, both in the sense of 'offer' and that of 'demand', between the institution on which they were dependent and other institutions and/or between the latter and private persons. It was indeed by the shifting and handling of money (in the broadest sense) that they managed to situate themselves differently in society. *Emporoi, kapeloi, naucleroi* and *endocheis* took over this role in the Ptolemaic and Roman periods. The evolution of the juridical and administrative management of commerce and the status of the professionals of maritime commerce, as well as the development of terminology, all explain the multiform character of commerce and an increase in the complexity of exchanges in the Hellenistic and Roman periods. It was in the Roman period that organised commercial structures were to be realised, extending across the known world. Indeed, with the development of the large-scale commerce necessitated by the existence of very big conurbations and in the first instance by the enormous Roman market, differentiated structures started to appear, that were not the same as the old ones. On the one hand, great commercial enterprises came into being, often specialised: those of the negotiators; on the other, in tandem with this great trade, there developed great enterprises of maritime transport, those of the shipowners who ran their vessels via a whole world of dependents; they had representatives in the great ports; were not specialised in particular types of transport and they loaded on to their ships whatever they were offered.

Permanence is marked by long-standing characteristics in the attitude people had towards traders. The sea has always inspired fear in men, and this explains the attitude of non-sailors towards sailors – they are not the same as other men, they live permanently face to face with danger, and even when they come ashore they still have certain personality traits that are difficult to understand. All of this explains the contradictory judgements that classical writers (or moralists) passed on navigation, commerce and the maritime trader. The latter is a man whom the fortunes of sea can ruin overnight, a man who will not hesitate to sink his ship that bears his cargo if he has made a bad bargain, so as not to have to reimburse his creditors, but he is also a man who can get rich overnight if he has had the good luck or the skill to arrive with a cargo of certain products in a country that was lacking in just those commodities at that very time and will grab them from him in exchange for gold. Thus Cicero weighs in against the interloping and cosmopolitan world of the merchants:[1]

> *Corruption and moral revolution are characteristic of maritime towns; they welcome new ideas and new kinds of behaviour and together with merchandise, foreign ways of life are imported into them, so that none of the ancestral rules can remain intact. Soon, those who dwell there lose their attachment to their own country; hope and imagination sweep them away on their wings, ever further from their dwelling, and even if their bodies remain there, their hearts go into exile and wander from place to place; […] finally, from the very charm of these places spring many seductions of the passions that lead to ruin or sloth.*

Permanence is evident in the divisions of commercial maritime spaces in the Mediterranean – simultaneously maritime zones that were privileged for a community of sailors, those where they had the ports to which they were attached, their habits, the best knowledge of the milieu, those in which they often sailed, and preferential markets, where most of the exchanges were carried out; but evolution within the maritime spaces known by the ancient Egyptians, which were different regional and interregional commercial circuits.

But this is already another story… a continuous story of the maritime relations between Egypt and the countries on her border, one that is related to maritime voyages via economic and institutional domains, and also via law, habit, the customs posts, and the Egyptian administration. The available documentation will then give us an opportunity to penetrate the system of relations between States – a system with its agents, its traditions, and its formulae – one that gives States the means to negotiate and conclude treaties, which (depending on the countries) are sanctioned by political marriages, or treaties of friendship, or are placed under the protection of the gods of the countries that are party to the contracts. Between these

---

1    Cicero, *On the Republic,* II, 167-168.

countries united by friendship, economic and financial relations are set up: treaties of commerce, protection of goods and persons, loans that give rise to diverse gifts in return. This international law is complemented by a veritable code of international courtesy. It possesses its language and its usages.

The investigation of the relations that Egypt may have had with the seas around it and the organisation of maritime exchanges between the Nile Valley and other regions cannot be envisaged without tackling the question of the nature of the merchandise embarked on the ships. If the products exchanged are largely the same over several millennia, there are perceptible changes too, multiple in their manifestations but responding to coherent historical causes: demographic variations, political fluctuations, modification of the environment, development of the areas of production and consumption, and so on. All of these circumstances and different factors weighed on the development of the interaction that is evident from the 3$^{rd}$ millennium BC.

Maritime voyage was, in short, a set of countless adventures, on different scales, consequences of the political, economic and social situation of the world as it then was. People moved from place to place, and materials, products and objects were transported. It is impossible to chart with any precision all these dispersed movements using multiple itineraries that could not be reduced to a few great 'routes', and that made up the wealth of inter-relational life. This world of ports was that of traders, but also that of exiles, pirates and mercenaries. It was also that of interpreters who allowed populations to understand each other and express themselves, that of all those who moved around, for diverse reasons, whether they were brokers, traffickers, or ambassadors, but also poets or artisans. They made many crossings, driven by innumerable motives. They were never-ending, these comings and goings, these circuits, these redistributions – these odysseys.

# Chronology

## Prehistory, 10,000–3300 BC

**5000 BC:** First sites occupied, first exchanges between Nubia and Egypt and between Palestine and northern Egypt.

**4000-3500 BC:** Nagada I or Amratian (3800-3500) in Upper Egypt, group 'A' culture in Lower Nubia, cultures of the north of the Nile Valley at Maadi, Wadi Digla, Heliopolis, Buto.

**3500-3300 BC:** Nagada II, progressive evolution and extension of the cultural characteristics of Nagada in the north of the Valley (Maadi); Nagada III, unification of the cultural characteristics in the Nile Valley and the Delta; development of the earliest cities and the earliest urban fortifications in Egypt, Syro-Palestine, Mesopotamia.

**3100-3000 BC:** Political unification between Upper and Lower Egypt by the sovereigns of Hierakonpolis, foundation of Memphis, hieroglyphic writing, relations between Egypt, the Near East and the Fertile Crescent.

## Pharaonic Egypt

**3150-2686 BC: Thinite era, 1ˢᵗ and 2ⁿᵈ Dynasties**

Thinis, the capital, has its necropolis at Abydos; development of Memphis and Saqqara; birth of the centralised state; architecture of unbaked bricks, first use of dressed stone; development of commercial relations between Egypt and Syro-Palestine.

**2686-2181 BC: Old Kingdom**

**2650-2575 BC:** 3ʳᵈ Dynasty, construction at Saqqara of the step-pyramid of King Djoser by the architect Imhotep; Memphis, capital of Egypt.

**2575-2465 BC:** 4ᵗʰ Dynasty, reign of Snefru (pyramids of Dashur and Meidum); the pharaohs Khufu, Khephren and Mykerinos build their pyramids at Giza; restructuring of the administration (the role of the vizir becomes important); expeditions to Nubia.

**2465-2323 BC:** 5ᵗʰ Dynasty, appearance of the Pyramid Texts in the pyramid of Unas; development of the bureaucracy.

**2323-2150 BC:** 6ᵗʰ Dynasty, pyramids of the pharaohs Teti, Pepi I, Merenra and Pepi II, at Saqqara; height of the vogue for autobiographical inscriptions by functionaries; rise of provincial autonomy; significant expansion into Nubia; colonisation of the oases of the Libyan Desert

**2180-2040 BC: First Intermediate Period**

Wakening of central royal power and development of local governments; 8ᵗʰ–10ᵗʰ Dynasties; division of the country, unrest, Asiatic invasions of the eastern Delta; struggle for power, then open war between the 10ᵗʰ Dynasty of Hierakonpolis and a Theban 11ᵗʰ Dynasty.

2040-1782 BC: **Middle Kingdom**

2040-1990 BC: 10th Dynasty; reign of Montuhotep I, who completes the reunification of Egypt; appearance of the Coffin Texts.

2000 BC: 12th Dynasty, rise to power of Amenemhat I; reigns of Sesostris I, Amenemhat II, Sesostris II and III, Amenemhat III; capital at Lisht; reorganisation of the centralised State; great period of literary creation; increasing importance of Fayum; construction of the Labyrinth; annexation of Lower Nubia (construction of fortresses); control of the Delta frontiers; military expeditions to Palestine.

1782-1570 BC: Second Intermediate Period

Anarchy and weakening of royal power; infiltration of the Hyksos, who found their capital at Avaris, in the north-east of the Delta; introduction of iron, the horse and chariots.

An independent 17th Dynasty in existence at Thebes and in Upper Egypt.

1560 BC: Open struggle between Thebes (Kamose and Ahmosis) and Avaris; attempted alliance between the Hyksos and Kerma; Theban reconquest, expulsion of the Hyksos and reunification of Egypt.

1570-1070 BC: **New Kingdom**

1560-1490 BC: Ahmosis I founds the 18th Dynasty. Thebes is the capital; Amenophis I, Thutmose I; Asiatic campaign; Thutmose II.

1490-1468 BC: Hatshepsut, pharaoh-queen, expedition to the land of Punt, construction of the temple of Deir el-Bahari.

1468-1436 BC: Thutmose III, seventeen campaigns in Asia, battle of Megiddo, Egyptian domination of Sudan, then Amenophis II and Thutmose IV.

1402-1364 BC: Amenophis III. Period of peace and apogee of Egyptian power and influence; temple of Luxor.

1364-1347 BC: Amenophis IV-Akhenaten, relocation of the capital to Amarna; solar cult of the god Aten; weakening of the Egyptian empire in Asia.

1347-1338 BC: Tutankhamun, restoration of the cult of Amun and return to Thebes.

1333-1306 BC: Horemheb, the traditional order is re-established.

1306 BC: 19th Dynasty: Seti I (1304-1290): aggressive policies in Asia, construction of the temple of Abydos.

1290-1224 BC: Rameses II, wars against the Hittites and in particular fights the battle of Kadesh; construction of numerous temples, Abu Simbel and the city of Piramesse in the east of the Delta.

1224 BC: Reign of Merenptah, war against the Hittites and the Libyans.

1186 BC: 20th Dynasty, Rameses III (1184-1153): conflict with the Libyans and the Sea Peoples; construction of the temple of Medinet Habu; palace plots.

1153-1069 BC: Reigns of Rameses IV to Rameses XI, progressive weakening of royal power; pillaging of the tombs in the Valley of the Kings; Herihor holds power in Thebes, power-struggles between royal power and the priests of Amon-Ra in Thebes.

| | |
|---|---|
| **1069-525 BC:** | **Third Intermediate Period** |
| 1069-722 BC: | Division of Egypt into two, then several kingdoms; 21st Dynasty (Tanite); Tanis is the capital in the reign of King Psusennes I; 22nd and 23rd Dynasties [Libyan] (945-722). |
| 730 BC: | Egypt is conquered by the Ethiopian sovereign Piankhi. |
| 725-713 BC: | 24th Dynasty at Sais, Tefnakht and Bocchoris resist the Kushites. |
| 715-664 BC: | 25th Dynasty (Kushite or Ethiopian); empire of the kings of Napata (Shabaka, Taharqa, Tanutamun); artistic renaissance (Djebed Barkal, Nuri and Kuri); opposition to the Assyrians in Asia. |
| 671 BC: | Conquest of northern Egypt by Esarhaddon and capture of Memphis. |
| 664 BC: | Assyrian conquest (sack of Thebes), then withdrawal after alliance with the princes of Sais. |
| 664-525 BC: | 26th Dynasty (Saite), reunification of Egypt by Psamtek I; Memphis again capital; Greek influence, cultural and artistic traditionalism; economic development; growth of the Persian threat. |

| | |
|---|---|
| **525-332 BC:** | **Late Period** |
| 525-404 BC: | 27th Dynasty, beginnings of Persian domination (reign of Cambyses III, Darius I, Xerxes); Egypt becomes a Persian province (satrapy); digging of the Red Sea canal (516-513); Herodotus in Egypt. |
| 404-343 BC: | 28th to 30th Dynasties, last independent dynasties; Nectanebo I consolidates royal power. |
| 343 BC: | Second period of Persian domination. |
| 333-332 BC: | Alexander conquers Egypt. |
| 331 BC: | Foundation of Alexandria. |

| | |
|---|---|
| **331 BC-AD 395: Graeco-Roman period** | |
| 311-30 BC: | Ptolemaic Dynasty founded by Ptolemy I; Ptolemy I to XIII, wars against the Seleucids; construction of numerous temples (end of the construction of the temple of Edfu, beginning of the construction of the temple of Kom Ombo, Dendera and Esna); construction of the Pharos of Alexandria; Queen Cleopatra associates with Pompey, Caesar, and then Antony: Battle of Actium; suicide of Antony and Cleopatra. |
| 30 BC-AD 305: | Egypt is a Roman province under the rule of prefects; Kiosk of Philae, decoration of mammisi at Dendera, foundation of Antinoe, portico of Hadrian at Philae. 250: last hieroglyphic inscriptions; growth of Christianity. |
| AD 383: | Edict of the Roman Emperor Theodosius, decreeing the closing of the pagan temples. |
| AD 395: | Death of Theodosius, Egypt is incorporated into the Eastern Empire. Start of the Byzantine Period. |

# Lexicon of nautical terms

## A

**Anchorage.** Place occupied by a ship held by one or more anchors. The ship's anchoring system.

## B

**Beams.** Principal beams placed across the ship to link its two sides, keep them apart and support the deck planking. The main-beam is the beam located at the ship's widest point.

**Bilge.** Part of the hull between the bottom and the side. Also the lowest part of the hull, situated above the keel, where the water gathers.

**Bilge-keel.** Piece located in the prolongation of the keel, under the stern, to increase the anti-drift surface area of the ship.

**Bill.** Point of each of the flukes of an anchor.

**Bolt rope.** Rope sewn around the edges of a ship to strengthen it against stresses transmitted from the rigging.

**Bottom planking.** Second strake on the planking, counting from the keel, and situated after the garboard.

**Bowline.** Rope made fast to the drop edge of a square sail enabling this sail to be hoisted fore to position it more effectively.

**Bowsprit.** Oblique mast placed at the fore of the ship, fixed on the stem and carrying a spritsail.

**Brace.** Rope used to position a yard.

**Brail.** Rope used to furl a sail to reduce its area, or to take it in.

## C

**Capstan.** Upright winch used to heave the moorings.

**Cast anchor.** To drop the anchor and let out the length of chain necessary for the ship's safe harbouring.

**Cathead.** Big piece of wood, projecting out on either side of the prow and helping to manoeuvre the anchor.

**Centre of effort** or **Centre of sail.** The centre of effort is the centre of gravity of all the sails when these are imagined on their respective masts, opened and extended longitudinally.

**Cleat.** Piece of hard wood bearing two gaffs and fixed to different places of the ship to fasten ropes to.

**Close to the wind.** Point of sailing corresponding to the direction closest to that of the wind. A ship is sailing 'close to the wind' when it is trying to move forward in the direction from which the wind is blowing, as when tacking.

**Cutwater.** Section at the front of the stem that cuts through the water when the ship is underway.

## D

**Dead-eye.** Block of wood, flat and circular, pierced by several holes through which pass the ropes used to tighten the shrouds.

**Dead wood.** Piece of reinforcing wood placed in the angle formed by the keel with the stern or the stem.

**Deck.** Set of plankings fixed on the beams and covering them.

**Deck-beam.** Transversal beam holding up the decks.

**Drag anchor.** Rough-and-ready piece of equipment, often composed of two spars in the shape of a cross on which a square canvas is stretched, or, simply, made from any available floating body. This arrangement, linked to a vessel by a cable, is used to control drifting in heavy seas.

**Draught.** Measure of how low a ship rests in the water, from the keel to the waterline.

## E

**Edge.** Narrowest surface of a piece of wood lengthwise.

## F

**False keel.** Reinforcement placed under the keel to protect it, especially in case of running aground.

**Floor timber.** Piece of the frame placed astraddle the keel and symmetrical to the axis of the ship. The floor timber constitutes the central part of a timber and its shape affects that of the bottom of the hull.

**Fluke.** More or less open arm situated at the lower end of the anchor, opposite the stock, and used to gain purchase on the seabed. An ancient anchor was generally fitted with two flukes, but examples of asymmetrical anchors with a single fluke are also known.

**Fore-and-aft sail.** Axial sail in the shape of a quadrilateral. The spritsail is a fore-and-aft sail.

**Fore-foot.** Piece of curved wood forming the junction between the keel and the stem.

**Foresail.** Mast placed forward on a ship in front of the main mast. The term also designates the sail carried by this mast.

**Frame.** The set of curved pieces of the transverse woodwork covered by the planking. An element of the transversal woodwork of a ship.

**Freeboard.** Distance from the waterline to the upper edge of a vessel's side.

## G

**Garboard.** The lowest strake of the planking, situated against the keel. A ship is said to be garboard return when its transversal section presents a counter-curve on the level of the junction of the keel and the garboard.

**Griping.** A ship is said to be griping when it has a tendency to come a-weather.

**Gunwale.** Set of horizontal pieces covering the heads of the summit timbers of the frame.

## H

**Half-timber.** In ancient shipbuilding, each of the two curved pieces brought together either side of the keel to form a timber.

**Halyard.** Rope used to hoist the yard.

**Hawsers.** Ropes used to moor the ship.

**Hull.** The whole framework of a ship and its external envelope. The hull of a ship is formed by two closely attached parts: the skeleton and the planking – the external covering of the skeleton. It also often includes the inner planking – the lining of the frame.

## I

**Inner plank.** Planking covering the inner face of the timbers.

**Inner planking.** Set of planks comprising the floor of a ship.

**Inner stem-post.** Piece reinforcing the stem from inside.

## J

**Jettisoning.** Action of throwing overboard a part of the cargo when a vessel is in difficulty.

## K

**Keel.** Long member used in the construction of the ship and acting as its base. It bears the stern at its rear and the stem at its front. It is the main piece of the axial woodwork of the ship's hull.

**Keelson.** Piece parallel to the keel and reinforcing it from within. The keelson rests on the frame.

**Knot.** Unit of measurement of a ship's speed. A speed of 1 knot corresponds to that of a ship travelling 1 nautical mile per hour.

## L

**Landmark.** Any fixed, characteristic and visible object that serves as a means of finding where you are off a coast.

**Large.** Point of sailing corresponding to a wind direction between a cross-wind and three-quarters behind (quartering wind).

**Lateen sail.** Triangular sail fixed to the mast by an oblique yard called a 'latten yard', situated in the axis of the ship.

**Lay out.** To run out a mooring in a given direction lengthwise.

**Lift.** Rope which goes up to the top of the mast bearing the yard and then comes back down to the deck. This rope is designed to support the ends of the yards, to raise them, peak them and manoeuvre them in a vertical direction, if required.

## M

**Mast.** Long piece of wood set up in greater or lesser numbers on the ship, to receive the yards, gaffs or stays that carry one or several sails designed to transmit to the ship the action of the wind, so as to make it move forward and help the rudder in steering. Masts in general have more or less the shape of a very long cylinder. In the Old Kingdom, the mast was almost regularly doubled - composed of two oblique shafts linked at the top and movable (derrick-mast).

**Mast-head.** Reinforced end of the mast that receives the pulleys of the yard ropes.

**Sea mile.** Unit of distance used in the navy: a French sea mile is the equivalent of 1852m.

**Moor broadside on.** To maintain a ship in a definite fixed direction by means of anchors dropped fore and aft.

**Mortice.** Notch made in the thickness of a piece of wood and designed to receive the tenon.

# P

**Peaking.** The deliberate peaking of a yard and its sails on ships rigged with a square sail allows the centre of effort to be brought back to the aft of the centre of drift so that the ship can carry a weather helm and sail into the wind.

**Peg.** Stem of wood used to assemble the different construction elements of a vessel.

**Pirate.** From the Greek 'pirates', the man who tries his fortunes at sea, a name given to sailors and ships that go round pillaging, in times of peace or war, other ships without the endorsement of any regular government.

**Planking.** Planks that make up the ship's sides. The planking forms the external envelope of the ship. 'Planking first' is when the planking is assembled before the frame is put in place.

**Point of sailing.** Direction followed by a ship with regard to the wind. By extension, the disposition of the sails. The main points of sailing are: following wind, quartering wind, free wind, beam wind, and close wind.

**Poop.** Rear part of the ship. It can be round or flat.

**Poop-deck.** Superstructure situated on the aft deck of a ship, extending to each side.

**Prow.** Forward part of the ship.

# R

**Rabbet.** Groove with ridges on either side, generally running the length of the keel to receive the edges of the planking.

**Rigging.** Everything concerned with the mast system and in particular the ropes; also, everything which is necessary for the propulsion of sailing ships (masts, yards, sails, ropes, and so on).

**Ropes.** The set of ropes comprising the rigging. Standing rigging, used to hold up the masts, is distinguished from running rigging, which enables the yards to be controlled and the sails furled.

**Rowing port.** Opening made in the side of a ship to allow an oar to pass through.

**Rudder chain.** Used to fasten the rudder to the side of the ship so as to prevent it from being carried away.

# S

**Scarf.** Halved-joint assemblage, more or less complex in form, between two pieces of woodwork.

**Shank.** Long straight piece of the anchor which goes from the stock to the junction of the flukes. Its upper part is often equipped with a ring, called the anchor ring, designed to receive the cable of the anchor.

**Sheave.** Pulley wheel.

**Sheaveless block.** Block of wood with a single hole (see **dead-eye**) used to stiffen ropes.

**Sheet.** Rope used to control a sail and to attach it at its lower corner when in the wind.

**Shroud.** A standing rope serving to maintain masts laterally.

**Side.** On board a ship, the side includes everything that constitutes the thickness of the flank, either ribs and timbers, or else planking, extending from the waterline to the gunwale on both sides.

**Sounding line.** Device serving to determine the depth and nature of the sea floor. An ancient sounding line was composed of a lead weight, hollowed out at its base and smeared with resin or soot, and a line from which it was suspended.

**Spar.** General term used to designate a long piece of wood used in the mast system.

**Sprit.** Spar or pole, fixed to the foot of the mast and maintaining under the wind, diagonally and pointing aft, the upper point of an ancient sail called a 'spritsail'.

**Square sail.** Rectangular sail situated perpendicular to the axis of the ship. It is carried by a yard.

**Stanchion.** Pieces of construction that are used to extend another piece by being added on to it at one end, or an upright used to support the deck-beams. However, in ancient ship building, the frame stanchions were generally not assembled on to the bottom frames.

**Stay.** Ropes designed to keep the mast firm in the longitudinal direction.

**Stem.** Piece of curved wood fixed in the prolongation of the keel which constitutes the forward extremity of the ship.

**Step.** Wooden block with a cavity into which the foot of the stem is lodged the foot of the mast. In ancient shipbuilding, the keelson often played this role.

**Stern post.** Piece of woodwork situated in the sheer plan of the ship and rising at the stern in the prolongation of the keel.

**Stern rudder.** Placed in the axis of the ship, the stern rudder was invented at the end of the 12th century. It is stronger than the lateral rudder and considerably facilitates manoeuvres.

**Stock.** The cross bar of an anchor, fixed or movable, situated in the upper part of the shank and perpendicular to the flukes. In antiquity, the anchor stock could be in stone, lead or iron.

**Strake.** The row of planking extending all along the side of the ship or the deck.

**Stringer.** Long reinforcing piece extending lengthways above the timbers and linking them together.

**Strop.** Rope collar used for several purposes, especially to maintain movable pieces (pulley, oar, yard, rudder, and so on).

**Superstructure.** Construction built on the upper deck of a ship, fore or aft, sometimes with several storeys.

**Swing at anchor.** Said of a ship at anchor which changes its bearing under the effect of winds or tides.

## T

**Tack** (noun). A rope holding the lower point of a sail on the windward side.

**Tack** (verb). To navigate in the direction from which the wind is coming, by zig-zagging from side to side. To tack is to change direction in such a way that the ship goes about.

**Tenon.** The tenon is a projection designed to fit into a mortice or any corresponding hollowed-out piece to form a joint between two members.

**Thole pin.** Stem in iron or wood that is planted in the gunwale of a vessel. The thole pin serves to keep in place a strop fixed to the oar's handle, and to support the latter while rowing.

**Timber.** Curved piece of the transversal woodwork of the hull, rising from the keel to the gunwale. The 'main-timber' is the timber situated at the greatest breadth of the ship. In the form of construction known as 'on timbers', these are the first members laid on the keel to receive the planking.

**Toggle-pin.** Wooden pin crossing the belaying-pin rack to which the running rigging is attached. Also, a wooden peg in the shape of a truncated cone used to bring together two ropes.

**Treenail.** Long peg of wood used in particular to fix the frame to the planking.

## W

**Wale.** Thicker strake of the planking, designed to protect the ship's side.

**Wash strakes.** Protections in canvas or wood placed above the gunwale to prevent the water from getting into the ship.

## Y

**Yard.** Spar carrying a sail, most often square in shape. The ancient yard was often made of two pieces joined in the middle.

# Glossary

## I. General vocabulary

*I.1 In Egyptian transliteration*

*jʿꜣ.w*, chiefs of foreign troops
181

*(j)m(y)-r(ꜣ) js.t ẖnw.w*, director of the team of rowers
147

*(j)m(y)-r(ꜣ) js.wt*, director of the crews
147

*(j)m(y)-r(ꜣ) ʿpr.w*, director of the crews
147

*(j)m(y)-r(ꜣ) ʿpr(.w) (n) ʿḥʿw n(y)-sw(.t)*, director of the crews of the royal fleet
147

*(j)m(y)-r(ꜣ) wp.wt n ʿš*, director of the cedar expeditions
175

*(j)m(y)-r(ꜣ) mšʿ*, director of the troops
148, 164, 175, 181

*(j)m(y)-r(ꜣ) md̲*, head of ten men
147

*(j)m(y)-r(ꜣ) md̲ wjꜣ*, head of ten men aboard the royal barque
148

*(j)m(y)-r(ꜣ) r(ꜣ)-ḥꜣw.t nb.t n(y).t wꜣd̲ wr*, director of all the mouths of *Wadj Wer*
177

*(j)m(y)-r(ꜣ) ẖnw.w*, director of the rowers
147

*(j)m(y)-r(ꜣ) smntj.w*, director of the explorers
179

*(j)m(y)-r(ꜣ) srsw wjꜣ*, director of the six (sailors?) of the royal barque
148

*(j)m(y)-r(ꜣ) kꜣ.t nb.t n(y).t n(y)-sw.t*, directors of the king's works
177

*Jnw*, presents
84, 85, 139

*Jrj šw.t*, to do trade
163, 181

*(J)r(y) pʿt*, prince
177

*Jry mḫꜣ*, controller of weighings
139

*(J)r(y) ḥꜣ.t*, the man at the prow, the *proreute*
148, 150

*(J)r(y) ḥmy*, the man at the poop
149, 150

*Js.t*, crew
30, 94, 143

*ʿpr wjꜣ*, fitter-out of the royal boat
147, 148

*ʿpr wjꜣ jmy jrty*, admiral
148, 181

*ʿpr.w n n(y)-sw(.t) wjꜣ*, crews of the royal barques
143

*ʿnty*, incense
83, 84, 178

*ʿḥʿ ʿpr ks.w*, manager of the kesou-barques
147

*ʿḥʿ ʿpr nfr.w*, manager of the crew of recruits
147, 148

*ʿš*, Pine of Cilicia
109

*Wpwty*, messenger
146, 166, 175-9, 181, 182, 184, 187

*Wpwty n(y)-sw(.t)*, royal messenger
175, 177, 178, 179, 182

*Wpwty n Jmn*, messenger of Amun
187

*Wḫr.w*, naval dockyard
47, 83

*Bꜣkw*, tributes
139, 146, 163

*Bjꜣy.t n Pwn.t*, marvels of Punt
181, 182

*Bnry.w*, suppliers of dates
159

*Br*, type of boat
84, 85, 94

*Btty*, basket maker
159

*Pr*, domain
145, 146, 155, 163, 164, 165

*Pd̲.t*, troop
143

*Mfk.t*, turquoise
181

*Mnj.t*, mooring stake
195

*Mnš*, menech-boat
47, 84, 85, 94, 95, 96, 110, 116, 140, 145, 151, 152, 155, 163

*Mry*, cedar of Lebanon
109

*Mry.t*, shore, port
47, 86, 189, 195

*Mḥʿw*, linen
119

*Mḫr*, purchase
119, 159

*Mšʿ*, troop
143, 164, 178, 181, 195

*Mškb.w*, escorters
135, 146, 166

*Mkrj*, vendor
159, 166

*Mdḥ*, to construct (in wood)
82, 83

*Nꜥy*, traveller
193, 194

*Nfw*, boatman, navigator
135, 149, 150, 151

*Nfw n rmṯ js.t*, boatman of the crew
142

*Rꜣ*, outlet
65

*Rꜣ-ꜣḥ.wt*, outlet for crops
15, 16

*Rꜣ-jꜣb.t*, outlet for the East
65

*Rꜣ-wꜣt.y*, outlet of the two ways
65

*Rwḏ.w*, controllers
84, 148, 164

*Ḥꜣty*, pilot
193

*Ḥꜣty-ꜥ*, governor
177

*Ḥꜥw*, fleet
83

*Ḥꜥty rḫ mw*, pilot who knows the waters
192

*Ḥwty.w*, non-commissioned officers
84, 148

*Ḥry wsḫ*, captain of an *ousekh*-boat
135, 151, 152

*Ḥry pḏ.t*, commander of a troop
94, 143, 148, 177

*Ḥry.w pḏ.wt n mnš*, chiefs of the troops of a *menech*-boat
84, 143, 148

*Ḥry mnš*, ship's captain
67, 94, 96, 151, 152

*Ḥry mškb.w*, chief of the escorters
146

*Ḥry nfw*, principal boatman
128, 150, 151

*Ḥbpꜣr*, commercial association
155, 156

*Ḫ.t*, goods
84, 85, 94

*Ḫntš*, forests of Lebanon
109

*Ḫny.t*, rower, oarsman
144

*Sꜣw.w*, overseers
135, 145, 146, 166

*Swn*, trade, to trade
159

*Sp*, to assemble
83

*Smntj.w*, explorers
179, 181

*Smr wꜥty*, sole friend
177

*Smsm hꜣj(.t) n pr Jmn*, keeper of the portico of the temple of Amun
184, 185

*Sḥḏ n wjꜣ*, inspector of the royal barque
181

*Sš*, scribe
163, 177

*Sš ꜥpr*, scribe of the crew
147

*Sš n(y)-sw(.t)*, royal scribe
177

*Sqd.w*, sailors
143, 192

*Šꜣy.t*, tax
146

*Šꜥty*, standard weight, monetary unit
165

*Šwj*, to unload
168

*Šw(.t)*, lack, penury
163

*Šwty.w*, traders
135, 140, 155-168, 169, 170, 189

*Šwty.w n ḫꜣs.t*, traders from abroad
161

*Štꜣ.w*, woodland
108

*Qwr.w*, transporters, dockers
137

*Kpn.wt/kbn.wt*, 'Giblite' boats?
82, 92, 100

*Krr*, type of boat
94

*Kftj.w*, Cretan boat?
93

*Tp-ḫ.t*, keel?
103

*Dp.t*, boat
39, 143, 192, 195

*Dmj(.t)*, city, port
30, 192

## I.2 In Semitic transliteration

*Bidal(u)/badal(u)*, vice-president, representative, intermediary
174

*Dwgy qnd/rʿ*, boat
127

*Hubur*, commercial association
156

*Ḫbr*, to ally oneself, to join
156

*Kzr*, boat originating in Asia Minor
127

*Maqqèbèt*, hammer
152

*Našu*, to raise, to be raised up
95

*Qardabbu*, cavalry officer
175

*Sa-rechi*, to convey, carry
174

*Šamallum*, broker
165

*Šulmanu*, courtesy gift
175

*Tám-kà-ri-ia / tamkaru*, trader
165, 176

*Tamkarum*, market square
165

*Ywny*, boat originating in Syro–Palestine
127

## II. Proper names

## II.1 In Egyptian transliteration

*Jmn*, Amun
139, 151, 192

*Jmn pꜣ ḥmy*, Amun the helmsman
192

*Jmn tꜣ mṯn*, Amun of the road
192

*Wn-Jmn*, Wenamun
184

*Mʿnwgꜣbwtj*, Mengabot
67, 152

*N(y)-sw-bꜣ-nb-ḏdw*, Smendes
67

*Tj-n(y).t-Jmn*, Tentamun
67

## III. Names of places and peoples

## III.1 In Egyptian transliteration

*J-r-sꜣ*, Cyprus
22, 29, 30

*Ym*, sea
12, 13, 30

*Ym ʿꜣ*, great sea
13, 30

*Ym ʿꜣ n Mw-qd*, great sea of Mou-qed
13, 84, 85

*Ym ʿꜣ n Ḫꜣrw*, great sea of Kharou
13, 22, 30, 67, 152

*ʿꜣm.w*, Asiatics
30, 33, 166, 167

*ʿꜣm.w ḥr(y).w šʿ*, Asiatics who dwell in the sands
26

*Wꜣḏ-wr*, Great Green
12, 13, 16, 34, 61, 143, 163, 178, 181, 191, 192

*Bjꜣ n Pwn.t*, Mines of Punt
41, 83

*Pꜣ mw n pꜣ Rʿ*, Waters of Ra
66

*Pwn.t*, Punt
83, 84, 178, 179, 181

*Pr-mry.t*, the house of the port, Naukratis
47, 62

*Prw-nfr*, arsenal of Memphis
66, 140, 142

*Pḥw*, hinterland
15, 16

*Pds.wt n(y.)wt š*
16

*Nwn*, primordial ocean
16

*Rꜣ-ḥꜣ.wt*
15, 16, 65

*Rꜣ-bꜣ-rꜣ*, Lebanon
22, 32

*Rṯnw*, Retenu
31

*Ḥꜣw-nb.wt*, Haunebut
13, 14, 34, 61

*Ḥn.t*, Thonis
16, 61, 62

*Ḫꜣrw*, Syria
22, 30, 67, 164

*Sww*, Mersa Gawasis
41, 76, 195

*Šn-ʿꜣ-šk*
16

*Šn-wr*, Great Circle
16

*Šn-rḫyt*
15

*Km.t*, Egypt
84, 85, 143

*Kp-pw-nw* / *Kp-pw-nꜣ* / *kpn* / *kbn*, Byblos
22, 31, 32, 40, 41

*Gbtjw*, Coptos
83, 84

*Tꜣ*, land, earth
30

*Tꜣ nṯr*, divine land
41, 84

*Tꜣ-qꜤḥ.t*, the elbow
13

*Tꜣ-kꜣ-r*, Sakal
22

*Dj-r*, Dor
22

*Ḏꜣ-r*, Tyre
22

*Ḏꜣhy*, Djahy
30, 31, 145

*ḎꜤn.t*, Tanis
22, 67

*Ḏd-dn-nꜣ*, Sidon
22

## III.2 In Semitic transliteration

*A-la-ch-ia*, Cyprus
29

*Gbl > Gebeil*, Byblos
31

*Ḫurri*, Hurrite
31

*Ḫurru > ḥor?* hurrite
30

*Karu(m)*, port, quay, trading centre
74

*Msry, Msrt*, Egyptian
160

*Rmn*, Lebanon
32

*Sōr*, Tyre
32

# Index

## I. Greek and Latin terms

*Custodes litorum*
142

*Customes nauium*
145

*Diaeta*
110

*Endocheus*
173

*Emporion*
vii, 45, 60, 61, 86, 109, 126, 152, 161, 162, 164, 166, 167

*Emporoi*
ix, 167, 168, 169, 172, 173

*Holkos*
100

*Kapeloi*
ix, 168, 169, 172

*Mare Aegyptiacum*
27, 28

*Mare Carpathicum*
27, 28

*Mare Cyprium*
27, 28

*Mare clausum*
22, 138

*Mare Libycum*
27, 28

*Mare Lycium*
27

*Mare Pamphylium*
27

*Mare Phoenicium*
27

*Mensores machinarii*
139

*Naucleroi*
ix, 152, 168, 169, 170, 171, 172, 173

*Negotiatores*
157, 206

*Negotiatores frumentarii*
157

*Negotiatores uinarii*
157

*Neoria*
100

*Palinkapelos*
167

*Phalangarii/falancarii*
137, 138

*Ploion*
100

*Prostatai*
161

*Pyknos*
106, 160

*Saburrarii*
140

*Societas unius negotiationis*
157

## II. Proper names

### II.1 Deities and divine beings

Amun
ix, xvi, 1, 23, 32, 62, 67, 68, 69, 84, 89, 96, 103, 128, 140, 141, 150, 151, 152, 155, 158, 165, 179, 184, 185, 186, 187, 189, 191, 192, 193, 202

Aphrodite
195

Apollo
61, 109

Astarte
11, 30, 140

Aten
165

Atum
78, 194

Baal
11, 74, 140, 161, 202

Bastet
198

Bes
40, 198, 199, 200

Haroeris
195

Harpocrates
62

Hathor
29, 85, 86, 143, 178, 193, 194, 198, 199, 200

Hephaistos
200

Hera
61

Herakles
50, 62, 109

Hermes
3, 4, 19, 202

Horus
16, 67, 70, 85, 86, 177, 179, 193, 194, 198, 200

Isis
xvi, 4, 6, 7, 11, 92, 109, 128, 161, 164, 200, 202

Khnum
162, 164, 166, 188, 191

Khonsu
xvi, 62

Khusor
200

Min
152, 165, 193, 194

Minerva
196

Neith
61

Osiris
xvi, 11, 92, 163, 194, 200

Ptah
45, 68, 128, 141, 151, 163, 194, 198, 199, 200

Ra
vii, 11, 13, 15, 16, 29, 65, 66, 84, 94, 95, 128, 146, 148, 160, 163, 164, 193, 194

Sekhmet
146, 194, 198

Serapis
200, 201, 202

Seth
11, 68, 192, 200

Shu
193

Typhon
11, 73

Yam
11, 16

Zeus
27, 61, 74, 75, 122, 200, 202

## II.2  Kings and queens

Alexander
xv, 4, 9, 36, 47, 60, 74, 83, 96

Amasis
61, 99, 161

Amenemhat I
41, 66

Amenemhat II
1, 30, 84

Amenemhat III
176, 195

Amenhotep II
34, 38, 47, 69

Amenhotep III
27, 32, 34, 181

Amenhotep IV/Akhenaten
47, 140, 161

Arsinoe Philadelphe
194

Augustus
73

Baal
11, 74, 140, 161, 202

Cheops – Khufu
xiii, 81, 83, 89, 90, 96, 103, 104, 105, 107, 108

Khephren
xiii

Cleopatra
4, 78, 157

Darius I
1 36, 73, 77, 81, 92

Djedkara-Isesi
1

Djoser
xiii, 47

Hatiba
30, 185

Hatshepsut
xvi, 12, 29, 34, 36, 38, 41, 79, 80, 81, 82, 83, 86, 89, 92, 93, 100, 101, 111, 112, 118, 119, 120, 121, 122, 123, 125, 137, 144, 145, 147, 148, 149, 150, 177, 179, 180, 181, 182, 191, 194

Hieron II
128

Hiram
126, 174

Huram
126

Kamosis
69

Lagides – Ptolemies
152, 156, 168, 172

Menelaus
60, 61, 191

Menkaura
xiii

Mentuhotep III
1, 82

Merenptah
27, 96

Merykara
16

Nectanebo I
61, 71, 192, 194

Nectanebo II
71

Nekau II
12, 36, 77, 78, 81, 82, 99, 156

Pepi I
109, 175

Pepi II
1, 25, 82, 175

Psammetichus I
61

Psusennes I
68

Ptolemy II Philadelphus
78, 79, 81, 86, 92, 100, 101, 152

Ptolemy III Euergetes
128, 157

Ptolemy IV Philopator
128

Ptolemy XII Auletes
78

Rameses II
xiii, 11, 27, 32, 34, 66, 68, 70, 82, 85, 94, 96, 98, 140, 141, 143, 152, 163, 175

Rameses III
5, 13, 26, 27, 32, 36, 41, 81, 82, 83, 84, 85, 94, 97, 98, 143, 146, 148, 152

Rameses IX
13

Sahure
1, 89, 92, 93, 100, 103, 107, 110, 111, 114, 121, 122, 123, 144, 147, 149

Sakarbaal
32, 152, 155, 185

Sargon II
74, 126, 127

Senusret I
1, 41, 82, 84, 105, 147, 181, 194

Senusret II
84, 194

Seti I
66, 69, 94, 146, 161, 162, 163

Snefru
1, 3, 5, 7, 9, 89, 133, 175

Solomon
86, 101

Teti
1, 194

Thutmose III
27, 30, 33, 34, 38, 47, 69, 83, 92, 96, 138, 140, 177, 193

Thutmose IV
69, 140

Zimri-Lim
93

## II.3  Names of individuals

Amennefer
164

Ameny
82, 83, 84, 147, 175

Anankha
82, 83

Antef
34

Antefoqer
41, 82, 83, 84, 147

Bias
xix

Chaeremon
11

Cornelius Gallus
65, 84

Eudoxus of Cyzicus
36, 157

Eumaeus
21

Helen
60, 61

Henu
39, 40, 41, 82, 146, 176

Hori
164

Izezi
128

Kenamun
95, 110, 115, 134, 137, 138, 142, 143, 149, 161, 188

Khaemwaset
129, 137, 141, 185, 186

Mark Antony
65

Mengabot
66, 67, 152

Nekhemhatef
163

Nessobek
163

Pepinakht
25, 26, 92

Rekhmira
34, 35, 149, 150, 187

Saint Paul
7

Senmut
150

Smendes
31, 32, 66, 67, 68, 69, 152, 155, 156, 185, 187

Sobek
163, 164

Tentamun
152, 187

Thon
61

Ulysses
xv, 21

Unas
1, 93, 102, 121, 122

Userkaf
1, 112

## II.4 Places and peoples

Aboukir
xvii, 4, 25, 50, 53, 60, 62

Abu Seifa (Tell)
65

Abusir
45, 63

Abydos
47, 94, 123, 140, 146, 152, 161, 163, 165

Achaean(s)
26

Actium
9, 65

Adoulis
42

Aegean
7, 9, 13, 15, 16, 19, 20, 26, 27, 33, 34, 53, 70, 71, 94, 170, 175

Aeolis
61

Africa
xv, xix, xx, 1, 13, 20, 21, 27, 36, 56, 58, 64, 66, 82, 86, 89, 99, 100, 108, 114, 156, 157, 182, 198

Akko
30, 33

Aksha
13, 32

Alasia
1, 22, 27, 29, 30, 96, 160, 161, 174, 184, 185

Aleppo
109

Alexandria
xv, xvi, 2, 4, 7, 8, 9, 19, 21, 23, 25, 28, 45, 50, 53, 54, 56, 59, 60, 62, 63, 64, 79, 82, 86, 118, 119, 128, 168, 169, 170, 171, 172, 173, 200

Al-Mina
13, 33, 156, 157, 161, 198

Almunecar
198

Amada
13

Amarna
13, 25, 29, 32, 47, 49, 92, 96, 109, 118, 161, 174, 175

Aqaba
37, 83, 101

Arab(s)
xv, 73, 74, 78, 79, 83, 86, 156, 157, 171

Arabia
xviii, 36, 40, 41, 78, 86, 100, 101, 162

Aramaean(s)
23

Asia
xv, xvi, xix, xx, 1, 9, 20, 21, 23, 25, 28, 29, 30, 33, 34, 35, 36, 50, 65, 66, 67, 69, 109, 123, 126, 140, 152, 156, 181

Asia Minor
xv, xx, 9, 20, 21, 23, 25, 28, 29, 30, 33, 34, 35, 109, 123, 126, 152

Aswan
76, 162

Assur
34, 126

Assyria(ns)
xix, 74, 142, 196

Athens
21, 28, 100

Athribis
122, 147, 194, 195

Avaris
vii, 66, 67, 68, 69

Bab el-Mandeb
40, 101, 156

Babylonia
xx, 33, 101

Bardawil (Lake)
vii, 72, 73, 74, 75

Beersheba
72

Berenice
xv, 38, 40, 42, 76, 82, 83, 84, 86, 128

Beirut
xvi, 32, 96, 171

Bitter Lakes
22, 76, 77, 78, 81, 85

Black Sea
9

Bubastis
38, 50, 78, 122

Busiris
14

Buto
17, 18, 59

Byblos
xvi, 1, 13, 22, 23, 30, 31, 32, 46, 47, 48, 49, 67, 83, 92, 96, 105, 123, 152, 155, 156, 181, 184, 185, 187, 191, 194

Byzantium
xvi, 21, 28

Canopic branch
53, 61, 62

Canopus
50, 53, 60, 62

Carpathic Sea
vii, 35, 127

Carthage
xv, 21, 28, 64, 160, 198

Caesarea
20, 21, 28, 31

Chasou
69

Chios
61, 161

Cyprus
xx, 8, 9, 21, 22, 23, 27, 28, 29, 30, 33, 34, 47, 69, 99, 109, 122, 160, 161, 174, 184, 185, 196, 198, 199

Cypriot Sea
vii, 33

Cilicia
28, 29, 33

Clazomenae
61

Cleopatris
84

Cnidus
36, 61, 101

Coptos
xv, 12, 13, 36, 47, 76, 80, 81, 82, 83, 84, 85, 86, 108, 128, 194, 195

Crete
7, 9, 18, 21, 26, 27, 30, 33, 34, 59, 93

Cyrenaica
18, 59, 63

Dahlak (Island)
38, 41

Damascus
30, 176

Damietta
xiv, 17

Deir el-Bahari
xviii, 79, 80, 81, 93, 112, 118, 119, 120, 121, 122, 125, 144, 147, 149, 150, 178, 179, 180, 194

Deir el-Medina
146, 148, 162, 167, 188

Delta of the Nile
xiv, 4, 14, 16, 18, 24, 25, 26, 27, 29, 30, 49, 50, 54, 55, 57, 59, 60, 64, 91

Delos
45, 171, 172, 173, 202

Diospolis
17, 18

Djahy
30, 31, 47, 93, 94, 145, 163, 192

Dor
1, 22, 29, 31, 47, 127, 152, 184, 185

Doris
61

Dura-Europos
xv

Edfu
13, 16, 82, 179, 181, 182, 192, 194, 200

Eilat
86

El-Arich (Wadi)
73, 74

El-Dab'a (Tell)
34, 66, 67, 69

El-Farama (Tell)
59, 65, 70, 72

El-Herr Tell
71, 72, 74

El-Kab
76

El-Kanais (Tell)
71

El-Makhzan (Tell)
71

El-Maskhuta (Tell)
78, 100

Elephantine
23, 109, 126, 152, 162, 164, 166

Erythraea
156

Ethiopia
38, 41, 86, 100, 157

Euphrates
31, 83, 94

Faqous

Farasan
38

Fayum
12, 16, 17, 76, 162, 164

Gasus (Wadi)
76, 80, 85, 194, 195

Gaza
72, 73, 74

Gerrha
xv, 65, 72, 75

Geziret Faraoun
86

Greece
xix, 9, 18, 33, 34, 59, 61, 161, 169

Greek(s)
x, xv, 4, 5, 7, 8, 9, 11, 13, 16, 17, 20, 21, 28, 33, 35, 36, 45, 50, 54, 60, 61, 62, 67, 70, 72, 73, 74, 75, 84, 94, 98, 99, 100, 127, 142, 145, 147, 148, 152, 156, 157, 159, 161, 167, 168, 171, 173, 202

Halicarnassus
61

Hammamat (Wadi)
36, 39, 40, 76, 80, 82, 85, 92, 148, 176, 179, 193

Haunebut
vii, 13, 15, 16, 19, 33, 55

Hebua (Tell)
69, 70

Heliopolis
69, 76, 78, 81, 85, 95, 141, 146, 189

Herakleion
4, 50, 60, 62, 63

Hermopolis
47, 118

Hittite(s)
xix, 13, 29, 96, 98, 109, 175

Hyksos
66, 68, 69

India
xv, 36, 38, 40, 78, 79, 101, 127, 157

Ionia
61

Iran
xvi

Ismailia
22, 76, 78

Israel
13, 33, 75, 160

Italy
ii, 7, 20, 53, 58, 61, 161

Jaffa
25, 30, 47, 126

Jerusalem
22, 95, 109, 126, 156

Joppa
126

Karnak
xiii, 69, 81, 84, 140, 185, 187, 189, 192

Kasios (Mount)
73, 74, 75, 122, 200, 202

Kefty(ou)
30, 33

Kharou
152

Khent-she
30

Kition
29, 33, 100, 122, 199

Lebanon
xix, 1, 8, 13, 22, 28, 31, 32, 46, 48, 49, 109, 126, 185, 193

Leukos Limen
6

Libya
xvi, 21, 25, 27, 28, 36, 50

Libyans
16, 27

Loukki (island of)
27

Luxor
xiii, 41, 75, 140

Lycia
27, 28

Malta
21, 28, 198

Mari
29, 30, 93

Massaoua
38

Medinet Habu (temple of)
7, 26, 32, 84, 94, 97, 139

Mediterranean
v, vii, xiii, xv, xvi, xix, xx, 1, 3, 5, 7, 8, 9, 12, 13, 16, 18, 19, 20, 21, 22, 23, 25, 26, 27, 28, 29, 30, 31, 32, 33, 35, 36, 39, 47, 49, 50, 55, 60, 64, 66, 68, 69, 70, 71, 72, 73, 74, 77, 79, 81, 92, 93, 94, 95, 96, 99, 101, 105, 107, 108, 110, 117, 122, 123, 127, 147, 156, 167, 173, 187, 196, 198, 199, 200, 202

Medjai
69, 182

Memphis
42, 45, 47, 49, 50, 53, 59, 65, 66, 68, 85, 89, 95, 128, 140, 141, 142, 160, 161, 165, 170, 171, 176, 188, 189, 194, 200

Mendes
14, 17, 18, 59, 194

Menzala (Lake)
xiv, 17

Egyptian Sea
vii, 28, 29, 33, 89, 92, 94, 108

Phoenician Sea
vii, 30, 33

Mersa Gawasis
38, 40, 41, 76, 80, 81, 82, 83, 84, 85, 121, 122, 128, 147, 194, 195

Mersa Matruh
63

Mesopotamia
109, 165

Miletus
21, 28, 161

Mitanni
31

Milesians
61

Minoans
34

Moeris (Lake)
17, 164

Mohamedia
65, 71, 72

Mons Claudianus
76

Mons Porphyrites
76

Mou-qed
13, 85

Mycenae/Mycenaean(s)
27, 64, 116, 122

Myos Hormos
40, 76, 86, 128

Nabataeans
xviii

Naukratis
vii, 4, 16, 35, 45, 47, 50, 53, 60, 61, 62, 70, 109, 161

Near East
ix, xv, xix, xx, 33, 45, 66, 67, 70, 71, 126, 134, 156, 160, 161, 164, 166, 174, 187, 188, 194

Negev
72, 76, 86

Nine Bows
15

Nile
xiii, xiv, xv, xvi, xvii, 4, 9, 11, 12, 13, 14, 15, 16, 17, 18, 21, 22, 23, 24, 25, 26, 27, 29, 30, 34, 41, 45, 46, 47, 49, 50, 53, 54, 55, 56, 57, 58, 59, 60, 61, 62, 63, 64, 65, 66, 67, 68, 69, 70, 71, 72, 73, 74, 76, 77, 78, 79, 81, 82, 85, 86, 89, 91, 93, 94, 95, 96, 100, 101, 102, 103, 105, 106, 108, 109, 110, 111, 112, 116, 117, 119, 121, 122, 124, 125, 137, 138, 142, 145, 146, 148, 149, 158, 160, 162, 169, 170, 171, 188, 189, 192, 194, 196, 198

Nun
16, 191

Nubia
41, 91, 108, 109, 161, 176, 179, 181, 184, 194

Oasis
xv, 59, 62, 109, 148, 158

Ophir
86

Opone
41

Ostracine
65, 72

Palestine
xix, xx, 1, 12, 13, 21, 22, 23, 28, 29, 31, 33, 34, 47, 65, 67, 69, 70, 71, 73, 76, 79, 95, 109, 126, 127, 140, 144, 152, 160, 163, 175, 196

Palmyra
xviii

Paraetonium
9, 25

Pe
14

Pelusium
vii, 50, 59, 64, 65, 66, 70, 71, 72, 73, 74

Pelusiac branch
17, 59, 65, 66, 67, 68, 69, 70, 71, 72, 73, 74, 76, 95

Peru-nefer
96, 140

Persia(ns)
xix, 61, 71, 73, 126, 129, 161, 162, 176, 194, 202

Persian Gulf
36, 40, 101

Pharos
25, 45, 128

Phoenicia(n)
vii, x, xv, xix, 4, 5, 12, 21, 22, 23, 30, 31, 32, 33, 34, 35, 36, 45, 49, 69, 70, 73, 74, 75, 78, 83, 95, 98, 99, 100, 105, 106, 109, 122, 146, 152, 156, 160, 169, 170, 171, 173, 174, 184, 187, 193, 196, 198, 199, 200

Pheselis
61

Philistine(s)
71

Philotera
86

Phocaea
61

Pillars of Hercules
36

Piramesse
vii, 66, 67, 68, 69, 85, 95, 128, 141

Pi-Sopdu
76

Pithom
78, 92, 100

Punt
xviii, 1, 12, 13, 26, 36, 38, 39, 40, 42, 79, 80, 81, 82, 83, 84, 85, 92, 93, 100, 119, 120, 121, 122, 123, 125, 128, 137, 143, 144, 148, 149, 150, 176, 177, 178, 179, 180, 181, 182, 183, 184, 191, 194, 195

Puntites (inhabitants of Punt)
85, 125, 179, 182

Port Sudan
38, 41

Ptolemais-Theron
42

Qadech
70, 95

Qantir
30, 65, 66, 67

Quseir
38, 81, 82, 83, 84, 194

Red Sea
vii, viii, xiii, xv, xvi, xix, xx, 1, 7, 12, 13, 16, 18, 26, 36, 37, 38, 39, 40, 42, 66, 76, 77, 78, 79, 80, 81, 82, 83, 84, 85, 86, 92, 99, 100, 101, 122, 128, 146, 156, 181, 182, 191, 194

Retenu
31

Rhinocoroura
73

Rhodes
xv, 7, 9, 34, 61

Rhodian Sea
35

Rome
xv, 7, 21, 28, 127, 157, 200

Rosetta
17, 25, 53

Ruqueich (Tell)
vii, 74

Sais
14, 19, 35, 47, 61, 62

Sakal
29

Salamis
96, 99

Samos
8, 45, 161

San el-Hagar
55, 59, 68

Santorini
34, 93

Saqqara
xiii, xviii, 17, 18, 45, 57, 99, 102, 111, 115, 140, 150, 151, 165, 188

Sebennytos
59, 194

Sea Peoples
12, 13, 26, 27, 34, 94, 97, 98, 159, 171

Seleucia
28

Serabit el-Khadim
69, 80, 86, 194

Shirdana
27

Shosu
13, 109

Sicily
8, 21, 61, 96, 161, 198

Sidon
22, 32, 47, 49, 99, 155, 160, 196

Sile
30, 31, 65, 67, 70

Sinai
vii, 12, 13, 24, 26, 37, 42, 65, 67, 70, 72, 73, 74, 75, 76, 79, 80, 81, 85, 86, 92, 148, 175, 181, 182, 194

Sirbonis (Lake)
72, 73

Somalia
41

Spain
21

Sudan
12, 38, 41, 114, 181

Suez (Gulf of)
12, 24, 37, 38, 42, 72, 73, 76, 77, 78, 81, 82, 83, 84, 85, 86, 194

Susa
139, 162

Syene
xv

Syria
xvi, xix, 9, 11, 12, 25, 28, 29, 30, 31, 70, 73, 75, 109, 156, 161, 163, 176, 199

Syrian Sea
vii, 30

Syro-Palestine
xx, 1, 13, 21, 23, 34, 47, 67, 71, 95, 109, 126, 140, 144, 152, 160, 163, 175

Syrtis (Major)
21

Tanis
v, vii, I, 13, 22, 30, 32, 53, 59, 64, 65, 66, 67, 68, 69, 71, 96, 152, 155, 184, 187

Tartessus
8

Teos
61

Thebes
xvi, 14, 22, 26, 32, 35, 39, 47, 68, 81, 82, 94, 95, 97, 101, 108, 120,
125, 137, 141, 149, 150, 162, 164, 165, 188, 189, 191

Thera
34, 93

Thonis
vii, 16, 17, 60, 61, 62

Tigris
31

Timna
85, 86, 194

Timsa (Lake)
22, 76, 78

Tjaru
vii, 30, 69, 70, 194

Tumilat (Wadi)
22, 26, 65, 76, 77, 78, 80, 81, 82, 100, 194

Tyre
21, 22, 28, 30, 32, 47, 49, 99, 110, 126, †155, 156, 160, 171, 196

Ugarit
x, 11, 30, 93, 94, 96, 163, 176, 200

Upper Egypt
1, 22, 59, 81, 91, 108, 109, 184, 189, 199

Via Hadriana
76

Wadj Wer
vii, 12, 13, 16, 19, 33, 61, 83, 100, 122, 143, 163, 177, 178, 179, 181, 191, 192, 193

Yam
11, 16

Yemen
38, 101

## III. *Res notabiles*

Economy, institutions, law, society, history, natural sciences, art and technology, religion, worship and abstract concepts

Acacia
102, 106, 108, 109

Administration
xx, 26, 45, 61, 73, 74, 93,134, 135, 141, 142, 148, 159, 162, 165, 168, 169, 171, 174, 175, 176, 179, 187

Almond tree
109

Anchor
25, 27, 41, 55, 121, 122, 123, 139, 143, 195

Annona (or tax paid in kind, often in corn)
142, 172, 200

Barley
xix

Barque of Amun
1, 32, 103, 184, 193

Beer
176, 188

Beliefs
x, xix, 191, 193, 195, 196, 197, 198, 199, 200, 201

Bitumen
96, 105, 109

Boats
xv, xvi, 5, 8, 9, 12, 16, 18, 22, 23, 36, 38, 39, 40, 41, 47, 55, 56, 61, 73, 82, 83, 84, 85, 91, 92, 93,
94, 95, 96, 100, 101, 103, 105, 106, 109, 112, 118, 120, 121, 122, 126, 127, 137, 138, 140, 144,
147, 149, 155, 170, 182

*Boghâz*
25

Captain
ix, xxi, 4, 5, 7, 8, 23, 29, 36, 66, 67, 94, 110, 117, 126, 128, 129, 143, 147, 148, 149, 151, 152,
155, 164, 166, 169, 172, 196

Cargo
xxi, 1, 3, 25, 39, 46, 61, 75, 82, 100, 106, 107, 110, 123, 125, 127, 128, 135, 137, 141, 144, 145,
146, 156, 157, 158, 163, 168, 169, 170, 171, 172, 185

Carob tree
109

Carpenter
140

Caulking
102, 109, 140

Cedar
49, 103, 108, 109, 126, 127, 175

Ceremonies and thank-offerings
x, 195, 196

Chaos
13, 16

Coast
vii, xiv, xvi, 2, 4, 7, 9, 15, 16, 17, 18, 19, 20, 21, 23, 25, 26, 27, 28, 29, 30, 31, 32, 33, 34, 36, 38, 39,
47, 49, 53, 57, 59, 62, 63, 64, 65, 67, 68, 69, 73, 74, 75, 76, 81, 82, 83, 84, 85, 86, 94, 96, 103,
105, 125, 126, 148, 157, 195, 200

Coinage
xx, 199

Commercial associations
ix, xx, 155, 156

Container(s)
123, 164

Copper
84, 107, 123, 159, 162, 163, 181, 188

Corn
8, 142, 157, 162, 164, 166, 169, 170, 171, 172, 187, 195, 196, 200

Crew
ix, xix, 1, 29, 30, 39, 42, 84, 92, 95, 128, 137, 140, 141, 142, 143, 144, 145, 146, 147, 148, 149,
155, 163, 166, 184, 185, 192, 195

Customs
xvi, xx, 23, 61, 70, 72, 109, 126, 129, 139, 141, 142, 152, 160, 185, 187, 188, 191

Cypress
108, 109

Date palm
108, 119

Director of all the mouths of Wadj Wer
177

Director of foreign lands
70

Director of the khetem of Tjaru
70

Director of the Treasury
39

Dockers
125, 137

Domains (of the pharaoh, the temples, estates, and so on)
xxi, 133, 135, 163, 164, 179

Donkey
58, 59

Ebony
86, 109, 128

Economy
x, xxi, 61, 91, 94, 133, 135, 158, 159, 168, 170, 172, 174, 179, 187, 188, 189

Elephant
101, 128

Emporion
161, 167

Eritrea
38

Fabrics
xvi, 46, 119, 125, 138, 159, 163, 164

Fir tree
109

Fish
29, 55, 56, 57, 59, 80, 81, 120, 141, 169, 188, 189

Frontier(s)
vii, xv, xvi, xix, 12, 15, 22, 30, 31, 47, 60, 61, 69, 70, 73, 75, 76, 194, 196, 200

Gift/counter-gift/trade gifts
xiii, xv, xvii, xix, 16, 35, 85, 174, 175, 178, 179, 185

Giraffe
12, 42, 86

Gold
xviii, 7, 22, 31, 41, 42, 77, 86, 99, 159, 162, 163, 165, 166, 172, 179, 181, 193, 194, 198

Governor of Tjaru
69

Great Intendant
39

Hemp
119

Honey
164, 189

Hull
93, 96, 103, 105, 106, 107, 108, 109, 110, 111, 112, 140

Incense
xviii, 41, 42, 137, 178, 191, 194

Institution(s)
128, 135, 150, 156, 158, 160, 162, 163, 164, 165

Ivory
45, 86, 91

Jujube tree
108

Juniper
109

Khetem
69, 70

Kyrenia (wreck of)
127

Lapis lazuli
194

Law
xix, 22, 59, 151, 152, 157, 158, 165, 172

Linen
119, 189

Maple
109

Market
ix, 28, 29, 41, 45, 46, 47, 61, 128, 134, 157, 161, 162, 168, 171, 188, 189

Marx (theory)
5, 98

Measurers, weighers
ix, 138, 139

Messenger(s), ambassador(s)
ix, 23, 31, 69, 70, 161, 167, 174, 175, 176, 177, 178, 179, 182, 184, 185, 186, 187

Migration
xxi

Modernist (theory)
xxi

Money
xx, 126, 133, 162, 166, 167, 168, 172, 179, 181, 185

Monopoly, State
9, 61, 70, 138, 158, 161, 189

Monsoon
36, 40

Mooring
xx, 16, 21, 23, 38, 40, 45, 46, 47, 63, 74, 75, 82, 84, 85, 86, 121, 124, 141, 195

Myrrh
39, 41, 42, 85, 86

Natron
158

Naucleros
169, 170, 172

Naval architecture
viii, 89, 93, 96, 102, 103, 107, 139

Naval dockyard(s)
47, 66, 75, 82, 83, 108, 139, 140

Navigation
vii, xiii, xv, xvi, xx, xxi, 1, 3, 4, 5, 7, 8, 9, 11, 12, 13, 18, 20, 21, 22, 23, 25, 27, 28, 29, 30, 35, 36, 38, 39, 40, 42, 45, 47, 49, 79, 80, 83, 84, 89, 98, 99, 101, 104, 105, 106, 111, 112, 116, 119, 120, 121, 123, 127, 128, 134, 138, 140, 142, 143, 144, 147, 148, 149, 150, 155, 156, 166, 169, 172, 189, 191, 196, 202

Oak
108, 109

Obsidian
xix

Offer/demand
9, 15, 59, 158, 159, 161, 169, 202

Officials, harbour
141

Oil
30, 75, 126, 138, 141, 165, 168

Olive/Olive tree
xix, 108, 109

Oracle
77, 161, 185

Oxherds (Bucoloi)
152, 168

Persea
108, 109

Pharaoh
xvi, 4, 15, 16, 26, 27, 30, 36, 61, 68, 77, 86, 89, 92, 96, 109, 134, 135, 156, 158, 163, 176, 179

Pilot
5, 7, 25, 60, 147, 149, 157, 170, 191, 192, 193

Pine
v, 108, 109

Pirates
xv, 5, 27, 101

Port(s)
vii, viii, ix, xx, 4, 17, 18, 23, 25, 28, 31, 35, 38, 40, 45, 46, 47, 49, 50, 51, 53, 55, 57, 59, 61, 63, 65, 67, 69, 71, 73, 74, 75, 76, 77, 79, 81, 82, 83, 84, 85, 86, 101, 122, 133, 135, 137, 138, 140, 141, 142, 143, 145, 147, 149, 151, 152, 157, 160, 161, 166, 169, 170, 173, 202

Pottery
v, 34, 62, 64, 66, 69, 71, 72, 74, 75, 76, 86, 123, 133, 188

Aegean pottery
30, 60, 64, 71

Cypriot pottery
29, 69

Phoenician pottery
71

Syro-palestinian pottery
71

Production/consumption
ii, xx, xxi, 45, 109, 135, 146, 158, 161, 168, 171, 188, 189, 196

*Proreutes*
ix, 137, 144, 147, 148, 149

Rigging
viii, 3, 83, 93, 110, 114, 115, 116, 117, 118, 119, 150, 182

Routes (maritime)
128, 156, 176, 179, 181, 193, 194

Royal messenger for all foreign lands
69, 175, 178, 179

Rudder
xxi, 4, 5, 7, 8, 89, 92, 102, 117, 119, 120, 121, 125, 149

Sailor(s)
v, xiv, xvi, xviii, xix, 1, 4, 5, 7, 8, 9, 16, 21, 22, 23, 27, 28, 29, 30, 31, 33, 36, 38, 39, 40, 42, 55, 64, 66, 74, 84, 102, 116, 117, 128, 137, 140, 143, 144, 145, 147, 148, 151, 155, 156, 163, 167, 191, 192, 195, 196, 200, 202

Salt
57, 58, 59, 141, 158, 169

Scarab
xix

Seal
47

Shore
1, 5, 16, 19, 25, 36, 38, 42, 60, 64, 75, 76, 83, 84, 85, 95, 102, 122, 144, 149, 178, 179, 188, 195

Silk Road
xv, xvi

State
xv, xix, xx, 3, 4, 11, 12, 15, 18, 22, 23, 29, 34, 53, 54, 60, 61, 73, 76, 80, 81, 96, 105, 128, 133, 134, 135, 142, 148, 151, 152, 155, 156, 159, 160, 161, 162, 167, 168, 170, 171, 172, 174, 176, 179, 187, 189, 194, 195, 200

Stone(s), precious
41, 42, 158, 181

Stowing
123, 125

Sycamore
108, 109, 188

Syncretism
196

Technology
xxi, 102

Tenon and mortice
105

Tension cable
89, 93, 111, 112, 119, 121

Thank-offering
195

Tonnage
viii, 3, 4, 106, 123, 126, 127, 128, 170, 171

Trade
v, ix, xviii, xix, xx, xxi, 3, 12, 23, 25, 35, 38, 41, 45, 46, 49, 61, 62, 66, 69, 74, 77, 78, 79, 94, 98, 101, 106, 123, 126, 133, 135, 155, 156, 158, 159, 160, 161, 162, 163, 165, 167, 169, 170, 172, 174, 184, 188, 189, 194, 196, 200

Treasure
135, 141

Treasury
39, 61, 146, 160, 163, 177, 179, 194

Tribute
140, 161, 175, 179, 181

Turquoise
69, 86

Ulu Burun (wreck of)
94, 105, 123

Underwater archaeology
x, 1, 3, 4, 5, 7, 9, 60, 123

Vine/wine
xix

Vizir
147, 148, 176, 187

Voyage, journey
xv, xvi, xviii, xix, xx, xxi, 1, 3, 7, 9, 20, 22, 25, 28, 31, 32, 38, 41, 42, 75, 83, 84, 85, 93, 129, 141, 147, 157, 166, 169, 191, 194

War
xiii, xx, xxi, 22, 27, 41, 60, 68, 75, 92, 94, 96, 98, 99, 100, 128, 140, 146, 170, 179, 181

Warship
5, 27, 96, 98, 100, 200

Waters, territorial
28

Willow
108, 109, 137, 138, 141, 149, 157, 165, 167, 176, 188, 196

Wood
1, 22, 32, 42, 49, 82, 83, 84, 91, 92, 101, 102, 103, 106, 107, 108, 109, 115, 116, 125, 126, 127, 140, 158, 174, 184, 185, 186, 191, 193

Wool
55

Wrecks
3, 4, 25, 106, 108, 191

Yew
109

# Sources

## I. Egyptian sources

| | |
|---|---|
| Abydos (temple of Seti I) | 94, 163 |
| Abu Simbel (temple of) | XIII, 34 |
| Annals of Thutmose III | 30, 69 |
| Amara-West (list of) | 32 |
| Barque of Lisht (Senusret I) | 105 |
| Barque of Khufu | 81, 83, 96, 103, 104, 105, 109 |
| Barque of Dashur (Senusret III) | 106 |
| Customs register of the satrapy of Egypt (P. Elephantine, TAD C, 3, 7) | |
| 23, 109, 126, 127 | |
| *DAE* (*Aramaean documents of Egypt*) | 109, 151, 152, 162, 176 |
| — 14 | 152 |
| — 17 | 152 |
| — 26 | 152 |
| — 54 | 152, 162 |
| — 55 | 162 |
| — 60 | 162 |
| — 61 | 109 |
| — 67 | 176 |
| — 71 | 162 |
| — 72 | 162 |
| — 109 | 152, 162 |
| Decree of Pepi I | 175 |
| Deir el-Bahari (temple of Hatshepsut) | |
| 79, 80, 81, 93, 112, 120, 121, 122, 125, 137, 143, 144, 145, 147, 149, 150, 178, 179, 180, 194 | |
| Dendera | |
| —, II, 131, 10 | 65 |
| —, V, 30, 12 | 194 |
| —, IX, 135, 4 | 15 |
| Dendera, Mammisi, 28, 2f | 192 |
| *Dipinti* of Alexandria | 118, 119 |
| *EA* (El Amarna, letters of) | 32, 49, 92, 109, 161, 174, 175 |
| — 7 | 174 |
| — 39 | 29, 96, 161, 174 |
| — 40 | 96, 161 |
| — 77 | 96 |
| — 105 | 26 |
| — 110 | 96 |
| — 113 | 26 |
| — 114 | 26 |
| — 129 | 96 |
| — 143 | 96 |
| — 153 | 96 |
| — 155 | 96 |
| — 161 | 96 |
| — 265 | 174 |
| — 287 | 174 |
| — 369 | 174 |

| | |
|---|---|
| Edfu | |
| —, I, 329, 10 | 16 |
| —, II, 202, 13-14 | 182 |
| —, IV, 183, 7 | 15 |
| —, IV, 196, 3 | 16 |
| —, VII, 106, 7 | 194 |
| Esna | |
| —, III, 378, 20-21 | 191 |
| —, III, 277, 23-24 | 191 |
| Hammamat (Wadi) | 82, 92, 146, 176, 179, 181 |
| —, n° 114 | 92, 146, 176 |
| *Instruction text of Ankhsheshonq* | |
| — 16, 5 | 167 |
| — 19, 8 | 167 |
| — 28, 4 | 167 |
| Kom el-Hetan (List of) | 33 |
| *KRI* | 42, 69, 84, 85, 94, 139, 146, 152, 166 |
| — I, 271, 4, 15 | 166 |
| — I, 332, 15 - 333, 1 | 94, 163 |
| — II, 12-16 | 69 |
| — II, 333, 1 | 159, 163 |
| — II, 406 | 85 |
| — II, 617-628 | 41 |
| — II, 800, 7 | 159, 163 |
| — II, 801, 7 | 159, 163 |
| — II, 802, 5 | 159, 163 |
| — II, 907 | 152 |
| — III, 330, 11 | 139 |
| — III, 330, 14-15 | 139 |
| — IV, 80, 2 | 152 |
| — IV, 445, 16 | 152 |
| — V, 93, 5-6 | 84 |
| — V, 97, 8-9 | 84 |
| — V, 225, 1 | 84 |
| — V, 272, 11 | 85 |
| — V, 318, 2-10 | 139 |
| — V, 396, 2-12 | 146 |
| *LdM* | |
| —, 30b | 150 |
| Mastaba of Nefer-nesout | 175 |
| Mastaba of Ty (Saqqara) | 17, 18, 57, 115, 140, 141, 147 |
| Maxim of Ptahotep, 8 | 175 |
| Medinet Habu (temple of) | 7, 26, 32, 84, 94, 97, 139 |
| *Medinet Habu* | |
| — II, 101, 13-14 | 84 |
| — II, 102, 15 | 84 |
| — V, 320 | 139 |
| — V, 229-235 | 94 |
| Mersa Gawasis (Stele of the vizir Antefoqer) | 41, 84, 129, 147 |
| Naukratis (Stele of) | 4, 16, 34, 45, 46, 47, 50, 53, 60, 61, 62, 70, 109, 161 |

Nauri (decree of) 94, 161, 163

Onomastica 31, 150, 166

*Onomasticon of Amenemope* 68

O. Berlin P.11292 137

Palette of Zizinia (Alexandria) 179

Paramessu (statue of) 177

P. Abbott Docket 164, 166

P. Anastasi III, 1, 9-10 30

P. Anastasi VIII, v° III, 4 95

P. Bankes I 165

P. Berlin 5883-5853 157

P. Berlin 10460 163, 164

P. BM 10052, r° 5, 1 + 5, 11-12 103, 162, 166, 167

—, r° 8, 2 164

P. BM 10053 162, 164, 166

—, r° 3, 1 164

—, r° 4, 10 164

—, r° 7, 18 159, 166

P. BM 10056 103

P. BM 10068 163, 164

P. BM 10383, 3, 1-7 165, 166, 167

P. BM 10508 167

P. Bologna 1094 160, 161

P. Boulaq XII, r° 6-7 146

P. Brooklyn 35.1453 46, 153, 159

P. Cairo 65.739, 3 164

P. Cairo Zenon I 59012 72, 152

P. Chester Beatty V 145

P. Columbia Zenon II 72

P. E3226 du Louvre 159

P. Geneva D.407 176

P. Harris I 94, 152

—, 7, 7 84

—, 7, 8 94, 152

—, 28, 5 146

—, 48, 6 94

—, 77, 8 - 78, 1 84, 85, 143, 148

P. Insinger 167

P. Lansing, 4, 8 - 4, 9 47, 140, 145, 159, 164, 182

—, 4, 10 - 5, 2 162, 192

—, 7, 1 163

P. Leiden I 350 94, 129, 135, 141, 143, 145, 146

P. London VII 1930, 205-211 72

P. Mathematics Rhind 69

P. Mayer A 163, 164

P. Michigan Zenon, 2, 5-6 72

P. Oxyrhynchus XII 1544, 1-11 72

P. Oxyrhynchus XXXIV 2732, 2-11 72

P. Oxyrhynchus XL 2926, 1-7 72

P. Oxyrhynchus L 3576, 7-15 72

P. Oxyrhynchus L 3602, 1-12 72

P. Prisse, 7, 3 175

P. Revenue Laws 72, 168

P. Sallier II, 5, 5-6 159

P. Turin 1887, v° 1, 8-11 166

—, 2, 9-11 164

P. Turin 2008 + 2016 46, 135, 142, 146, 147, 150, 159, 164

P. Turin Taxation, 3, 16 188

—, 4, 3 188

—, 4, 5 188

P. Zenon I, 59021 1 73

*Peasant (Tale of the Eloquent)* XV, 158

Palermo Stone 89

Pithom (Stele of, Tell el-Maskhuta, CGC 22183) 78, 92, 100

*Predestined Prince (Tale of the)* XVI

*Prophecy of Neferti* 4

*Pyramid Texts* 12, 13, 16

Sahure (temple of) 89, 92, 93, 100, 103, 107, 110, 111, 115, 121, 123, 144, 147, 149

*Satire on Trades* 47, 140, 158, 159, 160, 167, 192, 193

Sinai (inscriptions of), n° 112 179

—, n° 181 86

—, n° 211 181

*Sinuhe (Adventures of)* XVI, 16

—, B 94-95 176

—, B 156-160 191

Soleb (List of), funerary temple of Amenhotep III at Kom el-Hitam 13, 32, 34

Statue BM 290 146

Statue BM 1183 146

Stele Ashmolean 1947. 294 146

Stele Budapest 51.2145 146

Stele Cairo JE 8781 151

Stele Cairo JE 36861 159

Stele CGC 34182 165

Stele Florence 2576 176

Stele Philadelphia 61-13-1 146

Stele of Sinai (Thutmose III) 177

*Shipwrecked Sailor (Tale of the)* XVI, 1, 16, 39, 42, 143, 192, 195

—, 2-3 195

—, 25-30 42, 143

—, 31-135 42, 143

—, 33 39

—, 119-124 192

—, 134-135 192

—, 155-157 42

—, 160-167 42

—, 170-171 143, 195

—, 170-174 195

—, 173-175 42

*Talatat* (of Heliopolis) 118, 119

Thonis-Herakleion (Stele of) 61, 62

Tomb of Ameny (Beni-Hassan) 175

Tomb of Antef 34

Tomb of Benia (TT 178) 139

Tomb of Djedimeniouf-ankh (oasis of Bahariya) 158

Tomb of Huy (TT 40) 137

Tomb of Ipuy (TT 217) 137, 188

Tomb of Kenamun (TT 162) 95, 110, 115, 134, 137, 138, 142, 143, 161, 188

| | |
|---|---|
| Tomb of Khaemhat (TT 57) | 46, 137, 149, 189 |
| Tomb of Khamawaset (TT 261) | 129, 137, 141, 185, 186 |
| Tomb of Menna (TT 69) | 149 |
| Tomb of Menkheperraseneb | 34 |
| Tomb of Nebamun (TT 17) | 95, 149 |
| Tomb of Neferrebpet (TT 178) | 139 |
| Tomb of Niankhkhnum and of Khnumhotep (Saqqara) | |
| 107, 149, 150, 188 | |
| Tomb of Pashed | 151 |
| Tomb of Payri (TT 139) | 147, 149 |
| Tomb of Pouimra (TT 39) | 34 |
| Tomb of Rekhmira (TT 100) | 34, 35, 139 149 |
| Tomb of Senmut (TT 71) | 34 |
| Tomb of Sennefer (TT 96) | 149, 150 |
| Tomb of Si-Amun (oasis of Siwa) | 158 |
| Tomb of Useramun (TT 131) | 34 |
| *Two Brothers* (*Tale of the*) | XVI, 188 |
| Unas (temple of) | 102 |
| *Urk.* | |
| — I, 99, 13 | 147 |
| — I, 128, 17 - 129, 1 | 128 |
| — I, 131, 4-7 | 175 |
| — I, 134, 13-17 | 82 |
| — I, 210, 7-11 | 175 |
| — I, 214, 12-13 | 175 |
| — II, 4 | XVI |
| — II, 24, 6-7 | 194 |
| — II, 25, 3-6 | 194 |
| — II, 26, 1-2 | 194 |
| — II, 82, 5 | 65 |
| — II, 86, 10 | 100 |
| — II, 179 | 13 |
| — IV, 56, 11-15 | 15 |
| — IV, 304, 17 | 143 |
| — IV, 307, 15 | 143 |
| — IV, 323, 2 | 92, 178 |
| — IV, 325, 12-14 | 178 |
| — IV, 326, 2-3 | 178 |
| — IV, 344, 16 | 179 |
| — IV, 616, 1-2 | 33 |
| — IV, 647, 12-14 | 69 |
| — IV, 696 | 83 |
| — IV, 647, 12-14 | 69 |
| — IV, 706 | 93 |
| — IV, 886-888 | 177 |
| — IV, 1073, 3-6 | 187 |
| — IV, 1076, 17 - 1077, 2 | 150 |
| — IV, 1472-1473 | 182 |
| — IV, 2087 | 179 |
| — IV, 2175, 7-16 | 177 |
| — VII, 19,14 | 175 |

| | |
|---|---|
| *Wenamun* (*Report of*) | |
| IX, XVI, 1, 3, 8, 13, 20, 22, 23, 28, 29, 30, 31, 32, 33, 47, 67, 68, 69, 152, 156, 160, 166 | |
| —, 1, 3 | 67, 69 |
| —, 1, 5-6 | 155, 187 |
| —, 1, 6 | 187 |
| —, 1, 6-8 | 32, 67, 152, 187 |
| —, 1, 6 - 2 | 69 |
| —, 1, 7-8 | 13, 30, 31, 96 |
| —, 1, 8 | 32 |
| —, 1, 9-10 | 96, 187 |
| —, 1, 15 | 185 |
| —, 1, 16 | 32 |
| —, 1, 28 | 32 |
| —, 1, 29 | 32 |
| —, 1, 31-32 | 29 |
| —, 1, 33 | 32 |
| —, 1, 34 | 32 |
| —, 1, 39-40 | 184 |
| —, 1, 43-45 | 29 |
| —, 1, 49 | 31 |
| —, 1, 50 | 29 |
| —, 1, 51 | 29 |
| —, 1, 51-52 | 187 |
| —, 1, 54-55 | 30, 31, 152 |
| —, 1, 54-57 | 152 |
| —, 1, 57-58 | 96 |
| —, 1, 58 | 30 |
| —, 1, 58 - 2, 2 | 69, 96, 155 |
| —, 1, 59 | 32, 155 |
| —, 2, 1 | 96 |
| —, 2, 2 | 155 |
| —, 2, 3-5 | 32, 185 |
| —, 2, 14-24 | 193 |
| —, 2, 23-24 | 185 |
| —, 2, 25 | 32, 193 |
| —, 2, 25-26 | 186 |
| —, 2, 28 | 32, 193 |
| —, 2, 31-32 | 185 |
| —, 2, 32-34 | 185 |
| —, 2, 35 | 67, 69 |
| —, 2, 35-36 | 185 |
| —, 2, 39 | 31 |
| —, 2, 41-42 | 187 |
| —, 2, 43-44 | 126 |
| —, 2, 51-52 | 184 |
| —, 2, 55 | 184, 185 |
| —, 2, 58-59 | 184 |
| —, 2, 60-62 | 185 |
| —, 2, 65 | 29 |
| —, 2, 73 | 184, 185 |
| —, 2, 74-75 | 30 |
| —, 2, 75-76 | 29, 30 |
| —, 2, 75 | 30, 185 |
| —, 2, 77 | 29, 185 |

—, 2, 77-78     185
—, 2, 79     30, 185
—, 2, 81     185 30, 32, 185
*Wisdom of Ani*     14, 15

## II. Biblical sources

II Chronicles, 2, 15     126
Esdras, 3, 7     126
I Kings, 5, 15     174
—, 5, 22-23     126
—, 9, 26     86
—, 10     174
—, 17, 8-24     160
—, 20, 34     160

## III. Texts from Ugarit, classical authors and various sources...

Achilles Tatius, *Leucippus and Clitophon*, III, 5-6     54, 55, 56, 202
Agatharchides of Cnidus     36, 156
Akrotiri fresco     27
*Annals of Khorsabad*     74
*Antonine Itinerary*     70, 73, 75
Appian, *Civil War*, II, 12     75
Apuleius, *Metamorphoses*, XI, 5 and 16     22, 129, 200
Aristophanes, *Knights*, 541-543     149
Aristotle, *Meteorologica*     20
Athenagoras, *Embassy*, 22, 8     200
Athenaeus, *Deipnosophistes*, V, 206d-209     128
Basil of Caesarea, *Homily IV on the Hexaemeron*, 7     20
Cato, *On Agriculture*, XXI, 18, 9     92, 106
Cicero, *On the Republic*, II, 167-168     202
*Cosmography of Ravenna*     73
Demosthenes, *Against Athenodorus*, LVI, 30     23
—, *Against Dionysodoros*     173
*Digest*, VI, 1, 36     5, 22
—, XLVII, 5     145
Diodorus Siculus, *Bibliotheca historica*     25, 36, 73, 78
—, I, 15, 2     96
—, I, 19, 4     60
—, I, 33, 7-8     73
—, I, 168     99
—, I, 55     41
—, I, 55, 2     41
—, III, 44, 4     39
—, XV, 42, 14     71
—, XVI, 46, 4 - 49, 6     71
—, XVII, 52     45
—, XIX, 94, 4-5     78
—, XX, 74, 3     75
Dio Cassius, LI, 9, 1     65
Dom Joan de Castro     36
*Edict of Diocletian*, VII, 13     140
Euripides, *Iphigenia in Tauris*     137

Flavius Josephus, *Jewish War*, IV, 11, 5     59, 75
—, *Life*, 3     5
Heliodorus, *Aethiopica 5*     56
Herodotus, *History*
8, 33, 36, 42, 45, 53, 61, 62, 71, 73, 74, 75, 77, 78, 99, 100, 101, 102, 105, 106, 107, 151, 152, 156, 168, 176, 188, 200
—, I, 1     36, 156
—, I, 72     33
—, II, 6     75
—, II, 8     42
—, II, 35     188
—, II, 96     106
—, II, 112     45, 161
—, II, 113-119     61
—, II, 141     168
—, II, 154     100
—, II, 158     75, 77
—, II, 159     36, 99, 156
—, II, 164     152, 168
—, II, 178-180     61
—, II, 179     45, 161
—, II, 182     99
—, III, 5     73, 74, 75
—, III, 6     73
—, III, 11-16     71
—, III, 37     200
—, III, 60     45
—, IV, 42     36, 156
—, IV, 85-86     8
—, V, 52     176
—, VII, 89     36, 156
Hesiod, *Works and Days*, v. 663-665, 678-684     22
Homer, *Odyssey*     xv, 7, 27, 61, 105, 167
—, IV, 228     61
—, IV, 483     8
—, V, 244-245     105
—, V, 270-278     7
—, XIII, 19     25
—, XIV, 285-307     21
—, XIX     27
Horace, *Epistula*, I, v. 46     154
Jerome, *Commentary on Ezekiel*, IX, 27, 29, 30, 1     3, 72, 149
Libanus, *Discourse*, LXII, 46     7, 149
—, *Progymnasta sententiae*, I, 13     7
Lucian, *The Ship*, 5     129
—, *Toxaris*, 4     169
Map of Madaba     73
Mari Texts     29, 30, 93, 94
Mosaic of Praeneste     52, 53, 54
Mosaic of Susa     139
Orosius, VI, 12, 15     65
*Palatine Anthology*, XI, 480-538     191

*Periplus of the Erythrean Sea*    36, 40, 45, 83, 101

—, 6    40, 83

—, 14    40

—, 24    40, 83

—, 28    40

—, 49    40

—, 56    40

*Peutinger Table*    73

Philo of Alexandria, *De migratione Abrahami*    169

Philostratus, *Life of Apollonius*, IV, 9    143, 149

Pliny, *Natural History*    8, 9, 20, 38, 40, 42, 75, 83, 101, 108, 109, 141

—, II, 123–127    20

—, V, 32, 39    9

—, V, 68    75

—, VI, 26    101

—, VI, 33, 171–173    42

—, VI, 36, 104    40

—, VII, 52, 206    101

—, XII, 32, 58    41

—, XII, 35, 66–70    41

—, XIII, 63, 19    83, 109

—, XIII, 72    141

—, XVI, 203    109

Plutarch, *Agis and Cleomene*, 1    149

—, *Isis and Osiris*

—, 17    200

—, 32    11

—, *Life of Demetrius*, 43    128

Pollux, *Onomasticon*, I, 95    149

—, VII, 139 and 190    149

*Prism of Nimrod*    74

Ptolemy, *Tetrabiblos*, IV, 4    172

Relief from the Palace of Sargon II at Khorsabad (Louvre)    126, 127

*RS* (texts from Ras-Shamra–Ugarit)    151, 174, 191

— 15.109    174

— 16.257    174

— 17.112    174

— 17.131    174

— 17.137    174

— 17.144    174

— 17.244    174

— 17.289    174

— 17.383    174

— 17.422    174

— 20.184    174

Seneca, *Naturales quaestiones*, V, 10    20

Statius, *Silvae*, III, 2, 21–24    198

Strabo, *Geography*

9, 25, 26, 29, 36, 38, 42, 45, 50, 54, 60, 61, 62, 63, 64, 73, 75, 80, 86, 100, 101, 109

—, I, 44–45    86

—, II, 3, 4    36, 151

—, II, 5, 12    80

—, X, 4, 3    9

—, X, 4, 5    9

—, XIV, 6, 5    28, 109

—, XVI, 1, 16    60

—, XVI, 2, 30    73

—, XVI, 4, 2    100

—, XVI, 4, 5–14    42

—, XVI, 4, 18    101

—, XVII, 1, 6    45

—, XVII, 1, 14    9, 63

—, XVII, 1, 19    25

—, XVII, 794    45

Symmachus, *Letters*, IV, 54    22

Theodorus Lector, *Historia tripartita, Epitome* 362    72

Theophanes, *Chronography*, 106, 33    72

Theophrastus, *De historia plantarum*, vol. II, book II, 2, 8
20, 83, 108, 109

Vegetius, *Rei militaris instituta*, IV, 32    22

Virgil, *Aeneid*, VI, 413–414    107

Xenophon, *Oeconomicus*, VIII, 11    146

—, *Anabasis*, V, 8, 20    148

—, *Poroi*, 3    167

# Bibliography

Abdallah, M., Ahmed, A.M., William, A., Carrez-Maratray, J.Y., and Wagner, G., 'Timbres amphoriques grecs du Tell el-Moufariq', *CRIPEL* 18, 1996, pp. 143-151.

Abd el-Maksoud, M., 'Une nouvelle forteresse sur la route d'Horus: Tell Heboua 1987 (Nord Sinaï)', *CRIPEL* 9, 1987, pp. 13-16.

Abd el-Maksoud, M., *Tell Héboua I*, thesis presented at the University of Charles de Gaulle-Lille III, Lille, 1992.

Abd el-Maksoud, M., 'Tjarou, porte de l'Orient', *in* D. Valbelle and C. Bonnet (ed.), *Le Sinaï durant l'Antiquité et le Moyen Âge. 4000 ans d'histoire pour un désert*, 'Sinaï' UNESCO colloquium, 19–21 Sept. 1997, Errance, Paris, 1998, pp. 61-65.

Abel, F.-M., *Géographie de la Palestine*, vol. 2, Paris, 1933-1938.

Abel, F.-M., 'Les confins de la Palestine et de l'Égypte sous les Ptolémées', *RevBibl* 48, 1939, pp. 207-236, 530-548.

Abel, F.-M., 'Les confins de la Palestine et de l'Égypte sous les Ptolémées', *RevBibl* 49, 1940, pp. 55-75, 224-239.

Acquaro, A., *Amuleti Egiziani ed Egittizzanti del Museo Nazionale di Cagliari*, *CSF* 10, Rome, 1977.

Adam, S., 'Report on the Excavations of the Department of Antiquities at Ezbet Rushdi', *ASAE* LVI, 1959, pp. 207-226.

Adamson, P.B., 'The Possibility of sea trade between Mesopotamia and Egypt during the Predynastic Period', *Aula Orientalis* 10, 1992, pp. 175-179.

Ahituv, S., *Canaanite Toponyms in Ancient Egyptian Documents*, Jerusalem, 1984.

Aistleitner, J., *Wörterbuch der Ugaritischen Sprache*, Berichte über die Verhandlungen der Sächsischen Akademie der Wissenschaften zu Leipzig, Phil.-hist. Klasse, vol. 106/3, Berlin, 1963.

Albright, W.F., 'Exploring in Sinai with the University of California African Expedition', *BASOR* 109, 1948, pp. 5-20.

Albright, W.F., 'The Eastern Mediterranean about 1600 BC', *in* G.E. Mylonas (ed.), *Studies presented to D.M. Robinson*, I, Saint-Louis, Washington, 1951, pp. 223-231.

Albright, W.F., 'Syria, The Philistines and Phoenicia', *in* I.E.S. Edwards, C.J. Gadd, N.G.L. Hammond and E. Sollberger (eds), *History of the Middle East and the Aegean Region c. 1380-1000 BC*, *The Cambridge Ancient History*, vol. II, part 2, Cambridge, 1975.

Allam, S., *Hieratische Ostraka und Papyri aus den Ramessidenzeit, Urkunden zum Rechtsleben im alten Ägypten*, I, Tübingen, 1993.

Allam, S., 'Affaires et opérations commerciales', *in* N. Grimal and B. Menu (eds), *Le commerce en Égypte ancienne*, *BiÉtud* 121, IFAO, Cairo, 1998, pp. 133-156.

Allen, T.G., *Egyptian Stelae in the Field Museum of Natural History*, Chicago, 1936.

Alliot, M., *Rapport sur les fouilles de Tell Edfou*, *FIFAO* X, IFAO, Cairo, 1935.

Alliot, M., 'Un nouvel exemple de vizir divinisé dans l'Égypte ancienne', *BIFAO* XXXVII, 1937, pp. 99-101.

Alliot, M., *Le culte d'Horus à Edfou au temps des Ptolémées*, *BiÉtud* XX, vol. 3, IFAO, Cairo, 1949-1954.

Almagro, Gorbea M.J., *Corpus de las Terracotas de Ibiza*, *BPH* VIII, Madrid, 1980.

Alt, A., 'Ägyptisch-Ugaritisches', *Archiv für Orientforschung* 15, 1945-1951, pp. 70-71.

Altenmüller, H., *in* *LÄ* III, 1980, *s.v.* 'Market', cols 1191-1194.

Altenmüller, H., and Moussa, A.M., 'Die Inschrift Amenemhats II. aus dem Ptah-Tempel von Memphis. Ein Vorbericht', *SAK* 18, 1991, pp. 1-48.

Amigues, S., 'L'expédition d'Anaxicrate en Arabie Occidentale', *Topoi. Orient-Occident* 6/2, 1996, pp. 674-675.

Amouretti, M.-Cl., and Brun J.-P., 'Les rendements', *in* M.-Cl. Amouretti, J.-P. Brun and D. Eitam (eds), *Actes du symposium international organisé par le centre Camille Jullian (Université de Provence-CNRS) et le centre archéologique du Var, Aix-en-Provence et Toulon, 20-22 Novembre 1991*, *BCH suppl.* XXVI, École Française d'Athènes, Paris, 1993, pp. 551-562.

Amouretti, M.-Cl., 'Technique et économie', *in* M.-Cl. Amouretti, J.-P. Brun and D. Eitam (eds), *Actes du symposium international organisé par le centre Camille Jullian (Université de Provence-CNRS) et le centre archéologique du Var, Aix-en-Provence et Toulon, 20-22 Novembre 1991*, *BCH suppl.* XXVI, École Française d'Athènes, Paris, 1993, pp. 563-585.

Amouretti, M.-Cl., 'Introduction', *in* D. Meeks and D. Garcia (eds), *Techniques et économie antiques et médiévales: le temps de l'innovation, Colloque international (CNRS) Aix-en-Provence 21-23 Mai 1996*, Errance, Paris, 1997, pp. 7-12.

Ampolo, C., 'Due novi documenti ed il loro apporto allo studio del commercio aracaico e classico: l'ostrakon di Kerkinitis ed il Registro doganale di Elephantina', *in Magna Grecia, Etruschi, Fenici, Taranto 8-13 octobre 1993*, Tarente, 1996, pp. 245-247.

André, J.-M., and Baslez M.-Fr., *Voyager dans l'Antiquité*, Fayard, Paris, 1993.

Andréadès, A., 'Les droits de douane prélevés par les Lagides sur le commerce extérieur', *in Mélanges Glotz*, I, Paris, 1932, pp. 7-48.

Anthes, R., *Die Felseninschriften von Hatnub*, Leipzig, 1928.

Arnaud, D., 'Les ports de la 'Phénicie'à la fin de l'Âge du Bronze récent (XIVᵉ-XIIIᵉ s.) d'après les textes cunéiformes de Syrie', *Studi Micenei & Egeo-Anatolici* xxx, 1992, pp. 179-194.

Arnaud, P., 'Naviguer entre Égypte et Grèce: les principales lignes de navigation d'après les données numériques des géographes anciens', *in Entre Égypte et Grèce, Actes du Colloque du 6-9 octobre 1994, Cahiers de la villa 'Kérylos'* 5, Paris, 1995, pp. 94-107.

Arnaud, P., 'La navigation hauturière en Méditerranée ancienne d'après les données des géographes anciens: quelques exemples', *in* É. Rieth (ed.), *Méditerranée antique. Pêche, navigation, commerce*, national congress of the sociétés historiques et scientifiques: 120ᵗʰ, Aix-en-Provence, 23-29 Oct. 1995; 121ᵗʰ, Nice, 26-31 Oct. 1996, CTHS, Paris, 1998, pp. 75-87.

Artzy, M., Perlman I., and Asaro, F., 'Alasiya of the Amarna Letters', *JNES* 35, 1976, pp. 171-182.

Ascher E., 'The Timetables of the Periplus Maris Erythaei and of Pliny's Voyage to India', *The Journal of Tropical Geography* 28, 1969, pp. 1 *ff.*

Assmann, E., 'Die Schiffsbilder', *in* L. Borchardt, *Das Grabdenkmal des Königs Sahure II, Die Wandbilder, Wissenschaftliche Veröffentlichung der Deut. Orient-Gesellschaft* 26, *Ausgrabungen der Deut. Orient-Gesellschat in Abusir 1902-1908*, VII, J.C. Hinrichs'sche Buchhandlung, Leipzig, 1913.

Assmann, J., *Ägyptische Hymnen und Gebete*, Die Bibliothek der Alten Welt, Artemis Verlag, Zurich, Munich, 1975.

Assmann, J., and Blumenthal, E. (ed.), *Literatur und Politik im pharaonischen und ptolemäischen Ägypten, Vorträge der Tagung zum Gedenken an Georges Posener, 5-10 September 1996 in Leipzig, BiÉtud* 127, IFAO, Cairo, 1999.

Aufrère, S.H., *L'univers minéral dans la pensée égyptienne, BiÉtud* CV, vol. 2, IFAO, Cairo, 1991.

Aufrère, S.H., Golvin, J.-C., and Goyon, J.-C., *L'Égypte restituée, tome 2: Sites et temples des déserts*, Errance, Paris, 1994.

Aufrère, S.H., 'Les expéditions au pays de *Pount* au Moyen Empire', *Égypte. Afrique & Orient* 1, 1996, pp. 23-27.

Aufrère, S.H., 'L'Univers minéral dans la pensée égyptienne: essai de synthèse et perspectives (Autour de l'univers minéral x)', *Archéo-Nil* 7, octobre 1997, pp. 113-144.

Aufrère, S.H., 'Un prolongement Méditerranéen du mythe de la Lointaine à l'époque tardive', *in* N. Grimal and B. Menu (eds), *Le commerce en Égypte ancienne, BiÉtud* 121, IFAO, Cairo, 1998, pp. 19-39.

Aupert, P., 'Amathonte, le Proche-Orient et l'Égypte', *in* V. Karageorghis (ed.), *Cyprus between the Orient and the Occident, Acts of the International Archaeological Symposium, Nicosia, 8-14 Sept. 1985*, Nicosia, 1986, pp. 368-382.

Austin, M.M., *Greece and Egypt in the Archaic Age*, Cambridge, 1970.

Austin, M.M., *The Hellenistic World, from Alexander to the Roman Conquest: A Selection of Ancient Sources in Translation*, Cambridge, 1981.

Avner, R., and Eshel, E., 'A juglet with Phoenician Inscription from a Recent Excavation in Jaffa', *Transeuphratène* 12, 1996, pp. 59-63.

Baines, J., and Malek, J., *Atlas of Ancient Egypt*, Phaidon, Oxford, 1980.

Baines J., 'Interpreting the Story of the Shipwrecked Sailor', *JEA* 76, 1990, p. 55.

Bakir, A. el-M., *Slavery in Pharaonic Egypt, CASAE* 18, 1952.

Bakr, M.I., *Tell Basta I*, Cairo, 1995.

Bakr, M.I., 'The Old Kingdom at Bubastis: Excavations since 1978 Outline', *DE* special number 1, 1989, pp. 39-49.

Bakr, M.I., 'New Excavations of Zagazig University', *in L'Égyptologie en 1979. Axes pioritaires de recherche*, Paris, CNRS, 1982, pp. 154-167.

Bakr, M.I., and Nibbi, A., 'Three stone anchors from Tell Basta', *RdÉ* 42, 1991, pp. 3-10, pl. i.

Ballard, G.A., 'The Sculptures of Deir el-Bahari', *The Mariner's Mirror* 6, 1920, pp. 149-212.

Ballet, P., 'De la Méditerranée à l'océan Indien. L'Égypte et le commerce de longue distance à l'époque romaine: les données céramiques', *Topoi. Orient-Occident* 6/2, 1996, pp. 809-840.

Ballet, P., 'Routes septentrionales du Sinaï, de l'époque hellénistique au Bas-Empire. Les témoignages céramiques', *in* D. Valbelle and C. Bonnet (eds), *Le Sinaï durant l'Antiquité et le Moyen Âge. 4000 ans d'histoire pour un désert*, "Sinaï" UNESCO colloquium, 19–21 Sept. 1997, Errance, Paris, 1998, pp. 102-106.

Ballet, P., Galliano, G., Élaign S., Grataloup, C., Boutantin, C., and Nenna, M.-D., 'La ville de Coptos à l'époque romaine', *in Coptos. L'Égypte antique aux portes du désert, Lyon, musée des Beaux-Arts, 3 février-7 mai 2000*, Musée des Beaux-Arts de Lyon, RMN, Paris, 2000, pp. 176-187.

Baqués, L., 'Escarabeos egipcios de Ibiza', *Ampurias* 36–37, 1974–1975, pp. 87–146.

Barbour, K.M., *The Republic of the Sudan*, London, 1961.

Barns, J., 'Three Hieratic Papyri in the Duke of Northumberland's Collection', *JEA* 34, 1948, p. 39.

Barnett, J.D., 'The Sea Peoples', *in* I.E.S. Edwards, C.J. Gadd, N.G.L. Hammond and E. Sollberger (eds.), *History of the Middle East and the Aegean Region c. 1380-1000 BC, CAH* II, part 2, Cambridge, 1975 (3rd ed.), pp. 188–216.

Barta, W., *in LÄ* IV, 1982, *s.v.* 'Opferliste', cols 586–587.

Barucq, A., and Daumas, Fr., *Hymnes et prières de l'Égypte ancienne, LAPO* 10, Le Cerf, Paris, 1980.

Basch, L., 'Phoenician Oared Ships', *The Mariner's Mirror* 55, 1969, p. 142.

Basch, L., 'Another Punic Wreck in Sicily: its ram', *IJNA* 4/2, 1975, p. 201.

Basch, L., 'Les bateaux-corbeilles des Haou Nebout', *CRIPEL* 4, 1976, pp. 11–51.

Basch, L., 'Trières grecques, phéniciennes et égyptiennes', *JHS* 97, 1977, pp. 1–10.

Basch, L., 'Le navire *mnš* et autres notes de voyage en Égypte', *The Mariner's Mirror* 64, 1978, pp. 115–118.

Basch, L., 'M. le Professeur Lloyd et les trières: quelques remarques', *JHS* 100, 1980, pp. 198–199.

Basch, L., 'Carthage and Rome: tenons and mortises', *The Mariner's Mirror* 67/3, 1981, pp. 245–250.

Basch, L., 'When is a Ram not a Ram', *The Mariner's Mirror* 69, 1983, pp. 129–142.

Basch, L., 'Anchors in Egypt', *The Mariner's Mirror* 71, 1985, pp. 453–467.

Basch, L., *Le musée imaginaire de la marine antique*, Athens, 1987.

Basch, L., 'Navires et bateaux coptes: état des questions en 1991', *Graeco-Arabica* V, Athens, 1993, p. 51.

Basch, L., 'Some remarks on the use of stone anchors and pierced stones in Egypt' *IJNA* 23, n° 3, August 1994, pp. 219–227.

Basch, L., 'La construction navale égyptienne', *Égypte. Afrique & Orient* 1, 1996, pp. 2–7.

Basch, L., 'L'apparition de la voile latine en Méditerranée', *in* D. Meeks and D. Garcia (eds), *Techniques et économie antiques et médiévales : le temps de l'innovation, Colloque international (CNRS) Aix-en-Provence 21-23 Mai 1996*, Errance, Paris, 1997, pp. 214–223.

Basch, L., 'Construction privée et construction d'État dans l'Antiquité', *in* E. Rieth (ed.), *Concevoir et construire les navires, de la trière au picoteux*, Paris, 1998, pp. 22–31.

Baslez, M.-F., *Recherche sur les conditions de pénétrations et de diffusion des religions orientales à Délos (IIᵉ-Iᵉʳ s. avant notre ère)*, Paris, 1977.

Baslez, M.-Fr., *Les étrangers à Délos. Formes et évolution de la vie de relations dans un sanctuaire panhellénique*, thesis, Paris, 1982.

Baslez, M.-F., 'Cultes et dévotions des Phéniciens en Grèce: les divinités marines', *Studia Phoenicicia* IV, 1986, pp. 289–305.

Baslez, M.-F., 'Le rôle et la place des Phéniciens dans la vie économique des ports de l'Égée', *in* E. Lipinski (ed.), *Phoenicia and the East Mediterranean in the First Millennium BC, Studia Phoenicia* V, Louvain, 1987, pp. 267–285.

Baslez, M.-F., 'Les communautés d'orientaux dans la cité grecque: forme de sociabilité et modèles associatifs', *in* R. Lonis (ed.), *L'étranger dans le monde grec*, Nancy, 1988, pp. 139–158.

Bass, G.-F., 'The Cape Gelidonya Wreck: Preliminary Report', *AJA* 65, 1961, pp. 270–271.

Bass, G.F., 'Cape Gelidonya: a Bronze Age Shipwreck', *Transactions of the American Philosophical Society* 57, Philadelphia, 1967, p. 48.

Bass, G.F., and van Doorninck F.H., *'A Fourth-Century Shipwreck at Yassi Ada'*, *AJA* LXXV, 1971, pp. 27–37.

Bass, G.F. (ed.), *A History of Seafaring*, London, 1972.

Bass, G.F., 'Cape Gelidonya and Bronze Age Maritime Trade', *in* H.A. Hoffner (ed.), *Orient and Occident, Essays presented to Cyrus H. Gordon on the Occasion of his Sixty-fifth Birthday, AOAT* 22, 1973, Kevelaer, 1973, pp. 29–37.

Bass, G.F., *Archaeology Beneath the Sea*, New York, 1975.

Bass, G.-F., 'Recent archaeological research', *in Turkey, Underwater Archaeology*, 1984.

Bass, G.-F., 'Underwater Archaeology, 1984, Ulu Burun (Kas)', *Anatolian Studies* 35, 1985, pp. 211–212.

Bass, G.F., 'A Bronze Age Shipwreck at Ulu Burun (Kaç): 1984 Campaign', *AJA* 90, 1986, pp. 269–296.

Bass, G.-F., 'Oldest known shipwreck reveals splendors of the Bronze Age', *National Geographic* 172, December 1987, pp. 692–733.

Bass, G.F., 'Excavations at Ulu Burun (Kas) 1987 Campaign', *X. Kazi Sonuçlari Toplantisi* I, Ankara, 1989, pp. 307-321.

Bass, G.F., and Pulak, C., 'Excavations at Ulu Burun in 1986', *AJA* 73, 1989, pp. 1-12.

Bass, G.F., 'Construction of a seafaring vessel of the Late Bronze Age', *in Hellenic Trust for preservation of Nautical Traditions, TROPIS* 1, Athens, 1989, pp. 25-35.

Bass, G.F., 'Evidence of Trade from Bronze Age Shipwrecks', *in* N.H. Gale (ed.), *Bronze Age Trade in the Mediterranean, Papers presented at the Conference held at Rewley House, Oxford, in December 1989, SIMA* XC, Paul Åstroms Förlag, Jonsered, 1991, pp. 69-82.

Beaudouin, F., 'Une famille de voiles égyptiennes de l'antiquité à nos jours', *L'Ethnographie*, 60-61, 1966-1967, pp. 53-54.

Beckerath, J. von, *Tanis und Theban. Historische Grundlagen der Ramessidenzeit in Ägypten, ÄgyForsch* 16, Glückstadt, 1951.

Beckerath, J. von, *Handbuch der ägyptischen Königsnamen, MÄS* 20, Munich, 1984.

Beckerath, J. von, *in LÄ* v, 1984, *s. v.* 'Smendès', cols 991-992.

Beinlich, H., *in LÄ* VI, 1986, *s.v.* 'Wallfahrt', cols 1145-1146.

Bell, B., 'The dark ages in Ancient History, I, The first dark ages in Egypt', *AJA* 75, 1971, pp. 3-26.

Bell, B., *Interpreters and egyptianized Nubians in ancient Egyptian foreign policy: Aspects of the history of Egypt and Nubia*, PhD. thesis, University of Pennsylvania, 1976.

Bell, L., Johnson J., and Whitcomb, D., 'The Eastern Desert of Upper Egypt: Routes and Inscriptions', *JNES* 43, 1984, pp. 47-86.

Benz, F.L., *Personal Names in the Phoenician and Punic Inscriptions, StudPohl* 8, Rome, 1972.

Berlandini, J., 'Ptah-démiurge et l'exaltation du ciel', *RdÉ* 46, 1995, pp. 19-46.

Bernand, A., *Le Delta égyptien d'après les textes grecs*, 1, *Les confins libyques*, vol. 4, *MIFAO* 91, IFAO, Cairo, 1970.

Bernand, A., *De Koptos à Kosseir*, Leiden, 1972.

Bernand, A., *Pan du désert*, E.J. Brill, Leiden, 1977.

Berry, L., 'The Red Sea Coasts of the Sudan', *Sudan Notes and Records* 45/1, 1964, pp. 148-154.

Bickel, S., 'Commerçants et bateliers au Nouvel Empire. Mode de vie et statut d'un groupe social', *in* N. Grimal and B. Menu (eds), *Le commerce en Égypte ancienne, BiÉtud* 121, IFAO, Cairo, 1998, pp. 157-172, fig. 1-5.

Bietak, M., *Tell el-Dab'a* II. *Der Fundort im Rahmen einer archäologische-geographischen Untersuchung über das ägyptische Ostdelta, Untersuchungen der Zweigstelle Kairo des Österreichischen Archäologischen Institutes* I, Österreichische Akademie der Wissenschaften, vol. 2, Vienna, 1975.

Bietak, M., 'Avaris and Piramesse, Archaeological Exploration in the Eastern Nile Delta', *Proceedings of the British Academy* 65, London, 1979.

Bietak, M., 'Ceramics on the C-Group Culture', *Meroitica* 5, 1979, pp. 107-127.

Bietak, M., 'Eine Palastanlage aus der Zeit des späten Mittleren Reiches und andere Forschungsergebnisse aus dem östlichen Nildelta (Tell el-Dab'a 1979-1984)', *Anzeiger der Philosophisch-historischen Klasse der Österreichischen Akademie der Wissenschaften* 121, 1984, pp. 312-349.

Bietak, M., *in LÄ* V, 1984, *s.v.*, 'Ramsesstadt', cols 128-146.

Bietak, M., *Avaris and Piramesse: Archaeological Exploration in the Eastern Nile Delta*, Mortimer Wheeler Archaeological Lecture 1979, Oxford University Press, Oxford, 1986.

Bietak, M., *in LÄ* VI, Wiesbaden, 1986, *s.v.,* 'Tell el-Jahudija Keramik', cols 335-348.

Bietak, M., 'Zur Marine des Alten Reiches', *in Pyramid Studies and other Essays, Presented to I.E.S. Edwards*, EES, London, 1988, pp. 35-40, pls 5-9.

Bietak, M., 'Un projet d'archéologie urbaine à Tell el-Dab'a', *in* M. Baud (ed.), *Cités disparues*, Série 'monde'HS n° 35, Autrement, Paris, 1989, pp. 115-125.

Bietak, M., 'Archäologischer Befund und historische Interpretation am Beispiel der Tell el-Yahudiya Ware', *in* S. Schoske (ed.), *Papers of the 4th International Congress of Egyptology, Munich, 1985*, Hamburg, 1989, pp. 7-34.

Bietak, M., 'Zur Herkunft des Seth von Avaris', *ÄgLev* I, 1990, pp. 9-16.

Bietak, M., Mlinar, Chr., and Schwab, A., *Tell el-Dab'a* V, *DÖAW* 1, Vienna, 1991.

Bietak, M., 'Der Friedhof in einem Palastgarten aus der Zeit des späten Mittleren Reiches und andere Forschungsergebnisse aus dem östlichen Nildelta (Tell el Dab'a 1984-1987)', *ÄgLev* II, 1991, pp. 47-55.

Bietak, M., 'Avaris. Tell el-Dab'a', *in L'Égypte du Delta. Les capitales du Nord, Dossiers d'Archéologie* n° 213, March 1996, pp. 16-23.

Bietak, M., *Avaris: The Capital of the Hyksos. Recent Excavations at Tell el-Dab'a*, British Museum Press, London, 1996.

Bietak, M., 'Avaris and Piramesse: Archaeological Exploration in the Eastern Nile Delta, 1986', revised reprint from the *Proceedings of the British Academy* 65, London, 1997.

Bietak, M., 'Une citadelle royale à Avaris de la première moitié de la XVIIIᵉ dynastie et ses liens avec le monde minoen', *in* A. Caubet (ed.), *L'acrobate au taureau. Les découvertes de Tell el-Dabca (Égypte) et l'archéologie de la Méditerranée orientale (1800-1400 av. J.-C.),* proceedings of a colloquium held at the Louvre, 3 Dec. 1994, La documentation française & musée du Louvre, Paris, 1999, pp. 29-81, pls i-xi, figs 1-22.

Bietak, M., 'Regional Projects: Egypt', *in* M. Bietak (ed.), *The Synchronisation of Civilisations in the Eastern Mediterranean in the Second Millennium BC*, proceedings of an international symposium at Schloß Haindorf, 15ᵗʰ-17ᵗʰ of November 1996 and at the Austrian Academy, Vienna, 11ᵗʰ-12ᵗʰ of May 1998, Österreichische Akademie der Wissenschaften, *Denkschriften der Gesamtakademie*, vol. XIX, Vienna, 2000, pp. 83-95.

Bietak, M., and Kopetzky, K., 'Regional Projects: Israel/Palestine', *in* M. Bietak (ed.), *The Synchronisation of Civilisations in the Eastern Mediterranean in the Second Millenium BC,* proceedings of an international symposium at Schloß Haindorf, 15ᵗʰ-17ᵗʰ of November 1996 and at the Austrian Academy, Vienna, 11ᵗʰ-12ᵗʰ of May 1998, Österreichische Akademie der Wissenschaften, *Denkschriften der Gesamtakademie*, vol. XIX, Vienna, 2000, pp. 96-135.

Bissing, F.W. von, *Die Mastaba des Gem-ni-kai*, in association with A.E.P. Weigall, published by F.W. von Bissing, vol. 1, Alexander Duncker, Berlin, 1905.

Björkman, G., 'Neby, the Mayor of Tjaru in the Reign of Tuthmosis IV', *JARCE* XI, 1974, pp. 43-51.

Black, E., and Samuel D., 'What were Sails made of?', *The Mariner's Mirror* 77, 1991, pp. 217-226.

Blackman A.M., and Apted, M.R., *The Rock Tombs of Meir, Part v, The Tomb-Chapels, A, n° 1 (that of Ni-'Ankh-Pepi the Black), A, n° 2 (that of Pepi'onkh with the Good Name of Heny the Black), A, n° 4 (that of Hepi the Black), D, n° 1 (that of Pepi), and E, n° 1-4 (those of Meniu, Nenki, Pepi'onkh and Tjetu), Archaeological Survey of Egypt, EEF Memoir XXVIII*, London, 1953.

Blackman, D.J., *Ancient Harbours in the Mediterranean*, Part I, *IJNA* 11/2, 1982, pp. 79-104, pp. 185-211.

Blackman, M.J. (ed.), *Proceedings of the 24th International Archaeometry Symposium*, Washington, 1986.

Blumenthal, E., *Atägyptische Reiseerzählungen. Die Lebensgeschichte des Sinuhe. Der Reisebericht des Wen-Amun*, Leipzig, 1984 (2ⁿᵈ ed.).

Boardman, J., *The Greeks Overseas, Their Colonies and Trade*, London, 1980 (revised edition).

Boardman, J., *Escarabeos de piedra procedentes de Ibiza, Catálogos y Monografías del Museo Arqueológico Nacional 8*, Madrid, 1984.

Boardman, J., *Les Grecs outre-mer, colonisation et commerce archaïque*, Centre Jean Bérard, Naples, 1995.

Bonnefoux, P.-M.-J. de, and Pâris, F.-E., *Dictionnaire de marine à voiles*, Éditions du Layeur, Paris, [1859] 1999.

Borchardt, L., *Das Grabdenkmal des Königs Sah3re' II, Die Wandbilder, Wissenschaftliche Veröffentlichung der Deut. Orient-Gesellschaft 26, Ausgrabungen der Deut. Orient-Gesellschat in Abusir 1902-1908*, VII, J.C. Hinrichs'sche Buchhandlung, Leipzig, 1913.

Borchardt, L., *Statuen und Statuetten Königen und Privatleuten, CGC* n° 1-1294, vol. 2, Berlin, 1925.

Borchardt, L., *Denkmäler des Alten Reiches (usser den Statuen) im Museum von Kairo, Nr. 1295-1808*, part 2, *Text und Tafeln zu Nr. 1542-1808 (Manuskript Abgeschlossen 1899)*, CGC, Cairo, 1964.

Boreux, C., *Études de nautique égyptienne. L'art de la navigation en Égypte jusqu'à la fin de l'Ancien Empire, MIFAO* l, IFAO, Cairo, 1925.

Botta, P.E., and Flandin, E., *Monuments de Ninive* I, Paris, 1849.

Bouineau, J., 'Rapport de synthèse', *in* N. Grimal and B. Menu (eds), *Le commerce en Égypte ancienne, BiÉtud* 121, IFAO, Cairo, 1998, pp. 289-297.

Bowen, R., and Jux, U., *Afro-Arabian Geology*, London-New York, 1987.

Boyaval, B., 'La vieillesse et la mort du matelot Ménélaos', *CRIPEL* 19, 1998, pp. 57-58.

Bradbury, L., 'Reflections on Travelling to "God's Land" and Punt in the Middle Kingdom', *JARCE* XXV, 1988, pp. 127-156.

Bradbury, L., '*Kpn*-boats, Punt Trade, and a Lost Emporium', *JARCE* XXXIII, 1996, pp. 37-60.

Braemer, F., 'Éléments naturels (vents, courants: avantages, inconvénients et itinéraires maritimes', *in* É. Rieth (ed.), *Méditerranée antique. Pêche, navigation, commerce*, national congress of the sociétés historiques et scientifiques: 120ᵗʰ, Aix-en-Provence, 23-29 Oct. 1995; 121ᵗʰ, Nice, 26-31 Oct. 1996, CTHS, Paris, 1998, pp. 61-73.

Braudel, F., *La Méditerranée et le monde Méditerranéen à l'époque de Philippe II*, A. Colin, Paris, 1949.

Braudel, F., *Civilisation matérielle, économie et capitalisme, XVᵉ-XVIIᵉ siècle*, A. Colin, Paris 1979.

Braudel, F., *Grammaire des civilisations*, Flammarion, Paris, 1993.

Breasted, J.H., *History of Egypt*, London, 1905.

Breasted, J.H., *Ancient records of Egypt, Historical Documents, from the earliest Times to the Persian Conquest, collected, edited and translated with commentary*, I, *The First to the Seventeenth Dynasties*, The University of Chicago Press, Chicago, 1906.

Breasted, J.H., *Ancient Records of Egypt, Historical Documents, from the earliest Times to the Persian Conquest, collected, edited and translated with commentary*, II, *The Eighteenth Dynasty*, The University of Chicago Press, Chicago, 1906.

Breasted, J.H., *Ancient Records of Egypt, Historical Documents from the Earliest Times to the Persian Conquest, collected, edited and translated with commentary*, III, *The Nineteenth Dynasty*, The University of Chicago Press, Chicago, 1906.

Breasted, J.H., *Ancient Records of Egypt, Historical Documents, from the earliest Times to the Persian Conquest, collected, edited and translated with commentary*, IV, *The Twentieth to the Twenty-sixth Dynasties*, The University of Chicago Press, Chicago, 1906.

Breasted, J.H., 'The Earliest Boats on the Nile', *JEA* IV, 1917, pp. 174-176, 255.

Breasted, J.H., *A History of Ancient Egyptian*, John Murray, London, 1920.

Brecht, C., *Zur Haftung der Schiffer im antiken Recht*, Münch. Beitr. 45, Munich, 1962.

Bresciani, E., 'I semitici nell'Egitto di età saitica e persiana', *in Egitto e società antica*, Milan, 1985, pp. 93-104.

Bresciani, E., 'L'étranger', *in* S. Donadoni (ed.), *L'Homme égyptien*, Le Seuil, Paris, Chicago, 1992, pp. 267-303.

Briand, F., and Maldonado, A. (eds), *Transformations and evolution of the Mediterranean coastline*, Bulletin de l'Institut Océanographique 18, ciesm Science Series, Monaco, 1997.

Briant, P., *Histoire de l'Empire perse. De Cyrus à Alexandre*, Paris, 1996.

Briant, P., and Descat, R., 'Un registre douanier de la satrapie d'Égypte à l'époque achéménide (*TAD* C 3, 7)', *in* N. Grimal and B. Menu (eds), *Le commerce en Égypte ancienne*, BiÉtud 121, IFAO, Cairo, 1998, pp. 59-104.

Briquel-Chatonnet, F., *Les relations entre les cités de la côte phénicienne et les royaumes d'Israël et de Juda*, Studia Phoenicia XII, *OLA* 46, Leuven, 1992.

Briquel-Chatonnet, F., 'Les inscriptions proto-sinaïtiques', *in* D. Valbelle and C. Bonnet (eds.), *Le Sinaï durant l'Antiquité et le Moyen Âge. 4000 ans d'histoire pour un désert*, 'Sinaï' UNESCO colloquium, 19–21 Sept. 1997, Errance, Paris, 1998, pp. 56-60.

Briquel-Chatonnet, F., 'Le Liban à l'âge du Fer, les cités phéniciennes' *in Liban, l'autre rive, Exposition présentée à l'Institut du monde arabe du 27 octobre 1998 au 2 mai 1999*, Institut du monde arabe, Flammarion, Paris, 1998, pp. 100-110.

Briquel-Chatonnet, F., 'Le miracle phénicien', *in 3000 ans sur le mer*, Les collections de L'Histoire 8, June 2000, pp. 16-17.

Briquel-Chatonnet, F., 'Le cèdre a une patrie: le Liban', *L'Histoire* 248, Sept. 2000, pp. 20-21.

Brissaud, P., 'Tanis', in *L'Égypte du Delta. Les capitales du Nord*, Dossiers d'Archéologie 213, March 1996, pp. 66-75.

Brissaud, P., and Zivie-Coche, C. (eds), *Tanis, Travaux récents sur le Tell Sân el-Hagar, Mission française des fouilles de Tanis 1987-1997*, Noêsis, Paris, 1998.

Brissaud, P., and Zivie-Coche, C. (eds), *Tanis, Travaux récents sur le Tell Sân el-Hagar, 2, Mission française des fouilles de Tanis 1988-2000*, Noêsis, Paris, 2000.

Broerner, E., *Der staatliche Korntransport im griechisch-römischen Ägyptens*, Hamburg, 1939, pp. 42-43.

Brookner, J.B., Redford, D.B., and Holladay, J.S., *Cities of the Delta, Part III. Tell el-Maskouta, Preliminary Report on the Wadi Tumilat Project 1978-1979*, ARCE Reports 6, Undena Publications, Malibu, 1982.

Brown, F., Driver, S.R., and Briggs, C.A., *An Hebrew and English Lexikon of the Old Testament based on the Lexikon of W. Gesenius as translated by E. Robinson*, Oxford, 1976.

Brown, R., 'Ancient Egyptian Hull Forms', *The Mariner's Mirror* 46, 1920, pp. 303-306.

Bruce, J., *Travels to discover the Source of the Nile, 1768-1773*, London-Edinburgh, 1813.

Brunner, H., *Die Lehre des Cheti, Sohnes des Duauf*, Gluckstadt, 1944.

Brunton, G., *British Museum Expedition to Middle Egypt 1929-1931*, Matmar, London, 1948.

Bruyère, B., *Fouilles de Clysma-Qolzoum (Suez), 1930-1932*, FIFAO XXVII, IFAO, Cairo, 1966.

Bülow-Jacobsen, A., Cuvigny, H., and Fournet, J.-L., 'The Identification of Myos Hormos. New Papyrological Evidence', *BIFAO* 94, 1994, pp. 27–42, pls i–iv.

Bunnens, G., 'La mission d'Ounamon en Phénicie. Point de vue d'un non-égyptologue', *Revista di Studi Fenici* 6, 1978, pp. 1–16.

Bunnens, G., *L'expansion phénicienne en Méditerranée. Essai d'interprétation fondé sur une analyse des traditions littéraires, Études de philologie, d'archéologie et d'histoire anciennes* 17, Brussels-Rome, 1979.

Bunnens, G., 'Tyr et la mer', *in* E. Gubel, E. Lipinski and B. Servais-Soyez, *Redt Tyrus/Sauvons Tyr, Studia Phoenicia* I, *OLA* 15, Leuven, 1983, pp. 7–21.

Bunnens, G., 'Le luxe phénicien d'après les inscriptions royales assyriennes', *in* E. Lipinski and E. Gubel, *Phoenicia and its Neighbours, Proceedings of the Colloquium held on the 9th and 10th of December 1983 at the 'Vrije Universiteit Brussel', in cooperation with the 'Centrum voor Mycense en Archaïsch-Griekse Cultuur', Studia Phoenicia* III, Peeters, Leuven, 1985, pp. 121–133.

Burchardt, M., *Die alkanaanäische Fremdworte und Eigennamen im Ägyptischen*, vol. 2, Leipzig, 1909–1910.

Burstein, S.M., *Agatharchides of Cnidus. On the Erythraean Sea, translation and commentary*, London, 1989.

Butzer, K.W., *Studien zum vor- und frühgeschichtlichen Landschaftswandel der Sahara*, III, *Die Naturlandschaft Ägyptens während der Vorgeschichte und der Dynastischen Zeit*, Wiesbaden, 1959.

Butzer, K.W., *in LÄ* V, 1983, *s.v.* 'Rotes Meer', cols 311–313.

Calderini, A., and Daris, D., *Dizionario dei nomi geografici e topografici dell'Egitto greco-romano*, Cons. Sup. de Investig. Cientificas-Inst. 'Antonio de Nebrija', Madrid, 1935–1996.

Calvet, Y., and Robin, C. (eds), *Arabie heureuse, Arabie déserte, Les antiquités arabiques du musée du Louvre*, RMN, Paris, 1997.

Caminos, R.A., *Late-Egyptian Miscellanies, Brown Egyptological Studies* I, Oxford University Press, London, 1954.

Caminos, R.A., 'Le paysan', *in* S. Donadoni (ed.), *L'Homme Égyptien*, Paris, 1992, pp. 15–49.

Camps, G. (ed.), *Chronologie et synchronisme dans la préhistoire circum-Méditerranéenne*, Union internationale des Sciences préhistoriques et protohistoriques, Nice, 1976.

Camps, G., 'La navigation en France au néolithique et à l'âge du bronze', *in La Préhistoire française*, vol. 2, CNRS, Paris, 1976, pp. 192–201.

Camps, G., 'Les premiers navigateurs méditerranéens', *L'Histoire* 13, June 1979, pp. 6–13.

Camps, G., 'Les premiers navigateurs', *in 3000 ans sur le mer, Les collections de L'Histoire* 8, June 2000, pp. 12.

Cannuyer, C., 'Encore sur le naufrage du Naufrage', *BSEG* 14, 1990, pp. 15–21.

Cannuyer, C., Ries, J., and Van Tongerloo, A. (eds), *Les voyages dans les civilisations orientales, Acta Orientalia Belgica* XI, Leuven, 1998.

Cannuyer, C., 'Le voyage dans le Proche-Orient ancien. Quelques données et textes en guise d'avant-propos', 'Le voyage comme tension eschatologique dans l'Égypte ancienne. Les leçons du Naufragé', *in* C. Cannuyer, J. Ries and A. Van Tongerloo (eds), *Les voyages dans les civilisations orientales, Acta Orientalia Belgica* XI, Leuven, 1998, pp. 1–13, 27–42.

Capart, J., *Recueil de monuments égyptiens, Cinquante planches phototypiques avec texte explicatif*, vol. 1, A. Vromant & Co., Brussels, 1902.

Capart, J., *Memphis à l'ombre des Pyramides*, Vromant & Co., Brussels, 1930.

Capart, J., *L'Art égyptien*, III, Les arts graphiques, Paris, 1942.

Carr, G.G., *Sailing Barges*, London, 1951.

Carre, M.-B., 'La survivance de l'assemblage par ligatures après l'époque archaïque', *in* D. Meeks and D. Garcia (ed.), *Techniques et économie antiques et médiévales : le temps de l'innovation, Colloque international (CNRS Aix-en-Provence 21-23 Mai 1996)*, Errance, Paris, 1997, pp. 204–205.

Carrez-Maratray, J.-Y., and Wagner G., 'Tell el-Kanaïs', *CRIPEL* 15, 1993, pp. 105–110.

Carrez-Maratray, J.-Y., 'Pelusium robur Aegypti, de l'état des sources à l'état des lieux', *BAGB* 2, 1995, pp. 140–151.

Carrez-Maratray, J.-Y., and Defernez, C., 'Premières données sur l'occupation ancienne du site de Péluse (la stratigraphie de Farama Ouest)', *CRIPEL* 18, 1996, pp. 33–49.

Carrez-Maratray, J.-Y., Wagner, G., El-Taba'i, Ahmed, and El-Gindi, R., 'Timbres amphoriques de Tell Farama (tafe) et de Tell el-Herr (tateh)', *CRIPEL* 18, 1996, pp. 179–195.

Carrez-Maratray, J.-Y., 'Le Sinaï des Grecs et des Romains: un passage méconnu de Diodore', *in* D. Valbelle and C. Bonnet (ed.), *Le Sinaï durant l'Antiquité et le Moyen Âge. 4000 ans d'histoire pour un désert*, 'Sinaï' UNESCO colloquium, 19–21 Sept. 1997, Errance, Paris, 1998, pp. 88–92.

Carrez-Maratray, J.-Y., *Péluse et l'angle oriental du delta égyptien aux époques grecque, romaine et byzantine, BiÉtud* 124, IFAO, Cairo, 1999.

Carrez-Maratray, J.-Y., 'La 'monopole de Naucratis'et la 'bataille de Péluse': ruptures ou continuités de la présence grecque en Égypte des Saïtes aux Perses', *in La Transeuphratène à l'époque perse: économie, commerce et monnaie, Actes du IVᵉ colloque international, Institut Catholique de Paris, 20-22 novembre 1997, Transeuphratène* 19, 2000, pp. 159-172.

Cassanelli, L., *The Shaping of Somali Society*, Philadelphia, 1982.

Casson, L., 'Bishop Synesius'Voyage to Cyrene', *American Neptune* XII, n° 4, Oct. 1952, pp. 294-296.

Casson, L., 'The Size of Ancient Merchant Ships', *in Studi in onore di A. Calderini e R. Paribeni*, Milan, 1956, pp. 231-238.

Casson, L., 'Odysseus' boat', *American Journal of Philology* 85, 1964, pp. 61-64.

Casson, L., *Ships and Seamanship in the Ancient World*, Princeton, 1971.

Casson, L., *The Periplus Maris Erythaei*, Text with introduction, translation, and commentary, Princeton University Press, Princeton, 1989.

Casson, L., 'New Light on Maritime Loans: P. Vindob. G 40822', *Zeitschrift für Papyrologie und Epigraphik* 84, 3, 1990, pp. 195-206.

Casson, L., *The Ancient Mariners. Seafarers and Sea Fighters of the Mediterranean in Ancient Times*, Princeton University Press, Princeton, 1991 (2nd ed.).

Casson, L., *Ships and Seafaring in Ancient times*, British Museum Press, London, 1994.

Castle, E.W., 'Shipping and Trade in Ramesside Egypt', *JESHO* 35, 1992, pp. 249-256.

Catling, H.W., 'Cyprus in the Late Bronze Age', *in* I.E.S. Edwards, C.J. Gadd, N.G.L. Hammond and E. Sollberger (eds), *History of the Middle East and the Aegean Region c. 1380-1000 BC, CAH* , vol. 2, part 2, Cambridge, 1975 (3ʳᵈ ed.), pp. 188-216.

Catling, H.W., 'The Date of the Cape Gelidonya Ship and Cypriot Bronze-work', *RDAC*, 1986, pp. 68-71.

Caubet, A., 'Introduction', *in* A. Caubet (ed.), *L'acrobate au taureau. Les découvertes de Tell el-Dabca (Égypte) et l'archéologie de la Méditerranée orientale (1800-1400 av. J.-C.),* proceedings of a colloquium held at the Louvre, 3 Dec. 1994, La documentation française & musée du Louvre, Paris, 1999, pp. 9-26, figs 1-16.

Cerny, J., and Gardiner, A.H., *Hieratic Ostraca*, vol. 1, Oxford, 1957.

Cerny, J., *A Community of Workmen at Thebes in the Ramesside Period*, Cairo, 1973.

Cerny, J., *Papyrus hiératique de Deir el-Medineh, n° I-XVII, DFIFAO* VIII, IFAO, Cairo, 1978.

Cerulli, E., 'Sur Storia d'Etiopia di C. Conti Rossini, Bergamo, 1928', *RSO* 12, 3, 1929, pp. 353-359.

Cerulli, E., 'Il Mar Rosso nella storia della navigazione medievale', *in* E. Cerulli, *L'Islam di ieri e di oggi*, Rome, 1971, pp. 39-58.

Chantraine, P., *Dictionnaire étymologique de la langue grecque*, Paris, 1968.

Charpentier, G., *Recueil de matériaux épigraphiques relatifs à la botanique de l'Égypte antique*, Paris, 1986.

Charpin, D., 'Une mention d'Alasiya dans une lettre de Mari', *Revue d'Assyriologie* 84, 1990, pp. 125-127.

Charpin, D., and Joannès, F. (eds), *Marchands, Diplomates et Empereurs, Études sur la civilisation mésopotamienne offertes à Paul Garelli*, ERC, Paris, 1991.

Charpin, D., and Joannès, F. (eds), *La circulation des biens, des personnes et des idées dans le Proche-Orient ancien, Actes de la XXXVIIIᵉ Rencontre Assyriologique Internationale (Paris, 8-10 juillet 1991)*, ERC, Paris, 1992.

Chartier-Raymond, M., and Traunecker, Cl., 'Reconnaissance archéologique à la pointe orientale du delta. Campagne 1992', *CRIPEL* 15, 1993, pp. 45-69.

Charvet, P., Gompertz, S., and Yoyotte, J., *Strabon, Le Voyage en Égypte*, Nil éditions, Paris, 1997.

Chevereau, P.M., *Prosopographie des cadres militaires égyptiens de la Basse Époque, Carrières Militaires et Sacerdotales en Égypte du XIᵉ au IIᵉ siècle avant J.-C.*, Cybèle, Paris, 1985.

Chevereau, P.M., *Prosopographie des cadres militaires égyptiens au Nouvel Empire*, Antony (published by the author), 1994.

Chevereau, P.M., *Prosopographie des cadres militaires égyptiens du Nouvel Empire, Études et Mémoires d'Égyptologie* 3, Cybèle, Paris, 2001.

Christophe, L.A., 'La stèle de l'an III de Ramsès IV au Ouâdi Hammâmât (n°12) (avec une planche)', *BIFAO* XLVIII, 1949, pp. 1-38.

Christophe, L.A., 'Le pylône ramesside d'Edfou', *ASAE* LV, 1958, pp. 1-23, pls i-ix.

Chuvin, P., and Yoyotte, J., 'Documents relatifs au culte pélusien de Zeus Casios', *RevArch* I, 1986, pp. 41-63.

Cintas, P., *Amulettes puniques*, Tunis, 1946.

Cintas, P., *Contribution à l'étude de l'expansion carthaginois au Maroc, Publication de l'Institut des Hautes Études marocain* LVI, Paris, 1954.

Clarke, B.D., *Models in Archaeology*, Methuen, London, 1972.

Clarysse, W., 'Aratomenes, Brother of Komanos', *CdÉ* LVI, 1981, pp. 347-349.

Clerc, G., Karageorghis, V., Lagarce, E., and Leclant, J., *Fouilles de Kition*, II, *Objets égyptiens et égyptisants*, Nicosia, 1976.

Clerc, G., 'Aegyptiaca', *La Nécropole d'Amathonte, Tombes 110-385, EtudChypr* XIII, Nicosia, 1991, pp. 1-157.

Clerget, M., *Les types de temps en Méditerranée, Annales de Géographie* XLVI, 1937, pp. 225-246.

Cline, E.H., 'Amenhotep III and the Aegean: a reassessment of Egypto-Aegean relations in the 14th century BC', *Orientalia* 56, 1987, pp. 1-36.

Condon, V., 'Two Account Papyri of the Late Eighteenth Dynasty (Brooklyn 35.1453 A and B)', *RdÉ* 35, 1984, pp. 57-82, pls 4-7.

Condon, V., 'Two Variant Accounts? by Janssen? (*VA* 1, 1985, pp. 109-112)', *VA* 2, 1986, pp. 23-29.

Cornu, G., 'La circumnavigation de l'Arabie au IXᵉ-Xᵉ siècles', *in* J.-F. Salles (ed.), *L'Arabie et ses mers bordières*, I, *Itinéraires et voisinages, Séminaires 1985-1986, TMO* 16, Lyon, 1988, pp. 103-110.

Couroyer, B., 'L'origine des phéniciens', *RB* 80, 1973, pp. 264-276.

Couyat, J., 'La route de Myos-Hormos et les carrières de pophyre rouge', *BIFAO* VII, 1909, pp. 1-19.

Couyat, J., 'Ports gréco-romains de la mer Rouge et grandes routes du désert arabique', taken from *CRAIBL*, 1910, pp. 1-18.

Couyat, J., and Montet, P., *Les inscriptions hiéroglyphiques et hiératiques du Ouadi Hammâmât, MIFAO* XXXIV, IFAO, Cairo, 1912-1913.

Cowley, A., *Aramaic Papyri of the Fifth Century BC*, Oxford, 1923.

Crone, P., *Meccan Trade and the Rise of Islam*, Princeton, 1987.

Cuvigny, H., 'Coptos, plaque tournante du commerce érythréen, et les routes transdésertiques', *in Coptos. L'Égypte antique aux portes du désert, Lyon, musée des Beaux-Arts, 3 février-7 mai 2000*, musée des Beaux-Arts de Lyon, RMN, Paris, 2000, pp. 158-175.

Dainelli, G., 'La condizioni fisiche dell'Africa Orientale', *in L'Africa Orientale*, Bologne, 1936, pp. 69-194.

Dalongeville, R., and Sanlaville, P., 'Les marsas du littoral soudanais de la mer Rouge', *Bulletin de la Société Languedocienne de Géographie* 15, 1981, pp. 39-48.

D'Amicone, E., *in LÄ* VI, 1986, *s.v.* 'Stoffe und Webarten', cols 57-63.

Danelius, E., and Steinitz, H., 'The Fishes and Other Aquatic Animals on the Punt Reliefs at Deir el-Bahari', *JEA* 53, 1967, pp. 15-24.

Daressy, G., 'Stèle de l'an III d'Amasis', *RT* 22, 1900, pp. 1-8.

Daressy, G., 'Notes et remarques', *RT* 16, 1910, pp. 42-60.

Daressy, G., 'Sarcophages d'El-Qantarah', *BIFAO* XI, 1911, pp. 29-38.

Darnell, J.C., 'The *Kbn.wt* Vessels of the Late Period', *in* J.H. Johnson (ed.), *Life in a Multicultural Society: Egypt from Cambyses to Constantine and beyond, SAOC* 51, Chicago, 1992, pp. 67-89.

Daszewski, W.A., 'Excavations at Marina el-Alamein (1987-1988)', *MDAIK* 46, 1990, pp. 15-36.

Daszewski, W.A., 'Témoignage de l'urbanisation de la côte Méditerranéenne de l'Égypte à l'époque hellénistique et romaine à la lumière des fouilles de Marina el-Alamein', *BSFE* 132, 1995, pp. 11-29.

Daumas, F., *Les Mammisis de Dendera*, IFAO, Cairo, 1959.

Davies, N. de. G., *The Rock Tombs of Deir el-Gabrâwi, Archaeological Survey of Egypt* 12, EEF, London, 1902.

Davies, N. de G., *The Rock Tombs of el-Amarna, Part I, The Tomb of Meryra, The Archaeological Survey of Egypt* 13, EEF, London, 1903.

Davies, N. de G., *Five Theban Tombs (being those of Mentuherkhepeshef, User, Daga, Neheimawäy and Tati), Archaeological Survey of Egypt* 21, EEF, London, 1913.

Davies, N. de G., *The Tomb of Nakht at Thebes*, MMA, New York, 1917.

Davies, N. de G., Gardiner A.H., *The Tomb of Antefoker vizier of Sesostris I, and of his wife, Senet, The Theban Tombs Series*, EES, London, 1920.

Davies, N. de G., *The Tomb of Puyemra at Thebes*, MMA, New York, 1922.

Davies, N. de G., Gardiner A.H., *The Tomb of Huy, Viceroy of Nubia in the Reign of Tutankhamun (n° 40), The Theban Tombs Series*, IV, *EES*, London, 1926.

Davies, N. de G., *Two Ramesside Tombs at Thebes*, Robb de Payster Tytus Memorial Series, vol. 5, MMA, New York, 1927.

Davies, N. de G., 'The town house in ancient Egypt', *Metropolitan Museum Studies* I, part 2, 1928-1929, pp. 232-240.

Davies, N. de G., *The Tomb of Ken-Amun at Thebes*, Egyptian Expedition V, MMA, New York, 1930.

Davies, N. de G., *The Tomb of Nefer-hotep at Thebes*, vol. 1, Publication 9, MMA, New York, 1933.

Davies, N. de G., 'Trading with the Land of Punt', *BMMA*, 1934-1935, pp. 46-48.

Davies, N. de G., *Paintings from the tomb of Rekh-mi-re' at Thebes*, Egyptian Expedition 10, MMA, New York, 1935.

Davies, N. de G., 'The Works of the Graphic Branch of the Expedition: 1934-1935', *BMMA*, 1935, part 2, pp. 46-49, figs 2-3.

Davies, N. de G., 'The Tomb of Amenmose (N° 89) at Thebes', *JEA* XXVI, 1940, p. 136.

Davies, N. de G., *The Tomb of Rekh-mi-re' at Thebes*, PMMA Egyptian Expedition 11, New-York, 1943.

Davies, N. de G., and Faulkner, R.O., 'A Syrian Trading Venture to Egypt', *JEA* 33, 1947, pp. 40-46, pl. viii.

Davies, N. de G., *La peinture dans l'Égypte ancienne*, vol. 2, Paris, 1953.

Davies, N. de G., 'A fragment of a Punt scene', *JEA* 47, 1961, pp. 19-23.

De Bruyn, M.J., 'Falcon graffiti in the Eastern Desert', *JEA* 44, 1958, pp. 97-98.

De Buck, A., 'Egyptische Litteraire Papyri', *Jaarbericht Ex Oriente Lux* V, 1937-1938, pp. 295.

De Cénival, F., 'Un acte de renonciation consécutif à un partage de revenus lithurgiques memphites (P. Louvre E 3266)', *BIFAO* 71, 1972, pp. 33-54.

De Cenival, F., *Cautionnements démotiques du début de l'époque ptolémaïque*, Paris, 1973.

Defernez, C., 'Le Sinaï et l'Empire perse', *in* D. Valbelle and C. Bonnet (eds), *Le Sinaï durant l'Antiquité et le Moyen Âge. 4000 ans d'histoire pour un désert*, 'Sinaï' UNESCO colloquium, 19–21 Sept. 1997, Errance, Paris, 1998, pp. 67-74.

Degas, J., 'Dom Juan de Castro sur l'itinéraire de Pount (1541)', *RdÉ* 46, 1995, pp. 215-237.

Degas, J., 'Naviguer sur le Nil', 'Les pharaons et la mer', *Égypte. Afrique & Orient* 1, 1996, pp. 8-12, pp. 18-22.

Deger-Jalkotzy, S. (ed.), *Griechenland, die Aegäis und die Levante während der 'Dark Ages' vom 12. bis zum 9. Jh. v. Ch., Akten des Symposiums von Stift Zwettl (N), 11.-14. Oktober 1980*,

Oesterreichische Akademie der Wissenschaften, Philosophische-Historische Klasse, *Sitzungsberichte*, vol. 418, Vienna, 1983.

Del Olmo Late, G., 'Pervivencias Cananeas (Ugaríticas) en el Culto Senicio-III', *Seafared* 51, 1991, pp. 99-114.

Deman, A., 'Présence des Égyptiens dans la seconde guerre médique (480-479 av. J.-C.)', *CdÉ* LX, 1985, pp. 56-74.

Dequin, W., *Arabische Republik Jemen*, Riyadh, 1976.

Derchain, Ph., *Elkab I, Les monuments religieux à l'entrée de l'ouady Hellal*, Brussels, 1971.

De Romanis, F., and Tchernia, A. (eds), *Crossings. Early Mediterranean Contacts with India*, Centre de Sciences Humaines New Delhi, Italian Embassy Cultural Centre, Manohar, New Delhi, 1997.

Désanges, J., *Recherches sur l'activité de Méditerranéens aux confins de l'Afrique (VIe siècle avant J.-C. - IVe siècle après J.-C.)*, doctoral thesis presented at the Université de Paris-Sorbonne, École Française de Rome, Rome, 1978.

Dewachter, M., 'Le grand coude du Nil à Amada et le toponyme *t³ ḳ'ḥ(t)*', *RdÉ* 38, 1987, pp. 190-193.

De Wit, H.E., 'The Evolution of the Eastern Nile Delta as a factor in the development of human culture', *in* L. Krzyzaniak, M. Kobusiewicz and J. Alexander (eds), *Environmental Change and Human Culture in the Nile Basin and Northern Africa until the Second Millenium BC*, Poznan, 1993, pp. 305-320.

De Young, M., 'An African Emporium, The Addi Markato', *Journal of Ethiopian Studies* 4, 1966, pp. 104.

Dixon, D.M., 'The Transplantation of Punt Incense Trees in Egypt', *JEA* 55, 1969, pp. 55-65.

Dothan, M., 'The Fortress at Kadesh Barnea', *IEJ* 15, 1965, pp. 134-151.

Dothan, M., 'An Archaeological Survey of Mt. Casius and its Vicinity', *ErIsr* 9, 1969, pp. 47-59.

Doumet-Serhal, C., 'Discoveries around the harbour of Sidon', *in* Cl. Doumet-Serhal (ed.), *Sidon, National Museum News* 10, 1999, pp. 40-41.

Drenkhahn, R., *Die Handwerker und ihre Tätigkeiten im Alten Ägypten*, ÄgAbh 31, Otto Harrassowitz, Wiesbaden, 1976.

Drioton, É., *Le texte dramatique d'Edfou*, CASAE 11, LeCaire, 1948.

Drioton, É., *L'organisation économique de l'Égypte ancienne*, CHE III/3, Cairo, March 1951.

Drioton, É., and Vandier, J., *L'Égypte. Des origines à la conquête d'Alexandrie*, Paris, 1984 (6th ed).

Ducros, H., 'Étude sur les balances égyptiennes', *ASAE* IX, 1908, pp. 32-53.

Ducros, H., 'Deuxième étude sur les balances égyptiennes', *ASAE* X, 1910, pp. 240-253.

Duell, P., *The Mastaba of Mereruka*, vol. 2, The Oriental Institute, University of Chicago, Chicago, 1938.

Dunand, M., *Fouilles de Byblos I, 1926-1932*, vol. 2, Librairie orientaliste Paul Geuthner, Paris, 1939.

Dunand, M., in *Dictionnaire de la Bible*, suppl. VIII, Paris, 1966, *s.v.* 'Phénicie', col. 1186.

Dunand, M., *Byblos, son histoire, ses ruines, ses légendes*, Catholic Printers, Beruit, 1973.

Dunham, D., Janssen, J.M.A., *Second Cataract Forts*, vol. 1, *Semna Kumma, Excavated by G.A. Reisner*, Museum of Fine Arts, Boston, 1960.

Durrbach, F., *Choix d'inscriptions de Délos*, Paris, 1921.

Duval, M., *Ni morts, ni vivants: marins!, Pour une ethnologie du huis clos*, PUF, Paris, 1999.

Durand, J.-M., *Les documents épistolaires du palais de Mari*, vols 1–3, *LAPO* 16-18, 1997-2000.

Durand, J.-M., 'La façade occidentale du Proche-Orient d'après les textes de Mari', in A. Caubet (ed.) *L'acrobate au taureau. Les découvertes de Tell el-Dabca (Égypte) et l'archéologie de la Méditerranée orientale (1800-1400 av. J.-C.)*, proceedings of a colloquium held at the Louvre, 3 Dec. 1994, La documentation française & musée du Louvre, Paris, 1999, pp. 149-164.

Dürring, N., *Materialien zum Schiffbau im Alten Ägypten*, *ADAIK*, Ägyptologische Reihe 11, Achet Verlag, Berlin, 1995.

Dussaud, R., *Topographie historique de la Syrie antique et médiévale*, *BAH* IV, Paris, 1927.

Edel, E., *Die Ortsnamenlisten aus dem Totentempel Amenophis III*, *Bonner Biblische Beiträge* 25, Peter Hanstein Verlag, Bonn, 1966.

Edel, E., 'Ein neues Beleg für 'Niniveh' in hieroglyphischer Schreibung', *Orientalia* 37, 1968, pp. 417-420.

Edel, E., 'Neue Identification', *GM* 11, 1974, pp. 19-21.

Edel, E., 'Beiträge zu den ägyptischen Sinaiinschriften', *NAWG* 1983, pp. 176-185.

Edel, E., 'Der Seevölker-bericht aus dem 8. Jahr Ramses III', *in Mélanges Gamal Eddin Mokhtar*, *BiÉtud* 97/1, IFAO, Cairo, 1985, pp. 223-237.

Edel, E., *Die ägyptisch-hethitische Korrespondenz aus Boghazköi in babylonischer und hethitischer Sprache*, vol. 2, Opladen, 1994.

Edel, E., *Der Vertrag zwischen Ramses II von Ägypten und Hattusil III von Hatti*, Berlin, 1997.

Edgar, C.C., 'Selected Papyri from the Archives of Zenon', *ASAE* XXIII, 1923, pp. 73-84.

Edgar, C.C., *Zenon Papyri*, *CGC*, Cairo, 1925.

Edgerton, W., 'Ancient Egyptian Ships and Shipping', *AJSL* 39, 1922-1923, pp. 109-129.

Edgerton, W., 'Ancient Egyptian Steering Gear', *AJSL* 43, 1926-1927, pp. 155-162.

Edgerton, W., 'Dimensions of Ancient Egyptian Ships', *AJSL* XLVI, 1930, pp. 145-149.

Edgerton, W., 'Egyptian Seagoing Ships of One Hundred Cubits', *AJSL* 47, 1931, pp. 50-51.

Edgerton, W., and Wilson, J.A., *Historical Records of Ramsès III. The Texts in Medinet Habu*, vol. 2, *SAOC* 12, The University of Chicago Press, Chicago, 1936.

Edgerton, W., 'The Nauri Decree of Seti I, A translation and analysis of the Legal Portion', *JNES* VI, 1947, pp. 217-230.

Edwards, I.E.S., 'The Bankes Papyri I and II', *JEA* 68, 1982, pp. 126-133.

Egberts, A., 'The Chronology of the *Report of Wenamun*', *JEA* 77, 1991, pp. 57-67.

Eisler, R., 'Barakhel Sohn & Cie., Rheidereigesellschaft in Tanis', *ZDMG*, 1924, pp. 61-63.

Eissfeldt, O., 'Baal-Zephon, Zeus Kasios und der Durchzug der Israeliten durchs Meer', *Beitrage zur Religiogeschichte des Altertums* 1, 1932, Halle, p. 30.

Elat, M., 'Trade and Commerce', in *World History of Jewish People* IV, 2, *Jerusalem*, 1979, p. 178.

Elayi, J., 'The Phoenician Cities in the Persian Period', *JANES* 12, 1980, pp. 13-28.

Elayi, J., *Pénétration grecque en Phénicie sous l'empire perse*, Nancy, 1988.

Elayi, J., *Sidon, cité autonome de l'Empire perse*, Paris, 1989.

Elayi, J., 'L'exploitation des cèdres du Mont-Liban par les rois assyriens et néo-babyloniens', *JESHO* 31, 1988, pp. 14-41.

Elayi, J., 'La présence grecque dans les cités phéniciennes sous l'Empire perse achéménide', *REG* 105, 1992, pp. 305-327.

El-Fakharani, Fawzi, 'The Pharaonic Port on the Mediterranean: Its Shape, Development, and Importance', *in Egyptology at the Dawn of the Twenty-first Century, Proceedings of the Eighth International Congress of Egyptologists, 2000*, vol. 2: *History, Religion*, AUC Press, Cairo, New York, 2003, pp. 203-208.

El-Saady, Hassan, 'The External Royal Envoys of the Ramessides: A Study on the Egyptian Diplomats', *MDAIK* 55, 1999, pp. 411-425.

Elsasser, A.B., and Fredrickson V.-M., *Ancient Egypt. An exhibition at the Robert H. Lowie Museum of Anthropology of the University of California, Berkeley, March 25-October 23, 1966*, Berkeley, 1966.

El-Sawi, A., *Excavations at Tell Basta, Report of Seasons, 1967-1971, and Catalogue of Finds*, Prague, 1979.

El-Taba'i, A., and Carrey-Maratray J.-Y., 'Aux portes de Péluse: Farama Ouest. Campagne de sauvetage 1992', *CRIPEL* 15, 1993, pp. 111-118.

El-Yahky, Farid, 'Clarifications on the Gerzean Boat Scenes', *BIFAO* 85, 1985, pp. 187-195, pls xxxiii-xxxiv.

Eph'al, I., *The Ancient Arabs. Nomads on the Borders of the Fertile Crescent 9th-5th Centuries BC*, Leiden, 1982.

Epron, L., Daumas, Fr., and Wild, H., *Le tombeau de Ti*, *MIFAO* 65, fasc. 1-3, Cairo, 1939-1966.

Erichsen, W., *Papyrus Harris I, Hieroglyphische Trankription*, *Bibliotheca Aegyptiaca* v, Fondation Égyptologique Reine Élisabeth, Brussels, 1933.

Erichsen, W., *Demotisches Glossar*, Ejnar Munksgaard, Copenhagen, 1954.

Erman, A., *Life in Ancient Egypt*, Macmillan & Co., London, 1894 (reprinted, New York, 1971).

Erman, A., and Ranke, H., *Aegypten und Aegyptisches Leben im Altertum*, Tübingen, 1923.

Erman, A., *Die Literatur der Ägypter. Gedichte, Erzählungen und Lehrbücher aus dem 3. und 2. Jahrtausend v. Chr.*, J.C. Hinrichs'sche Buchhandlung, Leipzig, [1923] 1978.

Erman, A., and Lange, H., *Papyrus Lansing, eine ägyptische Schulhandschrift der 20. Dynastie*, Herausgegeben und erklärt, Det Kgl. Danske Videnskabernes Selskab X, 3, Copenhagen, 1925.

Erman A., and Ranke, H., *La civilisation égyptienne*, C. Mathien (trans.), Bibliothèque historique, Payot, Paris, 1952.

Esse D.L., and Hopke, P.K., 'Levantine Trade in the Early Bronze Age', *in* J.S. Olin and M.J. Blackman (eds), *Proceedings of the 24th International Archaeometry Symposium*, Washington, 1986, pp. 334-337.

Eyre, C., 'Work and the Organisation of Work in the Old Kingdom', 'Work and the Organisation of Work in the New Kingdom', *in* M.A. Powell (ed.), *Labor in the Ancient Near East*, American Oriental Society, New Haven, 1987, pp. 5-47, pp. 167-221.

Eyre, C., R. Ventura, *Living in the City of the Dead. A Selection of Topographical and Administrative Terms in the Documents of the Theban Necropolis*, Freiburg (Switzerland). Universitätsverlag/Göttingen, Vandenhoeck & Ruprecht, 1986; *CdÉ* LXVII, 1992, pp. 277-281.

Eyre, C., 'The Market Women of Pharaonic Egypt', *in* N. Grimal and B. Menu (eds), *Le commerce en Égypte ancienne*, *BiÉtud* 121, IFAO, Cairo, 1998, pp. 173-191, figs 1-2.

Eyre, C., 'Irony in the Story of Wenamun: the Politics of Religion in the 21st Dynasty', *in* J. Assmann and E. Blumenthal (eds), *Literatur und Politik im pharaonischen und ptolemäischen Ägypten, Vorträge der Tagung zum Gedenken an Georges Posener, 5-10 September 1996 in Leipzig*, *BiÉtud* 127, IFAO, Cairo, 1999, pp. 235-252.

Fabre, D., *Le dieu Seth en Égypte de la fin du Nouvel Empire à l'époque gréco-romaine*, Mémoire de DEA 'Histoire et Civilisation', dissertation written under the supervision of Prof. J.-C. Grenier, Institut d'Égyptologie François Daumas, Université Paul Valéry - Montpellier III, Montpellier, 1999.

Fabre, D., 'Compte rendu de lecture: N. Grimal, B. Menu (éd.), *Le commerce en Égypte ancienne*, *BiÉtud* 121, IFAO, Cairo, 1998', *Égypte. Afrique & Orient* n° 17, May 2000, pp. 57-58.

Fabre, D., 'Compte rendu de lecture: Chr. Cannuyer, J. Ries, A. Van Tongerloo (éd.), *Les voyages dans les civilisations orientales*, *Acta Orientalia Belgica* XI, la Société Belge d'Études Orientales, avec le concours de la Fondation Universitaire de Belgique, Brussels, Leuven-la-Neuve, 1998', *Égypte. Afrique & Orient* n° 17, May 2000, pp. 35-40.

Fabre, D., 'Le dieu Seth de la fin du Nouvel Empire à l'époque gréco-romaine. Entre mythe et histoire', 'De Seth à Typhon, et *vice versa*', *Égypte, Afrique & Orient* n° 22, Sept. 2001, pp. 19-40, pp. 41-55.

Fabre, D., *L'organisation du commerce maritime dans l'Égypte ancienne*, doctoral thesis, Paul Valéry – Montpellier III, Montpellier, 2003, XII.

Fabre, D., 'Le *Voyage d'Ounamon* et les temps de la navigation', publication of the 129th national congress of the sociétés historiques et scientifiques, CTHS, Besançon 19–24 April 2004, on the topic of time.

Fahd, T. (ed.), *L'Arabie préislamique et son environnement historique et culturel, Actes du Colloque de Strasbourg, 24-27 juin 1987*, Université des Sciences humaines de Strasbourg, Travaux du Centre de Recherche sur le Proche-Orient et la Grèce antiques 10, Brill, Leiden, 1989.

Fakhry, Ahmed, *The Egyptian Deserts, Baharia Oasis*, I, Cairo, 1942.

Fakhry, Ahmed, *The Egyptian Deserts: Siwa Oasis. Its History and Antiquities*, Egyptian Antiquities Organisation, Cairo, 1944.

Fakhry, Ahmed, *The Egyptian Deserts, Baharia Oasis*, II, Egyptian Antiquities Organisation, Cairo, 1950.

Farout, D., 'La carrière du *whmw* Ameny et l'organisation des expéditions au ouadi Hammamat au moyen Empire', *BIFAO* 94, 1994, pp. 143-172, pls i-iv.

Faulkner, R.O., 'Egyptian Seagoing Ships', *JEA* XXVI, 1940, pp. 3-9, pls ii-iv.

Faulkner, R.O., 'Egyptian Seagoing Ships: a correction', *JEA* XXVII, 1942, p. 158.

Faulkner, R.O., 'Egyptian Military Organization', *JEA* 39, 1953, pp. 32-47.

Faulkner, R.O., *A Concise Dictionary of Middle Egyptian*, Oxford, 1962.

Faure, P., *La vie quotidienne des colons grecs de la mer Noire à l'Atlantique au siècle de Pythagore, VI<sup>e</sup> siècle avant J.-C.*, Paris, 1978.

Favard-Meeks, C., 'La Delta égyptien et la mer jusqu'à la fondation d'Alexandrie', *in Herausgegeben von Hartwig Altenmüller und Dietrich Wildung, SAK* 16, 1989, pp. 39-63.

Favre, S., and Nogara, G., 'Prospection systématique de surface à l'est de Péluse et lever de la carte archéologique', *CRIPEL* 16, 1994, pp. 129-133.

Fernández, J.H., and Padró, J., *Escarabeos del Museo Arqueológico de Ibiza, TMAI* 7, Madrid, 1982.

Fernández, J.H., and Padró, J., *Amuletos de tipo egipcio del Museo Arqueológico de Ibiza, TMAI* 16, Ibiza, 1986.

Figueras, P., 'The North Sinai Road in the Graeco-Roman Period', *SCI* 8-9, 1985-1988, pp. 57-58.

Finkelstein, M.I., Ἔμπορος, ναυχληρος and χαπηλος: a prolegomena to the study of Athenian trade', *Class. philology* XXX, 1935, pp. 320-336.

Fischer, H.G., 'Sur les routes de l'Ancien Empire', *in Mélanges Jacques Jean Clère, CRIPEL* 13, 1991, pp. 59-64.

Flinder, A., 'The Island of Jezirat Fara'un. Its ancient harbour, anchorage and marine defense installation', *IJNA* 19, 1990, pp. 135-139.

Foster, L., 'Oriental Institute Ostracon # 12O74: 'Menna's Lament' or 'Letter to a Wayward Son'', *JSSEA* 14, 1984, pp. 88-98.

Foster, W. (ed.) *The Red Sea and Adjacent countries at the Close of the Seventeenth century, as described by Joseph Pitts, William Daniel and Charles Jacques Poncet*, Hakluyt Society, London, 1948.

Fourquin, N., 'Lexicographie et archéologie navale médiévales', *in Medieval Ships and the Birth of Technological Societies, II, The Mediterranean Area and European Integration*, European Coordination Centre for Research and Documentation in the Social Sciences, Foundation for International Studies, University of Malta, Malta, 1991, p. 431.

Franco, L., 'Ancient Mediterranean Harbours: a Heritage to Preserve', *Ocean and Coastal Management* 30, 2-3, 1996, pp. 115-151.

Frankfort, H., 'Egypt and Syria in the First Intermediate Period', *JEA* XII, 1926, pp. 80-99.

Frankfort, H., Buck, A. de, and Gunn, B., *The Cenotaph of Seti I at Abydos, The Egypt Exploration Society thirty-ninth memoir*, vol. 2, Antrim, New York, 1933.

Fraser, P.M., *Ptolemaic Alexandria*, Oxford, 1972.

Frösen, J., 'Le transport du blé et le rôle des ἐπιπλοοι', *in Arctos, Acta Philologica Fennica* 12, 1978, pp. 5-17.

Frösen, J., 'Chi è reponsabile? Il trasporto del grano nell'Egitto greco e romano', *Annali della Facoltà di Lettere e Filosofia, Università degli Studi di Perugia*, 18, n.s. 4, 1, *Studi Classici*, 1980-1981, pp. 161-176.

Frost, H., 'Bronze age stone anchors from the Eastern Mediterranean', *The Mariner's Mirror* 56, 1970, pp. 377-394.

Frost, H., 'Some Cypriot stone-anchors from land sites and from the sea', *Report of the Department of Antiquities*, Nicosia, 1970, pp. 14-23.

Frost, H., 'Mediterranean Harbours and Ports of Call in the Bronze and Iron Ages', *in Les Grandes escales I: Antiquité et Moyen Âge, Recueils de la Société Jean Bodin pour l'histoire comparative des institutions* 32, Brussels, 1974, pp. 35-41.

Frost, H., 'Egypt and Stone Anchors', *The Mariner's Mirror* 65, 1979, pp. 153.

Frost, H., 'Harbours and proto-harbours: early Levantine engineering', *in* V. Karageorghis and D. Michaelidis (eds), *Cyprus and the Sea, Proceedings of the International Symposium, Nicosia, 25-26 Oct. 1993*, Nicosia, 1995, pp. 1-22.

Frost, H., 'Ports, cairns and anchors. A Pharaonic outlet on the Red Sea', *Topoi. Orient-Occident* 6, 1996, pp. 869-902.

Frost, H., 'Byblos Wen-Amon's Harbour', *National Museum News* 8, 1998, p. 29.

Frost, H., 'Recent Marine Archaeological Findings at Byblos', *in* F. Van Voorden, *et al.* (eds), *Byblos-Lebanon, Project identification and implementation, Proceedings of the International Workshop, Delft University of Technology, Netherlands, 27-29 Apr. 1999*, UNESCO-DUT, 1999, pp. 23-26.

Frost, H., and Morhange, C., 'Proposition de localisation des ports antiques de Byblos (Liban)', *in Ports antiques et paléoenvironnements littoraux, Méditerranée. Revue géographique des pays méditerranéens* 1/2, 2000, pp. 101-105.

Frost, H, and Morhange, C., 'Mission de prospection marine à Byblos', *Bulletin d'Archéologie et d'Architecture libanaises*, in preparation.

Gaballa, G.A., *The Memphite Tomb Chapel of Mose*, Warminster, 1977.

Gaballa, G.A., 'False-door Stelae of some Memphite Personnel', *SAK* 7, 1979, pp. 42-44.

Gabolde, M., *D'Akhenaton à Toutânkhamon*, Collection de l'Institut d'Archéologie et d'Histoire de l'Antiquité 3, Université Lumière-Lyon 2, Lyon-Paris, 1998.

Gabolde, M., 'Le site de Coptos. La situation et l'historique du site', 'La cité religieuse. Le temple de Min et Isis', 'La cité économique. Les ateliers de sculpture de Coptos', *in Coptos. L'Égypte antique aux portes du désert, Lyon, musée des Beaux-Arts, 3 février-7 mai 2000*, musée des Beaux-Arts de Lyon, RMN, Paris, 2000, pp. 18-24, pp. 60-91, pp. 188-191.

Gabolde, M., 'Les forêts de Coptos', *in Autour de Coptos,* proceedings of the colloquium organised by the musée des Beaux-Arts de Lyon (17-18 March 2000), *Topoi, Orient-Occident*, suppl. 3, Lyon, 2002, pp. 137-145.

Gachet, J., 'P. Cairo Zénon IV 59649: un mémoire à Zénon. Trois propositions pour l'exploitation commerciale d'un navire', *CRIPEL* 12, 1990, pp. 101-129.

Gamer-Wallert, I., *Ägyptische und ägyptisierende Funde von der iberischen Halbinsel, TAVO* 21, Wiesbaden, 1978.

García Martinez, M.A., *Documentos preromanos de tipo egipcio de la vertiente atlantica hispano-mauritana*, vol. 2, *OrMonsp.* XIII, Montpellier, 2001.

Gardiner, A.H., 'Hymns to Amon from Leiden Papyrus', *ZÄS* 42, 1905, pp. 12-42.

Gardiner, A.H., 'The Stele of Bilgai', *ZÄS* 50, 1912, pp. 49-57.

Gardiner, A.H., 'The Delta Residence of the Ramessides', *JEA* v, 1918, pp. 179-200.

Gardiner, A.H., 'The Ancient Military Road between Egypt and Palestine', *JEA* VI, 1920, pp. 99-116.

Gardiner, A.H., 'The Autobiography of Rekhmire', *ZÄS* 60, 1925, pp. 62-76.

Gardiner, A.H., *Late-Egyptian Stories, Bibliotheca Aegyptiaca* I, Brussels, 1932.

Gardiner, A.H., 'A lawsuit arising from the purchase of two slaves', *JEA* XXI, 1935, pp. 140-146, pls xiii-xvi.

Gardiner, A.H., *Late-Egyptian Miscellanies, Bibliotheca Aegyptiaca* VII, Brussels, 1937.

Gardiner, A.H., 'Adoption Extraordinary', *JEA* XXVI, 1940, pp. 23-29.

Gardiner, A.H., 'Ramesside Texts relating to the Taxation and Transport of Corn', *JEA* xxvii, 1941, pp. 19-73, pls vii-viii.

Gardiner, A.H., *Ancient Egyptian Onomastica*, Oxford University Press, Oxford, 1947.

Gardiner, A.H., *Ramesside Administrative Documents*, Griffith Institute, Ashmolean Museum, Oxford University Press, Oxford, 1948.

Gardiner, A.H., *The Wilbour Papyrus*, II, *Commentary*, Oxford University Press, Oxford, 1948.

Gardiner, A.H., Peet E, and Cerny J, *The Inscriptions of Sinai, Part I, Introduction and Plates*, EES - Geoffrey Cumberlege, London, 1952.

Gardiner, A.H., Peet, T., and Cerny, J., *The Inscriptions of Sinai, Part II, Translations and Commentary, Memoirs of the EES* 45, EES - Geoffrey Cumberlege, London, 1955.

Gardiner, A.H., *The Kadesh Inscriptions of Ramses II*, Oxford, 1960.

Gardiner, A.H., *Egypt of the Pharaohs. An Introduction,* Oxford, 1961.

Gauthier, H., 'La grande inscription dédicatoire d'Abydos', *ZÄS* XLVIII, 1911, pp. 52-66.

Gauthier, H., *La grande inscription dédicatoire d'Abydos, BiÉtud* IV, IFAO, Cairo, 1912.

Gauthier, H., *Le livre des rois d'Égypte, Recueil des titres et protocoles royaux, noms propres de rois, reines, princes, princesses et parents de rois, suivi d'un index alphabétique*, vol. 4, *De la XXV᷎ dynastie à la fin des Ptolémées, MIFAO* xx, IFAO, Cairo, 1916.

Gauthier, H., *Dictionnaire des Noms Géographiques contenus dans les Textes hiéroglyphiques*, Cairo, 1975.

Gelb, I.J., *Hurrians und Subarians*, SAOC 22, Chicago, 1944, pp. 52-70.

Germer, R., *Flora des Pharaonischen Ägyptischen*, SDAIK 14, Mainz am Rhein, 1985.

Gianfrotta, P.A., 'Commerci e pirateria: prime testimonianze archeologiche sottomarine', *MEFRA* 93, 1981, pp. 227-242.

Gianfrotta, P.A., 'Les dangers de la navigation. La piraterie', 'Les marins et les passagers', *in* P. Pomey (ed.), *La navigation dans l'Antiquité*, Centre Camille Jullian, CNRS, Université de Provence, Maison Méditerranéenne des Sciences de l'Homme, published with the support of the Centre national du livre, Édisud, Aix-en-Provence, 1997, pp. 46-57, pp. 102-113.

Gil-Artagnan, A., 'Projet Pount. Essai de reconstitution d'un navire et d'une navigation antiques', *BSFE* 73, June 1975, pp. 28-43.

Gil-Artagnan, A., *Expedition Pount (Autour de l'Afrique sur la route des Phéniciens). Essai de reconstitution d'un navire et d'une navigation antiques (1975-1991)*, Paris, 1994.

Giveon, R., *Les bédouins Shosou des documents égyptiens*, Documenta et Monumenta Orientis Antiqui 22, Leiden, 1971.

Giveon, R., *in LÄ* II, 1977, *s.v.* 'Hapiru', cols 952-955.

Giveon, R., *The Impact of Egypt on Canaan*, OBO 20, Freiburg-Göttingen, 1978.

Giveon, R., *LÄ* III, 1980, *s.v.* 'Libanon', cols 1013-1014.

Giveon, R., *in LÄ* V, 1984, *s.v.* 'Sidon', cols 922-923.

Giveon, R., *in LÄ* VI, 1986, *s.v.* 'Syrien', cols 132-133.

Giveon, R., 'Dating the Cape Gelidonya Shipwreck', *Anatolian Studies* 35, 1985, pp. 99-101.

Giveon, R., *in LÄ* VI, 1986, *s.v.* 'Tyrus', cols 817-820.

Glanville, S.R.K., 'Records of the Royal Dockyard of the time of Thutmosis III: Papyrus British Museum 10056. Part. I', *ZÄS* 66, 1930, pp. 105-121.

Glanville, S.R.K., 'Records of the Royal Dockyard of the time of Thutmosis III: Papyrus British Museum 10056. Part. II', *ZÄS* 68, 1932, pp. 7-41.

Glanville, S.R.K., *Catalogue of Demotic Papyri in the British Museum*, vol. 2, *The Instructions of 'Onchsheshonqy (British Museum Papyrus 10508), Part I: Introduction, transliteration, translation, notes and plates*, The Trustees of the British Museum, London, 1955.

Godart, L., *Le pouvoir de l'écrit*, Paris, 1990.

Goddio, F., 'Cartographie des vestiges archéologiques submergés dans le port Est d'Alexandrie et dans la rade d'Aboukir', *in Alessandria e il mondo ellenistico-romano, Atti del II Congresso Internazionale Italo-Egiziano*, 'L'Erma'di Bretschneider, Rome, 1995, pp. 172-175.

Goedicke, H., *Königliche Dokumente aus dem Alten Reich*, ÄgAbh 14, Harrassowitz, Wiesbaden, 1967.

Goedicke, H., 'The Inverted Water', *GM* 10, 1974, pp. 13-17.

Goedicke, H., *The Report of Wenamun*, Baltimore, London, 1975.

Goedicke, H., 'Yam - More', *GM* 101, 1988, pp. 35-42.

Goedicke, H., 'The northeastern Delta and the Mediterranean', *in* E.C.M. Van den Brink (ed.), *The Archaeology of the Nile Delta, Problems and Priorities*, Amsterdam, 1988, pp. 165-175.

Golenischeff, W., 'Papyrus hiératique de la collection W. Golénischeff contenant la description du Voyage de l'Égyptien Ounou-Amon en Phénicie', *RT* 21, 1899, p. 74.

Golenischeff, W., 'Le papyrus n° 11158 de l'Ermitage Imperial de Saint Petersbourg', *RT* 28, 1906, p. 73.

Görg, M., 'Der Ekstatiker von Byblos', *GM* 23, 1977, pp. 31-33.

Görg, M., 'Das Ratespiel um *Mw-ḳd*', *GM* 32, 1979, pp. 21-22.

Görg, M., *Fremdformen im Wenamun, in* W. Voigt (ed.), *Vorträge: XX. Deutscher Orientalistentag, 1977, ZDMG* suppl. 4, Wiesbaden, 1980, pp. 69-72.

Görg, M., 'Namenstudien VI: drei weitere Belege für bekannte asiatische Ortsnamen aus Ägypten', *BN* 11, 1980, pp. 14-17.

Görg, M., 'Dor, die Teukrer und die Girgasiter', *BN* 28, 1985, pp. 7-14.

Görg, M., 'Sidon in Hieroglyphen. Zum Problem eines Namensidentification', *BN* 28, 1985, p. 15.

Görg, M., 'Sinaï und Zypern als Regionen der Erzgewinnung. Beobachtungen zur Namengebung nach Mineralien in Ägypten und im Alten Orient', *in The Intellectual Heritage of Egypt, Studies presented to Lázlo Kákosy by Friends and Colleagues on the Occasion of his 60th Birthday, Studia Aegyptiaca* XIV, Budapest, 1992, pp. 215-222.

Gouder, T., and Rocco, B., 'Un Talismano bronzeo da Malta contenente un nastro di papiro con inscrizione fenicia', *Studi Magrebini*, 7, Naples, 1975, pp. 1-18.

Goyon, G., 'Le papyrus de Turin dit 'des mines d'or'et le Wadi Hammamat', *ASAE* XLIX, 1949, pp. 337-392.

Goyon, G., *Nouvelles inscriptions rupestres du Wadi Hammamat*, Paris, 1957.

Goyon, G., 'Les navires de transport de la chaussée monumentale d'Ounas', *BIFAO* 69, 1971, pp. 11-41, pls i-vii.

Grandet, P., *Ramsès III, L'histoire d'un règne*, Bibliothèque de l'Égypte ancienne, Pygmalion, Paris, 1993.

Grandet, P., *Le papyrus Harris I*, *BiÉtud* 109, vol. 2, IFAO, Cairo, 1994.

Grandet, P., 'Pi-Ramsès', 'La bataille de Qadesh', 'Ramsès iii face aux Peuples de la mer', *in L'Égypte ancienne, L'Histoire*, Éditions du Seuil, points Histoire, Paris, 1996, pp. 73-86, pp. 87-101, pp. 103-120.

Grandet, P., Mathieu, B., *Cours d'Égyptien hiéroglyphique*, Khéops, Paris, 1997.

Grandet, P., *Contes de l'Égypte ancienne*, Hachette, Paris, 1998.

Grapow, H., *Die bildlichen Ausdrücke des Aegyptischen*, Leipzig, 1924.

Gras, M., Rouillard, P., and Teixidor, J., *L'univers phénicien*, Paris, 1979.

Gras, M., *La Méditerranée archaïque*, Armand Colin, Paris, 1995.

Green, M., 'Wenamun's Demand for Compensation', *ZÄS* 106, 1979, pp. 116-120.

Green, M., '*m-k-m-r*' und '*w-r-k-t-r*' in der Wenamun-Geschichte', *ZÄS* 113, 1986, pp. 115-119.

Greene, K., 'Reflexions on 'Le temps de l'innovation'. A Personal Response to the Colloquium's Principal Themes', *in* D. Meeks and D. Garcia (eds), *Techniques et économie antiques et médiévales: le temps de l'innovation, Colloque international (CNRS) Aix-en-Provence 21-23 Mai 1996*, Errance, Paris, 1997, pp. 227-229.

Grelot, P., *Documents araméens d'Égypte*, LAPO 5, Paris, 1972.

Griffith, F.L., 'The Abydos Decree of Seti I at Nauri', *JEA* XIII, 1927, pp. 193-208, pls xxxviii-xliii.

Griffith, J.G., *in LÄ* III, cols 164-172, *s.v.* 'Interpretatio graeca'.

Grimal, N., *Histoire de l'Égypte ancienne*, Paris, 1988.

Grimal, N., 'L'Égypte et le monde égéen préhellénique: entre commerce et histoire', *in Entre Égypte et Grèce, Actes du Colloque du 6-9 octobre 1994, Cahiers de la villa 'Kérylos'* 5, Paris, 1995, pp. 94-107.

Grimal, N., and Menu, B. (eds), *Le commerce en Égypte ancienne*, *BiÉtud* 121, IFAO, Cairo, 1998.

Grimal, P., and Monod, T., 'Sur la véritable nature du *garum*', *Revue des Études anciennes* LIV, 1952, pp. 27-52.

Groll, S.I., 'The Egyptian Background of the Exodus and the Crossing of the Reed Sea. A New Reading of Papyrus Anastasi VIII', *Jerusalem Studies in Egyptology = ÄuAT* 40, Wiesbaden, 1995, pp. 173-192.

Gubel, E., Lipinski, E., and Servais-Soyez, B., *Redt Tyrus/Sauvons Tyr, Studia Phoenicia* I, OLA 15, Leuven, 1983, pp. 7-21.

Gubel, E., Lipinski, E., and Servais-Soyez, B., *Histoire phénicienne/Fenicische Geschiedenis, Studia Phoenicia* II, OLA 15, Leuven, 1983.

Guibal, F., and Pomey, P., 'L'utilisation du matériau-bois dans la construction navale antique: analyse anatomique et dendrochronologique', *in* É. Rieth (ed.), *Méditerranée antique. Pêche, navigation, commerce*, national congresses of the sociétés historiques et scientifiques: 120th, Aix-en-Provence, 23-29 Oct. 1995; 121st, Nice, 26-31 Oct. 1996, CTHS, Paris, 1998, pp. 159-175.

Guilaine, J., *Premiers bergers et paysans de l'Occident Méditerranéen*, Paris, 1976.

Guilaine, J., *La mer partagée*, Nathan, Paris, 1994.

Guillerm, A., *La marine dans l'Antiquité*, coll. Que Sais-je? n° 2995, PUF, Paris, 1995.

Guillerm, A., *La marine à voiles*, coll. Que Sais-je? n° 3257, PUF, Paris, 1997.

Guilleux de la Roerie, C[dt]., 'Les transformations du gouvernail', *Annales d'Histoire économique et sociale*, 1935, pp. 564-583.

Gunlach, R., *in LÄ* VI, 1985, *s.v.* 'Wadi Hammamat', cols 1099-1113.

Habachi, L., *Tell Basta*, Cairo, 1957.

Hakem, A.M., Ali Elissef, H., Sanlaville, P., Tahir, M., Bazana, A., Dalongville, R., Montmessin, I., Dumas, B., and Verignieux, R., 'Preliminary Report on the Multi-disciplinary Mission of the Joint Sudanese-French Mission to the Red Sea, 1981', *Sudan Notes and Records* 60, 1979, pp. 97-109.

Haldane, C.W., 'Archaeobotanical remains from four shipwrecks off Turkey's southern shore', *in Fifth Conference of the Organization for the Phyto-Taxonomic Investigation of the Mediterranean Area*, Istanbul, 1986.

Haldane, C.W., 'Boat Timbers from el-Lisht: A New method of Ancient Egyptian Hull Construction', *The Mariner's Mirror* 74, 1988, pp. 141-152.

Haldane, C.W., 'Shipwrecked Plant Remains', *Biblical Archaeologist* 53, 1990.

Haldane, C.W., 'Egyptian hulls and the evidence for caulking', *IJNA* 19, 1990, pp. 135–137.

Haldane, C.W., 'A Fourth Dashour Boat', *JEA* 71, 1995, pp. 174–175.

Haldane, C.W., 'Ancient Egyptian Hull Construction', *in Proceedings of the 4ᵗʰ International Symposium on Ship Construction in Antiquity, Athens 1991, Tropis* IV, Athens, 1996, pp. 235-244.

Hall, R., *Egyptian Textiles*, Princes Risborough, 1986.

Hallo, W.W., and Simpson, W.K., *The Ancient Near East. A History*, New York, 1971.

Hallo, W.W., 'Trade and Traders in the Ancient Near East: Some New Perspectives', *in* D. Charpin and F. Joannès (eds), *La circulation des biens, des personnes et des idées dans le Proche-Orient ancien, Actes de la XXXVIIIᵉ Rencontre Assyriologique Internationale* (Paris, 8-10 July 1991), ERC, Paris, 1992, pp. 351–356.

Hani, J., *La religion égyptienne dans la pensée de Plutarque*, PhD. thesis, University of Paris IV, 1971.

Hari, R., *Horemheb et la reine Moutnedjemet ou la fin d'une dynastie*, Geneva, 1964.

Harris, Z.S., *A Grammar of the Phoenician Language, American Oriental Series* 8, New Haven, 1936.

Hassan, Selim Bey, 'Excavations at Saqqara, 1937-1938', *ASAE* XXXVIII, 1938, pp. 503–522, pls xciv–xcvii.

Hauben, H., 'An Annotated List of Ptolemaic Naukleroi with a Discussion of *BGU x 1933*', *ZPE* 8, 1971, pp. 259–275.

Hauben, H., 'Le transport fluvial en Égypte pharaonique. Les bateaux du roi et de la reine', *in Actes du XVᵉ Congrès International de Papyrologie IV, Papyrologica Bruxellensia* 19, Brussels, 1979, pp. 68–77.

Hauben, H., 'A Jewish Shipowner in Third-Century Ptolemaic Egypt', *Ancient Society* 10, 1979, pp. 167-170.

Hauben, H., 'Nauclères classiques et nauclères du Nil', *CdÉ* LVIII, 1983, pp. 237-247.

Hauben, H., 'The Guard Posts of Memphis', *ZPE* 60, 1985, pp. 183-187.

Hauben, H., 'Les nauclères 'phéniciens'de Memphis (63 av. J.-C)', *in* T. Hackens and G., Moucharte (eds), *Numismatique et économique phéniciennes et puniques, Actes du Colloque tenu à Louvain-la-Neuve, 13-16 Mai 1987, Publications d'Histoire de l'Art et d'Archéologie de l'Université Catholique de Louvain* LVIII, *Studia Phoenicia* ix, *Numismatica Lovaniensia* 9, Leuven, 1992, pp. 321-331.

Haudricourt, A.G., *La technologie. Science humaine*, Paris, 1987, pp. 9-32.

Hayes, W.C., 'Career of the Great steward Henenu under Nebhepetre Mentuhotpe', *JEA* 35, 1949, pp. 43-49.

Hayes, W.C., 'The Middle Kingdom in Egypt. Internal History from the Rise of the Heracleopolitans to the Death of Ammenemes III', *in* I.E.S. Edwards, C.J. Gadd and N.G.L. Hammond (eds), *Early History of the Middle East, CAH*, vol. I, part 2, Cambridge, 1971 (3ʳᵈ ed.), pp. 464-531.

Helck, W., 'Die Sinai-Inschrift des Amenmose', *MIO* 2, 1954, pp. 188-193.

Helck, W., Otto E, *Kleines Wörterbuch der Aegptologie*, Otto Harrassowitz, Wiesbaden, 1956.

Helck, W., *Zur Verwaltung des Mittleren und Neuen Reiches, ProÄg* III, Brill, Leiden, 1958.

Helck, W., *Materialien zur Wirtschaftsgeschichte des Neuen Reiches, Teil II, (i.) Die Eigentümer, die Provinztempel und säkulare Institutionen, (ii.) Eigentum und Besitz von Grund und Boden*, Akademie der Wissenschaften und der Literatur in Mainz, Wiesbaden, 1961.

Helck, W., *Die Beziehungen Ägyptens zu Vorderasien im 3. und 2. Jahrtausend v. Chr.*, Wiesbaden, 1962.

Helck, W., 'Eine Briefsammlung aus der Verwaltung des Amuntempels', *JARCE* VI, 1967, pp. 135-152.

Helck, W., 'Compte rendu de E. Edel, *Die Ortsnamenlisten aus dem Totentempel Amenophis III*, Bonn, 1966', *GGA* 221, 1969, pp. 72-86.

Helck, W., *Die Prophezeiung des Nfr.tj*, Kleine Ägyptische Texte, Wiesbaden, 1970.

Helck, W., *Die Beziehungen Ägyptens zu Vorderasien im 3. und 2. Jahrtauzend v. Chr., ÄgAbh* 5, 1971 (2ⁿᵈ ed.).

Helck, W., *Wirtschaftsgeschichte des Alten Ägypten im 3. und 2. Jahrtausend vor Chr., Handbuch der Orientalistik. Erste Abteilung, Der nahe und der mittlere Osten, 1. Ägyptologie* 5, Brill, Leiden and Cologne, 1975.

Helck, W., *Historisch-biographische Texte der 2. Zwischenzeit und neue Texte der 18. Dynastie*, KÄT, Wiesbaden, 1975.

Helck, W., *in LÄ* I, 1972, *s.v.* 'Ägäis' and 'Aegypten', cols 69-76.

Helck, W., *in LÄ* I, 1972, *s.v.* 'Byblos', cols 889-891.

Helck, W., *in LÄ* III, 1975, *s.v.* 'Hurriter', cols 86-87.

Helck, W., *Die Beziehungen Ägyptens und Vorderasiens zur Ägäis bis ins 7. Jahrhundert v. Chr.*, Erträge der Forschung 120, Wissenschaftliche Buchgesellschaft, Darmstadt, 1979.

Helck, W., *in LÄ* III, 1980, *s.v.* 'Imker', col. 151.

Helck, W., *in LÄ* III, 1980, *s.v.* 'Meer', cols 1276-1279.

Helck, W., 'Schwachstellen der Chronologie-Diskussion', *GM* 67, 1983, pp. 43-46.

Helck, W., *in LÄ* IV, 1982, *s.v.* 'Postwesen', cols 1080-1081.

Helck, W., 'Schwachstellen der Chronologie-Diskussion', *GM* 67, 1983, pp. 43-46.

Helck, W., *in LÄ,* VI, 5, 1985, *s.v.* 'Transportwesen', cols 743-744.

Helck, W., *in LÄ* VI, 1986, *s.v.* 'Wenamun', cols 1215-1216.

Helck, W., *in LÄ* VI, 1986, *s.v.* 'Zypern und Ägypten', 'Wadi'n-Natrun', cols 1452-1455, cols 1114-1116.

Helck, W., 'Zur Keftiu-Alasia- und Ahhijawa-Frage', *in* H.G. Buchholz (ed.), *Ägäische Bronzezeit*, Darmstadt, 1987, pp. 218-226.

Hellbing, L., 'Alasia Problems', *Studies in Mediterranean Archaeology* 57, Gothenburg, 1979, pp. 51-79.

Hengstl, J., *Private Arbeitverhältnisse freier Personen in den hellenistischen Papyri bis Diokletian*, Bonn, 1972.

Hepper, F.N., 'Arabian and African Frankincense Trees', *JEA* 55, 1969, pp. 66-72, pls xii-xiii.

Hermary, A., 'Un nouveau chapiteau hathorique trouvé à Amathonte', *BCH* CIX, 1985, pp. 657-701.

Herzog, R., *Punt*, ADAIK, Ägyptologische Reihe 6, Gluckstadt, 1968.

Hoch, J.E., *Semitic Words in Egyptian Texts of the New Kingdom and the Third Intermediate Period*, Princeton, 1994.

Hodjash, H., and Berlev, O., *The Egyptian Reliefs and Stelae in the Pushkin Museum Moscow*, Aurora Art Publishers, Leningrad, 1982.

Hodjash, S.I., and Berlev, O.D., 'A Market-Scene in the Mastaba of *Dꜣdꜣ-m-ꜥnḫ (Tp-m-ꜥnḫ)*', *Altor Forsch* 7, Berlin, 1980, pp. 31-49.

Hoffmann, I., '*pꜣ jm ꜥꜣ n mw kd*', *GM* 4, 1973, pp. 19-22.

Hohlwein, N., *Le blé d'Égypte*, *Étude de Papyrologie* 4, 1938, pp. 33-120.

Holladay, J.S., 'The Wadi Tumilat Project − 1977 and 1978 Seasons', *Qadmoniot* 12, 1979, pp. 85-89.

Holladay, J.S., *Tell el-Maskhouta. Preliminary Report on the Wadi Tumilat Project 1978-1979, ARCE*, Report 6, Malibu, 1982.

Holladay, J.S., 'Maskhuta, Tell el-', *The Anchor Bible Dictionary* IV, 1992, pp. 588-592.

Hornell, J., 'Origins of Plank-built Boats', *Antiquity* 13, 1939, pp. 35-44.

Hornell, J., 'Sea Trade in Early Times', *Antiquity* 15, 1941, p. 241.

Hornell, J., 'Origins of Plank-built Boats', *Antiquity* 17, 1943, pp. 32-36.

Hornell, J., 'Floats and Buoyed Rafts in Military Operations', *Antiquity* 19, 1945, pp. 72-79.

Hornell, J., *Water Transport. Origins and Early Evolution*, Cambridge, 1946 (reprinted, Newton Abbot, 1970).

Hughes, G.H., 'Are there two demotic writings of *šw?*', *in Festschrift zum 70. Geburtstag von Professor Dr Hermann Kees*, *MDAIK* 14, 1956, pp. 80-88.

Hulin, L., 'Marsah Matruh 1987: Preliminary Report', *JARCE* XXVI, 1989, pp. 115-126.

Humbert, G., *in* Ch. Daremberg, E. Saglio and E. Pottier, *Dictionnaire des antiquités grecques et romaines*, Paris, 1877-1918, *s.v.* 'negotiator'.

Hunt, A.S., and Edgar, C.C., *Select Papyri, with an English Translation*, Loeb Classical Library, William Heinemann, Harvard University Press, Cambridge, London, 1956 (2nd ed.).

Ilan, Z., and Yosef, A., 'Ancient Settlements on the Bardawil Reef', *Qadmoniot* 10, 1977, pp. 77-79.

James, T.G.H., *Corpus of Hieroglyphic Inscriptions in the Brooklyn Museum*, I, *From the Dynasty I to the End of Dynasty XVIII*, Wilbour Monographs VI, The Brooklyn Museum, New York, 1974.

Janssen, J.J., *Two Ancient Egyptian Ship's Logs*, Leiden, 1961.

Janssen, J.J., *Commodity Prices from the Ramessid Period, An Economic Study of the Village of Necropolis Workmen at Thebes*, Brill, Leiden, 1975.

Janssen, J.J., 'Prolegomena to the Study of Egypt's Economic History during the New Kingdom', *SAK* 3, 1975, pp. 127-185.

Janssen, J.J., 'Two Personalities', *in Gleanings from Deir el-Medina*, Leiden, 1982, pp. 116-123.

Janssen, J.J., 'Two Variant Accounts?', *VA* 1, 1985, pp. 109-112.

Janssen, J.J., 'The Cost of Nile-Transport', *BSEG* 18, 1994, pp. 41-47.

Jaritz, H., Favre, S., Nogara, G., and Rodziewicz M., *Pelusium. Prospections archéologiques et topographiques de la région de Tell el-Kana'is 1993 et 1994, BÀBA* 13, Stuttgart, 1996, pp. 24, pp. 30-31, pp. 209-210.

Jean, C.F., and Hoftijzer, J., *Dictionnaire des inscriptions sémitiques de l'Ouest*, Leiden, 1965.

Jidejian, N., *Byblos through the Ages*, Beirut, 1968.

Jidejian, N., *Sidon through the Ages*, Beirut, 1977.

Jidejian, N., *Byblos à travers des âges*, Beirut, 1977.

Jollois, P., 'Notice sur la ville de Rosette, comprenant la description de la traversée par mer d'Alexandrie dans cette ville et du voyage par le Nil de Rosette au Caire', *in Description de l'Égypte, Texte, État moderne*, 2, Paris, 1822, pp. 333-360.

Jones, D., *A Glossary of Ancient Egyptian Nautical Titles and Terms*, London and New York, 1988.

Jones, H., *A Greek-English Lexikon*, Oxford, 1961.

Jones, R., *et al.*, 'A Second Nabataean Inscription from Tell el-Shuqafiyah, Egypt', *BASOR* 269, 1988, pp. 47-57.

Jones, R.E., and Vagnetti, L., 'Traders and Craftsmen in the Central Mediterranean: archaeological evidence and archaeometric research', *in Bronze Age in the Mediterranean*, Jonsered, 1991, pp. 127-147.

Junker, H., *Gîza Grabungen auf dem Friedhof des Alten Reiches bei den Pyramiden von Gîza*, Oesterreichische Akademie der Wisseschaften, Philosophische-Historische Klasse, Hölder-Pichler, Tempsky, Vienna and Leipzig, 1938.

Kallai, Z., *Historical Geography of the Bible. The Tribal Territories of Israel*, Jerusalem, 1986.

Kammerer, A., *Pétra et la Nabatène, L'Arabie Pétrée et les Arabes du Nord dans leurs rapports avec la Syrie et la Palestine jusqu'à l'Islam, Texte*, Paris, 1929.

Kaplony, P., *Die Inschriften der ägyptischen Frühzeit*, vol. 3, Harrassowitz, Wiesbaden, 1963-1964.

Karageorghis, V., *Kition, Mycenaean and Phoenician discoveries in Cyprus*, London, 1976.

Karageorghis, V., 'Chronique des fouilles et découvertes à Chypre en 1975', *BCH* 100, 1976, pp. 839-906.

Karageorghis, V., 'Chypre entre l'Égypte et l'Égée', *in Entre Égypte et*

Grèce, *Actes du Colloque du 6-9 octobre 1994, Cahiers de la villa 'Kérylos'* 5, Paris, 1995, pp. 108-118.

Kasher, A., *The Jews in Hellenistic and Roman Egypt, The Struggle for Equal Rights*, Tübingen, 1985, pp. 184-185.

Katzenstein, H.J., *The History of Tyre. From the Beginning of the Second Millennium BCE until the Fall of the Neo-Babylonian Empire in 538 BCE*, Jerusalem, 1973.

Katzenstein, H.J., 'The Phoenician term *hubûr* in the Report of Wen-Amon', *in Atti del I Congresso Internazionale di Studi Fenici e Punici*, Rome, 1983, pp. 598-602.

Katzenstein, H.J., 'Gaza in the Persian Period', *Transeuphratène* 1, 1989, pp. 67-86.

Kees, H., *Kulturgeschichte des Alten Orients, Erster Abschnitt, Ägypten*, Handbuch der Altertumswissenschaft, C.H. Beck'sche Verlagsbuchhandlung, Munich, 1933.

Kees, H., 'Ein Handelsplatz des MR im Nordostdelta', *MDAIK* 18, 1962, pp. 1-13.

Keimer, L., *Die Gartenpflanzen im Alten Ägypten*, Hamburg, 1924.

Kemp, B.J., and O'Connor, D., 'An Ancient Nile Harbour; University Museum Excavations at 'Birket Habu'', *IJNA* 3, 1974, pp. 101-136.

Kemp, B.J., 'J.J. Janssen, *Commodity Prices from the Ramesside Period. An Economic Study of the Village of Necropolis Workmen at Thebes*, pp. xxvi + 601, 90 tables, Leiden, E.J. Brill, 1975', *JEA* 65, 1979, pp. 182-187.

Kemp, B.J., *Ancient Egypt: Anatomy of a Civilization*, London and New York, 1989.

Kestermont, G., *Diplomatique et droit international en Asie occidentale (1600-1200 av. J.C.)*, Louvain-la-Neuve, 1974.

Kestermont, G., 'Le panthéon des instruments hittites de droit public', *Orientalia* 45, 1976, pp. 153-169.

Kestermont, G., 'Remarques sur les aspects juridiques du commerce dans le Proche-Orient du XIVe siècle avant notre ère', *in* J.D. Hawkins (ed.), *Trade in the Ancient Near East, Papers presented to the 23rd Rencontre Assyriologique Internationale, Birmingham University, 5-9 July 1976*, British School of Archaeology in Iraq, London, 1977, pp. 191-201.

Kestermont, G., 'Accords internationaux relatifs aux ligues hittites (1600-1200 av. J.-C.)', *OLP* 12, 1981, pp. 54-55.

Kienitz, F.K., *Die politische Geschichte Aegyptens vom 7. bis zum 4. Jahrhundert vor der Zeitwende*, Akademie-Verlag, Berlin, 1953.

Kitchen, K.A., 'Theban Topographical Lists, Old and New', *Orientalia* 34, 1965, pp. 1-9.

Kitchen, K.A., 'Byblos, Egypt and Mari in the Early Second Millennium BC', *Orientalia* n. 36, 1967, pp. 39-54.

Kitchen, K.A., *Ramesside Inscriptions, Historical and Biographical*, Oxford, 1968-1988.

Kitchen, K.A., 'Punt and How to Get There', *Orientalia* 20, 1971, pp. 184-207.

Kitchen, K.A., *The Third Intermediate Period (1100-650 BC)*, Warminster, 1972.

Kitchen, K.A., in *LÄ* I, Wiesbaden, 1975, *s.v.* 'Barke', cols 619-625.

Kitchen, K.A., *Ancient Egypt: A Cultural Topography*, Chicago, 1977.

Kitchen, K.A., '*The Sea Peoples and Egypt* by A. Nibbi, pp. xiv + 161, 20 figures, frontispieces, xvi pls, Noyes Press, New Jersey, 1975', *JEA* 64, 1978, pp. 169-171.

Kitchen, K.A., in *LÄ* V, 1984, *s.v.* 'Ramses V-XI', cols 124-128.

Kitchen, K.A., in *LÄ* VI, 1986, *s.v.* 'Tanitendynastie', cols 209-210.

Kitchen, K.A., 'The Land of Punt', in T. Shaw, P. Sinclair, B. Andah and A. Okpoko (eds), *The Archaeology of Africa. Food, Metals and Towns*, London, 1993, pp. 587-608.

Kitchen, K.A., 'Punt, l'Égypte en quête des résines', in *Yémen, au pays de la reine de Saba', Exposition présentée à l'Institut du monde arabe du 25 octobre 1997 au 28 février 1998*, Flammarion, Paris, 1997, p. 49.

Kitchen, K.A., 'Ramesside Egypt's delta defense routes – the SE sector', *Studi di egittologia e di antichità puniche* 18, 1998, pp. 34–35.

Kitchen, K.A., 'Further thoughts on Pount and its neighbours', in A. Leahy and J. Tait (eds), *Studies on Ancient Egypt in honour of H.S. Smith*, London, 1999, pp. 173-178.

Klebs, L., *Die Reliefs und Malereien des Neuen Reiches (XVIII.-XX. Dynastie ca 1580-1100 v. Chr.), Material zur ägyptischen Kulturgeschichte, Abhandlungen der Heidelberger Akademie der Wissenschaften*, Carl Winters Universitätsbuchhandlung, Heidelberg, 1934.

Kœnig, Y., 'Livraisons d'or et de galène au trésor du temple d'Amon sous la XXᵉ dynastie', in *Hommages à Serge Sauneron*, I, *Égypte pharaonique*, BiÉtud 81, 1979, pp. 185-220, pls xxx-xxxviia.

Köster, A., 'Zur Seefahrt der alten Ägypten', *ZÄS* 58, 1923, pp. 125-132.

Kruchten, J.-M., 'L'évolution de la gestion domaniale sous le Nouvel Empire égyptien', in E. Lipinski (ed.), *State and Temple Economy in the Ancient Near East, Proceedings of the international Conference organised by the Katholieke Universiteit Leuven from the 10th to the 14th of April 1978*, Part 2, OLA 6, Leuven, 1979, pp. 517-525.

Kuentz, C., *La bataille de Qadech. Les textes ('Poème de Pentaour'et 'Bulletin de Qadech') et les bas-reliefs*, MIFAO LV, IFAO, Cairo, 1928.

Kueny, G., and Yoyotte, J., *Grenoble, musée des Beaux-Arts, Collection égyptienne*, Paris, 1979.

Kuhlmann, K., *Das Ammoneion: Archäologie, Geschichte und Kultpraxis des Orakels von Siwa mit einem Beitrag von W. Brashear, Im Memoriam Ahmed Fakhry et Georg Steindorff, Archäologische Veröffentlichungen* 75, Mainz, 1988.

Kunkel, W., 'Verwaltungsakten aus spätptolamaïscher Zeit', *Archiv für Papyrusforschung*, 8, 1927, pp. 169-215.

Labrousse, H., *Récits de la Mer Rouge et de l'Océan Indien, Études d'Histoire Maritime* 10, Paris, 1992.

Lacau, P., *Stèles du Nouvel Empire, CGC n° 34001-34064*, Cairo, 1909.

Lacau, P., *Stèles du Nouvel Empire, CGC n° 34065-34186*, Cairo, 1926.

Lackenbacher, S., 'Les relations entre Ugarit et l'Égypte, à propos d'un texte inédit', in *Les relations internationales, Actes du Colloque de Strasbourg 15-17 juin 1993*, Paris, 1995, pp. 107-118.

Lafont, B., 'Un homme d'affaire à Karkémish', in D. Charpin and F. Joannès (eds), *Marchands, Diplomates et Empereurs, Études sur la civilisation mésopotamienne offertes à Paul Garelli*, ERC, Paris, 1991, pp. 275-282.

Lagarce, E., and Lagarce, J., 'Regional Projects: Coastal Syria and Lebanon', in M. Bietak (ed.), *The Synchronisation of Civilisations in the Eastern Mediterranean in the Second Millennium BC*, proceedings of an International Symposium at Schloß Haindorf, 15th-17th of November 1996 and at the Austrian Academy, Vienna, 11th-12th of May 1998, Österreichische Akademie der Wissenschaften, *Denkschriften der Gesamtakademie*, vol. XIX, Vienna, 2000, pp. 140-146.

Landström, B., *The Ship*, New York, 1961.

Landström, B., *Ships of the Pharaos. 4000 years of Egyptian Shipbuilding*, Allen & Unwin, London, 1970.

Lapidus, M., *La quête de l'île merveilleuse (le conte du Naufragé), Texte égyptien traduit et commenté*, La Maison de vie, Château-Gontier, 1995.

Leclant, J., 'Les relations entre l'Égypte et la Phénicie du voyage d'Ounamon à l'expédition d'Alexandre', *in* W. Ward (ed.), *The Role of the Phoenicians in the Interaction of Mediterranean Civilizations*, American University Centennial Publications, 1968, pp. 9-31, pls viii-xii.

Leclant, J., 'Lexikon der Ägyptologie', *in LÄ* I, 1972, *s.v.* 'Biene', cols 786-789

Leclant, J., 'L'exploration des côtes de la Mer Rouge à la quête de Pount et des secrets de la Mer Érythrée', *Annales d'Éthiopie* 11, 1978, pp. 69-74.

Leclant, J., 'Le nom de Chypre dans des textes hiéroglyphiques', *in Salamine de Chypre. Histoire et archéologie, Colloque CNRS, n° 578*, Paris, 1980, pp. 131-135.

Leclant, J., 'Le rayonnement de l'Égypte au temps des rois tanites et libyens', *in Tanis, l'or des Pharaons*, Paris, 1987, pp. 77-84.

Leclant, J., 'Les Phéniciens et l'Égypte', *in Atti del II Congresso Internazionale di Studi Fenici e Punici*, vol. 1, Consiglio Nazionale delle Ricerche Istituto per la civilta Fenicia e Punica, Consiglio Nazionale delle Ricerche, Rome, 1991, pp. 9-17.

Leclant, J., *in* E. Lipínski (ed.), *Dictionnaire de la civilisation phénicienne et punique*, Brepols, 1992, pp. 146-147.

Leclant, L., 'Carthage et l'Égypte', *in Actes du III<sup>e</sup> congrès international des études phéniciennes et puniques, Tunis, 11-16 novembre 1991*, vol. 1, Institut national du patrimoine, Tunis, 1995, pp. 41-50.

Leclant, J., 'L'Égypte et l'Égée au second millénaire', *in Atti et memorie del secundo congresso internazionale di micenologia, Roma-Napoli*, 14-20 Oct. 1991, GET, Rome, 1996, pp. 613-625.

Lefebvre, G., *Inscriptions concernant les grands prêtres d'Amon Romê-Roy et Amenhotep*, Paris, 1929.

Lefebvre, G., 'Sur trois dates dans les Mésaventures d'Ounamon', *CdÉ* XXI, Jan. 1936, p. 97.

Lefebvre, G., *Romans et contes égyptiens d'époque pharaonique*, Paris, 1949.

Lefebvre, G., 'Les richesses inconnues de la littérature égyptienne', *RdÉ* VI, 1951, p. 41.

Lefevre, A., 'Leurs navires, de véritables marqueteries', *in Hommes, sciences et techniques au temps des pharaons, Science & Vie*, suppl., n° 197, Dec. 1997, pp. 118-126.

Lehmann, G.A., 'Die Sikalaju – ein neues Zeugnis zu den 'Seevölker'– Herrfahrten im späten 13. Jh. v. Chr. (RS 34. 129)', *UgForsch* 11, 1979, pp. 481-494.

Lehmann, G.A., 'Zum Auftreten von "Seevölker"-Gruppen im östlichen Mittelmeerraum – eine Zwischenbilanz', *in* S. Deger-Jalkotzy (ed.), *Griechenland, die Ägäis und die Levante während der 'Dark Ages' vom 12. bis zum 9. Jh. v. Chr.*, Veröffentlichungen der Kommission für Mykenische Forschung 10, Österreichische Akademie der Wissenschaften, Vienna, 1983, pp. 79-92.

Leibovitch, J., 'Un nouveau dieu égypto-canaanéen', *ASAE* XLVIII, 1948, pp. 435-444.

Lemaire, A., 'Les Phéniciens et le commerce entre la mer Rouge et la mer Méditerranée', *in* E. Lipinski, *Phoenicia and the East Mediterranean in the First Millenium BC*, Proceedings of the Conference held in Leuven from the 14<sup>th</sup> to the 16<sup>th</sup> of November 1985, *Studia Phoenicia* V, *OLA* 22, Leuven, 1987, pp. 49-60.

Lenger, M.-Th., *Corpus des ordonnances des Ptolémées*, Brussels, 1980.

Lesko, L.H. (ed.), *A Dictionary of Late Egyptian* I, Berkeley-Providence, 1982.

Lexa, F., *Papyrus Insinger: Les enseignements moraux d'un scribe égyptien du premier siècle après J.-C. Texte démotique avec transcription, traduction française, etc.*, vol. 2, Paris, 1926.

Lichtheim, M., *Ancient Egyptian Literature*, I, *The Old and Middle Kingdoms*, University of California Press, Berkeley, Los Angeles and London, 1973.

Lichtheim, M., *Ancient Egyptian Literature*, II, *The New Kingdom*, University of California Press, Berkeley, Los Angeles and London, 1976.

Lichtheim, M., 'The Naucratis Stela once again', *in Studies in Honor of G.H. Hughes, January 12 1977, SAOC* 39, The Oriental Institute of the University of Chicago, Chicago, 1977, pp. 139-146.

Lichtheim, M., *Ancient Egyptian Literature*, III, *The Late Period*, University of California Press, Berkeley, Los Angeles and London, 1980.

Lichtheim, M., *Late Egyptian Wisdom Literature in the International Context, OBO* 52, Freiburg, 1983.

Liesker, W.H.M., and Tromp, A.M., 'Zwei Ptolemäische Papyri aus der Wiener Papyrussammlung', *ZPE* 66, 1986, pp. 85-89.

Linder, E., 'Ma'agan Mikha'el', *in* E. Stern (ed.), *The New Encyclopaedia of Archaeological Excavations in the Holy Land*, vol. 3, Jerusalem, 1993, pp. 918-919.

Lipinski, E., 'Recherches ugaritiques, 2, Amarrage à Tyr'', *Syria* 44, 1967, pp. 282-284.

Lipinski, E., 'Deux marchands de blé phéniciens à Ninive', *Revista di Studi Fenici* 3, 1975, pp. 1-6.

Lipinski, E., 'An Ugaritic Letter to Amenophis III concerning Trade with Alasiya', *in* J.D. Hawkins (ed.), *Trade in the Ancient Near East, Papers presented to the 23rd Rencontre Assyriologique Internationale, Birmingham University, 5-9 July 1976,* British School of Archaeology in Iraq, London, 1977, pp. 213-217.

Lipinski, E. (ed.), *State and Temple Economy in the Ancient Near East, Proceedings of the International Conference organised by the Katholieke Universiteit Leuven from the 10th to the 14th of April 1978*, parts I-II, *OLA* 5-6, Leuven, 1979.

Lipinski, E., 'Egyptian Aramaic Coins from the Fifth and Fourth Centuries BC', *in* S. Scheers (ed.), *Studia Paulo Naster oblata*, I, *Numismatica antiqua*, Leuven, 1982, pp. 23-28.

Lipinski, E., 'Products and Brokers of Tyre According to Ezechiel 27', *Studia Phoenicia* III, Leuven, 1983, pp. 213-220.

Lipinski, E., 'Vestiges phéniciens d'Andalousie', *OLP* 15, 1984, pp. 81-132.

Lipinski, E., and Gubel, E., 'Phoenicia and its Neighbours', Proceedings of the Colloqium held on the 9th and 10th of December 1983 at the Vrije Universiteit Brussel, in cooperation with the Centrum voor Mycense en Archaïsch-Griekse Cultuur, *Studia Phoenicia* III, Peeters, Leuven, 1985.

Lipinski, E. (ed.), 'Phoenicia and the Bible', Proceedings of the Conference held at the University of Leuven on the 15th and 16th of March 1990, *Studia Phoenicia* XI, *OLA* 44, Leuven, 1991.

Lipinski, E. (ed.), *Dictionnaire de la civilisation phénicienne et punique*, Brepols, 1992.

Lipinski, E., 'Aramaic Documents from Ancient Egypt', *OLP* 29, 1994, pp. 61-68.

Lipke, P., 'Retrospective on the Royal Ship of Cheops', *in* S. McGrail, E. Kentley (ed.), *Sewn plank boats, Archaeological and ethnographic papers based on those présented to a conference at Greenwich in November 1984*, *BAR IS* 276, Archaeopress, Oxford, 1985, pp. 19-34.

Liverani, M., *Prestige and Interest. International Relations in the Near East ca. 1600-1100 BC, History of the Ancient Near East Studies* I, Padua, 1990.

Lloyd, A.B., 'Triremes and the Saite Navy', *JEA* 58, 1972, pp. 268-279.

Lloyd, A.B., 'Were Necho's Triremes Phoenician?', *JHS* 95, 1975, p. 55.

Lloyd, A.B., *Herodotus. Book II, Introduction*, *EPRO* 43, Brill, Leiden, 1975.

Lloyd, A.B., 'Necho and the Red Sea: Some Considerations', *JEA* 63, 1977, pp. 142-155.

Lloyd, A.B., 'Two Figured Ostraca from North Saqqara', *JEA* 64, 1978, pp. 108-109.

Lloyd, A.B., 'The Trireme Controversy', *JHS* 100, 1980, pp. 195-198.

Lopez, J., *Las inscripciones rupestres faraonicas entre Korosko y Kasr Ibrim (Orilla oriental del Nilo)*, *Memorias de la Mision Arqueologica* IX, Comite Español de la UNESCO para Nubia, Madrid, 1966.

Lopez, J., 'Inscriptions de l'Ancien Empire à Khor El-Aquiba', *RdÉ* 19, 1967, pp. 51-66.

Loprieno, A., *La pensée et l'écriture. Pour une analyse sémiotique de la culture égyptienne*, Cybèle, Paris, 2001.

Lorton, D., *The Juridical Terminology of International Relations in Egyptian Texts, Through Dynasty XVIII*, The Johns Hopkins Near Eastern Studies, Baltimore and London, 1974.

Lorton, D., 'Compte rendu 'Where was Ancient Egypt's *Kpn(j)*?'', *DE* 6, 1986, pp. 89-99.

Lucas, A., *Ancient Egyptian Materials and Industries*, London, [1926] 1948 (3rd ed.).

Lucas, A., 'Cosmetics, Perfumes and Incense in Ancient Egypt', *JEA* XVI, 1930, pp. 41-53.

Lucas, A., and Harris, J.R., *Ancient Egyptian Materials and Industries*, London, 1962 (4th ed.).

Lüddeckens, E., *Ägyptische Eheverträge*, Harrassowitz, Wiesbaden, 1960.

Mackay, E., 'Note on a New Tomb (n° 260) at Drah Abu'l Naga, Thebes', *JEA* III, 1916, pp. 125-126, pl. xiv.

Malaise, M., 'Sésostris, pharaon de légende et d'histoire', *CdÉ* XLI, n° 81, Jan. 1966, pp. 244-272.

Malaise, M., 'Pèlerinages et pèlerins dans l'Égypte ancienne', *in* J. Chélini and H. Branthomme (eds), *Histoire des pèlerinages non chrétiens. Entre magique et sacré : le chemin des dieux*, Paris, 1987, pp. 55-82.

Malinine, M., Posener, G., and Vercoutter, J., *Catalogue des stèles du Sérapéum de Memphis, I, Texte*, Éditions des musées nationaux, Paris, 1968.

Mallet, D., *Les premiers établissements des Grecs en Égypte (VII<sup>e</sup>-VI<sup>e</sup> siècles)*, MMAF XII, 1, Ernest Leroux, Paris, 1893.

Mallet, D., *Les rapports des Grecs avec l'Égypte (de la conquête de Cambyse, 525, à celle d'Alexandre, 331)*, MIFAO XLVIII, IFAO, Cairo, 1922.

Maltzer, E., 'The Setting of the Shipwrecked Sailor', *GM* 22, 1976, pp. 47-49.

Marcolongo, B., 'Évolution du paléo-environnement dans la partie orientale du Delta du Nil depuis la transgression flandrienne (8000 BP) par rapport aux modèles de peuplement ancien', *in CRIPEL* 14, 1992, pp. 23-31.

Mariette, A., *Deir el-Bahari, Documents topographiques, historiques et ethnographiques*, Hinrichs, Leipzig, 1877.

Mariette, A., *Catalogue général des monuments d'Abydos découverts pendant les fouilles de cette ville*, Paris, 1880.

Mariette, A., *Monuments divers recueillis en Égypte et en Nubie*, Paris, 1889.

Marinatos, S., and Hirmer, M., *Kreta, Thera und das mykenische Hellas*, Munich, 1973.

Martin, G.T., *The Tomb of Hetepka and other Reliefs and Inscriptions from the Sacred Animal Necropolis, North Saqqara, 1964-1973, Texts from Excavations*, Memoir 4, EES, London, 1979.

Martin-Pardey, E., *in LÄ* V, 1984, *s.v.* 'Schiff', cols 601-610.

Marx, E., 'The First Recorded Sea Battle', *The Mariner's Mirror* 32, 1946, pp. 242-251.

Marx, E., 'The Origin of the Ram', *The Mariner's Mirror* 34, 1948, pp. 118-119.

Maspero, G., 'De quelques navigations des Égyptiens sur les côtes de la mer Erythrée', *Revue historique* 9, Paris, 1874.

Masson, O., *Inscriptions Chypriotes syllabiques, Recueil critique et commenté*, Paris, 1961.

Masson, O., 'À propos de l'île d'Alasia', *Kadmos* 12, 1973, pp. 98-99.

Masson, O., *Carian Inscriptions from North Saqqâra and Buhen*, London, 1978.

Mathieu, B., *La poésie amoureuse de l'Égypte ancienne*, BiÉtud 115, IFAO, Cairo, 1996.

Mathieu, B., 'La 'Satire des métiers', Dossier bibliographique', *Grafma newletter* 2, Dec. 1998, pp. 37-40.

Matthiae Scandone, G., 'Scarabei egiziani del Museo Nazionale di Palermo', *Oriens Antiquus* 10, 1971, pp. 21-46, fig. 5 and pl. 5.

Matthiae Scandone, G., *Scarabei e Scaraboidi Egiziani ed Egittizznti del Museo Nazionale di Cagliari*, Collezione di Studi Fenici 7, Rome, 1975.

Mayerson, P., 'Aelius Gallus at Cleopatris (Suez) and on the Red Sea', *Greek, Roman and Byzantine Studies* 36, 1995, pp. 17-24.

Mayerson, Ph., 'The Port of Clysma (Suez) in transition from Roman to Arab rule', *JNES* 55, 1996, pp. 119-120.

McGrail, S., *Rafts, Boats and Ships*, HMSO, London, 1981.

McGrail, S., 'Boatbuilding techniques, technological change and attribute analysis', *in* S. McGrail, *Woodworking Techniques before 1500*, BAR 127, Oxford, 1982, pp. 25-72.

McGrail, S. (ed.), *Aspects of Maritime Archaeology and Ethnography*, Greenwich, 1984.

McGrail, S., 'Maritime Archaeology – present and future', *in* S. McGrail (ed.), *Aspects of Maritime Archaeology and Ethnography*, Greenwich, 1984, pp. 11-40.

McGrail, S., 'Towards a classification of water transport', *World Archaeology* 16, 1985, pp. 289-303.

McGrail, S, and Kentley, E. (ed.), *Sewn Plank Boats*, BAR 276, Oxford, 1985.

McGrail, S., 'Experimental boat archaeology, Some methodological considerations', *in* O. Crumlin-Pendersen and M.Viner (eds), *Sailing into the past*, Viking Ship Museum, Roskilde, 1986, pp. 8-17.

McGrail, S., 'Shipment of traded goods and of ballast in Antiquity', *OJA* 8, 1989, pp. 353-358.

McGrail, S., 'Bronze Age Seafaring in the Mediterranean: a view from N W Europe', *in* N.H. Gale (ed.), *Bronze Age Trade in the Mediterranean, Papers presented at the Conference held at Rewley House, Oxford, in December 1989*, SIMA XC, Paul Åstroms Förlag, Jonsered, 1991, pp. 83-91.

Meeks, D., 'Génies, anges et démons en Égypte', *in Génies, anges et démons*, Sources Orientales 8, Paris, 1971.

Meeks, D., *Le grand texte des donations au temple d'Edfou*, BiÉtud LIX, IFAO, Cairo, 1972.

Meeks, D., '*jwn-n-pt* = ΑΥΑΝUΠЄ = Le lin', *RdÉ* 24, 1974, 116-119.

Meeks, D., 'Une fondation memphite de Taharqa (Stèle du Caire JE 36861)', *in Hommages à S. Sauneron* I, *Égypte pharaonique*, BiÉtud 81, IFAO, Cairo, 1979, pp. 221-239, pl. xxxviii.

Meeks, D., 'Les donations aux temples dans l'Égypte du I$^{er}$ Millénaire avant J.-C.', in E. Lipiński (ed.), *State and Temple Economy in the Ancient Near East* II, OLA 6, Leuven, 1979, pp. 605-687.

Meeks, D., and Favard-Meeks, Chr., *La vie quotidienne des dieux égyptiens*, Paris, 1993.

Meeks, D., and Garcia, D. (eds), *Techniques et économie antiques et médiévales : le temps de l'innovation,* International Colloquium (CNRS) Aix-en-Provence 21-23 May 1996, Centre Camille Jullian et Recherches d'Antiquités Africaines (CNRS, Université de Provence), Temps, Espaces, Langages Europe Méridionale Méditerranée (CNRS, Université de Provence), Direction régionale des Affaires culturelles Provence Côte d'Azur, Centre Archéologique du Var, Errance, Paris, 1997.

Meeks, D., 'Coptos et les chemins de Pount', in *Autour de Coptos,* proceedings of the colloquium organised by the musée des Beaux-Arts de Lyon (17-18 March 2000), *Topoi, Orient-Occident*, suppl. 3, Lyon, 2002, pp. 267-335.

Megally, M., 'À propos du Papyrus CGC 58070 (Papyrus Boulaq XI)', *BIFAO* 74, 1974, pp. 161-169, pls xxi-xxii.

Megally, M., 'Le Papyrus CGC 58081, suite du Papyrus CGC 58070 (Papyrus Boulaq XI)', *BIFAO* 75, 1975, pp. 165-181, pls xxviii.

Megally, M., *Recherches sur l'économie, l'administration et la comptabilité égyptiennes à la XVIII$^e$ dynastie, d'après le papyrus E. 3226 du Louvre,* BiÉtud LXXI, IFAO, Cairo, 1977.

Meigs, P., *Geography of Coastal Deserts*, UNESCO, Paris, 1966.

Menu, B., 'Compte-rendu du livre de M. Valloggia, *Recherche sur les 'Messagers' (Wpwtyw) in les sources égyptiennes profanes'*, doctoral thesis n° 212, presented at the Faculty of Arts, University of Geneva, Éditions Droz, Geneva, 1976, *Revue de l'historique du droit français et étranger* 55, 1977, p. 413.

Menu, B., 'Ventes de maisons sous l'Ancien Empire Égyptien', in *Mélanges offerts à Jean Vercoutter*, published with the support of CNRS, Éditions Recherche sur les Civilisations, Paris, 1985, pp. 249-262.

Menu, B., 'Le commerce extérieur. Introduction', 'Le commerce intérieur. Introduction', 'Les échanges portant sur le travail d'autrui', in N. Grimal and B. Menu (eds), *Le commerce en Égypte ancienne*, BiÉtud 121, IFAO, Cairo, 1998, pp. 3-4, pp. 129-131, pp. 193-206.

Meredith, D., 'The Roman Eastern Remains in the Eastern Desert of Egypt', *JEA* 38, 1952, pp. 94-111.

Meredith, D., 'The Roman Eastern Remains in the Eastern Desert of Egypt (continued)', *JEA* 39, 1953, pp. 95-106, pl. vi.

Merrillees, R.S., 'Aegean Bronze Age Relations with Egypt', *AJA* 76, 1972, pp. 281-294.

Merrillees, R.S., 'Alasia', in V. Karageorghis and A. Christodoulos (eds), *Praktika tou Protou Diethnous Kiprologikou Synedriou, Nicosia, 1969*, Nicosia, 1972, pp. 111-119.

Merrillees, R.S., 'Alashia Revisited', *Cahiers de la Revue Biblique* 22, Paris, 1987.

Merzagora, M., 'La navigazione in Egitto nell'età greco-romano', *Aegyptus* 10, 1929, p. 111.

Meshel, Z., and Finkelstein, I. (eds), *Sinai in Antiquity: Researches in the History and Archaeology of the Peninsula*, Tel Aviv, 1980, pp. 181-198.

Meyer, P.M., *Juristische Papyri, Erklärung von Urkunden zur Einführung in die juristische Papyruskunde*, Berlin, 1920.

Meyer-Termeer, A.J.M., *Die Haftung der Schiffer im griechischen und römischen Recht*, Zutphen, 1978, pp. 3-52.

Midant-Reynes, B., *Préhistoire de l'Égypte. Des premiers hommes aux premiers pharaons*, Armand Colin, Paris, 1992.

Miege, J.-L. (ed.), *Navigation et migrations en Méditerranée. De la Préhistoire à nos jours*, Collioure 1983 - Sète 1985, Institut de Recherches Méditerranéennes, Commissions française d'Histoire maritime, CNRS, Paris, 1990.

Miroschedji, P. de, 'Les Égyptiens au Sinaï du nord et en Palestine au Bronze ancien', in D. Valbelle and C. Bonnet (eds), *Le Sinaï durant l'Antiquité et le Moyen Âge. 4000 ans d'histoire pour un désert,* 'Sinaï' UNESCO colloquium, 19–21 Sept. 1997, Errance, Paris, 1998, pp. 20-32.

Miroschedji, P. de, 'La Palestine, Gaza et l'Égypte au Bronze ancien', in J.-B. Humbert (ed.), *Gaza méditerranéenne, Histoire et archéologie en Palestine*, Errance, Paris, 2000, pp. 27-30.

Moers, G., 'Travel as narrative in Egyptian Literature', in G. Moers (ed.), *Definitely: Egyptian Literature, Lingua Aegyptia. Studia monographica* 2, Seminar für Ägyptologie und Koptologie, Göttingen, 1999, pp. 43-61.

Mogensen, M., *Le mastaba égyptien de la Glyptothèque Ny Carlsberg*, Copenhagen, 1921.

Mohr, P.A., *The geology of Ethiopia*, Addis Ababa, 1971.

Möller, A., 'Naukratis or how to identify a Port of Trade', *Document de travail de l'Institut Karl Polanyi d'économie politique*, Montreal, 1996, p. 4.

Möller, A., *Naukratis. Trade in Archaic Greece*, Oxford Monographs on Classical Archaeology, London, 2000.

Montet, P., *Les scènes de la vie privée dans les tombeaux égyptiens de l'Ancien Empire*, Publications de la Faculté des Lettres de l'Université de Strasbourg, fasc. 76, Strasbourg, 1925.

Montet, P., *Byblos et l'Égypte, quatre campagnes de fouilles à Gebeil, 1921-1924, BAH* XI, Paris, 1928.

Montet, P., *Tanis, Douze années de fouilles dans une capitale oubliée du Delta égyptien*, Bibliothèque historique, Payot, Paris, 1942.

Montet, P., *La vie quotidienne en Égypte au temps des Ramsès -1300/-1100*, Hachette, [1946] 1989.

Montet, P., 'Le nom des Grecs en égyptien et l'antiquité des Grecs en Égypte', *Revue Archéologique* 28, 2, 1947, pp. 129-144.

Montet, P., 'Nouvelles études sur les Haou-nebout et sur leur activité', *Revue Archéologique* 34, 2, 1949, p. 129.

Montet, P., 'Nouvelles études sur les Haou-nebout et sur leur activité', *Revue Archéologique* 48, 2, 1956, pp. 1-11.

Montet, P., *Géographie de l'Égypte ancienne, Première partie Tò-Mehou La Basse Égypte*, Paris, 1957.

Montet, P., *Géographie de l'Égypte ancienne, Deuxième partie Tò-chemâ La Haute Égypte*, Paris, 1961.

Moore, H.L., *Feminism and Anthropology*, Oxford, 1988.

Moran, W.L., *Les lettres d'El-Amarna, Correspondance diplomatique du pharaon, LAPO* 13, W.L. Moran, V. de Haas and G. Wilhelm (trans.), French translation by D. Collon and H. Gazelles, published with the support of CNRS, Le Cerf, Paris, 1987.

Morenz, S., 'Ptah-Hephaistos, der Zwerg', *in Festschrift F. Zucker*, Berlin, 1954, pp. 275-290.

Morenz, S., *Religion und Geschichte des alten Ägypten*, Cologne, Vienna, 1975, pp. 496-509.

Moret, A., 'De quelques voyages légendaires des Égyptiens en Asie', *Journal Asiatique*, Nov.–Dec. 1909, pp. 381-393.

Moret, A., 'La création d'une propriété privée sous le Moyen Empire égyptien', *CRAIBL*, 1915, pp. 1-10.

Morhange, C., Dubuquoy, O., Prunet, N., Ribes, E., Beaulieu, J.-L. de, Bourcier, M, Carbonel, P., Oberlin, C., and Doumet-Serhal, C., 'Étude paléoenvironnementale du port antique de Sidon. Premiers résultats du programme cedre', *in Ports antiques et paléoenvironnements littoraux, Méditerranée. Revue géographique des pays Méditerranéens* 1/2, 2000, pp. 91-100.

Morhange, C., Dubuquoy, O., Prunet, N., Beaulieu, J.-L. de, Bourcier, M., Carbonel, P., Le Campion, J., Oberlin, C., and Frost, H., 'Nouvelles données paléoenvironnementales sur le port antique de Sidon, proposition de datation', *National Museum News* 10, 2000, pp. 42-48.

Morhange, C., Dubuquoy, O., Prunet, N., Beaulieu, J.-L. de, Bourcier, M., Carbonel, P., Le Campion, J., Oberlin, C., Frost, H., and Doumet-Serhal, C., 'Étude des paléoenvironnements du port de Sidon (Liban) depuis 4000 ans, Résultats préliminaires', *Bulletin d'Archéologie et d'Architecture Libanaises*, in preparation.

Morrison, J., and Williams, R., *Greek oared Ships 900-322 BC*, Cambridge, 1968.

Morschauer, S.N., 'Crying to the Lebanon: A Note on Wenamun 2, 13-14', *SAK* 18, 1991, pp. 317-330.

Moscati, S., *et al.*, *An Introduction to the Comparative Grammar of the Semitic Languages*, Wiesbaden, 1964.

Moscati, S. (ed.), *The Phoenicians*, Bompiani, Milan, 1988.

Moscati, S. (ed.), *Les Phéniciens*, Stock, Milan, 1997.

Moussa, A.M., and Altenmüller, H., *Das Grab des Nianchchnum und Chnumhotep, Old Kingdom Tombs at the causeway of king Unas at Saqqara, Archäologische Veröffentlichungen* 21, Mainz am Rhein, 1977.

Müller, C., *Periplus Maris Erythraei, Geographi Graeci Minores*, Paris, 1853.

Müller-Wollermann, R., 'Warenaustausch im Ägypten des Alten Reiches', *JESHO* 28, 1985, pp. 121-168.

Murnane, W., 'In Defense of the Middle Kingdom Double Dates', *BES* 3, 1981, pp. 73-82.

Murray, G.W., and Myers, O.H., 'Some Pre-dynastic Rock Drawings', *JEA* XIX, 1933, pp. 129-132.

Nallino, C.A., 'L'Égypte avait-elle des relations directes avec l'Arabie méridionale avant l'âge des Ptolémées?', *BIFAO* XXX, 1930, pp. 465-475.

Navailles, R., Neveu, F., 'Une ténébreuse affaire: P. Bankes I', *GM* 103, 1988, pp. 51-60.

Naville, E., *Das Aegyptische Todtenbuch der XVIII. bis XX. Dynastie*, Mit Unterstützung des Königlich Preussischen der Geistlichen, Unterrichts- und Medicinal-Angelegenheiten, Verlag von A. Asher & Co, Berlin, 1886.

Naville, E., *The temple of Deir el-Bahari*, parts 1-4, EEF, London, 1894-1898.

Naville, E., 'Le pays de Pount et les Chamites', *Revue d'Archéologie* 22, pp. 112-121.

Negueruela, I., Pinedo, J., Gomez, M., Minano, A., Arellano, I., and Barba, J.S., 'Seventh-century BC Phoenician vessel discovered at Playa de la Isla, Mazzaron, Spain', *IJNA* 24/3, 1995, pp. 189-197.

Newberry, E., 'Notes on Seagoing Ships', *JEA* XXVIII, 1942, pp. 64-66.

Nibbi, A., *The Sea Peoples: A Re-examination of the Egyptian Sources*, Oxford, 1972.

Nibbi, A., *The Sea Peoples and Egypt*, Park-Ridge, 1975.

Nibbi, A., 'Egyptian Anchors', *JEA* 61, 1975, pp. 38-41.

Nibbi, A., 'The Wadi Tumilat, Atika and *mw-ḳd*', *GM* 16, 1975, pp. 33-38.

Nibbi, A., 'Henu of the Eleventh Dynasty and *wꜣḏ-wr*', *GM* 17, 1975, p. 43.

Nibbi, A., 'Remarks on the two stelae from Wadi Gasus', *JEA* 62, 1976, pp. 45-56, pls ix-x.

Nibbi, A., 'Ancient Egyptians in the Sinai', *PEQ* 109, 1977, pp. 125-128.

Nibbi, A., 'The *stt* Sign', *JEA* 64, 1978, pp. 56-64.

Nibbi, A., 'Some Remarks on the Assumption of Ancient Egyptian Sea-Going', *MM* 65, 1979, pp. 204-206.

Nibbi, A., *Ancient Egypt and Some Eastern Neighbours*, New Jersey, 1981.

Nibbi, A., 'Some Evidence from Scientists Indicating the Vegetation of Lower and Middle Egypt during the Pharaonic Period', *in L'Égyptologie en 1979. Axes prioritaires de recherches*, vol. 1, CNRS Colloquia, n° 595, Paris, 1982, pp. 247-254.

Nibbi, A., 'Gold and Silver from the Sinai', *GM* 57, 1982, pp. 35-40.

Nibbi, A., 'A Note on the Lexikon Entry: Meer', *GM* 58, 1982, pp. 53-58.

Nibbi, A., 'Rakotis on the Shore of the Great Green of the Haunebut', *GM* 69, 1983, pp. 69-80.

Nibbi, A., 'Some early dynastic clues relating to the environment of Ancient Egypt', *in* L. Krzyzaniak and M. Kousiewicz (eds), *Origin and early Development of Food-producing Cultures in North-Eastern Africa*, Poznan, 1984, pp. 287-293.

Nibbi, A., 'Ancient Egyptian anchors: a focus on the facts', *The Mariner's Mirror* 70, 1984, p. 259.

Nibbi, A., *Wenamun and Alashiya Reconsidered*, DE Publications, Oxford, 1985.

Nibbi, A., *Ancient Egypt and some Eastern Neighbours*, Park Ridge, 1985.

Nibbi, A., *Ancient Byblos Reconsidered*, DE Pubications, Oxford, 1985.

Nibbi, A., 'Some Middle Kingdom Oxhide-Shaped Ingots in the Egyptian Iconography and their Name: *nmś* and Ashmolean Ingot 1892-919', *DE* 4, 1986, p. 48.

Nibbi, A., 'Hatiba of Alasia and a Correction to my Proposed Area for that Country', *DE* 5, 1986, pp. 47-54.

Nibbi, A., *Ancient Egyptian Pot Bellows and the Oxhide Ingot Shape*, Oxford, 1987.

Nibbi, A., 'Byblos (sic) and Wenamun. A Reply to Some Recent Unrealistic Criticism', *DE* 11, 1988, pp. 31-42.

Nibbi, A., 'Some further remarks on the Haunebut', *ZÄS* 116, 1989, pp. 153-160.

Nibbi, A., 'Five stones anchors from Alexandria', *IJNA* 20, 1991, pp. 185-194.

Nibbi, A., 'A group of stone anchors from Mirgissa on the Upper Nile', *IJNA* 21, 1992, pp. 259-267.

Nibbi, A., 'Stone anchors: the evidence reassessed', *The Mariner's Mirror* 79, 1993, pp. 5-26.

Nibbi, A., 'Marsa Matruh as a Harbour and as a Measure of the Size of ancient Ships', *SAK* 26, 1998, pp. 203-212.

Niwinski, A., 'Problems in Chronology and Genealogy of the 21st Dynasty: New Proposals of their Interpretation', *JARCE* XVI, 1979, pp. 49-64.

Niwinski, A., 'Le passage de la XXe à la XXIe dynastie: chronologie et histoire politique', *BIFAO* 95, 1995, pp. 329-360.

Noth, M., *Die israelitischen Personennemen im Rahmen der gemeinsemitischen Namengebung, Beiträge zur Wissenschaft vom Alten und Neuen Testament* 46, Hildesheim, [1928] 1980.

Obsomer, Cl., *Les campagnes de Sésotris dans Hérodote, Essai d'interprétation du texte grec à la lumière des réalités égyptiennes, Connaissance de l'Égypte ancienne* 1, Brussels, 1989.

Obsomer, Cl., *Sésostris Ier Étude chronologique et historique du règne, Connaissance de l'Égypte ancienne* 5, Brussels, 1995.

Oren, E.D., 'The Overland Route between Egypt and Canaan in the Early Bronze Age. Preliminary Report', *IEJ* 23, 1973, pp. 198-200.

Oren, E.D., 'Land Bridge between Asia and Africa: Archaeology of Northern Sinai until the Classical Period', *in* B. Rothenberg, H. Weyer, *In Sinai: Pharaohs, Miners, Pilgrims and Soldiers*, Bern, 1979, pp. 181-192.

Oren, E.D., 'Bir el-'Abed', 'Harrouvit', 'La période perse', 'Migdol', 'Les premières colonies grecques', *Le Monde de la Bible* 24, 1982, pp. 10-13, 14, 16, 18.

Oren, E.D., 'Migdol: A New Fortress on the Edge of the Eastern Delta', *BASOR* 256, 1984, pp. 7-44.

Oren, E.D., 'The 'Ways of Horus' in North Sinai', *in* A.F. Rainey (ed.), *Egypt, Israel, Sinai: Archaeological and Historical relationship in the Biblical Period*, Tel Aviv, 1987, pp. 69-119.

Oren, E.D., 'Early Bronze Age Settlement in North Sinai: A Model for Egypto-Canaanite Interconnection', *in* P. de Miroschedji (ed.), *L'urbanisation de la Palestine à l'âge du Bronze ancien: Bilan et perspectives des recherches actuelles. Actes du Colloques d'Emmaüs, 20-24 octobre 1986*, vol. 2, *BAR IS* 527, Oxford, 1989, pp. 389-405.

Oren, E.D., and Yekutieli, Y., 'Taur Ikhbeineh: Earliest Evidence for Egyptian Interconnections', *in* E.C.M. Van den Brink (ed.), *The Nile Delta in Transition, 4th to 3rd Millenium BC*, Tel Aviv, 1992, pp. 361-384.

Oren, E.D., 'Ruqeish', 'Sinai: Northern Sinai', *in* E. Stern (ed.), *The New Encyclopedia of Archaeological Excavations in the Holy Land*, vol. 4, Jerusalem, 1993, pp. 1293-1294, 1334.

Oren, E.D., 'Ethnicity and Regional Archaeology: The Western Negev under Assyrian Rule', *in Proceedings of the Second International Congress of Biblical Archaeology, Jerusalem June-July 1990, Biblical Archaeology*, 1990, Jerusalem, 1993, pp. 102-105.

Oren, E.D., 'Le Nord-Sinaï à l'époque perse. Perspectives archéologiques', *in* D. Valbelle and C. Bonnet (eds), *Le Sinaï durant l'Antiquité et le Moyen Âge. 4000 ans d'histoire pour un désert*, 'Sinaï' UNESCO colloquium, 19–21 Sept. 1997, Errance, Paris, 1998, pp. 75-82.

Oren, E. D., *The Sea Peoples and their World: A Reassessment*, University Museum Monograph 108, University of Pennsylvania, Philadelphia, 2000.

Oren, E.D., 'Sinai: Northern Sinai', *in* E. Stern (ed.), *The New Encyclopaedia of Archaeological Excavations in the Holy Land*, vol. 4, Jerusalem, 1993, pp. 1387-1388.

Oren, E.D., and Yekutieli, Y., 'North Sinai during the MB I Period. Pastoral Nomadism and Sedentary Settlement', *ErIsr* 21, pp. 6-22 (in Hebrew) and 10★ (English abstract).

Oren, E.D., *et al.*, 'A Phoenician Emporium on the Border of Egypt', *Qadmoniot* 19, pp. 83-91.

Orrieux, Cl., *Les papyrus de Zénon. L'horizon d'un Grec d'Égypte au IIIe siècle av. n. è.*, Paris, 1983.

Orrieux, Cl., *Zénon de Caunos, parépidèmos, et le destin grec*, Paris, 1985.

Osing, J., 'Zum ägyptishen Namen für Zypern', *GM* 40, 1980, pp. 45-51.

Osing, J., 'La liste des toponymes égéens du temple funéraire d'Aménophis III', *Aspects de la culture pharaonique, Quatre leçons au Collège de France, février-mars 1989*, Mémoires de l'Académie des Inscriptions et Belles-Lettres, *n.s.* XII, 1992, pp. 25-36, figs 4-6.

Osing, J., 'Zu zwei geographischen Begriffen der Mittelmeerwelt', *in Gegengabe. Festschrift für Emma Brunner-Traut*, Tübingen, 1992, pp. 279-280.

Otto, E., *in LÄ* I, 1974, *s.v.* 'Bote (*jpwtj*)', col. 846.

Padró, J., 'À propos des trouvailles égyptiennes dans la péninsule ibérique: Considérations sur les relations de l'Égypte avec l'occident de l'Europe à la Basse Époque', *in Acts of the First International Congress of Egyptology, Cairo, 1976, SGKAO* 14, Berlin, 1979, pp. 507-514).

Padró, J., 'El déu Bes: Introducció al Seu Estudi', *Fonaments* 1, Barcelona, 1978, pp. 67-75.

Padró, J., *Egyptian-Type Documents from the Mediterranean Littoral of the Iberian Peninsula, before the Roman Conquest*, I, *Study of the Material, Introductory Survey*, *EPRO* LXV, Brill, Leiden, 1980.

Padró, J., *Egyptian-Type Documents from the Mediterranean Littoral of the Iberian Peninsula, before the Roman Conquest*, II, *Study of the Material, From Western Languedoc to Murcia*, *EPRO* LXV, Brill, Leiden, 1983.

Padró, J., *Egyptian-Type Documents from the Mediterranean Littoral of the Iberian Peninsula, before the Roman Conquest*, III, *Study of the Material, Andalusia*, *EPRO* LXV, Brill, Leiden, 1985.

Padró, J., *Egyptian-Type Documents from the Mediterranean Littoral of the Iberian Peninsula Before the Roman Conquest*, III, *Orientalia Monspeliensia* VIII, Montpellier, 1995.

Padró, J., 'Las divinidades egipcias en la Hispania romana y sus precedentes', *La Religión Romana en Hispania*, Madrid, 1981, pp. 337-352.

Padró, J., 'Los Fenicios y la distrubucíon de Objectos Egiptios en el Extremo Occidente Mediterráneo', *in Atti del I Congresso Internazionale di Studi Fenici e Punici*, Roma, 1979, I, Rome, 1983.

Padró, J., 'Hathor dans l'Hispanie préromaine', *in Hommages à J. Leclant*, *BiÉtud* 106/3, Cairo, 1994, pp. 397-404.

Padró, J., 'Les relations commerciales entre l'Égypte et le monde phénico-punique', *in* N. Grimal and B. Menu (eds), *Le commerce en Égypte ancienne*, *BiÉtud* 121, IFAO, Cairo, 1998, pp. 41-58, figs 1-10.

Pages, J., and Nied, A., *Itinéraires de la Mer Rouge. Antiquité-Moyen Âge*, *Études d'Histoire Maritime* 8, Paris, 1991.

Pankhurst, R., 'The Trade of Northern Ethiopia in the Nineteenth and Early Twentieth Centuries', *Journal of Ethiopian Studies* 2, 1964, pp. 66-102.

Pankhurst, R., 'The Trade of Northern Ethiopia in the Nineteenth and early Twentieth Centuries', *Journal of Ethiopian Studies* 11, 1964, pp. 70-75.

Pantalacci, L., and Traunecker, C., *Le temple d'el-Qal'a, I, Relevés des scènes et des textes, Sanctuaire central, Sanctuaire nord - Salle des offrandes*, IFAO, Cairo, 1990.

Parker, A.J., *Ancient Shipwrecks of the Mediterranean and the Roman provinces*, Oxford, 1992.

Parker, P., *The Calendars of Ancient Egypt*, SAOC 26, Chicago, 1950, Excursus C.

Parrot, A., 'La scène maritime de Khorsabad', *Sumer* 6, 1950, pp. 115-117.

Parrot, A., *Assur*, Paris, 1961.

Partridge, R., *Transport in Ancient Egypt*, The Rubicon Press, London, 1996.

Peet, T.E., *The Great Tomb-Robberies of the Twentieth Egyptian Dynasty, being a critical study, with translations and commentaries, of the papyri in which these are recorded*, Clarendon Press, Oxford, 1930.

Peet, T.E., 'The Unit of Value *š't̠y* in Papyrus Boulaq 11', *in Mélanges Maspero*, I, Orient Ancien, *MIFAO* LXVI, IFAO, Cairo, 1934, pp. 185-199.

Peremans, W., and Van't Dack, E., *Prosopographia Ptolemaica* V, *Studia Hellenistica* 13, Leuven, 1963.

Petrie, W.M.F., *Naukratis, Part I, 1884-1885*, EEF Memoir III, London, 1886.

Petrie, W.M.F., *Tanis I*, EEF, 2nd edition, London, 1888-1889.

Petrie, W.M.F., *Tanis II, 1886: Nebesheh (Am) and Defenneh (Tahpanhes)*, EEF Memoir IV, London, 1888.

Petrie, W. M. F., and Griffith, F. L, *Deshasheh 1897*, *EEF Memoir* XV, London, 1898.

Petrie, W.M.F., *Memphis*, I, London, 1909.

Petrie, W.M.F., *Social Life in Ancient Egypt*, Constable, London, 1923.

Petrie, W.M.F., *Gerar*, BSAE XIII, Bernard Quaritch, London, 1928.

Phytian-Adams, W.J., 'Report on the Stratfication of Gaza', *PEQ*, 1923, pp. 11-36.

Picard, C., 'Les navigateurs de Carthage vers l'Ouest. Carthage et le pays de Tarsis aux VIIIᵉ-VIᵉ siècles', *in* H.G. Niemeyer (ed.), *Phönizier im Western*, Mayence, 1982, pp. 169-171,

Pierce, R.H., *Three Demotic Papyri in the Brooklyn Museum, A Contribution to the Study of Contacts and their Instruments in Ptolémaic Egypt*, Universitetsforlaget, Oslo, 1972.

Pirenne, J., 'Un problème-clef pour la chronologie de l'Orient: la date du 'Périple de la mer Érythrée', *Journal Asiatique* CCXLIX, 1961, pp. 441-459.

Pirenne, J., *Le Royaume Sud-Arabe de Qatabân et sa datation d'après l'Archéologie et les sources classiques jusqu'au Périple de la mer Érythrée*, *Bibliothèque du Muséon* 48, Leuven, 1961.

Pirenne, J., and Van de Walle, B., *Documents juridiques égyptiens* I, *Archives d'Histoire du Droit Oriental* I, 1937.

Pirenne, J., 'La désagrégation de l'empire égyptien sous les règnes de Séthi Iᵉʳ et de Ramsès II', *AHDO & RIDA* I, 1952, p. 23.

Pirenne, J., 'À propos du droit commercial phénicien antique', Académie royale de Belgique, *Bulletin de la Classe des lettres et des sciences morales et politiques*, 5ᵗʰ series, 41, 1955, pp. 604-609.

Pirenne, J., *Histoire de la civilisation de l'Égypte ancienne, Deuxième cycle, De la fin de l'Ancien Empire à la fin du Nouvel Empire (± 2200-1085 av. J.-C.)*, La Baconnière, Neuchâtel, 1962, pp. 502-505.

Pirenne, J., 'Les escales phéniciennes dans la navigation égyptienne', *in Les Grandes escales I : Antiquité et Moyen Âge, Recueils de la Société Jean Bodin pour l'histoire comparative des institutions* XXXII, Brussels, 1974, pp. 43-50.

Pischilova, E.V., ''Mistakes' in the Representations of Objects in Saite Reliefs of Daily Life', *GM* 139, 1994, pp. 74-77.

Poidebard, A., and Lauffray, J., *Sidon, aménagements antiques du port de Saïda, étude aérienne, au sol et sous-marine (1946-1950)*, Republic of Lebanon, Ministry of Public Works, Beirut, 1951.

Polanyi, K., Arensberg, C.M., and Pearson, H.W. (eds), *Trade and Market in the Early Empires*, New York and London, 1957.

Polanyi, K., 'The economy as instituted process', *in* K. Polanyi, C.M. Arensberg, and H.W. Pearson (eds), *Trade and Market in the Early Empires*, New York and London, 1957.

Polanyi, K., *Primitive, Archaic and Modern Economies: Essays of Karl Polanyi*, New York, 1968.

Polanyi, K., 'Port of Trade in Early Societies', *in* G. Dalton (ed.), *Primitive, Archaic and Modern Economies*, Boston, 1968, pp. 238-260.

Polanyi, K., and Arensberg C.M. (eds), *Les systèmes économiques dans l'histoire et la théorie*, Paris, 1975.

Polanyi, K., 'Le commerce sans marché au temps d'Hammourabi', 'Aristote découvre l'économie', 'L'économie en tant que procès institutionnalisé', *in* K. Polanyi and C.M. Arensberg (eds), *Les systèmes économiques dans l'histoire et la théorie*, Paris, 1975, pp. 51-62, pp. 93-117, pp. 239-260.

Polanyi, K., 'Traders and Trade', *in* J.A. Sabloff and C.C. Lamberg-Karlowsky (eds), *Ancient Civilizations and Trade*, Albuquerque, 1975, pp. 133-154.

Pomey, P., and Tchernia, A., 'Le tonnage maximum des navires de commerce romains', *Archeonautica* 2, 1978, pp. 233-251.

Pomey, P., 'Comment naviguait-on dans la Méditerranée romaine?', *L'Histoire* 36, July-August 1981, pp. 96-101.

Pomey, P., 'L'épave de Bon-Porté et les bateaux cousus de Méditerranée', *The Mariner's Mirror* 67, 1981, pp. 235-237.

Pomey, P. (ed.), *La navigation dans l'Antiquité*, Centre Camille Jullian, CNRS, Université de Provence, Maison Méditerranéenne des Sciences de l'Homme, published with the support of the Centre national du livre, Édisud, Aix-en-Provence, 1997.

Pomey, P., 'Introduction', 'Le voyage de Saint Paul', 'Les conditions de la navigation', 'Les navires', 'Les épaves et leur cargaison', *in* P. Pomey (ed.), *La navigation dans l'Antiquité*, Centre Camille Jullian, CNRS, Université de Provence, Maison Méditerranéenne des Sciences de l'Homme, published with the support of the Centre national du livre, Édisud, Aix-en-Provence, 1997, pp. 5-6, pp. 10-17, pp. 18-35, pp. 60-101, pp. 161-191.

Pomey, P., 'Un exemple d'évolution des techniques de construction navale antique: de l'assemblage par ligatures à l'assemblage par tenons et mortaises', *in* D. Meeks and D. Garcia (eds), *Techniques et économie antiques et médiévales : le temps de l'innovation*, International Colloquium of the CNRS, Aix-en-Provence 21-23 May 1996, Errance, Paris, 1997, pp. 195-203.

Pomey, P., 'Comment naviguaient les Romains', *in 3000 ans sur le mer, Les collections de L'Histoire* 8, June 2000, pp. 24-27.

Porten, B., *Archives from Elephantine. The Life of an Ancient Jewish Military Colony*, Berkeley, Los Angeles, 1968.

Porten, B., and Yardeni, A., *Textbook of Aramaic Documents from Ancient Egypt*, III: *Litterature, Accounts, Lists*, Jerusalem, 1993.

Porten, B. (ed.), *The Elephantine Papyri in English, Three Millennia of Cross-Cultural Continuity and Change*, Leiden, 1996.

Posener, G., *La Première Domination Perse en Égypte*, BiÉtud XI, IFAO, Cairo, 1936.

Posener, G., 'Le canal du Nil à la mer Rouge avant les Ptolémées', *CdÉ* XIII, n° 26, July 1938.

Posener, G., 'La Légende de la Mer Insasiable', *AIPHO* XIII, 1953, pp. 461-478.

Posener, G., *Littérature et politique dans l'Égypte de la XIIᵉ dynastie*, Paris, 1956.

Posener, G., '*Mwk̠d - v*', *GM* 11, 1974, p. 39.

Posener, G., 'L'or de Punt', *Ägypten und Kush, SGKAO* 13, Berlin, 1977, pp. 337-342.

Posener, G., Sauneron, S., and Yoyotte, J., *Dictionnaire de la civilisation égyptienne*, Paris, 1992.

Posener-Kriéger, P., 'Le prix des étoffes', *in* M. Görg and E. Push (eds), *Festschrift Elmar Edel*, Bamberg, 1979, pp. 318-331.

Pottier, E., *Catalogue des antiquités assyriennes*, Musée du Louvre, Paris, 1924.

Poujade, J., *La route des Indes et ses navires*, Paris, 1946.

Préaux, C., *L'économie royale des Lagides*, Brussels, 1939.

Pritchard, J.B. (ed.), *Ancient Near Eastern Texts in Pictures Relating to the Old Testament*, Princeton.

Provansal, M., 'Environnements portuaires en Méditerranée', *in Ports antiques et paléoenvironnements littoraux, Méditerranée. Revue géographique des pays Méditerranéens* 1/2, 2000, pp. 3-5.

Pulak, C., and Frey, D.A., 'The Search for a Bronze Age Shipwreck', *Archaeology* 38/4, 1985, pp. 19-24.

Pulak, C., 'The Bronze Age Shipwreck at Ulu Burun, Turkey: 1985 Campaign', *AJA* 92/1, 1988, pp. 1-37.

Pulak, C., and Haldane, C., 'Ulu Burun. The Late Bronze Age Shipwreck: The Fourth Excavation Campaign', *INA Newsletter* 15/1, 1988, pp. 1-4.

Pulak, C., 'The Shipwreck at Ulu Burun, Turkey: 1992 excavation campaign', *INA Quarterly* 19, 1992, pp. 4-11.

Pulak, C., *et al.*, '1994 Excavations at Ulu Burun. The final Campaign', *INA Quarterly* 21/4, 1994, pp. 8-16.

Pusch, E.B., 'Pi-Ramesse-geliebt-von-Amun, Hauptquartier deiner Streitwagentruppe'. Ägypter und Hethiter in der Delta-Residenz der Ramessiden', *in* A. Eggebrecht (ed.), *Antike Welt im Pelizaeus Museum. Die Ägyptische Sammlung*, Mayence, 1993, pp. 126-143.

Pusch, E.B., 'Qantir/Pi-Ramsès', *in L'Égypte du Delta. Les capitales du Nord, Dossiers d'Archéologie* 213, March 1996, pp. 54-59.

Putter, T. de, 'Les routes vers les mines et les carrières: Coptos, la ville du 'Souverain à la tête des mines', *in Coptos. L'Égypte antique aux portes du désert, Lyon, musée des Beaux-Arts, 3 février-7 mai 2000*, musée des Beaux-Arts de Lyon, RMN, Paris, 2000, pp. 144-156.

Quack, J., *Die Lehren des Ani. Ein neuägyptischer Weinsheitstext in seinem kulturellen Umfeld, OBO* 141, Universitätsverlag Freiburg-Vandenhoeck & Ruprecht, Freiburg, Göttingen, 1994.

Raban, A. (ed.), *Harbour archaeology, Proceedings of the first workshop 'Ancient mediterranean harbours', BAR IS* 257, Oxford, 1985.

Raban, A., 'The Harbor of the Sea Peoples at Dor', *Biblical Archaeology* 50, 1987, pp. 118-127.

Raban, A. (ed.), *Archaeology of coastal change, Procceedings of the first international symposium 'Cities on the sea-past and present', BAR IS* 404, Oxford, 1988.

Raban, A., 'The Constructive Maritime Role of the Sea Peoples in the Levant', *in* M. Heltzer and E. Lipinski (eds), *Society and Economy in the Eastern Mediterranean (c. 1500-1000 B. C.), OLA* 23, 1988, Leuven, pp. 261-294.

Raepsaet, G., 'Réflexions sur l'innovation en matière de transport terrestre: l'exemple de la Gaule sous le Haut-Empire', *in* D. Meeks and D. Garcia (eds), *Techniques et économie antiques et médiévales : le temps de l'innovation,* International Colloquium of the CNRS, Aix-en-Provence 21-23 May 1996, Errance, Paris, 1997, pp. 137-141.

Rainey, A.F., 'Asiru and asiru in Ugarit and the Land of Canaan', *JNES* 26, 1967, pp. 296-301.

Rainey, A.F., 'Business Agents at Ugarit', *IEJ* 13, 1963, pp. 313-321.

Ramond, P., *Les stèles égyptiennes du musée Labit à Toulouse, BiÉtud* 62, IFAO, Cairo, 1977.

Ranke H, *Die ägyptishen Personennamen*, Glückstadt, 1935-1952.

Rappaport, U., 'Les Iduméens en Égypte', *RevPh* 43, 1969, pp. 73-82.

Rathbone, D., 'The 'Muziris'papyrus (SB XVIII 13167): financing Roman trade with India', *in Alexandrian Studies ii in Honour of Mostafa el Abbadi, BSAA* 46, 2000, p. 46

Rathbone, D., 'Koptos the *Emporion*. Economy and Society', *in Autour de Coptos,* proceedings of the colloquium organised by the musée des Beaux-Arts de Lyon (17-18 March 2000), *Topoi, Orient-Occident*, suppl. 3, Lyon, 2002, pp. 179-198.

Ray, H.P., and Salles, J.-Fr. (eds), *Tradition and Archaeology. Early Maritime Contacts Indian Ocean*, Proceedings of the New Delhi Colloquium, 1994, *Techno-Archaeological perspectives of Seafaring in the Indian Ocean, 4th cent. BC – 15th cent. A.D.*, New Delhi, 1996.

Reddé, M., and Bauzou, T., 'Pistes caravanières de Syrie, d'Arabie et d'Égypte: quelques éléments de comparaison', *in* T. Fahd (ed.), *L'Arabie Préislamique et son environnement historique et culturel*, Strasbourg, 1989, pp. 485-498.

Redford, D.B., *in LÄ* II, 1977, s.v. 'Herihor', cols 1129-1133.

Redford, D.B., 'Egypt and Western Asia in the Old Kingdom', *JARCE* XXIII, 1986, pp. 125-143.

Redford, D.B., *in* J. Weinstein, A. Ben-Tor, M. Bietak, E.D. Oren, W.G. Dever, J.S. Holladay, and Ward W.A, *Egypt and Canaan in the Bronze Age (1988), BASOR* 281, Chicago, 1991, pp. 1-79.

Redford, D.B., *Egypt, Canaan, and Israel in Ancient Times*, Princeton, 1992.

Redford, D.B., 'Le Wadi Tumilat', 'Mendès', *in L'Égypte du Delta. Les capitales du Nord, Dossiers d'Archéologie* 213, March 1996, pp. 78-81.

Redford, S., and Redford, D.B., 'Graffiti and Petroglyphs. Old and New from the Eastern Desert', *JARCE* XXVI, 1989, pp. 3-49.

Redmount, C., 'The Wadi Tumilat and the 'Canal of the Pharaohs', *JNES* 54/2, 1995, pp. 127-135.

Reekmans, T., 'Archives de Zénon: situation et comportement des entrepreneurs indigènes', *Proceedings of the International Colloquium*, Leuven, 1983, pp. 325-350.

Reich, R., 'The Identification of the 'Sealed *Karu*'of Egypt', *IEJ* 34, 1984, pp. 32-38.

Reinecke, W.F., 'Waren die *šwtj.w* wirklich Kaufleute?', *AltorForsch* 6, 1979, pp. 5-14.

Reisner, G.A., *Models of Ships and Boats, CGC n° 4798-4976 & 5034-5200*, IFAO, Cairo, 1913.

Renfrew, C., Dixon, J.E., and Cann, J.R., 'Obsidian and Early Cultural Contact in the Near East', *Proceedings of the Prehistoric Society* 32, 1966, pp. 30-72.

Renfrew, C., Dixon, J.E., and Cann, J.R., 'Further Analysis of Near Eastern Obsidian', *Proceedings of the Prehistoric Society* 32, 1968, pp. 319-331.

Renfrew, C., *The Emergence of Civilization*, Methuen, London, 1972.

Renfrew, C., *The Explanation of Culture Change, Models in Prehistory*, Duckworth, London, 1973.

Renfrew, C., 'Regression Analysis of some trade and marketing patterns', *World Archaeology* 6, 1, 1974, pp. 172-189.

Renfrew, C., 'Trade as Action at a Distance: question of integration and communication', *in* J.A. Sabloff and C.C. Lamberg-Karlowsky (eds), *Ancient Civilizations and Trade*, Albuquerque, 1975, pp. 3-60.

Renfrew, C., 'Alternative Models for Exchange and Spatial Distribution', *in* T.K. Earle, and J.E. Ericson, *Exchange systems in Prehistory*, New York, San Francisco and London, 1977, pp. 71-90.

Renfrew, C., and Bahn, P., *Archaeology – Theories, Methods and Practice*, Thames and Hudson, London, 1996.

Renfrew, C., 'Commerce et société pendant la préhistoire', *La Recherche* 331, May 2000, pp. 48-50.

Revere, R.B., 'Les ports de commerce de la Méditerranée orientale et la neutralité des côtes', *in* K. Polanyi and C.M. Arensberg (eds), *Les systèmes économiques dans l'histoire et la théorie*, Paris, 1975, pp. 71-92.

Rey Coquais, J.-P., 'L'Arabie et les routes du commerce', *in* T. Fahd (ed.), *L'Arabia Préislamique et son environnement historique et culturel*, Strasbourg, 1989, pp. 225-239.

Richter, W., *Phönizische Hafenstädte im öslichen Mittelmeerraum und ihre Bedeutung in heutinger Zeit. Die Biespiele: Saïda, Soúr, Akko, Geographische Luftbildinterpretation* 4, Bonn - Bad Godesberg, 1975.

Roccati, A., *La littérature historique sous l'Ancien Empire égyptien*, LAPO 11, Le Cerf, Paris, 1982.

Rodziewicz, M., *Les habitations romaines tardives d'Alexandrie à la lumière des fouilles polonaises à Kôm el-Dikka, Alexandrie* III, Éditions scientifiques de Pologne, Warsaw, 1984, p. 221.

Roquet, G., 'Inscriptions d'Ancien Empire articulées à l'image. Le dit du 'savetier'du mastaba de Ti', *in Mélanges H. Wild*, BSEG 9-10, 1984-1985, pp. 227-244.

Roquet, G., 'Avant le désert, savanes, véneries et caravanes. Réflexions sur une inscription d'Ancien Empire', *in* Fr. Geus and Fl. Thill (eds), *Mélanges offerts à Jean Vercoutter*, published with the support of the CNRS, Éditions Recherche sur les Civilisations, Paris, 1985, pp. 291-311.

Römer, H., *in LÄ* VI, 1986, *s.v.* 'Tanis', cols 194-209.

Römer, M., 'Der Handel und die Kaufleute im alten Ägypten', *SAK* 19, 1992, pp. 257-284.

Rostovtzeff, M., 'Foreign Commerce of Ptolemaic Egypt', *Journal of Economic and Business History* 4, 1932, p. 762.

Rostovtzeff, M., 'Πλοια θαλασσια on the Nile', *in Études dédiées à la mémoire d'A.M. Andréadès*, Athens, 1940, pp. 367-376.

Rostovtzeff, M., *The Social and Economic History of the Hellenistic World*, I, Oxford, 1941.

Rouch, J., *La Méditerranée*, Paris, 1946.

Rougé, J., 'La navigation hivernale sous l'Empire romain', *Revue des Études Latines* LIV, 1952, p. 316.

Rougé, J., 'Voyages officiels en Méditerranée orientale à la fin de la République et au Ier siècle de l'Empire', *Revue des Études anciennes* LV, 1953, p. 294.

Rougé, J., 'Ad ciconias nixas', *Revue des Études anciennes* LIX, 1957, p. 320-328.

Rougé, J., 'Le navire de Carpathos', *Cahiers d'histoire* VIII, 1963, pp. 253-268.

Rougé J, *Recherches sur l'organisation du commerce en Méditerranée sous l'empire romain*, Université de Paris, Faculté de Lettres et Sciences Humaines, École Pratique des Hautes Études, Imprimerie Nationale, Paris, 1966.

Rougé, J., *La marine dans l'Antiquité*, PUF, Paris, 1975.

Rougé J, 'Prêt et sociétés maritimes en droit romain', *in* J.H. D'Arms and E.C. Kopff (eds), *The Seaborne Commerce of Ancient Rome: Studies in Archaeology and History, Memoirs of the American Academy in Rome* 36, 1980, pp. 291-303.

Rougé, J., 'Routes et ports de la Méditerranée antique', *Revue d'Études Ligures*, 1987, pp. 151-160.

Rougé, J., 'la navigation en mer Érythrée dans l'Antiquité', *in* J.-Fr. Salles (ed.), *L'Arabie et ses mers bordières*, I, *Itinéraires et voisinages, Séminaires 1985-1986, TMO* 16, Lyon, 1988, pp. 59-74.

Roussel, D., and Marchand, S., 'Tanis. La céramique d'un bâtiment de la XXXe dynastie', *BCE* XVIII, 1994, pp. 12-18.

Roussel, P., *Délos, colonie athénienne*, Paris, 1916.

Rowe, A., *A Catalogue of Egyptian Scarabs, Scaraboids, Seals and Amulets in the Palestine Archaeological Museum*, Cairo, 1936.

Ruiz-Fernandez, A., *Almuñécar en la antigüedad fenicia*, Granada, 1979.

Ryhiner, M.L., *L'offrande du Lotus dans les temples égyptiens de l'époque tardive, Rites égyptiens* VI, Bruxellles, 1986.

Said, R., *The Geology of Egypt*, Amsterdam, 1962.

Said, R., *Explanatory notes to accompany the geological map of Egypt*, Cairo, 1971.

Said, R., *The Geological evolution of the River Nile*, New York, 1981.

Said, R., *The Geology of Egypt*, Balkema, 1990.

Saidah, R., 'Fouilles de Sidon-Dakerman: l'agglomération chalcolithiques', *Berytus* 27, 1979, pp. 29-55.

Saint-Denis, E. de, '*Mare Clausum*', *Revue des Études Latines* XXV, 1947, p. 106.

Saleh, A.-A., 'The GNBTYW of Thutmosis III's Annals and the South Arabian GEB(B)ANITAE of the Classical Writers', *BIFAO* 72, 1972, pp. 247-248.

Saleh, A.-A., 'Some Problems Relating to the Pwenet reliefs at Deir el-Bahari', *JEA* 58, 1972, pp. 140-150.

Salles, J.-F., 'The Arab-Persian Gulf under the Seleucids', *in*, A. Kuhrt and S. Sherwin-White (eds), *Hellenism in the East: The Interaction of Greek and Non-Greek Civilizations from Syria to Central Asia after Alexander*, London, Berkeley and Los Angeles, 1987, pp. 75-109.

Salles, J.-F., 'La circumnavigation de l'Arabie dans l'Antiquité', *in* J.-F. Salles (ed.), *L'Arabie et ses mers bordières*, I, *Itinéraires et voisinages, Séminaires 1985-1986*, TMO 16, Lyon, 1988, pp. 75-102.

Salles, J.-F., 'Les échanges commerciaux et culturels dans le golfe arabo-persique au Ier millénaire av. J.-C. Réflexions sur Makkam et Meluhha', *in* T. Fahd (ed.), *L'Arabie pré-islamique et son environnement culturel, Actes du Colloque de Strasbourg 1987*, Travaux du CRPOGA, Leiden, 1989, pp. 67-96.

Salles, J.-F., 'Du blé, de l'huile et du vin... (Notes sur les échanges commerciaux en Méditerranée orientale vers le milieu du Ier millénaire av. J.-C.)', *in* H. Sancisi-Weerdenburg and A. Kuhrt (eds), *Asia Minor and Egypt: Old Cultures in the New Empire*, Proceedings of the Groningen 1988 Achaemenid History Workshop, *AchHist* VI, Leiden, 1991, pp. 207-236.

Salles, J.-F., 'Du blé, de l'huile et du vin... (Notes sur les échanges commerciaux en Méditerranée orientale vers le milieu du Ier millénaire av. J.-C.)', *in* H. Sancisi-Weerdenburg and A. Kuhrt (eds), *Continuity and Change*, Proceedings of the Last Achaemenid History Workshop, April 6-8, 1990, Ann Arbor, Michigan, *AchHist* VIII, Leiden, 1994, pp. 193-215.

Salles, J.-F., 'La mer rouge, du IVe siècle av. J.-C. au milieu du premier siècle de notre ère', *in* D. Valbelle and C. Bonnet (eds), *Le Sinaï durant l'Antiquité et le Moyen Âge. 4000 ans d'histoire pour un désert*, 'Sinaï' UNESCO colloquium, 19–21 Sept. 1997, Errance, Paris, 1998, pp. 93-101.

Salles, J.-F., 'Byblos, métropole maritime', *in Liban, l'autre rive, Exposition présentée à l'Institut du monde arabe du 27 octobre 1998 au 2 mai 1999*, Institut du monde arabe, Flammarion, Paris, 1998, pp. 66-70.

Sandars, N.K., *Les peuples de la mer*, Paris, 1981.

Sander-Hansen, C.E., *Historische Inschriften der 19. Dynastie*, vol. 1, *Bibliotheca Aegyptiaca* 4, Brussels, 1933.

Sanlaville, P., 'Les bas niveaux marins pléistocènes du Liban', *Méditerranée* 34, 1969, pp. 257-292.

Sanlaville, P., 'Les variations holocènes du niveau de la mer au Liban', *Méditerranée* 35, 1970, pp. 279-304.

Sanlaville, P., *Étude géomorphologique de la région littorale du Liban*, vol. 3, Publications de l'Université Libanaise, Section des Études géographiques, Beirut, 1977.

Sanlaville, P., 'Des mers au milieu d'un désert: mer Rouge et Golfe arabo-persique', *in* J.F. Salles (ed.), *L'Arabie et ses mers bordières*, I, TMO 16, Lyon, 1988, pp. 9-26.

Sanlaville, P., Dalongeville, R., Bernier, P., and Evin, J., 'The Syrian Coast: a model of Holocene coastal evolution', *Journal of Coastal Research* 13/2, 1997, pp. 385-396.

Sass, B., 'Wenamun and his Levant – 1075 BC or 925 BC?', *ÄgLev* XII, 2002, pp. 247-256.

Sasson, J., 'Canaanite Maritime Involvement in the Second Millenium BC', *JAOS* 86, 1966, pp. 128-138.

Satzinger, H., 'Übersetzungsvorschläge und Anmerkungen zu einigen neuägyptischen Texten', *in* B.M. Bryan and D. Lorton (eds), *Essays in Egyptology in Honor of H. Goedicke*, Van Siclen Books, San Antonio, 1994, pp. 233-242.

Sauneron, S., 'La manufacture d'armes de Memphis', *BIFAO* LIV, 1954, pp. 7-12.

Sauneron, S., 'La justice à la porte des temples', *BIFAO* LIV, 1954, pp. 119-123.

Sauneron, S., 'Une page de géographie physique: le cycle agricole égyptien', *BIFAO* LX, 1960, pp. 11-17.

Sauneron, S., *Les fêtes religieuses d'Esna aux derniers siècles du paganisme*, Esna V, IFAO, Cairo, 1962.

Sauneron, S., *Villes et légendes d'Égypte*, BiÉtud 90, IFAO, Cairo, 1983 (2nd ed.).

Säve-Söderbergh, T., *The Navy of the Eighteenth Egyptian Dynasty, Recueil de travaux publiés par l'Université d'Uppsala* 6, Uppsala, 1946.

Sayed, Abdel Monem A.H., 'Discovery of the Site of the 12th Dynasty Port at Wadi Gawasis on the Red Sea Shore (Preliminary report on the excavations of the Faculty of Arts, University of Alexandria, in the Eastern Desert of Egypt – March 1976) [Plates 8-16]', *RdÉ* 29, 1977, pp. 138-178.

Sayed, Abdel Monem A.H., 'The Recently Discovered Port on the Red Sea Shore', *JEA* 64, 1978, pp. 69-71.

Sayed, Abdel Monem A.H., 'Observations on recent discoveries at Wâdi Gawâsîs', *JEA* 66, 1980, pp. 154-171.

Sayed, Abdel Monem A.H., 'New Light on the Recently Discovered Port on the Red Sea Shore', *CdÉ* LVIII, fasc. 115-116, 1983, pp. 23-37.

Sayed, Abdel Monem A.H., 'D.S. Whitcomb, J.H. Johnson, *Quseir al-Qadim 1980: Preliminary Report*. Malibu, Undena Publications, 1982. vol. 1, xii-406 pp., 29 figs, 5 tabls, 74 pls, (American Research Center in Egypt: Reports, vol. 7)', *CdÉ* LIX, 117, 1984, pp. 293-297.

Sayed, Abdel Monem A.H., 'Were there direct Relation ships between Pharaonic Egypt and Arabia?', *Proceedings of the Seminar for Arabian Studies*, vol. 19, 1989, pp. 155-166.

Scandone-Matthiae, G., 'Vasi iscritti di Chephren at Pepi I nel Palazzo Reale G di Ebla', *Studi Eblaiti* I / 3-4, 1979, pp. 33-43.

Scandone-Matthiae, G., 'The Mace of Pharaoh Hotepibre and the Connections between Egypt and Syria-Palestine in the XIIIᵉ dynasty', *in Studies in the History and Archaeology of Palestine*, Aleppo, 1985, pp. 49-58.

Schaeffer, C., *Ugaritica* IV, Paris, 1962.

Schaeffer, C., *Le palais Royal d'Ugarit*, vol. 6, *Mission de Ras Shamra* 12, Paris, 1970.

Schaefer, H., 'Ein Phönizier auf einem ägyptischen Grabstein der Ptolemäerzeit', *ZÄS* 40, 1902-1903, pp. 31-35.

Scheepers, A., 'Anthroponymes et toponymes du récit d'Ounamon', *in* E. Lipinski (ed.), *Phoenicia and the Bible*, Proceedings of the Conference held at the University of Leuven on the 15th and 16th of March 1990, *Studia Phoenicia* XI, *OLA* 44, Leuven, 1991, pp. 17-83.

Scheepers, A., 'Le voyage d'Ounamon: un texte 'littéraire'ou 'non-littéraire'?', *in Amosiadès, Mélanges offerts au Professeur Claude Vandersleyen par ses anciens étudiants*, Leuven-la-Neuve, 1992, pp. 355-363.

Schenkel, W., *Memphis, Hierakonpolis, Theben, Die epigraphischen Zeugnisse der 7.-11 Dynastie Ägyptens*, *ÄgAbh* 12, Harrassowitz, Wiesbaden, 1965.

Schenkel, W., *in LÄ* II, 1976, *s.v.* 'Götterverschmelzung', cols 720-725.

Scherer, J., 'Reçu de loyer à un nauclère', *BASP* 15, 1978, pp. 95-101.

Schoff, W.H., *The Periplus of the Erythrean Sea*, New York, 1912.

Schule, G., 'Navigaciones primitivas y visibilidad de la tierra en el Mediterraneo', *in IX Congresso nacional de Arqueologia*, Merida, 1968, p. 449.

Schulman, A.R., 'Alessandra Nibbi, *Ancient Egypt and Some Eastern Neighbours*, Park Ridge, New Jersey, Noyes Press, 1981', *BiOr* XLI, n° 5/6, 1984, cols 607-612.

Schulmann, A.R., *Military Rank, Title and Organization in the Egyptian New Kingdom*, *MÄS* 6, Berlin, 1964.

Schulmann, A.R., '*Mhr* and *Mškb*, Two Egyptian Military Titles of Semitic Origin', *ZÄS* 93, 1966, pp. 123-132.

Schumacher, I.W., *Der Gott Sopdu der Herr der Fremdländer*, Freiburg, 1988.

Schwab-Schlott, A., *Die Ausmasse Ägyptens nach altägyptischen Texten*, *AÄT* 3, 1981.

Segal, J.B., *Aramaic Texts from North Saqqâra with Some Fragments in Phoenician, Excavations at North Saqqara, Documentary Series*, London, 1983.

Sestini, G., 'Geomorphology of the Nile Delta', *in Proceedings of the Seminar on the Delta Sedimentology*, UNESCO, Alexandria, 1976, pp. 12-24.

Sethe, K., *Urkunden der 18. Dynastie* IV, *Urkunden des ägyptisvhen Altertums* 4, Berlin and Leipzig, [1927] 1961.

Sidebotham, S.E., *Roman Economic Policy in the Erythra Thalassa 30 BC - A.D. 217*, Leiden, 1986.

Sidebotham, S.E., 'From Berenike to Koptos: recent results of the desert route Survey', *in Autour de Coptos,* proceedings of the colloquium organised by the musée des Beaux-Arts de Lyon (17-18 March 2000), *Topoi, Orient-Occident*, suppl. 3, Lyon, 2002, pp. 199-233.

Sidebotham, S.E., and Wendrich, W.Z., *Berenike 1996, Report on the 1996 Excavations at Berenike (Egyptian Red Sea Coast) and the Survey of the Eastern Desert, Research School CNWS*, Leiden, 1998.

Sijpesteijn, P.J., 'Trajan and Egypt', *Studia Papyrologica Varia, Papyrological Lugduno-Batava* 14, Leiden, 1965, pp. 106-113.

Simpson, W.K., *Papyrus Reiner II, Accounts of the Dockyards Workshop at This in the Reign of Sesostris I*, Boston, 1965.

Simpson, W.K., 'A Tomb Chapel Relief of the Reign of Amunemhet III and Some Observations on the Length of the Reign of Sesostris III', *CdE* 47, 1972.

Simpson, W.K. (ed.), *The Literature of Ancient Egypt. An Anthology of Stories, Instructions and Poetry*, New Haven and London, 1973 (2nd ed.).

Simpson, W.K., *in LÄ* V, 1985, *s.v.* 'Sesostris III', cols 903-906.

Simpson, W.K., *in LÄ* V, 1985, *s.v.* 'Schiffbrüchiger', cols 619-622.

Sion, J., 'Les péninsules Méditerranéennes', *in* L. Gallois and P. Vidal de la Blache (eds), *Géographie universelle*, vol. 7, Paris, 1934.

Sleeswyk, A.W., 'Phoenician joints, *coagmenta punicana*', *IJNA* 9/3, 1980, pp. 243-244.

Sleeswyk, A.W., 'On the location of the Land of Pount on two Renaissance maps', *IJNA* 12/4, 1983, pp. 279-291.

Smith, H.S., 'The making of Egypt: A review of the influence of Susa and Sumer on Upper Egypt and Lower Nubia in the 4th millennium BC', *in The Followers of Horus, Studies dedicated to Michael Allen Hoffman*, Exeter, 1992, pp. 235-246.

Smith, J.S., 'Oren E.D, *The Sea Peoples and their World: a Reassessment*', *BiOr* LIX, 3/4, May–August 2002, pp. 399-405.

Smith, K.C., 'A Remarkable discovery, the bronze Age shipwreck at Kas', *INA Newsletter* 12/1, College Station, 1985, pp. 2-5.

Smither, P.C., 'An Old Kingdom letter concerning the Count Sabni', *JEA* XXVIII, 1942, pp. 16-19.

Smither, P.C., 'The Semnah Despatches', *JEA* XXXI, 1945, pls i-vii, pp. 3-10.

Smyth, F., 'Égypte-Canaan: quel commerce?', *in* N. Grimal and B. Menu (eds), *Le commerce en Égypte ancienne*, BiÉtud 121, IFAO, Cairo, 1998, pp. 5-18.

Snell, D.C., 'Marketless trading in our time', *JESHO* 34, 1991, pp. 129-141.

Solver, C.V., 'Egyptian Shipping of about 1500 BC', *The Mariner's Mirror* 22, 1936, pp. 430-444.

Spens, R. de, 'Droit international et commerce au début de la XXIe dynastie. Analyse juridique du rapport d'Ounamon', *in* N. Grimal and B. Menu (eds), *Le commerce en Égypte ancienne*, BiÉtud 121, IFAO, Cairo, 1998, pp. 105-126.

Spiegel, J., *in LÄ* I, 1980, *s.v.* 'Ätiologie. Ätiologische Mythen', cols 80-83.

Spiegelberg, W., 'Varia', *RT* 15, 1893, pp. 142-143.

Spiegelberg, W., *Hieratic Ostraka & Papyri found by J.E. Quibell in the Ramesseum, 1895-1896*, BSAE, extra vol., Quaritch, London, 1896.

Spiegelberg, W., *Rechnungen aus der Zeit Setis' I mit anderen Rechnungen des Neuen Reiches*, Strasbourg, 1896.

Spiegelberg, W., 'Die Stele 119 C des Louvre und das Τυριφν στρατοπεδον', *Kêmi* 2, 1929, pp. 107-112.

Stadelmann, R., *Syrisch-Palästinische Gottheiten in Ägypten*, ProbÄg V, Leiden, 1967.

Stadelmann, R., *in LÄ* V, 1984, *s.v.* 'Seevölker', cols 815-816.

Steffy, J.R., 'The Kyrénia Ship: an interim report on its hull construction', *AJA*, 1985, pp. 71-101.

Steffy, J.R., *Wooden ship building and the interpretation of shipwrecks*, Texas A & M University Press, College Station, 1994.

Steffy, J.R., 'Ancient scantlings; the projection and control of Mediterranean hull shapes', *in Tropis* III, 3rd International Symposium on Ship Construction in Antiquity, Athens *1989*, Athens, 1995, pp. 417-428.

Steiner, R.C., 'Northwest Semitic Incantations in an Egyptian Medical papyrus of the Fourteenth Century BCE', *JNES* 51, 1992, pp. 191-200.

Sternquist, B.B., *Models of Commercial Diffusion in Prehistoric Times*, Lund University, Lund, 1965-1966.

Stevenson Smith, W., *Interconnections in the Ancient Near East. A Study of the Relationships between the Arts of Egypt, the Aegean, and Western Asia*, New Haven and London, 1965.

Stewart, H.M., *Egyptian Stelae, Reliefs and Paintings, Part 2: Archaic Period to Second Intermediate Period*, Aris & Phillips Ltd., Warminster, 1979.

Störk, L., "*pꜣ jm ꜥꜣ n mw ḳd*'zum dritten?', *GM* 9, 1974, pp. 39-40.

Strange, J., 'Caphtor/Keftiu. A New Investigation', *Acta Théologica Danica* 14, Leiden, 1980, pp. 172-184.

Stronk, J.P., 'Sailing Merchant-Ships, *c.* 500–300 BC A Preliminary Analysis', *Talanta* 24-25, 1992-1993, pp. 117-140.

Suys, E.S.J., 'La théologie personnelle', *in Miscellanea Biblica* II, 1934, pp. 6-9.

Suys, E.S.J., *La Sagesse d'Ani, texte, traduction et commentaire*, Analecta Orientalia 11, Rome, 1935.

Swiderek, A., 'La société indigène en Égypte au IIIe siècle avant notre ère d'après les archives de Zénon', *JJP* 7-8, 1954, p. 245.

Swiderek, A., 'La société indigène en Égypte au IIIe siècle avant notre ère d'après les archives de Zénon. Sources des revenus privés de Zénon et de son entourage grec', *JJP* 9-10, 1956, p. 385.

Swiderek, A., 'Sarapis et les Hellénomemphites', *in* J. Bingen, G. Cambier and G. Masson (eds), *Le monde grec, Hommage à Claire Préaux*, Brussels, 1975, pp. 670–675.

Täckolm, V.L., and Drar, M., *Flora of Egypt*, Cairo, 1950–1954.

Tadmor, H., 'The Campaigns of Sargon II of Assur', *JCS* 12, 1958, p. 34.

Tchernia, A., Pomey, P., and Hesnard, A., *L'épave romaine de la Madrague de Giens (Var), Gallia*, suppl. 34, 1978, pp. 101–107.

Tchernia, A., 'Moussons et monnaies: les voies du commerce entre le monde gréco-romain et l'Inde', *Annales. Histoire, Sciences Sociales* 5, 50th year, Sept.-Oct. 1995, pp. 991–1009.

Tchernia, A., 'Le voyage de Saint Paul', 'Les dangers de la navigation. Tempêtes et naufrages', 'Le commerce maritime dans la Méditerranée romaine', *in* P. Pomey (ed.), *La navigation dans l'Antiquité*, Centre Camille Jullian, CNRS, Université de Provence, Maison Méditerranéenne des Sciences de l'Homme, published with the support of the Centre national du livre, Édisud, Aix-en-Provence, 1997, pp. 10–17, pp. 36–46, pp. 116–145.

Tchernia, A., 'Winds and Coins: From the Supposed Discovery of the Monsoon to the *Denarii* of Tiberius', *in* F. De Romanis and A. Tchernia (eds), *Crossings. Early Mediterranean Contacts with India*, Human Sciences Centre, New Delhi, Italian Embassy Cultural Centre, Manohar, New Delhi, 1997, pp. 250–276.

Teixidor, J., *The Pagan god: popular religion in the Greco-Roman Near East*, Princeton, 1977.

Teixidor, J., 'Les Nabatéens du Sinaï', *in* D. Valbelle and C. Bonnet (eds), *Le Sinaï durant l'Antiquité et le Moyen Âge. 4000 ans d'histoire pour un désert*, 'Sinaï' UNESCO colloquium, 19–21 Sept. 1997, Errance, Paris, 1998, pp. 83–87.

Te Velde, H., *Seth, God of Confusion, Study of his role in Egyptian Mythology and Religion, ProÄg* 6, Leiden, 1967.

Thalmann, J.-P., 'La civilisation des palais levantins à l'âge du bronze ancien et du bronze récent', *in* A. Caubet (ed.) *L'acrobate au taureau. Les découvertes de Tell el-Dabca (Égypte) et l'archéologie de la Méditerranée orientale (1800-1400 av. J.-C.),* proceedings of a colloquium held at the Louvre, 3 Dec. 1994, La documentation française & musée du Louvre, Paris, 1999, pp. 101–121, figs 1-9.

Théodoridès, A., 'À propos de *Pap. Lansing,* 4,8-5,2 et 6,8-7,5', *RIDA*, 3rd series, vol. 5, Brussels, 1958, pp. 65–119.

Théodoridès, A., 'Acte de 'sounet (vente) dans la stèle juridique de Karnak", *RIDA*, 3rd series, vol. 6, 1959, pp. 126–127.

Théodoridès, A., 'La 'Satire des métiers'et les marchands', *AIPHO* XV, 1960, pp. 39–40.

Théodoridès, A., 'Le Papyrus des Adoptions', *RIDA*, 3rd series, vol. 7, Brussels, 1965, pp. 79–142.

Théodoridès, A., *in LÄ* II, 1977, *s.v.* 'Frau', cols 280–295.

Thissen, H.-J., *Die Lehre des Anchscheschonqi (P. BM 10508)*, Bonn, 1984.

Thissen, H.-J., *in* O. Kaiser (ed.), *Texte aus der Umwelt des Alten Testaments* iii, 1991, pp. 251.

Thompson, D., 'Hellenistic Memphis: City and Necropolis', *in Alessandria e il mundo ellenistico-romano, Studi in onore di Achille Adriani*, Rome, 1983, pp. 16–24.

Thompson, D., 'Nile Grain Transports under the Ptolemies', *in* P. Garnsey, K. Hopkins, and C.R. Whittaker (eds), *Trade in the Ancient Economy*, London, 1983, pp. 64–75, 190–192.

Thompson, D., 'The Idumaeans of Memphis and the Ptolemaic Politeumata', *in Atti del XVII Congresso Internazionale di Papyrologia*, Naples, 1984, pp. 1069–1075.

Thompson, D., *Memphis under the Ptolemies*, Princeton, 1988.

Tomback, R.S., *A Comparative Semitic Lexicon of the Phoenician and Punic Languages*, Missoula, 1978.

Traunecker, C., 'Le panthéon du Ouadi Hammâmât (Inscription n° 58)', *in Autour de Coptos,* proceedings of the colloquium organised by the musée des Beaux-Arts de Lyon (17–18 March 2000), *Topoi, Orient-Occident*, suppl. 3, Lyon, 2002, pp. 355–381.

Tregenza, L.A., *The Red Sea Mountains of Egypt*, Oxford, 1955.

Tucker, J., *Women in Nineteenth-Century Egypt*, Cambridge, 1985.

Tuplin, C., 'Darius' Suez canal and Persian Imperialism', *in* H. Sancisi-Werdenburg and A. Kuhrt, *Achemenid History* VI, Leiden, 1991, pp. 237–283.

Tvedtnes, J.A., 'The Origin of the Name 'Syria', *JNES* 40, 1981, pp. 139–140.

U.S. Naval Oceanographic Office, *Sailing Direction for the Red Sea and Gulf of Aden*, Waschington, D.C., 1965.

Valbelle, D., *Les ouvriers de la tombe, Deir el-Medineh à l'époque ramesside, BiÉtud* XCVI, IFAO, Cairo, 1985.

Valbelle, D., 'Entre l'Égypte et la Palestine, Tell el-Herr', *BSFE* 109, June 1987, pp. 24–38.

Valbelle, D., *Les Neuf Arcs, l'Égyptien et les étrangers de la préhistoire à la conquête d'Alexandre*, Paris, 1990.

Valbelle, D., 'L'Égypte pharaonique', *in* J.-L. Huot, J.-P Thalmann and D. Valbelle, *Naissances des cités*, collection origines, Nathan, Paris, 1990, pp. 257-322.

Valbelle, D., Le Saout, F., Chartier-Raymond, M., Abd el-Samie, M., Traunecker, Cl., Wagner, G., Carrey-Maratrey, J.-Y., and Zigniani, P., 'Reconnaissance archéologique à la pointe orientale du Delta. Rapport préliminaire sur les saisons 1990 et 1991', *CRIPEL* 14, 1992, pp. 11-22.

Valbelle, D., 'La (les) Route(s)-d'Horus', *in Hommages à Jean Leclant*, vol. 4, *BiÉtud* 106/4, IFAO, Cairo, 1994, pp. 379-386.

Valbelle, D., 'Les niveaux hellénistiques de Tell el-Herr', *BSFE* 132, 1995, pp. 30-42.

Valbelle, D., and Defernez, C., 'Les sites de la frontière égypto-palestinienne à l'époque perse', *Transeuphratène* 9, 1995, pp. 93-100.

Valbelle, D., and Bonnet, C., *Le sanctuaire d'Hathor, maîtresse de la turquoise. Sérabit el-Khadim au Moyen Empire*, Paris, 1996.

Valbelle, D., and Abd el-Maksoud, M., 'La Marche du nord-est', *in L'Égypte du Delta. Les capitales du Nord*, *Dossiers d'Archéologie* 213, March 1996, pp. 60-65.

Valbelle, D., and Bonnet, C. (eds), *Le Sinaï durant l'Antiquité et le Moyen Âge. 4000 ans d'histoire pour un désert*, 'Sinaï' UNESCO colloquium, 19–21 Sept. 1997, Errance, Paris, 1998.

Valbelle, D., Abd el-Maksoud, M.), 'La frontière orientale du delta depuis le bronze moyen jusqu'au bronze récent', *in* A. Caubet (ed.), *L'acrobate au taureau. Les découvertes de Tell el-Dabca (Égypte) et l'archéologie de la Méditerranée orientale (1800-1400 av. J.-C.)*, proceedings of a colloquium held at the Louvre, 3 Dec. 1994, La documentation française & musée du Louvre, Paris, 1999, pp. 85-98, fig. 1-10.

Valloggia, M., *Recherche sur les 'Messagers' (Wpwtyw) dans les sources égyptiennes profanes*, doctoral thesis n° 212, presented at the Faculty of Arts, University of Geneva, Droz, Geneva, 1976.

Valloggia, M., 'Rapport préliminaire sur la troisième campagne de fouilles du mastaba V à Balat (oasis de Dakhla)', *BIFAO* 80, 1980, pp. 97-128.

Valloggia, M., *in LÄ* IV, Wiesbaden, 1980, *s.v.* 'Nachrichtenübermittlung', cols 287-291.

Valloggia, M., 'La stèle d'un chef d'expédition de la Première Période Intermédiaire', *BIFAO* 85, 1985, pp. 259-266, pls xlii-xliii.

Valloggia, M., 'Les amiraux de l'oasis de Dakhleh', *in* Fr. Geus and Thill, F., *Mélanges offerts à Jean Vercoutter*, published with the support of CNRS, Éditions Recherche sur les Civilisations, Paris, 1985, pp. 355-364.

Valloggia, M., *Vie quotidienne et voies de communication en Égypte ancienne*, Les civilisations orientales, Vie quotidienne, Université de Liège, Faculté de Philosophie et Lettres, Faculté ouverte, conférences, débats, dossiers, Section d'Histoire et Littératures orientales, Liège, 1986, pp. 1-13.

Valloggia, M., 'Chanceliers du dieu et messagers du roi à l'est de l'Égypte', *in* D. Valbelle and C. Bonnet (eds), *Le Sinaï durant l'Antiquité et le Moyen Âge. 4000 ans d'histoire pour un désert*, 'Sinaï' UNESCO colloquium, 19–21 Sept. 1997, Errance, Paris, 1998, pp. 39-43.

Van Beek, G.W., 'Frankincense and Myrrh', D. Freedman and E. Campbell (eds), *The Biblical Archaeologist Reader II*, New York, 1964, pp. 99-117.

Van Beek, G.W., 'Tell Jemmeh', *in* E. Stern (ed.), *The New Encyclopaedia of Archaeological Excavations in the Holy Land*, vol. 4, Jerusalem, 1993.

Van der Boorn, G.P.F., *The Duties of the Vizier. Civil Administration in the Early New Kingdom*, London, 1988, pp. 42-53.

Vandersleyen, C., *Les guerres d'Amosis, fondateur de la XVIIIᵉ dynastie*, Monographies Reine Élisabeth, Fondation Égyptologique Reine Élisabeth, Brussels, 1971.

Vandersleyen, C., 'Le sens de ouadj-our (w3ḏ-wr)', *in* S. Schoske (ed.), *Akten des Vierten Internationalen Ägyptologen Kongresses, München*, vol. 4, Hamburg, 1985, pp. 345-352.

Vandersleyen, C., 'Le dossier égyptien des Philistins', *in* E. Lipinski (ed.), *The Land of Israel: Cross-Roads of Civilizations*, proceedings of the conference held in Brussels from the 3ᵗʰ to the 5ᵗʰ of December 1984 to mark the twenty-fifth anniversary of the Institute of Archaeology Queen Elisabeth of Belgium at the Hebrew University of Jerusalem, *OLA* 19, Leuven, 1985, pp. 39-53.

Vandersleyen, C., 'Ouadj-Our ne signifie pas 'mer': qu'on se le dise!', *GM* 103, 1988, pp. 75-80.

Vandersleyen, C., 'Pount sur le Nil', *DE* 12, 1988, pp. 75-80.

Vandersleyen, C., 'n° 114 et 1 du Ouadi Hammamât (11ᵉ dynastie)', *CdÉ* XLIV, 127-128, 1989, pp. 148-158.

Vandersleyen, C., 'En relisant le Naufragé', *in* S.J. Groll (ed.), *Study in Egyptology presented to Miriam Lichtheim*, vol. 2, Jerusalem, 1990, pp. 1020-1023.

Vandersleyen, C., *L'Égypte et la vallée du Nil, vol. 2, De la fin de l'Ancien Empire à la fin du Nouvel Empire*, Nouvelle Clio, PUF, Paris, 1995.

Vandersleyen, C., 'Les monuments de l'Ouadi Gaouasis et la possibilité d'aller au pays de Pount par la mer Rouge', *RdÉ* 47, 1996, pp. 107-115.

Vandersleyen, C., 'Oublier l'Euphrate', *in* C. Cannuyer, J. Ries and A. Van Tongerloo (eds), *Les voyages dans les civilisations orientales, Acta Orientalia Belgica* XI, published with the support of the Fondation Universitaire de Belgique, la Société Belge d'Études Orientales, Brussels, Louvain-la-Neuve and Leuven, 1998, pp. 17-25.

Vandersleyen, C., *Ouadj our w³ḏ wr. Un autre aspect de la vallée du Nil, Connaissance de l'Égypte ancienne* 7, Brussels, 1999.

Vandier, J., *Manuel d'Archéologie égyptienne*, vol. 1, *Les époques de formation, la préhistoire, les trois premières dynasties*, Paris, 1952.

Vandier, J., *Manuel d'Archéologie égyptienne*, vol. 2, *Les grandes époques, L'architecture funéraire*, Paris, 1954.

Vandier, J., *Manuel d'Archéologie égyptienne*, vol. 4, *Bas-reliefs et peintures, scènes de vie quotidienne*, part I, *Les tombes*, Paris, 1964.

Vandier, J., *Manuel d'Archéologie égyptienne*, vol. 5, *Bas-reliefs et peintures, scènes de vie quotidienne*, part II, Paris, 1969.

Vandorpe, K., 'The Dockyard Workshop or the Toarchis Village', *Enchoria* 22, 1995, pp. 158-168.

Van't Dack, E., and Hauben, H., 'L'apport égyptien à l'armée navale lagide', *in* H. Maelher and V.M. Strocka (eds), *Das Ptolemäische Ägypten, Akten des Internationalen Symposiums 27-29 September 1976, Berlin*, Mayence, 1978, pp. 59-94.

Vélissaropoulos, J., 'Le monde de l'emporion', *DHA* 25, 1977, pp. 61-75.

Vélissaropoulos, J., *Les nauclères grecs. Recherches sur les institutions maritimes en Grèce et dans l'Orient hellénisé*, Geneva and Paris, 1980.

Ventura, R., *Living at the City of the Dead, A Selection of Topograpgical and Administrative Terms in the Documents of the Theban Necropolis, OBO* 69, Vandenhoeck & Ruprecht, Universitätsverlag/Gottingen and Freiburg, 1986.

Vercoutter, J., *Les objets égyptiens et égyptisants du mobilier funéraire carthaginois, BAH* XL, Paris, 1945.

Vercoutter, J., 'Les Haou-Nebout', *BIFAO* XLVI, 1947, pp. 125-158.

Vercoutter, J., 'Les Haou-Nebout (suite)', *BIFAO* XLVIII, 1949, pp. 107-209, pls i-ii.

Vercoutter, J., *L'Égypte et le monde égéen préhellénique*, Étude critique des sources égyptiennes (du début de la XVIIIᵉ à la fin de XIXᵉ dynastie), *BidÉtud* XXII, IFAO, Cairo, 1956.

Vercoutter, J., 'The Gold of Kush. Two Gold-washing Stations at Faras East', *KUSH* VII, 1959, pp. 120-153, pls xxviii-xxxv.

Vercoutter, J., 'The Gold of Kush', *KUSH* VII, 1959, pp. 120-153.

Vercoutter, J., 'Shelley Wachsmann, *Aegeans in the Theban Tombs, OLA* 20, Peeters, Leuven, 1987', *BiOr* XLV, 1988, cols 551-556.

Vercoutter, J., *L'Égypte et la vallée du Nil*, vol. 1, *Des origines à la fin de l'Ancien Empire 12000-2000 av. J.-C.*, Nouvelle Clio, PUF, 1992.

Vergote, J., *Phonique historique de l'Égyptien. Les consonnes, Bibliothèque du Muséon* 19, Leuven, 1945.

Verner, M., *Preliminary Report on Czechoslovak Excavations in the Mastaba of Ptahshepses at Abusir*, Charles University, Prague, 1976.

Vernus, P., 'Le mot št³w, 'branchage, bosquet, bois'', *RdÉ* 29, 1977, pp. 179-193.

Vernus, P., *Athribis, Textes et documents relatifs à la géographie, aux cultes et à l'histoire d'une ville du Delta pharaonique, BiÉtud* LXXIV, IFAO, Cairo, 1978.

Vernus, P., 'Choix de textes illustrant le temps des rois tanites et libyens', *in Tanis, l'or des Pharaons*, Paris, 1987, pp. 102-111.

Vernus, P., *Sagesses de l'Égypte pharaonique*, La Salamandre, Imprimerie nationale, Paris, 2001.

Villard, P., 'Un roi de Mari à Ougarit', *UgForsch* 18, 1986, pp. 387-412.

Vinson, S., 'The Earliest Representations of Brailed Sails', *JARCE* XXX, 1993, pp. 133-150.

Vinson, S., *Egyptian Boats and Ships*, Shire Egyptology, London, 1994.

Vinson, S., 'ΠΑΚΤΟΝ and ΠΑΚΤϬΣΙΣ as Ship-Construction terminology in Herodotus, Pollux and Documentary Papyri', *ZPE* 113, 1996, p. 202.

Volokhine, Y., 'Les déplacements pieux en Égypte pharaonique: sites et pratiques cultuelles', *in* D. Frankfurter (ed.), *Pilgrimage and Holy Space in Late Antique Egypt, Religions in the Graeco-Roman World* 134, Brill, Leiden, Boston and Cologne, 1998, pp. 51-97.

Vycichl, W., 'Notes on the Story of the Shipwrecked Sailor', *KUSH* V, 1957, pp. 70-72.

Wachsmann, S., *Aegeans in the Theban Tombs, OLA* 20, Leuven, 1987.

Wainwright, G., 'Zeberged/The Shipwrecked Sailor's Island', *JEA* XXXII, 1946, pp. 31-38.

Wallinga, H.T., 'Nautika I, The Unit of Capacity for Ancient Size', *Mnemosyne* XVII, 1964, pp. 1-40.

Wallinga, H.T., 'The Ancient Persian navy and its predecessors', *AchHist* I, 1987, pp. 47-77.

Warburton, D., *State and Economy in Ancient Egypt, Fiscal Vocabulary of the New Kingdom*, OBO 151, University Press - Vandenhoeck & Ruprecht, Göttingen and Freiburg, 1997.

Ward, W.A., *Egypt and the East Mediterranean World 2200-1900 BC*, Beirut, 1971.

Ward, W.A., *Index of Egyptian Administrative and Religious Title of the Middle Kingdom and Related Subjects*, American University of Beirut, Beirut, 1986.

Ward, W.A., 'Alessandra Nibbi, *Ancient Byblos Reconsidered*, Oxford, DE Publications, 1981', *BiOr* XLIII, n° 5/6, 1986, cols 689-692.

Ward, W.A., 'Scarab Typology and Archaeological Context', *AJA* 91, 1987, pp. 527-528.

Ward, W.A., 'Early Contacts between Egypt, Canaan, and Sinai: Remarks on the Paper by Amnon Ben-Tor', *BASOR* 281, 1991, pp. 11-26.

Wathelet, P., 'Les Phéniciens et la tradition homérique', *in* E. Gubel, E. Lipinski, and B. Servais-Soyez, *Histoire phénicienne/Fenicische Geschiedenis, Studia Phoenicia* II, OLA 15, Peeters, Leuven, 1983, pp. 235-243.

Watrin, L., *Les échanges entre la Palestine et l'Égypte au IVᵉ millénaire : état de la question*, dissertation, Université de Paris I Panthéon-Sorbonne, Paris, 1995.

Watrin, L., 'The Relationship between the Nile Delta and Palestine during the 4th Millennium: from Early Exchange (Naqada I-II) to the colonisation of Southern Palestine (Naqada III)', *in* C. Eyre (ed.), *Abstracts of papers, Seventh International Congress of Egyptologists, Cambridge, 3-9 September 1995*, Oxford, 1995, pp. 197-199.

Weigall, A., *Travels in the Upper Egyptians Deserts*, London, 1909.

Weill, R., 'Les ports antiques submergés de la Méditerranée orientale et le déplacement du niveau marin', *RdÉ* 5, 1946, pp. 137-187.

Wente, E.F., *Late Ramesside Letters*, SAOC 33, The Oriental Institute of the University of Chicago, Chicago, 1967.

Wente, E.F., 'The Report of Wenamun', *in* W.K. Simpson (ed.), *The Literature of Ancient Egypt. An Anthology of Stories, Instructions and Poetry*, New Haven and London, 1973 (2nd ed.), pp. 144-150.

Whitcomb, D., and Johnson, J.H., *Quseir al-Qadim 1980: Preliminary Report*, ARCE Report 7, Undena Publications, Malibu, 1982.

White, D., 'Excavations at Marsa Matruh, Summer 1985', *JARCE Newsletter* 131, 1985, pp. 3-17.

White, D., '1985 Excavations on Bates's Island, Marsa Matruh', *JARCE* XXIII, 1986, pp. 51-84.

White, D., '1987 Excavations on Bate's island, Marsa Matruh. Second preliminary report', *JARCE* XXVI, 1989, pp. 87-114.

Whitehead, D., *Early Aramaic Epistolography: The Arsames Correspondence*, doctoral thesis, Chicago, 1974.

Wiercinska, J., 'La procession d'Amon dans la décoration du temple de Thoutmosis III à Deir el-Bahari', *Études et Travaux* 14, Warsaw, 1990, pp. 72-85.

Wilcken, U., *Urkunden der Ptolemäerzeit*, I, Berlin, Leipzig, 1927, pp. 341-342.

Wilcken, U., *Urkunden der Ptolemäerzeit (ältere Fund). Herausgegeben von Ulrich Wilcken*, II, *Papyri aus Oberägypten,* Walter de Gruyter & Co., Berlin and Leipzig, 1935.

Wild, H., *Le tombeau de Ti*, fasc. III, *La chapelle (deuxième partie)*, MIFAO LXV, IFAO, Cairo, 1939.

Wild, H., 'Contributions à l'iconographie et à la titulature de Qen Amon', *BIFAO* LVI, 1957, pp. 229-230.

Wild, H., *La tombe de Neferhotep (I) et Neb-nefer*, MIFAO 103/2, IFAO, Cairo, 1979.

Wild, H., 'Une stèle memphite du règne d'Aménophis III à Lausanne', *Hommages à Serge Sauneron*, I, *Égypte pharaonique*, BiÉtud LXXXI, IFAO, Cairo, 1979, pp. 305-318, pl. xlviii.

Williams, B.B., 'The Qustul Incense Burner and the Case for a Nubian Origin of Ancient Egyptian Kindship', *in* Th. Celenko, *Egypt in Africa*, Indianapolis, 1996, pp. 95-96.

Wilson, J.A., *The Burden of Egypt: An Interpretation of Ancient Egyptian Culture*, Chicago, 1957 (3rd ed.).

Wilson, J.A., 'The Journey of Wen-Amon to Phoenicia', *in* J.B. Pritchard, *ANET*, Princeton, 1969, pp. 25-29.

Wilson, V., 'The Iconography of Bes in Cyprus and the Levant', *Levant* VII, 1975.

Winand, J., 'Derechef Ounamon 2, 13-14', *GM* 139, 1994, pp. 95-108.

Winlock, H., *The Rise and Fall of the Middle Kingdom in Thebes*, New York, 1947.

Wreszinski, W., *Atlas zur altaegyptische Kulturgeschichte*, vol. 36, Hinrichs'sche Buchhandlung, Leipzig, 1923-1935.

Yadin, Y., *The Art of Warfare in Biblical Land in the Light of Archaeological Discoveries*, London, 1963.

Yardeni, A., 'Maritime Trade and Royal Accountancy in an Erased Customs Account from 475 BC on the Ahiqar Scroll from Elephantine', *BASOR*, 293, 1994, pp. 67-87.

Yon, M., 'Le royaume de Kition. Époque classique', *in* T. Hackens and G. Moucharte (eds), *Numismatique et économique phéniciennes et puniques,* proceedings of a colloquium held at Louvain-la-Neuve, 13-16 May 1987, Publications d'Histoire de l'Art et d'Archéologie de l'Université Catholique de Louvain LVIII, *Studia Phoenicia* IX, *Numismatica Lovaniensia* 9, Leuven, 1992, pp. 243-260, pls xxv-xxxviii.

Yon, M., 'La Syrie et Chypre au bronze récent', *in* A. Caubet (ed.), *L'acrobate au taureau. Les découvertes de Tell el-Dabca (Égypte) et l'archéologie de la Méditerranée orientale (1800-1400 av. J.-C.),* proceedings of a colloquium held at the Louvre, 3 Dec. 1994, La documentation française & musée du Louvre, Paris, 1999, pp. 123-147, figs 1-3.

Yoyotte, J., 'Les stèles de Ramsès II à Tanis', *Kêmi* X, 1949, pp. 58-74.

Yoyotte, J., 'Une épithète de Min comme explorateur des régions orientales', *RdÉ* 9, 1952, pp. 125-137.

Yoyotte, J., 'Un corps de police de l'Égypte pharaonique', *RdÉ* 9, 1952, pp. 139-151.

Yoyotte, J., 'Égypte ancienne', *in Histoire universelle*, I, *Des origines à l'Islam, Encyclopédie de la Pléiade*, Gallimard, Paris, 1956, pp. 103-285.

Yoyotte, J., *in Dictionnaire de la Bible*, suppl. 6, Paris, 1958, *s.v.* 'Néchao ou Néko', cols 363-392.

Yoyotte, J., 'Notes de toponymie égyptienne', *in Festschrift zum 80. Geburgstag von Professor Dr Hermann Junker, MDAIK* 16, 1958, pp. 414-430.

Yoyotte, J., *Les pèlerinages en Égypte ancienne, in* Esnoul, A.-M. (ed.), *Les Pèlerinages. Égypte ancienne - Israël - Islam - Perse - Inde - Tibet - Indonésie - Madagascar - Chine - Japon, Sources Orientales* III, Le Seuil, Paris, 1960, pp. 19-74.

Yoyotte, J., 'Processions géographiques mentionnant le Fayoum et ses localités', *BIFAO* 61, 1962, pp. 79-138, pl. vii.

Yoyotte, J., Lopez J, 'L'organisation de l'armée et les titulatures de soldats au Nouvel Empire', *BiOr* XXVI, 1969, pp. 3-19.

Yoyotte, J., 'Les Sementiou et l'exploitation des régions minières à l'Ancien Empire', *BSFE* 73, June 1975, pp. 44-55.

Yoyotte, J., and Chuvin, P., 'Le delta du Nil au temps des pharaons', *L'Histoire* 54, March 1983, pp. 52-62.

Yoyotte, J., and Chuvin, P., 'Les hors-la-loi qui ont fait trembler Rome', *L'Histoire* 88, April 1986, pp. 40-48.

Yoyotte, J., and Chuvin, P., 'L'Égypte des marais', *in L'Égypte ancienne, L'Histoire*, Le Seuil, Paris, 1996, pp. 153-168.

Yoyotte, J., 'Tanis', 'Pharaons, Grands Prêtres et Guerriers libyens. 'La Troisième Période Intermédiaire', *in Tanis, l'or des Pharaons*, Paris, 1987, pp. 25-46, pp. 51-76.

Yoyotte, J., 'Le roi Mer-Djefa-Rê et le dieu Sopdou. Un monument de la XIV$^e$ dynastie', *BSFE* 114, April 1989, pp. 17-63.

Yoyotte, J., 'L'Égypte pharaonique. Société, économie, culture', *in* G. Mokhtar (ed.), *Histoire générale de l'Afrique*, II, *Afrique ancienne*, UNESCO/NEA, Paris, 1989, pp. 107-131.

Yoyotte, J., 'Naucratis, ville égyptienne', *ACF*, 92$^{nd}$ year, 1991-1992, pp. 634-645.

Yoyotte, J., 'L'Égypte du Delta. La problématique actuelle', 'Le Nouvel Empire (1550-1080 environ). Sites bibliques et sites moins connus', 'Les métropoles royales du Nord', *in L'Égypte du Delta. Les capitales du Nord, Dossiers d'Archéologie* 213, March 1996, pp. 6-11, pp. 24-29, pp. 30-33.

Yoyotte, J., and Bakr, M. I., 'Tell Basta/Boubastis', *in L'Égypte du Delta. Les capitales du Nord, Dossiers d'Archéologie* 213, March 1996, pp. 44-49.

Yoyotte, J., von der Way, T., 'De Bouto historique à Bouto archaïque', *in L'Égypte du Delta. Les capitales du Nord, Dossiers d'Archéologie* 213, March 1996, pp. 76-77.

Yoyotte, J., 'Les rivages d'Alexandrie', *in Les cités antiques, Pour la Science*, HS, Oct. 1999, pp. 44-49.

Yoyotte, J., 'Le second affichage du décret de l'an 2 de Nekhtnebef et la découverte de Thônis-Héracleion', *Égypte, Afrique & Orient* 24, Dec. 2001, pp. 24-34.

Zaba, Z., *Les maximes de Ptahhotep*, Académie Tchéchoslovaque des Sciences, Prague, 1956.

Zaba, Z., *The Rock Inscriptions of Lower Nubia*, Czechoslovak Concession, Prague, 1974.

Zaba, Z., 'Tafa and The Rock Inscriptions in Korosko', *ASAE* 81, 1981, p. 41.

Zaccagnini, C., *Lo scambio dei doni nel Vicino Oriente durante i secoli XV-XIII, Orientis Antiqui Collectio*, XI, Rome, 1973.

Zaccagnini, C., 'Tyre and the ceddar of Lebanon', *in* E. Acquaro (ed.), *Alla soglie della classicità. Il Mediterraneo tra tradizione e ihnovazione Studi in onore di S. Moscati*, I, Rome, 1996, pp. 451-466.

Zandee, J., *De Hymnen aan Amon van Papyrus Leiden I 350, Bijlage* I, *Hiëroglyphische Tekst, OMRO* XXVIII, Leiden, 1947.

Zarins, J., 'Obsidian and the Red Sea Trade Prehistoric Aspects', *in* M. Taddei and P. Callieri (eds), *South Asian Archaeology 1987*, part 1, Rome, 1990, pp. 507-541.

Zibelius, K., *Afrikanische Orts- und Völkernamen in hieroglyphischen und hieratischen Texten*, *TAVO*, suppl., vol. 1, Wiesbaden, 1972.

Zilliacus, H., 'Neue Ptolemäertexye zum Korntransport und Saatdarlehen', *Aegyptus* 19, 1939, pp. 59-76.

Zivie, A.P., *La tombe de Pached à Deir el-Medineh*, *MIFAO* 99, IFAO, Cairo, 1979.